A/CN.4/SER.A/2009/Add.1 (Part 1)

AF708238

YEARBOOK OF THE INTERNATIONAL LAW COMMISSION

2009

Volume II
Part One

Documents of the sixty-first session

United Nations
New York and Geneva, 2015

NOTE

Symbols of United Nations documents are composed of capital letters combined with figures. Mention of such a symbol indicates a reference to a United Nations document.

References to the *Yearbook of the International Law Commission* are abbreviated to *Yearbook* ..., followed by the year (for example, *Yearbook ... 2008*).

The *Yearbook* for each session of the International Law Commission comprises two volumes:

Volume I: summary records of the meetings of the session;

Volume II (Part One): reports of special rapporteurs and other documents considered during the session;

Volume II (Part Two): report of the Commission to the General Assembly.

All references to these works and quotations from them relate to the final printed texts of the volumes of the *Yearbook* issued as United Nations publications.

*

* *

The reports of the special rapporteurs and other documents considered by the Commission during its sixty-first session, which were originally issued in mimeographed form, are reproduced in the present volume, incorporating the corrigenda issued by the Secretariat and the editorial changes required for the presentation of the final text.

A/CN.4/SER.A/2009/Add.1 (Part 1)

UNITED NATIONS PUBLICATION

Sales No.: E.14.V.11 (Part 1)
ISBN: 978-92-1-133832-4
e-ISBN: 978-92-1-057128-9

ISSN: 0082-8289

CONTENTS

ABBREVIATIONS

ASEAN	Association of Southeast Asian Nations
EBRD	European Bank for Reconstruction and Development
EC	European Community
EEC	European Economic Community
EU	European Union
FAO	Food and Agriculture Organization of the United Nations
GATS	General Agreement on Trade in Services
IAEA	International Atomic Energy Agency
IASC	Inter-Agency Standing Committee
ICAO	International Civil Aviation Organization
ICJ	International Court of Justice
INTERPOL	International Criminal Police Organization
ICRC	International Committee of the Red Cross
IDRL	International Disaster Response Laws
IFRC	International Federation of Red Cross and Red Crescent Societies
ILC	International Law Commission
ILO	International Labour Organization
IMCO	Intergovernmental Maritime Consultative Organization (now IMO)
IMF	International Monetary Fund
IMO	International Maritime Organization
IOM	International Organization for Migration
NATO	North Atlantic Treaty Organization
NGO	non-governmental organization
OAS	Organization of American States
OAU	Organization of African Unity
OCHA	Office for the Coordination of Humanitarian Affairs
OECD	Organization for Economic Cooperation and Development
OPCW	Organization for the Prohibition of Chemical Weapons
PCIJ	Permanent Court of International Justice
TRIPS	Agreement on Trade-Related Aspects of Intellectual Property Rights
UNECE	United Nations Economic Commission for Europe
UNESCO	United Nations Educational, Scientific and Cultural Organization
UNHCR	Office of the United Nations High Commissioner for Refugees
UNITAR	United Nations Institute for Training and Research
UPU	Universal Postal Union
WHO	World Health Organization
WTO	World Trade Organization

*

* *

AC	Appeals Court
AFDI	*Annuaire français de droit international* (Paris)
AJIL	*American Journal of International Law* (Washington, D.C.)
BYBIL	*British Year Book of International Law* (London)
ECHR	European Court of Human Rights
GC	Grand Chamber
I.C.J. Pleadings	ICJ, *Pleadings, Oral Arguments, Documents*
I.C.J. Reports	ICJ, *Reports of Judgments, Advisory Opinions and Orders*
ILM	*International Legal Materials* (Washington, D.C.)
LGDJ	Librairie générale de droit et de jurisprudence (Paris)
OJ L	*Official Journal of the European Communities*, L Series
P.C.I.J., Series A	PCIJ, *Collection of Judgments* (Nos. 1–24: up to and including 1930)

P.C.I.J., Series B	PCIJ, *Judgments, Orders and Advisory Opinions* (Nos. 1–18: up to and including 1930)
P.C.I.J., Series A/B	PCIJ, *Collection of Advisory Opinions* (Nos. 40–80: beginning in 1931)
RGDIP	*Revue générale de droit international public* (Paris)
SLR	*Sri Lanka Law Reports*
UKHL	United Kingdom House of Lords
UNRIAA	United Nations, *Reports of International Arbitral Awards*
U.S.C.	United States Code
WLR	*Weekly Law Reports*

*

* *

In the present volume, the "International Tribunal for the Former Yugoslavia" refers to the International Tribunal for the Prosecution of Persons Responsible for Serious Violations of International Humanitarian Law Committed in the Territory of the Former Yugoslavia since 1991.

*

* *

NOTE CONCERNING QUOTATIONS

In quotations, words or passages in italics followed by an asterisk were not italicized in the original text.

Unless otherwise indicated, quotations from works in languages other than English have been translated by the Secretariat.

*

* *

The Internet address of the International Law Commission is **www.un.org/law/ilc**.

FILLING OF CASUAL VACANCIES IN THE COMMISSION (ARTICLE 11 OF THE STATUTE)

[Agenda item 2]

DOCUMENT A/CN.4/613

Note by the Secretariat

[*Original: English*]
[*1 April 2009*]

1. By a letter dated 25 March 2009 addressed to the Legal Counsel of the United Nations, Mr. Chusei Yamada submitted his resignation from the International Law Commission. There is therefore one casual vacancy in the membership of the Commission.

2. In this instance, article 11 of the statute of the Commission is applicable. The article prescribes that:

> In the case of a vacancy, the Commission itself shall fill the vacancy having due regard to the provisions contained in articles 2 and 8 of this statute.

Article 2 reads:

> 1. The Commission shall consist of thirty-four members who shall be persons of recognized competence in international law.
>
> 2. No two members of the Commission shall be nationals of the same State.
>
> 3. In case of dual nationality a candidate shall be deemed to be a national of the State in which he ordinarily exercises civil and political rights.

Article 8 reads:

> At the election the electors shall bear in mind that the persons to be elected to the Commission should individually possess the qualifications required and that in the Commission as a whole representation of the main forms of civilization and of the principal legal systems of the world should be assured.

3. The term of the member to be elected by the Commission will expire at the end of 2011.

RESERVATIONS TO TREATIES

[Agenda item 3]

DOCUMENT A/CN.4/614 and Add.1–2*

Fourteenth report on reservations to treaties, by Mr. Alain Pellet, Special Rapporteur

[Original: French]
[2 April, 22 May and 7 August 2009]

CONTENTS

* Incorporating A/CN.4/614/Corr.1.

Multilateral instruments cited in the present report

	Source
Convention on Certain Questions relating to the Conflict of Nationality Laws (The Hague, 12 April 1930)	League of Nations, *Treaty Series*, vol. CLXXIX, No. 4137, p. 89.
Revised General Act for the Pacific Settlement of International Disputes (New York, 28 April 1949)	United Nations, *Treaty Series*, vol. 71, No. 912, p. 101.
Convention on Road Traffic (Geneva, 19 September 1949)	*Ibid.*, vol. 125, No. 1671, p. 22.
Convention for the Protection of Human Rights and Fundamental Freedoms (European Convention on Human Rights) (Rome, 4 November 1950)	*Ibid.*, vol. 213, No. 2889, p. 221.
Convention (No. 102) concerning Minimum Standards of Social Security (Geneva, 28 June 1952)	*Ibid.*, vol. 210, No. 2838, p. 131.
Convention concerning Customs Facilities for Touring (New York, 4 June 1954)	*Ibid.*, vol. 276, No. 3992, p. 191.
Additional Protocol to the Convention concerning Customs Facilities for Touring, relating to the importation of tourist publicity documents and material (New York, 4 June 1954)	*Ibid.*, p. 266.
Convention on the Recovery Abroad of Maintenance (New York, 20 June 1956)	*Ibid.*, vol. 268, No. 3850, p. 3.
European Convention for the Peaceful Settlement of Disputes (Strasbourg, 29 April 1957)	*Ibid.*, vol. 320, No. 4646, p. 243.
European Convention on Extradition (Paris, 13 December 1957)	*Ibid.*, vol. 359, No. 5146, p. 273.
Convention on the Continental Shelf (Geneva, 29 April 1958)	*Ibid.*, vol. 499, No. 7302, p. 311.
Convention on the Recognition and Enforcement of Foreign Arbitral Awards (New York, 10 June 1958)	*Ibid.*, vol. 330, No. 4739, p. 3.
Vienna Convention on Diplomatic Relations (Vienna, 18 April 1961)	*Ibid.*, vol. 500, No. 7310, p. 95.
Vienna Convention on Consular Relations (Vienna, 24 April 1963)	*Ibid.*, vol. 596, No. 8638, p. 261.
European Code of Social Security (Strasbourg, 16 April 1964)	*Ibid.*, vol. 648, No. 9281, p. 235.
International Convention on the Elimination of All Forms of Racial Discrimination (New York, 21 December 1965)	*Ibid.*, vol. 660, No. 9464, p. 195.
International Covenant on Civil and Political Rights (New York, 16 December 1966)	*Ibid.*, vol. 999, No. 14668, p. 171.
Optional Protocol to the International Covenant on Civil and Political Rights (New York, 16 December 1966)	*Ibid.*
International Covenant on Economic, Social and Cultural Rights (New York, 16 December 1966)	*Ibid.*, vol. 993, No. 14531, p. 3.
Treaty for the Prohibition of Nuclear Weapons in Latin America and the Caribbean (Treaty of Tlatelolco) (with annexed Additional Protocols I and II) (Mexico, Federal District, 14 February 1967)	*Ibid.*, vol. 634, No. 9068, p. 281.

	Source
Convention (No. 128) concerning Invalidity, Old-Age and Survivors' Benefits (Geneva, 29 June 1967)	*Ibid.*, vol. 699, No. 10030, p. 185.
Convention on Road Signs and Signals (Vienna, 8 November 1968)	*Ibid.*, vol. 1091, No. 16743, p. 3.
Vienna Convention on the Law of Treaties (Vienna, 23 May 1969)	*Ibid.*, vol. 1155, No. 18232, p. 331.
American Convention on Human Rights: "Pact of San José, Costa Rica" (San José, 22 November 1969)	*Ibid.*, vol. 1144, No. 17955, p. 123.
Convention on Special Missions (New York, 8 December 1969)	*Ibid.*, vol. 1400, No. 23431, p. 231.
Agreement on the International Carriage of Perishable Foodstuffs and on the Special Equipment to be used for such Carriage (ATP) (Geneva, 1 September 1970)	*Ibid.*, vol. 1028, No. 15121, p. 121.
Convention on Psychotropic Substances (Vienna, 21 February 1971)	*Ibid.*, vol. 1019, No. 14956, p. 175.
Convention on the Elimination of All Forms of Discrimination against Women (New York, 18 December 1979)	*Ibid.*, vol. 1249, No. 20378, p. 13.
United Nations Convention on the Law of the Sea (Montego Bay, 10 December 1982)	*Ibid.*, vol. 1833, No. 31363, p. 3.
Convention against Torture and Other Cruel, Inhuman or Degrading Treatment or Punishment (New York, 10 December 1984)	*Ibid.*, vol. 1465, No. 24841, p. 85.
Vienna Convention on the Law of Treaties between States and International Organizations or between International Organizations (Vienna, 21 March 1986)	A/CONF.129/15.
Convention on the Rights of the Child (New York, 20 November 1989)	United Nations, *Treaty Series*, vol. 1577, No. 27531, p. 3.
European Charter for Regional or Minority Languages (Strasbourg, 5 November 1992)	*Ibid.*, vol. 2044, No. 35358, p. 575.
Framework Convention for the Protection of National Minorities (Strasbourg, 1 February 1995)	*Ibid.*, vol. 2151, No. 37548, p. 243.
European Social Charter (revised) (Strasbourg, 3 May 1996)	*Ibid.*, vol. 2151, No. 37549, p. 277.
International Convention for the Suppression of Terrorist Bombings (New York, 15 December 1997)	*Ibid.*, vol. 2149, No. 37517, p. 256.
Rome Statute of the International Criminal Court (Rome, 17 July 1998)	*Ibid.*, vol. 2187, No. 38544, p. 3.
International Convention for the Suppression of the Financing of Terrorism (New York, 9 December 1999)	*Ibid.*, vol. 2178, No. 38349, p. 197.
United Nations Convention against Corruption (New York, 31 October 2003)	*Ibid.*, vol. 2349, No. 42146, p. 41.

Works cited in the present report

ANZILOTTI, Dionisio

Corso di diritto internazionale. 4th ed. Padua, CEDAM, 1955. Vol. I: Introduzione—teorie generali. 438 p.

AUST, Anthony

Modern Treaty Law and Practice. 2nd ed. Cambridge, Cambridge University Press, 2007.

BARATTA, Roberto

Gli effetti delle riserve ai trattati. Milan, Giuffrè, 1999.

BOWETT, Derek William

"Reservations to non-restricted multilateral treaties", BYBIL, 1976–1977, vol. 48, pp. 67–92.

COCCIA, Massimo

"Reservations to multilateral treaties on human rights", *California Western International Law Journal*, vol. 15, 1985, pp. 1–51.

COMBACAU, Jean and Serge SUR

Droit international public. 8th ed. Paris, Montchrestien, 2008.

DAILLIER, Patrick and Alain PELLET

Droit international public. 7th ed. Paris, LGDJ, 2002.

DE CESARI, Patrizia

"Riserve, dichiarazioni e facoltà nelle convenzioni dell'Aja di diritto internazionale privato", *Communicazioni e Studi*, vol. 22, 2002, pp. 149–174.

FITZMAURICE, Sir Gerald

The Law and Procedure of the International Court of Justice. Cambridge, Grotius, 1986. 860 p.

GAJA, Giorgio

"Il regime della Convenzione di Vienna concernente le riserve inammissibili", *Studi in onore di Vincenzo Starace*. Naples, Editoriale Scientifica, 2008, vol. I, pp. 349–361.

"Unruly treaty reservations", *International Law at the Time of its Codification: Essays in Honour of Roberto Ago*. Milan, Giuffrè, 1987. Vol. I, pp. 307–330.

GORMLEY, W. Paul

"The modification of multilateral conventions by means of 'negotiated reservations' and other 'alternatives': a comparative study of the ILO and Council of Europe—part one", *Fordham Law Review*, vol. XXXIX, 1970–1971, pp. 59–80.

GREIG, D.W.

"Reservations: equity as a balancing factor?", *Australian Year Book of International Law 1995*, vol. 16, pp. 21–172.

HEYMANN, Monica

Einseitige Interpretationserklärungen zu multilateralen Verträgen (Unilateral interpretative declarations to multilateral treaties). Berlin, Duncker & Humblot, 2005.

HORN, Frank

Reservations and Interpretative Declarations to Multilateral Treaties. The Hague, T.M.C. Asser Instituut, Swedish Institute of International Law, Studies in International Law, 1988.

HYLTON, Daniel N.

"Default breakdown: the Vienna Convention on the Law of Treaties' inadequate framework on reservations", *Vanderbilt Journal of Transnational Law*, vol. 27, 1994, pp. 419–451.

IMBERT, Pierre-Henri

"À l'occasion de l'entrée en vigueur de la Convention de Vienne sur le droit des traités: Réflexions sur la pratique suivie par le Secrétaire général des Nations Unies dans l'exercice de ses fonctions de dépositaire", AFDI, vol. 26, 1980, pp. 524–541.

"La question des réserves dans la décision arbitrale du 30 juin 1977 relative à la délimitation du plateau continental entre la République française et le Royaume-Uni de Grande-Bretagne et d'Irlande du Nord", AFDI, vol. 24, 1978, pp. 29–58.

Les réserves aux traités multilatéraux: évolution du droit et de la pratique depuis l'avis consultatif donné par la Cour internationale de Justice le 28 mai 1951. Paris, Pedone, 1978. 503 p.

KELSEN, Hans

Pure Theory of Law. Translation from the 2nd (revised and enlarged) German ed. by Max Knight. Berkeley, University of California, 1967.

KOH, Jean Kyongun

"Reservations to multilateral treaties: How international legal doctrine reflects world vision", *Harvard International Law Journal*, vol. 23, 1982, pp. 71–116.

MAJOROS, Ferenc

"Le régime de réciprocité de la Convention de Vienne et les réserves dans les Conventions de La Haye", *Journal du droit international*, vol. 101, 1974, pp. 73–109.

MÜLLER, Daniel

"Article 20" and "Article 21", in Olivier Corten and Pierre Klein, eds., *Les Conventions de Vienne sur le droit des traités: commentaire article par article.* Vol. I. Brussels, Bruylant, 2006, pp. 797–882 and 883–934, respectively.

PARISI, Francesco and Catherine ŠEVČENKO

"Treaty reservations and the economics of article 21 (1) of the Vienna Convention", *Berkeley Journal of International Law*, vol. 21, 2003, pp. 1–26.

PELLET, Alain

"Article 19 (1969)", in Olivier Corten and Pierre Klein, eds., *Les Conventions de Vienne sur le droit des traités: commentaire article par article.* Vol. I. Brussels, Bruylant, 2006, pp. 641–788.

REDGWELL, Catherine

"Universality or integrity? Some reflections on reservations to general multilateral treaties", BYBIL, 1993, vol. 64, pp. 245–282.

RIQUELME CORTADO, Rosa

Las reservas a los tratados: Lagunas y ambigüedades del régimen de Viena. Murcia, University of Murcia, 2004.

ROUSSEAU, Charles

Droit international public, vol. I: *Introduction et sources.* Paris, Sirey, 1970.

SAPIENZA, Rosario

Dichiarazioni interpretative unilaterali e trattati internazionali. Milan, Giuffrè, 1996.

SCHERMERS, Henri G.

"The suitability of reservations to multilateral treaties", *Netherlands International Law Review*, vol. VI, 1959, pp. 350–361.

SIMMA, Bruno

Das Reziprozitätselement im Zustandekommen völkerrechtlicher Verträge. Berlin, Duncker & Humblot, 1972. 347 p.

SINCLAIR, Sir Ian

The Vienna Convention on the Law of Treaties. 2nd ed. Manchester, Manchester University Press, 1984.

SUCHARIPA-BEHRMANN, Lilly

"The legal effects of reservations to multilateral treaties", *Austrian Review of International and European Law*, vol. 1, 1996, pp. 67–88.

SZAFARZ, Renata

"Reservations to multilateral treaties", *Polish Yearbook of International Law*, vol. 3, 1970, pp. 293–316.

SZTUCKI, Jerzy

"Some questions arising from reservations to the Vienna Convention on the Law of Treaties", *German Yearbook of International Law*, vol. 20, 1977, pp. 277–305.

TOMUSCHAT, Christian

"Admissibility and legal effects of reservations to multilateral treaties", *Heidelberg Journal of International Law*, vol. 27, 1967, p. 466.

VIRALLY, Michel

"Le principe de réciprocité dans le droit international contemporain", *Collected Courses of The Hague Academy of International Law*, 1967–III, vol. 122, pp. 1–105.

WALDOCK, Sir Humphrey

"General course on public international law", *Collected Courses of The Hague Academy of International Law*, 1962–II, vol. 106, pp. 1–251.

Introduction

1. The eleventh report on reservations to treaties (*Yearbook ... 2006*, vol. II (Part One), document A/CN.4/574), submitted at the fifty-eighth session of the Commission, contained a brief summary of the work of the Commission on the subject (paras. 1–43). In a continuation of this tradition, deemed helpful by the members of the Commission, this year's report summarizes briefly the lessons to be drawn from the completion of the consideration of the tenth report in 2006 (*Yearbook ... 2005*, vol. II (Part One), document A/CN.4/558 and Add.1–2), and from the consideration of the eleventh, twelfth (*Yearbook ... 2007*, vol. II (Part One), document A/CN.4/584) and thirteenth (*Yearbook ... 2008*, vol. II (Part One), document A/CN.4/600) reports in 2007 and 2008 by the Commission and by the Sixth Committee of the General Assembly. These last three reports constitute a single text, all three of

them relating to the procedure for the formulation of reactions to reservations (acceptance and objection) and to interpretative declarations (approval, opposition, reclassification and silence).[1] This summary is supplemented by a presentation of the main developments concerning reservations that have occurred in recent years and have come to the attention of the Special Rapporteur.

A. Tenth report on reservations to treaties and the outcome

1. Completion of consideration of the tenth report by the Commission

2. At its fifty-eighth session, the Commission completed its consideration of the second part of the tenth report on reservations to treaties[2] which, owing to lack of time, had not been discussed in depth at the preceding session.[3] This part of the tenth report, devoted entirely to the question of the validity of reservations, related to the concept of the object and purpose of the treaty, competence to assess the validity of reservations and the consequences of the invalidity of a reservation. The Commission also had before it a note by the Special Rapporteur on draft guideline 3.1.5 (Definition of the object and purpose of the treaty)[4] in which he proposed two alternative formulations, taking into account the preliminary discussion that had taken place at the fifty-seventh session (2005).[5]

3. The discussion of the definition of the object and purpose of a treaty was fruitful and productive.[6] The idea of formulating a definition was favourably received, although the wording gave rise to questions and doubts. Nevertheless, the Commission and the Special Rapporteur considered that the three alternative versions of guideline 3.1.5 served as a basis for a definition, bearing in mind the element of subjectivity inherent in the concept.

4. Guidelines 3.1.7 to 3.1.13, which provide specific examples of reservations that are incompatible with the object and purpose of the treaty, generally met with support among the members of the Commission and the pragmatic approach they represented was deemed judicious.

5. The Commission welcomed guidelines 3.2 and 3.2.1 to 3.2.4, on competence to assess the validity of reservations, including that of dispute settlement bodies and treaty monitoring bodies.[7]

6. With regard to the effects of the invalidity of a reservation, the Commission referred guidelines 3.3 and 3.3.1 to the Drafting Committee, indicating that there was no reason to distinguish between the different types of invalidity in article 19 of the Vienna Convention on the Law of Treaties (hereinafter referred to as the 1969 Vienna Convention) and the Vienna Convention on the Law of Treaties between States and International Organizations or between International Organizations (hereinafter referred to as the 1986 Vienna Convention) and that invalidity applied only within the restricted context of treaty law and did not involve engaging the international responsibility of its author. However, the Commission preferred to defer its consideration of guidelines 3.3.2 to 3.3.4 pending its consideration of the effect of reservations, objections to reservations and acceptances of reservations.[8] The Special Rapporteur supported this position.[9]

7. The Commission decided to refer guidelines 3.1.5 to 3.1.13, 3.2, 3.2.1 to 3.2.4, 3.3 and 3.3.1 to the Drafting Committee.[10]

8. In addition, the Commission adopted seven guidelines[11] and their commentaries which had been referred to the Drafting Committee at the preceding session.[12]

2. Consideration of chapter VIII of the 2006 report of the Commission by the Sixth Committee

9. Chapter VIII of the Commission's report on the work of its fifty-eighth session[13] deals with reservations to treaties. As is customary, a very brief summary of it is given in chapter II[14] and the "specific issues on which comments would be of particular interest to the Commission" are set out in chapter III. In the perspective of the meeting it was planning to have with experts in the field of human rights in order to hold a discussion on issues relating to reservations, the Commission wished to know the views of Governments that are necessary or useful adjustments to the "preliminary conclusions" of 1997.[15]

10. The idea of exchanging views with human rights experts, including the monitoring bodies, met with wide support in the Sixth Committee.[16] It was maintained that the establishment of a special regime relating to

---

[1] See the thirteenth report on reservations to treaties, *Yearbook ... 2008*, vol. II (Part One), document A/CN.4/600, para. 7.

[2] *Yearbook ... 2005*, vol. II (Part One), document A/CN.4/558 and Add.1–2.

[3] See *Yearbook ... 2005*, vol. II (Part Two), p. 64, para. 345. See also the eleventh report on reservations to treaties, *Yearbook ... 2006*, vol. II (Part One), document A/CN.4/574, para. 28.

[4] *Yearbook ... 2006*, vol. II (Part One), document A/CN.4/572 and Corr.1.

[5] See *Yearbook ... 2005*, vol. I, 2856th, 2857th and 2858th meetings, pp. 177–204.

[6] *Yearbook ... 2006*, vol. II (Part Two), p. 137, para. 144.

[7] *Ibid.*, p. 136, paras. 130–136, and pp. 137–138, paras. 153–155.

[8] *Ibid.*, p. 136, para. 139.

[9] *Ibid.*, p. 138, para. 157.

[10] *Ibid.*, p. 134, para. 103.

[11] Guidelines 3.1 (Permissible reservations), 3.1.1 (Reservations expressly prohibited by the treaty), 3.1.2 (Definition of specified reservations), 3.1.3 (Permissibility of reservations not prohibited by the treaty) and 3.1.4 (Permissibility of specified reservations). In addition, the Commission provisionally adopted guidelines 1.6 (Scope of definitions) and 2.1.8 [2.1.7 *bis*] (Procedure in case of manifestly invalid reservations). See the text of and commentary to these guidelines (*ibid.*, para. 159).

[12] *Yearbook ... 2005*, vol. II (Part Two), p. 64, para. 345. See also the eleventh report on reservations to treaties, *Yearbook ... 2006*, vol. II (Part One), document A/CN.4/574, para. 30.

[13] *Yearbook ... 2006*, vol. II (Part Two), pp. 133–158, paras. 92–159.

[14] *Ibid.*, p. 19, para. 17.

[15] *Ibid.*, p. 21, para. 29. For the preliminary conclusions, see *Yearbook ... 1997*, vol. II (Part Two), p. 56, para. 157.

[16] Sweden, on behalf of the Nordic countries (*Official Records of the General Assembly, Sixty-first Session, Sixth Committee*, 16th meeting (A/C.6/61/SR.16), para. 44); Austria (*ibid.*, para. 48); Netherlands (*ibid.*, para. 57); Portugal (*ibid.*, para. 83); Japan (*ibid.*, para. 87); Chile (19th meeting (A/C.6/61/SR.19), para. 6); New Zealand (*ibid.*, para. 11). See, however, United Kingdom (16th meeting (A/C.6/61/SR.16), para. 91).

reservations to human rights treaties was not desirable.[17] Other delegations wished the preliminary conclusions to be reviewed by the Commission, particularly with respect to the role, functions and powers of the monitoring bodies. In the view of some delegations, views consistently expressed by those bodies regarding the validity of a certain category of reservations could become authoritative.[18]

11. On the whole, the work of the Special Rapporteur was favourably received.[19] However, in one view the work of the Commission and its Special Rapporteur was too far advanced in relation to the actual practice followed by States, and could lead to amendment of the 1969 and 1986 Vienna Conventions.[20]

12. A number of delegations felt that the question of reservations incompatible with the object and purpose of a treaty was the most important aspect of the topic.[21] Nevertheless, it was maintained that the proposed definition, which was too loose, would hardly contribute to clarifying the definition of that concept.[22] According to another view, definition of the object and purpose of a treaty was necessary,[23] but must be sufficiently broad that it could be applicable on a case-by-case basis in accordance with the rules of treaty interpretation.[24] Few delegations commented on guidelines 3.1.7 to 3.1.13 designed to provide more specific examples of reservations incompatible with the object and purpose of a treaty.[25]

13. Regarding the guidelines on competence to assess the validity of reservations, some delegations pointed out that, although their overall approach was commendable,[26] they lacked consistency.[27] It was recalled that the competence of monitoring bodies could stem only from the functions assigned to them in the treaty that itself established them.[28] Some States expressed doubts as to the competence of monitoring bodies in that respect, and asserted that it was not their task to assess the validity of reservations.[29] In one view, only the States parties concerned possessed such competence.[30] Greater caution was also urged with regard to the functions of the depositary and its role with respect to manifestly invalid reservations,[31] particularly because of the vagueness of the concept of object and purpose of a treaty.

14. With regard to the consequences of the non-validity of a reservation, it was said that this was an issue central to the study.[32] According to some delegations, such reservations must be regarded as null and void,[33] but the view was expressed that the specific consequences of that nullity should be specified.[34] Doubts were expressed regarding the desirability of guideline 3.3.4 regarding the unanimous acceptance of an invalid reservation.[35]

B. Eleventh and twelfth reports on reservations to treaties and the outcome

1. Consideration of the eleventh and twelfth reports by the Commission

15. The eleventh report on reservations to treaties had been submitted at the fifty-eighth session, in 2006, but the Commission decided to consider it at its fifty-ninth session, owing to a lack of time.[36] Therefore in 2007, the Commission had before it the eleventh report on reservations to treaties, which in fact constitutes the second part of the eleventh report, from which it carries on.

16. The majority of the guidelines relating to the formulation of objections and the withdrawal and modification of objections proposed in the eleventh report were approved without objection by the Commission.[37]

17. However, there were major divergences of views among members of the Commission as to the author of an objection (guideline 2.6.5), including as to whether any State or international organization that was entitled to become a party to the treaty might also formulate an objection to a reservation. The view was expressed that

[17] Sweden, on behalf of the Nordic countries (*ibid.*, para. 46); Belgium (*ibid.*, para. 69); Romania (19th meeting (A/C.6/61/SR.19), para. 61).

[18] Netherlands (*ibid.*, 16th meeting (A/C.6/61/SR.16), para. 57). See, however, Canada (*ibid.*, para. 58).

[19] Japan (*ibid.*, para. 86); Germany (*ibid.*, para. 88); Russian Federation (18th meeting (A/C.6/61/SR.18), para. 72); New Zealand (19th meeting (A/C.6/61/SR.19), para. 11).

[20] Portugal (*ibid.*, 16th meeting (A/C.6/61/SR.16), paras. 76 and 78).

[21] Sweden, on behalf of the Nordic countries (*ibid.*, para. 42).

[22] Sweden, on behalf of the Nordic countries (*ibid.*); Netherlands (*ibid.*, para. 55); United Kingdom (*ibid.*, para. 92); Israel (17th meeting (A/C.6/61/SR.17), para. 16).

[23] Spain (*ibid.*, 16th meeting (A/C.6/61/SR.16), para. 73).

[24] Mexico (*ibid.*, para. 47).

[25] See, for example,United Kingdom (*ibid.*, para. 92).

[26] Spain (*ibid.*, para. 74); Romania (19th meeting (A/C.6/61/SR.19), para. 61).

[27] Austria (*ibid.*, 16th meeting (A/C.6/61/SR.16), paras. 51–53); Spain (*ibid.*, para. 74); Israel (17th meeting (A/C.6/61/SR.17), para. 20).

[28] France (*ibid.*, para. 2); United States of America (*ibid.*, para. 8); Israel (*ibid.*, paras. 17–19). Although the Special Rapporteur does not wish to start an argument with the States which held this view, he does wish to state as clearly as possible that they are implicitly attributing to him intentions he did not have and that he never claimed that the competence of those bodies with respect to reservations could be based on a legal foundation other than the treaty establishing them (see tenth report on reservations to treaties, *Yearbook ... 2005*, vol. II (Part One), document A/CN.4/558 and Add.1–2, pp. 181–182, paras. 169–171; second report on reservations to treaties, *Yearbook ... 1996*, vol. II (Part One), document A/CN.4/477 and Add.1, pp. 75 and 79, paras. 209 and 234 respectively; and *Yearbook ... 2006*, vol. II (Part Two), pp. 134–135, para. 111).

[29] China (*Official Records of the General Assembly, Sixty-first Session, Sixth Committee*, 16th meeting (A/C.6/61/SR.16), para. 63). See also Russian Federation (18th meeting (A/C.6/61/SR.18), para. 73) or Australia (19th meeting (A/C.6/61/SR.19), para. 17).

[30] Ethiopia (*ibid.*, 14th meeting (A/C.6/61/SR.14), para. 94).

[31] Ethiopia (*ibid.*); Canada (16th meeting (A/C.6/61/SR.16), para. 60); Spain (*ibid.*, para. 72); United Kingdom (*ibid.*, para. 93); South Africa (*ibid.*, para. 96); France (17th meeting (A/C.6/61/SR.17), para. 1); Poland (*ibid.*, para. 13); Russian Federation (18th meeting (A/C.6/61/SR.18), para. 72); Australia (19th meeting (A/C.6/61/SR.19), para. 17). See also China (16th meeting (A/C.6/61/SR.16), para. 64).

[32] France (*ibid.*, 17th meeting (A/C.6/61/SR.17), para. 5).

[33] Sweden, on behalf of the Nordic countries (*ibid.*, 16th meeting (A/C.6/61/SR.16), para. 43); Austria (*ibid.*, para. 51); France (17th meeting (A/C.6/61/SR.17), para. 7). See, however, China (16th meeting (A/C.6/61/SR.16), paras. 65–67).

[34] Canada (*ibid.*, para. 59).

[35] Portugal (*ibid.*, para. 79) and Austria (*ibid.*, para. 54).

[36] *Yearbook ... 2007*, vol. II (Part Two), pp. 15–16, para. 43.

[37] *Ibid.*, p. 22, paras. 102–105.

such States and international organizations did not have the same rights as contracting States and contracting international organizations and might therefore not formulate objections in the strict sense of the term. Therefore, the statements formulated by States and international organizations which were only entitled to become parties to the treaty, should not be referred to as objections. According to that view, to provide for such a possibility would create a practical problem for, where an open treaty was concerned, the parties thereto might not have been aware of some objections.

18. However, according to the majority opinion, the provisions of article 20, paragraphs 4 (*b*) and 5, of the 1969 and 1986 Vienna Conventions not only in no way excluded, but indeed implied, the entitlement of States and international organizations that were entitled to become parties to the treaty to formulate objections. Article 21, paragraph 3, of the Vienna Conventions on the effects of objections on the application of the treaty in cases where the author of the objection had not opposed the entry into force of the treaty between itself and the reserving State provided for no limitation on the potential authors of an objection. Furthermore, as article 23, paragraph 1, of the 1986 Convention clearly states, reservations, express acceptances of and objections to reservations must be communicated not only to the contracting States and contracting organizations but also to "other States and international organizations entitled to become parties to the treaty". Such notification had meaning only if those other States and other international organizations could, in fact, react to the reservation by way of an express acceptance or an objection. In the opinion of the Commission, that approach alone was consistent with the letter and spirit of guideline 2.6.1, which defined objections to reservations not on the basis of their legal effects but according to the effects *intended* by the objecting States or international organizations.

19. Concerns were also expressed as to whether preemptive or late objections could be formulated (guidelines 2.6.14 and 2.6.15). The view was expressed that such objections did not have the effects of an objection *per se*. Therefore, such phenomena, which did occur in State practice, should be referred to differently.

20. The guidelines on procedure did not raise any concerns and were widely endorsed by members of the Commission.[38] In particular, the introduction of a guideline on the statement of reasons for objections and the suggestion by the Special Rapporteur that a similar draft guideline should be proposed on the reasons for reservations[39] were welcomed.

21. Few concerns were raised with respect to the guidelines concerning acceptance of reservations. Such concerns were often of an editorial nature or related to the translation of the guidelines into languages other than French.[40]

[38] *Ibid.*

[39] See note by the Special Rapporteur on draft guideline 2.1.9, "Statement of reasons for reservations", *Yearbook ... 2007*, vol. II (Part One), document A/CN.4/586.

[40] *Yearbook ... 2007*, vol. II (Part Two), p. 25, para. 141.

22. The Commission decided to refer guidelines 2.6.3 to 2.6.6, 2.6.7 to 2.6.15, 2.7.1 to 2.7.9, 2.8 and 2.8.1 to 2.8.12 to the Drafting Committee, and to review the wording of guideline 2.1.6.[41]

23. The Commission also adopted nine guidelines[42] that had been referred to the Drafting Committee in 2006[43] together with commentaries thereto.[44]

24. Pursuant to General Assembly resolution 61/34 of 4 December 2006, the Commission convened a meeting with representatives of United Nations human rights treaty bodies. The meeting took place on 15 and 16 May 2007. The following bodies were represented: the Committee on Economic, Social and Cultural Rights; the Human Rights Committee; the Committee against Torture; the Committee on the Rights of the Child; the Committee on the Elimination of Racial Discrimination; the Committee on the Elimination of Discrimination against Women; the Committee on Migrant Workers; the Council of Europe (European Court of Human Rights and the Committee of Legal Advisers on Public International Law (CAHDI)); and the Subcommission on the Promotion and Protection of Human Rights. The meeting provided an opportunity for a fruitful exchange of views that was welcomed by all participants.[45] There was consensus among representatives of human rights treaty bodies and some members of the Commission on the lack of a special regime applicable to reservations to human rights treaties which, like all other treaties, continued to be governed by the 1969 and 1986 Vienna Conventions and by individual norms and rules provided for under a particular treaty. However, there might arise under human rights treaties specific issues calling for specific solutions, such as whether treaty monitoring bodies had the power to rule on reservations formulated by States parties.

2. Consideration of chapter IV of the 2007 report of the Commission by the Sixth Committee

25. Chapter IV of the Commission's report on the work of its fifty-ninth session[46] deals with the topic of reservations to treaties. As is customary, a very brief summary is given in chapter II[47] and "specific issues on which comments would be of particular interest to the Commission" are set out in chapter III. In 2007, the Commission posed the following four questions on the invalidity of reservations and the effects thereof:

[41] *Ibid.*, p. 16, para. 45.

[42] Guidelines 3.1.5 (Incompatibility of a reservation with the object and purpose of the treaty), 3.1.6 (Determination of the object and purpose of the treaty), 3.1.7 (Vague or general reservations), 3.1.8 (Reservations to a provision reflecting a customary norm), 3.1.9 (Reservations contrary to a rule of *jus cogens*), 3.1.10 (Reservations to provisions relating to non-derogable rights), 3.1.11 (Reservations relating to internal law), 3.1.12 (Reservations to general human rights treaties) and 3.1.13 (Reservations to treaty provisions concerning dispute settlement or the monitoring of the implementation of the treaty).

[43] See paragraph 7 above.

[44] *Yearbook ... 2007*, vol. II (Part Two), pp. 33 *et seq.*, para. 154.

[45] For a more detailed account of this meeting, see the annex to the present report.

[46] *Yearbook ... 2007*, vol. II (Part Two), pp. 15–55, paras. 34–154.

[47] *Ibid.*, p. 11, para. 13.

"(*a*) What conclusions do States draw if a reservation is found to be invalid for any of the reasons listed in article 19 of the 1969 and 1986 Vienna Conventions? Do they consider that the State formulating the reservation is still bound by the treaty without being able to enjoy the benefit of the reservation? Or, conversely, do they believe that the acceptance of the reserving State is flawed and that that State cannot be considered to be bound by the treaty? Or do they favour a compromise solution and, if so, what is it?

"(*b*) Are the replies to the preceding questions based on a position of principle or are they based on practical considerations? Do they (or should they) vary according to whether the State has or has not formulated an objection to the reservation in question?

"(*c*) Do the replies to the above two sets of questions vary (or should they vary) according to the type of treaty concerned (bilateral or normative, human rights, environmental protection, codification, etc.)?

"(*d*) More specifically, State practice offers examples of objections that are intended to produce effects different from those provided for in article 21, paragraph 3 (objection with minimum effect), or article 20, paragraph 4 (*b*) (maximum effect), of the Vienna Conventions, either because the objecting State wishes to exclude from its treaty relations with the reserving State provisions that are not related to the reservation (intermediate effect), or because it wishes to render the reservation ineffective and considers the reserving State to be bound by the treaty as a whole and that the reservation thus has no effect ("super-maximum" effect). The Commission would welcome the views of States regarding these practices (irrespective of their own practice)."[48]

26. Some States replied in writing to these questions[49] while others responded to them in greater[50] or less[51] detail during the debates of the Sixth Committee.

27. Delegations reiterated their support for the work of the Commission and for its Special Rapporteur[52] although some expressed concern that the guidelines and the commentaries thereto[53] were too complex.

28. The difficulty of defining the object and purpose of a treaty was stressed once again.[54] Some States generally endorsed the Commission's approach, as reflected in guidelines 3.1.5 and 3.1.6[55] and in the guidelines intended to provide examples of the types of reservations that were incompatible with the object and purpose of the treaty,[56] despite some of the criticisms and suggestions made.[57]

29. The guidelines on objections and the formulation of objections were welcomed by the delegations which spoke on that issue. It was also stated that, while a State might raise an objection for any reason whatsoever,[58] such reason must be in conformity with international law.[59]

30. Concerning guideline 2.6.5 (Author of an objection), several delegations were of the view that the phrase "any State and any international organization that is entitled to become a party to the treaty" referred to signatory States and international organizations, since a State or international organization that had no intention of becoming a party to a treaty should not have the right to object to a reservation made by a State party.[60] It was also argued that such objections should be subsequently confirmed because of the considerable time which would have elapsed between when the objection was formulated and when the author of the objection expressed its consent to be bound by the treaty.[61]

31. The guidelines on the formulation of reservations were endorsed.[62] It was pointed out, however, that the provision for written form should also take account of modern means of communication.[63] Guideline 3.1.10 recommending that reservations should be justified[64] was also endorsed. Support was also expressed for the suggestion that a similar guideline should be elaborated for reservations, since a statement of reasons for reservations and objections to reservations promoted dialogue between the parties directly concerned.[65] However, some delegations found pre-emptive objections unacceptable.[66]

---

[48] *Ibid.*, p. 13, para. 23.

[49] The Czech Republic, Mauritius and South Africa.

[50] Germany (*Official Records of the General Assembly, Sixty-second Session, Sixth Committee*, 19th meeting (A/C.6/62/SR.19), paras. 21–27); Sweden, on behalf of the Nordic countries (22nd meeting (A/C.6/62/SR.22), paras. 27–30); France (23rd meeting (A/C.6/62/SR.23), paras. 64–67); Romania (24th meeting (A/C.6/62/SR.24), paras. 16 and 17); Japan (*ibid.*, paras. 88–90); Belgium (25th meeting (A/C.6/62/SR.25), paras. 20–22); Greece (*ibid.*, paras. 28 and 29).

[51] India (*ibid.*, 22nd meeting (A/C.6/62/SR.22), para. 37); Austria (*ibid.*, para. 50); Egypt (*ibid.*, para. 66); Hungary (23rd meeting (A/C.6/62/SR.23), para. 38); Belarus (*ibid.*, para. 43).

[52] Canada (*ibid.*, 19th meeting (A/C.6/62/SR.19), para. 53); Sweden, on behalf of the Nordic countries (*ibid.*, 22nd meeting (A/C.6/62/SR.22), para. 27); India (*ibid.*, para. 37); Germany (*ibid.*, paras. 78 and 79); Hungary (23rd meeting (A/C.6/62/SR.23), para. 37); Czech Republic (*ibid.*, para. 52); Cuba (*ibid.*, para. 72); New Zealand (25th meeting (A/C.6/62/SR.25), para. 11).

[53] Italy (*ibid.*, 22nd meeting (A/C.6/62/SR.22), para. 85); Hungary (23rd meeting (A/C.6/62/SR.23), para. 37); Poland (26th meeting (A/C.6/62/SR.26), para. 17).

[54] Austria (*ibid.*, 22nd meeting (A/C.6/62/SR.22), para. 40). See also United Kingdom (24th meeting (A/C.6/62/SR.24), para. 56) and New Zealand (25th meeting (A/C.6/62/SR.25), para. 11).

[55] Austria (*ibid.*, 22nd meeting (A/C.6/62/SR.22), paras. 40 and 41); Belarus (23rd meeting (A/C.6/62/SR.23), para. 46); Cuba (24th meeting (A/C.6/62/SR.24), para. 72); New Zealand (25th meeting (A/C.6/62/SR.25), para. 11); Slovakia (26th meeting (A/C.6/62/SR.26), para. 15). See, however, United States of America (22nd meeting (A/C.6/62/SR.22), para. 87); United Kingdom (24th meeting (A/C.6/62/SR.24), paras. 57–59); Republic of Korea (26th meeting (A/C.6/62/SR.26), para. 2).

[56] Italy (*ibid.*, 22nd meeting (A/C.6/62/SR.22), para. 86); Slovakia (26th meeting (A/C.6/62/SR.26), para. 16).

[57] Austria (*ibid.*, 22nd meeting (A/C.6/62/SR.22), paras. 40–42); China (*ibid.*, para. 60); Belarus (23rd meeting (A/C.6/62/SR.23), paras. 47–50); Australia (25th meeting (A/C.6/62/SR.25), para. 9).

[58] Argentina (*ibid.*, 22nd meeting (A/C.6/62/SR.22), para. 56); Malaysia (23rd meeting (A/C.6/62/SR.23), para. 1); Slovakia (26th meeting (A/C.6/62/SR.26), para. 13). See, however, Egypt (22nd meeting (A/C.6/62/SR.22), para. 66).

[59] Argentina (*ibid.* (A/C.6/62/SR.22), para. 56); China (*ibid.*, para. 60); Islamic Republic of Iran (25th meeting (A/C.6/62/SR.25), para. 41).

[60] Malaysia (*ibid.*, 23rd meeting (A/C.6/62/SR.23), para. 2); Canada (*ibid.*, para. 15); Russian Federation (24th meeting (A/C.6/62/SR.24), paras. 57 and 58); Portugal (*ibid.*, para. 101); Greece (25th meeting (A/C.6/62/SR.25), para. 31); Islamic Republic of Iran (*ibid.*, para. 42). See, however, Mexico (24th meeting (A/C.6/62/SR.24), para. 12).

[61] Malaysia (*ibid.*, 23rd meeting (A/C.6/62/SR.23), para. 2); Greece (25th meeting (A/C.6/62/SR.25), para. 12).

[62] Mexico (*ibid.*, 24th meeting (A/C.6/62/SR.24), para. 12).

[63] Belarus (*ibid.*, 23rd meeting (A/C.6/62/SR.23), para. 45).

[64] Argentina (*ibid.*, 22nd meeting (A/C.6/62/SR.22), para. 56); Czech Republic (23rd meeting (A/C.6/62/SR.23), para. 52); Democratic Republic of the Congo (24th meeting (A/C.6/62/SR.24), para. 26); Portugal (*ibid.*, para. 101). See also Mexico (*ibid.*, para. 14); New Zealand (25th meeting (A/C.6/62/SR.25), para. 13).

[65] Argentina (*ibid.*, 22nd meeting (A/C.6/62/SR.22), para. 56). For the action taken on this proposal, see paragraphs. 34 and 35 below.

[66] Malaysia (*ibid.*, 23rd meeting (A/C.6/62/SR.23), para. 4). See also Czech Republic (*ibid.*, para. 54); France (*ibid.*, para. 61); Portugal (24th meeting (A/C.6/62/SR.24), para. 101); Greece (25th meeting (A/C.6/62/SR.25), para. 31); Islamic Republic of Iran (*ibid.*, para. 43). For an opposing view, see Slovakia (26th meeting (A/C.6/62/SR.26), para. 14).

32. The Commission's general approach to late objections (guideline 2.6.15) was endorsed,[67] although it was suggested that late objections could be equated with simple interpretative declarations.[68] It was suggested that the legal effects, if any, of late objections should be further clarified.[69]

33. Few comments were made on the guidelines on acceptance. In general, delegations expressed support for them. However, several delegations were of the view that the distinction between tacit acceptance and implicit acceptance was superfluous and should be deleted.[70] There was support for the view that acceptance was irreversible.[71]

C. Thirteenth report on reservations to treaties and the outcome

1. Consideration of the thirteenth report by the Commission

34. At its sixtieth session, in 2008, the Commission had before it the thirteenth report on reservations to treaties,[72] which was devoted entirely to the subject of interpretative declarations. The Commission also considered the note by the Special Rapporteur on the statement of reasons for reservations,[73] which had been submitted in 2007 but had not been discussed owing to lack of time.

35. The Special Rapporteur's proposal to include, in the Guide to Practice, a guideline on the statement of reasons for reservations was received positively by the members of the Commission. Guideline 2.1.9 was referred to the Drafting Committee, and later was provisionally adopted.

36. There was no major opposition to the Special Rapporteur's thirteenth report. The majority of Commission members approved the various categories of reactions to interpretative declarations and the terminology proposed by the Special Rapporteur.[74] The Commission also agreed that it would be useful to include, in the Guide to Practice, guidelines on the formulation of, reasons for and communication of responses to interpretative declarations.

37. Generally speaking, the most vexatious problem was that of silence as a response to an interpretative declaration, as addressed in guidelines 2.9.8[75] and 2.9.9.[76] While the majority of Commission members approved the language used in guideline 2.9.8, whereby silence is not to be interpreted as either approval of or opposition to an interpretative declaration, the wording of guideline 2.9.9, particularly paragraph 2, was challenged. In stating that "in certain specific circumstances", silence could be construed as consent to an interpretative declaration, the guideline is intended solely to allow greater flexibility in applying the principle of neutrality set out in guideline 2.9.8; nevertheless, a number of members expressed reservations regarding the validity of the expression "in certain specific circumstances", which they considered too general, and suggested providing specific examples of such circumstances.

38. With regard to guideline 2.9.10[77] on reactions to conditional interpretative declarations, members voiced doubts about the relevance of such a distinction, given that, according to a majority of Commission members, the legal regime of conditional interpretative declarations was indistinguishable from that of reservations.[78] Nevertheless, in line with the proposal of the Special Rapporteur—who shares that position *a priori*—it was decided that it would be premature to do away with the intermediate category of conditional interpretative declarations as the Commission had not yet considered the effects of such declarations.[79]

39. At its 2978th meeting, the Commission decided to refer all the guidelines proposed in the thirteenth report, that is, guidelines 2.9.1 (including the second paragraph of guideline 2.9.3) to 2.9.10, to the Drafting Committee, while emphasizing that guideline 2.9.10 was without prejudice to the subsequent retention or otherwise of the guidelines on conditional interpretative declarations.

40. The Commission also provisionally adopted 23 guidelines and the commentaries thereto.[80] In addition, it

[67] Mexico (*ibid.*, 24th meeting (A/C.6/62/SR.24), para. 15).

[68] Czech Republic (*ibid.*, 23rd meeting (A/C.6/62/SR.23), para. 53).

[69] France (*ibid.*, para. 61); Portugal (24th meeting (A/C.6/62/SR.24), para. 101); Australia (25th meeting (A/C.6/62/SR.25), para. 9).

[70] Argentina (*ibid.*, 22nd meeting (A/C.6/62/SR.22), para. 56); France (23rd meeting (A/C.6/62/SR.23), para. 62).

[71] Argentina (*ibid.*, 22nd meeting (A/C.6/62/SR.22), para. 56); El Salvador (23rd meeting (A/C.6/62/SR.23), para. 33).

[72] *Yearbook ... 2008*, vol. II (Part One), document A/CN.4/600.

[73] *Yearbook ... 2007*, vol. II (Part One), document A/CN.4/586.

[74] *Yearbook ... 2008*, vol. II (Part Two), para. 94.

[75] Guideline 2.9.8 reads as follows:

"**2.9.8** *Non-presumption of approval or opposition*

"Neither approval of nor opposition to an interpretative declaration shall be presumed."

[76] Guideline 2.9.9 reads as follows:

"**2.9.9** *Silence in response to an interpretative declaration*

"Consent to an interpretative declaration shall not be inferred from the mere silence of a State or an international organization in response to an interpretative declaration formulated by another State or another international organization in respect of a treaty."

"In certain specific circumstances, however, a State or an international organization may be considered as having acquiesced to an interpretative declaration by reason of its silence or its conduct, as the case may be."

[77] Guideline 2.9.10 reads as follows:

"**2.9.10** *Reactions to conditional interpretative declarations*

"Guidelines 2.6 to 2.8.12 shall apply to reactions of States and international organizations to conditional interpretative declarations."

[78] *Yearbook ... 2008*, vol. II (Part Two), para. 108.

[79] *Ibid.*, paras. 109–110.

[80] *Ibid.*, paras. 75, 76 and 78: guidelines 2.1.6 (Procedure for communication of reservations) (as amended), 2.1.9 (Statement of reasons [for reservations]), 2.6.5 (Author [of an objection]), 2.6.6 (Joint formulation [of objections to reservations]), 2.6.7 (Written form), 2.6.8 (Expression of intention to preclude the entry into force of the treaty), 2.6.9 (Procedure for the formulation of objections), 2.6.10 (Statement of reasons), 2.6.11 (Non-requirement of confirmation of an objection made prior to formal confirmation of a reservation), 2.6.12 (Requirement of confirmation of an objection made prior to the expression of consent to be bound by a treaty), 2.6.13 (Time period for formulating an objection), 2.6.14 (Conditional objections), 2.6.15 (Late objections), 2.7.1 (Withdrawal of objections to reservations), 2.7.2 (Form of withdrawal of objections to reservations), 2.7.3 (Formulation and communication of the withdrawal of objections to reservations), 2.7.4 (Effect on reservation of withdrawal of an objection), 2.7.5 (Effective date of withdrawal of an objection), 2.7.6 (Cases in which an objecting State or international organization may unilaterally set the effective date of withdrawal of an objection to a reservation), 2.7.7 (Partial withdrawal of an objection), 2.7.8 (Effect of a partial withdrawal of an objection), 2.7.9 (Widening of the scope of an objection to a reservation) and 2.8 (Forms of acceptance of reservations).

took note of guidelines 2.8.1 to 2.8.12 as provisionally adopted by the Drafting Committee.[81]

2. Consideration of chapter VI of the 2008 report of the Commission by the Sixth Committee

41. Chapter VI of the Commission's report on the work of its sixtieth session[82] deals with reservations to treaties. As usual, a very brief summary is provided in chapter II[83] and the "specific issues on which comments would be of particular interest to the Commission" are dealt with in chapter III. The Commission asked several questions regarding the role of silence as a reaction to an interpretative declaration[84] as well as the potential effects of interpretative declarations.[85] The Secretariat has received written responses to the questions from Germany and Portugal.

42. Regarding the role of silence, the views expressed by the Sixth Committee supported the general approach of the Special Rapporteur appointed by the Commission. Several delegations argued that mere silence could not be considered as either approval of or opposition to an interpretative declaration and that, in theory, the consent of a State or international organization to an interpretative declaration should not be presumed.[86] The argument that silence can, in certain specific circumstances, be interpreted as consent was also approved.[87] Therefore, although it would seem that the principle has been accepted, the specific circumstances in which mere silence may be interpreted as acquiescence or consent have yet to be determined. Some members contended that it was not possible to identify in the abstract those situations in which the silence of a State or international organization constituted acquiescence or consent to an interpretative declaration. Because an enumeration of such situations would be difficult and possibly futile, the circumstances of a State's reaction of silence should be examined on a case-by-case basis.[88] Another view was that the legal consequences of such silence should be assessed in the light of article 31, paragraph 3 (*a*), of the Vienna Convention; consequently, the general rules for entering into an agreement were sufficient to resolve the issue.[89] It was also agreed that silence had a legal effect in cases where a protest against the interpretation given in an interpretative declaration would be expected from the State or international organization directly concerned. The arbitral award in the *North Atlantic Coast Fisheries Case (Great Britain, United States)*[90] was cited as an example. It was further argued that silence on the part of a Contracting Party must be considered to play a role in the event of a dispute between that party and the author of the interpretative declaration.[91] Likewise, one delegation maintained that consent could be inferred from silence in the case of treaties the subject matter of which would require a prompt reaction to any interpretative declaration.[92]

43. The second question, which dealt with the legal effects of an interpretative declaration on its author and on a State or an international organization having approved or objected to the declaration, produced a wide range of reactions and positions. It was generally stressed that a distinction must be drawn between the legal effect of interpretative declarations and that of reservations, and that that distinction should be borne in mind when considering the question of reactions to declarations and to reservations and their respective effects.[93] It was stated that the general rules governing the interpretation of treaties were sufficient to establish the effects of an interpretative declaration and the reactions it might prompt. According to the same view, a reference to those customary rules could resolve the issue within the framework of the Guide to Practice[94] without prejudice to the flexibility of those rules or to the essential role played by the intention of the parties. Some delegations specifically referred to article 31, paragraph 3 (*a*), of the 1969 Vienna Convention.[95] According to another point of view, the consequences of an interpretative declaration should be considered in the light of the principle of estoppel.[96] Thus, the author of an interpretative declaration was bound by the interpretation expressed only if another Contracting Party came to rely on the declaration.[97] It was also suggested that interpretative declarations could act as an aid to interpretation.[98] As far as reactions of opposition were concerned, it was stressed that, although they could limit the potential legal consequences of interpretative declarations, they could not in any way exclude application of the provision in question in the relationship between the author of the declaration and the party having expressed opposition.[99]

---

[81] *Ibid.*, para. 77.

[82] *Ibid.*, paras. 67–124.

[83] *Ibid.*, paras. 16–18.

[84] *Ibid.*, para. 26.

[85] *Ibid.*, paras. 27–28.

[86] France (*Official Records of the General Assembly, Sixty-third Session, Sixth Committee*, 19th meeting (A/C.6/63/SR.19), para. 19); Belarus (*ibid.*, para. 51); Argentina (*ibid.*, para. 74); Netherlands (20th meeting (A/C.6/63/SR.20), para. 9); Portugal (*ibid.*, para. 21); New Zealand (22nd meeting (A/C.6/63/SR.22), para. 7); Japan (23rd meeting (A/C.6/63/SR.23), para. 45); Greece (24th meeting (A/C.6/63/SR.24), para. 2).

[87] Argentina (*ibid.*, 19th meeting (A/C.6/63/SR.19), para. 74); Qatar (24th meeting (A/C.6/63/SR.24), para. 77). See, however, China (19th meeting (A/C.6/63/SR.19), para. 67); Netherlands (20th meeting (A/C.6/63/SR.20), para. 9); Sweden, on behalf of the Nordic countries (19th meeting (A/C.6/63/SR.19), para. 40); United Kingdom (21st meeting (A/C.6/63/SR.21), para. 18).

[88] Spain (*ibid.*, 22nd meeting (A/C.6/63/SR.22), para. 4). See, however, New Zealand (*ibid.*, para. 7); Japan (23rd meeting (A/C.6/63/SR.23), para. 45).

[89] Sweden (*ibid.*, 19th meeting (A/C.6/63/SR.19), para. 39); Germany (*ibid.*, para. 80).

[90] Arbitral award of 7 September 1910, UNRIAA, vol. XI, pp. 173–226.

[91] France (*Official Records of the General Assembly, Sixty-third Session, Sixth Committee*, 19th meeting (A/C.6/63/SR.19), para. 19).

[92] Romania (*ibid.*, 21st meeting (A/C.6/63/SR.21), para. 55).

[93] France (*ibid.*, 19th meeting (A/C.6/63/SR.19), para. 18); Romania (*ibid.*, 21st meeting (A/C.6/63/SR.21), para. 54).

[94] Austria (*ibid.*, 18th meeting (A/C.6/63/SR.18), para. 79); France (*ibid.*, 19th meeting (A/C.6/63/SR.19), para. 20); Belarus (*ibid.*, para. 49); Belgium (*ibid.*, 21st meeting (A/C.6/63/SR.21), para. 46); Greece (*ibid.*, 24th meeting (A/C.6/63/SR.24), para. 1).

[95] Sweden, on behalf of the Nordic countries (*ibid.*, 19th meeting (A/C.6/63/SR.19), para. 39); Germany (*ibid.*, paras. 81 and 83).

[96] Belarus (*ibid.*, para. 52); Germany (*ibid.*, para. 81).

[97] Austria (*ibid.*, 18th meeting (A/C.6/63/SR.18), para. 79); Germany (*ibid.*, 19th meeting (A/C.6/63/SR.19), para. 81).

[98] United Kingdom (*ibid.*, 21st meeting (A/C.6/63/SR.21), para. 19).

[99] Germany (*ibid.*, 19th meeting (A/C.6/63/SR.19), para. 82).

44. Aside from the suggestions and criticisms made with regard to the wording of the guidelines already approved by the Commission that the Special Rapporteur and the Commission would consider during their second reading, it was suggested more generally that the subject of reactions to interpretative declarations was not sufficiently ripe for codification and that, therefore, drafting guidelines in that respect would go beyond the mandate of the Commission.[100] Other delegations, however, expressed support for the inclusion of such guidelines in the Guide to Practice.[101]

45. Several delegations expressed reservations about the concept of "reclassification", which they believed did not reflect reality. According to that view, it was pointless to change the classification of a declaration, since it could be assessed objectively according to criteria already agreed by the Commission.[102] Other delegations expressed support for the guideline presented by the Special Rapporteur.[103]

46. Other reservations were expressed with regard to the issue of "conditional interpretative declarations" and the separate treatment given to them in the study. Like the majority of Commission members,[104] several delegations argued that there was no reason to distinguish such declarations from reservations, since they obeyed the same rules.[105] According to another view, the pure and simple assimilation of conditional interpretative declarations with reservations nevertheless remained premature as long as the specific legal effects of those declarations had not been analysed by the Commission.[106]

D. Recent developments with regard to reservations and interpretative declarations

47. On 3 February 2009, ICJ rendered a unanimous judgment in the case concerning *Maritime Delimitation in the Black Sea (Romania v. Ukraine)*. In that dispute, Romania invoked paragraph 3 of its interpretative declaration made upon signature and confirmed upon ratification of the United Nations Convention on the Law of the Sea of 1982. That declaration concerns article 121 of the Convention and reads as follows:

> 1. As a geographically disadvantaged country bordering a sea poor in living resources, Romania reaffirms the necessity to develop international cooperation for the exploitation of the living resources of the economic zones, on the basis of just and equitable agreements that should ensure the access of the countries from this category to the fishing resources in the economic zones of other regions or subregions.
>
> 2. The Socialist Republic of Romania reaffirms the right of coastal States to adopt measures to safeguard their security interests, including the right to adopt national laws and regulations relating to the passage of foreign warships through their territorial sea.
>
> The right to adopt such measures is in full conformity with articles 19 and 25 of the Convention, as it is also specified in the Statement by the President of the United Nations Conference on the Law of the Sea in the plenary meeting of the Conference on April 26, 1982.
>
> 3. The Socialist Republic of Romania states that according to the requirements of equity—as it results from articles 74 and 83 of the Convention on the Law of the Sea—the uninhabited islands and without economic life can in no way affect the delimitation of the maritime spaces belonging to the main land coasts of the coastal States.[107]

48. According to Romania, Ukraine accepted the applicability of article 121, paragraph 3, of the Montego Bay Convention in the delimitation of the continental shelf and exclusive economic zones, as interpreted by Romania when signing and ratifying it, and therefore Serpents' Island, which lies off the coasts of Romania and Ukraine, could not affect the delimitation between the two States.[108]

49. For its part, Ukraine stated, invoking the Commission's work on interpretative declarations, that its silence could not amount to consent to Romania's declaration because there is no obligation to respond to such a declaration.[109]

50. The Court seems to have admitted that point of view:

> Regarding Romania's declaration, quoted in paragraph 35 above, the Court observes that under Article 310 of UNCLOS, a State is not precluded from making declarations and statements when signing, ratifying or acceding to the Convention, provided these do not purport to exclude or modify the legal effect of the provisions of UNCLOS in their application to the State which has made a declaration or statement. The Court will therefore apply the relevant provisions of UNCLOS as interpreted in its jurisprudence, in accordance with Article 31 of the Vienna Convention on the Law of Treaties of 23 May 1969. Romania's declaration as such has no bearing on the Court's interpretation.[110]

51. The concrete implications of that judgment will be discussed in the study of the effects of an interpretative declaration and the responses to which it might give rise.

52. For their part, the bodies created within the United Nations or by international human rights conventions have continued to develop and harmonize their approaches to this issue at inter-committee meetings. Those meetings provide a forum for the bodies to exchange their views on the subject of their experiences in reservations. Their respective practices in the field were presented and discussed at the meeting between the Commission and the representatives of human rights

---

[100] United States of America (*ibid.*, 21st meeting (A/C.6/63/SR.21), paras. 4–6); United Kingdom (*ibid.*, para. 16). See also Islamic Republic of Iran (*ibid.*, 24th meeting (A/C.6/63/SR.24), para. 32).

[101] France (*ibid.*, 19th meeting (A/C.6/63/SR.19), para. 18); Sweden, on behalf of the Nordic countries (*ibid.*, para. 35); Spain (*ibid.*, 22nd meeting (A/C.6/63/SR.22), para. 2); Greece (*ibid.*, 24th meeting (A/C.6/63/SR.24), para. 1). See, however, Poland (*ibid.*, 21st meeting (A/C.6/63/SR.21), para. 31).

[102] Austria (*ibid.*, 18th meeting (A/C.6/63/SR.18), para. 80); Sweden, on behalf of the Nordic countries (*ibid.*, 19th meeting (A/C.6/63/SR.19), para. 36). See also Portugal (*ibid.*, 20th meeting (A/C.6/63/SR.20), para. 19); Greece (*ibid.*, 24th meeting (A/C.6/63/SR.24), para. 3). For another critical view on "reclassifications", see Republic of Korea (*ibid.*, 19th meeting (A/C.6/63/SR.19), para. 62).

[103] Mexico (*ibid.*, 20th meeting (A/C.6/63/SR.20), para. 4); Romania (*ibid.*, 21st meeting (A/C.6/63/SR.21), para. 54).

[104] See paragraph 38 above.

[105] Belarus (*Official Records of the General Assembly, Sixty-third Session, Sixth Committee*, 19th meeting (A/C.6/63/SR.19), paras. 49 and 50); Republic of Korea (*ibid.*, para. 62); Estonia (*ibid.*, para. 88); Netherlands (*ibid.*, 20th meeting (A/C.6/63/SR.20), para. 8); Spain (*ibid.*, 22nd meeting (A/C.6/63/SR.22), para. 2).

[106] Portugal (*ibid.*, 20th meeting (A/C.6/63/SR.20), para. 22).

[107] United Nations, *Treaty Series*, vol. 1835, No. 31363, pp. 88–89.

[108] *Maritime Delimitation in the Black Sea (Romania v. Ukraine), Judgment, I.C.J. Reports 2009*, p. 76, para. 35; CR 2008/18, 2 September 2008, paras. 39–41 (M. Aurescu); CR 2008/20, 4 September 2008, paras. 73–79 (M. Lowe).

[109] *Ibid.*, p. 77, para. 39. See also CR 2008/29, 12 September 2008, paras. 63–68 (Mme Malintoppi).

[110] *Ibid.*, p. 78, para. 42.

bodies, held in May 2007 pursuant to General Assembly resolution 61/34 of 4 December 2006.[111] At the meeting, the practice of human rights bodies was said to be relatively uniform and characterized by a high level of pragmatism.[112]

53. At the December 2006 meeting of the Working Group on Reservations to examine the report on the practice of human rights treaty bodies with respect to reservations to international human rights treaties and report on its work to the inter-committee meeting, the recommendations adopted in June[113] were modified. The sixth inter-committee meeting welcomed the report of the working group on reservations[114] and accepted the recommendations thus modified:[115]

1. The working group welcomes the report on the practice of human rights treaty bodies with respect to reservations to international human rights treaties (HRI/MC/2005/5) and its updated version (HRI/MC/2005/5/Add.1) which the secretariat had compiled for the fourth inter-committee meeting.

2. The working group recommends that while any statement made at the time of ratification may be considered as a reservation, however it was termed, particular care should be exercised before concluding that the statement should be considered as a reservation, when the State party has not used that term.

3. The working group recognizes that, despite the specific nature of the human rights treaties which do not constitute a simple exchange of obligations between States but are the legal expression of the essential rights that each individual must be able to exercise as a human being, general treaty law remains applicable to human rights instruments; however, that law can only be applied taking fully into account their specific nature, including their content and monitoring mechanisms.

4. The working group considers that when reservations are permitted, whether explicitly or implicitly, they can contribute to the attainment of the objective of universal ratification. Reservations which are not permitted, including those that are incompatible with the object and purpose of the treaty, do not contribute to attainment of the objective of universal ratification.

5. The working group considers that for the purpose of discharging their functions, treaty bodies are competent to assess the validity of reservations and, in the event, the implications of a finding of invalidity of a reservation, particularly in the examination of individual communications or in exercising other fact-finding functions in the case of treaty bodies that have such competence.

6. The working group considers that the identification of criteria for determining the validity of reservations in the light of the object and purpose of a treaty may be useful not only for States when they are considering making reservations, but also for treaty bodies in the performance of their functions. In this regard, the working group notes the potential significance of the criteria contained in the draft guidelines included in the tenth report of the Special Rapporteur of the International Law Commission on reservations to treaties (A/CN.4/558/Add.1). The working group appreciated its dialogue with the International Law Commission and welcomes the prospect of further dialogue.

7. As to the consequences of invalidity, the working group agrees with the proposal of the Special Rapporteur of the International Law Commission according to which an invalid reservation is to be considered null and void. It follows that a State will not be able to rely on such a reservation and, unless its contrary intention is incontrovertibly established, will remain a party to the treaty without the benefit of the reservation.

8. The working group welcomes the inclusion of a provision on reservations in the draft harmonized guidelines on reporting under the international human rights treaties, including the common core document and treaty-specific reports (HRI/MC/2006/3).

9. The working group recommends that:

(*a*) Treaty bodies should request in their lists of issues information, especially when it is provided neither in the common core document (where available), nor in the treaty-specific report, about:

(i) the nature and scope of reservations or interpretative declarations;

(ii) the reason why such reservations were considered to be necessary and have been maintained;

(iii) the precise effect of each reservation in terms of national law and policy;

(iv) any plans to limit the effect of reservations and ultimately withdraw them within a specific time frame.

(*b*) Treaty bodies should clarify to States parties their reasons for concern over particular reservations in light of the provisions of the treaty concerned and, as relevant, its object and purpose.

(*c*) Treaty bodies should in their concluding observations:

(i) welcome the withdrawal, whether total or partial, of a reservation;

(ii) acknowledge ongoing reviews of reservations or expressions of willingness to review;

(iii) express concern for the maintenance of reservations;

(iv) encourage the complete withdrawal of reservations, the review of the need for them or the progressive narrowing of scope through partial withdrawals of reservations.

(*d*) Treaty bodies should highlight the lack of consistency among reservations formulated to certain provisions protected in more than one treaty and encourage the withdrawal of a reservation on the basis of the availability of better protection in other international conventions resulting from the absence of a reservation to comparable provisions.

10. The working group recommends that the inter-committee meeting and the meeting of chairpersons decide whether another meeting of the working group should be convened taking into account the reactions and queries of treaty bodies on the recommendations of the working group, the outcome of the meeting with the International Law Commission and any further developments in the International Law Commission on the subject of reservations to treaties.[116]

54. The most remarkable change relates to paragraph 7, on the consequences the formulation of an invalid reservation has for the convention obligation of the author of the reservation. The previous text placed the emphasis on the intention of the State "at the time it enters its reservation", an intention which must be determined "during a serious examination of the available information, with the presumption, which may be refuted, that a State would prefer to remain a party to the treaty without the benefit of the reservation".[117] The new formulation of paragraph 7 places the emphasis solely on the presumption that the State entering an invalid reservation has the intention to remain bound by the treaty without the benefit of the reservation as long as its contrary intention has not been "incontrovertibly"

[111] See, in the annex to the present report, the account of the meeting prepared by the Special Rapporteur. See also paragraph 24 above.

[112] See paragraph 7 of the annex to the present report.

[113] HRI/MC/2006/5, para. 16; see also the eleventh report on reservations to treaties, *Yearbook ... 2006*, vol. II (Part One), document A/CN.4/574, para. 55.

[114] HRI/MC/2007/5 and Add.1.

[115] See the report of the nineteenth meeting of chairpersons of human rights treaty bodies, (A/62/224, annex, subpara. 48 (*v*)).

[116] HRI/MC/2007/5, para. 19.

[117] HRI/MC/2006/5, para. 16 (7).

established—which perhaps goes a little far (and in any case does not reflect the Special Rapporteur's position).

55. In the context of the universal periodic review mechanism, the Human Rights Council has raised the issue of reservations with States under review, and a number of them have been urged to withdraw their reservations to international human rights instruments.[118]

56. At the regional level, the Inter-American Court of Human Rights has again had to face the issue of reservations. In *Boyce et al. v. Barbados*, the Court had to rule on the effects of the respondent State's reservation to the American Convention on Human Rights. This reservation reads:

In respect of 4(4), the criminal code of Barbados provides for death by hanging as a penalty for murder and treason. The Government is at present reviewing the whole matter of the death penalty which is only rarely inflicted but wishes to enter a reservation on this point in as much as treason in certain circumstances might be regarded as a political offence and falling within the terms of section 4(4).

In respect of 4(5) while the youth or old age of an offender may be matters which the Privy Council, the highest Court of Appeal, might take into account in considering whether the sentence of death should be carried out, persons of 16 years and over or over 70 years of age may be executed under Barbadian law.[119]

57. Barbados maintained *inter alia* that its reservation to the Convention prevented the Court from ruling on the question of capital punishment, on the one hand, and the means of carrying it out, on the other.

58. Citing its advisory opinions of 1982 and 1983,[120] the Court recalled:

Firstly, in interpreting reservations the Court must first and foremost rely on a strictly textual analysis. Secondly, due consideration must also be assigned to the object and purpose of the relevant treaty which, in the case of the American Convention, involves the "protection of the basic rights of individual human beings". In addition, the reservation must be interpreted in accordance with Article 29 of the Convention, which implies that a reservation may not be interpreted so as to limit the enjoyment and exercise of the rights and liberties recognized in the Convention to a greater extent than is provided for in the reservation itself.[121]

59. Having considered the reservation of Barbados from this standpoint, the Court concluded that:

The text of the reservation does not explicitly state whether a sentence of death is mandatory for the crime of murder, nor does it address whether other possible methods of execution or sentences are available under Barbadian law for such a crime. Accordingly, the Court finds that a textual interpretation of the reservation entered by Barbados at the time of ratification of the American Convention clearly indicates that this reservation was not intended to exclude from the jurisdiction of this Court neither the mandatory nature of the death penalty nor the particular form of execution by hanging. Thus the State may not avail itself of this reservation to that effect.[122]

60. The Court emphasizes, moreover, that it "has previously considered that 'a State reserves no more than what is contained in the text of the reservation itself' ".[123] These findings relate to the interpretation of reservations, an issue hitherto neglected in the work of the Commission, and the effects of reservations; they are very useful, and should be taken into consideration when the Committee considers these issues.

61. The European Court of Human Rights, for its part, has also had occasion to rule on the extent of the effects of a valid reservation. In two cases against Finland, the Court referred to and considered the application of the reservation of Finland to the European Convention for the Protection of Human Rights and Fundamental Freedoms.[124] The reservation reads as follows:

For the time being, Finland cannot guarantee a right to an oral hearing insofar as the current Finnish laws do not provide such a right. This applies to:

1. Proceedings before the Supreme Court in accordance with Chapter 30, Section 20, of the Code of Judicial Procedure and proceedings before the Courts of Appeal as regards the consideration of petition, civil and criminal cases to which Chapter 26 (661/1978), Sections 7 and 8, of the Code of Judicial Procedure are applied if the decision of a District Court has been made before 1 May 1998, when the amendments made to the provisions concerning proceedings before Courts of Appeal entered into force;

And the consideration of criminal cases before the Supreme Court and the Courts of Appeal if the case has been pending before a District Court at the time of entry into force of the Criminal Proceedings Act on 1 October 1997 and to which existing provisions have been applied by the District Court; ...

3. Proceedings, which are held before the Insurance Court as the Court of Final Instance, in accordance with Section 9 of the Insurance Court Act, if they concern an appeal which has become pending before the entry into force of the Act Amending the Insurance Court Act on 1 April 1999;

4. Proceedings before the Appellate Board for Social Insurance, in accordance with Section 8 of the Decree on the Appellate Board for Social Insurance, if they concern an appeal which has become pending before the entry into force of the Act Amending the Health Insurance Act on 1 April 1999.

62. According to the Court, the application of this reservation deprives the applicant of the right, otherwise guaranteed in the context of article 6 of the Convention, to be heard:

In view of the above and having regard to the terms of Finland's reservation, Finland was under no Convention obligation to ensure in respect of the Court of Appeal that an oral hearing was held on count 9. While it is true that the effect of the reservation was to deny the applicant a right to an oral hearing as to the charge in dispute before the Court of Appeal, this result must be considered compatible with the Convention as a consequence of the operation of a valid reservation" (see *Helle v. Finland*, Judgment of 19 December 1996, *Reports 1997*, pp. 2925–2926, §§ 44 and 47).[125]

[118] HRI/MC/2008/5, para. 3. See the reports of the Working Group on the Universal Periodic Review, Bahrain (A/HRC/8/19, para. 6 (2)), Tunisia (A/HRC/8/21, para. 83 (3)), Morocco (A/HRC/8/22, para. 75 (3)), Indonesia (A/HRC/8/23, para. 76 (2)), United Kingdom (A/HRC/8/25, para. 56 (24) to (26)), India (A/HRC/8/26, para. 86 (9)), Algeria (A/HRC/8/29, para. 69 (10)) and Netherlands (A/HRC/8/31, para. 78 (10)).

[119] United Nations, *Treaty Series*, vol. 1298, (No. A-17955) p. 441.

[120] Advisory opinion OC-2/82, 24 September 1982, *Effect of Reservations on the Entry into Force of the American Convention on Human Rights (Arts. 74 and 75), Series A, No. 2*, para. 35; advisory opinion OC-3/83, 8 September 1983, *Restrictions to the Death Penalty (Arts. 4(2) and 4(4)) American Convention on Human Rights, Series A, No. 3*, paras. 62–66.

[121] *Boyce et al. v. Barbados*, Series C, No. 169, para. 15 (footnotes omitted).

[122] *Ibid.*, para. 17.

[123] *Ibid.* See also advisory opinion OC–3/83 (footnote 120 above), para. 69.

[124] United Nations, *Treaty Series*, vol. 2158, No. A-2889, p. 140.

[125] Judgement of 12 April 2007, *Laaksonen v. Finland* (Application No. 70216/01), para. 24—the judgement is available only in English. See also judgement of 24 April 2007, *V. v. Finland* (Application No. 40412/98), para. 61.

63. Nevertheless—and on this point the decisions of the European Court of Human Rights are reminiscent of the decision of the Inter-American Court[126]—the application of the reservation does not release Finland from the obligation to respect the other guarantees associated with the right to a fair trial. As the reservation relates only to the issue of the right to an oral hearing before certain courts, Finland remains bound by its obligation to ensure a fair trial. The reservation of Finland could thus not exclude the applicability of article 6 as a whole, and the Court remains competent to rule on the obligations that are not covered by the reservations.[127]

64. In the context of the Council of Europe (in the Committee of Legal Advisers on Public International Law), the member States are continuing to consider and, where necessary, react collectively or at least in a concerted manner to invalid reservations, in conformity with Recommendation No. 12 (99) 13 on responses to inadmissible reservations to international treaties.[128] Since 2004, the European Observatory of Reservations to International Treaties has been considering from a more sectoral standpoint the reservations and declarations to the international treaties relating to the fight against terrorism. It is interesting to note in this respect that the list submitted periodically by the European Observatory to the Committee containing the reservations and declarations to international treaties that are likely to give rise to objections not only reproduces reservations formulated less than 12 months previously, the limit set by article 20, paragraph 5 of the 1969 and 1986 Vienna Conventions, but also draws the attention of member States to certain reservations formulated more than 12 months earlier.[129] This practice appears to suggest that the Observatory does not consider that these reservations whose validity it deems to be open to dispute can no longer be the subject of objections, and that a response, belated though it may be, remains not only possible but also desirable. This confirms that guideline 2.6.15 (late objections), adopted in 2008, probably meets a need.[130]

E. Plan of the fourteenth report on reservations[131]

65. Following a rapid presentation of certain additional points relating to the procedure with respect to the formulation of interpretative statements in accordance with the wishes of the Commission,[132] the present report will deal with the third and fourth parts of the Guide to Practice, that is to say with issues relating to the validity of reservations,[133] interpretative declarations and reactions to reservations and interpretative declarations, on the one hand, and the effects of reservations, acceptances of reservations, objections to reservations, interpretative declarations and the reactions to them, on the other hand. If possible, a fourth part will deal with the guidelines that might be adopted by the Commission on the basis of the valuable study drawn up by the Codification Division on "reservations in the context of the succession of States".

66. Furthermore, the Special Rapporteur has decided to propose to the Commission the addition of two annexes to the Guide to Practice. The first of these might consist of a recommendation relating to the "reservations dialogue", since, upon reflection, it seems difficult to incorporate provisions relating to this in the body of the Guide: it is more, however, a state of mind that is reflected in a desirable diplomatic practice than an exercise in codification, however flexible the latter may be. As for the second annex, it could deal with the implementation mechanism that might be incorporated in the Guide to Practice. These two draft annexes will be the subject of two separate parts of the present report.

[126] See paragraphs 56–60 above.

[127] Judgement of 12 April 2007, *Laaksonen v. Finland* (Application No. 70216/01), para. 25; judgement of 24 April 2007, *V. v. Finland* (application No. 40412/98), para. 61.

[128] See also the third report on reservations to treaties, *Yearbook ... 1998*, vol. II (Part One), document A/CN.4.491 and Add.1–6, paras. 28–29; the eighth report, *Yearbook ... 2003*, vol. II (Part One), document A/CN.4/535, para. 23; and the eleventh report, *Yearbook ... 2006*, vol. II (Part One), document A/CN.4/574, para. 56.

[129] See, for example, the United States reservation to the United Nations Convention against Corruption, formulated in 2003, CAHDI (2008) 15, 7 October 2008, appendix VII, No. C.5.

[130] *Yearbook ... 2008*, vol. II (Part Two), para. 124.

[131] The Special Rapporteur wishes to express his most profound gratitude to Daniel Müller, doctoral student and researcher at the International Law Centre (CEDIN) of Université Paris Ouest, Nanterre-La Défense, for the decisive role he played in drafting the present report.

[132] See paragraph 36 above.

[133] One part of this problem has already been the subject of the tenth report on reservations (*Yearbook ... 2005*, vol. II (Part One), document A/CN.4/558 and Add.1–2). A number of draft guidelines in the third part have already been provisionally adopted by the Commission (see paragraph 23 above).

CHAPTER I

Procedure for the formulation of interpretative declarations (*continuation and conclusion*)

67. At its sixtieth session, in 2008, the Commission asked the Special Rapporteur to prepare guidelines on the form, statement of reasons for and communication of interpretative declarations in order to fill a gap in the second part of the Guide to Practice.[134]

68. The Commission has already adopted a set of rules on the procedure for the formulation of interpretative declarations, contained in section 2.4 of the Guide to Practice. These guidelines concern the authorities competent to formulate an interpretative declaration (guideline 2.4.1[135]), formulation of an interpretative declaration at the internal level (guideline 2.4.2 [2.4.1 *bis*][136]), time

[134] *Yearbook ... 2008*, vol. II (Part Two), paras. 74 and 117; see also the position taken by the Special Rapporteur in his thirteenth report on reservations to treaties (*Yearbook ... 2008*, vol. II (Part One), document A/CN.4/600), para. 46. See also paragraph 36 above.

[135] *Yearbook ... 2002*, vol. II (Part Two), p. 46.

[136] *Ibid.*, p. 47.

at which an interpretative declaration may be formulated (guideline 2.4.3[137]), non-requirement of confirmation of interpretative declarations made when signing a treaty (guideline 2.4.4 [2.4.5][138]), late formulation of an interpretative declaration (guideline 2.4.6 [2.4.7][139]) and modification of an interpretative declaration (guideline 2.4.9[140]). This section also includes other guidelines on conditional interpretative declarations.[141]

69. There is no guideline on the form of interpretative declarations, on their communication (contrary to what has been decided in the case of conditional interpretative declarations[142]) or on modification of interpretative declarations. This is not an oversight, but a deliberate decision on the Special Rapporteur's part.[143] As he explained in his sixth report:

> There seems to be no reason to transpose the rules governing the communication of reservations to simple interpretative declarations, which may be formulated orally; it would therefore be paradoxical to insist that they be formally communicated to other interested States or international organizations. By refraining from such communication, the author of the declaration runs the risk that the declaration may not have the intended effect, but this is a different problem altogether. It does not seem necessary, therefore, to include a clarification of this point in the Guide to Practice.[144]

70. There is no reason to reconsider this conclusion. There would be no justification for requiring a State or an international organization to follow a given procedure in giving its interpretation of a convention to which it is a party or a signatory or to which it intends to become a party. It would thus be incongruous to propose guidelines that made the formal validity of an interpretative declaration conditional upon respect for such a procedure.[145]

71. Nevertheless, while there is no legal obligation in that regard, it seems appropriate to ensure, to the extent possible, that interpretative declarations are publicized widely. Their influence will, in practice, depend to a great extent on their dissemination. Without discussing, at this stage, the legal implications of these declarations for the interpretation and application of the treaty in question, it goes without saying that such unilateral statements are likely to play a role in the life of the treaty; this is their *raison d'être* and the purpose for which they are formulated by States and international organizations. ICJ has highlighted the importance of these statements in practice:

> Interpretations placed upon legal instruments by the parties to them, though not conclusive as to their meaning, have considerable probative value when they contain recognition by a party of its own obligations under an instrument.[146]

72. Mr. Rosario Sapienza also underlined the importance of reactions to interpretative declarations, which:

> Will contribute usefully to the settlement [of a dispute]. Statements will be still more useful to the interpreter when there is no dispute, but only a problem of interpretation.[147]

73. In her study, *Einseitige Interpretationserklarungen zu multilateralen Verträgen* (Unilateral interpretative declarations to multilateral treaties), Ms. Monika Heymann has rightly stressed:

> In that regard, it should be noted that a simple written interpretative declaration can take on greater importance because the other contracting parties take note of it and, in the event of a dispute, it has greater probative value.[148]

74. Moreover, in practice, States and international organizations endeavour to give their interpretative declarations the desired publicity. They transmit them to the depositary and the Secretary-General of the United Nations, in turn, disseminates the text of such declarations[149] and publishes them in *Multilateral Treaties Deposited with the Secretary-General.*[150] Clearly, this communication procedure, which ensures wide publicity, presupposes that declarations are made in writing.

75. If the authors of interpretative declarations want their position to be taken into account in the treaty's application, particularly when there is a dispute, it would doubtless be in their interest to:

(*a*) Formulate the reaction in writing to meet the requirements of legal security and to ensure notification of the declaration; and

(*b*) Follow, in making such statements, the same communication and notification procedure applicable to the communication and notification of other declarations in respect of the treaty (reservations, objections or acceptances).

---

[137] *Yearbook ... 2001*, vol. II (Part Two), p. 192.

[138] *Ibid.*, p. 193.

[139] *Ibid.*, p. 194.

[140] *Yearbook ... 2004*, vol. II (Part Two), pp. 108–109.

[141] Guidelines 2.4.5 [2.4.4], 2.4.7 [2.4.2, 2.4.9], 2.4.8 and 2.4.10.

[142] See guideline 2.4.7 [2.4.2, 2.4.9] on the formulation and communication of interpretative declarations. This guideline reads:

"**2.4.7 [2.4.2, 2.4.9]** *Formulation and communication of conditional interpretative declarations*

"1. A conditional interpretative declaration must be formulated in writing.

"2. Formal confirmation of a conditional interpretative declaration must also be made in writing.

"3. A conditional interpretative declaration must be communicated in writing to the contracting States and contracting organizations and other States and international organizations entitled to become parties to the treaty.

"4. A conditional interpretative declaration regarding a treaty in force which is the constituent instrument of an international organization or a treaty which creates an organ that has the capacity to accept a reservation must also be communicated to such organization or organ."

[143] *Yearbook ... 2001*, vol. II (Part Two), p. 157, para. 154.

[144] *Yearbook ... 2001*, vol. II (Part One), document A/CN.4/518 and Add.1, para. 130.

[145] See also Heymann, *Einseitige Interpretationserklärungen zu multilateralen Verträgen* (*Unilateral interpretative declarations to multilateral treaties*), p. 117.

[146] Advisory opinion of 11 July 1950, *International Status of South-West Africa, I.C.J. Reports 1950*, pp. 135–136.

[147] *Dichiarazioni interpretative unilaterale e trattati internazionali*, p. 275.

[148] *Op. cit.*, p. 118.

[149] *Summary of Practice of the Secretary-General as Depositary of MultilateralTreaties* (United Nations publication, Sales No. E.94.V.15), document ST/LEG/7/Rev.1, para. 218.

[150] To give just one example, while article 319 of the United Nations Convention on the Law of the Sea does not explicitly require its depositary to communicate interpretative declarations made under article 311 of the Convention, the Secretary-General publishes them systematically in chapter XXI (No. 6) of *Multilateral Treaties Deposited with the Secretary-General* (http://treaties.un.org/).

76. The Commission has considered that it would be useful to include guidelines to that effect in the Guide to Practice.[151] However, these could consist only of recommendations modelled on those adopted, for example, with respect to statements of reasons for reservations[152] and objections to reservations.[153] Guidelines recommending the written form and the procedure for communication could draw upon those concerning the procedure for other types of declarations in respect of a treaty, as, for example, contained in guidelines 2.1.1[154] and 2.1.5 to 2.1.7[155] on reservations, although their wording cannot be fully aligned with these models. It is therefore proposed that these guidelines should be worded as follows:[156]

[151] See footnote 134 above.

[152] Guideline 2.1.9 (Statement of reasons [for reservations]) (*Yearbook ... 2008*, vol. II (Part Two), para. 124); see also the note by the Special Rapporteur on draft guideline 2.1.9, "Statement of reasons for reservations" (*Yearbook ... 2007*, vol. II (Part One), document A/CN.4/586).

[153] Guideline 2.6.10 (Statement of reasons [for objections]) (*Yearbook ... 2008*, vol. II (Part Two), para. 124); see also the eleventh report on reservations to treaties (*Yearbook ... 2006*, vol. II (Part One), document A/CN.4/574), paras. 110–111.

[154] This guideline reads:

"**2.1.1** *Written form*

"A reservation must be formulated in writing."

[155] These guidelines read:

"**2.1.5** *Communication of reservations*

"1. A reservation must be communicated in writing to the contracting States and contracting organizations and other States and international organizations entitled to become parties to the treaty.

"2. A reservation to a treaty in force which is the constituent instrument of an international organization or to a treaty which creates an organ that has the capacity to accept a reservation must also be communicated to such organization or organ.

"**2.1.6 [2.1.6, 2.1.8]** *Procedure for communication of reservations*

"1. Unless otherwise provided in the treaty or agreed by the contracting States and international contracting organizations, a communication relating to a reservation to a treaty shall be transmitted:

"(*a*) If there is no depositary, directly by the author of the reservation to the contracting States and contracting organizations and other States and international organizations entitled to become parties to the treaty; or

"(*b*) If there is a depositary, to the latter, which shall notify the States and international organizations for which it is intended as soon as possible.

"2. A communication relating to a reservation shall be considered as having been made with regard to a State or an international organization only upon receipt by that State or organization.

"3. Where a communication relating to a reservation to a treaty is made by electronic mail or by facsimile, it must be confirmed by diplomatic note or depositary notification. In such a case the communication is considered as having been made at the date of the electronic mail or the facsimile.

"**2.1.7** *Functions of depositaries*

"1. The depositary shall examine whether a reservation to a treaty formulated by a State or an international organization is in due and proper form and, if need be, bring the matter to the attention of the State or international organization concerned.

"2. In the event of any difference appearing between a State or an international organization and the depositary as to the performance of the latter's functions, the depositary shall bring the question to the attention of:

"(*a*) The signatory States and organizations and the contracting States and contracting organizations; or

"(*b*) Where appropriate, the competent organ of the international organization concerned."

[156] The numbering of these guidelines will certainly need to be reviewed during the second reading.

"**2.4.0** *Written form of interpretative declarations*

"Whenever possible, an interpretative declaration should be formulated in writing.

"**2.4.3 *bis*** *Communication of interpretative declarations*

"Whenever possible, an interpretative declaration should be communicated, *mutatis mutandis*, in accordance with the procedure established in guidelines 2.1.5, 2.1.6 and 2.1.7."

77. This raises the question of whether the depositary can initiate a consultation procedure in cases where an interpretative declaration is manifestly invalid, in which case guideline 2.1.8[157] should also be mentioned in guideline 2.4.3 *bis*. Since, on the one hand, guideline 2.1.8 has met with criticism[158] and, on the other, it is far from clear that an interpretative declaration can be "valid" or "invalid", it seems unnecessary to make such a mention.

78. Notwithstanding the position expressed by some members of the Commission at its sixtieth session, in 2008, with which the Special Rapporteur had unwisely agreed in his thirteenth report on reservations to treaties,[159] statements of reasons for interpretative declarations do not appear to correspond to the practice of States and international organizations or, in essence, to meet a need. In formulating interpretative declarations, States and international organizations doubtless wish to set forth their position concerning the meaning of one of the treaty's provisions or of a concept used in the text of the treaty and, in general, they explain the reasons for this position. It is not necessary, or even possible, to provide explanations for these explanations. Thus, a guideline, even in the form of a simple recommendation, is not needed.

79. The situation is different with respect to reactions to interpretative declarations. In this case, the authors of an approval, opposition or reclassification may indeed explain the reasons that led them to react to the interpretative declaration in question, for example by explaining why the proposed interpretation does not correspond to the parties' intention, and it is doubtless useful for them to do so. Guideline 2.9.6 (Statement of reasons for approval, opposition and reclassification), proposed in the thirteenth report[160] and sent to the Drafting Committee in 2008,[161] is thus of continuing value.

[157] This guideline reads:

"**2.1.8 [2.1.7 *bis*]** *Procedure in case of manifestly invalid reservations*

"1. Where, in the opinion of the depositary, a reservation is manifestly invalid, the depositary shall draw the attention of the author of the reservation to what, in the depositary's view, constitutes the grounds for the invalidity of the reservation.

"2. If the author of the reservation maintains the reservation, the depositary shall communicate the text of the reservation to the signatory States and international organizations and to the contracting States and international organizations and, where appropriate, the competent organ of the international organization concerned, indicating the nature of legal problems raised by the reservation."

[158] *See Yearbook ... 2006*, vol. II (Part Two), pp. 157–158, paras. (2)–(3) of the commentary to draft guideline 2.1.8. See also paragraph 36 above.

[159] See footnote 134 above.

[160] *Yearbook ... 2008*, vol. II (Part One), document A/CN.4/600, para. 46.

[161] See paragraph 39 above.

CHAPTER II

Validity of reservations and interpretative declarations (*continuation and conclusion*)

80. The Special Rapporteur began his study of the validity of reservations and interpretative declarations in 2005 in his tenth report on reservations to treaties.[162] In the second part of this report, he plans to conclude this study, with a view to the full adoption on first reading of part III of the Guide to Practice on the topic "Validity of reservations and interpretative declarations".

81. The Commission has already adopted several guidelines in part III.[163] There can be no question of reopening the debate on these guidelines, which were adopted following a full discussion of the tenth report on reservations to treaties, nor would it seem useful to reconsider the terminology used in part III, particularly the term "validity", which was approved by the Commission after a lengthy discussion.[164] However, in order to understand the guidelines proposed in this report for inclusion in part III of the Guide to Practice, it seems appropriate to recall the context of the issue of the validity of reservations and to briefly review the guidelines already adopted by the Commission in 2006 and 2007[163] (sect. A), before addressing the related issue of the validity of reactions to reservations (sect. B). A study of the validity of interpretative declarations is included for the sake of completeness rather than for its practical implications (sect. C). The same is true for the study of the validity of reactions to interpretative declarations (sect. D). The issue of the validity of conditional interpretative declarations will be dealt with in a separate short study (sect. E).

82. The Commission has also already discussed the issues relating to determination of the validity of reservations, which were set forth by the Special Rapporteur in his tenth report.[165] The corresponding guidelines were referred by the Commission to the Drafting Committee in 2006[166] but have not yet been adopted by the Committee; it is to be hoped that they will be adopted this year at last. They may need to be supplemented with guidelines on determination of the validity of reactions to reservations, of interpretative declarations and of reactions to interpretative declarations (sect. F).

83. Guidelines 3.3 and 3.3.1, which were proposed by the Special Rapporteur in his tenth report[167] and deal with the consequences of the validity of reservations, have also been referred to the Drafting Committee;[168] it is therefore unnecessary to discuss them further. However, it may be appropriate to consider their place in the Guide to Practice since they relate more to the effects of reservations (or the lack thereof) than to their validity *per se*.[169]

84. Similarly, in 2006, the Special Rapporteur decided upon reflection that it was doubtless preferable to defer a decision on guidelines 3.3.2 to 3.3.4,[170] which also deal with the consequences of the (non-)validity of a reservation, until the Commission had considered the effects of reservations.[171] Accordingly, the Commission has not yet taken any action on these guidelines. They should be included in part IV of the Guide to Practice, on the effects of reservations and interpretative declarations, and will be considered again in chapter III of this report.

A. Validity of reservations (background)

85. Part III of the Guide to Practice begins with a study of the issue of the substantive validity of reservations. It does not consider the consequences of the validity or non-validity of a reservation; it merely addresses the issue of whether the basic conditions for the validity of

---

[162] *Yearbook ... 2005*, vol. II (Part One), document A/CN.4/558 and Add.1–2.

[163] *Yearbook ... 2006*, vol. II (Part Two), p. 134, para. 104; and *Yearbook ... 2007*, vol. II (Part Two), p. 16, para. 47. See also paragraphs 8 and 23 above.

[164] *Yearbook ... 2005*, vol. I, 2859th meeting, pp. 12–13; *Yearbook ... 2005*, vol. II (Part Two), p. 64, para. 345. For a summary of the Sixth Committee's discussion of this terminological issue, see the eleventh report on reservations to treaties, *Yearbook ... 2006*, vol. II (Part One), document A/CN.4/574, paras. 19 to 22.

[165] *Yearbook ... 2005*, vol. II (Part One), document A/CN.4/558 and Add.1–2. See also paragraphs 5 and 13 above.

[166] *Yearbook ... 2005*, vol. I, 2859th meeting, p. 204; *Yearbook ... 2005*, vol. II (Part Two), pp. 25–26, para. 103. See also paragraph 7 above.

[167] *Yearbook ... 2005*, vol. II (Part One), document A/CN.4/558 and Add.1–2, pp. 183–186, paras. 181–194. The text of these guidelines reads:

"**3.3** *Consequences of the non-validity of a reservation*

"A reservation formulated in spite of the express or implicit prohibition arising from the provisions of the treaty or from its incompatibility with the object and the purpose of the treaty is not valid, without there being any need to distinguish between these two grounds for invalidity.

"**3.3.1** *Non-validity of reservations and responsibility*

"The formulation of an invalid reservation produces its effects within the framework of the law of treaties. It shall not, in itself, engage the responsibility of the State or international organization which has formulated it."

[168] *Yearbook ... 2006*, vol. II (Part Two), p. 134, para. 104. See also paragraph 6 above.

[169] *Ibid.*, para. 157.

[170] The text of these guidelines, as proposed by the Special Rapporteur in his tenth report on reservations to treaties (*Yearbook ... 2005*, vol. II (Part One), document A/CN.4/558 and Add.1–2, paras. 195–208), reads:

"**3.3.2** *Nullity of invalid reservations*

"A reservation that does not fulfil the conditions for validity laid down in guideline 3.1 is null and void.

"**3.3.3** *Effect of unilateral acceptance of an invalid reservation*

"Acceptance of a reservation by a contracting State or by a contracting international organization shall not change the nullity of the reservation.

"**3.3.4** *Effect of collective acceptance of an invalid reservation*

"1. A reservation that is explicitly or implicitly prohibited by the treaty or which is incompatible with its object and purpose, may be formulated by a State or an international organization if none of the other Contracting Parties object to it after having been expressly consulted by the depositary.

"2. During such consultation, the depositary shall draw the attention of the signatory States and international organizations and of the contracting States and international organizations and, where appropriate, the competent organ of the international organization concerned, to the nature of legal problems raised by the reservation."

[171] *Yearbook ... 2006*, vol. II (Part Two), p. 138, para. 157.

reservations have been met. This is consistent with the underlying logic of the entire Guide to Practice: before the legal regime of a reservation can be considered, it must be determined whether a unilateral statement constitutes a reservation. In order for it to do so, the statement must be consistent with the definition provided in article 2, paragraph 1 (*d*), of the 1969 and 1986 Vienna Conventions, as specified and supplemented in part I of the Guide to Practice. Only after the reservation has been classified is it possible to assess the validity of its form—the subject of part II of the Guide to Practice—and content—the subject of part III of the Guide. The legal effects of a reservation may be determined only subsequently and, moreover, depend not only on its validity but on the reactions of other States and international organizations.

86. The substantive validity of reservations is determined primarily by article 19 of the 1969 and 1986 Vienna Conventions. For this reason, guideline 3.1 (Permissible reservations)[172] reproduces, verbatim, the provisions of article 19 of the 1986 Vienna Convention. The purpose of guidelines 3.1.1 to 3.1.13 is to set forth the conditions for substantive validity that are listed in this key provision of the reservations regime derived from the Vienna Conventions.

87. Guideline 3.1.1 (Reservations expressly prohibited by the treaty)[173] explains the meaning of the words "prohibited by the treaty" and specifies the meaning of article 19 (*a*) of the 1969 and 1986 Vienna Conventions.

88. Guideline 3.1.2 (Definition of specified reservations)[174] explains the concept of *specified* reservations, mentioned in article 19 (*b*) of the 1969 and 1986 Vienna Conventions. Where a treaty expressly allows only specified reservations to be made—or formulated,[175] in the case of specified reservations for which the content is not made explicit in the treaty[176]—any other reservation that does not meet the criteria established by the treaty is considered to be prohibited.

89. While guideline 3.1.5 (Incompatibility of a reservation with the object and purpose of the treaty)[177] does not establish a directly operational definition of the concept of the "object and purpose of the treaty", it does indicate when, as a general rule, a reservation should be considered as contrary to the object and purpose of the treaty and attempts to clarify the wording of article 19 (*c*) of the 1969 and 1986 Vienna Conventions. This occurs when a reservation has the potential to "affect an essential element of the treaty that is necessary to its general thrust, in such a way that the reservation impairs the *raison d'être* of the treaty".

90. Nevertheless, the guideline does not establish a solid criterion for determining whether a reservation is incompatible with the object and purpose of the treaty. Therefore, it seems appropriate to provide further clarification of the manner in which the object and purpose of a treaty should be determined and to illustrate this methodology through specific examples.[178]

91. Guideline 3.1.6 (Determination of the object and purpose of the treaty)[179] performs the first of these functions by establishing the method to be followed in determining the object and purpose of a treaty.

92. The role and function of guidelines 3.1.7 (Vague or general reservations),[180] 3.1.8 (Reservations to a provision reflecting a customary norm),[181] 3.1.9 (Reservations contrary to a rule of *jus cogens*),[182] 3.1.10 (Reservations to provisions relating to non-derogable rights),[183] 3.1.11 (Reservations relating to internal law),[184] 3.1.12 (Reservations to general human rights treaties)[185] and 3.1.13 (Reservations to treaty provisions concerning dispute settlement or the monitoring of the implementation of the treaty)[186] are to provide specific examples of reservations that for one reason or another (as explained in these guidelines) may be considered incompatible with the object and purpose of the treaty in question. These reasons may concern either the nature of the treaty or the specific provision to which the reservation refers, or the characteristics of the reservation itself (for example, its vague or general formulation or the fact that it relates to unspecified rules of domestic law).

93. In addition, guideline 3.1.3 (Permissibility of reservations not prohibited by the treaty) states that even where the treaty prohibits certain reservations, reservations which are not prohibited by the treaty must nevertheless be consistent with the object and purpose of the treaty. Guideline 3.1.4 (Permissibility of specified reservations) contains a similar rule for specified reservations where their content is not specified in the treaty. Such reservations must also meet the criterion established in article 19 (*c*) of the 1969 and 1986 Vienna Conventions.

B. Validity of reactions to reservations

94. Unlike the case of reservations, the 1969 and 1986 Vienna Conventions do not set forth any criteria or conditions for the substantive validity of reactions to reservations, although they deal extensively with acceptances and objections. Such reactions do not, however, constitute criteria for the validity of a reservation that can be evaluated objectively in accordance with the conditions established in article 19 of the Vienna Conventions. They are a way for States and international organizations to express their point of view regarding the validity of a reservation, but the validity (or non-validity) of a reservation must be evaluated independently of the acceptances or objections to which it gave rise. Moreover, this idea is

[172] For the text of this guideline and the commentaries thereto, see *Yearbook ... 2006*, vol. II (Part Two), pp. 145–147.

[173] *Ibid.*, pp. 147–150.

[174] *Ibid.*, pp. 150–154.

[175] See paragraph 93 below.

[176] Cf. guideline 3.1.4 and the commentary thereto (*Yearbook ... 2006*, vol. II (Part Two), pp. 155–156).

[177] *Yearbook ... 2007*, vol. II (Part Two), pp. 33–37.

[178] *Ibid.*, p. 37, para. (15) of the commentary.

[179] *Ibid.*, pp. 37–39.

[180] *Ibid.*, pp. 39–42.

[181] *Ibid.*, pp. 42–46.

[182] *Ibid.*, pp. 46–48.

[183] *Ibid.*, pp. 48–50.

[184] *Ibid.*, pp. 50–52.

[185] *Ibid.*, pp. 52–53.

[186] *Ibid.*, pp. 53–55.

clearly expressed in guideline 3.3 (Consequences of the non-validity of a reservation).[187]

95. The *travaux préparatoires* of the Vienna regime in respect of objections leave no doubt as to the lack of connection between the validity of a reservation and the reactions thereto.[188] It also follows that while it may be appropriate to refer to the substantive "validity" of an objection or acceptance, the term does not have the same connotation as in the case of reservations themselves. The main issue is whether the objection or acceptance can produce its full effects.

1. Validity of objections

96. In his eleventh report on reservations to treaties, the Special Rapporteur proposed the following wording for guideline 2.6.3:

2.6.3 *Freedom to make objections*

A State or an international organization may formulate an objection to a reservation for any reason whatsoever, in accordance with the provisions of the present Guide to Practice.[189]

97. The Commission referred this guideline to the Drafting Committee, which nevertheless decided to defer consideration of the matter.[190] Apart from the question of whether objections are a "freedom" or a genuine "right"—which the Drafting Committee could settle—the Committee preferred to wait until the Special Rapporteur submitted a study on the validity of objections before deciding on the final wording of the guideline. In other words, the guideline must take the issue of validity into account. The eleventh report (which justifies this provision)[191] should therefore be seen as a preface to the study on the issue of the validity of objections.

98. In its 1951 advisory opinion, ICJ made an analogy between the validity of objections and that of reservations. It considered that:

> The object and purpose of the Convention thus limit both the freedom of making reservations and that of objecting to them. It follows that it is the compatibility of a reservation with the object and purpose of the Convention that must furnish the criterion for the attitude of a State in making the reservation on accession as well as for the appraisal by a State in objecting to the reservation. Such is the rule of conduct which must guide every State in the appraisal which it must make, individually and from its own standpoint, of the admissibility of any reservation.[192]

99. This position was endorsed by the Commission in article 20, paragraph 2 (*b*) on the law of treaties, adopted on first reading in 1962. The paragraph provides that:

> An objection to a reservation by a State which considers it to be incompatible with the object and purpose of the treaty precludes the entry into force of the treaty as between the objecting and the reserving State, unless a contrary intention shall have been expressed by the objecting State.[193]

100. In subsequent *travaux*, the Commission and the United Nations Conference on the Law of Treaties removed this requirement that objections to reservations must be compatible with the object and purpose of the treaty.[194] In accordance with the principle of consent that underlies all treaty law, "[n]o State can be bound by contractual obligations it does not consider suitable".[195] Moreover, in its 1951 advisory opinion *Reservations to the Convention on the Prevention and Punishment of the Crime of Genocide*, ICJ had stressed that "it is well established that in its trade relations a State cannot be bound without its consent, and that consequently no reservation can be effective against any State without its agreement thereto".[196] In other words, a State may make an objection to any reservation, whether valid or invalid (including as a result of its incompatibility with the object and purpose of the treaty).

101. Does this absence of a link between the validity of a reservation and an objection mean that the substantive validity of objection is no longer an issue? Or is it possible to envisage a situation in which an objection might be incompatible with the object and purpose of the treaty or contrary to a treaty-based prohibition?

102. Regardless of whether the reservation is compatible or incompatible with the object and purpose of the treaty, any objection results, *a priori*, in exclusion of the application of the treaty as a whole (if the author has "clearly" stated that that is its intention) or, as stipulated

[187] See footnote 167 above.

[188] See the eleventh report on reservations to treaties (*Yearbook ... 2006*, vol. II (Part One), document A/CN.4/574), paras. 61–66.

[189] *Ibid.*, para. 67.

[190] *Yearbook ... 2008*, vol. II (Part Two), footnote 233. The Commission also referred guideline 2.6.4 (Freedom to oppose the entry into force of the treaty *vis-à-vis* the author of the reservation), which reads:

"**2.6.4** *Freedom to oppose the entry into force vis-à-vis the author of the reservation*

"A State or international organization that formulates an objection to a reservation may oppose the entry into force of the treaty as between itself and the reserving State or international organization for any reason whatsoever, in accordance with the provisions of the present Guide to Practice"

(*Yearbook ... 2006*, vol. II (Part One), document A/CN.4/574, para. 75).

[191] See the eleventh report on reservations to treaties (*Yearbook ... 2006*, vol. II (Part One), document A/CN.4/574), paras. 60–75.

[192] Advisory opinion of 28 May 1951, *Reservations to the Convention on the Prevention and Punishment of the Crime of Genocide, I.C.J. Reports 1951*, p. 24.

[193] *Yearbook ... 1962*, vol. II, p. 176.

[194] See the eleventh report on reservations to treaties (*Yearbook ... 2006*, vol. II (Part One), document A/CN.4/574), paras. 61 and 62.

[195] Tomuschat, "Admissibility and legal effects of reservations to multilateral treaties", p. 466; see also the second report on reservations to treaties (*Yearbook ... 1996*, vol. II (Part One), document A/CN.4/477 and Add.1), p. 57, paras. 97 and 99; and Müller, "Article 20", in *Les Conventions de Vienne sur le droit des traités: Commentaire article par article*, Corten and Klein, eds., pp. 809–811, paras. 20–24.

[196] See Advisory Opinion cited in footnote 192 above, p. 21. The dissenting judges also stressed this principle in their joint opinion: "The consent of the parties is the basis of treaty obligations. The law governing reservations is only a particular application of this fundamental principle, whether the consent of the parties to a reservation is given in advance of the proposal of the reservation or at the same time or later" (*ibid.*, pp. 31–32). The famous dictum of the Permanent Court of International Justice in the case of the *S.S. "Lotus"* confirms this position: "The rules of law binding upon States therefore emanate from their own free will as expressed in conventions or by usages generally accepted as expressing principles of law and established in order to regulate the relations between these co-existing independent communities or with a view to the achievement of common aims. Restrictions upon the independence of States cannot therefore be presumed." (*P.C.I.J., Series A*, No. 10, p. 18). The arbitral tribunal that settled the case concerning the *Delimitation of the Continental Shelf between the United Kingdom of Great Britain and Northern Ireland, and the French Republic* also stressed the importance of the "principle ... of the mutuality of consent in the conclusion of treaties" (decision of 30 June 1977, UNRIAA, vol. XVIII, p. 40, para. 57).

in article 21, paragraph 3, of the 1969 and 1986 Vienna Conventions, in exclusion of the application of the provision to which the reservation relates. Thus, the purpose and possible effect of any objection is to undermine the integrity of the treaty regime applicable between the author of the reservation and the author of the objection.

103. This does not, however, render the objection invalid. The potential effect of an objection is simply the total or partial deregulation,[197] of the bilateral relations between the author of the objection and the author of the reservation. The author of the objection has merely exercised a right (or freedom)[198] which is recognized under the Vienna Conventions since they expressly establish the possibility of excluding, in this bilateral relationship, the application not only of some provisions, but also of the treaty as a whole. Even if an objection could have the effect of undermining the object and purpose of the treaty by excluding, for example, the application of an essential provision, it should be borne in mind that its author has the *right* (or, in any event, the freedom) to exclude all treaty relations with the author of the reservation. "He who can do more, can do less". While certainly unsatisfactory, this result is nevertheless the corollary of the formulation of the reservation (not that of the objection). It is immediately rectified when the reservation is withdrawn in order to restore the integrity of the treaty relations. A strong case can be made that, even if the reservation has the undesirable effect of depriving the treaty of an essential part of its content in its application as between the reserving State (or international organization) and the objecting State (or international organization), it is better to accept that risk in the hope that the effect will be temporary.

104. This does not prevent the authors of a reservation to which objections have been made from expressing their displeasure. A particularly telling example is the reaction of the United States of America to the objections made by France and Italy in respect of the United States "declaration" regarding the Agreement on the International Carriage of Perishable Foodstuffs and on the Special Equipment to be used for such Carriage (ATP).[199] The protest by the United States reads:

> The United States considers that under the clear language of article 10 [of the Agreement], as confirmed by the negotiating history, any State party to the Agreement may file a declaration under that article. The United States therefore considers that the objections of Italy and France and the declarations that those nations will not be bound by the Agreement in their relations with the United States are unwarranted and regrettable. The United States reserves its rights with regard to this matter and proposes that the parties continue to attempt cooperatively to resolve the issue.[200]

It should nevertheless be noted that the author of the protest (reproduced in the United Nations publication, *Status of Multilateral Treaties Deposited with the Secretary-General* under the heading "objections") does not consider that the objections made by France and Italy are invalid, but "only" that they are "unwarranted and regrettable".

105. It is quite clear that if the effect of an objection is to modify the bilateral treaty relations between its author and the author of the reservation in a manner that proves to be contrary to a peremptory norm of international law (*jus cogens*), this result would be unacceptable. Such an eventuality would, however, seem to be impossible: an objection purports only to, and can only, exclude the application of one or more treaty provisions. Such an exclusion cannot "produce" a norm that is incompatible with a *jus cogens* norm. The effect is simply "deregulatory". Ultimately, therefore, the norms applicable as between the author of the reservation and the author of the objection are never different from those that predated the treaty and, unless application of the treaty as a whole is excluded, from treaty-based provisions not affected by the reservation. It is extremely difficult—and, in fact, impossible under these circumstances—to imagine an "objection" that would violate a peremptory norm.

106. Furthermore, when the definition of "objection" was adopted, the Commission refused to take a position on the question of the validity of objections that purport to produce a "super-maximum" effect.[201] These are objections in which the authors determine not only that the reservation is not valid but also that, as a result, the treaty as a whole applies *ipso facto* in the relations between the two States. The validity of objections with super-maximum effect has frequently been questioned,[202] including by the Special Rapporteur, primarily because the effect of such a statement is not to bar the application of the treaty as a whole or of the provisions to which the reservation refers in the relations between the two parties but to render the reservation null and void without the consent of its author. This greatly exceeds the consequences of the objections to reservations provided for in article 21, paragraph 3, and article 20, paragraph 4 (*b*), of the Vienna Conventions. Whereas "unlike reservations, objections express the attitude of a State, not in relation to a rule of law, but in relation to the position adopted by another State", in this case it is the rule itself advocated by the reserving State which is challenged, and this is contrary to the very essence of an objection.[203] It is not, however, the validity of the objection as such that is called into question; the issue raised by this practice is whether the objection is capable of producing the effect intended by its author,[204] and this is far from certain. A State (or an international organization) may well make an objection

[197] In this connection, see Horn, *Reservations and Interpretative Declarations to Multilateral Treaties*, pp. 175–176.

[198] See paragraph 97 above.

[199] In their objections, France and Italy considered that "only European States can formulate the declaration provided for in article 10 with respect to carriage performed in territories situated outside Europe". The two States thus raised "an objection to the declaration by the Government of the United States of America and, consequently, declare[d] that [they would] not be bound by the ATP Agreement in [their] relations with the United States of America" (*Multilateral Treaties Deposited with the Secretary-General*, available online from http://treaties.un.org/, chap. XI.B 22).

[200] *Ibid.*

[201] See paragraph (24) of the commentary to guideline 2.6.1 (Definition of objections to reservations) (*Yearbook ... 2005*, vol. II (Part Two), p. 81).

[202] See the eighth report on reservations to treaties (*Yearbook ... 2003*, vol. II (Part One), document A/CN.4/535 and Add.1), paras. 97–98, and footnote 153.

[203] *Ibid.*, para. 97.

[204] See paragraph 95 above.

and wish to give it super-maximum effect, but this does not mean that the objection is capable of producing such an effect, which is not envisaged by the Vienna regime. However, as the Commission has acknowledged in its commentary on guideline 2.6.1, where the definition of the term "objection" unquestionably includes objections with super-maximum effect:

> The Commission has endeavoured to take a completely neutral position with regard to the validity of the effects [and not of the objection] that the author of the objection intends its objection to produce. This is a matter to be taken up in the consideration of the effects of objections.[205]

107. The same is true in the case of objections with "intermediate effect",[206] through which a State or international organization "expresses the intention to be associated with the author of the reservation but considers that the exclusion of treaty relations should go beyond what is provided for in article 21, paragraph 3, of the 1969 and 1986 Vienna Conventions".[207]

108. While treaty practice provides relatively few specific examples of intermediate-effect or "extensive" objections, some do exist. It would seem, however, that this "*nueva generación*" (new generation)[208] of objections grew up exclusively around reservations to the 1969 Vienna Convention itself. The reservations formulated by a number of States in respect of article 66 of the Vienna Convention, concerning dispute settlement procedures,[209] caused a number of other States to make objections that were broader in scope than "simple" reservations, but without stating that they did not wish to be associated with the author of the reservation through the treaty. Although a number of States parties to the Vienna Convention made objections to these reservations that were limited to the "presumed" effects envisaged in article 21, paragraph 3, of the 1969 Vienna Convention,[210] other States—Canada,[211] Egypt,[212] Japan,[213] the Netherlands,[214] New Zealand,[215] Sweden,[216] the United Kingdom[217] and the United States[218]—intended their objections to produce more serious consequences but did not wish to exclude the entry into force of the Vienna Convention as between themselves and the reserving States.[219] Indeed, these States not only wanted to exclude the application of the obligatory dispute settlement provision or provisions "to which the reservation refers"; they also do not consider themselves bound by the substantive provisions to which the dispute settlement procedure or procedures apply in their bilateral relations with the reserving State. For example, the United States, in its objection to the reservation of Tunisia to article 66 (*a*) of the Vienna Convention, states that:

> The United States Government intends, at such time as it becomes a party to the Convention, to reaffirm its objection … and declare that it will not consider that Article 53 or 64 of the Convention is in force between the United States of America and Tunisia.[220]

109. Such limitations on treaty relations between the reserving State and the objecting State are not envisaged in the wording of the Vienna Convention and the legal basis for such an intermediate effect of an objection is not clearly established either in the Vienna Convention, which does not provide for it, or in doctrine. Some authors propose to consider that "these extended objections are, in fact, reservations (limited *ratione personae*).[221] This analysis is to some extent supported by the fact that other States have chosen to formulate reservations in the strict

---

[205] See paragraph (25) of the commentary to guideline 2.6.1 (Definition of objections to reservations) (*Yearbook … 2005*, vol. II (Part Two), pp. 81–82).

[206] Eighth report on reservations to treaties, *Yearbook … 2003*, vol. II (Part One), document A/CN.4/535 and Add.1, p. 47, para. 95. See also the eleventh report on reservations to treaties, *Yearbook … 2006*, vol. II (Part One), document A/CN.4/574, p. 215, footnote 309.

[207] *Yearbook … 2006*, vol. II (Part One), document A/CN.4/574, p. 215, footnote 309.

[208] Riquelme Cortado, *Las reservas a los tratados: Lagunas y ambigüedades del Régimen de Viena*, p. 293.

[209] See the reservations formulated by Algeria (*Multilateral Treaties Deposited with the Secretary-General*, available online at http://treaties.un.org/, chap. XXIII.1), Belarus (*ibid.*), China (*ibid.*), Cuba (*ibid.*), Guatemala (*ibid.*), the Russian Federation (*ibid.*), the Syrian Arab Republic (*ibid.*), Tunisia (*ibid.*), Ukraine (*ibid.*) and Viet Nam (*ibid.*). Bulgaria, the Czech Republic, Hungary and Mongolia had formulated similar reservations but withdrew them in the early 1990s (*ibid.*). The Democratic German Republic had also formulated a reservation excluding the application of article 66 (*ibid.*).

[210] This is the case with Denmark and Germany (*ibid.*).

[211] In respect of the reservation by the Syrian Arab Republic (*ibid.*).

[212] The objection of Egypt is directed not at one reservation in particular, but at any reservation that excludes the application of article 66 (*ibid.*).

[213] In respect of any reservation that excludes the application of article 66 or the annex to the Vienna Convention (*ibid.*).

[214] In respect of all States that had formulated reservations concerning the compulsory dispute settlement procedures. This general declaration was reiterated separately for each State that had formulated such a reservation (*ibid.*).

[215] In respect of the reservation of Tunisia (*ibid.*).

[216] In respect of any reservation that excludes application of the dispute settlement provisions, in general, and of the reservations made by Cuba, the Syrian Arab Republic and Tunisia, in particular (*ibid.*).

[217] As provided in its declaration of 5 June 1987 and with the exception of the reservation of Viet Nam.

[218] The objections made by the United States were formulated before it became a Contracting Party and concern the reservations made by the Syrian Arab Republic, Tunisia and Cuba (*ibid.*).

[219] The United Kingdom made maximum-effect objections, in due and proper form, to the reservations formulated by the Syrian Arab Republic and Tunisia. The effect of these objections seems, however, to have been mitigated *a posteriori* by the declaration of the United Kingdom of 5 June 1987, which constitutes in a sense the partial withdrawal of its earlier objection (see guideline 2.7.7 and the commentary thereto (*Yearbook … 2008*, vol. II (Part Two), pp. 101–102), since the author does not oppose the entry into force of the Convention as between the United Kingdom and a State that has made a reservation to article 66 or to the annex to the Vienna Convention and excludes only the application of part V in their treaty relations. This declaration, which the United Kingdom recalled in 1989 (with regard to the reservation of Algeria) and 1999 (with regard to the reservation of Cuba), states that "[w]ith respect to any other reservation the intention of which is to exclude the application, in whole or in part, of the provisions of article 66, to which the United Kingdom has already objected or which is made after the reservation by [the Union of Soviet Socialist Republics], the United Kingdom will not consider its treaty relations with the State which has formulated or will formulate such a reservation as including those provisions of Part V of the Convention with regard to which the application of article 66 is rejected by the reservation" (*Multilateral Treaties*…(see footnote 199 above), chap. XXIII.1). Nevertheless, in 2002, the United Kingdom again objected to the maximum-effect reservation made by Viet Nam by excluding all treaty relations with Viet Nam (*ibid.*). New Zealand also chose to give its objection to the Syrian reservation maximum effect (*ibid.*).

[220] *Multilateral Treaties* … (see footnote 199 above), chap. XXIII.1.

[221] See, *inter alia*, Sztucki, "Some questions arising from reservations to the Vienna Convention on the Law of Treaties", p. 297. The author suggests that such declarations should be viewed as "objections only to the initial reservations and own reservations of the objecting States in the remaining part" (*ibid.*, p. 291).

sense of the word in order to achieve the same result.[222] Thus, Belgium formulated a (late) reservation concerning the Vienna Convention, stating that:

> The Belgian State will not be bound by articles 53 and 64 of the Convention with regard to any party which, in formulating a reservation concerning article 66 (2), objects to the settlement procedure established by this article.[223]

110. On this issue, Gaja has written:

> As a partial rejection modifies the content of the treaty in relation to the reserving State to an extent that exceeds the intended effect of the reservation, acceptance or acquiescence on the part of the reserving State appear to be necessary for a partial rejection to take its effect; failing this, no relations under the treaty are established between the reserving State and an objecting State which partially rejects those relations.[224]

111. If we agree with this way of breaking down objections with intermediate effect, the logical conclusion is that they should meet the requirements for the substantive and formal validity of reservations; they would be "counter-reservations".

112. However, this approach seems debatable. It must be borne in mind that, like any objection, objections with intermediate effect are made in reaction to a reservation formulated by another State. They typically do not arise until after the objecting State has become a party to the treaty, which, generally speaking, prevents it from formulating a reservation within the time period established in the 1969 and 1986 Vienna Conventions and reproduced in guideline 1.1 of the Guide to Practice.[225] A contracting State that wished to react to a reservation through an objection of intermediate effect would inevitably be faced with the uncertainties that characterize the regime of late reservations. This is, moreover, true of the reservation of Belgium:[226] a simple objection on the grounds of the reservation's lateness would have sufficed for it to be deemed invalid as to form and without effect. Thus, the State that formulated the initial reservation would have had little difficulty in convincing other States; it would merely have had to formulate a (simple) objection in order to prevent the reservation from having effect.

113. Only the formulation of a "preventive" reservation in place of an anticipated "objection", as in the case of the reservation formulated by the United Republic of Tanzania upon accession to the Vienna Convention in 1976,[227] remains possible and appears capable of producing the desired result. It is, however, quite often difficult for States to anticipate, when expressing their consent to be bound by a treaty, all possible reservations and to evaluate their potential effects in order to formulate a preventive "counter-reservation" at that time.[228]

114. Thus, there can be no question of simply equating objections with intermediate effect to reservations; to do so would seriously undermine the principle of consent.[229] Furthermore, the Commission has already agreed that these are indeed objections, not reservations; the definition of "objection" in guideline 2.6.1[230] clearly establishes that not only unilateral declarations that purport to exclude the legal effects of the reservation or treaty as a whole, but also those that purport to "modify the legal effects of the reservation", constitute objections. This wording has been incorporated into the definition of "objection" specifically in order to reflect the actual practice in respect of objections with intermediate effect.[231] Except in the context of a "reservations dialogue", which can become complicated, the reserving State is not, in principle, in a position to respond effectively to such objections.

115. It should be noted that, while the 1969 and 1986 Vienna Conventions do not expressly authorize these objections with intermediate effect, they do not prohibit them. On the contrary, objections with intermediate effect, as their name indicates, may be entertained in that they fall midway between the two extremes envisaged under the Vienna regime: they purport to prohibit the application of the treaty to an extent greater than a minimum-effect objection (art. 21, para. 3, of the Vienna Conventions), but less than a maximum-effect objection (art. 20, para. 4 (*b*) of the Vienna Conventions).[232]

116. It would, however, be unacceptable for States and international organizations to use a reservation as an excuse for attaching intermediate-effect objections of their choosing, thereby excluding any provision that they do not like. A look back at the origins of objections with intermediate effect would be edifying.

117. This practice has been resorted to mainly, if not exclusively, in the case of reservations and objections to the provisions of part V of the 1969 Vienna Convention and makes clear the reasons which led objecting States to seek, in a sense, to expend the intended effects of their objections. Article 66 of the Vienna Convention and its annex relating to compulsory conciliation provide procedural guarantees which many States, at the time when the Convention was adopted, considered essential in order to prevent abuse of other provisions of part V.[233] This link was stressed by some of the States that formulated objections with intermediate effect in respect of reservations to article 66. For example:

[222] The reservation of Belgium quoted below is quite similar in spirit, purpose and technique to the conditional objections envisaged in guideline 2.6.14. See, *inter alia*, the objection of Chile to the 1969 Vienna Convention, quoted in the commentary to guideline 2.6.14 (*Yearbook ... 2008*, vol. II (Part Two), para. (2)).

[223] *Multilateral Treaties* ... (see footnote 199 above), chap. XXIII.1.

[224] Gaja, "Unruly treaty reservations", p. 326. See also Baratta, *Gli effetti delle riserve ai trattati*, p. 385.

[225] *Yearbook ... 1998*, vol. II (Part Two), pp. 99–100. See also guideline 1.1.2, *ibid.*, pp. 103–104.

[226] See paragraph 109 above.

[227] The reservation of the United Republic of Tanzania states: "Article 66 of the Convention shall not be applied to the United Republic of Tanzania by any State which enters a reservation on any provision of Part B or the whole of that part of the Convention" (*Multilateral Treaties* ... (see footnote 199 above), chap. XXIII.1).

[228] On that issue, see Horn, *op. cit.* (footnote 197 above), p. 179.

[229] See footnote 196 above.

[230] *Yearbook ... 2005*, vol. II (Part Two), p. 77.

[231] *Ibid.*, p. 81, para. (23) of the commentary to guideline 2.6.1. See also *Yearbook ... 2004*, vol. II (Part Two), p. 100, para. 293 (*d*).

[232] Müller, "Article 21", in Corten and Klein (eds.), *op. cit.* (footnote 195 above), pp. 925–926, paras. 67–69.

[233] Sztucki, *loc. cit.* (footnote 221 above), pp. 286–287 (see also the references provided by the author).

> The Kingdom of the Netherlands is of the view that the provisions regarding the settlement of disputes, as laid down in article 66 of the Convention, are an important part of the Convention and cannot be separated from the substantive rules with which they are connected.[234]

The United Kingdom stated even more explicitly that:

> Article 66 provides in certain circumstances for the compulsory settlement of disputes by the International Court of Justice … or by a conciliation procedure … These provisions are inextricably linked with the provisions of Part V to which they relate. Their inclusion was the basis on which those parts of Part V which represent progressive development of international law were accepted by the Vienna Conference.[235]

Thus, the reaction of several States to reservations to article 66 of the 1969 Vienna Convention was aimed at safeguarding the package deal which some States had sought to undermine through reservations and which could only be restored through an objection that went beyond the "normal" effects of the reservations envisaged by the Vienna Conventions.[236]

118. It is therefore clear from the practice concerning objections with intermediate effect that there is an intrinsic link between the provision which gave rise to the reservation and the provisions whose legal effect is affected by the objection. However, this is not a condition for the validity of the objection. On the one hand, there is no evidence that this is a "practice accepted as law". On the other hand, it would be contradictory to make objections with intermediate effect subject to conditions of validity while maximum-effect objections are not subject to such conditions. Indeed, determination and assessment of the necessary link between the provisions which could potentially be deprived of legal effect by the interaction between a reservation and a broad objection has more to do with the question of whether the objection with intermediate effect can produce the effect intended by its author. It is one thing to say that an objection with intermediate effect is not valid and quite another to maintain that such an objection cannot produce the effect intended by its author. Thus, the issue does not bear on the validity of an objection and should therefore be included not in the part of the Guide to Practice on the substantive validity of declarations in respect of treaties, but rather in the part dealing with the effects that an objection with intermediate effect can actually produce.

119. It follows from the foregoing that a State or organization has the right (or the freedom) to formulate an objection without this right (or freedom) being subject to conditions for substantive validity, as in the case of reservations. While some of the intended effects of an objection may appear undesirable—as, for example, the lack of any treaty-based relations between the author of the reservation and the author of the objection—this is simply a logical consequence of the principle of consent. It is the author of the reservation, not the reaction of the other Contracting Parties, that challenges the integrity of the treaty. As ICJ noted:

> It is well established that in its treaty relations a State cannot be bound without its consent, and that consequently no reservation can be effective against any State without its agreement thereto.[237]

120. Furthermore, it should be reiterated that one who has initially accepted a reservation to an objection may no longer properly formulate an objection thereto. While this condition may be understood as a condition for the substantive validity of an objection, it may also be viewed as a question of form or of formulation. Thus, guideline 2.8.12, of which the Commission took note in 2008[238] and which it is expected to finalize in 2009, provides:

"**2.8.12** *Final nature of acceptance of a reservation*

"Acceptance of a reservation cannot be withdrawn or amended."

There would seem to be no need to revisit this issue.

2. Validity of acceptances

121. With regard to acceptance, and in the light of the Commission's earlier work on the validity of reservations, it also seems unnecessary to address the issue of the validity of acceptances of a reservation.

122. It seems clear that contracting States or international organizations can freely accept a reservation that is valid and that the validity of such acceptances cannot be questioned. However, at least on the face of it, such is not the case where a State or international organization accepts a reservation that is substantively non-valid.

123. While acceptance cannot determine the validity of a reservation,[239] commentators have argued that:

> An acceptance of an inadmissible reservation is theoretically not possible. Directly or indirectly prohibited reservations under article 19 (1) (*a*) and (*b*) cannot be accepted by any confronted state. Such reservations and acceptances of these will not have any legal effects. (…) Similarly, an incompatible reservation under article 19 (1) (*c*) should be regarded as incapable of acceptance and as *eo ipso* invalid and without any legal effect.[240]

124. The Special Rapporteur shares this view. It does not follow, however, that acceptance of a non-valid reservation is *ipso facto* invalid. It seems more accurate to state that it simply cannot produce the legal effects intended by its author, not because of the non-validity of the acceptance but because of the non-validity of the reservation. The acceptance itself may not be characterized as valid or non-valid. In his tenth report on reservations to treaties, the Special Rapporteur has already maintained that "acceptance of a reservation by a contracting State or by a contracting international organization shall not change the nullity of the reservation",[241] but the issue in that case is not the validity of the acceptance, but that of the reservation.

---

[234] *Multilateral Treaties* ...(see footnote 199 above), chap. XXIII.1. See also footnote 214 above.

[235] United Kingdom, objection of 5 June 1987 in respect of a Soviet reservation to article 66 of the Vienna Convention (see footnote 219 above).

[236] Müller, "Article 21", *loc. cit.* (footnote 195 above), pp. 927–928, para. 70.

[237] *I.C.J. Reports 1951*, p. 21.

[238] *Yearbook ... 2008*, vol. II (Part Two), para. 77.

[239] See paragraphs 94–95 above.

[240] Horn, *op. cit.* (footnote 197 above), p. 121.

[241] Guideline 3.3.3 (Effect of unilateral acceptance of an invalid reservation), proposed in the tenth report (*Yearbook ... 2005*, vol. II (Part One), document A/CN.4/558 and Add.1–2, para. 202).

The aim of this draft guideline is not to determine the effects of acceptance of a reservation by a State, but simply to establish that, if the reservation in question is invalid, it remains null even if it is accepted. This observation accords with article 21, which envisages the effects of reservations only if they are "established" in accordance not only with articles 20 and 23 of the Vienna Conventions but also, explicitly, with article 19. Furthermore, the principle established in draft guideline 3.3.3 is in line with the provisions of article 20; in particular, it does not exclude the possibility that acceptance may have other effects, in particular, of allowing the entry into force of the treaty with regard to the reserving State or international organization.[242]

The response to the question as to the conditions under which, in these circumstances, a treaty may enter into force for the author of the reservation and what the content of its treaty obligations would then be is in no way affected by the acceptance; it is solely dependent on the validity of the reservation and on the effects that its author intended it to produce.

125. Furthermore, to argue that no acceptance of a non-invalid reservation may, in turn, be considered valid would prevent the Contracting Parties from collectively accepting such a reservation. Yet "it can be argued that the Parties always have a right to amend the treaty by general agreement *inter se* in accordance with article 39 of the 1969 and 1986 Vienna Conventions and that nothing prevents them from adopting unanimous agreement to that end on the subject of reservations".[243]

126. Moreover, in the light of the presumption contained in article 20, paragraph 5, of the 1969 and 1986 Vienna Conventions, States or international organizations which have remained silent on a reservation, whether valid or not,[244] are deemed to have "accepted" the reservation. If every acceptance were subject to conditions of validity, it would have to be concluded that the tacit acceptance that these States or international organizations are presumed to have expressed was not valid, which is absurd.[245]

3. Conclusions regarding reactions to reservations

127. In the light of the above, it is clear that, as in the case of objections, the 1969 and 1986 Vienna Conventions do not establish conditions for the substantive validity of acceptances and that it would be unwise to speak of the substantive validity of reactions to reservations, regardless of whether the latter are valid. Should the Commission deem it necessary to adopt a guideline to that effect, which strikes the Special Rapporteur as unnecessary,[246] it might read:

"**3.4**[247] *Substantive validity of acceptances and objections*

"Acceptances of reservations and objections to reservations are not subject to any condition of substantive validity."

C. Validity of interpretative declarations

128. The 1969 and 1986 Vienna Conventions do not contain any rule on interpretative declarations as such, or, of course, on the conditions for the validity of such unilateral declarations. From that point of view, and from many others as well, they are distinct from reservations and cannot simply be equated with them.

129. The definition of "interpretative declarations" provided in guideline 1.2 (Definition of interpretative declarations) is also limited to identifying the practice in positive terms:

"Interpretative declaration" means a unilateral statement, however phrased or named, made by a State or by an international organization whereby that State or that organization purports to specify or clarify the meaning or scope attributed by the declarant to a treaty or to certain of its provisions.[248]

However, this definition, as noted in the commentary, "in no way prejudges the validity or the effect of such declarations and ... the same precautions taken with respect to reservations must be applied to interpretative declarations: the proposed definition is without prejudice to the permissibility and the effects of such declarations from the standpoint of the rules applicable to them".[249] The term "permissibility", used in 1999, should now be understood, as in the case of reservations, to mean "validity", a word which, in the view of the Commission,[250] seems, in all cases, to be more appropriate.

130. There is, however, still some question as to whether an interpretative declaration can be valid, a question that is clearly different from that of whether a unilateral statement constitutes an interpretative declaration or a reservation. Indeed, it is one thing to determine whether a unilateral statement "purports to specify or clarify the meaning or scope attributed by the declarant to a treaty or to certain of its provisions"—which corresponds to the definition of "interpretative declarations"—and another to determine whether the interpretation proposed therein is valid, or, in other words, whether the "meaning or scope attributed by the declarant to a treaty or to certain of its provisions" is valid.

131. The issue of the validity of interpretative declarations can doubtless be addressed in the treaty itself;[251] while this is not very common in practice, it is still a

[242] *Ibid.*, para. 203.

[243] *Ibid.*, para. 205 (footnotes omitted). In this regard, see Greig, "Reservations: equity as a balancing factor?", pp. 56–57; and Sucharipa-Behrman, "The legal effects of reservations to multilateral treaties", p. 78. This is also the position of Bowett, but he considers that the possibility does not come under the law of reservations ("Reservations to non-restricted multilateral treaties", p. 84); see Redgwell, "Universality or integrity? Some reflections on reservations to general multilateral treaties", p. 269.

[244] See, however, the position of Gaja, who contends that article 20, paragraph 5—and, indeed, all of articles 20 and 21 of the Vienna Convention—are applicable only to valid reservations ("Il regime della Convenzione di Vienna concernente le riserve inammissibili", pp. 349–361).

[245] It could no doubt be argued that article 20, paragraph 5, does not apply to non-valid reservations (*ibid.*), but how can such non-invalidity be determined *ex ante*?

[246] Its adoption would nevertheless have the "pedagogical" advantage of justifying the inclusion in the Guide to Practice of commentaries corresponding to the elements of section A above.

[247] The numbering of the guidelines proposed in the present report continues from the numbering used previously; since it has been suggested that some of the previously adopted guidelines should be moved from part III to part IV (see paragraphs 83–84 above), the Drafting Committee would have to renumber the guidelines contained in part III of the Guide to Practice.

[248] *Yearbook ... 1999*, vol. II (Part Two), p. 97.

[249] *Ibid.*, p. 103, para. (33) of the commentary.

[250] *Yearbook ... 2005*, vol. II (Part Two), p. 64, para. 345.

[251] Heymann, *op. cit.* (footnote 145 above), p. 114.

possibility. Thus, a treaty's prohibition of any interpretative declaration would invalidate any declaration that purported to "specify or clarify the meaning or scope" of the treaty or certain of its provisions. Article XV.3 of the 2001 Canada–Costa Rica Free Trade Agreement[252] is an example of such a provision. Other examples exist outside the realm of bilateral treaties. The third draft agreement for the Free Trade Area of the Americas (FTAA) of November 2003, though still in the drafting stage, states in chapter XXIV, draft article 4:

> This Agreement shall not be subject to reservations [or unilateral interpretative declarations] at the moment of its ratification.[253]

132. It is also conceivable that a treaty might merely prohibit the formulation of certain interpretative declarations to certain of its provisions. To the Special Rapporteur's knowledge, no multilateral treaty contains such a prohibition in this form. But treaty practice includes more general prohibitions which, without expressly prohibiting a particular declaration, limit the parties' capacity to interpret the treaty in one way or another. It follows that, if the treaty is not to be interpreted in a certain manner, interpretative declarations proposing the prohibited interpretation are invalid. The European Charter for Regional or Minority Languages of 5 November 1992 includes examples of such prohibition clauses; article 4, paragraph 4, states:

> Nothing in this Charter shall be construed as limiting or derogating from any of the rights guaranteed by the European Convention on Human Rights.

And article 5 states:

> Nothing in this Charter may be interpreted as implying any right to engage in any activity or perform any action in contravention of the purposes of the Charter of the United Nations or other obligations under international law, including the principle of the sovereignty and territorial integrity of States.

Similarly, articles 21 and 22 of the Framework Convention for the Protection of National Minorities of 1 February 1995 also limits the potential to interpret the Convention:

Article 21

> Nothing in the present framework Convention shall be interpreted as implying any right to engage in any activity or perform any act contrary to the fundamental principles of international law and in particular of the sovereign equality, territorial integrity and political independence of States.

Article 22

> Nothing in the present framework Convention shall be construed as limiting or derogating from any of the human rights and fundamental freedoms which may be ensured under the laws of any Contracting Party or under any other agreement to which it is a Party.

133. With the exception of treaty-based prohibitions of unilateral interpretative declarations, it would seem impossible to identify any other criterion for the substantive validity of an interpretative declaration. By definition, such declarations do not purport to modify the legal effects of the treaty, but only to specify or clarify them.[254]

134. If, on the contrary, the effect of an "interpretative declaration" is to undermine the legal effect of one of the provisions of the treaty or of the treaty as a whole, it is not an interpretative declaration but a reservation which should be treated as such and should therefore meet the conditions for the substantive (and formal) validity of reservations.

135. The Court of Arbitration that settled the dispute between France and the United Kingdom concerning the delimitation of the continental shelf in the *English Channel* case confirmed this approach. In that case, the United Kingdom maintained that the third reservation of France to article 6 of the Geneva Convention on the Continental Shelf was merely an interpretative declaration and subsequently rejected this interpretation on the grounds that it could not be invoked against the United Kingdom. The Court rejected this argument and considered that the declaration of France was not simply an interpretation; it had the effect of modifying the scope of application of article 6 and was therefore a reservation, as France had maintained:

> This condition, according to its terms, appears to go beyond mere interpretation; for it makes the application of that regime dependent on acceptance by the other State of the French Republic's designation of the named areas as involving "special circumstances" regardless of the validity or otherwise of that designation under Article 6. Article 2 (1) (*d*) of the Vienna Convention on the Law of Treaties, which both Parties accept as correctly defining a "reservation", provides that it means "a unilateral statement, however phrased or named, made by a State… whereby it purports to exclude or modify the legal effect of certain provisions of the treaty in its application to that State". This definition does not limit reservations to statements purporting to exclude or modify the actual terms of the treaty; it also covers statements purporting to exclude or modify the *legal effect* of certain provisions in their application to the reserving State. This is precisely what appears to the Court to be the purport of the French third reservation and it, accordingly, concludes that this "reservation" is to be considered a "reservation" rather than an "interpretative declaration".[255]

136. While States often maintain or suggest that an interpretation proposed by another State is incompatible with the object and purpose of the relevant treaty,[256] an interpretative declaration, by definition, cannot be contrary to the treaty or to its object or purpose. Where this is not the case, the statement is, in fact, a reservation, as noted in

[252] Article XV.3—Reservations: "This Agreement shall not be subject to unilateral reservations or unilateral interpretative declarations" (available from www.sice.oas.org/Trade/cancr/English/text_e.asp#p7c15arXV.3 (accessed 8 December 2014)).

[253] See the FTAA website, www.ftaa-alca.org/FTAADraft03/ChapterXXIV_e.asp (accessed 8 December 2014); the square brackets are original to the text.

[254] *Yearbook ... 1999*, vol. II (Part Two), p. 100 (para. (16) of the commentary to guideline 1.2.). See also the famous ICJ dictum in *Interpretation of Peace Treaties with Bulgaria, Hungary and Romania, Advisory Opinion of 18 July 1950, I.C.J. Reports 1950*, p. 229; and the 27 August 1952 judgement of the Court in *Rights of Nationals of the United States of America in Morocco (France v. the United States of America), I.C.J. Reports 1952*, p. 196.

[255] Arbitral award of 30 June 1977, UNRIAA, vol. XVIII, p. 40, para. 55.

[256] See, for example, Germany's reactions to Poland's interpretative declaration to the European Convention on Extradition of 13 December 1957 (United Nations, *Treaty Series*, vol. 1862, No. A-5146, pp. 469 and 470) and to India's declaration interpreting article 1 of the International Covenant on Civil and Political Rights and the International Covenant on Economic, Social and Cultural Rights (*Multilateral Treaties Deposited with the Secretary-General*, available online from http://treaties.un.org/, chaps. IV.3 and IV.4 respectively).

many States' reactions to "interpretative declarations".[257] Spain's reaction to the "declaration" formulated by Pakistan in signing the 1966 International Covenant on Economic, Social and Cultural Rights also demonstrates the different stages of thought in cases where the proposed "interpretation" is really a modification of the treaty that is contrary to its object and purpose. The term "declaration" must first be defined; only then will it be possible to apply to it conditions for substantive validity (of reservations):

> The Government of the Kingdom of Spain has examined the Declaration made by the Government of the Islamic Republic of Pakistan on 3 November 2004 on signature of the International Covenant on Economic, Social and Cultural Rights, of 16 December 1966.
>
> The Government of the Kingdom of Spain points out that regardless of what it may be called, a unilateral declaration made by a State for the purpose of excluding or changing the legal effects of certain provisions of a treaty as it applies to that State constitutes a reservation.
>
> The Government of the Kingdom of Spain considers that the Declaration made by the Government of the Islamic Republic of Pakistan, which seeks to subject the application of the provisions of the Covenant to the provisions of the constitution of the Islamic Republic of Pakistan is a reservation which seeks to limit the legal effects of the Covenant as it applies to the Islamic Republic of Pakistan. A reservation that includes a general reference to national law without specifying its contents does not make it possible to determine clearly the extent to which the Islamic Republic of Pakistan has accepted the obligations of the Covenant and, consequently, creates doubts as to the commitment of the Islamic Republic of Pakistan to the object and purpose of the Covenant.
>
> The Government of the Kingdom of Spain considers that the Declaration made by the Government of the Islamic Republic of Pakistan to the effect that it subjects its obligations under the International Covenant on Economic, Social and Cultural Rights to the provisions of its constitution is a reservation and that that reservation is incompatible with the object and purpose of the Covenant.
>
> According to customary international law, as codified in the Vienna Convention on the Law of Treaties, reservations that are incompatible with the object and purpose of a treaty are not permissible.
>
> Consequently, the Government of the Kingdom of Spain objects to the reservation made by the Government of the Islamic Republic of Pakistan to the International Covenant on Economic, Social and Cultural Rights.
>
> This objection shall not preclude the entry into force of the Covenant between the Kingdom of Spain and the Islamic Republic of Pakistan.[258]

137. Therefore, the issue is not the "validity" of interpretative declarations. These unilateral statements are, in reality, nothing more than reservations and will be treated as such, including with respect to their substantive and formal validity. The European Court of Human Rights followed that reasoning in its judgment in the case of *Belilos v. Switzerland*. Having reclassified Switzerland's declaration as a reservation, it applied the conditions for substantive validity of the European Convention on Human Rights:

> In order to establish the legal character of such a declaration, one must look behind the title given to it and seek to determine the substantive content. In the present case, it appears that Switzerland meant to remove certain categories of proceedings from the ambit of Article 6 § 1 (art. 6–1) and to secure itself against an interpretation of that Article (art. 6–1) which it considered to be too broad. However, the Court must see to it that the obligations arising under the Convention are not subject to restrictions which would not satisfy the requirements of Article 64 (art. 64) as regards reservations. Accordingly, it will examine the validity of the interpretative declaration in question, as in the case of a reservation, in the context of this provision.[259]

138. It would therefore seem wise to specify in a guideline that any unilateral statement, which purports to be an interpretative declaration but which in fact constitutes a reservation is subject to the conditions for the validity of a reservation.

"**3.5.1** *Conditions of validity applicable to unilateral statements which constitute reservations*

"The validity of a unilateral statement which purports to be an interpretative declaration but which constitutes a reservation must be assessed in accordance with the provisions of guidelines 3.1 to 3.1.15."

139. But it must still be determined whether a true interpretative declaration, which purports to explain the meaning of the treaty or of its provisions, can be valid or invalid where the treaty is silent.[260]

140. It goes without saying that an interpretation may be held to be with or without merit although, in absolute terms, it is difficult to determine whether the author is right or wrong until a competent body rules on the interpretation of the treaty. Interpretation remains an eminently subjective process and it is rare that a legal provision, or a treaty as a whole, can be interpreted in only one way. "The interpretation of documents is to some extent an art, not an exact science."[261]

141. As Kelsen has noted:

> If "interpretation" is understood as cognitive ascertainment of the meaning of the object that is to be interpreted, then the result of a legal interpretation can only be the ascertainment of the frame which the law that is to be interpreted represents, and thereby the cognition of several possibilities within the frame. The interpretation of a statute, therefore, need not necessarily lead to a single decision as the only correct one, but possibly to several, which are all of equal value …[262]

Jean Combacau and Serge Sur consider that:

> The process of interpretation [in international law] is, in fact, only occasionally centralized, either through a judicial body or in some other way. Competence to interpret lies with all subjects and, individually, with each one of them. The resulting proliferation of forms

[257] In addition to the aforementioned example of the reservation of Spain, see the objection of Austria to the "interpretative declaration" formulated by Pakistan in respect of the 1997 International Convention for the Suppression of Terrorist Bombings and the comparable reactions of Australia, Canada, Denmark, Finland, France, Germany, India, Israel, Italy, Japan, the Netherlands, New Zealand, Norway, Spain, Sweden, the United Kingdom and the United States of America (*Multilateral Treaties Deposited with the Secretary-General*, available online from http://treaties.un.org/, chap. XVIII.9). See also the reactions of Germany and the Netherlands to the unilateral statement of Malaysia (*ibid.*) and the reactions of Finland, Germany, the Netherlands and Sweden to the "interpretative declaration" formulated by Uruguay in respect of the Statute of the International Criminal Court (*ibid.*, chap. XVIII.10). For other examples of reclassifications, see the thirteenth report on reservations to treaties (*Yearbook ... 2008*, vol. II (Part One), document A/CN.4/600), p. 9, para. 26.

[258] *Multilateral Treaties Deposited with the Secretary-General*, available online from http://treaties.un.org/, chap. IV.3.

[259] Judgment, 29 April 1988, *Series A*, vol. 132, para. 49, p. 18.

[260] For cases in which a treaty excludes certain interpretations, see paragraphs 131–132 above.

[261] *Yearbook ... 1966*, vol. II, p. 218, para. (4) of the commentary. See also Aust, *Modern Treaty Law and Practice*, p. 230.

[262] Kelsen, *Pure Theory of Law*, p. 351.

of interpretation is only partially compensated for by their hierarchy. Unilateral interpretations are, in principle, of equal value, and the agreed forms are optional and consequently unpredictable. However, the practical difficulties must not be overestimated. It is not so much a question of an essential flaw in international law as an aspect of its nature, which guides it in its entirety towards an ongoing negotiation that can be rationalized and channelled using the rules currently in force.[263]

142. Thus, it is accepted that "on the basis of its sovereignty, every State has the right to indicate its own understanding of the treaties to which it is party".[264] If States have the right to interpret treaties unilaterally, they must also have the right to let their point of view be known as regards the interpretation of a treaty or of certain of its provisions.

143. International law does not, however, provide any criterion allowing for a definitive determination of whether a given interpretation has merit. There are, of course, methods of interpretation (see, initially, articles 31 to 33 of the 1969 and 1986 Vienna Conventions), but they are only guidelines as to the ways of finding the "right" interpretation; they do not offer a final test of whether the interpretation has merit. Thus, article 31, paragraph 1, of the Vienna Conventions specifies that "a treaty shall be interpreted in good faith in accordance with the ordinary meaning to be given to the terms of the treaty in their context and *in the light of its object and purpose**". This specification is in no way a criterion for merit, and still less a condition for the validity of the interpretations of the treaty, but a means of deriving *one* interpretation. That is all.

144. In international law, the value of an interpretation is assessed not on the basis of its content, but of its authority. It is not the "right" interpretation that wins out, but the one that was given either by all the parties to the treaty—in which case it is called an "authentic" interpretation—or by a body empowered to interpret the treaty in a manner that is binding on the parties. In that regard, the instructive 1923 opinion of the Permanent Court of International Justice in the *Jaworzina* case is noteworthy. Although the Court was convinced that the interpretation reached by the Conference of Ambassadors lacked merit, it did not approach the problem as a question of validity, but rather of opposability. The Court stated:

And even leaving out of the question the principles governing the authoritative interpretation of legal documents, it is obvious that the opinion of the authors of a document cannot be endowed with a decisive value when that opinion has been formulated after the drafting of that document and conflicts with the opinion which they expressed at that time. There are still stronger grounds for refusing to recognize the authority of such an opinion when, as in the present case, a period of more than two years has elapsed between the day on which it was expressed and the day on which the decision to be interpreted was itself adopted.[265]

145. International law in general and treaty law in particular do not impose conditions for the validity of interpretation in general and of interpretative declarations in particular. It has only the notion of the opposability of an interpretation or an interpretative declaration which, as far as it is concerned, comes into full play in the context of determination of the effects of an interpretative declaration. In the absence of any condition for validity, "simple interpretative declarations are therefore, in principle, admissible",[266] although this does not mean that it is appropriate to speak of validity or non-validity unless the treaty itself sets the criterion.[267]

146. Thus, Heymann therefore was right in stating:

International law knows no limits to the formulation of a simple interpretative declaration since treaties, regardless of the hierarchical place of their provisions in international law, are in principle interpreted in a decentralized manner and, for the entire period of their existence, must be applied and consequently interpreted. Thus, restrictions on the admissibility of simple interpretative declarations may only derive from the treaty itself. This means that a simple interpretative declaration is not prohibited, or that its formulation is not time-limited, unless the treaty in question contains special rules in that regard (translated for the report).[268]

147. In the light of these remarks, the Special Rapporteur thinks that it would be useful to include in the Guide to Practice a guideline highlighting the lack of conditions for the substantive validity of an interpretative declaration unless, of course, the treaty provides otherwise. Such a guideline could be based on article 19 of the 1969 and 1986 Vienna Conventions, which is reflected in guideline 3.1 (Permissible reservations), in so far as paragraphs (*a*) and (*b*) of the guideline cover the explicit or implicit prohibition of certain reservations by the treaty itself. This idea could be transposed to the case of interpretative declarations.

148. To the Special Rapporteur's knowledge, however, no treaty expressly authorizes "specified" interpretative declarations with a meaning corresponding to that of "specified reservations".[269] While this possibility cannot be entirely ruled out, it is difficult to imagine the purpose of such a clause or how it could be worded. Thus, in the light of its transposition to interpretative declarations, the wording of guideline 3.3 could be simplified and might simply state that the treaty-based prohibition on formulating an interpretative declaration may be express or implicit (as, for example, in the case of a treaty that permits interpretative declarations to only some of its provisions).

"**3.5** *Substantive validity of interpretative declarations*

"A State or an international organization may formulate an interpretative declaration unless the interpretative declaration is expressly or implicitly prohibited by the treaty."

149. It should also be stressed that guideline 3.3 does not include the temporal limitations on the formulation of reservations contained in article 19 of the 1969 and 1986 Vienna Conventions, which guideline 3.1

[263] Combacau and Sur, *Droit international public*, p. 171.

[264] Daillier and Pellet, *Droit international public*, 7th ed., p. 254. See also Rousseau, *Droit international public*, vol. I, *Introduction et Sources*, p. 250.

[265] Advisory opinion of 6 December 1923, *P.C.I.J., Series B*, No. 8, p. 38.

[266] Heymann, *op. cit.* (footnote 145 above), p. 113.

[267] See paragraphs 131–132 above.

[268] Heymann, *op. cit.* (footnote 145 above), p. 116.

[269] See guidelines 3.1.2 (Definition of specified reservations) and 3.1.4 (Validity of specified reservations) and the commentaries thereto (*Yearbook ... 2006*, vol. II (Part Two), pp. 150–154 and 155–156).

simply reproduces in accordance with the Commission's consistent practice. There is no such limitation in respect of interpretative declarations, as the Commission has noted elsewhere.[270] It is therefore unnecessary to mention it again in guideline 3.3.

150. Ultimately, determining the validity of interpretative declarations is infinitely more complex than in the case of reservations. A treaty-based prohibition on formulating interpretative declarations should not raise major assessment issues. A guideline specifying the rules to be followed in such cases seems unnecessary.

D. Validity of reactions to interpretative declarations (approval, opposition or reclassification)

151. The question of the validity of reactions to interpretative declarations—approval, opposition or reclassification—must be considered in the light of the study of the validity of interpretative declarations themselves. Since any State, on the basis of its sovereign right to interpret the treaties to which it is a party, has the right to make interpretative declarations, there seems little doubt that the other Contracting Parties also have the right to react to these interpretative declarations without any potential for assessment of the "validity" of their reactions.

1. Validity of approval

152. In approving an interpretative declaration, the author expresses agreement with the interpretation proposed and, in so doing, conveys its own point of view regarding the interpretation of the treaty or of some of its provisions. Thus, a State or international organization which formulates an approval does exactly the same thing as the author of the interpretative declaration.[271] It is difficult to see how this reaction could be subject to different conditions of validity than those applicable to the initial act.

153. Furthermore, the relationship between an interpretation and its acceptance is mentioned in article 31, paragraph 3 (*a*), of the 1969 and 1986 Vienna Conventions, which speak of "any subsequent agreement between the parties regarding the interpretation of the treaty or the application of its provisions".[272]

154. Logically, where the interpretative declaration itself is non-valid owing to a treaty-based prohibition, the approval will have no effect and there will be no need to declare it invalid. Without prejudice to the issue of the effects of an interpretative declaration, it seems clear that no subsequent agreement within the meaning of article 31, paragraph 3 (*a*), of the 1969 and 1986 Vienna Conventions can be established. Furthermore, the treaty-based prohibition deprives individual interpretations by States of all authority.

155. The question of whether the interpretation proposed by the author of the interpretative declaration, on the one hand, and accepted by the author of the approval, on the other, is the "right" interpretation and, as such, is capable of producing the effects desired by the key players in relation both to themselves and to other parties to the treaty[273] is, however, different from that of the validity of the declaration and the approval.[274] The first of these questions cannot be resolved until the effects of interpretative declarations are considered.

2. Validity of oppositions

156. The validity of a negative reaction—an opposition—is no more predicated upon respect for any specific criteria than is that of interpretative declarations or approvals.

157. This conclusion is particularly evident in the case of opposition expressed through the formulation of an interpretation different from the one initially proposed by the author of the interpretative declaration.[275] There is no reason to subject such a "counter-interpretative declaration", which simply proposes an alternate interpretation of the treaty or of some of its provisions, to stricter criteria and conditions for validity than the initial interpretative declaration. While it is clear that in the event of a conflict, only one of the two interpretations, at best,[276] could prevail, both interpretations should be presumed valid unless, at some point, it becomes clear to the key players that one interpretation has prevailed. In any event, the question of whether one of them, or neither of them, actually expresses the "correct" interpretation of the treaty is a different matter and has no impact on the validity of such declarations.[277]

158. This is also true in the case of a simple opposition, where the author merely expresses its refusal of the interpretation proposed in an interpretative declaration without proposing another interpretation that it considers

---

[270] In that regard, see guideline 2.4.3:

"**2.4.3** *Time at which an interpretative declaration may be formulated*

"Without prejudice to the provisions of guidelines 1.2.1, 2.4.6 [2.4.7], and 2.4.7 [2.4.8], an interpretative declaration may be formulated at any time."

(*Yearbook ... 2001*, vol. II (Part Two), pp. 192–193. See also *Yearbook ... 1999*, vol. II (Part Two), p. 101, paras. (21) and (22) of the commentary to guideline 1.2.)

[271] See the thirteenth report on reservations to treaties (*Yearbook ... 2008*, vol. II (Part One), document A/CN.4/600), pp. 12–13, paras. 42–48; see also Heymann's position (*op. cit.*, footnote 145 above, pp. 119–123).

[272] See also the thirteenth report on reservations to treaties (*Yearbook ... 2008*, vol. II (Part One), document A/CN.4/600), p. 6, para. 10. This issue was the subject of a discussion between the parties during the oral arguments in the *Dispute regarding Navigational and Related Rights*, when Costa Rica maintained that two identical interpretations in the same language by the parties constituted such an agreement (CR 2009/2 (2 March 2009), pp. 56–57, paras. 47–48 (Mr. Kohen)). Nicaragua contested this position (CR 2009/4 (5 March 2009), p. 56, paras. 28–29 (Mr. Pellet)); at the time when this report was written, the Court had not yet issued a judgement in the case.

[273] This question must be considered, in particular, in the context of article 41 of the 1969 and 1986 Vienna Conventions (Agreements to modify multilateral treaties between certain of the parties only).

[274] See paragraphs 140–144 above.

[275] See guideline 2.9.2 in the thirteenth report on reservations to treaties (*Yearbook ... 2008*, vol. II (Part One), document A/CN.4/600), para. 23.

[276] In fact, it is not impossible that a third party might not agree with either of the interpretations proposed individually and unilaterally by the parties to the treaty if, through the application of methods of interpretation, it concludes that another interpretation arises from the provisions of the treaty. See, for example, *Rights of Nationals of the United States of America in Morocco (France v. United States of America)*, Judgment of 27 August 1952, *I.C.J. Reports 1952*, p. 211.

[277] See paragraphs 140–144 above.

more "correct". Such oppositions are certainly not subject to any condition of validity. The position expressed by the author of an opposition may prove ineffective, particularly when the interpretation proposed in the interpretative declaration proves to be the most "correct", but this does not call the validity of the opposition into question and concerns only its possible effects.

3. Validity of reclassifications

159. The question of the validity of reclassifications of interpretative declarations must be approached from a slightly different angle. In the case of a reclassification, the author does not call into question[278] the content of the initial declaration, but rather its legal nature and the regime applicable to it.[279]

160. It must be borne in mind that the question of whether to use the term "reservation" or "interpretative declaration" must be determined objectively, taking into account the criteria that the Commission set forth in guidelines 1.3 and 1.3.1 to 1.3.3. Guideline 1.3 states:

> The character of a unilateral statement as a reservation or an interpretative declaration is determined by the legal effect it purports to produce.[280]

The "objective" test takes into account only the declaration's potential effects on the treaty as intended by its author. In other words:

> only an analysis of the potential—and objective—effects of the statement can determine the purpose sought. In determining the legal nature of a statement formulated in connection with a treaty, the decisive criterion lies in the effective result that implementing the statement has (or would have). If it modifies or excludes the legal effect of the treaty or certain of its provisions, it is a reservation "however phrased or named"; if the statement simply clarifies the meaning or scope that its author attributes to the treaty or certain of its provisions, it is an interpretative declaration.[281]

161. Without prejudice to the Commission's future position on the effects of these unilateral statements, it is clear that they are an important factor in determining the legal nature of the initially formulated act: in order to determine whether such statements constitute interpretative declarations or reservations, they must be taken into account as expressing the position of parties to a treaty on the nature of the "interpretative declaration" or "reservation", with all the consequences that this entails. Nevertheless, the author of a reclassification is simply expressing its opinion on this matter. That opinion may prove to be justified or unjustified when the test of guideline 1.3 is applied, but this in no way implies that the reclassification is valid or invalid; once again, these are two different questions.

162. Furthermore, the reclassification is, in itself, simply an interpretation of the "interpretative declaration" itself. As noted above, it is impossible to assess the validity of such an interpretation.[282] Except where the treaty itself prohibits an interpretation, international law establishes only the methods of interpretation, not the conditions of validity.

163. Furthermore, reclassifications, whether justified or unjustified in their use of the term "interpretative declaration" or "reservation", are not subject to criteria for validity. Abundant State practice[283] shows that Contracting Parties consider themselves entitled to make such declarations, often in order to ensure the integrity of the treaty or in response to treaty-based prohibitions of reservations.[284]

4. Conclusions regarding reactions to interpretative declarations

164. It follows from these considerations that the very idea that the concept of validity applies to reactions to interpretative declarations is unwarranted. While such reactions may prove to be "correct" or "erroneous", this does not imply that they are "valid" or "non-valid".

165. In the light of these observations, the Special Rapporteur wonders whether it would be appropriate to include guidelines specifying that there are no conditions for the validity of reactions to interpretative declarations; a detailed presentation of the matter could be provided in the commentary on guideline 2.9.4.[285] If the Commission deems it useful to include such a guideline in the Guide to Practice, it could be worded:

"**3.6** *Substantive validity of an approval, opposition or reclassification*

"Approval of an interpretative declaration, opposition to an interpretative declaration and reclassification of an interpretative declaration shall not be subject to any conditions for substantive validity."

E. Validity of conditional interpretative declarations

166. According to the definition contained in guideline 1.2.1, a conditional interpretative declaration is:

> a unilateral statement formulated by a State or an international organization when signing, ratifying, formally confirming, accepting, approving

---

[278] It may *simultaneously* call into question and object to the content of the reclassified declaration by making an objection to it; in such cases, however, the reclassification and the objection remain conceptually different from one another; see the thirteenth report on reservations to treaties (*Yearbook ... 2008*, vol. II (Part One), document A/CN.4/600), paras. 29–30.

[279] *Ibid.*, para. 25.

[280] For the guideline and the commentary thereto, see *Yearbook ... 1999*, vol. II (Part Two), p. 107.

[281] *Ibid.*, para. (3) of the commentary to guideline 1.3.1.

[282] See paragraphs 140–144 above.

[283] See, *inter alia*, the thirteenth report on reservations to treaties (*Yearbook ... 2008*, vol. II (Part One), document A/CN.4/600), para. 26.

[284] For a particularly telling example, see the reactions of several States to the Philippines' "interpretative declaration" to the 1982 United Nations Convention on the Law of the Sea (*Multilateral Treaties Deposited with the Secretary-General* available online from http://treaties.un.org, chap. XXI.6).

[285] This guideline, proposed by the Special Rapporteur in his thirteenth report on reservations to treaties (*Yearbook ... 2008*, vol. II (Part One), document A/CN.4/600, para. 48), reads:

"**2.9.4** *Freedom to formulate an approval, protest or reclassification*

"An approval, opposition or reclassification in respect of an interpretative declaration may be formulated at any time by any contracting State or any contracting international organization and by any State or any international organization that is entitled to become a party to the treaty."

or acceding to a treaty, or by a State when making a notification of succession to a treaty, whereby the State or international organization subjects its consent to be bound by the treaty to a specific interpretation of the treaty or of certain provisions thereof.[286]

Thus, the key feature of a conditional interpretative declaration is not that it proposes a certain interpretation, but that it constitutes a condition for its author's consent to be bound by the treaty.[287] It is that element of conditionality that brings a conditional interpretative declaration closer to being a reservation.

167. *A priori*, however, the question of the validity of conditional interpretative declarations seems little different from that of "simple" interpretative declarations and it would seem unwarranted to make formulation of a conditional interpretative declaration subject to conditions for validity other than those applicable to "simple" interpretative declarations.[288] It is clear from the definition of a conditional interpretative declaration that it does not purport to modify the treaty, but merely to interpret one or more of its provisions in a certain manner.

168. The situation changes significantly, however, where the interpretation proposed by the author of a conditional interpretative declaration does not correspond to the interpretation of the treaty established by agreement between the parties. In that case, the condition formulated by the author of the declaration, stating that it does not consider itself to be bound by the treaty in the event of a different interpretation, brings this unilateral statement considerably closer to being a reservation. Horn has stated that:

> If a state does not wish to abandon its interpretation even in the face of a contrary authoritative decision by a court, it may run the risk of violating the treaty when applying its own interpretation. In order to avoid this, it would have to qualify its interpretation as an absolute condition for participation in the treaty. The statement's nature as a reservation is established at the same time the propagated interpretation is established as the incorrect one.[289]

169. Thus, any conditional interpretative declaration potentially constitutes a reservation: a reservation conditional upon a certain interpretation. This can be seen from one particularly clear example of a conditional interpretative declaration; the declaration that France attached to its expression of consent to be bound by its signature of Additional Protocol II to the Treaty for the Prohibition of Nuclear Weapons in Latin America and the Caribbean (Treaty of Tlatelolco) stipulates that:

> In the event that the interpretative declaration thus made by the French Government should be contested wholly or in part by one or more Contracting Parties to the Treaty or to Protocol II, these instruments shall be null and void in relations between the French Republic and the contesting State or States.[290]

In other words, France intends to exclude the application of the treaty in its relations with any States parties that do not accept its interpretation of the treaty, exactly as if it had made a reservation.

170. While this scenario is merely a potential one, it seems clear that the declaration in question is subject to the conditions for substantive validity set out in article 19 of the 1969 and 1986 Vienna Conventions. Although it might be thought *prima facie* that the author of a conditional interpretative declaration is merely proposing a specific interpretation (not subject to conditions for validity), the effects of such unilateral statements are, in fact, made conditional by their authors upon one or more provisions of the treaty not being interpreted in the desired manner.

171. The deliberate decision of the Netherlands to formulate reservations, rather than interpretative declarations, to the International Covenant on Civil and Political Rights clearly shows the considerable similarities between the two approaches:

> The Kingdom of the Netherlands clarif[ies] that although the reservations are partly of an interpretational nature, it has preferred reservations to interpretational declarations in all cases, since if the latter form were used doubt might arise concerning whether the text of the Covenant allows for the interpretation put upon it. By using the reservation form the Kingdom of the Netherlands wishes to ensure in all cases that the relevant obligations arising out of the Covenant will not apply to the Kingdom, or will apply only in the way indicated.[291]

172. *A priori*, there is therefore no alternative to the application to these conditional interpretative declarations of the same conditions for substantive (and, moreover, formal) validity as those that apply to reservations. The (precautionary) application of the conditions set out in article 19 of the 1969 and 1986 Vienna Conventions is not easy, however, unless it has been established that the interpretation proposed by the author is unwarranted and does not correspond to the authentic interpretation of the treaty. For example, although a treaty may prohibit the formulation of reservations to its provisions, it does not follow that a State cannot subject its consent to be bound by the treaty to a certain interpretation of that treaty. If the interpretation proves to be warranted and in accordance with the authentic interpretation of the treaty, it is a genuine interpretative declaration that must meet the conditions for the validity of interpretative declarations, but only those conditions. If, however, the interpretation does not express the correct meaning of the treaty and is rejected on that account, the author of the "interpretative declaration" does not consider itself bound by the treaty unless the treaty is *modified* in accordance with its wishes. In that case, the "conditional declaration" is indeed a reservation and must meet the corresponding conditions for the validity of reservations.

173. It follows that, so long as its status as to correctness has not been, or cannot be, determined, such a conditional interpretative declaration must meet both the conditions for the validity of an interpretative declaration (in the event that the interpretation is ultimately shared by the other parties or established by a competent body) and the conditions for the validity of a reservation (in the event that the proposed interpretation is rejected). So long as the correct interpretation has not been established, the conditional interpretative declaration remains in a legal vacuum and it is impossible to determine

---

[286] *Yearbook ... 1999*, vol. II (Part Two), pp. 103–106.

[287] *Ibid.*, p. 105, para. (16) of the commentary.

[288] See paragraphs 128–148 above.

[289] Horn, *op. cit.* (footnote 197 above), p. 326.

[290] This declaration was confirmed in 1974 at the time of ratification (United Nations, *Treaty Series*, vol. 936, No. 9068, p. 419).

[291] *Multilateral Treaties Deposited with the Secretary-General*, available online from http://treaties.un.org/, chap. IV.4.

whether it is a mere interpretation or a reservation. Either case is still possible.

174. However, the problem remains largely theoretical. Where a treaty prohibits the formulation of interpretative declarations, a conditional interpretative declaration that proposes the "correct" interpretation must logically be considered non-valid, but the result is exactly the same: the interpretation of the author of the declaration is accepted (otherwise, the conditional declaration would not be an interpretative declaration). Thus, the validity or non-validity of the conditional interpretative declaration as an "interpretative declaration" has no practical effect. Whether or not it is valid, the proposed interpretation is identical with the authoritative interpretation of the treaty.

175. If, on the other hand, the treaty prohibits reservations, but not interpretative declarations, a conditional interpretative declaration is considered non-valid since it does not meet the conditions for the validity of a reservation. But, here again, if the proposed interpretation is ultimately accepted as the correct and authoritative interpretation, the author of the conditional interpretative declaration has achieved its aim, despite the non-validity of its declaration.

176. The question of whether a conditional interpretative declaration meets the conditions for the validity of an interpretative declaration does not actually affect the interpretation of the treaty. The "interpretation" element is merely the condition that transforms the declaration into a reservation. However, in the event that the conditional interpretative declaration is indeed transformed into a reservation, the question of whether it meets the conditions for the validity of reservations does have a real impact on the content (and even the existence) of treaty relations.

177. In the light of these observations, there is no reason to think that conditional interpretative declarations are subject to the same conditions for the validity as "simple" interpretative declarations. Instead, they are subject to the conditions for the validity of reservations, as in the case of conditions for formal validity.[292] The conditional interpretative declaration is in fact a conditional reservation.

"**3.5.2** *Conditions for the substantive validity of a conditional interpretative declaration*

"The validity of a conditional interpretative declaration must be assessed in accordance with the provisions of draft guidelines 3.1 and 3.1.1 to 3.1.15."

178. No specific new provision needs to be adopted, at this stage of the study, regarding the issue of assessment of the validity of conditional interpretative declarations. In the light of the observations concerning their validity, it would seem that the issue must be resolved in the same way as that of competence to assess the validity of reservations. In accordance with the Commission's consistent practice regarding these specific interpretative declarations, and pending its final decision as to whether to maintain the distinction—which cannot be made until it has considered the effects of these declarations—the Special Rapporteur proposes the provisional inclusion in the Guide to Practice of a guideline consisting of a simple cross-reference to other guidelines, which could be worded:

"**3.5.3** *Competence to assess the validity of conditional interpretative declarations*

"Guidelines 3.2, 3.2.1, 3.2.2, 3.2.3 and 3.2.4 apply, *mutatis mutandis*, to conditional interpretative declarations."

[292] See guidelines 2.4.5 to 2.4.8 and 2.4.10 (*Yearbook ... 2001*, vol. II (Part Two), pp. 194–195; *Yearbook ... 2002*, vol. II (Part Two), pp. 47–48; and *Yearbook ... 2004*, vol. II (Part Two)), p. 109.

Chapter III

Effects of reservations and interpretative declarations

179. The fourth part of the Guide to Practice, as provided for in the general outline of the study,[293] covers the effects of reservations, acceptances and objections, to which the effects of interpretative declarations and reactions thereto (approval, opposition, recharacterization or silence) should also be added. This part follows the logic of the Guide to Practice, in which an attempt is made to present, as systematically as possible, all of the legal issues concerning reservations and related unilateral declarations, as well as interpretative declarations: after defining the issues (in the first part of the Guide) and establishing the rules for assessing the validity (second part of the Guide) and permissibility (third part of the Guide) of these various declarations, the fourth part is concerned with determining the legal effects of the reservation or interpretative declaration.[294]

180. Although it was initially planned that the fourth part would address issues relating to "The prohibition of certain reservations",[295] it does not seem to be the appropriate place for this section of the provisional outline. Those issues have in fact been addressed in the context of permissibility of reservations, in the third part of the Guide. The study should therefore concentrate on the effects of reservations, acceptances and objections, on the one hand, and on the effects of interpretative declarations and reactions to them, on the other.

[293] Second report on reservations to treaties, *Yearbook ... 1996*, vol. II (Part One), document A/CN.4/477 and Add.1, pp. 48–49, para. 37.

[294] The fifth and final part of the Guide to Practice will address the succession of States in relation to reservations.

[295] Second report on reservations to treaties, *Yearbook ... 1996*, vol. II (Part One), document A/CN.4/477 and Add.1, pp. 48–49, para. 37, sect. IV.A.

181. First of all, it is worth recalling a point that is crucial to understanding the legal effects of a reservation or interpretative declaration. It is now accepted by the International Law Commission that both reservations and interpretative declarations are defined in relation to the legal effects that their authors intend them to have on the treaty. Accordingly, guideline 1.1 (Definition of reservations) provides as follows:

"Reservation" means a unilateral statement, however phrased or named, made by a State or an international organization when signing, ratifying, formally confirming, accepting, approving or acceding to a treaty or by a State when making a notification of succession to a treaty, whereby the State or organization purports to exclude or to modify the legal effect of certain provisions of the treaty in their application to that State or to that international organization.[296]

In the same spirit, guideline 1.2 (Definition of interpretative declarations) states that:

"Interpretative declaration" means a unilateral statement, however phrased or named, made by a State or by an international organization whereby that State or that organization purports to specify or clarify the meaning or scope attributed by the declarant to a treaty or to certain of its provisions.[297]

182. Although the potential legal effects of a reservation or interpretative declaration are thus a "substantive element"[298] of its definition,[299] this does not at all mean that a reservation or interpretative declaration actually produces those effects. The fourth part of the Guide is not intended to determine the effects that the author of a reservation or the author of an interpretative declaration purported it to have—this issue was dealt with in the first part on the definition and identification of reservations and interpretative declarations. The fourth part, in contrast, deals with determining the legal effects that reservations and interpretative declarations actually produce in relation to eventual reactions from other Contracting Parties. The purported effects and the effects actually achieved are not necessarily identical and depend on the one hand on the validity and permissibility of the reservations and interpretative declarations and, on the other hand, on the reactions of other interested States or international organizations.

A. Effects of reservations, acceptances and objections

1. The rules of the 1969 and 1986 Vienna Conventions

183. Despite the relevant provisions set out in the 1969 and 1986 Vienna Conventions, the effects of a reservation or of an acceptance of or objection to a reservation remain one of the most controversial issues of treaty law. Article 21 of the two Conventions refers exclusively to the "legal effects of reservations and of objections to reservations". The drafting of this provision was relatively simple compared to that of the other provisions on reservations. Neither the International Law Commission nor the United Nations Conference on the Law of Treaties, held at Vienna in 1969, seem to have had any particular difficulty in formulating the rules presented in the first two paragraphs of article 21 concerning the effects of reservations (whereas paragraph 3 deals with the effects of objections).

184. The Commission's first Special Rapporteur on the law of treaties, J. L. Brierly, had already suggested in his draft article 10, paragraph 1, that a reservation be considered as:

limiting or varying the effect of [a] treaty in so far as concerns the relation of [the] State or organization [author of the reservation] with one or more of the existing or future parties to the treaty.[300]

Fitzmaurice made the first proposal for a separate provision on the legal effects of a reservation, which largely prefigured the first two paragraphs of the current article 21.[301] It is interesting that these draft provisions seemed to smack of the obvious: Fitzmaurice did not make any comment on the draft and only noted that "it is considered useful to state these consequences, but they require no explanation".[302]

185. At the outset, Sir Humphrey Waldock suggested a provision on the effects of a reservation deemed "admissible",[303] and since then his proposal has undergone only minor drafting changes.[304] Neither Sir Humphrey[305] nor the Commission considered it necessary to comment at length on that rule, the Commission merely stating that:

These rules, which appear not to be questioned, follow directly from the consensual basis of the relations between parties to a treaty.[306]

Nor did the issue give rise to observations or criticisms from States between the two readings by the Commission or at the United Nations Conference on the Law of Treaties.

---

[296] *Yearbook ... 1998*, vol. II (Part Two), p. 99.

[297] *Yearbook ... 1999*, vol. II (Part Two), p. 92.

[298] *Yearbook ... 1998*, vol. II (Part Two), p. 94, para. 495. The Special Rapporteur has emphasized that "it is generally recognized that the function of reservations is to purport to produce legal effects" (Third report on reservations to treaties, *Yearbook ... 1998*, vol. II (Part One), document A/CN.4/491 and Add.1–6, p. 248, para. 144). Horn, *op cit.* (footnote 197 above), p. 41, maintains that the fact that reservations purport to produce certain specific legal effects is the "*differentia specifica*" of this type of unilateral act. See also the statements of Ruda and Rosenne, who have emphasized the close link between the definition of the reservation and the legal effects that it is likely to produce (*Yearbook ... 1965*, vol. I, 799th meeting, p. 167, para. 46, and 800th meeting, p. 171, para. 8).

[299] For a definition of reservations in general, see draft guidelines 1.1, *Yearbook ... 1998*, vol. II (Part Two), pp. 108–110, and 1.1.1 (*Yearbook ... 1999*, vol. II (Part Two), pp. 93–95).

[300] [First] Report on the law of treaties, *Yearbook ... 1950*, vol. II, document A/CN.4/23, p. 222.

[301] Report on the law of treaties, *Yearbook ... 1956*, vol. II, document A/CN.4/101, pp. 115–116.

[302] *Ibid.*, p. 127, para. 101.

[303] This is the term that was used in draft article 18, paragraph 5, as presented in Sir Humphrey Waldock's first report, *Yearbook ... 1962*, vol. II, document A/CN.4/144, p. 61.

[304] The text proposed by Sir Humphrey for article 18, paragraph 5, became article 18 *ter*, entirely devoted to the legal effect of reservations, with a few editorial changes from the Drafting Committee (see *Yearbook ... 1962*, vol. I, 664th meeting, p. 234, para. 63). Subsequently, the Committee made other changes to the draft (*ibid.*, 667th meeting, p. 253, para. 71). It ultimately became article 21, as adopted by the Commission on first reading in 1962 (*ibid.*, vol. II, p. 181). The text underwent changes made necessary by the rephrasing of other provisions on reservations. The changes were purely editorial, except for the change to subparagraph 1 (*b*) (on this point, see paragraph 279 below).

[305] *Ibid.*, p. 68, para. 21.

[306] See the commentary in 1962 (*Yearbook ... 1962*, vol. II, p. 181 (commentary to article 21)) and the commentary to draft article 19 adopted on second reading in 1965 (*Yearbook ... 1966*, vol. II, p. 209, para. 1).

186. The drafting of the current article 21, paragraph 3, posed greater difficulties. This provision, logically absent from Sir Humphrey's first proposals, had to be included in the article on the effects of reservations and objections when the Commission accepted that a State objecting to a reservation could nevertheless establish treaty relations with the author of the reservation.[307] A United States proposal to that effect convinced Sir Humphrey of the logical need for such a provision,[308] but its drafting by the Commission was nevertheless time-consuming.[309] The Conference made only a relatively minor change in order to harmonize paragraph 3 with the reversal of the presumption of article 20, paragraph 4 (*b*).[310]

187. The resumed consideration of article 21 during the drafting of the 1986 Vienna Convention did not pose any significant difficulties. During the very brief discussion of draft article 21, two members of the Commission emphasized that the provision in question "followed logically" from draft articles 19 and 20.[311] Even more clearly, Mr. Calle y Calle stated that:

> If reservations were admitted, their legal effect was obviously to modify the relations between the reserving party and the party with regard to which the reservation was established.[312]

The Commission, and then several years later the United Nations Conference on the Law of Treaties, adopted article 21 with only the drafting changes required by the broader scope of the 1986 Vienna Convention.

188. One might think that the widespread acceptance of article 21 during adoption of the draft articles on the law of treaties between States and international organizations or between international organizations showed that the provision was even then accepted as reflecting international custom on the subject. The arbitral ruling made concerning the delimitation of the continental shelf in the *English Channel* case corroborates this analysis. The Court of Arbitration recognized:

> … that the law governing reservations to multilateral treaties was then undergoing an evolution which crystallized only in 1969 in Articles 19 to 23 of the Vienna Convention on the Law of Treaties.[313]

189. Nevertheless, the effects of a reservation, acceptance or objection are not fully addressed by article 21 of the 1969 and 1986 Vienna Conventions. This provision concerns only the effect of those instruments on the content of the treaty relationship between the reserving party and the other Contracting Parties. The separate issue of the effect of the reservation, acceptance or objection on the consent of the reserving party to be bound by the treaty is covered not by article 21 of the two Vienna Conventions, but by article 20, entitled "Acceptance of and objection to reservations":

190. This provision is the result of draft article 20 adopted by the Commission on first reading in 1962, entitled "The effects of reservations":

> 1. (*a*) A reservation expressly or impliedly permitted by the terms of the treaty does not require any further acceptance.
>
> (*b*) Where the treaty is silent in regard to the making of reservations, the provisions of paragraphs 2 to 4 below shall apply.
>
> 2. Except in cases falling under paragraphs 3 and 4 below and unless the treaty otherwise provides:
>
> (*a*) Acceptance of a reservation by any State to which it is open to become a party to the treaty constitutes the reserving State a party to the treaty in relation to such State, as soon as the treaty is in force;
>
> (*b*) An objection to a reservation by a State which considers it to be incompatible with the object and purpose of the treaty precludes the entry into force of the treaty as between the objecting and the reserving State, unless a contrary intention shall have been expressed by the objecting State.
>
> 3. Except in a case falling under paragraph 4 below, the effect of a reservation to a treaty which has been concluded between a small group of States shall be conditional upon its acceptance by all the States concerned unless:
>
> (*a*) The treaty otherwise provides; or
>
> (*b*) The States are members of an international organization which applies a different rule to treaties concluded under its auspices.
>
> 4. Where the treaty is the constituent instrument of an international organization and objection has been taken to a reservation, the effect of the reservation shall be determined by decision of the competent organ of the organization in question, unless the treaty otherwise provides.[314]

191. This provision was appropriate to its title, as it did indeed cover the effects of a reservation and the reactions to a reservation on the entry into force of the treaty for the reserving State. In 1965, however, it was included in the

[307] See Müller, "Article 21", *loc. cit.* (footnote 195 above), p. 888, paras. 7–8.

[308] Fourth report on the law of treaties, *Yearbook … 1965*, vol. II, document A/CN.4/177 and Add.1, pp. 47 and 55. See also the comments of Denmark (*ibid.*, p. 46).

[309] Although Sir Humphrey considered that the case of a reservation to which a simple objection had been made was "not altogether easy to express" (*Yearbook … 1965*, vol. I, 813th meeting, p. 270, para. 96), most of the members (see Mr. Ruda (*ibid.*, para. 13); Mr. Ago (*ibid.*, 814th meeting, p. 271, paras. 7 and 11); Mr. Tunkin (*ibid.*, para. 8) and Mr. Briggs (*ibid.*, p. 272, para. 14) were convinced that it was necessary, and even "indispensable" (Mr. Ago, *ibid.*, p. 271, para. 7) to introduce a provision on that subject "in order to forestall ambiguous situations" (*ibid.*, p. 271, para. 7). However, members had different opinions as to the basis of the paragraph proposed by the United States and the Special Rapporteur: whereas Sir Humphrey's proposal emphasized the consensual basis of the treaty relationship established despite the objection, the paragraph proposed by the United States seemed to suggest that the intended effect originated only from the unilateral act of the objecting State, that is, from the objection, without the reserving State having a real choice. The two positions had their supporters within the Commission (see the positions of Mr. Yasseen (*ibid.*, 800th meeting, p. 171, para. 7 and pp. 172–173, paras. 21–23 and 26), Mr. Tunkin (*ibid.*, 800th meeting, p. 172, para. 18) and Mr. Pal (*ibid.*, para. 24) and those of Sir Humphrey (*ibid.*, p. 173, para. 31), Mr. Rosenne (*ibid.*, p. 172, para. 10) and Mr. Ruda (*ibid.*, p. 172, para. 13)). The text that the Commission finally adopted on a unanimous basis (*ibid.*, 816th meeting, p. 284), however, is very neutral and clearly shows that the issue was left open by the Commission (see also the Special Rapporteur's summing-up, *ibid.*, 800th meeting, p, 173, para. 31).

[310] *Official Records of the United Nations Conference on the Law of Treaties, Second Session, Vienna, 9 April to 22 May 1969, Summary records of the plenary meetings and of the meetings of the Committee of the Whole* (A/CONF.39/11/Add.1), 33rd plenary meeting, 21 May 1969, p. 181.

[311] Cf. Mr. Tabibi, *Yearbook … 1977*, vol. I, 1434th meeting, p. 98, para. 7; Mr. Dadzie, *ibid.*, p. 99, para. 18.

[312] *Ibid.*, p. 98, para. 8.

[313] *Case concerning the delimitation of the continental shelf between the United Kingdom of Great Britain and Northern Ireland and the French Republic*, decision of 30 June 1977, UNRIAA, vol. XVIII (Sales No. E/F.80.V.7), p. 32, para. 38.

[314] *Yearbook … 1962*, vol. II, p. 176.

new draft article 19 entitled "Acceptance of and objection to reservations"[315] (which later became article 20 of the 1969 Vienna Convention), after significant reworking out of concern for clarity and simplicity.[316] In the context of that reworking, the Commission also decided to abandon the link between objections and the conditions for permissibility of a reservation, including its compatibility with the object and purpose of the treaty.

192. At the United Nations Conference on the Law of Treaties, the first paragraph of this provision underwent substantial amendment,[317] and paragraph 4 (*b*) was then altered by a Soviet amendment.[318] This latter amendment was very significant as it reversed the presumption of article 4 (*b*): any objection would in future be considered a simple objection unless its author had clearly expressed an intention to the contrary. Furthermore, despite the inappropriate title of article 20, it is clear from the origin of this provision that it was intended to cover, *inter alia*, the effects of a reservation of it, any acceptance and of objections to that reservation.

193. Nevertheless, articles 20 and 21 of the 1969 and 1986 Vienna Conventions have some unclear elements and some gaps. In State practice, the case foreseen by article 21, paragraph 3, is no longer seen as "unusual"[319] as the Commission had initially envisaged; on the contrary, owing to the presumption of article 20, paragraph 4 (*b*), it has become the most frequent type of objection.

194. The practice of States is not limited to recourse to the effects set out in paragraph 3. They are increasingly trying to have their objections produce different effects. The absence of a firm position on the part of the Commission, which intentionally opted for a neutral solution that was acceptable to everyone, far from resolving the problem, created others that should be resolved in the Guide to Practice.

195. Nor do articles 20 and 21 respond to the question of what effects are produced by a reservation that does not meet the conditions of substantial permissibility set out in article 19 or of formal permissibility (contained in article 23 and elsewhere). In other words, neither article 20 nor article 21 set out the consequences of the non-permissibility of a reservation, at least not expressly. It is also of particular concern that the application of paragraph 3 on the combined effects of a reservation and an objection is not limited to cases of permissible reservations, that is, reservations established in accordance with article 19, contrary to the provision of paragraph 1. Gaja is therefore quite right to consider that "Article 21 is somewhat obscure".[320]

196. Under these conditions, it seems logical to begin the study by examining the legal effects of a permissible reservation, which are set out—at least partially—in the two 1969 and 1986 Vienna Conventions. The issue of the legal effects of a non-permissible reservation, which has—in part—already been addressed by a section of the tenth report on reservations to treaties[321] and on which the Commission has already adopted two guidelines,[322] should also be given further consideration, so as to give some guidance to the author of such a reservation and to other Contracting Parties.

2. Permissible reservations

197. The legal effects of a permissible reservation depend to a large extent on the reactions that it has received. A permissible and accepted reservation has different legal effects to those of a permissible reservation to which objections have been made. Article 21 of the 1969 and 1986 Vienna Conventions establishes this distinction clearly. In its 1986 version, which is fuller in that it includes the effects of reservations and reactions from international organizations:

> 1. A reservation established with regard to another party in accordance with articles 19, 20 and 23:
>
> (*a*) Modifies for the reserving State or international organization in its relations with that other party the provisions of the treaty to which the reservation relates to the extent of the reservation; and
>
> (*b*) Modifies those provisions to the same extent for that other party in its relations with the reserving State or international organization.
>
> 2. The reservation does not modify the provisions of the treaty for the other parties to the treaty *inter se*.
>
> 3. When a State or an international organization objecting to a reservation has not opposed the entry into force of the treaty between itself and the reserving State or organization, the provisions to which the reservation relates do not apply as between the reserving State or organization and the objecting State or organization to the extent of the reservation.

While paragraph 1 of this provision concerns the legal effects of an established reservation, a concept that should be clarified, paragraph 3 covers the legal effects

[315] *Yearbook ... 1965*, vol. II, p. 162.

[316] Fourth report on the law of treaties (*Yearbook ... 1965*, vol. II, document A/CN.4/177 and Add.1–2), p. 50, paras. 4–5.

[317] See the amendments by Switzerland (A/CONF.39/C.1/L.97), France and Tunisia (A/CONF/39/C.1/L.113) and Thailand (A/CONF.39/C.1/L.150), *Official Records of the United Nations Conference on the Law of Treaties, First and Second Sessions, Vienna, 26 March–24 May 1968 and 9 April–22 May 1969, Documents of the Conference* (A/CONF.39/11/Add.2, United Nations publication, Sales No. E.70.V.5), Report of the Committee of the Whole on its work at the first session of the Conference (A/CONF.39/14), p. 135, para. 179(ii) (b)–(d). These amendments were adopted by a large majority (*ibid., First Session, Vienna, 26 March–24 May 1968, Summary records of the plenary meetings and of the meetings of the Committee of the Whole* (A/CONF.39/11, United Nations publication, Sales No. E.68.V.7), 25th meeting of the Committee of the Whole, p. 135, para. 30.

[318] A/CONF/39/L.3, *Official Records of the United Nations Conference on the Law of Treaties, First and Second Sessions, Vienna, 26 March–24 May 1968 and 9 April–22 May 1969, Documents of the Conference* (A/CONF.39/11/Add.2, United Nations publication, Sales No. E.70.V.5), Report of the Committee of the Whole on its work at the first session of the Conference (A/CONF.39/L.3), pp. 265–266. This amendment was adopted by 49 votes to 21, with 30 abstentions (*ibid., Second Session, Vienna, 9 April–22 May 1969, Summary records of the plenary meetings and of the meetings of the Committee of the Whole* (A/CONF.39/11/Add.1, United Nations publication, Sales No. E.70.V.6), 10th plenary meeting, p. 35, para. 79). See also Müller, "Article 20", *loc. cit.* (footnote 195 above), pp. 806–807, para. 14.

[319] See the fourth report on the law of treaties, *Yearbook ... 1965*, vol. II, document A/CN.4/177 and Add.1–2, p. 55.

[320] Gaja, "Unruly treaty reservations", p. 330.

[321] *Yearbook ... 2005*, vol. II (Part One), document A/CN.4/558 and Add.1–2, pp. 183–189, paras. 181–208.

[322] These are guidelines 3.3 (Consequences of the non-permissibility of a reservation) and 3.3.1 (Non-permissibility of reservations and international responsibility). See *Yearbook ... 2009*, vol. II (Part Two), chap. V, sect. C.2.

of a reservation to which an objection has been made. A distinction should therefore be made between the case of a permissible and accepted reservation—that is, an "established" reservation, on the one hand, and that of a permissible reservation[323] to which an objection has been made, on the other hand. Paragraph 2 of article 21 does not, properly speaking, address the legal effects of a reservation, but rather the absence of legal effects of the reservation on the legal relations between Contracting Parties other than the author of the reservation, independently of its established or permissible nature. This issue will be examined below in the section on the effects of reservations on treaty relations between other Contracting Parties.

(a) *Established reservations*

198. According to the chapeau of article 21, paragraph 1, only an established reservation—in accordance with the provisions of articles 19, 20 and 23—has the legal effects set out in that paragraph and, in particular, in its subparagraphs (*a*) and (*b*). As for the scope of application of article 21, paragraph 1, the 1969 and 1986 Vienna Conventions merely make a rather clumsy reference to provisions concerning the substantial permissibility of a reservation (art. 19), consent to a reservation (art. 20) and the form of a reservation (art. 23), without explaining the interrelation of those provisions in greater detail. It therefore seems appropriate, before considering the legal effects produced by an established reservation, to return to the concept of established reservation, which is essential for determining the "normal" legal effects of a reservation.

(i) *The "establishment" of a reservation*

a. The general rule

199. Under the terms of the chapeau of article 21 of the 1969 and 1986 Vienna Conventions, a reservation is established "with regard to another party in accordance with articles 19, 20 and 23". The phrase, which appears clear on the surface and which is often understood as referring to permissible reservations accepted by a Contracting Party, contains many uncertainties and imprecisions which are the result of a significant recasting undertaken by the Commission during the second reading of the draft articles on the law of treaties in 1965, on the one hand, and changes introduced to article 20, paragraph 4 (*b*) of the Convention during the United Nations Conference on the Law of Treaties in 1969.

200. First of all, the reference to article 23 as a whole is awkward, to say the least, since the provisions of article 23, paragraphs 3 and 4, have no effect on the establishment of a reservation. They concern only its withdrawal and the fact that, in certain cases, the formulation of an acceptance or an objection does not require confirmation.

201. Secondly, it is difficult, indeed, impossible, to determine what connection might exist between the establishment of a reservation and the effect on the entry into force of the treaty of an objection provided for in article 20, paragraph 4 (*b*). The objection cannot be considered as consent to the reservation since, to the contrary, it aims to "exclude or to modify the legal effects of the reservation, or to exclude the application of the treaty as a whole, in relations with the reserving State or organization".[324] Accordingly, a reservation to which an objection has been made is obviously not established within the meaning of article 21, paragraph 1.

202. Consultation of the *travaux préparatoires* provides an explanation for this "contradiction". In the draft articles adopted by the Commission, which contained in article 19 (later art. 21) the same reference, the presumption of article 17 (future art. 20), para. 4 (*b*)) established the principle that a treaty did not enter into force between a reserving State and a State which had made an objection. Since the treaty was not in force, there was no reason to determine the legal effects of the reservation on the content of treaty relations. Moreover, the comments of the Commission specified: "Paragraphs 1 and 2 of this article set out the rules concerning the legal effects of a reservation which has been established under the provisions of articles 16, 17 and 18, *assuming that the treaty is in force.**"[325] The "contradiction" was introduced only during the Conference through the reversal of the presumption of article 20, paragraph 4 (*b*), following the adoption of the Soviet amendment.[326] Because of this new presumption, a treaty does remain in force for the reserving State even if a simple objection is formulated. However, this could not mean that the reservation is established under article 21.

203. In his first report, Sir Humphrey Waldock took into account the condition of consent to a reservation for it to be able to produce its effects. The draft article 18 that he proposed to devote to "Consent to reservations and its effects" specified that:

> A reservation, since it purports to modify the terms of the treaty as adopted, shall only be effective against a State which has given, or is presumed to have given, its consent thereto in accordance with the provisions of the following paragraphs of this article.[327]

In its advisory opinion on reservations to the Convention on the Prevention and Punishment of the Crime of Genocide, ICJ also highlighted this basic principle of the law of reservations, and of treaty law as well:

> It is well established that in its treaty relations a State cannot be bound without its consent and that consequently no reservation can be effective against any State without its agreement thereto.[328]

It is this idea to which paragraph 1 of article 21 of the 1969 and 1986 Vienna Conventions refers, and this is the meaning which must be given to the reference to article 20.

[323] It should be noted that paragraph 3 of article 21 does not refer only to a permissible reservation which has been the subject of an objection. It is therefore possible that this provision also applies to the case of an objection to a non-permissible reservation.

[324] See guideline 2.6.1 (Definition of objections to reservations), *Yearbook ... 2005*, vol. II (Part Two), pp. 77–82.

[325] *Yearbook ... 1966*, vol. II, p. 209, para. (1) of the commentary to article 19.

[326] See paragraph 192 above.

[327] *Yearbook ... 1962*, vol. II, p. 61.

[328] Advisory opinion of 28 May 1951, *I.C.J. Reports 1951*, p. 17. See also Müller, "Article 20", *loc. cit.* (footnote 195 above), pp. 809–811, paras. 20–24.

204. Consent to the reservation is therefore a *sine qua non* for the reservation to be considered established and to produce its effects. But contrary to what has been maintained by certain partisans of the opposability school,[329] consent is not the only condition. The chapeau of article 21, paragraph 1, cumulatively refers to consent to the reservation (the reference to art. 20), permissibility (art. 19) and validity (art. 23). Consent alone is thus not sufficient for the reservation to produce its "normal" effects. Moreover, the reservation must be permissible within the meaning of article 19 and have been so formulated that it complies with the rules of procedure and form set forth in article 23. Only this combination can "establish" the reservation.

205. This necessary combination of permissibility and consent results also from the phrase in article 21, paragraph 1, which states that a reservation is established "with regard to another party". Logically, a reservation cannot be permissible only with regard to another party. Either it is permissible or it is not. This is a question which in principle is not subject to the will of the other Contracting Parties[330] unless, of course, they decide by common accord to "permit" the reservation.[331] On the other hand, a reservation which is objectively permissible is opposable only to the parties which have, in one way or another, consented to it. It is a bilateral link which is created, following acceptance, between the reserving State and the Contracting Party which has consented thereto. The reservation is established only in regard to that party and it is only in relations with that party that it produces its effects.

206. As a consequence, it seems necessary to emphasize once again in the Guide to Practice that the establishment of a reservation results from the combination of its permissibility and of consent. To simply reproduce article 21, paragraph 1, which defines the notion of an established reservation, does not seem feasible precisely because of the references to other provisions of the 1969 and 1986 Vienna Conventions. The fourth part, on the legal effects of reservations and interpretative declarations, could open with a guideline 4.1 reading as follows:

"**4.** *Legal effects of reservations and interpretative declarations*

"**4.1** *Establishment of a reservation*

"A reservation is established with regard to another Contracting Party if it meets the requirements for permissibility of a reservation and was formulated in accordance with the form and procedures specified for the purpose, and if the other Contracting Party has accepted it."

b. Special situations

207. Guideline 4.1 relates only to the general rule, and does not fully answer the question of whether a reservation is established. Article 20, which embodies in its paragraph 4 the general rule regarding consent to a reservation and hence constitutes the cornerstone of the "flexible" Vienna system,[332] does in fact contain exceptions as regards the expression of consent to the reservation by the other Contracting Parties. Moreover, paragraph 4 clearly specifies that it applies only in "cases not falling under the preceding paragraphs and unless the treaty otherwise provides". The establishment of the reservation, and particularly the requirement of consent, may thus be modified depending on the nature of the reservation or of the treaty, but also by any provision incorporated in the treaty to that effect.

i. Expressly authorized reservations

208. According to article 20, paragraph 1, expressly authorized reservations need not be accepted "subsequently" by the other Contracting Parties. However, this paragraph 1 does not mean that the reservation is exempt from the requirement for the Contracting Parties' assent; it simply expresses the idea that, since the parties have given their assent even before the formulation of the reservation, and have done so in the text of the treaty itself, subsequent acceptance is superfluous. Moreover, the expression "unless the treaty so provides" which appears in the text of this provision[333] clearly requires this interpretation. Only reservations that are actually covered by this prior agreement do not require subsequent acceptance, and are thus, logically established from the moment they are permissibly made.[334]

209. It should be recalled that the draft articles adopted by the Commission on second reading did not continue the possibility of *a priori* acceptance solely to reservations "expressly" authorized by the treaty, but also included reservations "impliedly" authorized; however, the work of the Commission sheds no light on the meaning to be attributed to this concept.[335] At the United Nations Conference on the Law of Treaties, a number of delegations expressed their doubts regarding this solution[336] and

[329] On these two schools, see First report on the law and practice relating to reservations to treaties, *Yearbook ... 1995*, vol. II (Part One), document A/CN.4/470, pp. 142–143, paras. 101–105. See also Koh, "Reservations to multilateral treaties: how international legal doctrine reflects world vision", pp. 71–116; Redgwell, *op. cit.* (footnote 243 above), pp. 263–269; Cortado, *op. cit.* (footnote 208 above), pp. 73–82; Sir Ian Sinclair, *The Vienna Convention on the Law of Treaties*, p. 81, footnote 78; and Pellet, "Article 19 (1969)", pp. 696 *et seq.*, paras. 111 *et seq.*

[330] See the tenth report on reservations to treaties, *Yearbook ... 2005*, vol. II (Part One), document A/CN.4/558 and Add.1–2, pp. 187–188, paras. 201–203.

[331] *Ibid.*, pp. 188–189, paras. 205–208.

[332] See *Yearbook ... 1966*, vol. II, p. 207, para. (21) of the commentary to article 17. See also Bowett, "Reservations to non-restricted multilateral treaties", p. 84; Müller, "Article 20" (footnote 195 above), p. 799, para. 1.

[333] The words "unless the treaty so provides" were added by the Special Rapporteur in order to take account of "the possibility ... that a treaty may specifically authorize reservations but on condition of their acceptance by a specified number or fraction of the parties" (Fourth report on the law of treaties, *Yearbook ... 1965*, vol. II, document A/CN.4/177 and Add.1–2, p. 50). This wording was slightly modified by the Drafting Committee (*Yearbook ... 1965*, vol. I, 813th meeting, p. 265, para. 30). In 1966, the wording was once again slightly modified, but the summary records of the meetings shed no light on the reasons for this change.

[334] "Made", not "formulated", because they produce their effects without any additional formality being required. See the commentary to guideline 3.1 (Permissible reservations), *Yearbook ... 2006*, vol. II (Part Two) p. 146, para. (6).

[335] *Yearbook ... 1966*, vol. II, p. 202 and the commentary, which is not particularly illuminating on this point, p. 207, para. (18).

[336] See the statements by the representatives of India (*Summary records of the plenary meetings and of the meetings of the Committee of*

proposed amendments aimed at deleting the words "or impliedly",[337] and the change was accepted.[338] Sir Humphrey Waldock, Expert Consultant at the Conference, had himself recognized that "the words 'or impliedly' in article 17, paragraph 1, seemed to have been retained in the draft articles as a relic from earlier and more detailed drafts which dealt with implied prohibition and implied authorization of reservations".[339] It is thus with good reason that reservations implicitly authorized by the treaty are not mentioned in article 20, paragraph 1.

210. Had it been held, as Horn suggests,[340] that where a treaty prohibits certain reservations or certain categories of reservations, it *ipso facto* authorizes all others, which amounts to a reversal of the presumption of article 19 (*b*), this interpretation would clearly place article 20, paragraph 1, in direct contradiction to article 19. Assuming this to be the case, the inclusion in the treaty of a clause prohibiting reservations to a specific provision would suffice to institute total freedom to make any reservation whatsoever other than those that were expressly prohibited; the criterion of the object and purpose of the treaty would then be rendered inapplicable.[341] The Commission has already ruled out this interpretation in guideline 3.1.3 (Permissibility of reservations not prohibited by the treaty), which makes it clear that reservations not prohibited by the treaty are not *ipso facto* permissible and hence can with still greater reason not be regarded as established and accepted by the terms of the treaty itself.

211. By the same token, and despite the regrettable lack of precision in the 1969 and 1986 Vienna Conventions on this point, a general authorization of reservations in a treaty cannot constitute *a priori* acceptance on the part of the Contracting Parties. To say that all the parties have the right to formulate reservations to the treaty cannot imply that this right is unlimited, still less that all reservations so formulated are, by virtue of the simple general clause included in the treaty, established within the meaning of the chapeau to article 21, paragraph 1. To accept this way of looking at things would render the Vienna regime utterly meaningless. Such general authorizations do no more than refer to the general regime, of which the Vienna Conventions constitute the expression, and which is based on the fundamental principle that the parties to a treaty have the power to formulate reservations.

212. Nor is the notion of an expressly authorized reservation identical or equivalent[342] to the concept of a specified reservation. This was very clearly established by the arbitral tribunal in the *English Channel* case in relation to the interpretation of article 12 of the 1958 Convention on the Continental Shelf, paragraph 1 of which provides that:

> At the time of signature, ratification or accession, any State may make reservations to articles of the Convention other than to articles 1 to 3 inclusive.

213. There can be no doubt that, pursuant to this provision, any State may make its consent to be bound by the Convention on me Continental Shelf subject to the formulation of a reservation so "specified", that is to say any reservation relating to articles 4 to 15, in accordance with article 19 (*b*) of the 1969 and 1986 Vienna Conventions. This authorization does not however imply that any reservation so formulated is necessarily valid,[343] nor, *a fortiori*, that the other parties have consented, under article 12, paragraph 1, to any and every reservation to articles 4 to 15. The Court of Arbitration considered that this provision:

> ... cannot be read as committing States to accept in advance any and every reservation to articles other than Articles 1 to 3 ... Such an interpretation ... would amount almost to a license to contracting States to write their own treaty.[344]

214. State practice supports the solution used by the Court of Arbitration. The fact that 11 States objected to reservations made to the Convention on the Continental Shelf,[345] although those reservations only concern articles other than articles 1 to 3, as provided for in article 12, paragraph 1, of the Convention, is moreover revealing as regards the interpretation to be followed.

215. The term "reservations expressly authorized" by the treaty must be interpreted restrictively in order to meet the objective of article 20, paragraph 1. In the *English Channel* case, the Court of Arbitration rightly considered that:

> ... only if the Article had authorised the making of specific reservations could parties to the Convention be understood as having accepted a particular reservation in advance.

216. In order to determine which "expressly authorized" reservations do not require subsequent unilateral acceptance, it is thus appropriate to determine which reservations the parties have already consented to in the treaty. In this regard, Horn emphasized that "where the contents

the Whole (A/CONF.39/11) (footnote 317 above), 24th meeting, p. 128, para. 30), the United States (*ibid.*, p. 130, para. 53) and Ethiopia (*ibid.*, 25th meeting, p. 134, para. 15).

337 See the amendments by France and Tunisia (A/CONF.39/C.1/L.113), Switzerland (A/CONF.39/C.1/L.97) and Thailand (A/CONF.39/C.1/L.150) (*Documents of the Conference* (A/CONF.39/11/Add.2 (footnote 318 above), p. 135)).

338 The three amendments aimed at deleting "or impliedly" (see footnote 337 above) were adopted by 55 votes to 18, with 12 abstentions (*Summary Records* ... (A/CONF.39/11) (footnote 317 above), 25th meeting, p. 135, para. 30).

339 *Ibid.*, 24th meeting, pp. 126–127, para. 14.

340 Horn, *op. cit.* (footnote 197 above), p. 132.

341 See, *inter alia*, the criticisms by Tomuschat (*loc. cit.* (footnote 195 above)), p. 475.

342 Imbert nevertheless maintains that specified reservations are included within the term "expressly authorized reservation". In support of this interpretation he suggests that article 20, paragraph 1, in no way limits the right of contracting States to object to an expressly authorized reservation, but expresses only the idea that the reserving State becomes a Contracting Party upon the deposit of its instrument of ratification or accession ("La question des réserves dans la décision arbitrale du 30 juin 1977 relative á la délimitation du plateau continental entre la République française et le Royaume-Uni de Grande-Bretagne et d'Irlande du Nord", pp. 52–57). He does not deny that this solution openly contradicts the provisions of article 20, but justifies his approach by referring to the work of the United Nations Conference on the Law of Treaties. See also the commentary to guideline 3.1.2, *Yearbook ... 2006*, vol. II (Part Two), p. 153, para. (11).

343 See on this question guideline 3.1.4 (Permissibility of specified reservations) and the commentary thereto, *Yearbook ... 2006*, vol. II (Part Two), pp. 155–156.

344 Arbitral award of 30 June 1977, UNRIAA, vol. XVIII, p. 32, para. 39.

345 *Multilateral Treaties Deposited with the Secretary-General*, available online from http://treaties.un.org/ (Status of treaties), chap. XXI.4.

of authorized reservations are fixed beforehand, acceptance can reasonably be construed as having been given in advance, at the moment of consenting to the treaty".[346]

217. In line with this opinion, the scope of article 20, paragraph 1, contains two types of prior authorizations through which parties do not simply accept the abstract possibility of formulating reservations, but determine in advance exactly what reservations may be made. On the one hand, a reservation made pursuant to a reservations clause that authorizes the parties purely and simply to exclude the application of a provision[347] or an entire part of the treaty[348] must be deemed to be an "expressly authorized reservation". In this case, the other Contracting Parties may appreciate exactly, when the treaty is concluded, what contractual relations they will have with the parties that exercise the option of making reservations pursuant to the exclusion clause. On the other hand, "negotiated"[349] reservations can also be regarded as specified reservations. Indeed, certain international conventions do not purely and simply authorize State parties to make reservations to one provision or another, but contain an exhaustive list of reservations from among which States must make their choice.[350] This procedure also allows contracting States to gauge precisely and *a priori* the impact and effect of a reservation on treaty relations. By expressing its consent to be bound by the convention, a State or an international organization consents to any reservations permitted by the "list".

218. In these two cases, the content of the reservation is sufficiently predetermined by the treaty for these reservations to be able to be considered "expressly authorized" within the meaning of article 20, paragraph 1, of the Vienna Conventions. The Contracting Parties are aware in advance of the treaty relations that derive from the formulation of a given reservation and have agreed to it in the actual text of the treaty. There is no surprise and the principle of consent is not undermined.)

[346] Horn, *op. cit.* (footnote 197 above), p. 133.

[347] See, for example, article 20, paragraph 1, of the 1930 Hague Convention on Certain Questions relating to the Conflict of Nationality Laws: "Any High Contracting Party may, when signing or ratifying the present Convention or acceding thereto, append an express reservation excluding any one or more of the provisions of Articles 1 to 17 and 21." Treaties often authorize a reservation excluding the application of a provision concerning the settlement of disputes (see Imbert, *Les réserves aux traités multilatéraux*, p. 169, footnote 27, and Riquelme Cortado, *op. cit.* (footnote 208 above), pp. 135 and 136).

[348] Revised General Act for the Pacific Settlement of International Disputes of 1949, art. 38; European Convention for the Peaceful Settlement of Disputes of 1957, art. 34. The Convention concerning Minimum Standards of Social Security, No. 102, of the International Labour Organization (ILO) combines, moreover, this possibility of rejecting the application of entire chapters with a minimum number of chapters that must actually be applied (art. 2) (see also article 2 of ILO Convention No. 128 concerning Invalidity, Old-Age and Survivors' Benefits, article 20 of the European Social Charter or article 2 of the European Code of Social Security of 1964). See also Riquelme Cortado, *op. cit.* (footnote 208 above), p. 134.

[349] On this notion, see also *Yearbook ... 2000*, vol. II (Part Two), p. 116, para. (11) of the commentary to guideline 1.1.8. See also Gormley, "The modification of multilateral conventions by means of 'negotiated reservations' and other 'alternatives': a comparative study of the ILO and Council of Europe", p. 59 (1970–1971), pp. 75–76, and Imbert, *op. cit.* (footnote 347 above), pp. 196 *et seq.*

[350] For Council of Europe practice, see Riquelme Cortado, *op. cit.* (footnote 208 above), pp. 130 *et seq.*

219. The Commission has, moreover, provided a starting point for a definition of the notion of expressly authorized reservations in its guideline 3.1.4 (Permissibility of specified reservations). Pursuant to this provision:

> Where the treaty envisages the formulation of specified reservations without defining their content, a reservation may be formulated by a State or an international organization only if it is not incompatible with the object and purpose of the treaty.

A contrario, a specified reservation whose content is fixed in the treaty is considered *ipso facto* to be permissible and, given the provision expressly authorizing them, established.

220. Guideline 4.1.1 presents the exception to the general rule contained in article 20, paragraph 1, of the 1969 and 1986 Vienna Conventions while establishing a link to the notion of "established reservation". Indeed, since a reservation expressly authorized by the treaty is, by definition, permissible and accepted by the Contracting Parties, making it in a way that respects the rules applicable to the formulation and the communication of reservations is all that is required to establish it. That makes it binding on all the Contracting Parties.

"**4.1.1** *Establishment of a reservation expressly authorized by the treaty*

"A reservation expressly authorized by the treaty is established with regard to the other Contracting Parties if it was formulated in accordance with the form and procedure specified for the purpose.

"A reservation expressly authorized by a treaty does not require any subsequent acceptance by the other contracting States and organizations, unless the treaty so provides.

"The term 'reservation expressly authorized by the treaty' applies to reservations excluding the application of one or more provisions of the treaty or modifying the legal effect of one or more of its provisions or of the treaty as a whole, pursuant to and to the extent provided by an express provision contained in the treaty."

221. The first paragraph of guideline 4.1.1 sets forth the specific rule that applies to the establishment of reservations expressly authorized by the treaty, while the second recalls article 20, paragraph 1, of the 1986 Vienna Convention. While that reference may not be strictly necessary, as it follows from a close reading of guidelines 4.1 and 4.1.1, it is in line with the Commission's established and consistent practice of incorporating to the extent possible the provisions of the Convention. That is also why the Special Rapporteur has not changed the wording despite the fact that the phrase "unless the treaty so provides" states the obvious and, moreover, appears superfluous in this provision.[351] The third paragraph endeavours to define the concept of an "expressly authorized reservation".

222. It should also be emphasized that once it has been clearly established that a given reservation falls under article 20, paragraph 1, not only is its acceptance by the other parties not necessary, but they are deemed to have

[351] See Müller, "Article 20" (footnote 195 above), p. 888, para. 7.

effectively and definitively accepted it, with all the consequences that follow therefrom. One of the consequences of this particular regime is that the other parties cannot object to this type of reservation.[352] Accepting this reservation in advance in the text of the treaty itself effectively prevents the Contracting Parties from subsequently making an objection, as "[t]he Parties have already agreed that the reservation is permissible and, having made its permissibility the object of an express agreement, the Parties have abandoned any right thereafter to object to such a reservation".[353] An amendment[354] proposed by France at the United Nations Conference on the Law of Treaties expressed exactly the same idea, but was not adopted by the Drafting Committee.[355] Guideline 2.8.12 (Final nature of acceptance of a reservation) is therefore applicable *a fortiori* to expressly authorized reservations. They are deemed to have been accepted, and thus there can be no objection to them. The commentary on guideline 4.1.1 might draw attention to the matter.

ii. Reservations to treaties "with limited participation"

223. Another specific case provided for by the 1969 and 1986 Vienna Conventions, article 20, paragraph 2, is that of treaties "with limited participation". Paragraph 2 states that the flexible system shall not apply to any treaty whose application in its entirety between all the parties is an essential condition of the consent of each one to be bound by the treaty. In such cases, a reservation requires acceptance by all the parties.

224. Fitzmaurice made a distinction between plurilateral treaties, which were in his view closer to bilateral treaties, and multilateral treaties.[356] However, it was only in Sir Humphrey Waldock's first report that the usefulness of such a distinction became clearly apparent. What is now article 20, paragraph 2, resulted from a compromise between the members of the Commission who remained deeply convinced of the virtues of the traditional system of unanimity and the proponents of Sir Humphrey's flexible system.[357] At the time, the paragraph represented the last bastion which the proponents of unanimity refused to give up. During the second reading of the Waldock draft, the principle behind article 20, paragraph 2, no longer gave rise to debate in the Commission or at the United Nations Conference on the Law of Treaties.

225. However, the main issue is not the principle of unanimity, which has long been practised. Rather, the question is how to determine which treaties are not subject to the safeguard clause and are therefore excluded from the flexible system. Until 1965, the limited number of parties was the only criterion referred to by the special rapporteurs and the Commission.[358] Sir Humphrey's fourth report took into account the criticisms levelled against that criterion, and recognized that "to find a completely precise definition of the category of treaties in issue is not within the bounds of possibility".[359] At the same time, he proposed a reference to the intention of the parties: "the application of its provisions between all the parties is to be considered an essential condition of the treaty".[360] The parties' intention to preserve the integrity of the treaty was therefore the criterion for ruling out the "flexible" system and retaining the traditional unanimity system. The Commission adopted that idea, making minor drafting changes to what would become the present paragraph 2.[361]

226. It is worth noting, however, that the new provision addresses a completely different category of treaty than had been envisaged before 1962. The reference to intention has two advantages. First, it allows the flexible system to extend to treaties which, although ratified by only a small number of States, are otherwise more akin to general multilateral treaties. Secondly, it excludes treaties that have been ratified by a more significant number of States, but whose very nature requires that the integrity of the treaty be preserved. The concept of the plurilateral treaty has therefore shifted towards that of a treaty whose integrity must be ensured.[362]

227. The criterion of number was never completely discarded, and remains in paragraph 2. However, its function has changed. Before 1965, it was the sole factor in determining whether or not a given treaty belonged within the "flexible" system. Its purpose is now to shed light on the intention of the parties. As a result, it now carries less weight in determining the nature of a treaty, having become an auxiliary criterion in this respect while unfortunately remaining somewhat imprecise and difficult to apply.[363] The reference to the "limited number of the negotiating States" is particularly unusual, and does not allow a clear distinction between such treaties and multilateral treaties proper; the latter can also be concluded as a result of negotiations between only a few States. It seems

[352] Bowett, *loc. cit.* (see footnote 332 above), p. 84; Coccia, "Reservations to multilateral treaties on human rights", p. 9.

[353] Bowett, *loc. cit.* (see footnote 332 above), pp. 84–85.

[354] A/CONF.39/C.1/L.169. Paragraph 2 of the single article that, according to the French proposal, was to replace articles 16 and 17 of the draft of the Commission provided that "a reservation expressly authorized by the treaty cannot be the subject of an objection by other contracting States, unless the treaty so provides" (*Documents of the Conference* (A/CONF.39/11/Add.2) (see footnote 318 above), p. 133).

[355] With regard to the rejection of that amendment, Imbert concluded that the States represented at the Conference did not want to restrict the right to object to expressly authorized reservations (*op. cit.* (footnote 347 above), p. 55).

[356] First report on the law of treaties, *Yearbook ... 1956*, vol. II, document A/CN.4/101, p. 127, para. 97.

[357] The Special Rapporteur stressed that "paragraph [4] and paragraph 2 represented the balance on which the whole article was based" (*Yearbook ... 1962*, vol. I, 664th meeting, p. 230, para. 17). See also the statements made by Gros (*ibid.*, 663rd meeting, pp. 228–229, para. 97) and Ago (*ibid.*, p. 228, para. 87).

[358] This is true of Fitzmaurice (draft art. 38 in the Report on the law of treaties, *Yearbook ... 1956*, vol. II, document A/CN.4/101, p. 115) and of Sir Humphrey Waldock (draft art. 1 (*d*), First report on the law of treaties, *Yearbook ... 1962*, vol. II, document A/CN.4/144, p. 221). Draft article 20, paragraph 3, which was adopted by the Commission on first reading in 1962, refers to treaties concluded "between a small group of States" (*Yearbook ... 1962*, vol. II, p. 176).

[359] *Yearbook ... 1965*, vol. II, document A/CN.4/177 and Add.1–2, p. 51, para. 7.

[360] Draft art. 19, para. 2, *ibid.*, p. 50.

[361] *Yearbook ... 1965*, vol. I, 813th meeting, pp. 258–260, paras. 36–53, and 816th meeting, pp. 283–284, paras. 43–49.

[362] See Imbert, *op. cit.* (footnote 347 above), p. 115.

[363] See in particular the criticisms made by Imbert, *ibid.*, pp. 112–113. See also the United States proposal at the United Nations Conference on the Law of Treaties, to delete any reference to criteria other than intention, owing to those difficulties; *Summary records* (A/CONF.39/11) (see footnote 318 above), 21st meeting, p. 108, para. 9.

preferable to refer not to negotiating States, but rather to States authorized to become parties to the treaty.[364]

228. Sir Humphrey proposed other "auxiliary" criteria that could assist in the intrinsically problematic task of establishing the parties' intentions. In his fourth report, he also mentioned the nature of the treaty and the circumstances of its conclusion.[365] The change was never explained, and despite the proposals of the United States, which pressed for the definition to refer to the nature of the treaty,[366] the object and purpose of the treaty was the only other "auxiliary" criterion adopted by the Committee and subsequently at the United Nations Conference on the Law of Treaties. The criterion of object and purpose, like that of number, is far from clear-cut. The inclusion of such an enigmatic criterion[367] does not help clarify the interpretation of paragraph 2. Indeed, one could argue that it makes the task even more arbitrary and subjective.[368]

229. Paragraph 2 of article 20 is unclear, or at any rate difficult to interpret, not only in respect of its scope, but also in respect of the applicable legal regime. According to paragraph 2, reservations require acceptance by all parties. Only two things can be deduced for certain. First, such reservations are not subject to the "flexible" system set forth in paragraph 4. Indeed, paragraph 4 confirms that view, in that it applies only to "cases not falling under the preceding paragraphs". Secondly, the reservations are indeed subject to unanimous acceptance: they must be accepted "by *all** the parties".

230. However, paragraph 2 of article 20 does not clearly state who should actually accept the reservation. The text does refer to "the parties", but this is hardly satisfactory. It is questionable whether the acceptance of a reservation by all "parties" only should be a condition, a "party" being defined under article 2, paragraph 1 (*g*), as "a State or an international organization which has consented to be bound by the treaty and for which the treaty is in force". That would contradict the underlying idea, which is that the treaty should be implemented in its entirety by all current and future parties. To argue otherwise would, in no small measure, deprive unanimous consent of its meaning.

231. Moreover, although article 20, paragraph 5, connects the principle of tacit or implied consent to paragraph 2, it remains a mystery how implied acceptance could apply to the treaties referred to in the latter provision. It follows from article 20, paragraph 5, that a contracting State may make any objection only on becoming a party to the treaty. A signatory State could thus block unanimous acceptance even without formulating a formal objection to the reservation, because it is impossible to presume that State's assent before the 12-month deadline to elapse. Article 20, paragraph 5, would therefore have the exact opposite of the desired effect, namely the rapid stabilization of treaty relations and of the status of the reserving State.[369] For precisely that reason, the Special Rapporteur argued in 1962 that where States not yet parties to a treaty are concerned:

> [t]his qualification of the rule is not possible in the case of plurilateral treaties because there the delay of taking a decision does place in suspense the status of the reserving State *vis-à-vis* all the States participating in the treaty.[370]

232. Such lacunae and inconsistencies are particularly surprising given that article 18 as proposed by Sir Humphrey Waldock in 1962 made a clear distinction between the tacit or implied acceptance of "plurilateral treaties" on the one hand and of multilateral treaties on the other hand.[371] These clarifications described the legal regime for the treaties referred to in article 20, paragraph 2, perfectly well. They were nevertheless sacrificed in order to make the provisions on reservations less complex and more succinct.

233. It therefore seems appropriate and necessary to include in the Guide to Practice a guideline on how to establish a reservation to treaties with "limited participation":

"**4.1.2** *Establishment of a reservation to a treaty with limited participation*

"A reservation to a treaty with limited participation is established with regard to the other Contracting Parties if it meets the requirements for permissibility of a reservation and was formulated in accordance with the form and procedures specified for the purpose, and if all the other Contracting Parties have accepted it.

"The term 'treaty with limited participation' means a treaty of which the application in its entirety between the parties is an essential condition of the consent of each one to be bound by the treaty."

iii. Reservations to be bound by constituent instruments of international organizations

234. The other exception to the principle that tacit acceptance is sufficient to establish a reservation is provided for by article 20, paragraph 3, of the 1969 and 1986 Vienna Conventions and relates to constituent treaties of international organizations. Under the terms of this provision:

> When a treaty is a constituent instrument of an international organization and unless it otherwise provides, a reservation requires the acceptance of the competent organ of that organization.

235. A simple perusal of this provision shows that, in order to be established, a reservation to a constituent treaty of an international organization calls for the acceptance of the competent organ of the organization. The formulation

[364] Imbert, *op. cit.* (footnote 347 above), pp. 112–113.

[365] *Yearbook ... 1965*, vol. II, document A/CN.4/177 and Add.1–2, p. 51, para. 7.

[366] See amendment, A/CONF.39/C.1/L.127, *Official Records: Documents of the Conference* (A/CONF.39/11/Add.2) (footnote 318 above), p. 135.

[367] See guideline 3.1.5 (Incompatibility of a reservation with the object and purpose of the treaty) and 3.1.6 (Determination of the object and purpose of the treaty), *Yearbook ... 2007*, vol. II (Part Two), pp. 33–39.

[368] See Tomuschat, *loc. cit.* (footnote 195 above), p. 479; Imbert, *op. cit.* (footnote 347 above), pp. 114–115.

[369] See Müller, "Article 20" (footnote 195 above), pp. 820–821, paras. 46–47.

[370] *Yearbook ... 1962*, vol. II, document A/CN.4/144, p. 67, para. (16).

[371] *Ibid.*, pp. 61–62.

of this acceptance was the subject of a detailed study in the twelfth report on reservations to treaties,[372] which, *inter alia*, presents the *travaux préparatoires* of this provision. On the basis of that report, the Commission adopted a number of guidelines related to this exception to the rules. These are guidelines 2.8.7 to 2.8.11:

2.8.7 *Acceptance of a reservation to the constituent instrument of an international organization*

When a treaty is a constituent instrument of an international organization and unless it otherwise provides, a reservation requires the acceptance of the competent organ of that organization.

2.8.8 *Organ competent to accept a reservation to a constituent instrument*

Subject to the rules of the organization, competence to accept the reservation to a constituent instrument of an international organization belongs to the organ competent to decide on the admission of a member to the organization, or to the organ competent to amend the constituent instrument, or to the organ competent to interpret this instrument.

2.8.9 *Modalities of the acceptance of a reservation to a constituent instrument*

Subject to the rules of the organization, the acceptance by the competent organ of the organization shall not be tacit. However, the admission of the State or the international organization which is the author of the reservation is tantamount to the acceptance of that reservation.

For the purposes of the acceptance of a reservation to the constituent instrument of an international organization, the individual acceptance of the reservation by States or international organizations that are members of the organization is not required.

2.8.10 *Acceptance of a reservation to a constituent instrument that has not yet entered into force*

In the case set forth in guideline 2.8.7 and where the constituent instrument has not yet entered into force, a reservation is considered to have been accepted if no signatory State or signatory international organization has raised an objection to that organization by the end of a period of 12 months after they were notified of that reservation. Such a unanimous acceptance thus obtained is final.

2.8.11 *Reaction by a member of an international organization to a reservation to its constituent instrument*

Guideline 2.8.7 does not preclude States or international organizations that are members of an international organization from taking a position on the permissibility or appropriateness of a reservation to a constituent instrument of the organization. Such an opinion is in itself devoid of legal effects.[373]

236. It does not appear necessary to recall once again the reasons that led the Commission and the Conference to adopt the provisions contained in article 20, paragraph 3, of the 1969 Vienna Convention. Although guideline 2.8.7 is sufficient to express the need for the acceptance of the competent organ of the organization, it is nevertheless worth recalling this particular requirement in the section dealing with the effects of reservations, given that the acceptance of the competent organization is the *sine qua non* for the establishment of a reservation to the constituent instrument of an international organization. Only this collective acceptance can enable the reservation to produce all its effects. The individual acceptance of the other members of the organization is indeed not prohibited, but remains without effect on the establishment of the reservation. Guideline 4.1.3 could read as follows:

"**4.1.3** *Establishment of a reservation to a constituent instrument of an international organization*

"A reservation to a constituent instrument of an international organization is established with regard to the other Contracting Parties if it meets the requirements for permissibility of a reservation and was formulated in accordance with the form and procedures specified for the purpose, and if the competent organ of the organization has accepted it in conformity with guidelines 2.8.7 and 2.8.10."

(ii) *Effects of established reservations*

237. A reservation "established" within the meaning of guideline 4.1 produces all the effects purported by its author, that is to say, to echo the wording of guideline 1.1.1 (Object of reservations), "to exclude or modify the legal effect of certain provisions of a treaty or of the treaty as a whole with respect to certain specific aspects".[374] If that is done, the object of the reservation as desired or purported by its author is achieved.

238. However, modifying or excluding the legal effect of one or more provisions of the treaty is not the only effect of the establishment of the reservation; it also constitutes the author of the reservation a Contracting Party to the treaty. Following the establishment of the reservation, the treaty relationship is established between the author of the reservation and the Contracting Party or parties for which the reservation is established.

a. Entry into force of the treaty and status of the author of the reservation

239. The establishment of the reservation has a number of consequences for its author relating to the very existence of the treaty relationship and the author's status in relation to the other Contracting Parties. It may even result in the entry into force of the treaty for all of the contracting States or contracting international organizations. These consequences follow directly from article 20, paragraph 4 (*a*) and (*c*), of the 1969 and 1986 Vienna Conventions: the first of these provisions relates to the establishment of treaty relations between the author of the reservation and the Contracting Party which has accepted it (hence, the Contracting Party for which the reservation is established), whereas the second relates to whether the consent of the reserving State or reserving international organization takes effect, or in other words whether the author of the reservation becomes a Contracting Party to the treaty. They read as follows:

4. In cases not falling under the preceding paragraphs and unless the treaty otherwise provides:

(*a*) Acceptance by another contracting State of a reservation constitutes the reserving State a party to the treaty in relation to that other State if or when the treaty is in force for those States;

(*b*) ...

(*c*) An act expressing a State's consent to be bound by the treaty and containing a reservation is effective as soon as at least one other contracting State has accepted the reservation.

[372] *Yearbook ... 2007*, vol. II (Part One), document A/CN.4/584 and Corr.1, paras. 60–90.

[373] *Yearbook ... 2009*, vol. II (Part Two), para. 83.

[374] *Yearbook ... 1999*, vol. II (Part Two), p. 91.

240. The Commission's comments on draft article 17 (which becomes article 20) clearly explain the object of the provisions:

> Paragraph 4 contains the three basic rules of the "flexible" system which are to govern the position of the contracting States in regard to reservations to any multilateral treaties not covered by the preceding paragraphs. Subparagraph (*a*) provides that acceptance of a reservation by another contracting State constitutes the reserving State a party to the treaty in relation to that State if or when the treaty is in force. Subparagraph (*b*), on the other hand, states that a contracting State's objection precludes the entry into force of the treaty as between the objecting and reserving States, unless a contrary intention is expressed by the objecting State. Although an objection to a reservation normally indicates a refusal to enter into treaty relations on the basis of the reservation, objections are sometimes made to reservations for reasons of principle or policy without the intention of precluding the entry into force of the treaty between the objecting and reserving States. Subparagraph (*c*) then provides that an act expressing the consent of a State to be bound and containing a reservation is effective as soon as at least one other contracting State has accepted the reservation. This provision is important since it determines the moment at which a reserving State may be considered as a State which has ratified, accepted or otherwise become bound by the treaty.[375]

241. The rule that the acceptance of a permissible reservation establishes a treaty relationship between the author of the reservation and the State or international organization that has accepted it also makes good sense. It appears in various forms in the drafts by all the special rapporteurs on the law of treaties. The only difference between Sir Humphrey Waldock's approach and that of his predecessors lies in the number of acceptances needed in order to produce this effect. The attachment of the first three rapporteurs to the traditional regime of unanimity meant that they did not accept the establishment of a treaty relationship unless all the other Contracting Parties had accepted the reservations. In Sir Humphrey's flexible approach, each State (or international organization) not only decides individually whether a reservation is opposable to it or not; this individual acceptance also has effects independently of the reactions of the other States or international organizations, but logically, only in the bilateral relations between the author of the reservation and the author of the acceptance. The Commission explained in its commentary on draft article 20 as adopted on first reading that the application of this flexible system may:

> certainly have the result that a reserving State may be a party to the treaty with regard to State X, but not with regard to State Y, although States X and Y are mutually bound by the treaty. But in the case of a general multilateral treaty or of a treaty concluded between a considerable number of States, this result appears to the Commission not to be as unsatisfactory as allowing State Y, by its objection, to prevent the treaty from coming into force between the reserving State and State X, which has accepted the reservation.[376]

242. This system of "relative" participation in the treaty[377] is applicable, however, only in the "normal" instance of establishment of the reservation. Clearly, it cannot be applied in cases where unanimous acceptance is required in order to establish a reservation. For the reservation to be able to produce its effects, including the entry into force of the treaty for the author of the reservation, all of the Contracting Parties must consent to the reservation. Consequently, the treaty necessarily enters into force in the same way for all of the Contracting Parties, on the one hand, and the author of the reservation, on the other hand. A comparable solution is necessary in the case of a reservation to the constituent instrument of an international organization; only the acceptance of the competent organ can establish the reservation and constitute its author one of the circle of Contracting Parties. Once this acceptance is obtained, the author of the reservation establishes treaty relations with all the other Contracting Parties without their individual consent being required.

243. It should however be noted that once the reservation is established, in conformity with the rules described in guidelines 4.1 to 4.1.3 depending on the nature of the reservation and of the treaty, a treaty relationship is formed between the author of the reservation and the Contracting Party or parties in respect of whom the reservation is established: the Contracting Party which accepted the reservation (in the "normal" case), and all the Contracting Parties (in the other cases). It thus suffices to recall this rule which constitutes the core of the Vienna regime, without any need to distinguish again between the general rule and the exceptions to it, as the drafting of guidelines 4.1, 4.1.1, 4.1.2 and 4.1.3 makes it possible to determine in respect of whom the reservation is established and with whom the treaty relationship is constituted:

"**4.2** *Effects of an established reservation*

"**4.2.3** *Effects of the entry into force of a treaty on the status of the author of an established reservation*

"The establishment of a reservation constitutes its author a party to the treaty in relation to contracting States or international organizations in respect of which the reservation is established if or when the treaty is in force."

244. Guideline 4.2.3 does not resolve the issue of the date on which the author of the reservation may be considered to have joined the group of contracting States or contracting international organizations. Article 20, paragraph 4 (*c*), of the 1969 Vienna Convention was quite rightly inserted by the Commission in order to fill that gap. As Sir Humphrey Waldock explained in his fourth report:

> The point is not purely one of drafting, since it touches the question of the conditions under which a reserving State is to be considered a "party" to a multilateral treaty under the "flexible" system. Indeed, not only the Australian but also the Danish Government urges the Commission to deal explicitly with that question, since it may affect the determination of the date on which the treaty comes into force and may otherwise be of concern to a depositary. The Special Rapporteur understands the position under the "flexible" system to be that a reserving State is to be considered as a "party" if and at the moment when another State which has established its consent to be bound by the treaty accepts the reservation either expressly or tacitly under paragraph 3 of the existing article 19 (paragraph 4 of the new article 20 as given below).[378]

Sir Humphrey's explanation, which thus gave rise to article 20, paragraph 4 (*c*), of the 1969 Vienna Convention, is perhaps not entirely correct: indeed, it is impossible to determine whether the author of the reservation becomes a "party" to the treaty in the sense of article 2, paragraph 1 (*g*),

---

[375] *Yearbook ... 1966*, vol. II, p. 207, para. (21) of the commentary.

[376] *Yearbook ... 1962*, vol. II, p. 181, para. (23) of the commentary. See also *Yearbook ... 1966*, vol. II, pp. 207–208, para. (22) of the commentary to draft article 17.

[377] *Yearbook ... 1966*, vol. II, pp. 207–208, para. (22) of the commentary to draft article 17.

[378] *Yearbook ... 1965*, vol. II, pp. 52–53, para. 11.

of the 1969 Vienna Convention, as, independently of the establishment of the reservation, the treaty may not be in force owing to the low number of ratifications or acceptances. However, what can be determined with certainty is the issue of whether the author becomes a contracting State or contracting organization, that is, whether the author has "consented to be bound by the treaty, whether or not the treaty has entered into force" (art. 2, para. 1 (*f*)). It is also the subject of article 20, paragraph 4 (*c*), which merely states that the "act expressing … [the author of the reservation's] consent to be bound by the treaty and containing a reservation *is effective** when at least one other contracting State has accepted the reservation".

245. Although the rule seems to be clearly established by article 20, paragraph 4 (*c*), of the 1969 and 1986 Vienna Conventions—the author of a reservation becomes a contracting State or contracting organization as soon as the author's permissible reservation has been accepted by at least one contracting State or organization—its practical application is far from consistent and is even less coherent. The main parties concerned by the application of this rule, that is, depositaries, have applied and continue to apply it in a very approximate manner.

246. The Secretary-General of the United Nations, in his capacity as depositary of multilateral treaties, for example, agrees that any instrument expressing consent to be bound by a treaty which is accompanied by a reservation may be deposited and, refusing to adopt a position on the issue of the permissibility or effects of the reservation, "indicates the date on which, in accordance with the treaty provisions, the instrument would normally produce its effect, leaving it to each party to draw the legal consequences of the reservations that it deems fit".[379] In other words, the Secretary-General does not wait for at least one acceptance to be received before accepting the definitive deposit of an instrument of ratification or accession accompanied by a reservation, but treats such instruments in the same way as any other ratification or accession that is not accompanied by an objection:

> Since he is not to pass judgement, the Secretary-General is not therefore in a position to ascertain the effects, if any, of the instrument containing reservations thereto, *inter alia*, whether the treaty enters into force as between the reserving State and any other State, *a fortiori* between a reserving State and an objecting State if there have been objections. As a consequence, if the final clauses of the treaty in question stipulate that the treaty shall enter into force after the deposit of a certain number of instruments of ratification, approval, acceptance or accession, the Secretary-General as depositary will, subject to the considerations in the following paragraph, include in the number of instruments required for entry into force all those that have been accepted for deposit, whether or not they are accompanied by reservations and whether or not those reservations have met with objections.[380]

This position, which is entirely open to criticism[381] in view of the content of article 20, paragraph 4 (*c*), of the 1969 and 1986 Vienna Conventions (read in conjunction with article 20, paragraph 5), has been justified by the Secretary-General by the fact that:

> no objection had ever in fact been received from any State concerning an entry into force that included States making reservations. Finally, for a State's instrument not to be counted, it might conceivably be required that all other contracting States, without exception, would have not only objected to the participation of the reserving State, but that those objecting States would all have definitely expressed their intention that their objection would preclude the entry into force of the treaty as between them and the objecting State.[382]

247. To give a recent example, Pakistan has acceded to the International Convention for the Suppression of the Financing of Terrorism through a notification dated 17 June 2009. This instrument was accompanied by reservations to articles 11, 14 and 24 of the Convention. Despite the reservations, the Secretary-General noted in his depositary notification of 19 June 2009 that:

> The Convention will enter into force for Pakistan on 17 July 2009 in accordance with its article 26 (2) which reads as follows: "For each State ratifying, accepting, approving or acceding to the Convention after the deposit of the twenty-second instrument of ratification, acceptance, approval or accession, the Convention shall enter into force on the thirtieth day after deposit by such State of its instrument of ratification, acceptance, approval or accession."[383]

Pakistan's instrument is therefore considered by the depositary as taking immediate effect, notwithstanding article 20, paragraph 4 (*c*), of the 1969 Vienna Convention. For the depositary, Pakistan is one of the contracting States, and even a party to the International Convention for the Suppression of the Financing of Terrorism, independently of whether its reservations have been accepted by at least one other Contracting Party.

248. This practice, which seems to have been followed for many years and which existed well before the 1969 Vienna Convention,[384] has also been followed by other depositary institutions or States. Thus, both the Dominican Republic and the Council of Europe informed the Secretary-General of the United Nations in 1965 that, as a depositary, a reserving State was "counted among the number of countries necessary for bringing the convention into force"[385]—in other words, as soon as it acquired the status of a contracting State. Other depositaries, including the United States, the Organization of American States and the Food and Agriculture Organization of the United Nations, reported a more nuanced practice and do not in principle count reserving States as contracting States.[389]

249. However, the Special Rapporteur is of the view that although the application of article 20, paragraph 4 (*c*), of the 1969 and 1986 Vienna Conventions is hesitant, to say the least, the rule expressed in this provision has not lost its authority. It is certainly part of the reservations regime established by the Conventions and it has been a principle

[379] United Nations, *Summary of Practice of the Secretary-General as Depositary of Multilateral Treaties*, New York, 1999, (ST/LEG/7/Rev.1), para. 187.

[380] *Ibid.*, para. 184.

[381] Imbert, "*À l'occasion de l'entrée en vigueur de la Convention de Vienne sur le droit des traités, réflexions sur la pratique suivie par le Secrétaire général des Nations Unies dans l'exercice de ses fonctions de dépositaire*", pp. 524–541; Gaja, *loc. cit.* (see footnote 320 above), pp. 323–324; Riquelme Cortado, *op. cit.* (see footnote 208 above), pp. 245–250; or Müller, "Article 20" (see footnote 195 above), pp. 821 and 822, para. 48.

[382] *Summary of Practice of the Secretary-General as Depositary of Multilateral Treaties*, United Nations, New York, 1999 (ST/LEG/7/Rev.1), para. 186.

[383] *Multilateral Treaties Deposited with the Secretary-General*, available online from http://treaties.un.org/ (Status of treaties, chap. XVIII.11).

[384] See *Yearbook ... 1965*, vol. II, para. 109, p. 103.

[385] *Ibid.*, p. 98.

of the Commission to complement the provisions on reservations of these two Conventions, rather than to contradict them.[386] According to the terms of article 20, paragraph 4 (*c*), of the Conventions, the author of a reservation does not become a contracting State or organization until at least one other contracting State or other contracting organization accepts the reservation, either expressly—which seldom occurs—or tacitly on expiration of the time period set by article 20, paragraph 5, and referred to in guidelines 2.6.13[387] and 2.8.1.[388] In the worst case, the consequence of strict application of this provision is a delay of 12 months in the entry into force of the treaty for the author of the reservation. This delay may certainly be considered undesirable; nevertheless, it is caused by the author of the reservation, and it can be reduced by express acceptance of the reservation on the part of a single other contracting State or a single other contracting international organization.

250. In the light of the above, a guideline should be included in the Guide to Practice which expresses the idea of article 20, paragraph 4 (*c*), rather than reproducing it word for word. As soon as a valid reservation is accepted by at least one contracting State or one contracting international organization, the reservation is established as indicated in guidelines 4.1, 4.1.1, 4.1.2 and 4.1.3, and the instrument of ratification or accession of the author of the reservation takes effect and constitutes the author a contracting State or a contracting international organization. This has the consequence that the author of the reservation is one of the contracting States or contracting organizations even if the treaty has not yet entered into force. This is the idea reflected in guideline 4.2.1:

"**4.2.1** *Status of the author of an established reservation*

"As soon as the reservation is established, its author is considered a contracting State or contracting organization to the treaty."

251. Clearly, if the treaty is in force, the author of an established reservation also becomes a party to it.

252. Moreover, if the treaty has not yet entered into force, the establishment of the reservation and the permissibility of the instrument through which the author of the reservation has expressed consent to be bound by the treaty may have the consequence that the treaty enters into force for all contracting States and organizations, including the author of the reservation. That is the case if, following the establishment of the reservation, the addition of the author to the number of Contracting Parties has the result that the conditions for the entry into force of the treaty are fulfilled. This consequence then depends largely on the circumstances of the case, and in particular on the conditions for the entry into force of the treaty as established by the final clauses, the number of Contracting Parties and so on. It is thus scarcely possible to draw a general rule in this respect except that the author of the established reservation must be included in the number of contracting States or organizations that determines the entry into force of the treaty. This is made clear by guideline 4.2.2:

"**4.2.2** *Effect of the establishment of a reservation on the entry into force of a treaty*

"When a treaty has not yet entered into force, the author of a reservation shall be included in the number of contracting States or contracting organizations required for the treaty to enter into force once the reservation is established."

b. Effect of an established reservation on the content of treaty relations

253. The entry into force of the treaty between the author of the reservation and the parties to the treaty that have accepted it is not the only consequence of the establishment of the reservation. It also modifies the content of the treaty relationship thus constituted and thus achieves the object of the reservation in the sense that "the provisions of the treaty to which the reservation relates" will be modified "to the extent of the reservation" in the mutual relations between the two States concerned.[389] This effect follows, as the Commission pointed out, "directly from the consensual basis of the relations between parties to a treaty".[390] The reservation, which is nothing but an offer formulated by its author purporting to modify or exclude the application of certain provisions of the treaty, and its acceptance constitute an agreement between the protagonists, an agreement *inter partes*, which modulates their treaty relations deriving from the treaty.

254. Article 21, paragraph 1 (*a*), of the 1969 and 1986 Vienna Conventions specifies the effect an established reservation produces for its author on the content of treaty relations. In the 1986 Vienna Convention, this provision reads:

> A reservation established with regard to another party in accordance with articles 19, 20 and 23:
>
> (*a*) Modifies for the reserving State or international organization in its relations with that other party the provisions of the treaty to which the reservation relates to the extent of the reservation.

255. The term "modify" used in this provision must however be interpreted broadly. It seems strange that the texts of this provision and of article 2, paragraph 1 (*d*), should never have been harmonized. Article 2, paragraph 1 (*d*), of the 1969 and 1986 Vienna Conventions defines a reservation as any unilateral statement whereby a State "purports to exclude or to modify the legal effect of certain provisions of the treaty". However, this inconsistency scarcely affects the outcome, given that paragraphs 1 (*a*) and (*b*) clearly specify that the provision of the treaty will be modified "to the extent of the reservation". This wording includes both excluding reservations—whereby States purport purely and simply to exclude the application of one or more provisions of the treaty—and limiting reservations, which simply relate to a specific aspect of the provision in question, without completely excluding its application.

[386] First report on the law and practice relating to reservations to treaties, *Yearbook ... 1995*, vol. II (Part One), document A/CN.4/470, vol. pp. 151–154, paras. 153–169.

[387] *Yearbook ... 2008*, vol. II (Part Two), para. 123.

[388] *Yearbook ... 2009*, vol. II (Part Two), para. 83.

[389] On the principle of reciprocity, see paragraphs 272–290 below.

[390] *Yearbook ... 1966*, vol. II, p. 209, para. (1) of the commentary to article 19 [21].

256. Another inconsistency, and a more serious one, may be signalled between the definition of the term "reservation" in the 1969 and 1986 Vienna Conventions and the effects provided for by article 21, paragraph 1, two provisions that need to be juxtaposed:[391] whereas according to article 21 the reservation modifies "the provisions of the treaty", the object of the reservation under article 2, paragraph 1 (*b*), is to modify or exclude "the legal effect of certain provisions of the treaty". This problem did not go unnoticed during the discussions in the Commission: while some members stressed that the reservation could not change the provisions of the treaty, and that it would be preferable to replace "provisions" by "application",[392] other members paid little attention to the matter[393] or indicated their clear satisfaction with the text proposed by the Drafting Committee.[394]

257. In the literature, the question of whether it is the "provisions of the treaty" or their "legal effects" that are modified has been raised more forcefully. Imbert is of the view that:

> It is precisely the link which the drafters of the Vienna Convention established between reservations and the provisions of a convention that seems to be most open to criticism, in that a reservation is aimed at eliminating not a *provision* but an *obligation*.[395]

258. However, this view considers the effect of the reservation only from the standpoint of its author, and appears to overlook the fact that in modifying the author's obligation the reservation also affects the correlative rights of the States or international organizations that have accepted the reservation. It is thus more convincing to conclude that, with regard to this question:

> article 2, paragraph 1 (*b*), of the 1969 and 1986 Vienna Conventions is better drafted than article 21, paragraph 1. It is unclear how a reservation, which is an instrument *external* to the treaty, could modify *a provision of that treaty*. It might exclude or modify its application, i.e. its effect, but not the text itself, i.e. the provision.[396]

259. And yet the text of article 2, paragraph 1 (*d*), also does not appear to correspond fully to State practice with respect to reservations, in that it specifies that a reservation can purport to exclude or modify only "the legal effect of *certain provisions* of the treaty".[397] It is in fact not uncommon for States to formulate reservations in order to modify the application of a treaty as a whole, or at least of a substantial part of it. In some cases, such reservations can certainly not be regarded as permissible, in that they deprive the treaty of its object and purpose, so that they no longer have the status of "established reservations".[398] However, this is not always the case, and there are in practice many examples of such across-the-board reservations which were not the subject of objections or challenges by the other contracting States.[399] Article 21, paragraph 1, appears more open in this respect, in that it simply provides that the reservation modifies (or excludes) "the provisions of the treaty to which the reservation relates to the extent of the reservation". If a reservation can thus permissibly purport to modify the legal effects of all of the provisions of a treaty in certain specific aspects, as the Commission clearly acknowledged in guideline 1.1.1 (Object of reservations),[400] it will have the effect, once established, of modifying all these provisions in accordance with article 21, paragraph 1, or indeed, as the case may be, all of the provisions of the treaty.[401]

260. It follows that a permissibly established reservation affects the treaty relations of the author of the reservation in that it excludes or modifies the legal effect of a provision or provisions of the treaty, or even of the treaty as a whole, on a specific aspect and on a reciprocal basis.[402]

261. In accordance with the Commission's well-established practice in the context of the Guide to Practice, it is consequently appropriate to incorporate a guideline 4.2.4 which largely reproduces article 21, paragraph 1 (*a*), of the 1986 Vienna Convention while specifying that the reservation modifies not the provision of the treaty in question, but its legal effects:[403]

"**4.2.4** *Content of treaty relations*

"A reservation established with regard to another party modifies for the reserving State or international organization in its relations with that other party the legal effects of the provisions of the treaty to which the reservation relates, to the extent of the reservation."

262. In order to clarify further the content of the obligations and rights of the author of the reservation and of the State or international organization with regard to which the reservation is established, it is wise to distinguish between, as Horn terms them, on the one hand

---

[391] Third report on reservations to treaties, *Yearbook ... 1998*, vol. II (Part One), document A/CN.4/491 and Add.1–6, p. 249, para. 149.

[392] Mr. Rosenne (*Yearbook ... 1965*, vol. I, 800th meeting, p. 172, para. 9, and 814th meeting, p. 271, para. 2) and Mr. Tsuruoka (*ibid.*, p. 272, para. 16).

[393] Mr. Tunkin "considered it of no great importance whether the wording used was 'modifies the provisions of the treaty' or 'modifies the application of the provisions of the treaty'" (814th meeting, p. 271, para. 9). For a similar view, see Mr. Briggs (*ibid.*, p. 272, para. 13).

[394] Mr. Briggs (*ibid.*, 800th meeting, p. 173, para. 28).

[395] Imbert, *op. cit.* (footnote 347 above), p. 15.

[396] Third report on reservations to treaties, *Yearbook ... 1998*, vol. II (Part One), document A/CN.4/491 and Add.1–6, para. 150.

[397] Imbert, *op. cit.* (footnote 347 above), pp. 14–15; Szafarz, "Reservations to multilateral treaties", p. 296. See also Pellet (Third report on reservations to treaties, *Yearbook ... 1998*, vol. II (Part One), document A/CN.4/491 and Add.1–6, para. 156. See, however, Hylton, who maintains that "reservations modify a treaty only in regard to specific provisions" ("Default breakdown: the Vienna Convention on the Law of Treaties: inadequate framework on reservations," p. 422).

[398] See guideline 1.1.1 (Object of reservations), *Yearbook ... 1999*, vol. II (Part Two), p. 94, paras. (6) and (7) of the commentary.

[399] *Ibid.*, pp. 93–94, para. (5).

[400] Guideline 1.1.1 (Object of reservations) reads: "A reservation purports to exclude or modify the legal effect of certain provisions of a treaty or of the treaty as a whole with respect to certain specific aspects, in their application to the State or to the international organization which formulates the reservation" (*Yearbook ... 1999*, vol. II (Part Two), p. 93).

[401] De Cesari has written on this subject that "By means of reservations, States can reduce the material or subjective scope of application of a treaty to the point of exclusion of one or more provisions of the treaty or its non-application to specific subjects, or again they can demonstrate willingness to accept the provisions of the treaty in accordance with restrictive modalities or by attaching to the limitations of a temporal or territorial nature." ("Riserve, dichiarazioni e facoltà nelle convenzioni dell'Aja di diritto internazionale privato", p. 167, para. 8.)

[402] On the question of reciprocity, see paragraphs 272–290 below.

[403] See paragraph 258 above.

"modifying reservations" and on the other hand "excluding reservations".[404] The distinction is certainly not always easy to make. Thus, a reservation by which its author purports to limit the scope of application of a treaty obligation only to a certain category of persons may be understood equally well as a modifying reservation (it modifies the legal effect of the initial obligation by limiting the circle of persons concerned) or as an excluding reservation (it purports to exclude the application of the treaty obligation for all persons not forming part of the specified category).[405] The distinction does, however, permit a better insight into the two most common hypotheses. The vast majority of reservations may be classified in one or other of these categories, or at least understood by means of this distinction.

263. In the case of excluding reservations, the author of the reservation purports to exclude the legal effect of one or more provisions of the treaty. There are many examples of this.[406] An excluding reservation that is particularly frequently utilized is that relating to compulsory dispute settlement procedures. Thus Pakistan notified the Secretary-General of the following reservation when it acceded on 17 June 2009 to the International Convention for the Suppression of the Financing of Terrorism:

> The Government of the Islamic Republic of Pakistan does not consider itself bound by Article 24, Paragraph 1 of the International Convention for the Suppression of the Financing of Terrorism.
>
> The Government of Islamic Republic of Pakistan hereby declares that, for a dispute to be referred to the International Court of Justice, the agreement of all parties shall in every case be required.[407]

264. A large number of reservations also purport to exclude the application of material provisions of the treaty. Egypt, for example, formulated a reservation to the Vienna Convention on Diplomatic Relations purporting to exclude the legal effect of article 37, paragraph 2:

> Paragraph 2 of article 37 shall not apply.[408]

Cuba also made a reservation purporting to exclude the application of article 25, paragraph 1, of the Convention on special missions:

> The Revolutionary Government of the Republic of Cuba enters an express reservation with regard to the third sentence of paragraph 1, article 25 of the Convention and consequently does not accept the assumption of consent to enter the premises of the special mission for any of the reasons mentioned in that paragraph or for any other reasons.[409]

Or again, the Government of Rwanda formulated a reservation to the International Convention on the Elimination of All Forms of Racial Discrimination worded as follows:

> The Rwandese Republic does not consider itself as bound by article 22 of the Convention.[410]

265. Applying article 21, paragraph 1 (*a*), of the 1969 and 1986 Vienna Conventions to reservations of this kind is relatively easy. An established reservation modifies the legal effect of the treaty provision to which the reservation relates "to the extent of the reservation", that is to say by purely and simply excluding any legal effect of the treaty provision. Once the reservation is established, everything in the treaty relations between the author of the reservation and the parties that have accepted it takes place as if the treaty did not include the provision referred to in the reservation. Excluding reservations thus have a "contraregulatory effect".[411] The author of the reservation is no longer bound by the obligation stemming from the treaty provision in question, but is in no way prevented from complying with it (and being held to it if the treaty norm enunciates a customary obligation). Logically, the other States or international organizations with regard to which the reservation is established have, through their acceptance, waived their right to demand performance of the obligation stemming from the treaty provision in question in the context of their treaty relationship with the author of the reservation.

266. This shows, moreover, that the exclusion of an obligation stemming from a provision of the treaty by a reservation does not automatically mean that the author of the reservation refuses to fulfil the obligation. The author of the reservation may simply wish to exclude the application of the treaty obligation *within the legal framework established by the treaty*. A State or an international organization may be in full agreement with a norm contained in a provision of the treaty, but nevertheless reject the competence of a treaty body or a judicial authority with respect to the application and interpretation of that norm. Although remaining entirely free to comply with the obligation established within the treaty framework, the author nevertheless excludes the opposability of the control mechanisms established by the treaty.[412]

267. It thus seems appropriate to specify the exclusion effect produced by such reservations. This is the purpose of guideline 4.2.5, which is not an alternative to guidelines 4.2.3 but seeks to specify its meaning with respect to a particular category of reservations:

"**4.2.5** *Exclusion of the legal effect of a treaty provision*

"A reservation established with regard to another party which purports to exclude the legal effect of a treaty provision renders the treaty provision(s) inapplicable in relations between the author of the reservation and the other party.

---

[404] See Horn, *op. cit.* (footnote 197 above), pp. 80–87.

[405] See, for example the Egyptian reservation to the Vienna Convention on Consular Reservations: "Article 49 concerning exemption from taxation shall apply only to consular officers, their spouses and minor children. This exemption cannot be extended to consular employees and to members of the service staff".

[406] *Multilateral Treaties Deposited with the Secretary-General*, available online from http://treaties.un.org/ (Status of treaties), chap. III.6. See also guideline 1.1.8 and the commentary thereto (*Yearbook ... 2000*, vol. II (Part Two)), pp. 108–112.

[407] See also the comparable reservations of Algeria, Andorra, Bahrain, Bangladesh, China, Colombia, Cuba, Egypt, El Salvador, Saudi Arabia, the United Arab Emirates, the United States of America, etc. (*Multilateral Treaties Deposited with the Secretary-General*, available online from http://treaties.un.org/, chap. XVIII.11).

[408] *Ibid.*, chap. III.3. See also the reservation formulated by Morocco (*ibid.*).

[409] *Ibid.*, chap. III.9.

[410] *Ibid.*, chap. IV.2.

[411] Horn, *op. cit.* (footnote 197 above), p. 84.

[412] See also guideline 3.1.8 (Reservations to a provision reflecting a customary norm) and the commentary thereto, *Yearbook ... 2007*, vol. II (Part Two), pp. 42–46, and in particular para. (7) of the commentary.

"The author of the established reservation is not required to comply with the obligation imposed by the treaty provision(s) concerned in treaty relations between it and States and international organizations with regard to which the reservation is established.

"The State or international organization with regard to which the reservation is established cannot claim the right contained in the relevant provision in the context of its treaty relations with the author of the reservation."

268. The concrete effect of a modifying reservation is significantly different. In contrast to excluding reservations, the author of a reservation does not purport to be released from its obligations under one or more treaty provisions in order to regain freedom of action within the treaty legal framework. Rather, it purports to replace the obligation under the treaty with a different one. A clear example of this type of reservation is the reservation of the Federal Republic of Germany to the Convention on Psychotropic Substances:

> In the Federal Republic of Germany, manufacturers, wholesale distributors, importers and exporters are not required to keep records of the type described [in paragraph 2 of article 11 of the Convention] but instead to mark specifically those items in their invoices which contain substances and preparations in Schedule III. Invoices and packaging slips showing such items are to be preserved by these persons for a minimum period of five years.[413]

By this reservation, Germany thus purported not only to exclude the application of article 11, paragraph 2, of the Convention on Psychotropic Substances, but to replace the obligation under that provision with another, different one.

269. The reservation of Finland to article 18 of the Convention on Road Signs and Signals of 1968 is another example that clearly shows that the author of the reservation is not simply releasing itself from its obligation under the treaty, but is replacing the latter with another obligation:

> Finland reserves the right not to use signs E,9a or E,9b to indicate the beginning of a built-up area, nor signs E,9c or E,9d to indicate the end of such an area. Instead of them symbols are used. A sign corresponding to sign E,9b is used to indicate the name of a place, but it does not signify the same as sign E,9b.[414]

270. By such a modifying reservation the author, once the reservation is established, is not simply released from all treaty obligations covered by the reservation. The effect of the reservation is to replace the obligation initially provided for in the treaty by another one which is provided for in the reservation. In other words, the obligation under the treaty provision which is the subject of the reservation is replaced or modified, in the treaty relations between its author and the State or international organization in regard to which the reservation is established, by the one set forth in the reservation; or, more exactly, the established reservation leads to replacement of the obligation and the correlative right under the relevant treaty provision by the obligation and the correlative right provided for in the reservation or resulting from the treaty provision as modified by the reservation.

271. Guideline 4.2.6 clarifies guideline 4.2.2 by explaining the effect of a reservation with a modifying effect on the content of treaty relations:

"**4.2.6** *Modification of the legal effect of a treaty provision*

"A reservation established with regard to another party which purports to modify the legal effect of a treaty provision has the effect, in the relations between the author of the reservation and the other party, of substituting the rights and obligations contained in the provision as modified by the reservation for the rights and obligations under the treaty provision which is the subject of the reservation.

"The author of an established reservation is required to comply with the obligation under the treaty provision (or provisions) modified by the reservation in the treaty relations between it and the States and international organizations with regard to which the reservation is established.

"The State or international organization with regard to which the reservation is established can claim the right under the treaty provision modified by the reservation in the context of its treaty relations with the author of the reservation in question."

272. As soon as the reservation has been "established", it can be invoked not only by its author but also by any other party in regard to which it has acquired this status. The reservation creates between its author and the parties with regard to which it is established a special regulatory system which is applied on a reciprocal basis. In this regard, Sir Humphrey Waldock has explained that "reservations always work both ways".[415] This idea is also to be found in article 21, paragraph 1 (*b*), of the Vienna Convention, which, in its 1986 version, reads as follows:

> 1. A reservation established with regard to another party in accordance with articles 19, 20 and 23:
>
> (*a*) …
>
> (*b*) Modifies those provisions [of the treaty which is their subject] to the same extent for that other party in its relations with the reserving State or international organization.

273. It follows that the author of the reservation is not only released from compliance with the treaty obligations which are the subject of the reservation; it also loses the right to require the State or international organization with regard to which the reservation is established to fulfil the treaty obligations covered by the reservation.

274. This principle of reciprocity is based on common sense.[416] The regulatory system governing treaty relations between the two States concerned reflects the common denominator of their respective commitments resulting

[413] *Multilateral Treaties Deposited with the Secretary-General*, available online from http://treaties.un.org/, chap. VI.6.

[414] *Ibid.*, chap. XI.B.20.

[415] "General course on public international Law", p. 87.

[416] Anzilotti believed that "the effect of the reservation is that the reserving State is not bound by the provisions which are the subject of the reservation; *naturally**, the other parties are not bound in respect to it; thus, in relations between the reserving State and the others, it is as if the provisions which are the subject of the reservation are not part of the treaty" (*Corso di diritto internazionale*, p. 355).

from the overlap—albeit partial—of their wills.[417] It follows "directly from the consensual basis of treaty regulations", which has a significant influence on the general regime of reservations of the 1969 Vienna Convention. In his first report on treaty law, Sir Humphrey Waldock explains:

> A reservation operates reciprocally between the reserving State and any other party to the treaty, so that both are exempted from the reserved provisions in their mutual relations.[418]

ICJ has presented the problem of the reciprocal application of the optional declarations of acceptance of compulsory jurisdiction contained in article 36, paragraph 2, of the Statute of the Court in a comparable, although slightly different, way. In its judgment in the *Norwegian Loans* case, it stated:

> Since two unilateral declarations are involved, such jurisdiction is conferred upon the Court only to the extent to which the two Declarations coincide in conferring it. A comparison between the two Declarations shows that the French Declaration accepts the Court's jurisdiction within narrower limits than the Norwegian Declaration; consequently, the common will of the Parties, which is the basis of the Court's jurisdictions, exists within these narrower limits indicated by the French reservation.[419]

275. The reciprocity of the effects of the reservation also rebalances the inequalities created by the reservation in the bilateral relations between the author of the reservation and the other States or international organizations with regard to which the reservation is established. The latter cannot, through the reservations mechanism, be bound by more obligations towards the author of the reservation than the latter itself is ready to assume.[420] Simma believed the following in this regard:

> Whoever has withdrawn from certain treaty obligations by a reservation cannot claim treatment in accordance with the treaty provisions which are the subject of the reservation.[421]

276. The reciprocal application of a reservation follows directly from the idea of the reciprocity of international commitments and of give-and-take between the parties and conforms to the maxim *do ut des*.

277. Furthermore, the reciprocity of the effects of the reservation plays a regulatory, even a deterrent role, which is not unimportant in the exercise of the widely recognized freedom to formulate a reservation: the author of the reservation must have in mind that the effects of the reservation are not only to the author's benefit; the author also runs the risk of the reservation being invoked against it. On this subject, Sir Humphrey Waldock has written:

> There is of course another check upon undue exercise of the freedom to make reservations in the fundamental rule that a reservation always works both ways, so that any other State may invoke it against the reserving State in their mutual relations.[422]

Reciprocal application thus cuts both ways and "contributes significantly to resolving the inherent tension between treaty flexibility and integrity".[423] In a way, this principle appears to be a complement to, and is often far more effective than, the requirement of permissibility of the reservation, owing to the uncertain determination of permissibility in a good number of cases. The proliferation of reservations in human rights treaties, in which context the principle of reciprocity plays only a marginal role,[424] can probably be explained in part by the link between the formulation of reservations and their reciprocal application:[425] when reciprocity is not a factor, there are more reservations.

278. A number of reservation clauses thus make express reference to the principle of reciprocal application of reservation,[426] whereas other treaties recall the principle of reciprocal application in more general terms.[427] However, such express clauses appear to be superfluous.[428] The principle of reciprocity is recognized not only as a general principle,[429] but also as a principle that applies

[417] Baratta, *Gli effetti della riserve ai trattati*, p. 291: "We have seen, moreover, that the trend resulting from international practice seems to be linked with the consensual principle, a basic element of treaty law: the rule which is the subject of the reservation loses its juridical status, absent an agreement between subjects of law due to the fact of the formulation of the reservation itself."

[418] Sir Humphrey Waldock, First report on the law of treaties, *Yearbook ... 1962*, vol. II, document A/CN.4/144, p. 68, para. 21. The Commission endorsed this explanation in the comments on draft article 19 (which became article 21) adopted on second reading (*Yearbook ... 1966*, vol. II, p. 227, para. (1) of the commentary).

[419] Judgment of 6 July 1957, *Case of Certain Norwegian Loans, I.C.J. Reports 1957*, p. 23.

[420] See *Yearbook ... 1966*, vol. II, p. 206, para. (13) of the commentary on draft articles 16 and 17. Baratta has rightly maintained that the reciprocity of the effects of a reservation has proved to be a "compensatory mechanism in the mutual relations between contracting parties which has served to restore the balance in the *quantum* of reciprocally assumed treaty obligations that was unilaterally altered by a given reservation" (*op. cit.* (footnote 417 above), p. 292).

[421] *Das Reziprozitätselement im Zustandekommen völkerrechtlicher Verträge*, p. 60.

[422] Sir Humphrey Waldock, *loc. cit.* (footnote 415 above), p. 87. See also Parisi and Ševcenko, "Treaty reservations and the economics of article 21 (l) of the Vienna Convention", pp. 1–26.

[423] *Ibid.* See also Baratta, *op. cit.* (footnote 417 above), pp. 295–296.

[424] See paragraph 285 below.

[425] Parisi and Ševcenko, *loc. cit.* (footnote 422 above).

[426] This was already the case in article 20, paragraph 2, of The Hague Convention on Conflict of Nationality Laws of 1930 ("The provisions thus excluded cannot be applied against the Contracting Party who has made the reservation nor relied on by that Party against any other Contracting Party"). Other examples are found in The Hague Conventions on International Private Law (for these reservation clauses, see Majoros, "Le régime de réciprocité de la Convention de Vienne et les réserves dans les Conventions de La Haye", pp. 90 *et seq.*), in a number of conventions concluded within the Economic Commission for Europe (see Imbert, *op. cit.* (footnote 347 above), pp. 188–191 and p. 251) and in some conventions drawn up and concluded within the Council of Europe. The Model Final Clauses for Conventions and Agreements Concluded within the Council of Europe adopted by the Council of Ministers in 1980 proposes the following provision relating to reciprocity of the effects of reservation: "A Party which has made a reservation in respect of a provision of [the Agreement concerned] may not claim the application of that provision by any other Party; it may, however, if its reservation is partial or conditional, claim the application of that provision in so far as it has itself accepted it" (art. *e*, para. 3). See also Horn, *op. cit.* (footnote 197 above), pp. 146–147.

[427] See, for example, article 18 of the Convention on the Recovery Abroad of Maintenance ("A Contracting Party shall not be entitled to avail itself of this Convention against other Contracting Parties except to the extent that it is itself bound by the Convention") or article XIV of the New York Convention on the Recognition and Enforcement of Foreign Arbitral Awards ("A Contracting State shall not be entitled to avail itself of the present Convention against other Contracting States except to the extent that it is itself bound by the Convention").

[428] Imbert, *op. cit.* (see footnote 347 above), p. 252; Majoros, *op. cit.* (see footnote 426 above), pp. 83 and 109. Majoros's criticism of the suggestion that clauses reiterating the reciprocity principle should be introduced into treaties is "for reasons of clarity and legal stability" (*ibid.*, p. 81).

[429] Majoros, *op. cit.*, pp. 83 and 109; Baratta, *op. cit.* (footnote 417 above), p. 243 *et seq.*; Horn, *op. cit.* (footnote 197 above), p. 148; see also Simma, *op. cit.* (footnote 421 above), pp. 60–61.

automatically, requiring neither a specific clause in the treaty nor a unilateral declaration by the States or international organizations that have accepted the reservation to that effect.[430]

279. Draft article 21 adopted on first reading by the Commission in 1962 was, however, not very clear as regards the question of automaticity of the reciprocity principle, in that it provided that the reservation would operate "reciprocally to entitle any other State Party to the treaty to claim the same modification of the provisions of the treaty in its relations with the reserving State".[431] This formulation of the rule implied that the other contracting States should claim the reservation in order to benefit from the effects of reciprocity. Following the comments of Japan and the United States,[432] the text was recast so as to establish that the reservation produces *ipso jure* the same effect for the reserving State and the State accepting it.[433] The text finally adopted by the Commission in 1965 thus clearly expresses the idea of automaticity, although it still underwent a number of drafting changes.[434]

280. This does not mean, however, that the principle of reciprocity is absolute—far from it. Although today it constitutes, under cover of article 21, paragraph 1, the general rule, there are nevertheless major exceptions[435] which stem either from the content of the reservation itself or from the content or nature of the treaty.

281. The principle of reciprocity cannot find application in cases where a rebalancing between the obligations of the author of the reservation and the State or international organization with regard to which the reservation is established is unnecessary or proves impossible.

282. This situation arises, for example, in the case of reservations purporting to limit the territorial application of a treaty. Reciprocal application of such reservation is quite simply not possible in practice.[436] Similarly, reciprocal application of the effects of the reservation is also excluded if it was motivated by situations obtaining specifically in the reserving State.[437] Thus, a party to the 1971 Convention on Psychotropic Substances can certainly not invoke in its favour the reservation formulated by Canada purporting to exclude peyotl,[438] from the application of the Convention; it was formulated solely because of the presence in Canadian territory of groups which use in their magical or religious ceremonies certain psychotropic substances that would normally fall under the Convention regime.[439]

283. The principle of reciprocal application of reservations may also be limited by reservation clauses contained in the treaty itself. An example is the 1954 Convention on Customs Facilities for Touring and its Additional Protocol. Article 20, paragraph 7, of the Convention provides that:

> No Contracting State shall be required to extend to a State making a reservation the benefit of the provisions to which such reservation applies. Any State availing itself of this right shall notify the Secretary-General accordingly and the latter shall communicate its decision to all signatory and contracting States.[440]

Even though this particular clause does not in itself exclude the principle of reciprocal application, it deprives it of automaticity by making it subject to notification by the accepting State. Such notifications have been made by the United States in relation to the reservations formulated by Bulgaria, Romania and the Union of Soviet Socialist Republics to the dispute settlement mechanism provided for in article 21 of that Convention.[441]

284. In other cases, it is not the clauses or provisions of the treaty that invalidate the application of the principle of reciprocity, but the nature and object of the treaty and the obligations it contains. The principle of reciprocity is conditioned by the reciprocal application of the provisions and obligations of the treaty. If the treaty is not itself based on reciprocity of rights and obligations between the parties, a reservation can also produce no such reciprocal effect.

285. A typical example is afforded by the human rights treaties.[442] The fact that a State formulates a reservation excluding the application of one of the obligations contained in such a treaty does not release a State which accepts the reservation from respecting that obligation, despite the existence of the reservation, as these obligations apply not in an inter-State relationship between the reserving State and the State which has accepted the reservation, but simply in a State-human being relationship. The Human Rights Committee considered in this respect in its general comment No. 24 that:

---

[430] Baratta, *op. cit.* (footnote 417 above), pp. 227 *et seq.* and 291; Majoros, *op. cit.* (footnote 426 above), pp. 83 and 109; Parisi and Ševcenko, *loc. cit.* (see footnote 422 above). There have, however, been cases where, simply as a precaution, States have made their acceptance conditional upon the reciprocal application of the reservation. It is in this sense that we must understand the United States declarations in response to the reservation by Romania and the Union of Soviet Socialist Republics to the 1949 Convention on Road Traffic whereby the Government of the United States specified that it "has no objection to [these] reservation[s] but 'considers that it may and hereby states that it will apply [these] reservation[s] reciprocally with respect to [their respective author States]'". (*Multilateral Treaties Deposited with the Secretary-General*, available online from http://treaties.un.org/, chap. XI.B.1).

[431] *Yearbook ... 1962*, vol. II, p. 181.

[432] *Yearbook ... 1966*, vol. II, pp. 303 and 351. See also the comments by Austria, *ibid.*, p. 282.

[433] Fourth report on the law of treaties, *Yearbook ... 1965*, vol. II, document A/CN.4/177 and Add.1–2, p. 58.

[434] For the final text of draft article 19, see *Yearbook ... 1966*, vol. II, p. 227.

[435] Simma, *op. cit.* (footnote 421 above), p. 61; Baratta, *op. cit.* (footnote 417 above), p. 292; Greig, "Reservations: equity as a balancing factor?", p. 139; Horn, *op. cit.* (footnote 197 above), p. 148.

[436] Imbert, *op. cit.* (footnote 347 above), p. 258; Simma, *op. cit.* (footnote 421 above), p. 61.

[437] Horn, *op. cit.* (footnote 197 above), pp. 165–166; Imbert, *op. cit.* (footnote 347 above, pp. 258–260. See, however, the more cautious ideas relating to these assumptions formulated by Majoros, *op. cit.* (footnote 426 above), pp. 83–84).

[438] This is a species of small cactus which has hallucinogenic psychotropic properties.

[439] *Multilateral Treaties Deposited with the Secretary-General*, available online from http://treaties.un.org/, chap. VI.16.

[440] *Ibid.*, chap. XI.A.6.

[441] *Ibid.*, chap. XI.A.6 and A.7. See Riquelme Cortado, *op. cit.* (footnote 208 above), p. 212, footnote 44.

[442] First report on the law and practice relating to reservations to treaties (*Yearbook ... 1995*, vol. II (Part One), document A/CN.4/470, p. 148, para. 138.

Although treaties that are mere exchanges of obligations between States allow them to reserve *inter se* application of rules of general international law, it is otherwise in human rights treaties, which are for the benefit of persons within their jurisdiction.[443]

For this reason, the Committee continues, the human rights treaties, "and the Covenant [on Civil and Political Rights] specifically, are not a web of inter-State exchanges of mutual obligations. They concern the endowment of individuals with rights. The principle of inter-State reciprocity has no place".[444]

286. The human rights treaties are not, however, the only ones that do not lend themselves to reciprocity. This effect is also absent from treaties establishing obligations owed to the community of contracting States. Examples can be found in treaties on commodities,[445] in environmental protection treaties, in some demilitarization or disarmament treaties[446] and also in international private law treaties providing uniform law.[447]

287. In all of these situations, the reservation cannot produce a reciprocal effect in the bilateral relations between its author and the State or international organization with regard to which it is established. Such a bilateral relationship does not exist between the two States. A State party does not owe an individual obligation to another State party to respect the obligation, and the latter does not individually have a right for the obligation to be respected. Thus the reverse effect of the reservation has "nothing on which it can 'bite' or operate".[448]

288. This does not mean, however, that the principle of reciprocity plays no role in these exceptions. The reservation will nevertheless produce at least one effect: even if a State or international organization accepting the reservation, or for that matter a State or international organization formulating an objection to it, is required to discharge the obligations contained in the treaty, the reserving State is not entitled to call for compliance with these obligations which it does not assume on its own account. As Baratta has rightly pointed out:

Even on the assumption of reservations to the norms enunciated in the above-mentioned agreements, the effect of reciprocity is produced, as neither practice nor the principles applicable suggest that the reserving State would have a legal right to call for the application of the provision to which the reservation relates by a subject which is not the author of the reservation. There nonetheless remains the obligation for all subjects which have not formulated the reservation to apply in all cases the norm to which the reservation relates, by virtue of the regime of solidarity established by the agreement.[449]

289. This moreover was the thinking underlying the model clause on reciprocity adopted by the Council of Ministers of the Council of Europe in 1980:

A Party which has made a reservation in respect of a provision of [the agreement concerned] may not claim the application of that provision by any other Party; it may, however, if its reservation is partial or conditional, claim the application of that provision in so far as it has itself accepted it.[450]

290. Guideline 4.2.7 takes account of the reciprocal application of a reservation by reproducing in large measure article 21, paragraph 1, of the 1986 Vienna Convention. It nevertheless emphasizes that this general rule has major exceptions, contrary to what a reading of article 21 of the Vienna Conventions might suggest:

"**4.2.7** *Reciprocal application of the effects of an established reservation*

"A reservation modifies the content of treaty relations for the State or international organization with regard to which the reservation is established in their relations with the author of the reservation to the same extent as for the author, unless:

"(*a*) Reciprocal application of the reservation is not possible because of the nature or content of the reservation;

"(*b*) The treaty obligation to which the reservation relates is not owed individually to the author of the reservation; or

"(*c*) The object and purpose of the treaty or the nature of the obligation to which the reservation relates exclude any reciprocal application of the reservation."

---

[443] Report of the Human Rights Committee, *Official Records of the General Assembly, Fiftieth Session, Supplement No. 40* (A/50/40), vol. I, annex V, p. 120, para. 8. See also Coccia, *loc. cit.* (footnote 352 above), p. 37; Imbert, *op cit.* (footnote 347 above), p. 153; Virally, "Le principe de réciprocité dans le droit international contemporain", pp. 26 – 27.

[444] Report of the Human Rights Committee (see preceding footnote), annex V, p. 123, para. 17.

[445] Schermers, "The suitability of reservations to multilateral treaties", p. 356. See also Greig, *loc. cit.* (footnote 435 above), p. 140.

[446] Horn, *op. cit.* (footnote 197 above), pp. 164–165.

[447] On the conventions of The Hague Conference on International Private Law, see de Cesari, *loc. cit.* (footnote 401 above), pp. 149–174, and Majoros, *op. cit.* (footnote 426 above), pp. 73–109.

[448] Fitzmaurice, *The Law and Procedure of the International Court of Justice*, vol. 1, p. 412.

[449] Baratta, *op. cit.* (footnote 417), p. 294; Greig, *loc. cit.* (footnote 435), p. 140.

[450] See footnote 427 above.

Annex

MEETING WITH HUMAN RIGHTS BODIES, 15 AND 16 MAY 2007[a]

Report prepared by Mr. Alain Pellet, Special Rapporteur[b]

1. Pursuant to General Assembly resolution 61/34 of 4 December 2006, the International Law Commission convened a meeting with representatives of United Nations human rights treaty bodies and regional human rights bodies. The meeting took place on 15 and 16 May 2007 at the United Nations Office at Geneva and provided an opportunity for a fruitful exchange of views that was welcomed by all participants.

2. Mr. Ian Brownlie, Q.C., Chairman of the International Law Commission, chaired the meeting, the last segment of which was co-chaired by Sir Nigel Rodley, member of the Human Rights Committee and Chairperson-Rapporteur of the Working Group on reservations to treaties of the Meeting of chairpersons of the human rights treaty bodies. Mr. Brownlie welcomed the participants and explained that the meeting offered a unique opportunity to pursue a dialogue with the human rights bodies on the issue of reservations to treaties. Mr. Alain Pellet, Special Rapporteur of the International Law Commission on reservations to treaties, underscored the importance of such an exchange of ideas for strengthening mutual understanding between the Commission and the human rights expert bodies.

1. Introduction of the practice of the human rights bodies represented

3. The meeting began with brief presentations by the representatives of the human rights bodies participating in the meeting on the respective practice of each of the bodies represented, with the understanding that neither those presentations nor what was said during the meeting would in any way engage the responsibility of the bodies in question. The following bodies were represented: the Committee on Economic, Social and Cultural Rights; the Human Rights Committee; the Committee against Torture; the Committee on the Rights of the Child; the Committee on the Elimination of Racial Discrimination; the Committee on the Elimination of Discrimination against Women; the Committee on Migrant Workers; the Council of Europe (the European Court of Human Rights and the Committee of Legal Advisers on Public International Law (CAHDI));[c] and the Sub-Commission on the Promotion and Protection of Human Rights.

(a) *Reservations to human rights treaties*

4. The use of reservations in human rights treaties varied from treaty to treaty. For that matter, some conventions explicitly provided for the formulation of reservations (Convention against Torture, European Convention on Human Rights and Fundamental Freedoms). Two broad trends could be observed.

5. On the one hand, some treaties—in particular, those that had been widely ratified—had been the subject of numerous reservations. Significant examples included the Convention on the Elimination of All Forms of Discrimination against Women and the Convention on the Rights of the Child, but also the conventions against torture and the elimination of all forms of racial discrimination and the European Convention on Human Rights. Conversely, few reservations had been made to the International Covenant on Economic, Social and Cultural Rights.

6. On the other hand, reservations were too frequently made to fundamental or substantive provisions of human rights treaties. In that connection, the representative of the Committee on the Elimination of Racial Discrimination pointed to the large number of reservations made to article 4 of the International Convention on the Elimination of All Forms of Racial Discrimination, concerning the prohibition of incitement to hatred or to racial discrimination. The same comment was made with regard to the Convention on the Elimination of All Forms of Discrimination against Women.

(b) *The practice of human rights bodies with respect to reservations*

7. The practice of human rights bodies, as described by some representatives, was relatively uniform and was characterized by a high level of pragmatism. The question of reservations could arise in two situations: the consideration of periodic reports submitted by States and the examination of individual communications. However, the latter option was available only to bodies charged with receiving individual petitions or communications.

---

[a] The present report—which is not a "statement of conclusions"—was prepared on the sole responsibility of the Special Rapporteur on reservations to treaties. It was submitted for opinion to outside participants and to those members of the Commission who had made introductory presentations but in no way engages their responsibility. This annex is a very slightly revised version of document ILC(LIX)/RT/CRP.1, which appears on the website of the International Law Commission at http://legal.un.org/ilc/documentation/english/ilc_lix_rt_crp1.pdf (accessed on 8 September 2014).

[b] I wish to extend warm thanks to Céline Folsché, intern from New York University (LLM) during the fifty-ninth session of the International Law Commission, who wrote the first draft of this report.

[c] The other regional bodies invited were unable to send representatives.

8. In considering the periodic reports submitted by States, nearly all the various committees had taken a somewhat pragmatic approach to the question of reservations. Their chief position was that the formulation of reservations by States should be strictly limited. In practice, however, they were relatively flexible and showed great willingness to establish a dialogue with States, to which the latter were generally amenable. While encouraging and recommending the withdrawal of reservations, the committees engaged in discussions with States about the justification and the scope of their reservations. Although the objective of the dialogue was the complete withdrawal of reservations, the committees' position was flexible, owing to their goal of achieving universal ratification of their conventions. Only very rarely had the committees taken a formal position to declare a reservation invalid.

9. Some committees had considered the scope and even the validity of reservations when considering individual communications or requests. However, that practice was limited, if only because few bodies received such communications or requests. Currently, only the Human Rights Committee and the European Court of Human Rights followed it. In the case of the Human Rights Committee, the risk that the State whose reservation was declared invalid might withdraw from the Optional Protocol could not be overlooked.

2. Presentations

10. Presentations serving as a basis for the discussion were delivered by:

—Mr. Alain Pellet, Special Rapporteur of the Commission on reservations to treaties: "Codification of the right to formulate reservations to treaties";

—Ms. Françoise Hampson, member of the Sub-Commission on the Promotion and Protection of Human Rights: "Principal aspects of the problem";

—Mr. Enrique Candioti, member of the Commission: "Grounds for the invalidity of reservations to human rights treaties";

—Mr. Alexandre Sicilianos, member of the Committee on the Elimination of Racial Discrimination: "Assessment of the validity of reservations to human rights treaties";

—Mr. Giorgio Gaja, member of the Commission: "The consequences of the non-validity of reservations to human rights treaties".

(a) *Codification of the right to formulate reservations to treaties*

11. Mr. Alain Pellet, Special Rapporteur of the International Law Commission on reservations to treaties, described the history of the codification of the law of treaties. He began by recalling the Commission's mission of codification and presenting the 1969 Vienna Convention as its most significant achievement. He went on to describe the process used by the Commission in drawing up draft conventions or draft guidelines. Lastly, he described the Commission's consideration of the topic of reservations.

12. Although flexible and relatively detailed, the Vienna regime was vague and ambiguous with respect to the legal regime of reservations to treaties. Efforts to draft a Guide to Practice that would complement the provisions of the Vienna Conventions had been initiated in 1996. The lack of specific rules governing reservations to human rights treaties had been considered by the drafters of the Vienna Conventions. For one thing, human rights treaties had not been accorded the same importance at the time the Convention was drafted; for another, and most notably, the authors of the Convention, who had been cognizant of the specificity of certain types of treaties, including human rights treaties (see article 60, paragraph 5), had intended that the rules pertaining to reservations should be uniformly applied. However, as the Special Rapporteur had demonstrated in his second report (*Yearbook ... 1996*, vol. II (Part One), document A/CN.4/478), the considerable extent of practice in respect of reservations to human rights treaties could not be ignored, and the Commission was thus very interested in the practice of human rights bodies.

(b) *Principal aspects of the problem*

13. Ms. Françoise Hampson, member of the Sub-Commission on the Promotion and Protection of Human Rights, began by outlining those aspects of the problem on which there was general consensus. One point on which consensus had been reached was the principle that reservations that were incompatible with the object and purpose of a treaty produced no effects. An invalid reservation was null and void. In such cases it was assumed that the other Contracting Parties did not have the option of accepting such a reservation. Moreover, articles 20 to 23 of the 1969 Vienna Convention and, in particular, the rules concerning objections to reservations did not apply in the event of incompatibility. The "validity" or "effectiveness" of a reservation depended on an objective criterion and not on the potential acceptance or objection of States. Such a declaration of incompatibility could be made by the Contracting Parties—which were not compelled to take such action—or by any body whose functions required it to take such a decision.

14. There was also consensus that there was no special regime applicable to reservations to human rights treaties. Nevertheless, the possibility existed that certain specific situations might produce predictable results. In the case of human rights treaties, the bodies established by those instruments were competent to determine whether or not a reservation was compatible with the object and purpose of the treaty. That observation applied both to judicial bodies that were competent to hand down decisions having the authority of *res judicata* and to bodies whose monitoring of the implementation of treaties resulted in recommendations or opinions that were not legally binding.

15. Ms. Hampson next identified the areas in which problems remained. There were a number of unanswered questions with respect to the general regime of reservations and, in particular, with respect to the effects that a declaration of incompatibility of a reservation with the object and purpose of a treaty might have. In the case of human rights treaties, questions arose as to whether the treaty bodies were under an obligation to enter into

a "reservations dialogue" with States or simply had the option of doing so. Moreover, given the diversity of human rights bodies, it was difficult to adopt a general method for assessing a reservation's compatibility with the object and purpose of the treaty. Lastly, in cases involving incompatibility, the question arose as to the severability of the invalid reservation and whether or not the author of the reservation retained the status of Contracting Party. The precedents established by the human rights bodies and the reactions of the States that had taken the floor in the Sixth Committee of the General Assembly would seem to indicate that the rule of severability could stand to be revised in certain areas of international law and, in particular, in the area of human rights.

(c) *Grounds for the invalidity of reservations to human rights treaties*

16. Mr. Enrique Candioti, member of the Commission, emphasized that it was difficult to define objectively the grounds for the invalidity of reservations to treaties. He described the guidelines contained in the Guide to Practice that had been prepared by the Commission. The Special Rapporteur had proposed a general definition according to which a reservation was incompatible with the object and purpose of a treaty if it affected an essential element of the treaty. Another group of guidelines concerning non-derogable norms and human rights treaties were currently being considered by the Commission.

(d) *Assessment of the validity of reservations to human rights treaties*

17. Mr. Alexandre Sicilianos, member of the Committee on the Elimination of Racial Discrimination, generally approved of the principles contained in the tenth report on reservations to treaties (*Yearbook ... 2005*, vol. II (Part One), document A/CN.4/558 and Add.1–2) and in particular the assertion that human rights bodies were competent to assess a reservation's compatibility with the object and purpose of a treaty. He particularly supported the guideline which indicated that there were various bodies that were competent to determine the validity of a reservation.

18. Human rights bodies—for which the issue of human rights was not necessarily paramount—assessed reservations through two distinct procedures: the consideration of periodic reports and the examination of individual complaints.

19. In considering reports, committees exercised a quasi-"diplomatic" function. In some instances, the assessment of reservations was clear-cut. There were, however, situations in which it was not necessarily useful or desirable for the committee to make a "yes" or "no" pronouncement. For that reason, Mr. Sicilianos recommended that the realities of the situation should be taken into account: it was essential to deal with political considerations as well as with practical problems (such as the amount of time available to committees for considering reports). He stressed the importance of dialogue with States and of studying States' internal law, since reservations could not be considered in the abstract and their scope was dependent on internal law. It was therefore necessary to establish priorities for the purpose of determining the validity of reservations during the consideration of reports.

20. The individual complaints procedures of the human rights bodies conferred a quasi-judicial function on those bodies. Although the bodies' decisions were not binding, the States concerned were required to draw the appropriate conclusions from the opinions expressed by the bodies. Mr. Sicilianos stressed that a distinction should be made between reservations to jurisdictional clauses and reservations to substantive provisions. He drew attention in that connection to the ICJ judgment of 3 February 2006 in the case concerning *Armed Activities on the Territory of the Congo (Democratic Republic of the Congo v. Rwanda)*.

(e) *The consequences of the non-validity of reservations to human rights treaties*

21. Mr. Giorgio Gaja, member of the Commission, shared the view expressed by Ms. Hampson that articles 20 to 23 of the 1969 Vienna Convention did not apply to invalid reservations, and particularly to those that were incompatible with the object and purpose of the treaty. Nevertheless, in practice it was generally considered that even invalid reservations were subject to the general regime of reservations and could therefore be accepted by other contracting States.

22. The treaty bodies made use of their authority to play an active role in respect of reservations they considered invalid. They relied on two techniques to accomplish that end. The first was the approach taken by the European Court of Human Rights in the case of *Belilos v. Switzerland*. The Court had concluded that the willingness of Switzerland to be a party to the European Convention on Human Rights was "stronger" than its willingness to maintain the reservation in question. The invalidity of the reservation did not subsequently impair the status of Switzerland as a State party to the Convention.

23. The second approach was the one adopted by the Human Rights Committee in its general comment No. 24. The Committee did not seek to verify a State's willingness to be bound by the International Covenant on Civil and Political Rights. It maintained that reservations were severable from the treaty and produced no effects if they were incompatible with its object and purpose.

24. Mr. Gaja urged caution. A restrictive attitude towards the reserving State could lead to political difficulties, such as a State's withdrawal from the Optional Protocol to the International Covenant on Civil and Political Rights concerning individual communications. He welcomed the spirit of openness to dialogue that existed between the human rights treaty bodies and States. Even though the question of the validity of reservations was a difficult one, a "gentle" approach was called for. The reservations dialogue should be encouraged by the Commission.

3. Summary of the discussion

25. The members of the International Law Commission and the representatives of the human rights bodies had an opportunity to participate in a general discussion following each of the presentations. Mr. Roman Kolodkin and Ms. Hanqin Xue, members of the Commission,

summarized the discussions on grounds for and assessment of the validity of reservations and on the consequences of the non-validity of reservations, respectively. Their views are reflected in the present report, as are the conclusions of Sir Nigel Rodley, member of the Human Rights Committee and Chairperson-Rapporteur of the Working Group on Reservations of the Meeting of Chairpersons of Human Rights Treaty Bodies.

(a) *The specific nature of human rights treaties*

26. Some participants emphasized the special nature of human rights treaties. That specific nature did not, however, imply that the law of treaties was not applicable to them. Human rights treaties continued to be governed by treaty law.

27. The special nature of human rights treaties was reflected in the test provided for in article 19 (*c*) of the 1969 Vienna Convention, which concerned the incompatibility of a reservation with the object and purpose of the treaty. It was nevertheless pointed out that that specific feature was not unique and that environmental protection treaties and disarmament treaties also presented particular features that could have an impact in terms of reservations. The reason that human rights treaties were of special interest to the Commission was that they had treaty monitoring bodies. The representatives of the human rights bodies stressed the fact that it was not necessary to establish a separate regime governing reservations to human rights treaties. However, they did feel that the general regime should be applied in an appropriate and suitably adapted manner.

28. A number of participants highlighted the fact that the delicate balance between the integrity and the universality of the treaty lay at the heart of the debate on the specific nature of human rights treaties. According to some, the treaty bodies gave precedence to integrity; however, the opposing view was also expressed, i.e., that treaty bodies sought to work on the basis of reservations and to hold discussions with States, which showed a greater concern for universality.

(b) *The use of the term "validity"*

29. Several participants expressed uncertainty as to the terminology to be employed. All the members of the human rights bodies had used the term "validity". Nevertheless, notwithstanding the previous decision of the Commission on the matter, some Commission members were once again specifically opposed to the use of that term, owing to its objectivistic connotation and lack of neutrality.

(c) *Grounds for invalidity*

30. The participants were in general agreement that article 19 of the 1969 Vienna Convention set forth the conditions for the validity of a reservation. However, discussion focused on subparagraph (*c*), according to which a reservation was prohibited if it was "incompatible with the object and purpose of the treaty". While some participants were opposed to the use of the term "reservation" to designate a reservation that was prohibited under article 19 (*c*), others pointed to the practical problem that would arise if another term was used.

31. It was noted that because it was not possible to establish a standard criterion for the object and purpose, the guidelines of the Commission had been limited to identifying typical problems and attempting to illustrate article 19 (*c*).

32. Many participants noted the problematic nature of general and vague reservations. Although they were not considered to be incompatible with the object and purpose of the treaty, it was impossible to assess the validity of such reservations.

33. Participants also discussed the issue of reservations to provisions setting forth a rule of *jus cogens*. Some were of the view that any reservation to that type of clause should automatically be considered invalid, since it would inevitably affect the "quintessence" of the treaty. Others observed that the problem arose in much the same way that it did for reservations to provisions setting forth a customary norm—which could not be considered to be invalid *ipso jure*.

(d) *Assessment of validity*

34. All participants agreed that the competence of the human rights bodies to assess the validity of reservations was unquestionable. Many welcomed their reliance on political means of persuasion rather than on legal imperatives in their interactions with States.

35. The discussion focused in particular on the issue of the "reservations dialogue". It was observed that, in practice, such an approach was extremely useful for understanding the political considerations underlying reservations and that the pragmatism and discretion exercised by the human rights bodies had already met with success.

(e) *The consequences of non-validity*

36. To date, the human rights bodies had endeavoured, insofar as possible, to avoid taking a position on the validity of reservations. Examples of assessments of validity or declarations of invalidity of reservations were the exception and had occurred only in the rare cases in which such determinations were unavoidable. In any event, the consequences of the non-validity of a reservation were not obvious. The participants were unanimous in considering that a reservation that was incompatible with the object and purpose of a treaty was null and void. However, some disagreement was voiced as to whether there was any need for States to rule on that matter, and it was considered unnecessary for States to object to an invalid reservation. Conversely, several participants felt that States had an interest in taking a position owing both to a lack of monitoring bodies in certain areas or, where such bodies did exist, to the sometimes random manner in which they considered the matters referred to them.

37. The consequences of the non-validity of a reservation for the status of the treaty presented a major difficulty, one which was linked, more specifically, to the

consent of the author of the reservation to be bound by the treaty. The problem lay in determining whether or not the invalid reservation was severable from consent to be bound by the treaty. The participants stressed that the human rights bodies must act with caution. Their approach consisted in determining the State party's intention. If intention could not be discerned, a presumption would have to be made. In the view of several speakers, such a presumption should be in favour of severing the invalid reservation from consent to be bound by the treaty and firmly maintained by the human rights bodies (with the understanding that it must not constitute a conclusive presumption). Other participants, however, believed that the principle of State sovereignty must prevail. A reservation that was declared invalid altered the scope of the treaty for the reserving State, which should then have the option of withdrawing its consent to be bound by the treaty. Some participants pointed to the dangers inherent in the severance of an invalid reservation and considered that there was a risk that the reserving State might withdraw its participation in the optional protocol, or even in the treaty. According to one opinion, however, experience had shown that risk to be quite small.

RESERVATIONS TO TREATIES

[Agenda item 3]

DOCUMENT A/CN.4/616

Reservations to treaties in the context of succession of States: memorandum by the Secretariat

[*Original: French*]
[*6 May 2009*]

CONTENTS

Multilateral instruments cited in the present report

	Source
Special Protocol concerning Statelessness (The Hague, 12 April 1930)	United Nations, *Laws concerning nationality* (ST/LEG/SER.B/4) (United Nations publications, Sales No. 1954.V.1), New York, 1954, p. 577.
Convention on the Prevention and Punishment of the Crime of Genocide (New York, 9 December 1948)	United Nations, *Treaty Series*, vol. 78, No. 1021, p. 277.
Geneva Conventions for the protection of war victims (Geneva, 12 August 1949)	*Ibid.* vol. 75, Nos. 970–973, pp. 31 *et seq.*
Geneva Convention for the Amelioration of the Condition of the Wounded and Sick in Armed Forces in the Field	*Ibid.*, No. 970, p. 31.
Geneva Convention for the Amelioration of the Condition of the Wounded, Sick and Shipwrecked Members of the Armed Forces at Sea	*Ibid.*, No. 971, p. 85.
Geneva Convention relative to the Treatment of Prisoners of War	*Ibid.*, No. 972, p. 135.
Geneva Convention relative to the Protection of Civilian Persons in Time of War	*Ibid.*, No. 973, p. 287.
Convention relating to the Status of Refugees (Geneva, 28 July 1951)	*Ibid.*, vol. 189, No. 2545, p. 137.
International Convention on the Elimination of All Forms of Racial Discrimination (New York, 21 December 1965)	*Ibid.*, vol. 660, No. 9464, p. 195.
Vienna Convention on the Law of Treaties (Vienna, 23 May 1969)	*Ibid.*, vol. 1155, No. 18232, p. 331.
Vienna Convention on Succession of States in respect of Treaties (Vienna, 23 August 1978)	*Ibid.*, vol. 1946, No. 33356, p. 3.
Vienna Convention on the Law of Treaties between States and International Organizations or between International Organizations (Vienna, 21 March 1986)	A/CONF.129/15.

Works cited in the present report

BOKOR-SZEGŐ, Hanna

New States and International Law. Budapest, Akadémiai Kiadó, 1970. 116 p.

CAFLISCH, Lucius

"La pratique suisse en matière de droit international public 1996" (chronique), *Revue suisse de droit international et de droit européen*, vol. 7, 1997, pp. 637–707.

GAJA, Giorgio

"Reservations to treaties and the newly independent States", *Italian Yearbook of International Law*, vol. 1, 1975, pp. 52–68.

GONÇALVES PEREIRA, André

La succession d'États en matière de traité. Paris, Pedone, 1969. 232 p.

IMBERT, Pierre-Henri

Les réserves aux traités multilatéraux: Évolution du droit et de la pratique depuis l'avis consultatif donné par la Cour internationale de Justice le 28 mai 1951. Paris, Pedone, 1979. 503 p.

KLABBERS, Jan

"State succession and reservations to treaties", in Jan KLABBERS and René LEFEBER, eds., *Essays on the Law of Treaties: A Collection of Essays in Honour of Bert Vierdag*. The Hague, Martinus Nijhoff, 1998, pp. 107–120.

MARCOFF, Marco G.

Accession à l'indépendance et succession d'États aux traités internationaux. Fribourg, Editions universitaires, 1969. 388 p.

MENON, P. K.

"The newly independent States and succession in respect of treaties". *Korean Journal of Comparative Law*, vol. 18, 1990, pp. 139–173.

MIKULKA, Václav

"The dissolution of Czechoslovakia and succession in respect of treaties", in Mojmir MRAK, ed., *Succession of States*. The Hague, Martinus Nijhoff, 1999, pp. 100–125.

O'CONNELL, Daniel Patrick

State Succession in Municipal Law and International Law. Cambridge Studies in International and Comparative Law, VII, vol. II: International relations. Cambridge, Cambridge University Press, 1967. 592 p.

RUDA, José María

"Reservations to treaties", *Collected Courses of The Hague Academy of International Law, 1975–III*, vol. 146. The Hague, Martinus Nijhoff, 1975, pp. 95–218.

SZAFARZ, Renata

"Vienna Convention on Succession of States in respect of Treaties: a general analysis", *Polish Yearbook of International Law*, vol. X, 1979–1980, pp. 77–113.

ZEMANEK, Karl

"State succession after decolonization", *Collected Courses of The Hague Academy of International Law, 1965–III*, vol. 116. The Hague, Martinus Nijhoff, 1965, pp. 181–300.

Introduction

1. The Vienna Convention on the Law of Treaties, of 23 May 1969 (hereinafter "the 1969 Vienna Convention"), does not address the question of succession of States in respect of treaties. In fact, article 73 of that Convention contains a safeguard clause stipulating that "the provisions of the present Convention shall not prejudge any question that may arise in regard to a treaty from a succession of States ...". A similar safeguard clause appears in article 74, paragraph 1, of the Vienna Convention on the Law of Treaties between States and International Organizations or between International Organizations, of 21 March 1986 (hereinafter "the 1986 Vienna Convention").[1]

2. The Vienna Convention on Succession of States in respect of Treaties (hereinafter "the 1978 Vienna Convention"), lays down, in article 20, rules concerning reservations in the context of succession of States. However, this provision applies only to the case of a "newly independent State", meaning, according to the definition set out in article 2, paragraph 1 *(f)*, of the Convention, "... a successor State the territory of which immediately before the date of the succession of States was a dependent territory for the international relations of which the predecessor State was responsible". Thus, the rules governing reservations, as set out in the 1978 Vienna Convention, cover only cases of succession in which a State gains independence as a result of a decolonization process; this also includes new States whose territories had previously been under the mandate and/or trusteeship system. It should be noted, moreover, that the Convention contains no provisions on objections to reservations.

[1] This Convention is not yet in force.

3. The present study is divided into two chapters.

4. Chapter I provides an overview of the rules laid down in article 20 of the 1978 Vienna Convention, taking account of the debates held at the United Nations Conference on Succession of States in Respect of Treaties, 1977–1978, and of the work done prior to the Conference by the Commission. Some questions that are left unresolved by the 1978 Vienna Convention are also discussed.

5. Chapter II of the study reviews the practice in relation to reservations and objections to reservations in the context of succession of States. The practice in relation to treaties for which the Secretary-General of the United Nations serves as depositary is considered first. Some elements of the practice in relation to other treaties are then mentioned. This review also takes into account the replies to the two questionnaires which the Special Rapporteur addressed to States and to international organizations, respectively, in 1999.[2] It should be stated at the outset, however, that the vast majority of States or international organizations (34 in all) that replied to the questionnaires did not provide any information on their practice in this regard.

[2] Questionnaires prepared by the Special Rapporteur on reservations to treaties pursuant to paragraph 489 of the report of the International Law Commission on the work of its forty-seventh session (*Yearbook ... 1995*, vol. II (Part Two)), p. 108). For the text of the questionnaires, see *Yearbook ... 1996*, vol. II (Part One), document A/CN.4/477 and Add.1, annexes II and III, pp. 97 and 107.

CHAPTER I

The rules of the 1978 Vienna Convention

A. The case of newly independent States

6. In contrast to cases involving the uniting or separation of States, which are governed by the provisions of part IV of the 1978 Vienna Convention, the basic rule laid down in part III of the Convention with regard to newly independent States is that of "non-succession", i.e. the absence of automatic devolution to the newly independent State of treaties by which the predecessor State was bound. Nonetheless, the newly independent State may voluntarily notify its succession to any such treaty.

7. It is on this premise that article 20 of the 1978 Vienna Convention sets out rules on reservations to treaties in the context of succession to a treaty by a newly independent State. Except for a few minor differences in the wording, this provision mirrors draft article 19 adopted by the Commission at its twenty-sixth session, in 1974.[3]

[3] The text of the draft articles on succession of States in respect of treaties, with commentary, is reproduced in *Yearbook ... 1974*, vol. II (Part One), pp. 174 *et seq.*, para. 85.

1. Status of reservations formulated by the predecessor State

(a) *Presumption in favour of the maintenance of reservations*

8. Article 20, paragraph 1, of the 1978 Vienna Convention establishes, in the case of silence on the part of a newly independent State in its notification of succession, a presumption that it is maintaining any reservation formulated by the predecessor State which was applicable at the date of the succession of States in respect of the territory to which the succession relates.[4] This presumption

[4] This paragraph provides as follows: "When a newly independent State establishes its status as a party or as a contracting State to a multilateral treaty by a notification of succession under article 17 or 18, it shall be considered as maintaining any reservation to that treaty which was applicable at the date of the succession of States in respect of the territory to which the succession of States relates unless, when making the notification of succession, it expresses a contrary intention or formulates a reservation which relates to the same subject matter as that reservation."

is reversed, however, if the successor State expresses a "contrary intention" when making the notification of succession or if, at the same time, it formulates a reservation "which relates to the same subject matter".

9. The presumption in favour of the maintenance of reservations formulated by the predecessor State had already been proposed by D. P. O'Connell, Rapporteur of the International Law Association on the subject of "the Succession of New States to the Treaties and Certain Other Obligations of their Predecessors".[5] It had also been proposed at the outset by the Commission's first Special Rapporteur on the succession of States in respect of treaties, Sir Humphrey Waldock, who based his considerations, in particular, on a concern for respecting the actual intention of the successor State by avoiding the creation of an irreversible situation[6] and on a number of elements of practice that seemed to support such a presumption.[7] The second Special Rapporteur on the subject, Sir Francis Vallat, also supported the presumption in favour of the maintenance of reservations formulated by the predecessor State, despite the contrary view of a number of Governments, which had recommended the reversal of this presumption.[8]

10. A majority of the members of the Commission shared the view of the two Special Rapporteurs, and the commentary to article 19 as finally adopted by the Commission contains the following arguments supporting the presumption in favour of the maintenance of reservations formulated by the predecessor State:

> First, the presumption of an intention to maintain the reservations was indicated by the very concept of succession to the predecessor's treaties. Secondly, a State is in general not to be understood as having undertaken more onerous obligations unless it has unmistakably indicated an intention to do so; and to treat a newly independent State, on the basis of its mere silence, as having dropped its predecessor's reservations would be to impose upon it a more onerous obligation. Thirdly, if presumption in favour of maintaining reservations were not to be made, the actual intention of the newly independent State might be irrevocably defeated; whereas, if it were made and the presumption did not correspond to the newly independent State's intention, the latter could always redress the matter by withdrawing the reservations.[9]

11. At the United Nations Conference on Succession of States in Respect of Treaties of 1977–1978, the representative of the United Republic of Tanzania had proposed an amendment to reverse the presumption in favour of the maintenance of reservations formulated by the predecessor State. The wording of that amendment provided that the successor State was considered as discontinuing any reservations formulated by the predecessor State unless it expressed a contrary intention.[10] The representative of the United Republic of Tanzania expressed a preference for a "clean slate" in regard to reservations and pointed out that reservations formulated by the predecessor State were not necessarily in the interest of the successor State.[11] The amendment was rejected, however, by 26 votes to 14, with 41 abstentions,[12] and the presumption in favour of the maintenance of reservations was retained in the final text of article 20 as adopted at the Conference.[13]

12. This presumption is inferred logically, since succession to a treaty by a newly independent State, though voluntary, is a true succession that must be distinguished from accession. Because it is a succession, it seems reasonable to presume that treaty obligations are transmitted to the successor State as modified by the reservation formulated by the predecessor State.

[5] See *Yearbook ... 1969*, vol. II, p. 49, para. 17, "additional point" No. 10: "A successor State can continue only the legal situation brought about as a result of its predecessor's signature or ratification. Since a reservation delimits that legal situation it follows that the treaty is succeeded to (if at all) with the reservation."

[6] The Special Rapporteur indicated, in this regard, that "... if a presumption in favour of maintaining reservations were not to be made, the actual intention of the successor State might be irrevocably defeated; whereas, if it were made and the presumption did not correspond to the successor State's intention, the latter could always redress the matter by withdrawing the reservations" (*Yearbook ... 1970*, vol. II, document A/CN.4/224 and Add.1, p. 50).

This reasoning has been criticized in the literature. See, in particular, Imbert, *Les réserves aux traités multilatéraux: Évolution du droit et de la pratique depuis l'avis consultatif donné par la Cour internationale de Justice le 28 mai 1951*, p. 309; the author considers that "there is no reason to think that the State would not study the text of the convention carefully enough to know exactly which reservations it wished to maintain, abandon or formulate".

[7] *Yearbook ... 1970*, vol. II, document A/CN.4/224 and Add.1, pp. 47–49.

[8] *Yearbook ... 1974*, vol. II (Part One), document A/CN.4/278 and Add.1–6, pp. 52–54.

[9] *Ibid.*, p. 226, para. (17). One author has nonetheless questioned the soundness of these explanations, casting doubt in particular on the assumption that the predecessor State's reservations would be "necessarily advantageous to the newly independent State"; Imbert, *op. cit.* (footnote 6 above), p. 310. The author also suggests that "since reservations constitute derogations from or limitations on a State's commitments, they should not be a matter of presumption. On the contrary, it makes more sense to assume that, in the absence of a formal statement of its intention, a State is bound by the treaty as a whole".

[10] *Official Records of the United Nations Conference on Succession of States in Respect of Treaties. Vienna, 4 April–6 May 1977 and 31 July–23 August 1978*, vol. I, *Summary records of the plenary meetings and of the meetings of the Committee of the Whole* [1977 session], A/CONF.80/16, United Nations publication, Sales No. 78.V.8, 28th meeting, para. 37; and A/CONF.80/14, para. 118 (*c*) (reproduced in *Documents of the Conference*, A/CONF.80/16/Add.2, United Nations publication, Sales No. E.79.V.10 (hereinafter A/CONF.80/16/Add.2)). A preference for the opposite presumption had also been expressed by other delegations; see A/CONF.80/16, 28th meeting, para. 13 (Romania), para. 18 (India) and para. 33 (Kenya).

[11] A/CONF.80/16, 27th meeting, para. 79.

[12] *Ibid.*, 28th meeting, para. 41.

[13] While the presumption in favour of the maintenance of the predecessor State's reservations has been criticized in the literature (see, in particular, Imbert, *op. cit.* (footnote 6 above), pp. 307–318), a number of authors have supported this presumption; see O'Connell, *State Succession in Municipal Law and International Law*, p. 229, which states: "Since a State which makes a reservation to a multilateral convention commits itself only to the convention as so reserved, its successor State cannot, logically, succeed to the convention without reservations. Should the reservation be unacceptable to it the appropriate procedure would be to ask the depositary to remove it and notify all parties accordingly. It might be objected that to this extent the new State is becoming a party to new commitments without acceding, but in practice this is not likely to prove a difficulty, except in respect of close conventions" (note omitted). See also Gaja, "Reservations to treaties and the newly independent States", pp. 54–56 (the author states, in particular: "The opinion that the predecessor State's reservations are maintained is also based on the reasonable assumption that when a newly independent State elects to become a party to a treaty by means of a notification of succession, in principle it wants the treaty to continue to be applied to its territory in the same way as it did before independence" (p. 55)); Ruda, "Reservations to treaties", p. 206 ("... the solution given by the ILC seems to be more acceptable, in the absence of any clear existing customary rule or practice, because it affords better protection for the interests of the successor State"); also Menon, "The newly independent States and succession in respect of treaties", p. 152.

(b) *Formulation of a "reservation which relates to the same subject matter"*

13. The presumption in favour of the maintenance of reservations formulated by the predecessor State is reversed, under article 20, paragraph 1, of the 1978 Vienna Convention not only if a "contrary intention" is specifically expressed by the successor State when making the notification of succession, but also if that State formulates a reservation "which relates to the same subject matter" as the reservation formulated by the predecessor State. The exact wording of this second possibility was a subject of debate in the Commission.

14. Sir Humphrey Waldock had proposed, in his third report, a different formulation that provided for the reversal of the presumption that the predecessor State's reservations were maintained if the successor State formulated "reservations different from those applicable ... at the date of succession".[14]

15. In its draft article 15 provisionally adopted in 1972, the Commission had settled on a solution according to which the presumption that the predecessor State's reservations were maintained was reversed if the successor State formulated a new reservation "which relates to the same subject matter and is incompatible with [the reservation formulated by the predecessor State]".[15] However, in response to comments from some Governments, the Commission decided to delete, in its final draft article, the reference to the test of "incompatibility", which "might be difficult to apply"; the commentary to draft article 19 merely pointed out that "if the newly independent State were to formulate a reservation relating to the same subject-matter as that of the reservation made by the predecessor State, it could reasonably be presumed to intend to withdraw that reservation".[16]

16. The wording that was finally adopted by the Commission and reflected in the 1978 Vienna Convention has been criticized in the literature for omitting the test of "incompatibility" between a reservation formulated by the predecessor State and one formulated by the successor State.[17]

2. New reservations formulated by a successor State that is a newly independent State

17. Article 20, paragraph 2, of the 1978 Vienna Convention establishes that a successor State that is a newly independent State may formulate, when making a notification of succession, reservations that are not excluded by the provisions of subparagraphs (*a*), (*b*) or (*c*) of article 19 of the 1969 Vienna Convention.[18] Article 20, paragraph 3, of the 1978 Vienna Convention provides, further, that the rules set out in articles 20 to 23 of the 1969 Vienna Convention apply in respect of reservations formulated by a newly independent State in its notification of succession.[19]

18. As the Commission had noted in its commentary to draft article 19,[20] the existence of this capacity seems to have been confirmed in practice, including the practice regarding cases of succession to multilateral treaties for which the Secretary-General of the United Nations serves as depositary.[21] In his third report, the first Special Rapporteur, Sir Humphrey Waldock, based his views *inter alia* on the practice of the Secretary-General, who, on several occasions, seemed to have acknowledged that newly independent States have this capacity, without prompting any objections from States to this assumption.[22] The second Special Rapporteur was also in favour, for "practical" reasons, of acknowledging the right of a newly independent State to make new reservations when notifying its succession.[23]

19. The view of the two Special Rapporteurs prevailed in the Commission, which, as indicated in the commentary to draft article 19 as finally adopted, had a choice between two alternatives: "(*a*) to decline to regard any notification of succession made subject to new reservations as a true instrument of succession and to treat it in law as a case of accession, or (*b*) to accept it as having the character of a succession but at the same time apply to it the law governing reservations as if it were a wholly new expression of consent to be bound by the treaty".[24] Drawing upon the practice of the Secretary-General and wishing to take a "flexible" approach in this regard, the Commission opted for the second alternative, noting also that it might ease the access of a newly independent State to a treaty that was not, "... for technical reasons, open to its participation by any other procedure than succession".[25]

20. At the United Nations Conference on Succession of States in Respect of Treaties of 1977–1978, the Austrian delegation had proposed the deletion of paragraphs 2 and 3 of the provision that would become article 20 of the 1978 Vienna Convention.[26] That delegation considered that recognizing the capacity of a newly independent State to formulate new reservations when notifying its succession "seemed to be based on an erroneous concept of succession".[27] In the Austrian delegation's view, "[i]f a newly independent State wished to make reservations, it should use the ratification or accession procedure provided

[14] *Yearbook ... 1970*, vol. II, p. 47.

[15] *Yearbook ... 1972*, vol. II, p. 260.

[16] *Yearbook ... 1974*, vol. II (Part One), p. 226, para. (18). The removal of the reference to the test of "incompatibility" had been supported by the second Special Rapporteur (*ibid.*, pp. 53–54).

[17] See Gaja, *loc. cit.* (footnote 13 above) pp. 59–60.

[18] Article 20, paragraph 2, of the 1978 Vienna Convention provides as follows: "When making a notification of succession establishing its status as a party or as a contracting State to a multilateral treaty under article 17 or 18, a newly independent State may formulate a reservation unless the reservation is one the formulation of which would be excluded by the provisions of subparagraph (*a*), (*b*) or (*c*) of article 19 of the Vienna Convention on the Law of Treaties."

[19] Article 20, paragraph 3, of the 1978 Vienna Convention provides as follows: "When a newly independent State formulates a reservation in conformity with paragraph 2, the rules set out in articles 20 to 23 of the Vienna Convention on the Law of Treaties apply in respect of that reservation."

[20] *Yearbook ... 1974*, vol. II (Part One), pp. 224–225, paras. (7)–(12).

[21] See chapter II, section A, below.

[22] *Yearbook ... 1970*, vol. II, document A/CN.4/224 and Add.1, pp. 48–50.

[23] *Yearbook ... 1974*, vol. II (Part One), document A/CN.4/278 and Add.1–6, p. 54, paras. 291–294.

[24] Commentary to draft article 19, *Yearbook ... 1974*, vol. II (Part One), p. 227, para. (20).

[25] *Ibid.*

[26] A/CONF.80/16, 27th meeting, paras. 59–64.

[27] *Ibid.*, para. 60.

for becoming a party to a multilateral treaty".[28] However, the Austrian amendment was rejected by 39 votes to 4, with 36 abstentions.[29]

21. The delegations which, at the United Nations Conference on Succession of States in Respect of Treaties, had opposed the Austrian amendment had put forth various arguments, including the desirability of ensuring that the newly independent State would "not be obliged to conform with more complicated ratification procedures than those provided for by the International Law Commission",[30] the alleged incompatibility of the Austrian amendment with the principle of self-determination[31] or the principle of the "clean slate",[32] the need to be "realistic" rather than "puristic",[33] and the fact that a succession of States was not "a legal inheritance or a transmission of rights and obligations".[34]

22. While it has been criticized in the literature,[35] a newly independent State's capacity to formulate reservations when notifying its succession to a treaty is expressly acknowledged by some authors.[36] The recognition of this capacity may be considered a "pragmatic" solution that takes account of the "non-automatic", i.e. voluntary, nature of succession to treaties on the part of newly independent States.

23. However, a newly independent State's capacity to formulate reservations to a treaty to which it intends to succeed ought not to be unlimited over time. It seems reasonable to consider that a newly independent State should exercise this capacity when notifying its succession and that reservations formulated after that date should be subject to the legal regime for late reservations, as set out in draft guidelines 2.3.1, 2.3.2, 2.3.3 and 2.3.5 provisionally adopted so far by the Commission.[37]

3. Questions not covered by the Convention

(a) *Other types of declarations*

24. Article 20 of the 1978 Vienna Convention exclusively governs the issue of reservations.

25. At the United Nations Conference on Succession of States in Respect of Treaties, the delegation of the Federal Republic of Germany had proposed an amendment broadening the scope of this provision. The amendment would have prefaced the rules on reservations, as proposed by the Commission, with the indication that "... any statement or instrument made in respect to the treaty in connexion with its conclusion or signature by the predecessor State, shall remain effective for the newly independent State".[38] The delegation of the Federal Republic of Germany subsequently withdrew this proposed amendment, to which a number of delegations had objected for various reasons.[39]

(b) *Objections to reservations*

26. The 1978 Vienna Convention does not cover the issue of objections to reservations in the context of succession of States.[40] Despite a request to that effect from the representative of the Netherlands[41] and despite the concerns expressed,[42] the United Nations Conference on Succession of States in Respect of Treaties provided no solution to this question.

(i) *Status of objections formulated by the predecessor State*

27. More specifically with respect to the status of objections formulated by the predecessor State, the fact that the 1978 Vienna Convention is silent on this point seems to leave a gap, as the 1969 Vienna Convention does not deal with this issue either.[43]

[28] *Ibid.*, see also 28th meeting, para. 30.

[29] A/CONF.80/16, 28th meeting, para. 40.

[30] *Ibid.*, 27th meeting, para. 71 (Netherlands).

[31] *Ibid.*, para. 73 *in fine* (Algeria) and para. 89 (Guyana).

[32] *Ibid.*, para. 85 (Madagascar).

[33] *Ibid.*, para. 77 (Poland).

[34] *Ibid.*, 28th meeting, para. 7 (Israel). The representative of Israel went on to say: "A newly independent State ... would simply have the right of option to establish itself as a separate party to the treaty in virtue of the legal nexus established by its predecessor. Its right was to notify its own consent to be considered as a separate party to the treaty; that was not a right to step into the predecessor's shoes. The significance of article 19 was that a newly independent State should be 'considered' as maintaining its succession to the treaty. In other words, notification of succession was an independent act of the successor State's own volition."

[35] See Zemanek, "State succession after decolonization", pp. 234–235; Gonçalves Pereira, *La succession d'États en matière de traité*, pp. 175–176, footnote 50; and Bokor-Szegö, *New States and International Law*, p. 100, cited by Gaja, *loc. cit.* (footnote 13 above), p. 61, footnote 39.

[36] See Marcoff, *Accession à l'indépendance et succession d'États aux traités internationaux*, p. 346. According to the author, "The right to make reservations is not a right that is transmissible through inheritance, but a prerogative that is part of the set of supreme powers attributed by virtue of the protective principle to sovereign States"; the author further considers that "[t]he institution of State succession is not incompatible with the exercise of the right to make reservations insofar as it is recognized under general international law". See also Gaja, *loc. cit.* (footnote 13 above), pp. 60–65, and Ruda, *loc. cit.* (footnote 13 above), p. 206.

[37] See the report of the Commission on the work of its sixtieth session, 5 May–6 June and 7 July–8 August 2008, *Yearbook ... 2008*, vol. II (Part Two), para. 123.

[38] A/CONF.80/16, 28th meeting; and A/CONF.80/14, para. 118 (*b*) (reproduced in *Documents of the Conference*, A/CONF.80/16/Add.2).

[39] A/CONF.80/16, 27th meeting, para. 73 (Algeria, which considered that the proposed amendment seemed to bring the principle of self-determination into question); para. 78 (Poland, which believed that the amendment was not sufficiently clear); para. 87 (Madagascar, which felt that the wording of the amendment was "much too broad in scope"); para. 90 (Guyana); and para. 95 (Italy, which found the wording of the amendment "very strong and inflexible").

[40] At the United Nations Conference on Succession of States in Respect of Treaties, Mr. Y. Yasseen, Chairman of the Drafting Committee, explicitly raised this point; see A/CONF.80/16, 35th meeting, para. 17: "The Drafting Committee had paid particular attention to the question of objections to reservations and objections to such objections, which had been raised by the Netherlands representative. It had noted that, as was clear from the International Law Commission's commentary to article 19, particularly paragraph (15) (A/CONF.80/4, p. 66), the article did not deal with that matter, which was left to be regulated by general international law" (notes omitted). The Chairman of the Drafting Committee also stated that: "... it was clear from the wording of article 19 and the International Law Commission's commentary thereto that the question of objections to reservations should be resolved by reference to general international law. What precise solution general international law would provide, it was not within the Committee [of the Whole]'s competence to determine"; A/CONF.80/16, 35th meeting, para. 21.

[41] A/CONF.80/16, 27th meeting, para. 70; 28th meeting, para. 32; and 35th meeting, para. 19.

[42] *Ibid.*, 27th meeting, para. 85 (Madagascar).

[43] See, in this connection, Imbert, *op. cit.* (footnote 6 above), p. 320. But the author goes on to say, on the following page, that "[d]espite the absence of an express provision, it is on the presumption in favour of the maintenance of objections that article 20 [of the 1978 Vienna

28. Draft article 19, as adopted by the Commission, also did not address the question of objections to reservations in the context of succession of States. In this regard, the Commission noted, in the commentary to this draft article,

that it would be better, in accordance with its fundamental method of approach to the draft articles, to leave these matters to be regulated by the ordinary rules applicable to acceptances and objections on the assumption that, unless it was necessary to make some particular provision in the context of the succession of States, the newly independent State would "step into the shoes of the predecessor State".[44]

29. The final words of the above-cited paragraph could imply that the Commission considered that the transmission of objections should be the rule.[45]

30. In order to justify its silence on the question of objections to reservations, the Commission invoked an argument based on the legal effects of such objections. In its commentary, the Commission noted, on the one hand, that unless the objecting State has definitely indicated that by its objection it means to stop the entry into force of the treaty as between the reserving State and the objecting State, the legal position created by an objection to a reservation is "much the same as if no objection had been lodged"; and, on the other, that if such an indication is given, the treaty will not have been in force at all between the predecessor State and the reserving State at the date of the succession.[46]

31. It should be pointed out that the first Special Rapporteur on the succession of States in respect of treaties, Sir Humphrey Waldock, while highlighting the scarcity of practice in this regard, had suggested that the rules regarding reservations should apply *mutatis mutandis* to objections.[47] In particular, this meant that the same presumption that the Commission would later incorporate into its draft article 19, paragraph 1, which was reproduced in article 20, paragraph 1, of the 1978 Vienna Convention, would apply to objections.[48] The second Special Rapporteur, Sir Francis Vallat, also supported the presumption in favour of the maintenance of objections formulated by the predecessor State, while considering that there was "no need to complicate the draft by making express provisions with respect to objections". Sir Francis was of the view, on the one hand, that "on the whole, the reasoning which supports the retention of the presumption in favour of the maintenance of reservations also supports the presumption in favour of the maintenance of objections which is inherent in the present draft"; and, on the other, that it would "always be open to the successor State to withdraw the objection if it wishes to do so".[49]

32. Given the scarcity of practice in this area,[50] it may seem difficult to give a definitive answer to the question of whether or not objections formulated by a predecessor State are transmissible to a newly independent State.[51] It should be noted, however, that the maintenance of objections formulated by the predecessor State was proposed by D.P. O'Connell, Rapporteur of the International Law Association on the subject of "the Succession of New States to the Treaties and Certain Other Obligations of their Predecessors".[52] In addition, certain elements of recent practice, which will be discussed below, seem to support the maintenance of objections.[53]

(ii) *Formulation of objections by a successor State that is a newly independent State*

33. If the rules regarding reservations had applied *mutatis mutandis* to objections, as proposed by the first Special Rapporteur, Sir Humphrey Waldock, then a successor State could also have formulated its own objections to reservations "whether formulated before or after the date of succession", in line with the time limits set out in article 20, paragraph 5, of the 1969 Vienna Convention.[54]

34. Sir Humphrey Waldock had, however, intended to provide for an exception with respect to the treaties referred to in article 20, paragraph 2, of the 1969 Vienna Convention.[55] Such an exception was warranted, in the Special Rapporteur's view, by the fact that a reservation to a provision of such a treaty must be accepted by all States parties before the reserving State could participate in the treaty. Accordingly, the Special Rapporteur pointed out that allowing a successor State to object to a

Convention] is based" (note omitted). This author believes, however, that this presumption is erroneous, particularly in view of the alleged "*intuitu personae*" nature of objections.

[44] *Yearbook ... 1974*, vol. II (Part One), p. 226, para. (15); see also paragraph (23) of the commentary (p. 227). This explanation was recalled at the United Nations Conference on Succession of States in Respect of Treaties of 1977–1978 by Sir Francis Vallat, acting as an expert consultant; see A/CONF.80/16, 27th meeting, para. 83.

[45] See, in this connection, Imbert, *op. cit.* (footnote 6 above), p. 320, footnote 126.

[46] Commentary to article 19, *Yearbook ... 1974*, vol. II (Part One), p. 226, para. (14). This reasoning seems to be supported by Ruda, *loc. cit.* (footnote 13 above), pp. 207–208. See, however, the rather critical remarks of Klabbers, "State succession and reservations to treaties", pp. 109–110.

[47] The provision proposed by Sir Humphrey Waldock read as follows: "The rules laid down in paragraphs 1 and 2 regarding reservations apply also, *mutatis mutandis*, to objections to reservations" (*Yearbook ... 1970*, vol. II, p. 47).

[48] *Ibid.*, p. 51.

[49] *Yearbook ... 1974*, vol. II (Part One), document A/CN.4/278 and Add.1–6, p. 54, para. 289.

[50] This scarcity of practice was noted more than 30 years ago by Gaja, *loc. cit.* (footnote 13 above), p. 56; it seems that this observation remains valid today (see chapter II below).

[51] See, on this subject, Szafarz, "Vienna Convention on Succession of States in respect of Treaties: a general analysis", p. 96. See also the considerations of Gaja, *loc. cit.* (footnote 13 above), p. 57, who takes the view that practice does not contradict the presumption in favour of the maintenance of objections formulated by the predecessor State, but also does not suffice to support this presumption.

[52] See *Yearbook ... 1969*, vol. II, p. 49, para. 17, "additional point" No. 13: "Since a new State takes over the legal situation of its predecessor, it takes over the consequences of its predecessor's objections to an incompatible reservation made to a multilateral convention by another party. Therefore the reservation would not be effective against the new State unless the latter formally waives the objection."

[53] See chapter II below.

[54] *Yearbook ... 1970*, vol. II, document A/CN.4/224 and Add.1, p. 52. Article 20, para. 5, of the 1969 Vienna Convention provides as follows: "for the purposes of paragraphs 2 and 4 and unless the treaty otherwise provides, a reservation is considered to have been accepted by a State if it shall have raised no objection to the reservation by the end of a period of twelve months after it was notified of the reservation or by the date on which it expressed its consent to be bound by the treaty, whichever is later".

[55] This paragraph provides as follows: "When it appears from the limited number of the negotiating States and the object and purpose of a treaty that the application of the treaty in its entirety between all the parties is an essential condition of the consent of each one to be bound by the treaty, a reservation requires acceptance by all the parties."

reservation already accepted by all the parties to the treaty would have empowered that State to compel the reserving State to withdraw from the treaty.[56]

35. One author has expressly acknowledged the right of a newly independent State to formulate, when notifying its succession to a treaty, its own objections with respect to reservations formulated by other States parties.[57]

(iii) *Status of objections to reservations formulated by the predecessor State*

36. At the United Nations Conference on Succession of States in Respect of Treaties of 1977–1978, the representative of Japan indicated that he could accept the text of draft article 19, as proposed by the Commission, on the understanding, however, that "a State party which had objected to the original reservation which had been made by the predecessor State did not need to repeat the objection with regard to the successor State".[58] A similar view was expressed by the representative of the Federal Republic of Germany, who considered, with respect to both newly independent States and other successor States, that "[t]he successor State was bound *ipso jure* by the individual treaty relationship created by the predecessor State, including the reservations and other declarations made by that State *and the objections thereto entered by its treaty partners**"[59].

37. There is a divergence of views among the few authors who have considered the status of objections to reservations formulated by a predecessor State.[60] Nonetheless, it is hard to see why a State that has objected to a reservation made by a predecessor State should have to repeat the objection when the same reservation is maintained by the successor State.

(iv) *New objections to reservations maintained by a successor State that is a newly independent State*

38. Another question is whether, when a reservation formulated by a predecessor State is maintained by the successor State, the other States parties are entitled to formulate objections to that reservation which they had not formulated with regard to the predecessor State.

39. This right is explicitly denied by one author, who considers that there is no reason to allow a State party to revoke its acceptance of a reservation that applied to the territory to which the succession relates.[61]

(v) *Objections to reservations formulated by a successor State that is a newly independent State*

40. When a newly independent State, in notifying its succession to a treaty, formulates reservations which the predecessor State had not formulated, it seems logical to consider that the other States parties to the treaty have the capacity to object to those reservations under the general rules of the law of treaties.[62]

(c) *Effects* ratione temporis *of a declaration whereby a newly independent State announces, when notifying its succession to a treaty, that it is not maintaining a reservation formulated by the predecessor State*

41. Article 20 of the 1978 Vienna Convention does not directly address the effects *ratione temporis* of a declaration whereby a newly independent State announces, when notifying its succession to a treaty, that it is not maintaining a reservation formulated by the predecessor State. Neither practice nor the literature seems to provide a clear answer to this question.

42. It seems reasonable to consider that such a declaration will not become operative in relation to another contracting State until notice of it has been received by that State, in accordance with the solution reflected in article 22, paragraph 3 (*a*), of the 1969 Vienna Convention regarding the withdrawal of a reservation.

(d) *Effects* ratione temporis *of a reservation formulated by a newly in`dependent State when notifying its succession to a treaty*

43. Article 20 of the 1978 Vienna Convention does not specify the date of entry into force of a reservation formulated by a newly independent State when notifying its succession to a treaty.[63]

44. Draft article 19, as adopted by the Commission, is also silent on this issue. The Commission had decided that it would be better to leave the matter to be regulated by the ordinary rules of international law relating

[56] *Yearbook ... 1970*, vol. II, document A/CN.4/224 and Add.1, p. 52.

[57] See Gaja, *loc. cit.* (footnote 13 above), p. 66: "The admissibility of objections on the part of newly independent States notifying succession to a treaty can be founded on the same reason given when considering the admissibility of reservations in cases in which succession depends on acceptance of the treaty by the newly independent State. This State appears to be in the same position as any acceding State, and may therefore take any action open to an acceding State with regard to other States' reservations."

[58] A/CONF.80/16, 28th meeting, paras. 15–16.

[59] *Official Records of the United Nations Conference on Succession of States in Respect of Treaties. Vienna, 4 April–6 May 1977 and 31 July–23 August 1978*, vol. II, *Summary records of the plenary meetings and of the meetings of the Committee of the Whole* [resumed session, 1978], A/CONF.80/16/Add.1, United Nations publication, Sales No. E.79.V.9 (hereinafter A/CONF.80/16/Add.1), 43rd meeting, para. 11.

[60] The view that such objections are maintained is supported by Gaja, who explains his position as follows: "Objections made to the predecessor State's reservations continue to apply in relation to the newly independent State. The objecting State obviously may withdraw its objections. If it so wishes, it may do so with regard to the newly independent State only, while maintaining the objection to a similar reservation concerning the application of the treaty to other territories" (*loc. cit.* (footnote 13 above), p. 67). *Contra*: Imbert, *op. cit.* (footnote 6 above), p. 316.

[61] Gaja, *loc. cit.* (footnote 13 above), p. 67: "When a newly independent State maintains a reservation made by its predecessor State, the other States parties to the treaty can make no new objection to the reservation because it becomes applicable to the newly independent State. This would appear to be inconsistent with the acceptance of the reservation applicable to the same territory before independence. Such acceptance cannot be revoked with regard to the predecessor State, and no special reason justifies its becoming revocable in respect of the successor State."

[62] Arts. 20–23 of the 1969 Vienna Convention. See, in this regard, Gaja, *loc. cit.* (footnote 13 above), p. 67.

[63] See, on this issue, the interpretation given at the United Nations Conference on Succession of States in Respect of Treaties of 1977–1978 by the Austrian delegation, to the effect that "any new reservation made by the new State would become effective not at the date of the succession, but at a later date in accordance with the treaty provisions" (A/CONF.80/16, 28th meeting, para. 28).

to reservations, on the understanding that a reservation could not have retroactive effect.[64] It should be noted, however, that the second Special Rapporteur, Sir Francis Vallat, had proposed the adoption of a provision governing this question, in response to a request to that effect made by the United States of America.[65] The provision proposed by Sir Francis was worded as follows: "A new reservation established under paragraphs 2 and 3 shall not have any effect before the date of the making of the notification of succession".[66]

45. The Secretary-General of the United Nations has gone so far as to consider that a reservation formulated by a newly independent State when notifying its succession should become effective on the day when it would have done so had it been formulated in an instrument of accession, i.e. after a certain amount of time had elapsed, pursuant to the treaty concerned.[67] However, one author has expressed the view that there is no reason to delay, beyond the date of the notification of succession, the effects of a reservation formulated by a newly independent State.[68]

B. Other cases of succession

46. The 1978 Vienna Convention contains no provisions on the question of reservations in cases of succession other than those leading to the creation of a newly independent State. The fact that article 20 appears in part III of the Convention shows clearly that this provision relates only to newly independent States.[69] The question therefore arises as to how the Convention's silence on this issue should be interpreted.

47. At the United Nations Conference on Succession of States in Respect of Treaties of 1977–1978, it had been suggested that, with respect to other cases of succession, a provision regulating the issue of reservations should be included.[70] The delegation of the Federal Republic of Germany proposed a new article 36 *bis* that provided in particular for the transposition, to the cases of succession referred to in part IV of the Convention, of the rules on reservations applicable to newly independent States.[71] That delegation considered that "the situation with respect to succession, as distinct from accession, was identical for the States to which Parts III and IV of the draft referred".[72]

48. The delegation of the Federal Republic of Germany nonetheless withdrew its proposed amendment after a number of delegations objected to it.[73] Those delegations considered that giving a successor State the right to formulate new reservations was inconsistent with the principle of *ipso jure* continuity of treaties set out by the Convention for cases involving the uniting or separation of States.[74] On the other hand, regarding the presumption in favour of the maintenance of reservations formulated by the predecessor State, various delegations believed that that presumption was obvious in cases involving the uniting or separation of States, bearing in mind the principle of *ipso jure* continuity of treaties, which had been reflected in the Convention in relation to these kinds of succession.[75]

49. It seems that in the light of the regime established by the 1978 Vienna Convention for cases involving the uniting or separation of States, there are serious doubts as to whether a successor State other than a newly independent

[64] Commentary to article 19, *Yearbook ... 1974*, vol. II (Part One), p. 227, para. (22). The Commission refers here "to the general position that a reservation can only be effective at the earliest from the date when it is made". For another view in support of non-retroactivity, see also the position expressed by Austria (footnote 63 above).

[65] In the view of the United States of America, "the Commission should eliminate these complications by making it clear that new reservations take effect when made, that is, at the date of notification of succession"; reproduced in *Yearbook ... 1974*, vol. II (Part One), document A/CN.4/278 and Add.1–6, p. 52.

[66] *Ibid.*, p. 55, para. 298.

[67] Cf. letter dated 10 October 1969 from the Secretary-General to the Government of Zambia, the relevant passage of which is cited in the Commission's commentary to draft article 19 (*Yearbook ... 1974*, vol. II (Part One), pp. 224–225, para. (10)).

[68] See Gaja, *loc. cit.* (footnote 13 above), p. 68: "The newly independent State's interest may be considered to lie in applying the treaty in the same way from the date of acceptance of the treaty. This clearly cannot have the result that reservations, or withdrawals of reservations, made after notification of succession have a retroactive effect. On the other hand, there is no apparent reason why reservations, or withdrawals of reservations, made at the time of notification of succession should not take effect at the same time as the notification" (footnotes omitted).

[69] See also, in this regard, the explanations given at the United Nations Conference on Succession of States in Respect of Treaties of 1977–1978 by Sir Francis Vallat, expert consultant, on draft article 19 adopted by the Commission (A/CONF.80/16, 27th meeting, para. 84).

[70] A/CONF.80/16, 28th meeting, para. 17 (India), which pointed out that there was a gap in the Convention and, accordingly, a need to add an article on reservations to the part of the Convention which dealt with the uniting and separation of States.

[71] A/CONF.80/16/Add.1, 43rd meeting, paras. 9–12. The amendment proposed by the Federal Republic of Germany was worded as follows:

"1. When under articles 30, 31, 33 and 35 a treaty continues in force for a successor State or a successor State participates otherwise in a treaty not yet in force for the predecessor State, the successor State shall be considered as maintaining:

"(*a*) Any reservation to that treaty made by the predecessor State in regard to the territory to which the succession of States relates;

"(*b*) The consent of the predecessor State expressed, in conformity with the treaty, to be bound by part of the treaty;

"(*c*) The choice of the predecessor State made, in conformity with that treaty, between differing provisions in the application of the treaty.

"2. Notwithstanding paragraph 1, the successor State may however:

"(*a*) Withdraw or modify, wholly or partly, the reservation (paragraph 1 subparagraph (*a*)) or formulate a new reservation, subject to the conditions laid down in the treaty and the rules set out in articles 19, 20, 21, 22 and 23 of the Vienna Convention on the Law of Treaties;

"(*b*) Withdraw or modify the consent to be bound by part of the treaty (paragraph 1 subparagraph (*b*));

"(*c*) Alter the choice made between differing provisions in the application of the treaty (paragraph 1 subparagraph (*c*))"

(A/CONF.80/30, para. 118, reproduced in *Documents of the Conference*, A/CONF.80/16/Add.2).

[72] A/CONF.80/16/Add.1, 43rd meeting, para. 11.

[73] A/CONF.80/30, para. 119 (reproduced in *Documents of the Conference*, A/CONF.80/16/Add.2).

[74] A/CONF.80/16/Add.1, 43rd meeting, para. 14 (Poland), para. 15 (United States), para. 18 (Nigeria), para. 19 (Mali), para. 20 (Cyprus), para. 21 (Yugoslavia), para. 22 (Australia) and para. 24 (Swaziland, albeit in more nuanced terms).

[75] A/CONF.80/16/Add.1, 43rd meeting, para. 13 (Poland), para. 16 (France), para. 20 (Cyprus), para. 21 (Yugoslavia) and para. 22 (Australia).

State may formulate reservations.[76] These doubts are confirmed in a passage of the separate opinion annexed by Judge Tomka to the judgment of ICJ of 26 February 2007 in *Application of the Convention on the Prevention and Punishment of the Crime of Genocide (Bosnia and Herzegovina v. Serbia and Montenegro)*.[77] Indeed, if succession is considered to take place *ipso jure* in cases involving the uniting or separation of States, it is difficult to contend that a successor State may avoid or alleviate its obligations by formulating reservations.

50. This being the case, if a successor State formulates a reservation, it would seem appropriate to make that reservation subject to the legal regime for "late reservations", as provided for in the draft guidelines provisionally adopted so far by the Commission. Pursuant to draft guideline 2.3.1,[78] such a reservation may not be formulated unless none of the other Contracting Parties objects. This solution would have the advantage of placing the successor State in the same legal position that the predecessor State would have been in if it had sought to formulate a reservation after expressing its consent to be bound by the treaty.

51. The *ipso jure* nature of succession, as established in the 1978 Vienna Convention for cases involving the uniting or separation of States, also raises doubts as to whether the successor State may formulate objections to reservations to which the predecessor State had not objected. One author has explicitly denied that such a State may do so.[79]

52. Another question that merits consideration is that of the effects *ratione temporis* of a declaration whereby a successor State other than a newly independent State announces that it is not maintaining a reservation formulated by the predecessor State. Since, under the regime established in part IV of the 1978 Vienna Convention for cases involving the uniting or separation of States, succession to treaties takes place *ipso jure* on the date of the succession of States, such a declaration must necessarily be regarded as a *withdrawal* of the reservation in question and, as such, must be considered subject to the ordinary rules of the law of treaties, as reflected in article 22 of the 1969 Vienna Convention. Pursuant to paragraph 3 (*a*) of that article, "[u]nless the treaty otherwise provides, or it is otherwise agreed[,] the withdrawal of a reservation becomes operative in relation to another contracting State only when notice of it has been received by that State".

[76] See, however, Gaja, *loc. cit.* (footnote 13 above), pp. 64–65. While he refers specifically to newly independent States, the author makes observations that he believes can apply to other cases of succession. The author reasons as follows: even if a newly independent State were considered not to be entitled to make a reservation when notifying its succession, one should take the view that such a State may achieve practically the same result by making a partial withdrawal (if such a withdrawal is permitted) to the same extent that may be covered by a reservation. In the author's view, these considerations also apply to cases in which succession is considered not to depend on the acceptance of the treaty by the successor State.

[77] *Application of the Convention on the Prevention and Punishment of the Crime of Genocide (Bosnia and Herzegovina v. Serbia and Montenegro), Judgment of 26 February 2007*, separate opinion of Judge Tomka, para. 35:

"*There can be no doubt that this decision to notify of the accession to the Genocide Convention, with a reservation to Article IX and not succession (where no reservation is allowed) was motivated by the considerations relating to the present case.** It was intended to prevent a claim that Serbia and Montenegro had obligations under the Genocide Convention prior to June 2001 (in particular, substantive obligations in the period of 1992–1995, relevant for the claims of Bosnia and Herzegovina). This decision was also intended to avoid the jurisdiction of the Court under Article IX, not only for that period, but also for the future until the reservation was eventually withdrawn. Bosnia and Herzegovina timely objected to the Federal Republic of Yugoslavia's notification of accession to the Genocide Convention with a reservation to Article IX.

"That single notification of accession, in my view, was totally inconsistent with the succession by the Federal Republic of Yugoslavia—notified the very same day to the United Nations Secretary-General as accession to the Genocide Convention—to the Vienna Convention on Succession of States in Respect of Treaties, which in Article 34 provides that the treaties of the predecessor State continue in force in respect of each successor State. By the latter notification of succession, the Federal Republic of Yugoslavia became a contracting State of the Vienna Convention on Succession of States in Respect of Treaties as of April 1992. That Convention entered into force on 6 November 1996. Although not formally applicable to the process of the dissolution of the former Yugoslavia, which occurred in the 1991–1992 period, in light of the fact that the former Yugoslavia consented to be bound by the Vienna Convention already in 1980, and the Federal Republic of Yugoslavia has been a contracting State to that Convention since April 1992, one would not expect, by analogy to Article 18 of the Vienna Convention on the Law of Treaties, a State which, through notification of its accession, expresses its consent to be considered as bound by the Vienna Convention on Succession of States in Respect of Treaties to act in a singular case inconsistently with the rule contained in Article 34 of that Convention, while in a great number of other cases to acting in full conformity with that rule.

"These considerations, taken together, lead me to the conclusion that the Court should not attach any legal effect to the notification of accession by the Federal Republic of Yugoslavia to the Genocide Convention, and should instead consider it bound by that Convention on the basis of the operation of the customary rule of *ipso jure* succession codified in Article 34 as applied to cases of the dissolution of a State".

[78] See footnote 37 above.

[79] Gaja, *loc. cit.* (footnote 13 above), p. 67: "When, on the contrary, succession is considered to be automatic, the admissibility of objections on the part of the successor State must be ruled out. … If the predecessor State had accepted the reservation, such consent cannot be subsequently revoked either by the same State or by its successor."

CHAPTER II

Analysis of practice

A. Practice in relation to treaties deposited with the Secretary-General of the United Nations

53. The issue of the succession of States to treaties arose for the Secretary-General, as depositary, from the Organization's very beginnings, in connection with succession to treaties concluded under the auspices of the League of Nations. Newly independent States announced that they were assuming the rights and obligations created by the relevant treaty and that they considered

themselves parties to the treaty.[80] Practice was gradually built up through these notifications of succession. Starting in the 1960s, with the admission of a number of newly independent States to the United Nations (most of which were non-metropolitan territories that had become independent), the practice that had emerged since the 1950s became established. A number of points should be mentioned at the outset:

(*a*) In all cases, the Secretary-General was guided by practical considerations in the exercise of his depositary functions. Accordingly, he did not include a successor State (whether a newly independent State or a State resulting from a uniting or separation of States) in the list of States parties to a treaty deposited with him unless he had received either a notification concerning a particular treaty (most newly independent States deposited such notifications) or a notification accompanied by a list of treaties to which the State concerned was succeeding (as in the case of the Czech Republic and Slovakia);

(*b*) In cases where a notification of succession was silent on the subject of reservations and/or objections, the Secretary-General included the successor State (newly independent or other successor State) in the list of States parties to the treaty without making any mention of the reservations and/or objections formulated by the predecessor State. Exceptions can be found, however, with respect to some successor States of the former Yugoslavia.[81] Moreover, the practice shows that, in the absence of an indication on the part of the successor State concerning reservations formulated by the predecessor State, the Secretary-General does not request clarification on this point, leaving it to States parties to draw the legal conclusions they deem appropriate;

(*c*) Nonetheless, in his reply to the Special Rapporteur's questionnaire,[82] the Chief of the Treaty Section of the United Nations Office of Legal Affairs indicated that "[t]he Secretary-General has encountered difficulties in cases where, upon succession, the successor State makes no mention of the declarations/reservations made by the predecessor State. In these cases the Secretary-General presumes that the successor State is maintaining such declarations/reservations but is unable to take a definitive position". Similarly, in a memorandum addressed to the Regional Representative of the United Nations High Commissioner for Refugees regarding the succession of Jamaica to rights and obligations under the 28 July 1951 Convention relating to the Status of Refugees, the Office of Legal Affairs of the United Nations Secretariat assumed in principle that the reservations previously formulated by the United Kingdom remained applicable to Jamaica;[83]

(*d*) The Secretary-General always mentions any declarations concerning reservations, declarations, objections, etc. (repeating, confirming or amending them) that accompany a notification of succession.

54. Below are some examples that serve as a fairly representative typology of how the question of reservations and objections to reservations has been treated in the context of succession to treaties deposited with the Secretary-General.

1. Reservations

(a) *Successor States that are newly independent States*

55. The practice of newly independent States in relation to reservations in the context of succession to treaties deposited with the Secretary-General has varied widely:

(*a*) In a number of cases, newly independent States have deposited a notification of succession to a particular treaty without making any mention of the question of reservations. In such cases, the Secretary-General has included the newly independent State in the list of States parties to the treaty concerned without passing judgement upon the status of reservations formulated by the predecessor State;[84]

(*b*) Some newly independent States have expressly maintained the reservations formulated by the predecessor State;[85]

(*c*) In other cases, the newly independent State has essentially reformulated the same reservations made by the predecessor State;[86]

(*d*) There have been cases in which the newly independent State has maintained the reservations formulated by the predecessor State while adding new reservations;[87]

(*e*) There have also been cases in which the newly independent State has "reworked" reservations made by the predecessor State;[88]

(*f*) In a few cases, the newly independent State has withdrawn the predecessor State's reservations while formulating new reservations;[89]

(*g*) Lastly, there have been cases in which the newly independent State has formulated new reservations while maintaining those of the predecessor State.[90]

[80] This was the case of Pakistan in relation to the Special Protocol concerning Statelessness; see *Multilateral Treaties Deposited with the Secretary-General (Status as at 31 December 2005)* (United Nations publication, Sales No. E.06.V.2), ST/LEG/SER.E/24, vol. II, p. 561.

[81] See paragraph 60 below.

[82] See footnote 2 above.

[83] See United Nations, *Juridical Yearbook 1963*, p. 182: "Jamaica would have the right to avail itself of these reservations which were made by the United Kingdom under the terms of the Convention and it may be that in due course your office will wish to obtain a declaration by Jamaica which would withdraw these reservations. However, we think your main inquiry at present is answered by the conclusion that Jamaica is under the obligations of the Convention subject to the reservations made by the United Kingdom."

[84] See, for example, *Multilateral Treaties Deposited with the Secretary-General*, *op. cit.*, vol. I, chap. IV.2, p. 136 (Solomon Islands). The Solomon Islands succeeded to the International Convention on the Elimination of All Forms of Racial Discrimination without making any mention of the reservations made by the predecessor State (the United Kingdom), which are not reproduced in relation to the Solomon Islands. The same remark may be made in relation to the succession of Senegal and Tunisia to the Convention relating to the Status of Refugees (*ibid.*, chap. V.2, p. 376).

[85] *Ibid.*, chap. V.2, p. 379 and p. 389, footnote 18 (Cyprus); p. 631 (Fiji), p. 390, footnote 21 (Gambia); and vol. II, chap. XVI.1, p. 84 (Solomon Islands).

[86] *Ibid.*, chap. IV.2, pp. 138–139 (Fiji) and chap. V.3, pp. 394–395 (Kiribati).

[87] *Ibid.*, chap. V.3, p. 398, footnote 12 (Lesotho).

[88] *Ibid.*, chap. V.2, pp. 380 and 393 (Fiji).

[89] *Ibid.*, chap. V.3, p. 396 and p. 398, footnote 14 (Zambia).

[90] *Ibid.*, chap. V.3, p. 393 and p. 398, footnote 7 (Botswana).

(b) *Successor States other than newly independent States*

56. In these cases of succession, in particular those of the States that emerged from the former Yugoslavia and Czechoslovakia, the reservations of the predecessor State have been maintained.

57. It should be noted, in this regard, that the Czech Republic,[91] Slovakia,[92] the Federal Republic of Yugoslavia[93] and, subsequently, Montenegro[94] formulated general declarations whereby these successor States reiterated the reservations of the predecessor State.

58. In addition, in some cases the predecessor State's reservations have been expressly confirmed[95] or reformulated[96] by the successor State in relation to a particular treaty.

59. In the case of the Republic of Yemen [united], there was also a repetition of reservations by the successor State. In a letter dated 19 May 1990 addressed to the Secretary-General, the Ministers for Foreign Affairs of the Yemen Arab Republic and the People's Democratic Republic of Yemen communicated the following:

> As concerns the treaties concluded prior to their union by the Yemen Arab Republic or the People's Democratic Republic of Yemen, the Republic of Yemen (as now united) is accordingly to be considered as a party to those treaties as from the date when one of these States first became a party to those treaties. Accordingly the tables showing the status of treaties will now indicate under the designation "Yemen" the date of the formalities (signatures, ratifications, accessions, declarations and reservations, etc.) effected by the State which first became a party, those eventually effected by the other being described in a footnote.[97]

60. Lastly, there is the case of the other successors to the former Yugoslavia (apart from the Federal Republic of Yugoslavia), which appear in the list of successor States to various treaties deposited with the Secretary-General with the indication, in footnotes, of reservations formulated by the former Yugoslavia.[98]

2. Objections to reservations

(a) *Successor States that are newly independent States*

61. At the outset, mention should be made of a number of cases in which a newly independent State confirmed, in notifying its succession, the objections made by the predecessor State to reservations formulated by States parties to the treaty.[99]

62. There have also been a few cases in which objections formulated by the predecessor State have been withdrawn and, at the same time, new objections have been formulated.[100]

(b) *Successor States other than newly independent States*

63. In the case of the successor States to Czechoslovakia, objections made by the predecessor State to reservations formulated by other States parties were explicitly maintained by Slovakia.[101] Similarly, the Federal Republic of Yugoslavia stated that it maintained the objections made by the former Yugoslavia,[102] and Montenegro stated that it maintained the objections made by Serbia and Montenegro.[103]

B. Practice in relation to treaties deposited with other depositaries

64. The practice concerning these other treaties provides little guidance on the question of reservations and objections to reservations in the context of succession of States. The few elements that have been identified do not tend to contradict the lessons that can be drawn from the practice in relation to treaties for which the United Nations Secretary-General serves as depositary.

65. As to the status of reservations formulated by the predecessor State, it should first be noted that the Czech

[91] *See* https://treaties.un.org/Pages/Historicalinfo.aspx#"Czech%20 Republic". In a letter dated 16 February 1993 addressed to the Secretary-General and accompanied by a list of multilateral treaties deposited with the latter, the Czech Republic stated, among other things: "In conformity with the valid principles of international law and to the extent defined by it, the Czech Republic, as a successor State to the Czech and Slovak Federal Republic, considers itself bound, as of 1 January 1993, i.e., the date of the dissolution of the Czech and Slovak Federal Republic, by multilateral international treaties to which the Czech and Slovak Federal Republic was a party on that date, including reservations and declarations to their provisions made earlier by the Czech and Slovak Federal Republic".

[92] *See* https://treaties.un.org/Pages/Historicalinfo.aspx#"Slovakia". Slovakia declared, in a letter dated 19 May 1993 addressed to the Secretary-General and accompanied by a list of multilateral treaties deposited with the latter: "In accordance with the relevant principles and rules of international law and to the extent defined by it, the Slovak Republic, as a successor State, born from the dissolution of the Czech and Slovak Federal Republic, considers itself bound, as of 1 January 1993, i.e., the date on which the Slovak Republic assumed responsibility for its international relations, by multilateral treaties to which the Czech and Slovak Federal Republic was a party as of 31 December 1992, including reservations and declarations made earlier by Czechoslovakia, as well as objections by Czechoslovakia to reservations formulated by other treaty-parties."

[93] *See* https://treaties.un.org/Pages/Historicalinfo.aspx#"Yugoslavia". The notification of 8 March 2001 addressed to the Secretary-General by the Federal Republic of Yugoslavia contained the following indication: "The Government of the Federal Republic of Yugoslavia maintains the signatures, reservations, declarations and objections made by the Socialist Federal Republic of Yugoslavia to the treaties listed in the attached annex 1, prior to the date on which the Federal Republic of Yugoslavia assumed responsibility for its international relations."

[94] See https://treaties.un.org /Pages/HistoricalInfo.aspx?#"Montenegro". In a letter dated 10 October 2006, accompanied by a list of treaties deposited with the Secretary-General, Montenegro indicated that it would maintain "… the reservations, declarations and objections made by Serbia and Montenegro" in relation to the treaties concerned.

[95] *Multilateral Treaties Deposited with the Secretary-General, op. cit.*, vol. I, chap. VI.16, p. 448 (Serbia and Montenegro).

[96] *Ibid.*, chap. IV.11, p. 340, footnote 39 (Slovenia, which withdrew this reservation in 2004).

[97] *See* https://treaties.un.org/Pages/Historicalinfo.aspx#"Yemen".

[98] *Ibid.*, for example, vol. I, chap. VI.11, p. 335, footnote 3; chap. IV.16, p. 448, footnote 2; and chap. VI.17, p. 454, footnote 3; see also vol. II, chap. XVIII.5, p. 114, footnote 2; chap. XXI.4, p. 306, footnote 1; and chap. XXII.1, pp. 370–371, footnote 2.

[99] *Ibid.*, vol. I, chap. III.3, p. 95 (Malta), which repeated, upon succession, some objections formulated by the United Kingdom; *ibid.*, p. 97 (Tonga), which indicated that it "adopted" the objections made by the United Kingdom respecting the reservations and statements made by Egypt; vol. II, chap. XXI.1–XXI.2, pp. 292 and 298 (Fiji); and chap. XXI.4, p. 293 and p. 306, footnote 6 (Tonga).

[100] *Ibid.*, vol. II, chap. XXI.2, p. 298 (Fiji) and p. 299 (Tonga).

[101] See footnote 92 above.

[102] See footnote 93 above.

[103] See footnote 95 above.

Republic and Slovakia transmitted to a number of depositaries notifications of succession similar to those transmitted to the Secretary-General of the United Nations and providing for the maintenance of reservations formulated by the predecessor State.[104] Neither the depositaries in question nor the other States parties to the treaties concerned raised any objections to this practice.

66. On the issue of whether or not a successor State should be presumed to maintain reservations made by the predecessor State, the reply of the Universal Postal Union to the Special Rapporteur's questionnaire is worth mentioning.[105] That organization's practice is to consider that valid reservations applicable to a member State are automatically transferred to the successor State; the same is true in the case of States that have become independent by separating from a member State.

67. The Council of Europe applied the same presumption with respect to Montenegro. In a letter dated 28 June 2006 addressed to the Minister for Foreign Affairs of Montenegro, the Director General of Legal Affairs of the Council of Europe indicated that, in accordance with article 20 of the 1978 Vienna Convention, the Republic of Montenegro was considered "as maintaining these reservations and declarations because the Republic of Montenegro's declaration of succession does not express a contrary intention in that respect".[106] That letter also included a list of reservations and declarations that had been revised in places to remove references to the Republic of Serbia. By a letter dated 13 October 2006, the Minister for Foreign Affairs of Montenegro communicated his agreement on the wording of those reservations and declarations, as adapted by the depositary.

[104] See Václav Mikulka, "The dissolution of Czechoslovakia and succession in respect of treaties", in *Succession of States*, Mojmir Mrak, ed., The Hague/London/Boston, Nijhoff, 1999, pp. 111–112.

[105] See footnote 2 above.

[106] JJ55/2006, PJD/EC.

68. The practice followed by Switzerland as depositary of a number of multilateral treaties likewise does not reveal any fundamental contradiction with that of the Secretary-General of the United Nations. It is true that Switzerland had initially applied, to a successor State that made no reference to the status of the predecessor State's reservations, the presumption that such reservations were not maintained. Today, however, Switzerland no longer applies any presumption, as its practice is to invite the successor State to communicate its intentions as to whether or not it is maintaining reservations formulated by the predecessor State.[107]

69. Lastly, on the capacity of a successor State to formulate new reservations, it should be noted that the Council of Europe, in its letter to Montenegro of 28 June 2006,[108] took the position that that State was not entitled to make new reservations to treaties to which it had notified its succession.[109] This position seems to be consistent with the rule of *ipso jure* succession to treaties, as set out in the 1978 Vienna Convention for cases involving the uniting or separation of States.

[107] See the letter dated 3 May 1996 from the Directorate of Public International Law addressed to an individual, describing the practice of Switzerland as depositary State for the Geneva Conventions of 12 August 1949 for the Protection of Victims of War, in relation to the succession of States to treaties; reproduced in *Revue suisse de droit international et de droit européen*, 1997, 7th year, pp. 683–685, especially p. 684. This approach was confirmed in an opinion given on 6 February 2007 by the Directorate of Public International Law of the Federal Department of Foreign Affairs, entitled "Pratique de la Suisse en tant qu'Etat dépositaire: réserves aux traités dans le contexte de la succession d'Etats", reproduced in *Jurisprudence des autorités administratives de la Confédération (JAAC)*, 5 December 2007 edition, pp. 328–330, especially p. 330 (available from www.bk.admin.ch/dokumentation/02574/02600/index.html?lang=fr).

[108] See footnote 106 above.

[109] "[T]he Republic of Montenegro does not have the possibility, at this stage, to make new reservations to the treaties already ratified."

Annex

Selected bibliography

I. Treaties

Vienna Convention on the Law of Treaties (Vienna, 23 May 1969), United Nations, *Treaty Series*, vol. 1155, No. 18232, p. 331.

Vienna Convention on Succession of States in respect of Treaties (Vienna, 23 August 1978), *ibid.*, vol. 1946, No. 33356, p. 3.

Vienna Convention on the Law of Treaties between States and International Organizations or between International Organizations (Vienna, 21 March 1986), A/CONF.129/15 (not yet in force).

II. International conferences

Official Records of the United Nations Conference on Succession of States in Respect of Treaties. Vienna, 4 April–6 May 1977 and 31 July–23 August 1978, vol. I, *Summary records of the plenary meetings and of the meetings of the Committee of the Whole* [1977 session], A/CONF.80/16, United Nations publication, Sales No. 78.V.8; vol. II, *Summary records of the plenary meetings and of the meetings of the Committee of the Whole* [resumed session, 1978], A/CONF.80/16/Add.1, United Nations publication, Sales No. 79.V.9; and vol. III, *Documents of the Conference*, A/CONF.80/16/Add.2, United Nations publication, Sales No. 79.V.10.

III. International case law

International Court of Justice, *Application of the Convention on the Prevention and Punishment of the Crime of Genocide (Bosnia and Herzegovina v. Serbia and Montenegro), Judgment of 26 February 2007*, and separate opinion of Judge Tomka.

IV. Documents of the International Law Commission

Third report on succession in respect of treaties, by Sir Humphrey Waldock, Special Rapporteur, *Yearbook ... 1970*, vol. II, document A/CN.4/224 and Add.1, pp. 25–60.

First report on succession of States in respect of treaties, by Sir Francis Vallat, Special Rapporteur, *Yearbook ... 1974*, vol. II (Part One), document A/CN.4/278 and Add.1–6.

Questionnaires prepared by the Special Rapporteur on the topic of reservations to treaties, in accordance with paragraph 489 of the report of the Commission on the work of its forty-seventh session, *Yearbook ... 1996*, vol. II (Part One), document A/CN.4/477 and Add.1, annexes II and III, pp. 97 and 107 respectively.

V. Practice of treaty depositaries

Multilateral Treaties Deposited with the Secretary-General (Status as at 31 December 2005), vols. I and II, United Nations, ST/LEG/SER.E/24.

Letter dated 3 May 1996 from the Directorate of Public International Law addressed to an individual, describing the practice of Switzerland as depositary State for the Geneva Conventions of 12 August 1949 for the protection of victims of war, in relation to the succession of States to treaties; reproduced in *Revue suisse de droit international et de droit européen*, 1997, 7th year, pp. 683–685.

Opinion of the Directorate of Public International Law of the Federal Department of Foreign Affairs of Switzerland, entitled "Pratique de la Suisse en tant qu'Etat dépositaire: réserves aux traités dans le contexte de la succession d'Etats", given on 6 February 2007 and reproduced in *Jurisprudence des autorités administratives de la Confédération (JAAC)*, 5 December 2007 edition, pp. 328–330, especially p. 330 (www.bk.admin.ch/dokumentation/02574/02600/index.html?lang=fr).

Letter dated 28 June 2006 from the Director General of Legal Affairs of the Council of Europe addressed to the Minister for Foreign Affairs of Montenegro, JJ55/2006, PDJ/EC.

VI. Doctrine

A. Books

Bokor-Szegő, Hanna

New States and International Law. Budapest, Akadémiai Kiadó, 1970.

Gonçalves Pereira, André

La succession d'Etats en matière de traités. Paris, Pedone, 1969.

Imbert, Pierre-Henri

Les réserves aux traités multilatéraux. Evolution du droit et de la pratique depuis l'avis consultatif donné par la Cour internationale de Justice le 28 mai 1951. Paris, Pedone, 1979.

Marcoff, Marco G.

Accession à l'indépendance et succession d'Etats aux traités internationaux. Fribourg, Editions universitaires, 1969.

O'Connell, Daniel Patrick

State Succession in Municipal Law and International Law. Cambridge Studies in International and Comparative Law, VII (Vol. II: International relations). Cambridge, Cambridge University Press, 1967. 592 p.

B. Articles

Gaja, Giorgio

"Reservations to treaties and the newly independent States", *Italian Yearbook of International Law*, vol. 1, 1975, pp. 52–68.

Klabbers, Jan

"State succession and reservations to treaties", in *Essays on the Law of Treaties: A Collection of Essays in Honour of Bert Vierdag*, Jan Klabbers and René Lefeber, eds. The Hague, Martinus Nijhoff, 1998, pp. 107–120.

Menon, P. K.

"The newly independent States and succession in respect of treaties", in *Korean Journal of Comparative Law*, vol. 18, 1990, pp. 139–173.

Mikulka, Václav

"The dissolution of Czechoslovakia and succession in respect of treaties", in *Succession of States*, Mojmir Mrak, ed., The Hague, Martinus Nijhoff, 1999, pp. 100–125.

Ruda, J. M.

"Reservations to treaties", *Collected Courses of The Hague Academy of International Law, 1975–III*. Vol. 146. The Hague, Martinus Nijhoff, 1975, pp. 95–218.

Szafarz, Renata

"Vienna Convention on Succession of States in respect of Treaties: a general analysis", *Polish Yearbook of International Law*, vol. X, 1979–1980, pp. 77–113.

Zemanek, Karl

"State succession after decolonization", *Collected Courses of The Hague Academy of International Law, 1965–III*. Vol. 116. The Hague, Martinus Nijhoff, 1965, pp. 181–300.

RESPONSIBILITY OF INTERNATIONAL ORGANIZATIONS

[Agenda item 4]

DOCUMENT A/CN.4/610

Seventh report on responsibility of international organizations,* by Mr. Giorgio Gaja, Special Rapporteur

[Original: English]
[27 March 2009]

CONTENTS

Multilateral instruments cited in the present report

	Source
Articles of Agreement of the International Monetary Fund and Articles of Agreement of the International Bank for Reconstruction and Development (Washington, 27 December 1945)	United Nations, *Treaty Series*, vol. 2, No. 20, p. 39.
Convention for the Protection of Human Rights and Fundamental Freedoms (Rome, 4 November 1950)	*Ibid.*, vol. 213, No. 2889, p. 221.
Vienna Convention on the Law of Treaties between States and International Organizations or between International Organizations (Vienna, 21 March 1986)	A/CONF.129/15.

* The Special Rapporteur gratefully acknowledges the assistance given in the preparation of the present report by Paolo Palchetti (Associate Professor, University of Macerata, Italy), Stefano Dorigo (PhD, University of Pisa, Italy) and Nadia Kalb (LLM, New York University).

Works cited in the present report

BODEAU-LIVINEC, Pierre, G. P. BUZZINI and S. VILLALPANDO

"*Behrami & Behrami v. France; Saramati v. France, Germany & Norway*", Note, AJIL, vol. 102, No. 2 (2008), pp. 323–331.

D'ASPREMONT, Jean

"Abuse of the legal personality of international organizations and the responsibility of Member States", *International Organizations Law Review*, vol. 4 (2007), pp. 91–119.

DOMINICÉ, Christian

"La responsabilité internationale des Nations Unies", in J.-P. COT and A. PELLET, eds., *La Charte des Nations Unies, Commentaire article par article*, 3rd ed., Paris, Economica (2005), p. 141.

INSTITUTE OF INTERNATIONAL LAW

Yearbook, vol. 66, Part II, Session of Lisbon, Paris, Pedone (1996).

KLEIN, Pierre

"Responsabilité pour les faits commis dans le cadre d'opérations de paix et étendue du pouvoir de contrôle de la Cour européenne des droits de l'homme: quelques considérations critiques sur l'arrêt *Behrami et Saramati*", AFDI, vol. LIII (2007), pp. 43–64.

KUIJPER, Peter Jan and Esa PAASIVIRTA

"Further exploring international responsibility: the European Community and the ILC's project on responsibility of international organizations", *International Organizations Law Review*, vol. 1 (2004), p. 111.

LAGRANGE, Philippe

"Responsabilité des États pour actes accomplis en application du chapitre VII de la Charte des Nations Unies", RGDIP, vol. 112 (2008), p. 85.

LARSEN, Kjetil Mujezinović

"Attribution of conduct in peace operations: the 'ultimate authority and control' test", *European Journal of International Law*, vol. 19 (2008), p. 509.

MENDELSON, Maurice

"The definition of 'international organization' in the International Law Commission's current project on the responsibility of international organizations", in M. RAGAZZI, ed., *International Responsibility Today: Essays in Memory of Oscar Schachter.* Leiden/Boston, Nijhoff (2005), pp. 371–389.

MILANOVIĆ, Marko and Tatjana PAPIĆ

"As bad as it gets: the European Court of Human Rights' *Behrami and Saramati* decision and general international law", *International and Comparative Law Quarterly*, vol. 58 (2009), pp. 267–296.

ORAKHELASHVILI, Alexander

"*R (on the application of Al-Jedda) (FC) v. Secretary of State for Defence (Alexander Orakhelashvili)*", AJIL, vol. 102, No. 2, (April 2008), pp. 337–345.

PALCHETTI, Paolo

"Azioni di forze istituite o autorizzate dalle Nazioni Unite davanti alla Corte europea dei diritti dell'uomo: i casi Behrami e Saramati", *Rivista di Diritto Internazionale*, vol. 90 (2007), p. 681.

QUIGLEY, John

"State responsibility for ethnic cleansing", *University of California at Davis Law Review*, vol. 32 (1998–1999), p. 341.

REINISCH, August

"How necessary is necessity for international organizations?" (editorial), *International Organizations Law Review*, vol. 3 (2006), pp. 177–183.

RIVIER, Raphaële and Philippe LAGRANGE

"Travaux de la Commission du droit international et de la sixième commission" in AFDI, vol. 52 (2006), pp. 305–350.

SARI, Aurel

"Jurisdiction and international responsibility in peace support operations: the *Behrami* and *Saramati* cases", *Human Rights Law Review*, vol. 8 (2008), pp. 151–170.

SCHMALENBACH, Kristen

Die Haftung Internationaler Organisationen. Frankfurt, Peter Lang (2004).

STUMER, Andrew

"Liability of Member States for acts of international organizations: reconsidering the policy objections", *Harvard International Law Journal*, vol. 48, No. 2 (third trimester 2007), p. 553.

TALMON, Stefan

"Responsibility of international organizations: does the European Community require special treatment?" in M. RAGAZZI, ed., *International Responsibility Today: Essays in Memory of Oscar Schachter.* Leiden/Boston, Martinus Nijhoff (2005), p. 405.

THALLINGER, Gerhard

"The rule of exhaustion of local remedies in the context of the responsibility of international organizations", *Nordic Journal of International Law*, vol. 77 (2008), p. 401.

YAMADA, Chusei

"Revisiting the International Law Commission's draft articles on State responsibility", in M. RAGAZZI, ed., *International Responsibility Today: Essays in Memory of Oscar Schachter,* Leiden/Boston, Martinus Nijhoff, 2005, p. 117.

Introduction

1. The present report is intended to provide the basis for the International Law Commission to complete the adoption of its draft articles on responsibility of international organizations at first reading.

2. The Commission so far provisionally adopted 53 draft articles on responsibility of international organizations.[1] Articles 1 to 30 make up part one, concerning "The internationally wrongful act of an international organization"; articles 31 to 45 cover part two, on the "Content of the international responsibility of an international organization", while articles 46 to 53 constitute chapter I ("Invocation of the responsibility of an international organization") of part three, relating to "The implementation of the international responsibility of an international organization". At its sixtieth session, the Commission also

[1] The text of the draft articles so far provisionally adopted is reproduced in *Yearbook ... 2008*, vol. II (Part Two), chap. VII, sect. C, para. 164.

took note[2] of articles 54 to 60, which had been adopted by the Drafting Committee and are intended to build up chapter II of part three, concerning “Countermeasures”.

3. With regard to the articles so far adopted, there remain certain extant questions, such as the drafting of article 19 (“Countermeasures”) in chapter V (“Circumstances precluding wrongfulness”) of part one, and the placement of chapter (x) (“Responsibility of a State in connection with the act of an international organization”). The present report will address those questions and also propose a few provisions of a general nature to be placed in the part of the draft articles containing “General provisions”.

4. Moreover, as was indicated in earlier reports,[3] it seems advisable for the Commission to review the texts so far adopted before completing the first reading. This would enable the Commission to reconsider some of the draft articles in the light of comments subsequently made by States and international organizations and of later developments that occurred in judicial decisions and in practice. Also, the views expressed in legal literature may be taken into account. Thus, the present report will include a survey of all the relevant materials and make some proposals for amending the texts that were provisionally adopted or for adding some clarifications in the commentaries.

5. Certain comments were addressed by States and international organizations to the Special Rapporteur’s reports and original proposals rather than to the draft articles that had meanwhile been provisionally adopted by the Commission. Comments relating to texts that have been superseded will be considered in the present report only insofar as they may be relevant also for the Commission’s draft articles.

6. The present report is divided into sections that correspond to the partitions existing in the texts that were provisionally adopted. Proposals concerning the draft articles to be discussed in the following sections will be made at the end of each section. These proposals include the suggestion of some changes in the order of the existing partitions. In the present report, reference is always made to the current numbering of the draft articles. The numbering will be modified, if required, only at the time of the adoption of the draft articles on first reading.

[2] *Ibid.*, sect. A, para. 134. The text of the draft articles on countermeasures that were adopted by the Drafting Committee (A/CN.4/L.725/Add.1) may be found on the website of the International Law Commission, www.un.org/law/ilc.

[3] In Gaja’s second report (*Yearbook ... 2004*, vol. II (Part One), document A/CN.4/541), para. 1; and again in his third (*Yearbook ... 2005*, vol. II (Part One), document A/CN.4/553), para. 1; fifth (*Yearbook ... 2007*, vol. II (Part One), document A/CN.4/583), paras. 3–6; and sixth reports (*Yearbook ... 2008*, vol. II (Part One), document A/CN.4/597), para. 3.

Chapter I

Scope of the articles, use of terms and general principles

7. As stated in article 1, the present draft articles apply to the international responsibility of international organizations (para. 1) and also to “the international responsibility of a State for the internationally wrongful act of an international organization” (para. 2). This article reflects the position taken by the Commission in the articles on the responsibility of States for internationally wrongful acts.[4] This position was expressed in article 57, according to which “[t]hese articles are without prejudice to any question of the responsibility under international law of an international organization, or of any State for the conduct of an international organization”.

8. In the current draft articles, while issues concerning attribution of conduct, the breach of an international obligation and circumstances precluding wrongfulness are dealt with in part one so as to cover all cases in which the international responsibility of an international organization may arise, part two only concerns the content of responsibility of an international organization towards another international organization or a State and part three the invocation of responsibility of an international organization by another international organization or a State. Endorsing a view that had been expressed within the Commission at its sixtieth session and referred to in the Commission’s report,[5] some States suggested that part three should include also the invocation by an international organization of the international responsibility of a State.[6] However, this is a matter which lies outside the definition of the scope in article 1. Moreover, if it was felt necessary to specify the rules applying to the invocation of the responsibility of a State by an international organization, the appropriate place would be the articles on State responsibility and not the current draft articles. Various articles of part three on State responsibility, such as articles 42, 43, 45 to 50, 52 and 54, could conceivably be extended to cover also the invocation of responsibility by international organizations.

9. The same approach should be taken with regard to various other matters for which the articles on State

[4] *Yearbook ... 2001*, vol. II (Part Two), p. 26. The questions left aside by article 57 include that of the responsibility that a State may incur for the conduct of an international organization of which it is not a member. Thus, it is preferable not to follow the suggestion made by Pakistan (*Official Records of the General Assembly, Fifty-eighth Session, Sixth Committee*, 16th meeting (A/C.6/58/SR.16), para. 5) and Malaysia (*ibid., Fifty-ninth Session, Sixth Committee*, 23rd meeting (A/C.6/59/SR.23), para. 1) to restrict to “member” States the reference to States in article 1 of the current draft.

[5] *Yearbook ... 2008*, vol. II (Part Two), chap. VII, sect. B, para. 147.

[6] Thus the interventions by Austria (*Official Records of the General Assembly, Sixty-third Session, Sixth Committee*, 18th meeting (A/C.6/63/SR.18), para. 85), Belarus (*ibid*, 19th meeting (A/C.6/63/SR.19), para. 56), the Russian Federation (*ibid.*, 21st meeting (A/C.6/63/SR.21), para. 42) and Belgium (*ibid.*, para. 47). See also the interventions by Hungary (*ibid.*, 20th meeting (A/C.6/63/SR.20), para. 29) and Poland (*ibid.*, 21st meeting (A/C.6/63/SR.21), para. 32).

responsibility only consider inter-State relations, such as consent (art. 20), necessity (art. 25) or the content of international responsibility (part two, especially articles 33 and 41). For example, should the same conditions for considering consent a circumstance precluding wrongfulness apply to States and international organizations, article 20 on State responsibility could be amended as follows: "Valid consent by a State *or an international organization** to the commission of a given act by another State precludes the wrongfulness of that State in relation to the former State *or the international organization** to the extent that the act remains within the limits of that consent".

10. Article 2 defines the term "international organization" for the purposes of the draft articles. It seems clear, and has often been suggested, that also the definition of "rules of the organization" which is currently in article 4, paragraph 4, should be included in article 2 and made more general, so that it would refer to the purposes of all the draft articles and not only, as it presently reads, to those of article 4.

11. The definition of "international organization" in article 2 is more elaborate than the one contained in the Vienna Convention on the Law of Treaties between States and International Organizations or between International Organizations (hereinafter "the 1986 Vienna Convention"), which only describes it as "an intergovernmental organization".[7] While not insisting on that definition, some States would have preferred to consider only organizations that have States as their members.[8] The majority of the comments by States were, however, in favour of referring, as has been done in article 2, also to international organizations which include among their members entities other than States, as reflecting "current reality".[9]

12. In its comments, UNESCO noted that the reference in article 2 to the fact that an international organization may be established by "a treaty or other instrument governed by international law" "finds confirmation in the UNESCO practice concerning the creation of intergovernmental organizations through a simplified procedure whereby UNESCO governing bodies (the General Conference and the Executive Board) adopt their statutes and those Member States interested in their activities may notify the Director-General of their acceptance of the statutes".[10]

13. One State criticized the definition because it did not restrict responsibility of an international organization towards a State to the case in which that State recognized the legal personality of the organization.[11] The question of whether recognition is a precondition of personality is controversial,[12] but does not need to be settled for the purposes of the current draft. It does not appear necessary to state the conditions for the legal personality of an international organization to arise under international law and to add to the definition in article 2. Clearly, an international organization can be held responsible only if it has legal personality. Should recognition be considered an essential element for the organization's personality to arise, the organization would be responsible only towards those States that had recognized it and the organization's members would acquire responsibility towards the non-recognizing States. The requirement of recognition would not apply where an objective personality of the international organization can be said to exist.

14. As was noted above (see paragraph 10), article 2 should include in a second paragraph the definition of "rules of the organization" that is currently contained in article 4, paragraph 4. These rules are defined there as meaning "in particular: the constituent instruments;

[7] Art. 2, para. 1 (*i*) of the Convention. The use of this definition in the current text was advocated by the United Kingdom (*Official Records of the General Assembly, Fifty-eighth Session, Sixth Committee*, 15th meeting (A/C.6/58/SR.15), para. 10).

[8] See the interventions by China (*ibid.*, 14th meeting (A/C.6/58/SR.14), paras. 49 and 51), Israel (*ibid.*, 15th meeting (A/C.6/58/SR.15), para. 19), Cuba (*ibid., Fifty-ninth Session, Sixth Committee*, 23rd meeting (A/C.6/59/SR.23), para. 24) and Argentina (*Official Records of the General Assembly, Sixtieth Session, Sixth Committee*, 12th meeting (A/C.6/60/SR.12), para 79). Some doubts were expressed by the Russian Federation (*ibid., Fifty-eighth Session, Sixth Committee*, 15th meeting (A/C.6/58/SR.15), para. 29). See also the intervention by El Salvador (*ibid., Sixtieth Session, Sixth Committee*, 13th meeting (A/C.6/60/SR.13), para 65).

[9] Thus the intervention by Greece (*ibid., Fifty-eighth Session, Sixth Committee*, 15th meeting (A/C.6/58/SR.15), para. 11). Similar views were expressed by Chile (*ibid.*, para. 17), Pakistan (*ibid.*, 16th meeting (A/C.6/58/SR.16), para. 6), India (*ibid.*, para. 66), Bulgaria (*ibid.*, 20th meeting (A/C.6/58/SR.20), para. 62), Hungary (*ibid.*, 21st meeting (A/C.6/58/SR.21), para. 4), the Bolivarian Republic of Venezuela (*ibid.*, para. 23), Sierra Leone (*ibid.*, para. 25), Mexico (*ibid.*, para. 47) and Switzerland (*ibid., Sixtieth Session, Sixth Committee*, 13th meeting (A/C.6/60/SR.13), para. 41). While generally approving the definition, France (*ibid., Fifty-eighth Session, Sixth Committee*, 14th meeting (A/C.6/58/SR.14), para. 55) suggested the following wording: "An international organization is composed of States and may, as the case may be, include among its members entities other than States." Spain (*ibid.*, 15th meeting (A/C.6/58/SR.15), para. 38) found "merit in the alternative version proposed by France" and proposed the reference to "an international organization established by States and consisting basically of States". These two proposals are in substance very close to the text of article 2; it is not certain that they improve its drafting. The Netherlands (*ibid.*, 14th meeting (A/C.6/58/SR.14), para. 42), and Portugal (*ibid.*, 15th meeting A/C.6/58/SR.15, para. 26) pointed to the possible relevance, for the purposes of international responsibility, of the distinction between full members and associate or affiliate members. This remark does not appear to affect the definition of an international organization, but rather the question of the responsibility of the members of the organization.

[10] See *Yearbook ... 2006*, vol. II (Part One), document A/CN.4/568 and Add.1, sect. C. The Netherlands (*Official Records of the General Assembly, Fifty-eighth Session, Sixth Committee*, 14th meeting (A/C.6/58/SR.14), para. 40) queried the correctness of the reference, in paragraph 4 of the commentary to article 2, to resolutions of the General Assembly establishing an international organization. However, there is no need for the relevant resolution to be "binding", as the Netherlands suggested. An example of a resolution by the General Assembly establishing an international organization could be provided by resolution 1995 (XIX) that constituted the United Nations Conference on Trade and Development, although ostensibly as a subsidiary organ.

[11] See the interventions by Austria (*Official Records of the General Assembly, Sixty-first Session, Sixth Committee*, 13th meeting (A/C.6/61/SR.13), para. 36, and *ibid., Sixty-third Session, Sixth Committee*, 18th meeting (A/C.6/63/SR.18), para. 83). Some weight to recognition was given by China (*ibid., Fifty-eighth Session, Sixth Committee*, 14th meeting (A/C.6/58/SR.14), para. 50) and the European Commission (see A/CN.4/582, sect. J). On the other hand, Ireland (*Official Records of the General Assembly, Sixty-second Session, Sixth Committee*, 18th meeting A/C.6/62/SR.18, para. 90) maintained that international responsibility of an international organization does not depend on recognition of its legal personality.

[12] Among the authors that take the position that recognition is essential for legal personality to arise, see Mendelson, "The definition of 'international organization' in the International Law Commission's current project on the responsibility of international organizations", p. 371; and Schmalenbach, *Die Haftung Internationaler Organisationen*, pp. 63–68.

decisions, resolutions and other acts taken by the organization in accordance with those instruments; and established practice of the organization".

15. The definition above closely resembles the one contained in article 2, paragraph 1 (*j*), of the 1986 Vienna Convention, which reads as follows: " 'rules of the organization' means, in particular, the constituent instruments, decisions and resolutions adopted in accordance with them, and established practice of the organization". This definition had been considered adequate by several States that had previously expressed their views in the Sixth Committee at the request of the Commission.[13] Apart from some minor stylistic changes, the only amendment was the addition of a reference to "other acts" taken by the organization after the mention of decisions and resolutions.[14] This change allows the wide variety of terminology that is used for describing acts of international organizations to be taken into account.[15]

16. After article 4, paragraph 4, was adopted, some States expressly welcomed the new text.[16] UNESCO approved "the decision to enlarge the definition set forth in the 1986 Vienna Convention … to cover, together with 'decisions' and 'resolutions', 'other acts taken by the organization' ".[17] A few States expressed doubts about one aspect that was taken over from the Vienna Convention without change: the reference to "established practice".[18] Even if this reference may appear vague, it is hardly dispensable when considering functions and instruments of international organizations.

17. While articles 1 and 2, which respectively concern the scope of the draft articles and the use of terms, relate to the draft articles as a whole, article 3 concerns issues relating to the international responsibility of international organizations and not those relating to the responsibility of a State for the internationally wrongful act of an international organization. It would thus be more logical to include articles 1 and 2 in a short part one of the draft articles under the heading "Introduction" and start part two from article 3, with the title currently given to part one, "The internationally wrongful act of an international organization".

18. Article 3 states the conditions generally applying for the international responsibility of an international organization to arise. Like the parallel provisions in the articles on the responsibility of States for internationally wrongful acts,[19] article 3 is only intended to provide a general description of the preconditions. It is not meant to rule out exceptions and this is made clear in the commentary.[20] In particular, responsibility is not always conditional on the fact that conduct is to be attributed to the international organization. For instance, when an international organization coerces another organization or a State to commit an act that would, but for the coercion, be an internationally wrongful act of the latter organization or of that State, the former organization incurs responsibility even if the conduct is not attributable to it.[21]

19. The view has often been expressed that it should be stated that an international organization should abide by the applicable rules of that organization. While it is to be expected that an international organization does so consistently, the requirement that it should so conduct itself is imposed by the relevant primary rules and is not part of the law of international responsibility.

20. It would be difficult to state, as a general rule, that the breach by an international organization of its relevant rules entails as a consequence an international responsibility. Responsibility would in any case arise only with regard to members of the organization, since the rules of the organization cannot *per se* be invoked by non-members. Nor could one say, as has been suggested,[22] that an organization is free from international responsibility if it acts in compliance with its constituent instrument.

---

[13] See the interventions by Denmark, also on behalf of Finland, Iceland, Norway and Sweden (*Official Records of the General Assembly, Fifty-eighth Session, Sixth Committee*, 14th meeting (A/C.6/58/SR.14), para. 25), Austria (*ibid.*, para. 33), Japan (*ibid.*, paras. 36–37), Italy (*ibid.*, para. 45), Canada (*ibid.*, 15th meeting (A/C.6/58/SR.15), para. 2), Greece (*ibid.*, para. 12), Israel (*ibid.*, para. 20), Portugal (*ibid.*, para. 27) (though advocating "a more exhaustive definition"), the Russian Federation (*ibid.*, para. 30), Spain (*ibid.*, para. 40), Belarus (*ibid.*, para. 42), Egypt (*ibid.*, 16th meeting (A/C.6/58/SR.16), para. 1), Romania (*ibid.*, 19th meeting A/C.6/58/SR.19, para. 53), Bolivarian Republic of Venezuela (*ibid.*, 21st meeting A/C.6/58/SR.21, para. 21), Sierra Leone (*ibid.*, para. 25) and Mexico (*ibid.*, para. 47). See also the written comments of Mexico (*Yearbook … 2005*, vol. II (Part One), document A/CN.4/547, sect. F, p. 22), Poland (*ibid.*) and the Democratic Republic of the Congo (*Yearbook … 2005*, vol. II (Part One), document A/CN.4/556, sect. I, p. 42). The view that the definition in the Convention was "not satisfactory" was voiced by Gabon (*Official Records of the General Assembly, Fifty-eighth Session, Sixth Committee*, 15th meeting (A/C.6/58/SR.15), para. 4). France (*ibid.*, 14th meeting (A/C.6/58/SR.14), para. 58) suggested that one should "consider the clarifications on the subject given by the Institute of International Law in the resolution adopted in Lisbon in 1995" (see *Annuaire de l'Institut de Droit International, Session de Lisbonne*, vol. 66 (Part II), p. 447 (1996)).

[14] According to the Russian Federation, however, the definition in the current draft "had departed from the perfectly satisfactory definition given in article 2 (*j*)" of the Vienna Convention (*Official Records of the General Assembly, Fifty-ninth Session, Sixth Committee*, 23rd meeting (A/C.6/59/SR.23), para. 22).

[15] The definition provided by the Institute of International Law (see footnote 13 above) attempted to do this by referring to "constituent instruments of the organization and any amendments thereto, regulations adopted thereunder, binding decisions and resolutions adopted in accordance with such instruments and the established practice of the organization". The definition adopted by the Commission is shorter and appears to be more comprehensive.

[16] See especially the interventions by Greece (*Official Records of the General Assembly, Fifty-ninth Session, Sixth Committee*, 23rd meeting (A/C.6/59/SR.23), para. 38) and Romania (*ibid.*, 25th meeting (A/C.6/59/SR.25), para. 16).

[17] See *Yearbook … 2006*, vol. II (Part One), document A/CN.4/568 and Add.1, sect. E.

[18] Criticisms on this point were voiced by China (*Official Records of the General Assembly, Fifty-ninth Session, Sixth Committee*, 21st meeting (A/C.6/59/SR.21), para. 38) and the Republic of Korea (*ibid.*, 23rd meeting (A/C.6/59/SR.23), paras. 14–15). Portugal (*ibid.*, 22nd meeting (A/C.6/59/SR.22), para. 40) suggested a text that would have deleted any reference to practice. The European Commission (*ibid.*, 21st meeting (A/C.6/59/SR.21), para. 19) suggested replacing the term "established practice" with "generally accepted practice".

[19] Art. 1 and 2.

[20] *Yearbook … 2003*, vol. II (Part Two), chap. IV, sect. C, pp. 22–23.

[21] See article 14 of the current draft.

[22] IMF (see *Yearbook … 2007*, vol. II (Part One), document A/CN.4/582, sect. B) maintained that "the fundamental parameters within which all of an international organization's obligations must be constrained are established in the constituent agreement of the organization, since the outer limits of what the members have agreed to are set out in that charter".

21. The following proposals are made at the conclusion to this chapter of the present report:

(*a*) A new part one, headed "Introduction", should comprise articles 1 and 2;

(*b*) Article 4, paragraph 4, should be moved to article 2 as a new paragraph;

(*c*) The word "article" in that new paragraph should be rendered in the plural;

(*d*) The present title of part one should become the title of part two and start from article 3;

(*e*) Article 3 should be placed as the only article in chapter I of part two, the title of the chapter being "General principles".

Chapter II

Attribution of conduct

22. The general rule on attribution to an international organization, as expressed in article 4, elicited some favourable comments.[23] The fact that the conduct of an organ or agent may be attributed to the relevant international organization only if it is taken "in the performance of functions of that organ or agent" appears to imply that the organ or agent acts in an "official capacity"; it may thus not be necessary to refer to the fact that the person is acting in his or her official capacity, as one State suggested that one should specify.[24] When paragraph 3 states that "rules of the organization shall apply to the determination of the functions of its organs and agents", it does not say that attribution may only be based on the rules of the organization; as was noted by ILO, conduct of a person or entity could also be attributed to an international organization on a different, factual basis, when the person or entity is "acting on its instructions, or under its direction or control".[25]

23. ILO[26] and UNESCO[27] voiced concerns about the width of the definition of the term "agent" in paragraph 2 of article 4, which covers "officials and other persons or agents through whom the organization acts". As suggested by these international organizations, it would be appropriate to add some qualifications to this definition. In its comments, UNESCO considered that attribution should be precluded when the relations between an international organization and a private contractor are governed by a contract that includes a clause purporting to rule out that the contractor "be considered as an agent or member of the staff of UNESCO". However, this type of clause cannot exclude the possibility that, because of factual circumstances, the conduct of the private contractor would nevertheless be attributed to the organization under international law. In order to establish attribution when an international organization acts through a person or entity that is not an organ, according to ICJ in its advisory opinion on *Reparation for injuries suffered in the service of the United Nations*,[28] the decisive factor appears to be whether or not the person or entity has been charged by an organ of the international organization with carrying out, or helping to carry out, one of the functions of that organization. Paragraph 2 could be rephrased as follows:

> "2. For the purposes of paragraph 1, the term "agent" includes officials and other persons or entities through whom the international organization acts, when they have been charged by an organ of the organization with carrying out, or helping to carry out, one of its functions."

24. In recent years much attention has been devoted to the question of whether the conduct of a State organ may be attributed to an international organization when the State organ is put at the organization's disposal. Article 5 considers the case of a State organ retaining its character of State organ, but acting to a certain extent under the control of an international organization, at the disposal of which it has been placed. The criterion for attribution set out in article 5 is that of the "effective control" over the conduct in question.

25. Several States indicated their approval of the criterion of "effective or factual control" as adopted in article 5.[29] It

[23] See the interventions by Germany (*Official Records of the General Assembly, Fifty-ninth Session, Sixth Committee*, 21st meeting (A/C.6/59/SR.21), para. 20), France (*ibid.*, 22nd meeting (A/C.6/59/SR.22), para. 7), Belarus (*ibid.*, para. 43), Singapore (*ibid.*, para. 52), Greece (*ibid.*, 23rd meeting (A/C.6/59/SR.23), para. 38) and Romania (*ibid.*, 25th meeting (A/C.6/59/SR.25), para. 16).

[24] The United Kingdom (*ibid.*, 22nd meeting (A/C.6/59/SR.22), para. 30) would have preferred a reference to the person's "official capacity" rather than to "the performance of the functions". Austria (*ibid.*, para. 18) suggested a reference to both "official capacity" and "functions" and proposed the following text: "An 'agent' or 'organ' of an international organization is a person or entity that has been charged by that organization with carrying out, or helping to carry out, one of its functions, provided the agent or organ is acting in that capacity in the particular instance". Part of this proposal has been adopted in the rewording of article 4, paragraph 2, as suggested in paragraph 23 of the present report.

[25] *Yearbook ... 2006*, vol. II (Part One), document A/CN.4/568 and Add.1, sect. E. Jordan (*Official Records of the General Assembly, Fifty-ninth Session, Sixth Committee*, 23rd meeting (A/C.6/59/SR.23), para. 32) advocated a "factual test"; Austria (*ibid.*, 22nd meeting (A/C.6/59/SR.22, para. 20) suggested that the case of "a private person acting under the effective control of the organization" should also be considered. As was noted in paragraph 13 of the commentary on article 4, such a person would come within the definition of agent in article 4, paragraph 2. See *Yearbook ... 2004*, vol. II (Part Two), chap. V, sect. C, p. 49. This result would not be changed by the modification of article 4, paragraph 2, as suggested in this chapter.

[26] See *Yearbook ... 2006*, vol. II (Part One), A/CN.4/568 and Add.1, sect. E.

[27] *Ibid.*

[28] *I.C.J. Reports 1949*, p. 174 at p. 177. According to IMF (*Yearbook ... 2005*, vol. II (Part One), document A/CN.4/556, sect. E, p. 39), this dictum is not applicable to IMF, to which "only acts of officials performed in their official capacity would be attributable".

[29] Germany (*Official Records of the General Assembly, Fifty-ninth Session, Sixth Committee*, 21st meeting (A/C.6/59/SR.21), para. 21), Italy (*ibid.*, para. 32), China (*ibid.*, para. 39), the Islamic Republic of Iran (*ibid.*, 22nd meeting (A/C.6/59/SR.22), para. 6), France (*ibid.*, para. 8), New Zealand (*ibid.*, 23rd meeting (A/C.6/59/SR.23), para. 8), the Russian Federation (*ibid.*, para. 22), Mexico (*ibid.*, para. 26), Greece (*ibid.*,

was noted in one comment that this criterion was tailored for "military operations" and was "less adequate for deciding attribution in the case of other types of cooperation between international organizations and States or other international organizations".[30] It may well be that outside military operations it may be more difficult to establish which entity has an effective control.[31] However, this does not imply that the criterion set out in article 5 is inadequate, but that in many cases its application will lead to the conclusion that conduct has to be attributed both to the lending State and to the receiving international organization.

26. After article 5 was adopted, the European Court of Human Rights considered, first in *Behrami and Behrami v. France* and *Saramati v. France, Germany and Norway*, the issue of attribution of conduct in the case of forces placed in Kosovo at the disposal of the United Nations (United Nations Interim Administration Mission in Kosovo (UNMIK)) or authorized by the United Nations (Kosovo Force (KFOR)). These cases raised the question of the Court's jurisdiction *ratione personae* with regard to applications that challenged the lawfulness of conduct taken by national contingents. The Court quoted *in extenso* article 5 of the Commission's draft and summarized various paragraphs of the related commentary.[32] The Court's decision did not contain any criticism of the criterion that was stated by the Commission; however, the Court made use of a different notion of control for reaching its decision. It considered that the decisive point was whether "the United Nations Security Council retained ultimate authority and control so that operational command only was delegated".[33] While acknowledging "the effectiveness or unity of NATO command in *operational* matters",[34] the Court noted that the presence of KFOR in Kosovo was based on a resolution adopted by the Security Council and concluded that "KFOR was exercising lawfully delegated Chapter VII powers of the UNSC so that the impugned action was, in principle, 'attributable' to the UN within the meaning of the word outlined [in article 3 of the ILC draft]".[35] With regard to UNMIK, the Court stated that it was "a subsidiary organ of the UN created under Chapter VII of the Charter so that the impugned inaction was, in principle, 'attributable' to the UN in the same sense".[36] Several commentators rightly observed that, had the Court applied the criterion of effective control set out by the Commission, it would have reached the different conclusion that the conduct of national contingents allocated to KFOR had to be attributed either to the sending State or to NATO.[37]

27. In *Kasumaj v. Greece*[38] and *Gajić v. Germany*[39] the European Court of Human Rights reiterated its views concerning the attribution to the United Nations of conduct taken by national contingents allocated to KFOR. Likewise in *Berić and others v. Bosnia and Herzegovina*[40] the same Court quoted verbatim and at length its previous decision in *Behrami and Saramati* when reaching the conclusion that also the conduct of the High Representative in Bosnia and Herzegovina had to be attributed to the United Nations.

28. The judgement given by the House of Lords in *Al-Jedda* also contains ample references to article 5 of the Commission's draft and the related commentary.[41] One of the majority opinions stated that "[i]t was common ground between the parties that the governing principle [was] that expressed by the International Law Commission in article 5 of its draft articles on the Responsibility of International Organizations".[42] The House of Lords was confronted with a claim arising from the detention of a person by British troops in Iraq. In its resolution 1546 (2004), the Security Council had previously authorized the presence of the multinational force in that country. The majority of opinions appeared to endorse the views expressed by the European Court of Human Rights in *Behrami and Saramati*, but distinguished the facts of the case and concluded that "[i]t cannot realistically be said that US and UK forces were under the effective command and control of the UN, or that UK forces were under such command and control when they detained the appellant".[43]

---

para. 39) and Romania (*ibid.*, 25th meeting (A/C.6/59/SR.25), para. 16). Also IMF endorsed article 5 (*Yearbook ... 2005*, vol. II (Part One), document A/CN.4/556, sect. F). Japan (*Official Records of the General Assembly, Fifty-ninth Session, Sixth Committee*, 21st meeting (A/C.6/59/SR.21), para. 55) required "clarification" of the standard and Belarus (*ibid.*, 22nd meeting (A/C.6/59/SR.22), para. 44) a "clear definition of the term 'effective control'". Austria (*ibid.*, para. 19) suggested a reference to the fact that the State organ was exercising one of the functions of the organization; this could be taken as implied, but may be specified in the commentary. The Republic of Korea (*ibid.*, 23rd meeting (A/C.6/59/SR.23), paras. 16–17) proposed to take into consideration the criterion of overall control, that has been generally applied to the different issue of the attribution to a State of conduct by private persons.

[30] Thus Denmark, on behalf of the five Nordic countries (Denmark, Finland, Iceland, Norway and Sweden) (*ibid.*, 22nd meeting (A/C.6/59/SR.22), para. 62).

[31] ILO (see *Yearbook ... 2006*, vol. II (Part One), document A/CN.4/568 and Add.1, sect. F) noted that, when an official is seconded but is "kept under employment contract with the releasing State or international organization", the "issue of effective control over the official's conduct is not so obvious".

[32] Decision (Grand Chamber) of 2 May 2007 on the admissibility of applications No. 71412/01 and No. 78166/01, paras. 29–33.

[33] Para. 133.

[34] Para. 139.

[35] Para. 141.

[36] Para. 143.

[37] See Bodeau-Livinec, Buzzini and Villalpando, "*Behrami & Behrami v. France; Saramati v. France, Germany & Norway*", pp. 328–329; Klein, "Responsabilité pour les faits commis dans le cadre d'opérations de paix et étendue du pouvoir de contrôle de la Cour européenne des droits de l'homme: quelques considérations critiques sur l'arrêt *Behrami et Saramati*", p. 55; Lagrange, "Responsabilité des États pour actes accomplis en application du chapitre VII de la Charte des Nations Unies"; Larsen, "Attribution of conduct in peace operations: the 'ultimate authority and control' test", pp. 521–522; Milanović and Papić, "As bad as it gets: the European Court of Human Rights' *Behrami and Saramati* decision and general international law"; Orakhelashvili, "*R (on the application of Al-Jedda) (FC) v. Secretary of State for Defence (Alexander Orakhelashvili)*", p. 341; Palchetti, "Azioni di forze istituite o autorizzate dalle Nazioni Unite davanti alla Corte europea dei diritti dell'uomo: i casi *Behrami* e *Saramati*", pp. 689–690; Sari, "Jurisdiction and international responsibility in peace support operations: the *Behrami* and *Saramati* cases", p. 164.

[38] Decision of 5 July 2007 on the admissibility of application No. 6974/05.

[39] Decision of 28 August 2007 on the admissibility of application No. 31446/02.

[40] Decision of 16 October 2007 on the admissibility of applications Nos. 36357/04 and others.

[41] Judgement of 12 December 2007, *R (on the application of Al-Jedda) (FC) v. Secretary of State for Defence.*

[42] *Ibid.*, para. 5 of the opinion of Lord Bingham of Cornhill.

[43] Thus the opinion of Lord Bingham of Cornhill, paras. 22–24 (the quotation is taken from paragraph 23). Baroness Hale of Richmond (para. 124), Lord Carswell (para. 131) and Lord Brown of Eaton-under-Heywood (paras. 141–149, with his own reasons) concurred on this conclusion, while Lord Rodger of Earlsferry dissented.

29. More recently, a judgement by the District Court of The Hague concerned the attribution of the conduct of the Dutch contingent in the United Nations Protection Force (UNPROFOR) in relation to the massacre in Srebrenica. This judgement contained only a general reference to the Commission's draft.[44] The Court found that "the reprehended acts of Dutchbat should be assessed as those of an UNPROFOR contingent" and that "these acts and omissions should be attributed strictly, as a matter of principle, to the United Nations".[45] The Court then considered that if "Dutchbat was instructed by the Dutch authorities to ignore UN orders or to go against them, and Dutchbat behaved in accordance with this instruction from the Netherlands, this constitutes a violation of the factual basis on which the attribution to the UN rests".[46] The Court did not find that there was sufficient evidence for reaching such a conclusion.

30. The positive reaction generally adopted by States with regard to the criterion set out in article 5 and the absence of any criticism of that criterion in any of the judicial decisions referred to above give an indication that no change should be suggested to article 5. It is true that the European Court of Human Rights applied a different criterion for attribution and reached, with regard to attribution of conduct of national contingents allocated to a force authorized by the United Nations, a conclusion that differed from the one that would have been reached on the basis of article 5, as was specified in the commentary.[47] Without denying the importance of this jurisprudence, it would be difficult to accept, simply on the strength of the judgment in *Behrami and Saramati*, the criterion there applied as a potentially universal rule. Also as a matter of policy, the approach taken by the European Court is unconvincing. It would lead to attributing to the United Nations conduct which the organization has not specifically authorized and of which it may have little knowledge or no knowledge at all. It is therefore not surprising that in his report of June 2008 on the United Nations Interim Administration Mission in Kosovo, the United Nations Secretary-General distanced himself from that criterion and stated: "It is understood that the international responsibility of the United Nations will be limited to the extent of its effective operational control."[48]

31. Also with regard to the relations between an international organization and State organs that act for the organization, the European Commission suggested adding a rule on attribution so that, when implementing a binding act of the European Community or "other potentially similar organizations", the conduct of the organ of a member State would be attributed to that international organization.[49] The State organ would then act as a quasi-organ of the international organization. One could envisage a more general rule based on the same rationale, to the effect that conduct taken for the implementation of a binding act of an international organization would be attributed to that organization.

32. A WTO panel seemed receptive to this approach. In *European Communities—Protection of Trademarks and Geographical Indication for Agricultural Products and Foodstuffs*, the panel "accepted the European Communities' explanation of what amounts to its *sui generis* domestic constitutional arrangements that Community laws are generally not executed through authorities at Community level but rather through recourse to the authorities of its member States which, in such a situation, 'act *de facto* as organs of the Community, for which the Community would be responsible under WTO law and international law in general.'"[50]

33. With regard to the implementation of a regulation of the European Community by one of its member States, the European Court of Human Rights took a different view in *Bosphorus Hava Yollari Turizm ve Ticaret Anonim Şirketi v. Ireland*. The Court found that "a Contracting Party is responsible under article 1 of the [European Convention on Human Rights] for all acts and omissions of its organs regardless of whether the act or omission in question was a consequence of domestic law or of the necessity to comply with international legal obligations".[51] The same line was taken by the European Court of Justice in *Kadi, Al Barakaat International Foundation v. Council and Commission* when it considered the attribution of a regulation adopted by the European Community for complying with a binding resolution of the United Nations Security Council. According to this Court, "the contested regulation cannot be considered to be an act directly attributable to the United Nations as an action of one of its subsidiary organs created under Chapter VII of the Charter of the United Nations or an action falling within the exercise of powers lawfully delegated by the Security Council pursuant to that Chapter".[52] These judicial decisions, both of which examined the implementation of a binding act that left no discretion, clearly do not lend support to the proposal of considering that conduct implementing an act of an international organization should be attributed to that organization. This proposal would moreover conflict with the rule that conduct taken by any one of the State organs is attributed to the State, as set out in article 4 of the articles on the international responsibility of States for internationally wrongful acts.

34. Article 6 of the current draft considers that the conduct of one of the organs or agents of an international organization is attributed to that organization even when the organ or agent acts in "excess of authority or contravention of instructions". Attribution is considered to be

[44] Judgement of 10 September 2008, case No. 265615/HA ZA 06-1671, para. 4.8.

[45] *Ibid.*, para. 4.11.

[46] *Ibid.*, para. 4.14.1.

[47] *Yearbook ... 2004*, vol. II (Part Two), chap. V, sect. C, pp. 50 *et seq.*

[48] S/2008/354, para. 16.

[49] *Official Records of the General Assembly, Fifty-ninth Session, Sixth Committee*, 21st meeting (A/C.6/59/SR.21), para. 18. This view was developed by Kuijper and Paasivirta, "Further exploring international responsibility: the European Community and the ILC's project on responsibility of international organizations", p. 127; and by Talmon, "Responsibility of international organizations: does the European Community require special treatment?", pp. 412–414.

[50] Report of 15 March 2005 (WT/DS174/R), para. 7.725. Again with regard to a claim brought against the European Communities, the panel report of 29 September 2006 on *European Communities—Measures Affecting the Approval and Marketing of Biotech Products* (WT/DS291/R, WT/DS292/R and WT/DS293/R), para. 7.101, reiterated the same view.

[51] *Bosphorus Hava Yollarŏ Turizm ve Ticary Anonim Şirkyi (Bosphorus Airways) v. Ireland*, Judgment (Grand Chamber) of 30 June 2005, application No. 45036/98, para. 153.

[52] Judgment (Grand Chamber) of 3 September 2008, joined cases C-402/05 P and C-415/05 P, para. 314, *European Court Reports 2008*, p. I-06351.

conditional on the organ or agent acting "in that capacity", that is in connection with his or her functions. It is thus to be assumed that attribution does not occur "when the conduct ... clearly exceed[s] the authority of the organs or agents, or when it obviously contravene[s] the instructions of the organization".[53]

35. Various States approved the criterion set out in this article.[54] Some States suggested that a specific reference be added to the case of an organ or agent exceeding the competence of the organization.[55] As was indicated in the commentary on article 6, this conclusion is implied, "because an act exceeding the competence of the organization necessarily exceeds the organ's or agent's authority".[56]

36. The International Criminal Police Organization (INTERPOL) observed that, for the purposes of attribution, "when the *ultra vires* act exceeds the competence of the organization, the proposed rule becomes less persuasive".[57] A similar remark was made by ILO.[58] INTERPOL would have liked the text to specify that attribution be excluded when the violation of the rules on competence of the organization is "manifest".[59] However, the consideration that attribution is excluded when there is a manifest excess of authority applies more generally. In the presence of a manifest excess of authority, whether or not it affects the competence of the international organization, one cannot say that the organ or agent acted "in that capacity". This may not seem obvious from a reading of the text. While an attempt could be made to make the meaning of the text more transparent, on balance it seems preferable to keep the same wording that was used in article 7 of the articles on the responsibility of States for internationally wrongful acts.

37. Article 7 considers the case of an international organization acknowledging that a certain conduct should be attributed to it.[60] A few States expressed specific support for this article,[61] while one State found that the provision was "inconceivable in the context of international organizations"[62] and another that there was no "jurisprudence or practice to support that approach".[63] Acknowledgement of attribution is certainly not a frequent event, either by a State or by an international organization. Yet the commentary on article 7 gave some examples of practice relating to international organizations.[64] Article 7 could have been omitted, and so, arguably, could have been the corresponding provision in the articles on the responsibility of States for internationally wrongful acts. Once a provision on acknowledgement of attribution was included in the latter articles, it seems reasonable to adopt the same solution with regard to international organizations.

38. In conclusion to the present section (which comprises articles 4 to 7), the only suggested change concerns a new wording of paragraph 2 of article 4, as proposed in paragraph 23 above. It may be useful to recall that a proposal concerning article 4, paragraph 4, has been made in the previous chapter (paras. 10 and 21 above).

[53] This solution, which was advocated by Malaysia (*Official Records of the General Assembly, Fifty-ninth Session, Sixth Committee*, 23rd meeting (A/C.6/59/SR.23), para. 1), is arguably implied in article 6.

[54] See the interventions by Germany (*ibid.*, 21st meeting (A/C.6/59/SR.21), para. 21), Singapore (*ibid.*, 22nd meeting (A/C.6/59/SR.22), para. 52), Jordan (*ibid.*, 23rd meeting (A/C.6/59/SR.23), para. 32) and Romania (*ibid.*, 25th meeting (A/C.6/59/SR.25), para. 16). On the contrary, the Russian Federation (*ibid.*, 23rd meeting (A/C.6/59/SR.23), para. 22) would have preferred the application of the criterion set out in article 4, paragraph 1.

[55] France (*ibid.*, 22nd meeting (A/C.6/59/SR.22), para. 9) and Greece (*ibid.*, 23rd meeting (A/C.6/59/SR.23), para. 40).

[56] *Yearbook ... 2004*, vol. II (Part Two), chap. V, sect. C, p. 52, para. (1).

[57] *Yearbook ... 2005*, vol. II (Part One), document A/CN.4/556, p. 41, sect. G, second paragraph.

[58] See *Yearbook ... 2006*, vol. II (Part One), document A/CN.4/568 and Add.1, p. 133, sect. G.

[59] See *Yearbook ... 2005*, vol. II (Part One), document A/CN.4/556, pp. 41–42, sect. G, at p. 42.

[60] This rule is not intended to imply "a transfer of responsibility" which could "adversely affect the position of the injured State", contrary to what was suggested by Yamada, "Revisiting the International Law Commission's draft articles on State responsibility", at p. 122.

[61] France (*Official Records of the General Assembly, Fifty-ninth Session, Sixth Committee*, 22nd meeting (A/C.6/59/SR.22), para. 10), the Russian Federation (*ibid.*, 23rd meeting (A/C.6/59/SR.23), para. 22) and Romania (*ibid.*, 25th meeting (A/C.6/59/SR.25), para. 16).

[62] Thus Portugal (*ibid.*, 22nd meeting (A/C.6/59/SR.22), para. 42).

[63] Jordan (*ibid.*, 23rd meeting (A/C.6/59/SR.23), para. 32).

[64] *Yearbook ... 2004*, vol. II (Part Two), chap. V, sect. C, pp. 53–54.

Chapter III

Breach of an international obligation

39. The chapter on the breach of an international obligation in the current draft (arts. 8 to 11) has been basically modelled on the corresponding articles on the responsibility of States for internationally wrongful acts. Various States approved the approach taken on this matter by the Commission.[65] Moreover, no criticism was expressed in this regard.

40. The main question raised by the present chapter concerns the definition of obligations under international law as applied to an international organization. These include obligations that are imposed by rules of general international law and by treaties concluded by the organization

[65] France (*Official Records of the General Assembly, Sixtieth Session, Sixth Committee*, 11th meeting (A/C.6/60/SR.11), para. 76), Romania (*ibid.*, 12th meeting (A/C.6/60/SR.12), para. 75), Argentina (*ibid.*, para. 81), Denmark, on behalf of the five Nordic countries (Denmark, Finland, Iceland, Norway and Sweden) (*ibid.*, 13th meeting (A/C.6/60/SR.13), para. 18), Greece (*ibid.*, para. 25, with regard to article 8, paragraph 1), Poland (*ibid.*, paras. 58–59) and Nigeria (*ibid.*, 20th meeting (A/C.6/60/SR.20), para. 48, with reference to article 8). Guatemala (*ibid.*, 12th meeting (A/C.6/60/SR.12), para. 101) suggested specifying in article 8, paragraph 1, that the international obligation in question was "binding on the international organization". This seems implied by the fact that, according to article 8, paragraph 1, the act of the international organization has to be "not in conformity with what is required of it by the obligation". Although it has a different object, article 9 confirms that the organization is "bound by the obligation".

concerned.[66] They also comprise obligations under the rules of the organization; however, it is debatable to what extent these rules are part of international law. Article 8, paragraph 2, does not attempt to provide a clear-cut solution. As was approvingly noted by some States during the debates in the General Assembly, "[a]lthough article 8, paragraph 2, did not really clarify which rules [give rise to international responsibility], it provide[s] for a case-by-case determination of the international legal character of the various types of rules of international organizations".[67] Some other States endorsed article 8, paragraph 2.[68] Further States maintained that all the rules of the organization imposed obligations under international law and that article 8, paragraph 2, should be deleted.[69] Yet other States requested "more guidance" on what obligations under the rules of the organization actually constituted obligations under international law.[70]

41. The fact that a rule of the organization "bound, or granted rights to, persons or entities that were subjects of international law"[71] cannot be a decisive criterion for identifying which rules of the organization pertain to international law, because certain relations between subjects of international law could well be regulated by private law. Some States maintained that "rules which were merely procedural or administrative in nature" did not give rise to an international obligation.[72] WHO stated that it could not "share the view that the rules governing employment of the officials of an organization are rules of international law".[73] The difficulty with providing a general criterion is that the extent to which the breach of an obligation under the rules of the organization constitutes the breach of an obligation under international law is likely to vary according to the organization concerned.[74] Thus, although the subject matter may give some indication on the legal nature of the rules of the organization, it cannot be taken as decisive.

42. One State noted that the wording of paragraph 2 seemed to imply that "without paragraph 2, international obligations created by the rules of the organization would not be covered by the draft articles".[75] It would be useful to avoid any misunderstanding on this point. Moreover, paragraph 2 could be rephrased in order to state more clearly that the rules of the organization are in principle part of international law, thus conveying that there are certain exceptions. The paragraph could read as follows:

> "The breach of an international obligation by an international organization includes in principle the breach of an obligation under the rules of that organization."

43. IMF[76] and UNESCO[77] expressed doubts about whether an international organization could be required to take positive action: this in particular in view of the difficulty for the organization in complying with this type of obligation, since its decision-making process may not allow the organization to adopt the necessary action.[78] However, this difficulty cannot be a reason for generally excluding the possibility that international organizations may be the legal addressees of an international obligation to take positive action.

44. In conclusion to the present chapter, it is suggested that paragraph 2 of article 8 should be modified as indicated in paragraph 42 above.

[66] This is not the opinion of IMF, according to whom "the issue of whether there is a breach of an international obligation by an international organization can only be determined by reference to the rules of the organization (save in exceptional cases involving peremptory norms of general international law)" (see *Yearbook ... 2007*, vol. II (Part One), document A/CN.4/582, sect. C, p. 21).

[67] Thus Denmark, on behalf of the Nordic countries (Denmark, Finland, Iceland, Norway and Sweden) (*Official Records of the General Assembly, Sixtieth Session, Sixth Committee*, 13th meeting (A/C.6/60/SR.13), para. 18).

[68] Ireland (*ibid.*, 11th meeting (A/C.6/60/SR.11), para. 38), France (*ibid.*, para. 76) and the Russian Federation (*ibid.*, 12th meeting (A/C.6/60/SR.12), para. 66). The Russian Federation found that the solution provided by article 8, paragraph 2, was "elegant" and that "[t]he precise circumstances in which a breach of the rules gave rise to such responsibility obviously had to be decided in each specific case in the light of the type of rule in question".

[69] Austria (*ibid.*, 11th meeting (A/C.6/60/SR.11), para. 60), Portugal (*ibid.*, 12th meeting (A/C.6/60/SR.12), para. 34), Hungary (*ibid.*, 13th meeting (A/C.6/60/SR.13), para. 6) and Bulgaria (*ibid.*, *Sixty-second Session, Sixth Committee*, 18th meeting (A/C.6/62/SR.18), para. 82).

[70] Thus Greece (*ibid.*, *Sixtieth Session*, 13th meeting (A/C.6/60/SR.13), para. 25). Similar remarks were made by Canada (*ibid.*, 11th meeting (A/C.6/60/SR.11), para. 69), Argentina (*ibid.*, 12th meeting (A/C.6/60/SR.12), para. 83), Jordan (*ibid.*, 13th meeting A/C.6/60/SR.13, para. 13), Germany (*ibid.*, para. 33) and Spain (*ibid.*, para. 51).

[71] Thus Guatemala (*ibid.*, 12th meeting (A/C.6/60/SR.12), para. 99).

[72] Thus India (*ibid.*, 18th meeting (A/C.6/60/SR.18), para. 59). Similar proposals were made by Switzerland (*ibid.*, 13th meeting (A/C.6/60/SR.13, para. 43) and Indonesia (*ibid.*, 20th meeting (A/C.6/60/SR.20), para. 5).

[73] See *Yearbook ... 2008*, vol. II (Part One), document A/CN.4/593 and Add.1, sect. B; the same point had been made in an earlier comment, see *Yearbook ... 2006*, vol. II (Part One), document A/CN.4/568 and Add.1, sect. H, p. 135.

[74] A remark to this effect was made by Singapore (*Official Records of the General Assembly, Fifty-ninth Session, Sixth Committee*, 22nd meeting (A/C.6/59/SR.22), para. 56).The European Commission (*ibid., Sixtieth Session, Sixth Committee*, 12th meeting (A/C.6/60/SR.12), paras. 11–12) and Romania (*ibid.*, para. 76) stressed the particular situation of the European Community.

[75] Canada (*ibid.*, 11th meeting (A/C.6/60/SR.11), para. 68).

[76] See *Yearbook ... 2004*, vol. II (Part One), document A/CN.4/545, sect. D, pp. 25–26.

[77] See *Yearbook ... 2006*, vol. II (Part One), document A/CN.4/568 and Add.1, sect. D, pp. 129–130.

[78] See also the intervention of Bulgaria (*Official Records of the General Assembly, Sixty-second Session, Sixth Committee*, 18th meeting (A/C.6/62/SR.18), para. 81).

Chapter IV

Responsibility of an international organization in connection with the act of a State or another international organization

45. The first three articles of the chapter on "Responsibility of an international organization in connection with the act of a State or another international organization" (arts. 12 to 14) are parallel to articles 16 to 18 on the responsibility of States for internationally wrongful acts. They concern the cases of an international organization

aiding or assisting, or directing or controlling, or coercing a State or another international organization in the commission of an internationally wrongful act. Although these cases may rarely occur, several States accepted the idea that, if one of them takes place, an international organization should be responsible under the same conditions as a State aiding or assisting, or directing and controlling, or coercing another State.[79] This implies in particular that, for responsibility to arise, the act would have to be internationally wrongful if it had been committed by the international organization that, for instance, assists a State in the commission of the wrongful act.[80]

46. Certain States expressed concern about the possible overlap between articles 12 to 14 and article 15, which considers the responsibility of an international organization that circumvents an international obligation by binding its members to take a certain act, or by authorizing or recommending that conduct.[81] A partial overlap may not be excluded. However, an overlap would not lead to a conflict, because all the provisions concerned may lead, under different conditions, to establishing the responsibility of the same international organization.

47. Article 15 is designed to prevent an international organization from successfully circumventing one of its international obligations by availing itself of the separate legal personality of its members, whether States or other international organizations. The provision considers international responsibility only to the extent that the former international organization may incur it. Article 16 makes it clear that the draft does not address the question of the responsibility that members may incur in such circumstances, supposing that by their conduct they breach one of their obligations.

48. The idea that "an international organization should not be allowed to escape responsibility by 'outsourcing' its actors"[82] was welcomed by certain States,[83] when it was first mooted in a request for comments made by the Commission.[84] After article 15 was adopted, several States expressed their approval, albeit sometimes with comments.[85] Moreover, a few States and the European Commission made certain proposals that would imply an extension of the responsibility of an international organization as envisaged in article 15.[86]

49. On the other hand, a few States and ILO considered that the requirement that "the unlawful act in question should actually be committed" should apply not only, as paragraph 2 provides, in the case of recommendations or authorizations, but also in the case, considered in paragraph 1, that the international organization binds its members with a decision.[87]

50. With regard to circumvention through a non-binding act, some States and IMF argued that, since members are free not to act upon an authorization or recommendation, the international organization should not incur responsibility if they take the authorized or recommended action.[88] One State noted that it "might be necessary to

---

[79] France (*ibid.*, *Sixtieth Session, Sixth Committee*, 11th meeting A/C.6/60/SR.11, para. 78, with reference to articles 13 and 14), Romania (*ibid.*, 12th meeting (A/C.6/60/SR.12), para. 75), New Zealand (*ibid.*, para. 110), Denmark, on behalf of the Nordic countries (Denmark, Finland, Iceland, Norway and Sweden) (*ibid.*, 13th meeting (A/C.6/60/SR.13), para. 18), Germany (*ibid.*, para. 33), Poland (*ibid.*, para. 59, with regard to article 13, though requesting "further clarification") and Nigeria (*ibid.*, *Sixty-second Session, Sixth Committee*, 24th meeting (A/C.6/62/SR.24), para. 4).

[80] The United States (*ibid.*, *Sixtieth Session, Sixth Committee*, 12th meeting (A/C.6/60/SR.12), para. 24) raised the question whether an international organization assisting a State in the commission of a wrongful act would incur responsibility even if the obligation binding the organization was not the same as the one binding the assisted State. Article 12, as the corresponding article on the responsibility of States for internationally wrongful acts, appears to assume that the assisting and assisted entities are under the same obligation. See paragraph (6) of the commentary on article 16 on State responsibility, *Yearbook ... 2001*, vol. II (Part Two), p. 66. The Russian Federation (*Official Records of the General Assembly, Sixtieth Session, Sixth Committee*, 12th meeting (A/C.6/60/SR.12), para. 67) criticized the requirement in articles 12 and 13 of the current draft that the act be wrongful if committed by the international organization, for the reason that "some actions could be taken only by States and not by international organizations". This would not necessarily make the act lawful if performed by the international organization. Guatemala (*ibid.*, paras. 102–103) and Israel (*ibid.*, 16th meeting (A/C.6/60/SR.16), para. 55) made a more general criticism of the same requirement, involving also the articles on State responsibility.

[81] See thc interventions by the Russian Federation (*ibid.*, 12th meeting (A/C.6/60/SR.12), para. 68), Jordan (*ibid.*, 13th meeting (A/C.6/60/SR.13), para. 11) and Germany (*ibid.*, paras. 33–34). France (*ibid.*, 11th meeting (A/C.6/60/SR.11), para. 78) insisted on avoiding "any needless confusion over the differences between the necessary respect for binding decisions of an international organization and the idea of coercion". According to Portugal (*ibid.*, 12th meeting (A/C.6/60/SR.12), para. 33) there was "no situation that might be subject to the provisions of draft articles 12, 13 and 14 that was not also covered by draft article 15". This would be hard to prove, if only because the latter provision exclusively concerns the relations between an international organization and its members.

[82] Thus Austria (*Official Records of the General Assembly, Fifty-ninth Session, Sixth Committee*, 22nd meeting (A/C.6/59/SR.22), para. 24).

[83] New Zealand (*ibid.*, 23rd meeting (A/C.6/59/SR.23), para. 11), the Russian Federation (*ibid.*, para. 23) and Cuba (*ibid.*, para. 25).

[84] *Yearbook ... 2004*, vol. II (Part Two), chap. III, sect. B, p. 15, para. 25.

[85] China (*Official Records of the General Assembly, Sixtieth Session, Sixth Committee*, 11th meeting (A/C.6/60/SR.11), para. 51), Italy (*ibid.*, 12th meeting (A/C.6/60/SR.12), para. 3), the Netherlands (*ibid.*, paras. 16–17, considering, however, that "the meaning and scope of the criterion [of circumvention] were not clear"), Belarus (*ibid.*, para. 48), New Zealand (*ibid.*, para. 110), Hungary (*ibid.*, 13th meeting (A/C.6/60/SR.13), para. 7, with the request that the meaning of the word "circumvention" should be "further clarified"), Greece (*ibid.*, para. 26), Germany (*ibid.*, para. 34, with reference to paragraph 1) and India (*ibid.*, 18th meeting (A/C.6/60/SR.18, para. 60). See also the intervention by the European Commission (*ibid.*, 12th meeting (A/C.6/60/SR.12), para. 13).

[86] Guatemala (*ibid.*, para. 105) suggested the deletion in paragraphs 1 and 2 of the words "and would circumvent an international obligation of the former organization". The European Commission (*ibid.*, para. 14; see also *Yearbook ... 2006*, vol. II (Part One), A/CN.4/568 and Add.1, sect. I) wondered whether "the notion of circumvention was superfluous". A similar view was expressed by Greece (*Official Records of the General Assembly, Sixtieth Session, Sixth Committee*, 13th meeting (A/C.6/60/SR.13), para. 28). With reference to paragraph 2, the Russian Federation (*ibid.*, 12th meeting (A/C.6/60/SR.12), para. 69) considered that "the organization must incur responsibility, even when its members did not use its recommendation or authorization".

[87] France (*ibid.*, 11th meeting (A/C.6/60/SR.11), para. 79), Jordan (*ibid.*, 13th meeting (A/C.6/60/SR.13), para. 14, from which the quotation is taken) and ILO (see *Yearbook ... 2006*, vol. II (Part One), document A/CN.4/568 and Add.1, sect. I).

[88] United States (*Official Records of the General Assembly, Sixtieth Session, Sixth Committee*, 12th meeting (A/C.6/60/SR.12), para. 27), Denmark, on behalf of the Nordic countries (Denmark, Finland, Iceland, Norway and Sweden) (*ibid.*, 13th meeting (A/C.6/60/SR.13),

(*Continued on next page.*)

introduce some new element in [article 15] that would make it possible to take into consideration the variety of legal regimes that existed among international organizations".[89] Another State stressed the need for a "very close connection between the authorization or recommendation and the relevant act of the member State".[90]

51. In view of these suggestions, an attempt should be made to restrict responsibility in paragraph 2 by using a slightly different wording, that would emphasize the role played by the authorization or the recommendation in determining the member to act consistently with the act of the international organization. A possible improvement in this direction could be to rephrase paragraph 2 (*b*) of article 15 as follows:

> "(*b*) That State or international organization commits the act in question as the result of that authorization or recommendation."

52. Although the title refers to the responsibility of an international organization "in connection with the act of a State or another international organization", the chapter now under examination does not contain any provision relating to the possibility that an international organization incurs responsibility as a member of another international organization. The question of the responsibility of members is considered elsewhere in the draft with reference to the responsibility of member States (arts. 28–29). Since international organizations are not frequently members of other international organizations, it is understandable that the discussion on the responsibility of members has been centred on the responsibility of member States. However, as was noted by one State, "the responsibility of members could also be incurred by international organizations which were members of other international organizations".[91]

53. It would be difficult to assume that an international organization that is a member of another international organization would incur responsibility on conditions that are different from those applying to a member State. This could be reflected in a provision to be placed in the present chapter as draft article 15 *bis*, with the title "Responsibility of an international organization for the act of another international organization of which it is a member". The provision could simply contain a reference to the conditions set out in articles 28 and 29. The following text is suggested:

> "Responsibility of an international organization that is a member of another international organization may arise in relation to an act of the latter also under the conditions set out in articles 28 and 29 for States that are members of an international organization."

54. In conclusion to the present chapter, the following proposals are made:

(*a*) Article 15, paragraph 2 (*b*), is reworded as suggested above in paragraph 51;

(*b*) A new article 15 *bis*, as drafted in paragraph 53 above, is added.

(*Footnote 88 continued*)

para. 19), Germany (*ibid.*, para. 34), Switzerland (*ibid.*, para. 45), the Islamic Republic of Iran (*ibid.*, *Sixty-second Session, Sixth Committee*, 25th meeting (A/C.6/62/SR.25), para. 50 and *ibid.*, *Sixty-third Session, Sixth Committee*, 24th meeting (A/C.6/63/SR.24), para. 35) and IMF (see *Yearbook ... 2007*, vol. II (Part One), document A/CN.4/582, sect. I).

[89] Thus Spain (*Official Records of the General Assembly, Sixtieth Session, Sixth Committee*, 13th meeting (A/C.6/60/SR.13), para. 52).

[90] Austria (*ibid.*, 11th meeting (A/C.6/60/SR.11), paras. 61–62). The suggested rewording (to use the term "in compliance with" or "in conformity with" instead of "in reliance") does not seem to attain the intended result.

[91] Thus the Netherlands (*ibid.*, *Sixty-first Session, Sixth Committee*, 14th meeting (A/C.6/61/SR.14), para. 20).

Chapter V

Circumstances precluding wrongfulness

55. Several States expressed their general agreement with the draft articles included in chapter V of part one ("Circumstances precluding wrongfulness"), albeit sometimes with specific comments concerning certain provisions.[92]

56. Only a few remarks regarded article 17, relating to consent.[93] One State noted that an *ultra vires* act by an international organization would not be sufficient to determine consent.[94] Another State suggested that the Commission should define "what constituted valid consent, the limits of consent, and how those limits were determined".[95] However, as was noted in paragraph (4) of the commentary,[96] an elaboration of the questions raised by the use of the term "valid" as referring to consent would lead to a discussion on matters outside the framework of international responsibility. It would thus be preferable to refrain from further elaborating this question. The same

[92] See the interventions by Finland, on behalf of the European Union (*ibid.*, 13th meeting (A/C.6/61/SR.13), para. 27), Denmark, on behalf of the Nordic countries (Denmark, Finland, Iceland, Norway and Sweden) (*ibid.*, para. 30), Ireland (*ibid.*, para. 42), Argentina (*ibid.*, para. 48), Spain (*ibid.*, 14th meeting (A/C.6/61/SR.14), para. 48, with the exception of articles 18 and 22) and France (*ibid.*, para. 59). See also the interventions by Belarus (*ibid.*, para. 98) and Poland (*ibid.*, para. 103).

[93] The "vital importance" of consent to the European Union was stressed by Finland, on behalf of the European Union (*ibid.*, 13th meeting (A/C.6/61/SR.13), para. 25), and the European Commission in its written comments (see *Yearbook ... 2007*, vol. II (Part One), document A/CN.4/582, sect. K).

[94] Thus Poland (*Official Records of the General Assembly, Sixty-first Session, Sixth Committee*, 14th meeting (A/C.6/61/SR.14), para. 103).

[95] This view was expressed by Ethiopia (*ibid.*, para. 93). Comments on the validity and limits of consent were made by the Islamic Republic of Iran (*ibid.*, 15th meeting (A/C.6/61/SR.15), para. 51) and Jordan (*ibid.*, 16th meeting (A/C.6/61/SR.16), para. 2).

[96] *Yearbook ... 2006*, vol. II (Part Two), chap. VII, sect. C, p. 122.

approach had been taken by the Commission with regard to consent as a circumstance precluding wrongfulness in the articles on the responsibility of States for internationally wrongful acts.[97]

57. IMF stressed the importance of "consent that occurs upon a State's accession to an international organization's charter".[98] Consent given by a State when acceding to the constituent instrument of an international organization is no doubt relevant in order to exclude the responsibility of that organization with regard to an act of the organization that has been agreed to. However, the act of the organization would then be lawful on the basis of the applicable rules of international law and would not need to be justified by a circumstance precluding wrongfulness.

58. Article 18 on self-defence raised various critical comments. It was noted that "the concept of self-defence as applied to international organizations differed considerably from the concept of self-defence as applied to States".[99] It was also observed that "Article 51 of the Charter of the United Nations did not directly apply to the self-defence of international organizations".[100] Some States argued that "self-defence, by its nature, was applicable only to the actions of a State".[101] Also according to WHO, "a circumstance such as self-defence is by its very nature only applicable to the actions of a State".[102]

59. The instances in which self-defence could be relevant for an international organization as a circumstance precluding wrongfulness are limited and sometimes unclear, even if one may not agree with the remark that, when an international organization is administering a territory or deploying an armed force, "the State whose forces were in the territory or the individual members of those armed forces were the entities exercising self-defence".[103] Should no reference be made to self-defence in the current draft, an international organization would not necessarily be precluded from invoking self-defence as a circumstance precluding wrongfulness. This will be on the basis of a general provision (see draft article 62 below), that leaves unprejudiced questions of responsibility not regulated by the present draft. Thus, in view of the many critical comments expressed by States and international organizations, it would seem preferable for the Commission to delete article 18 and leave the matter of invocability of self-defence unprejudiced.

60. When the Commission discussed circumstances precluding wrongfulness at its fifty-eighth session, the question of whether to include in the pertinent chapter a provision on countermeasures was left open, pending the examination of countermeasures in the context of the invocation of responsibility of international organizations.[104] Chapter II of the current part three, which has not yet been provisionally adopted by the Commission, has been drafted by the Drafting Committee on the basis of the premise that international organizations, like States, may take countermeasures against a responsible international organization. When discussing circumstances precluding wrongfulness, one should therefore start from the same premise.

61. With regard to countermeasures that an international organization may take against another international organization, it would be coherent to consider that a circumstance precluding wrongfulness justifies an otherwise wrongful act subject to the conditions set out in chapter II of part three, which covers countermeasures taken both by international organizations and by States against an international organization.

62. However, countermeasures are more likely to be taken by an international organization against a responsible State. Practice shows a number of examples, particularly relating to the case of an international organization that, while not "injured" within the meaning of article 46, invokes responsibility according to article 52.[105]

63. IMF gave as an example of countermeasures the action that the Fund may take under article V, section 5, of the Articles of Agreement, "whenever IMF is of the opinion that a member is using the Fund's general resources in a manner contrary to the organization's purposes".[106] However, this pertains to the sanctions that an international organization may take against a member under the rules of the organization. In the relations between an international organization and one of its members, these sanctions are *per se* lawful and cannot be considered as countermeasures.

64. Since practice appears to point to the conclusion that international organizations are placed in substantially the same position as States when they take countermeasures against a State,[107] article 19 could contain a reference to the conditions that States need to comply with for their countermeasures to be considered lawful. However, such a reference could be made only in general terms, given the

[97] *Yearbook ... 2001*, vol. II (Part Two), p. 73.

[98] See *Yearbook ... 2007*, vol. II (Part One), document A/CN.4/582, sect. K.

[99] This is how this frequent remark was voiced by Spain (*Official Records of the General Assembly, Sixty-first Session, Sixth Committee*, 14th meeting (A/C.6/61/SR.14), para. 48).

[100] Thus Japan (*ibid.*, para. 57). Similar observations were made by Austria (*ibid.*, 13th meeting (A/C.6/61/SR.13), para. 38), Portugal (*ibid.*, 14th meeting (A/C.6/61/SR.14), para. 74), the United States (*ibid.*, para. 82), the United Kingdom (*ibid.*, 15th meeting (A/C.6/61/SR.15, para. 26) and the Islamic Republic of Iran (*ibid.*, para. 52).

[101] The quotation is from the intervention by India (*ibid.*, 16th meeting (A/C.6/61/SR.16, para. 8). Similar views were expressed by Jordan (*ibid.*, para. 2) and Bulgaria (*ibid.*, *Sixty-second Session, Sixth Committee*, 18th meeting (A/C.6/62/SR.18), para. 83). Doubts about the applicability of self-defence to international organizations were voiced also by Cuba (*ibid.*, *Sixty-first Session, Sixth Committee*, 16th meeting A/C.6/61/SR.16, para. 12) and Romania (*ibid*, 19th meeting (A/C.6/61/SR.19), para. 60).

[102] See *Yearbook ... 2006*, vol. II (Part One), document A/CN.4/568 and Add.1, sect. L.

[103] Thus Portugal (*Official Records of the General Assembly, Sixty-first Session, Sixth Committee*, 14th meeting (A/C.6/61/SR.14, para. 74). The contrary view that self-defence may be invoked by the United Nations when they administer a territory was expressed by Dominicé, "La responsabilité internationale des Nations Unies", at p. 157.

[104] *Yearbook ... 2006*, vol. II (Part Two), chap. VII, sect. C, p. 123.

[105] Some examples were given in the Special Rapporteur's sixth report (*Yearbook ... 2008*, vol. II (Part One), document A/CN.4/597), pp. 28–29, para. 58.

[106] See *Yearbook ... 2007*, vol. II (Part One), document A/CN.4/582, p. 25, sect. M.

[107] This was observed by Italy (*Official Records of the General Assembly, Sixty-third Session, Sixth Committee*, 19th meeting (A/C.6/63/SR.19), para. 96).

still undefined status of the articles on the responsibility of States for internationally wrongful acts. It would thus be preferable to allude to the conditions for the lawfulness of countermeasures by simply requiring their "lawful" character. This same term would also apply to the conditions under which an international organization may take countermeasures against another international organization.

65. The principle of cooperation that restricts recourse to countermeasures in the relations between an international organization and its members appears to be relevant, not only when a State or an international organization takes countermeasures against another international organization of which it is a member,[108] but also when an international organization takes countermeasures against one of its members. This principle should lead to a similar restriction to countermeasures in the latter case. Countermeasures would not be allowed if some reasonable means for ensuring compliance with the obligations of the member concerning cessation of a continuous wrongful act and reparation are available in accordance with the rules of the organization. It is clear that those rules may further restrict countermeasures or, on the contrary, allow them to be used more widely.

66. The following text of draft article 19 is here proposed:

"Draft article 19. Countermeasures

"1. Subject to paragraph 2, the wrongfulness of an act of an international organization not in conformity with an international obligation towards a State or another international organization is precluded if and to the extent that the act constitutes a lawful countermeasure on the part of the former international organization.

"2. An international organization is not entitled to take countermeasures against a responsible member State or international organization if, in accordance with the rules of the organization, reasonable means are available for ensuring compliance with the obligations of the responsible State or international organization concerning cessation of the breach and reparation."

67. Article 22 on necessity has proved controversial. In drafting it, the Commission took into account the diverse views that had been expressed by several States at the sixtieth session of the General Assembly, in response to a request for comments that was contained in the Commission's report.[109] According to article 22, necessity precludes wrongfulness of an act of an international organization only when there is an imminent peril to "an essential interest of the international community as a whole" and "the organization has, in accordance with international law, the function to protect that interest". Contrary to one interpretation given to article 22,[110] there is no indication in that article that a regional international organization would be precluded from protecting an essential interest of the international community. States that are members of an international organization, regional or other, may well confer on that organization functions that imply the task of protecting an essential interest of the international community.

68. The solution that was adopted by the Commission in article 22 was endorsed by several States.[111] However, some States would have preferred that "the essential interests of member States, or indeed the organization itself, could also be the basis for an international organization's invocation of necessity".[112] One State proposed to amend article 22 in order to refer to "an essential interest that the organization, in accordance with international law, has the function to protect".[113] Also, IMF urged "a broader construction of 'essential interest' than is suggested by the Commission's commentary on draft article 22".[114]

69. On the other hand, one State argued that "international practice did not provide sound support for the invocation of necessity by an international organization".[115] Another State "questioned whether it would ever be appropriate for an international organization to rely on necessity to violate its international obligations".[116] A third State suggested the deletion of the article.[117]

70. The concept of an essential interest that the organization has the function to protect was found by yet another State as "a vague and potentially expansive standard".[118] Some other States criticized the reference to an essential interest of the international community as a whole or argued that it was not clear.[119] However, this is not a new concept. It already appears in the corresponding text of the articles

---

[108] Reference is here made to article 55 as provisionally adopted by the Drafting Committee (see A/CN.4/L.725/Add.1).

[109] An overview of these replies may be found in paragraph (4) of the commentary to article 22, *Yearbook ... 2006*, vol. II (Part Two), chap. VII, sect. C, p. 125.

[110] See the intervention by France (*Official Records of the General Assembly, Sixty-first Session, Sixth Committee*, 14th meeting (A/C.6/61/SR.14), para. 59).

[111] Finland, on behalf of the European Union, acceding countries, candidate countries, countries in the process of stabilization and association, and Moldova and Ukraine (*ibid.*, 13th meeting (A/C.6/61/SR.13), para. 26); Denmark, on behalf of the Nordic countries (Denmark, Finland, Iceland, Norway and Sweden) (*ibid.*, para. 30, with the remark quoted immediately afterwards in the text); Austria (*ibid.*, para. 38); Argentina (*ibid.*, para. 48); and Germany (*ibid.*, 14th meeting (A/C.6/61/SR.14), para. 2).

[112] Thus Denmark, on behalf of the Nordic countries (Denmark, Finland, Iceland, Norway and Sweden) (*ibid.*, 13th meeting (A/C.6/61/SR.13), para. 30). A similar point was made by Ireland (*ibid.*, paras. 42–44), Spain (*ibid.*, 14th meeting (A/C.6/61/SR.14), para. 49) and France (*ibid.*, para. 59). Cuba (*ibid.*, 16th meeting (A/C.6/61/SR.16), para. 12) referred to the safeguard of "an essential interest of the organization". The same solution was advocated by Reinisch, "How necessary is necessity for international organizations?", p. 177.

[113] The proposal was made by France (*Official Records of the General Assembly, Sixty-first Session, Sixth Committee*, 14th meeting (A/C.6/61/SR.14), para. 59).

[114] See *Yearbook ... 2007*, vol. II (Part One), document A/CN.4/582, sect. O, p. 26.

[115] Thus China (*Official Records of the General Assembly, Sixty-first Session, Sixth Committee*, 14th meeting (A/C.6/61/SR.14), para. 8).

[116] See the intervention of the United Kingdom (*ibid.*, 15th meeting (A/C.6/61/SR.15), para. 28).

[117] This was the position of India (*ibid.*, 16th meeting (A/C.6/61/SR.16), para. 9).

[118] See the comment by the United States (*ibid.*, 14th meeting (A/C.6/61/SR.14), para. 82).

[119] These remarks were made by Austria (*ibid.*, 13th meeting (A/C.6/61/SR.13), para. 38), the United Kingdom (*ibid.*, 15th meeting (A/C.6/61/SR.15), para. 28), the Islamic Republic of Iran (*ibid.*, para. 53) and Jordan (*ibid.*, 16th meeting (A/C.6/61/SR.16), para. 3).

on the responsibility of States for internationally wrongful acts.[120] There is no specific reason for further elaborating in the present context the meaning of an essential interest of the international community as a whole.

71. Given the endorsement of article 22 by a certain number of States and the fact that the critical comments go in opposite directions and that a prevailing trend cannot be detected, it seems preferable not to propose any amendment of article 22.

[120] Art. 25 (1) (*b*).

72. The suggestions made in the present chapter may be summarized as follows:

(*a*) Article 18 on self-defence should be deleted;

(*b*) Article 19 on countermeasures should be drafted on the basis of the text reproduced above, in paragraph 66.

Chapter VI

Responsibility of a State in connection with the act of an international organization

73. Only a few States made a general endorsement of chapter (x) ("Responsibility of a State in connection with the act of an international organization").[121] Some further States[122] gave their approval of articles 25 to 27. These adapt to the relations between a State and an international organization the provisions concerning aid or assistance, direction and control, and coercion that were set out for the relations between States in the articles on the responsibility of States for internationally wrongful acts. The idea of including such an adaptation in the current draft had already been accepted by a larger group of States,[123] in response to a question raised by the Commission in its report to the General Assembly relating to its fifty-seventh session.[124]

74. Two States suggested an addition to the commentary to article 25, in order to distinguish the case of aid or assistance in the commission of an internationally wrongful act from the implementation by a State of a binding act of the organization[125] and the "mere involvement of a member State in the day-to-day functioning of an international organization".[126] The latter concern appears to be met by the observation made in paragraph (2) of the commentary to article 25, that "the influence that may amount to aid or assistance could not simply consist in participation in the decision-making process of the organization according to the pertinent rules of the organization".[127] With regard to the other comment, one may note that, when a wrongful act is taken by an international organization with the assistance or aid of a State, the act is attributed to the international organization, while the act of a State implementing a binding act of an organization is attributable to that State and represents an internationally wrongful act of the same State.[128]

[121] Denmark, on behalf of the Nordic countries (Denmark, Finland, Iceland, Norway and Sweden) (*ibid.*, 13th meeting (A/C.6/61/SR.13), para. 30), and Belarus (*ibid.*, 14th meeting (A/C.6/61/SR.14), para. 98).

[122] Argentina (*ibid.*, 13th meeting (A/C.6/61/SR.13), para. 48) and France (*ibid.*, 14th meeting (A/C.6/61/SR.14), para. 60), though wondering whether "a saving clause... would not have been sufficient" (a similar view had been voiced the previous year (*ibid.*, *Sixtieth Session, Sixth Committee*, 11th meeting (A/C.6/60/SR.11), para. 80). Also, the European Commission endorsed articles 25 to 27 (*ibid.*, *Sixty-first Session, Sixth Committee*, 16th meeting (A/C.6/61/SR.16), para. 15).

[123] See the interventions by China (*ibid.*, *Sixtieth Session, Sixth Committee*, 11th meeting (A/C.6/60/SR.11), para. 52), Austria (*ibid.*, para. 64), the Republic of Korea (*ibid.*, para. 86), Italy (*ibid.*, 12th meeting (A/C.6/60/SR.12), para. 4), Belarus (*ibid.*, paras. 49–50), the Russian Federation (*ibid.*, para. 70), Romania (*ibid.*, para. 77), Hungary (*ibid.*, 13th meeting (A/C.6/60/SR.13), para. 8), Denmark, on behalf of the Nordic countries (Denmark, Finland, Iceland, Norway and Sweden) (*ibid.*, para. 20), the Libyan Arab Jamahiriya (*ibid.*, 19th meeting (A/C.6/60/SR.19), para. 11) and Algeria (*ibid.*, 20th meeting (A/C.6/60/SR.20), para. 60).

[124] *Yearbook ... 2005*, vol. II (Part Two), chap. III, p. 13, sect. C, para. 26.

[125] See the comment made by France (*Official Records of the General Assembly, Sixty-first Session, Sixth Committee*, 14th meeting (A/C.6/61/SR.14), para. 60).

[126] Thus the intervention by Greece (*ibid.*, 15th meeting (A/C.6/61/SR.15), para. 37). Jordan (*ibid.*, 16th meeting (A/C.6/61/SR.16), para. 4) queried "whether a financial contribution to the annual budget of the organization would constitute aid or assistance to the commission of the wrongful act".

75. One difficulty in defining more precisely aid or assistance in the commission of an internationally wrongful act is that, for the purpose of assessing whether aid or assistance occurs, much depends on the content of the obligation breached and on the circumstances. Thus, it seems preferable not to modify the wording that was used in the provision (art. 16) included in the articles on the responsibility of States concerning aid or assistance given by a State to another State. However, some further clarifications could be given in the commentary to article 25. One State suggested adding that "relevant intention would be required, as had been specified in the commentary to the corresponding article on State responsibility".[129] Another suggestion would be to take over a further part of the commentary to article 16 on the responsibility of States, which aims at making it clearer that the aiding or assisting State "would have to play an active role in the commission of the wrongful act".[130]

76. Only a few remarks were specifically addressed to articles 26 and 27. These comments were requests for clarifications,[131] which are difficult to give at the present stage in the development of the law on international

[127] *Yearbook ... 2006*, vol. II (Part Two), chap. VII, sect. C, p. 127.

[128] If the conduct is attributed to the executing State, there is no need for a specific provision dealing with the case of a State "acting as an executing agent of an organization", as was suggested by Greece (*Official Records of the General Assembly, Sixty-first Session, Sixth Committee*, 15th meeting (A/C.6/61/SR.15), para. 40), apparently adopting a different premise.

[129] Thus Greece (*ibid.*, para. 37).

[130] See the comment by Romania (*ibid.*, 19th meeting (A/C.6/61/SR.19), para. 60).

[131] See the interventions by Austria (*ibid.*, 13th meeting (A/C.6/61/SR.13), para. 40) and Jordan (*ibid.*, 16th meeting (A/C.6/61/SR.16), para. 4).

responsibility. One State suggested adding a few words to subparagraph (*a*) in article 27 so that it would read: "The act would, but for the coercion, be an internationally wrongful act of the international organization or of the coercing State."[132] While the current text of article 27 only mentions the coerced international organization, this proposal would add a reference to the coercing State. Subparagraph (*a*), as does the parallel article 18 on the responsibility of States for internationally wrongful acts, envisages the possibility that the coerced entity would not incur responsibility because it was forced to act against its will. It seems difficult to understand why the fact of exercising coercion should come into reckoning in order to exonerate also the coercing State from an international responsibility which that State would otherwise incur.

77. Although arguably innovative, the idea underlying article 28, that a State cannot escape responsibility when it circumvents one of its obligations by availing itself of the separate legal personality of an international organization of which it is a member, was remarkably well received.[133] This is not to say that the wording of the provision was generally considered satisfactory. Several States argued that the Commission should amend article 28 in order to narrow down the responsibility of member States.[134]

78. Various suggestions were made for the purpose of restricting the responsibility of member States. One of them does not seem to address specifically the object of article 28. The European Commission proposed to take from the *Bosphorus* judgement of the European Court of Human Rights the conclusion that "there was no circumvention if the State transferred powers to an international organization which was not bound by the State's own treaty obligations but whose legal system offered a comparable level of guarantees".[135] However, the fact that an equivalent standard may be regarded as sufficient depends on the content of the international obligation concerned. If a treaty considers that an obligation to take a certain conduct may be satisfied by providing a comparable level of guarantees, there would be no breach of an international obligation and hence no international responsibility.

79. One State suggested that the "scope of application of the article … be limited to cases where the international organization was not itself bound by the obligation breached".[136] No doubt, circumvention is more likely to occur in one of those cases. However, there would be little justification for considering that the existence of an obligation also for the international organization should exonerate the circumventing State.

80. One could address a similar observation on the proposal that circumvention be considered relevant only when a transfer of competence is made by member States to an international organization in its constituent instrument.[137] The adoption of such a proposal would leave out those cases in which a transfer of functions occurs, as it often does, on the basis of rules of the organization other than the constituent instrument, while circumvention could be equally significant in the latter cases.

81. One State proposed to replace "circumvention" with "a more neutral term".[138] Other States seemed to point to a different direction when they suggested "the introduction of some element of bad faith, specific knowledge or deliberate intent"[139] or of "misuse".[140] If a reference to intent was inserted in article 28, intent should not necessarily be linked with the transfer of competence to the international organization.[141] That transfer could well have occurred in good faith, while the opportunity for circumventing an international obligation may have appeared only at a later stage.

82. A reference to intention or bad faith in article 28 would no doubt have the effect of restricting the international responsibility of member States. However, such a reference would introduce a subjective test which would be difficult to apply. It thus seems preferable to try to

[132] The proposal was made by Switzerland (*ibid.*, 15th meeting (A/C.6/61/SR.15), para. 2).

[133] See the favourable comments of Ireland (*ibid.*, 13th meeting (A/C.6/61/SR.13), paras. 45–46), Argentina (*ibid.*, para. 48), Germany (*ibid.*, 14th meeting (A/C.6/61/SR.14), para. 3), Belgium (*ibid.*, para. 39), Spain (*ibid.*, para. 50), France (*ibid.*, para. 61), Italy (*ibid.*, para. 67), Poland (*ibid.*, para. 105), Switzerland (*ibid.*, 15th meeting (A/C.6/61/SR.15), para. 3), the United Kingdom (*ibid.*, para. 30), Greece (*ibid.*, para. 38), New Zealand (*ibid.*, para. 43), Jordan (*ibid.*, 16th meeting (A/C.6/61/SR.16), para. 5), the Russian Federation (*ibid.*, 18th meeting (A/C.6/61/SR.18), para. 68) and Sierra Leone (*ibid.*, 19th meeting (A/C.6/61/SR.19), para. 68). See also the interventions by Denmark, on behalf of the Nordic countries (Denmark, Finland, Iceland, Norway and Sweden) (*ibid.*, 13th meeting (A/C.6/61/SR.13), para. 31), and the Netherlands (*ibid.*, 14th meeting (A/C.6/61/SR.14), para. 21). Finland, speaking on behalf of the European Union (*ibid.*, 13th meeting (A/C.6/61/SR.13), para. 27), expressed the "serious concerns" of the Union; this position was reiterated by the European Commission (*ibid.*, 16th meeting (A/C.6/61/SR.16), paras. 15–16). Doubts were expressed by Austria (*ibid.*, 13th meeting (A/C.6/61/SR.13), para. 40) and Japan (*ibid.*, 14th meeting (A/C.6/61/SR.14), para. 58).

[134] See the interventions by Denmark, on behalf of the Nordic countries (Denmark, Finland, Iceland, Norway and Sweden) (*ibid.*, 13th meeting (A/C.6/61/SR.13), para. 31), Ireland (*ibid.*, paras. 45–46), Germany (*ibid.*, 14th meeting (A/C.6/61/SR.14), para. 3), Netherlands (*ibid.*, para. 21), Belgium (*ibid.*, para. 39), Spain (*ibid.*, para. 50), France (*ibid.*, para. 61), Italy (*ibid.*, para. 67), Switzerland (*ibid.*, 15th meeting (A/C.6/61/SR.15), para. 3), the United Kingdom (*ibid.*, para. 30), Greece (*ibid.*, para. 38) and the Russian Federation (*ibid.*, 18th meeting (A/C.6/61/SR.18), para. 68). A similar suggestion was made by the European Commission (*ibid.*, 16th meeting (A/C.6/61/SR.16), paras. 15–16).

[135] *Ibid.*, 16th meeting (A/C.6/61/SR.16), para. 16.

[136] Thus Greece (*ibid.*, 15th meeting (A/C.6/61/SR.15), para. 38).

[137] This proposal was made by Belgium (*ibid.*, 14th meeting (A/C.6/61/SR.14), para. 39).

[138] Thus Switzerland (*ibid.*, 15th meeting (A/C.6/61/SR.15), para. 3).

[139] See the intervention by the United Kingdom (*ibid*, 15th meeting (A/C.6/61/SR.15), para. 30). Also Ireland (*ibid.*, 13th meeting (A/C.6/61/SR.13), paras. 45–46) insisted on the "requirement of intent" on the part of the member State that the obligation be breached. A similar view was expressed by Spain (*ibid., Sixth Committee*, 14th meeting (A/C.6/61/SR.14), para. 50).

[140] This suggestion was made by Germany (*ibid.*, 14th meeting (A/C.6/61/SR.14), para. 3).

[141] France (*ibid.*, para. 61) suggested that relevance be given to the member State's "intention in conferring competence … to avoid complying with its international obligations". See also the intervention by Denmark, on behalf of the Nordic countries (Denmark, Finland, Iceland, Norway and Sweden) (*ibid.*, 13th meeting (A/C.6/61/SR.13), para. 31), which expressed the view that only the transfers of competence "made with the intention to evade responsibility" should "give rise to responsibility". On the other hand, d'Aspremont, "Abuse of the legal personality of international organizations and the responsibility of member States", at p. 100, criticized the Commission for having given in article 28 "a very narrow understanding of the abuse of the legal personality at the *level of the creation of the organization**".

achieve a similar objective, instead of by requiring an assessment of intent, by referring to what may reasonably be assumed from the circumstances. It should in any case be clear that the transfer of competences to an international organization does not *per se* imply circumvention and thus responsibility for the member States concerned.

83. Paragraph 1 of article 28 could be recast as follows:

"A State member of an international organization incurs international responsibility if:

"(*a*) It purports to avoid compliance with one of its international obligations by availing itself of the fact that the organization has been provided with competence in relation to that obligation;

"(*b*) The organization commits an act that, if committed by the State, would have constituted a breach of the obligation."

84. Also, article 29, concerning the responsibility of member States of an international organization for the internationally wrongful act of that organization, attracted several comments. There was wide support for restricting the responsibility of member States, as provided in article 29, to the case that member States accepted responsibility or led the injured party to rely on their responsibility.[142]

85. As set out in the commentary, article 29 implies that, as a residual rule, "membership does not as such entail for member States international responsibility when the organization commits an internationally wrongful act".[143] Opinions of States were divided on the question of whether this residual rule should be expressed in the text.[144] While such an addition would arguably add clarity to the text, the current draft, like the articles on the responsibility of States for internationally wrongful acts, only sets out when responsibility arises and does not indicate when responsibility is not incurred.

86. Some States raised the issue of the relevance of the rules of the organization for the responsibility of member States.[145] This issue has to be considered on the basis of the assumption that the rules of the organization produce effects only in the relations between an international organization and one or more of its members or between members of the organization, and not with regard to non-members. Since this point, which already underlies article 35, is relevant for a number of issues, it will be addressed in a general provision, to be placed in the final part (see draft article 61 below). Thus, supposing that the rules of the organization restricted responsibility, they could not be opposed as such to a non-member State. Nor would rules providing for a wider responsibility of member States be of avail to a non-member State, which could rely on the rules of the organization only if member States had made them relevant in their dealings with the non-member. On the other hand, it is clear that the rules of the organization would prevail as special rules in the relations between the members of the organization.

87. The European Commission noted that "explicit acceptance of responsibility was severely curtained by the constitutional law of the organization".[146] This comment appears to refer to the fact that the rules of the organization may preclude member States from accepting responsibility when it falls on the organization. However, should a member State nevertheless accept responsibility in its relations with a non-member, the "constitutional law of the organization" would not prevent acceptance of responsibility from obtaining its intended effect.

88. One State suggested that the text should reflect a point made in the commentary, namely that "a State had to accept responsibility for the act of the organization *vis-à-vis* the victim of the act and not *vis-à-vis* the organization itself".[147] This could arguably be done by rephrasing the part of subparagraph 1 (*a*) preceding the semicolon as follows: "It has accepted responsibility for that act towards the injured party". However, it is not certain that the addition of these four final words is really necessary. Moreover, there would be a slight ambiguity in the text, because the acceptance of responsibility could be made "towards" the injured party but not necessarily be operative in the relations with that party.

89. A drafting suggestion was made also with regard to paragraph 2 of article 29. According to this proposal, wording should be added "to the effect that a State's international responsibility was subsidiary to that of the

[142] See the interventions by Argentina (*Official Records of the General Assembly, Sixty-first Session, Sixth Committee*, 13th meeting (A/C.6/61/SR.13), para. 48), Germany (*ibid.*, 14th meeting (A/C.6/61/SR.14), para. 4), the Netherlands (*ibid.*, para. 22), France (*ibid.*, para. 62, though with some criticism of subparagraph (*b*)), Italy (*ibid.*, para. 66), Portugal (*ibid.*, para. 76, advocating "a more precise language in order to preclude the consideration of implied action"), Switzerland (*ibid.*, 15th meeting (A/C.6/61/SR.15), para. 4, suggesting an extension of responsibility of member States in case of a criminal organization), New Zealand (*ibid.*, para. 44) and Sierra Leone (*ibid.*, 19th meeting (A/C.6/61/SR.19), para. 68). See also the interventions by Belgium (*ibid.*, 14th meeting (A/C.6/61/SR.14), para. 40), Spain (*ibid.*, para. 51), Belarus (*ibid.*, para. 99), the Republic of Korea (*ibid.*, 15th meeting (A/C.6/61/SR.15), paras. 20–21, criticizing the idea of an "implied acceptance"), the United Kingdom (*ibid.*, para. 31, considering the drafting "too broad"), Jordan (*ibid.*, 16th meeting (A/C.6/61/SR.16), para. 5).

[143] *Yearbook ... 2006*, vol. II (Part Two), chap. VII, sect. C, p. 130, para. (2).

[144] Germany (*Official Records of the General Assembly, Sixty-first Session, Sixth Committee*, 14th meeting (A/C.6/61/SR.14), para. 4) spoke against expressing a negative rule, while the Netherlands (*ibid.*, para. 22) and Greece (*ibid.*, 15th meeting (A/C.6/61/SR.15), para. 39) took the opposite view.

[145] See the interventions of Belarus (*ibid.*, 14th meeting (A/C.6/61/SR.14), para. 99), the United Kingdom (*ibid.*, 15th meeting (A/C.6/61/SR.15), para. 31) and Jordan (*ibid.*, 16th meeting (A/C.6/61/SR.16), para. 5). Stumer, "Liability of member States for acts of international organizations: reconsidering the policy objections", at pp. 563–564, considered that the Commission had left "unresolved" the question "whether a provision in the constituent instrument stating that member States would be liable for the debts of the organization could be relied upon by a third party".

[146] *Official Records of the General Assembly, Sixty-first Session, Sixth Committee*, 16th meeting (A/C.6/61/SR.16), para. 17. Acceptance of (presumably subsidiary) responsibility cannot be equated with acknowledgement of attribution of conduct, which is covered by article 7, contrary to what was suggested by Rivier, "Travaux de la Commission du droit international (cinquante-huitième session) et de la Sixième Commission (soixante et unième session)", at pp. 344–345.

[147] Thus Greece (*Official Records of the General Assembly, Sixty-first Session, Sixth Committee*, 15th meeting (A/C.6/61/SR.15), para. 39).

international organization".[148] While one could indeed specify that the responsibility of member States is presumed to be subsidiary "to that of the responsible organization", this is implied by the current text. It may thus not be necessary to spell it out.

90. Although it was also made with reference to article 29, a further proposal raises a different issue, by envisaging an additional case of responsibility of certain member States: those who "played a major or leading role in the commission of an act by an international organization". It is argued that the "main responsibility for the consequences of that act should be placed on the member State".[149] This view would entail not only an additional responsibility for member States, but may also affect the primary responsibility of the organization for the wrongful acts that are attributed to it. This proposal, which reflects the view of what seems to be a minority opinion among the States, finds only limited support in practice.[150]

[148] This proposal was made by Belgium (*ibid.*, 14th meeting (A/C.6/61/SR.14), para. 40).

[149] This point was elaborated by China (*ibid.*, para. 9).

[150] One instance of practice is provided by a claim made by Bosnia and Herzegovina against the United Kingdom in relation to action taken by the latter State in the Security Council. See Quigley, "State responsibility for ethnic cleansing", pp. 375–377.

91. A further question concerns the placement of chapter (x). The Commission has yet to settle this point. One element to consider is that chapter (x) contains the only provisions in the current draft that address the matters covered in paragraph 2 of article 1, that is, the international responsibility of States for the internationally wrongful act of an international organization. The preferable solution seems to be to place chapter (x) as part five, after the part (currently part three) relating to the implementation of the international responsibility of an international organization. One advantage of this solution would be to give continuity to the examination of the responsibility of international organizations within the draft.

92. In conclusion to this chapter, which concerns articles 25 to 30, the following proposals are made:

(*a*) Chapter (x) should be placed after the current part three as part five;

(*b*) Article 28, paragraph 1, should be recast as suggested in paragraph 83 above;

(*c*) Certain additions should be made to the commentary to article 25, as noted in paragraph 75 above.

Chapter VII

Content of international responsibility

93. Several States expressed their general agreement with the approach taken by the Commission in chapter I ("General principles") of part two ("Content of international responsibility").[151] Some States specifically endorsed article 35, which affirms that a responsible international organization cannot rely, in its relations to a non-member, on the rules of the organization as justification for its failure to comply with one of its obligations under international law.[152]

94. Leaving the question of the acceptability of article 43 aside, one may note that a certain number of States also expressed their general agreement with the provisions contained in chapter II ("Reparation for injury").[153]

95. Article 43 sets out that "[t]he members of a responsible international organization are required to take, in accordance with the rules of the organization, all appropriate measures in order to provide the organization with the means for effectively fulfilling its obligations under this chapter". This article elicited several comments. The majority of States that expressed views on the article indicated their basic agreement with the Commission's text.[154] Some States argued that there was no need

[151] See the interventions by Argentina (*Official Records of the General Assembly, Sixty-second Session, Sixth Committee*, 18th meeting (A/C.6/62/SR.18), para. 62), Denmark, on behalf of the Nordic countries (Denmark, Finland, Iceland, Norway and Sweden) (*ibid.*, para. 98), Greece (*ibid.*, 19th meeting (A/C.6/62/SR.19), para. 5), Guatemala (*ibid.*, para. 20), Germany (*ibid.*, para. 30), India (*ibid.*, para. 106), France (*ibid.*, 20th meeting (A/C.6/62/SR.20), para. 6), the Russian Federation (*ibid.*, 21st meeting (A/C.6/62/SR.21), para. 67), Romania (*ibid.*, para. 76), Switzerland (*ibid.*, para. 79) and Sierra Leone (*ibid.*, 24th meeting (A/C.6/62/SR.24), para. 98). See also the intervention by the European Commission (*ibid.*, 21st meeting (A/C.6/62/SR.21), para. 114). At a later session, the United States (*Official Records of the General Assembly, Sixty-third Session, Sixth Committee*, 21st meeting (A/C.6/63/SR.21), para. 8) expressed the view that the "general obligation to make reparation for injury, for example, might have the effect of diverting the resources of international organizations away from funding the internationally agreed functions of the organization towards protecting against unquantifiable litigation risks …". While this may conceivably occur, it is difficult to see on what basis the injured party should not be entitled, at least in principle, to receive full reparation.

[152] Argentina (*Official Records of the General Assembly, Sixty-second Session, Sixth Committee*, 18th meeting (A/C.6/62/SR.18), para. 62), Ireland (*ibid.*, para. 93), Greece (*ibid.*, 19th meeting (A/C.6/62/SR.19), para. 6), Germany (*ibid.*, para. 30), India (*ibid.*, para. 106), the Republic of Korea (*ibid.*, 21st meeting (A/C.6/62/SR.21), para. 35), the Russian Federation (*ibid.*, para. 67), Romania (*ibid.*, para. 76), Switzerland (*ibid.*, para. 79) and Belarus (*ibid.*, para. 95).

[153] See the interventions by Argentina (*ibid.*, 18th meeting (A/C.6/62/SR.18), para. 62), Denmark, on behalf of the Nordic countries (Denmark, Finland, Iceland, Norway and Sweden) (*ibid.*, para. 98), Guatemala (*ibid.*, 19th meeting (A/C.6/62/SR.19), para. 20), Germany (*ibid.*, para. 30), France (*ibid.*, 20th meeting (A/C.6/62/SR.20), para. 6), the Russian Federation (*ibid.*, 21st meeting (A/C.6/62/SR.21), para. 67) and Romania (*ibid.*, para. 76).

[154] Support for article 43 was expressed by Ireland (*ibid.*, 18th meeting (A/C.6/62/SR.18), para. 92), Guatemala (*ibid.*, 19th meeting (A/C.6/62/SR.19), para. 20), Germany (*ibid.*, para. 31), Sri Lanka (*ibid.*, para. 66), the Netherlands (*ibid.*, 20th meeting (A/C.6/62/SR.20), paras. 37–38), the Russian Federation (*ibid.*, 21st meeting (A/C.6/62/SR.21), para. 67), Romania (*ibid.*, para. 77) and Switzerland (*ibid.*, paras. 81–83). See also the interventions by the European Commission (*ibid.*, para. 115) and Sierra Leone (*ibid.*, 24th meeting (A/C.6/62/SR.24), para. 98), and the written comments by WHO (see

to include in the draft a provision such as article 43.[155] Some other States commented that the reference to the rules of the organization required elucidation.[156] Also, the words "all appropriate measures" and "required" prompted some queries.[157]

96. Only a few States favoured, as an alternative to article 43, the text that had been suggested by a minority within the Commission and had been reproduced as a footnote in the Commission's report and again in the commentary to article 43.[158]

97. Concerns were expressed that article 43 should not be understood as implying that member States or international organizations have a subsidiary obligation to provide reparation.[159] Although the current text does not appear to convey that there would be an obligation for members towards the injured entity, a clarification in this regard could be given by adding to article 43, as a second paragraph, a text such as the following one:

> "2. The preceding paragraph does not imply that members acquire towards the injured State or international organization any obligation to make reparation."

98. A further question concerns the placement of article 43. The European Commission suggested that it should be moved to chapter I so that it would be placed among the general principles.[160] However, since article 43 concerns the performance of the obligation of reparation, which is defined in chapter II, the current position seems more appropriate.

99. The content of chapter III ("Serious breaches of obligations under peremptory norms of general international law") reflects the views expressed by several States at the sixty-first session of the General Assembly,[161] in response to the question, raised by the Commission in its report,[162] whether this chapter should be drafted along the lines of the corresponding chapter In the articles on the responsibility of States for internationally wrongful acts. Some endorsements of the text of articles 44 and 45 were made at the following sessions of the General Assembly.[163]

100. One State observed that "the obligation of an international organization to cooperate to bring to an end through lawful means any serious breach must take into account the ability of the organization depending on its mandate".[164] This point may have been adequately addressed in the commentary to article 45, when it explains that this provision "is not designed to vest international organizations with functions that are alien to their respective mandates".[165]

101. In conclusion to the present chapter, which relates to the current part two (arts. 31–45), only one change is suggested: that of adding a second paragraph to article 43, as proposed in paragraph 97 above.

Yearbook ... 2008, vol. II (Part One), document A/CN.4/593 and Add.1, sect. D), and WTO (*ibid.*).

[155] This view was expressed by India (*Official Records of the General Assembly, Sixty-second Session, Sixth Committee*, 19th meeting (A/C.6/62/SR.19), para. 106), France (*ibid.*, 20th meeting (A/C.6/62/SR.20), para. 6) and Hungary (*ibid.*, 21st meeting (A/C.6/62/SR.21), para. 15). See also the comment by Italy (*ibid.*, 19th meeting (A/C.6/62/SR.19), para. 39).

[156] Switzerland (*ibid.*, 21st meeting (A/C.6/62/SR.21), para. 82) suggested that "the limits on the obligations of the members of a responsible international organization to contribute should be stated more clearly in the draft article". New Zealand (*ibid.*, para. 42) maintained that the reference to the rules of the organization "should not be interpreted as justifying inaction by the members of an organization in the absence of suitable rules". Romania (*ibid.*, para. 77) noted that "strict adherence to the internal rules of an organization might render timely reparation impossible". Ireland (*ibid.*, 18th meeting (A/C.6/62/SR.18), para. 92) referred to "a case where, for example, the rules expressly prohibited extraordinary financial contributions from members to finance operations". However, it would be difficult to base an obligation for member States to contribute on rules other than the rules of the organization.

[157] See, respectively, the interventions by the Republic of Korea (*ibid.*, 21st meeting (A/C.6/62/SR.21), para. 36) and Romania (*ibid.*, para. 77).

[158] The text was reproduced in *Yearbook ... 2007*, vol. II (Part Two), chap. VIII, sect. C, p. 85, footnote 441. Austria (*Official Records of the General Assembly, Sixty-second Session, Sixth Committee*, 18th meeting (A/C.6/62/SR.18), paras. 53–54) and Japan (*ibid.*, 19th meeting (A/C.6/62/SR.19), para. 99) favoured this text. See also the comments by Argentina (*ibid.*, 18th meeting (A/C.6/62/SR.18), para. 62) and Israel (*ibid.*, 21st meeting (A/C.6/62/SR.21), para. 100). Specific criticism of the alternative text was voiced by Hungary (*ibid.*, para. 15), which "shared the majority view that the alternative version of draft article 43 offered in footnote [441] of the report would be unnecessary, since the stated obligation was implied in the obligation of the responsible international organization to make full reparation".

[159] See in particular the interventions by Greece (*ibid.*, 19th meeting (A/C.6/62/SR.19, para. 7), Malaysia (*ibid.*, para. 74) and Israel (*ibid.*, 21st meeting (A/C.6/62/SR.21), para. 100). The possibility of a subsidiary responsibility of member States was admitted in this context by Belarus (*ibid.*, para. 96).

[160] *Ibid.*, 21st meeting (A/C.6/62/SR.21), para. 115 and *Yearbook ... 2008*, vol. II (Part One), document A/CN.4/593 and Add.1, sect. D. A similar proposal was made by the International Organization for Migration (*ibid.*).

[161] This view was expressed by Denmark, on behalf of the Nordic countries (Denmark, Finland, Iceland, Norway and Sweden) (*Official Records of the General Assembly, Sixty-first Session, Sixth Committee*, 13th meeting (A/C.6/61/SR.13), para. 33), Argentina (*ibid.*, para. 50), the Netherlands (*ibid.*, 14th meeting (A/C.6/61/SR.14), para. 25), Belgium (*ibid.*, paras. 43–46), Spain (*ibid.*, para. 54), France (*ibid.*, para. 64), Belarus (*ibid.*, para. 101), Switzerland (*ibid.*, 15th meeting (A/C.6/61/SR.15), para. 8), Jordan (*ibid.*, 16th meeting (A/C.6/61/SR.16), para. 5), the Russian Federation (*ibid.*, 18th meeting (A/C.6/61/SR.18), para. 68) and Romania (*ibid.*, 19th meeting (A/C.6/61/SR.19), para. 60).

[162] *Yearbook ... 2006*, vol. II (Part Two), chap. III, sect. B, para. 28.

[163] See in particular the interventions by Argentina (*Official Records of the General Assembly, Sixty-second Session, Sixth Committee*, 18th meeting (A/C.6/62/SR.18), para. 63), Malaysia (*ibid.*, 19th meeting (A/C.6/62/SR.19), para. 74) and Cuba (*ibid.*, *Sixty-third Session, Sixth Committee*, 24th meeting (A/C.6/63/SR.24), para. 26). Greece (*ibid.*, *Sixty-second Session, Sixth Committee*, 19th meeting (A/C.6/62/SR.19), para. 8) and Cyprus (*ibid.*, 21st meeting (A/C.6/62/SR.21), para. 37) insisted on the importance of the obligation of non-recognition as stated in article 45. A general endorsement of articles 44 and 45 was made also by the European Commission (*ibid.*, 21st meeting (A/C.6/62/SR.21), para. 116).

[164] Thus Argentina (*ibid.*, 18th meeting (A/C.6/62/SR.18), para. 63), Switzerland (*ibid.*, 21st meeting (A/C.6/62/SR.21), para. 84) expressed a similar concern.

[165] This statement in the commentary to article 45 (*Yearbook ... 2007*, vol. II (Part Two), chap. VIII, sect. C, p. 93, para. (4)) was welcomed by Ireland (*Official Records of the General Assembly, Sixty-second Session, Sixth Committee*, 18th meeting (A/C.6/62/SR.18), para. 95).

Chapter VIII

Implementation of international responsibility

102. The draft articles relating to the invocation of responsibility of an international organization (arts. 46 to 53) were adopted by the Commission at its sixtieth session and could thus be discussed only at the sixty-third session of the General Assembly. At that session, several States expressed their general approval of these draft articles, in particular those relating to the invocation of international responsibility by an injured State or international organization.[166] In later written comments also the Organization for the Prohibition of Chemical Weapons and UNESCO expressed support for articles 46 to 53, the latter organization subject to a few minor drafting suggestions.[167]

103. The inclusion of a provision on admissibility of claims (art. 48) was welcomed.[168] While it is clear, and need not be expressed, that the requirement of nationality does not apply to a claim put forward by an injured international organization,[169] the suggestion was made that the Commission examine in this context issues relating to functional protection: for instance, whether an international organization could bring a claim for the benefit of a former official.[170] However, there is only a limited analogy between the question of the admissibility of claim by a State on behalf of one of its nationals—to which article 48 refers—and that of the admissibility of functional protection by an international organization.[171] Moreover, it would be difficult to state on this matter a rule generally applying to all, or most, international organizations.[172]

104. With regard to the further requirement stated in article 48—exhaustion of local remedies—the use of the term "local" as applied to remedies raised a few comments.[173] As was explained in the commentary to article 48,[174] this provision is intended to include both remedies existing "within an international organization" and those "available before arbitral tribunals, national courts or administrative bodies when the international organization has accepted their competence to examine claims".[175] Some States observed that this "would include the various internal tribunals and bodies competent to address the relevant issues".[176] The "scope of individuals' entitlement" to remedies[177] cannot be usefully specified in the current articles, because it would depend on the international organization and on the injury.

105. Failing any indication to the contrary, the rules of the organization will determine whether an organ of an international organization is competent to waive a claim validly on behalf of the organization.[178] The fact that article 49 does not contain a reference to the rules of the organization is in line with the absence of any reference to the internal law of a State, both in the same article and in article 45 on the responsibility of States for internationally wrongful acts, when the valid waiver of a claim by a State is considered.

106. The question whether acquiescence has occurred may give rise to doubts, but it is difficult to state a general

[166] See the interventions by the Czech Republic (*ibid., Sixty-third Session, Sixth Committee*, 19th meeting (A/C.6/63/SR.19), para. 90, with reference to articles 46 to 51), Italy (*ibid.*, para. 96), the Russian Federation (*ibid.*, 21st meeting (A/C.6/63/SR.21), para. 39, with reference to articles 46, 47, 50 and 51), Belgium (*ibid.*, para. 47) and Romania (*ibid.*, para. 56). See also the intervention by the European Commission (*ibid.*, 22nd meeting (A/C.6/63/SR.22), para. 20). Austria (*ibid.*, 18th meeting (A/C.6/63/SR.18), para. 82) observed that there were "good reasons for accepting" that the right to invoke responsibility "could be based on the implied powers doctrine". This remark appears to concern competence under the rules of the organization rather than the entitlement of an international organization to invoke responsibility under international law.

[167] See document A/CN.4/609 of the present volume, p. 97, sects. B to D, F and G.

[168] The importance of introducing a provision on admissibility of claims was stressed by Argentina (*Official Records of the General Assembly, Sixty-third Session, Sixth Committee*, 19th meeting (A/C.6/63/SR.19), para. 76).

[169] The Russian Federation (*ibid.*, 21st meeting (A/C.6/63/SR.21), para. 39) proposed that the inapplicability of the requirement of nationality to a claim by an international organization be "made clear in the draft itself". However, like the articles on the responsibility of States for internationally wrongful acts, the current draft does not contain "negative" propositions and the need to introduce one exception in the context of article 48 is not self-evident.

[170] This was suggested by Austria (*ibid.*, 18th meeting (A/C.6/63/SR.18), para. 85).

[171] As ICJ noted in its advisory opinion on *Reparation for Injuries Suffered in the Service of the United Nations* (*I.C.J. Reports 1949*, p. 186), "the bases of the two claims are different".

[172] In its advisory opinion referred to in the previous footnote, ICJ developed an argument that specifically related to the United Nations (*ibid.*, pp. 181–184). Slovenia (*Official Records of the General Assembly, Fifty-eighth Session, Sixth Committee*, 17th meeting (A/C.6/58/SR.17), para. 9) said that it was "opposed to granting international organizations the right to exercise functional protection on behalf of their officials".

[173] The Russian Federation (*Official Records of the General Assembly, Sixty-third Session, Sixth Committee*, 21st meeting (A/C.6/63/SR.21), para. 39) would have preferred the use of the term "legal" instead of "local", but the latter term is more usual and may be considered a term of art.

[174] *Yearbook ... 2008*, vol. II (Part Two), chap. VII, sect. C, commentary to article 48, para. (9).

[175] France (*Official Records of the General Assembly, Sixty-third Session, Sixth Committee*, 20th meeting (A/C.6/63/SR.20), para. 39) observed that "the term 'local remedies' should be defined, because individuals could take action against a State before jurisdictions that were not national". The commentary arguably attempts to provide the necessary explanations.

[176] Thus Denmark, on behalf of the five Nordic countries (Denmark, Finland, Iceland, Norway and Sweden) (*ibid.*, para. 1). Thallinger, "The rule of exhaustion of local remedies in the context of the responsibility of international organizations", at p. 423, "suggested that the rule of exhaustion of local remedies should be adapted and 'softened' when applied to claims by states against international organizations". What appears to be meant is that the rule should be applied more strictly: "As long as the international organizations provide some adequate mechanism of legal redress, they should be given the means to rectify the wrongdoing of their organs" (p. 425).

[177] Japan (*Official Records of the General Assembly, Sixty-third Session, Sixth Committee*, 22nd meeting (A/C.6/63/SR.22), para. 18) suggested that this scope be defined.

[178] See the commentary to article 49, *Yearbook ... 2008*, vol. II (Part Two), chap. VII, sect. C, paras. (3)–(4). This point was stressed by Argentina (*Official Records of the General Assembly, Sixty-third Session, Sixth Committee*, 19th meeting (A/C.6/63/SR.19), para. 77). The Russian Federation (*ibid.*, 21st meeting (A/C.6/63/SR.21), para. 40) suggested the addition of a rule on competence.

rule with regard to "the appropriate time frame for a claim to be treated as having lapsed".[179]

107. Article 51 addresses the case of a plurality of responsible States or international organizations. It does not assume that when a State is responsible together with an international organization, the responsibility of a State would be necessarily subsidiary or concurrent. Whether responsibility is subsidiary or concurrent depends on the pertinent rules of international law.[180] When responsibility is concurrent, it was noted that the injured entity may "decide the order in which it [invokes] the responsibility of the responsible State or international organization".[181]

108. In its report on its fifty-ninth session, the Commission requested comments on the question of whether an international organization could invoke responsibility in case of a breach of an international obligation owed to the international community as a whole. The question was as follows: "Should a breach of an obligation owed to the international community as a whole be committed by an international organization, would the other organizations or some of them be entitled to make a similar claim?"[182] Some States gave, at least tentatively, an unqualified positive answer,[183] while other States indicated that the organization invoking responsibility had to be given the mandate to protect the general interest underlying the obligation breached.[184] The latter view was endorsed by the Commission and reflected in article 52. The solution adopted by the Commission attracted some favourable comments[185] at the following session of the General Assembly. A few doubts were also expressed.[186]

109. Two States suggested that the invocability of the international responsibility in the case in hand be further limited to those international organizations that have "a universal vocation".[187] However, since a State could individually invoke responsibility for the same breach, it seems more coherent to accept that even a small number of States could establish an international organization that includes among its functions the protection of the general interest underlying the obligations and that the same organization could do what the States are entitled to do individually.

110. Although the draft articles on countermeasures (arts. 54–60) were adopted only by the Drafting Committee and were thus not included in the Commission's report relating to its sixtieth session, a certain number of States referred to the text of those articles in the debates in the Sixth Committee at the sixty-third session of the General Assembly. Other States made some more general remarks.

111. Some States stressed the need to make a distinction between countermeasures and sanctions.[188] While countermeasures are acts that would *per se* be unlawful, sanctions are lawful measures that an international organization may take against its members according to the rules of the organization. Sanctions are therefore not considered in the chapter on countermeasures.

112. The main question under discussion was whether there should be a chapter on countermeasures at all. Several States had expressed a favourable view at the sixty-second session of the General Assembly, in response to a request for comments made by the Commission.[189] At the following session, various States gave their basic approval to the draft articles that had been meanwhile provisionally adopted by the Drafting Committee.[190]

---

[179] Israel (*ibid.*, 24th meeting (A/C.6/63/SR.24), para. 75) requested "further clarification" on this point.

[180] Argentina (*ibid.*, 19th meeting (A/C.6/63/SR.19), para. 78) referred instead to the rules of the organization.

[181] Thus China (*ibid.*, para. 69). While Greece rightly noted (*ibid.*, 21st meeting A/C.6/63/SR.21, para. 3) that "the subsidiary responsibility could be invoked only insofar as the invocation of primary responsibility had not led to reparation", this does not prevent the injured party from addressing a claim before the subsidiary responsibility is triggered, provided that the subsidiary character of the responsibility is acknowledged. See the commentary to article 51, *Yearbook ... 2008*, vol. II (Part Two), chap. VII, sect. C, para. (3).

[182] *Yearbook ... 2007*, vol. II (Part Two), chap. III, sect. D, para. 30 (*a*).

[183] See the interventions by Hungary (*Official Records of the General Assembly, Sixty-second Session, Sixth Committee*, 21st meeting (A/C.6/62/SR.21), para. 16), Cyprus (*ibid.*, para. 38), Belgium (*ibid.*, paras. 89–90) and Belarus (*ibid.*, para. 97). See also the intervention by Malaysia (*ibid.*, 19th meeting (A/C.6/62/SR.19), para. 75).

[184] Thus Argentina (*ibid.*, 18th meeting (A/C.6/62/SR.18), para. 64), Denmark, on behalf of the Nordic countries (Denmark, Finland, Iceland, Norway and Sweden) (*ibid.*, paras. 99–100), Italy (*ibid.*, 19th meeting (A/C.6/62/SR.19), para. 40), Japan (*ibid.*, para. 100), the Russian Federation (*ibid.*, 21st meeting (A/C.6/62/SR.21), para. 70) and Switzerland (*ibid.*, para. 85).

[185] By Argentina (*ibid., Sixty-third Session, Sixth Committee*, 19th meeting (A/C.6/63/SR.19), para. 78), Germany (*ibid.*, para. 84), the Russian Federation (*ibid.*, 21st meeting (A/C.6/63/SR.21), para. 41) and the European Commission (*ibid.*, 22nd meeting (A/C.6/63/SR.22), para. 23).

[186] According to China (*ibid.*, 19th meeting (A/C.6/63/SR.19), para. 70) there is "no established practice" to justify the Commission's text. Austria (*ibid.*, 18th meeting (A/C.6/63/SR.18), para. 84) considered that "the limited functions of many international organizations argued against their capacity to invoke responsibility for the breach of an obligation owed to the international community as a whole". This objection is arguably taken care of by the requirement set out in article 52 that the functions of the organization invoking responsibility include "safeguarding the interest of the international community underlying the obligation breached".

[187] Belarus (*ibid.*, 19th meeting (A/C.6/63/SR.19), para. 60) and Argentina (*ibid.*, para. 78, from which the quotation is taken).

[188] See the interventions by Germany (*ibid.*, 19th meeting (A/C.6/63/SR.19), para. 86), Portugal (*ibid.*, 20th meeting (A/C.6/63/SR.20), para. 25), Viet Nam (*ibid.*, para. 38), Greece (*ibid.*, 21st meeting (A/C.6/63/SR.21), para. 1) and Spain (*ibid.*, 22nd meeting (A/C.6/63/SR.22), para. 5).

[189] Argentina (*Official Records of the General Assembly, Sixty-second Session, Sixth Committee*, 18th meeting (A/C.6/62/SR.18), para. 64, for the case that the organization had "a close connection to the right protected by the obligation breached"), Denmark, on behalf of the Nordic countries (Denmark, Finland, Iceland, Norway and Sweden) (*ibid.*, para. 101), Italy (*ibid.*, 19th meeting (A/C.6/62/SR.19), para. 41), Malaysia (*ibid.*, para. 75), Japan (*ibid.*, para. 100), the Netherlands (*ibid.*, 20th meeting (A/C.6/62/SR.20), para. 40), the Russian Federation (*ibid.*, 21st meeting (A/C.6/62/SR.21), para. 71), Switzerland (*ibid.*, para. 86) and Belgium (*ibid.*, para. 91).

[190] Argentina (*ibid., Sixty-third Session, Sixth Committee*, 19th meeting (A/C.6/63/SR.19), para. 79), Germany (*ibid.*, paras. 85–86), Malaysia (*ibid.*, 20th meeting (A/C.6/63/SR.20), para. 36), Romania (*ibid.*, 21st meeting (A/C.6/63/SR.21), para. 56), Spain (*ibid.*, 22nd meeting (A/C.6/63/SR.22), para. 5) and Japan (*ibid.*, para. 18). The same view was expressed by the European Commission (*ibid.*, para. 24). The Russian Federation (*ibid.*, 21st meeting (A/C.6/63/SR.21), para. 41) maintained that international organizations may take countermeasures against other international organizations only to "the extent of their particular competence". This restriction seems implied. There is no indication in the draft articles that the taking of countermeasures would justify *ultra vires* acts.

113. As was noted by WHO,

there is no cogent reason why an international organization that breaches an international obligation should be exempted from countermeasures taken by an injured State or international organization to bring about compliance by the former organization with its obligations. Conversely, it would seem illogical to deprive an international organization injured by a breach of an international obligation by another international organization of the possibility of taking retaliatory measures to induce the latter organization to comply with its obligations.[191]

In the same vein, UNESCO wrote that it did not "have any objection to the inclusion of draft articles on countermeasures".[192]

114. Several States stressed the need for caution when considering countermeasures. The Commission is certainly aware of this need, since the manifest purpose of the chapter on countermeasures is to restrict them with a series of substantive and procedural rules. A few States nevertheless expressed doubts about the advisability of addressing the issue of countermeasures in the current draft.[193] Some other States suggested that recourse to countermeasures be further limited, by admitting as countermeasures only "withholding the performance of contractual obligations under treaty relationships".[194]

115. Concern was expressed that countermeasures taken against an international organization should not "impair the exercise of the functional competence of international organizations".[195] This concern appears to be met by article 54, paragraph 4, according to which "countermeasures shall, as far as possible, be taken in such a way as to limit their effects on the exercise by the responsible international organization of its functions".

116. Several remarks were addressed on the question whether an injured member of a responsible international organization could take countermeasures against that organization. In this matter the rules of the organization clearly have a significant role to play.[196] They take "precedence as *lex specialis* over general international law on countermeasures when the dispute [is] between the organization and one of its member States".[197] According to one view, "the rules of the organization determine whether an organization could … be the target of countermeasures" by its members.[198] However, the rules of the organization do not necessarily regulate the matter and there is therefore the need for a residual rule.

117. The view was expressed that "as a general rule, countermeasures had no place in the relations between an international organization and its members".[199] Some doubts were voiced about whether that principle and the limited exceptions are adequately stated in article 55.[200] This is a point that the Commission may wish to reconsider.

118. With regard to article 56, it has been observed that most of the obligations that, according to that provision, cannot be breached for the purpose of taking countermeasures against a responsible international organization are "owed to the international community at large, not to the international organization against which countermeasures might be taken".[201] A similar remark could be made with regard to States in relation to the parallel provision in the articles on the responsibility of States for internationally wrongful acts. The meaning of the restrictions on the obligations that may be breached when taking countermeasures is to say that a breach of the obligation would not be justified even in the relations between the injured State or international organization and the responsible organization.

119. In conclusion, no proposal for change is made to the draft articles (46 to 60) that are considered in the present chapter.

[191] See document A/CN.4/609 of the present volume, sect. I, p. 101.

[192] *Ibid.*

[193] Greece (*Official Records of the General Assembly, Sixty-third Session, Sixth Committee*, 21st meeting (A/C.6/63/SR.21), para. 1). See also the interventions by the United Kingdom (*ibid.*, para. 24) and Israel (*ibid.*, 24th meeting (A/C.6/63/SR.24), para. 75).

[194] Thus the Republic of Korea (*ibid.*, 19th meeting (A/C.6/63/SR.19), para. 64). A similar view was expressed by the Czech Republic (*ibid.*, para. 92).

[195] Thus Belarus (*ibid.*, *Sixty-second Session, Sixth Committee*, 21st meeting (A/C.6/62/SR.21), para. 98 and *ibid.*, *Sixty-third Session, Sixth Committee*, 19th meeting (A/C.6/63/SR.19), para. 58). A similar point was made by Israel (*ibid.*, 24th meeting (A/C.6/63/SR.24), para. 75).

[196] The need for compliance with the rules of the organization was stressed by Belgium (*ibid.*, 21st meeting (A/C.6/63/SR.21), para. 48). On a similar line, the Philippines (*ibid.*, 19th meeting (A/C.6/63/SR.19), para. 43) and Uruguay (*ibid.*, 21st meeting (A/C.6/63/SR.21), para. 45) referred to the "constituent instruments" of the organization.

[197] Denmark, on behalf of the Nordic countries (Denmark, Finland, Iceland, Norway and Sweden) (*ibid.*, 20th meeting (A/C.6/63/SR.20), para. 1). A similar statement was made in the written comments of the Legal Counsel of WHO (see A/CN.4/609 of the present volume, sect. I, p. 101).

[198] Thus India (*Official Records of the General Assembly, Sixty-third Session, Sixth Committee*, 23rd meeting (A/C.6/63/SR.23), para. 22).

[199] Germany (*ibid.*, 19th meeting (A/C.6/63/SR.19), para. 86). See also the interventions by France (*ibid.*, 20th meeting (A/C.6/63/SR.20), para. 40) and Greece (*ibid.*, 21st meeting (A/C.6/63/SR.21), para. 2).

[200] UNESCO supported the wording that had been suggested in the sixth report of the Special Rapporteur (see *Yearbook … 2008*, vol. II (Part One), document A/CN.4/597, para. 48) "only if this is not inconsistent with the rules of the injured organization". See A/CN.4/609, sect. I, p. 101.

[201] Thus Romania (*Official Records of the General Assembly, Sixty-third Session, Sixth Committee*, 21st meeting (A/C.6/63/SR.21), para. 56).

Chapter IX

General provisions

120. Like the articles on the responsibility of States for internationally wrongful acts, the current draft should be completed by a few general provisions. These are intended to apply to issues relating both to the international responsibility of international organizations and to the responsibility of States for the internationally wrongful act of an international organization. According to the suggestions made in paragraphs 21 and 92 above, parts two

to four will cover the international responsibility of international organizations and part five the responsibility of States for the internationally wrongful act of an international organization. If these suggestions are accepted, the general provisions will build up part six. Unlike the matters that have been considered in the preceding chapters of the present report, the general provisions are discussed here for the first time.

121. As many States and international organizations stressed in their comments, the great variety of international organizations makes it essential to acknowledge the existence of special rules on international responsibility that apply to certain categories of international organizations, or to one specific international organization, in their relations with some or all States and other international organizations.[202] These special rules (*lex specialis*) may supplement the more general rules that have been drafted in the current text or may replace them, in full or in part.

122. It would be an impossible task for the Commission to try to identify the content and the scope of application of these special rules. Thus, the opinions that have been voiced about the existence of special rules have not been examined in the previous reports and are not going to be discussed here. It may appear that there has been one exception, because some attention has been given to the issue, raised by the European Commission, of whether a "special rule of attribution of conduct" exists for the European Community and "other potentially similar organizations", with regard to the attribution of acts of member States implementing binding acts of the relevant organization to that organization.[203] This issue leads to a wider question, which needs to be considered in the context of the present draft: whether, as a general rule, conduct taken by a State or an international organization when implementing an act of another international organization of which it is a member is attributable to the latter organization. Also in view of some recent developments in judicial and other decisions, this question has been discussed again above, in paragraphs 31 to 33. The outcome of the discussion on the wider question does not settle the issue of the existence of a special rule on attribution concerning a category of international organizations, or even only an individual organization, in their relations to States and other international organizations.

123. The rules of the organization are likely to build a body of special rules affecting to a certain extent the application of the rules on international responsibility in the relations between an international organization and its members.[204] It is clear that the rules of the organization are relevant for a number of issues that have been considered in the present draft, so much so that various provisions could include the words "subject to the special rules of the organization". A provision on *lex specialis* would make this repeated proviso unnecessary, even if there was no specific mention of the rules of the organization. However, given the practical importance of the rules of the organization as a possible source of *lex specialis*, it seems appropriate to make an express reference to those rules.

124. The following text takes into account the wording of article 55 on the responsibility of States for internationally wrongful acts and adds a reference to the rules of the organization:

"*Draft article 61.* Lex specialis

"These articles do not apply where and to the extent that the conditions for the existence of an internationally wrongful act or the content or implementation of the international responsibility of an international organization, or a State for an internationally wrongful act of an international organization, are governed by special rules of international law, such as the rules of the organization that are applicable to the relations between an international organization and its members."

125. The present draft addresses issues relating to the international responsibility of States only to the extent that these issues are dealt with in what is currently chapter (x) and should become part five, according to the suggestion made in paragraph 92 above. As was noted above, in paragraph 8, given the definition of the scope of the current draft as outlined in article 1, other issues concerning State responsibility are not covered, even when they are not expressly covered in the articles on the responsibility of States for internationally wrongful acts. Since there would be no reason to infer that matters concerning State responsibility that are not addressed in the draft are not covered by other rules of international law, it may seem superfluous to state this in a general provision. However, if this point is made in a general provision with regard to the responsibility of international organizations, the fact of not adding a reference to States may lead to unintended implications.

126. The main purpose of a general provision concerning rules of international law other than those existing on matters regulated in the present draft seems to be to convey that the draft does not address all the issues of international law that may be relevant in order to establish whether an international organization is responsible and

[202] When the suggestion of including a provision on *lex specialis* was made in the fifth report of the Special Rapporteur (*Yearbook ... 2007*, vol. II (Part One), document A/CN.4/583, para. 3), it was welcomed by Ireland (*Official Records of the General Assembly, Sixty-second Session, Sixth Committee*, 18th meeting (A/C.6/62/SR.18), para. 96) and the United Kingdom (*ibid.*, 19th meeting (A/C.6/62/SR.19), para. 44).

[203] *Official Records of the General Assembly, Fifty-ninth Session, Sixth Committee*, 21st meeting (A/C.6/59/SR.21), para. 18. The European Commission also suggested some other possibilities: that of providing for "special rules of responsibility, so that responsibility could be attributed to the organization, even if organs of member States were the prime actors of a breach of an obligation borne by the organization" and that of making a "special exception or saving clause for organizations such as the European Community". The second alternative would be covered by a provision concerning *lex specialis* such as the one suggested in paragraph 124 below. The first alternative does not seem to require the existence of a special rule on responsibility. Responsibility would depend on the content of the obligation breached. Supposing that an international organization accepts an obligation towards a third State to ensure a certain result and that this result is not achieved because of the conduct of one of its member States, the organization would incur responsibility under the general rules, even if the relevant conduct was attributed to the member State. On the other hand, the member State would not incur responsibility if it has not acquired a parallel obligation under international law towards the third State.

[204] See on this point especially the intervention by Poland (*ibid.*, 22nd meeting (A/C.6/59/SR.22), para. 1).

what responsibility entails. A similar point was made with regard to States in article 56 on the responsibility of States for internationally wrongful acts.[205]

127. Article 56 on the responsibility of States for internationally wrongful acts may serve as a model for a text that would refer to the responsibility of both international organizations and States and may read as follows:

"Draft article 62. Questions of international responsibility not regulated by these articles

"The applicable rules of international law continue to govern questions concerning the responsibility of an international organization or a State for an internationally wrongful act to the extent that they are not regulated by these articles."

128. The present draft does not address questions of individual responsibility. While this may appear obvious, it seems nevertheless useful to include in the draft a general provision that is designed as a reminder of the fact that issues of individual responsibility may arise in connection with a wrongful act of an international organization. This would make it clear that the official position of an individual cannot exempt that individual from international responsibility that he or she may incur for his or her conduct. A similar course was taken in the articles on the responsibility of States for internationally wrongful acts by including article 58 among the general provisions.

129. When an internationally wrongful act of an international organization or a State is committed, the responsibility under international law of individuals acting on behalf of the international organization or the State cannot be taken as implied. There are, however, cases in which responsibility of certain individuals is likely, as in the case of those who are instrumental for the serious breach of an obligation under a peremptory norm of general international law that is envisaged in article 44 of the current draft and in article 40 of the responsibility of States for internationally wrongful acts.

130. It is therefore proposed to include a draft article that replicates article 58 on the responsibility of States for internationally wrongful acts, with the addition of four words in order to extend its scope to international organizations. The text would read as follows:

"Draft article 63. Individual responsibility

"These articles are without prejudice to any question of the individual responsibility under international law of any person acting on behalf of an international organization or a State."

131. The last provision in the articles on the responsibility of States for internationally wrongful acts sets out that the articles are "without prejudice to the Charter of the United Nations". This is meant to point to the impact that the Charter may have on issues of State responsibility. The impact may result directly from the Charter or from acts taken by one of the organs of the United Nations pursuant to the Charter. What applies to issues of State responsibility that are regulated by the pertinent articles also applies to questions of State responsibility that are covered in the present draft.

132. While Article 103 of the Charter only refers to conflicts between "obligations of the Members of the United Nations under the present Charter", on the one hand, and "their obligations under any other international agreement", on the other, the impact of the Charter is not limited to obligations of members of the United Nations. The Charter may well affect obligations, and hence the responsibility, of an international organization. Should, for instance, a resolution adopted by the Security Council under Chapter VII of the Charter exclude the adoption of countermeasures against a certain State, neither States nor international organizations could lawfully resort to those countermeasures.[206] It is not necessary, for the purpose of the present draft, to define the extent to which international responsibility of an international organization may be affected, directly or indirectly, by the Charter.[207]

133. Article 59 on the responsibility of States for internationally wrongful acts may be reproduced without change:

"Draft article 64. Charter of the United Nations

"These articles are without prejudice to the Charter of the United Nations."

134. In conclusion to this chapter, it is suggested to include in the draft the four articles presented in paragraphs 124, 127, 130 and 133 above.

---

[205] *Yearbook ... 2001*, vol. II (Part Two), p. 141.

[206] According to Poland (*Official Records of the General Assembly, Sixty-first Session, Sixth Committee*, 14th meeting (A/C.6/61/SR.14), para. 105), the provision on countermeasures as a circumstance precluding wrongfulness (art. 19) "should contain an explicit reference to the Charter and United Nations law, in order to indicate the possible scope and substantive and procedural limitations to countermeasures taken by an international organization". A general provision could fulfil the same function.

[207] Belgium (*ibid.*, para. 46) suggested that "a saving clause, modelled on article 59 of the articles on responsibility of States for internationally wrongful acts, should be added at the end of the draft articles on responsibility of international organizations".

RESPONSIBILITY OF INTERNATIONAL ORGANIZATIONS

[Agenda item 4]

DOCUMENT A/CN.4/609

Comments and observations received from international organizations

[*Original: English*]
[*13 March 2009*]

CONTENTS

Multilateral instruments cited in the present report

	Source
Convention on the Privileges and Immunities of the Specialized Agencies (New York, 21 November 1947)	United Nations, *Treaty Series*, vol. 33, No. 521, p. 261.
Vienna Convention on the Law of Treaties (Vienna, 23 May 1969)	*Ibid.*, vol. 1155, No. 18232, p. 331.

Introduction

1. At its fifty-fifth session, the International Law Commission asked the Secretariat to circulate, on an annual basis, the portions of its report relevant to the topic "Responsibility of international organizations" to international organizations for their comments.[1] Pursuant to that request, selected international organizations were invited to submit their comments on the relevant portions of the Commission's 2003, 2004, 2005, 2006, 2007 and 2008 reports.[2] Most recently, the Commission sought comments on chapter VII of its 2008 report[3] and on the issues of particular interest to it noted in paragraphs 29 and 30 of that report.[4]

2. As at 15 March 2009, written comments had been received from the following five international organizations (dates of submission in parentheses): International Maritime Organization (IMO) (15 January 2009); International Monetary Fund (27 February 2009); Organization for the Prohibition of Chemical Weapons (13 January 2009); United Nations Educational, Scientific and Cultural Organization (UNESCO) (12 January 2009); World Health Organization (WHO) (4 February 2009). Those comments are reproduced below, in a topic-by-topic manner. In a submission dated 6 January 2009, the International Atomic Energy Agency indicated that it did not have any comments to provide at this stage.

[1] *Yearbook ... 2003*, vol. II (Part Two), p. 18, para. 52.

[2] The written comments of international organizations received prior to 15 April 2008 are contained in *Yearbook ... 2004*, vol. II (Part One), document A/CN.4/545; *Yearbook ... 2005*, vol. II (Part One), document A/CN.4/556; *Yearbook ... 2006*, vol. II (Part One), document A/CN.4/568 and Add.1; *Yearbook ... 2007*, vol. II (Part One), document A/CN.4/582; and *Yearbook ... 2008*, vol. II (Part One), document A/CN.4/593 and Add.1.

[3] *Yearbook ... 2008*, vol. II (Part Two). The text of the draft articles on responsibility of international organizations provisionally approved by the Commission is contained in *ibid.*, para. 164. The text of the draft articles and corresponding comments approved by the Commission at its Sixtieth session I, in 2008, is contained in paragraph 165.

[4] *Ibid.*, chap. III. Paragraphs 29 and 30 of the 2008 report read as follows:

> 29. The Commission would welcome comments and observations from Governments and international organizations on draft articles 46 to 53, dealing with the invocation of the responsibility of an international organization.
>
> 30. The Commission would also welcome comments on issues relating to countermeasures against international organizations, taking into account the discussion of these issues, as reflected in chapter VII.

Comments and observations received from international organizations

A. General remarks

International Monetary Fund

1. We note the suggestion by the Special Rapporteur that, before completing the first reading, the texts of the draft articles provisionally adopted by the Commission should be reviewed in the light of all comments from States and international organizations. It will be recalled from our prior comments,[1] and from similar comments by a number of other international organizations, that a central issue when considering their international responsibility is that international organizations, unlike States, do not possess a general competence. As the Commission has recognized in two of the draft articles provisionally adopted, it follows that international organizations cannot be required to take actions that are outside their respective mandates.[2] In our view, that insight should be incorporated into a number of other draft articles, and the Special Rapporteur's suggestion of a review before completing the first reading presents a welcome opportunity to do so. We also believe that it follows that, since the mandates of international organizations are established by international agreement, their acts that are clearly pursuant to such treaties should normally be regarded as consistent with international law.

[1] See *Yearbook ... 2004*, vol. II (Part One), p. 19, document A/CN.4/545; *Yearbook ... 2005*, vol. II (Part One), p. 27, document A/CN.4/556; and *Yearbook ... 2007*, vol. II (Part One), document A/CN.4/582.

[2] *Yearbook ... 2007*, vol. II (Part Two), p. 93 (commentary to draft art. 45, para. (4)) and *Yearbook ... 2008*, vol. II (Part Two) (draft art. 52, para. 3 and commentary thereto, para. (10)).

2. We hope that the Commission will follow up on the suggestion to organize a meeting with legal advisers of international organizations to engage in a concrete discussion of the issues raised by these and other comments,[3] and we would be pleased to participate in such a meeting.

[3] *Yearbook ... 2008*, vol. II (Part Two).

World Health Organization

At the outset, let us express our congratulations to the Commission and to the Special Rapporteur for having almost reached the end of the first reading of the draft articles in only six years. At the same time, we applaud the invitation extended by the Commission to the legal advisers of a number of international organizations to engage in a discussion with the Commission on the entire set of draft articles on the responsibility of international organizations and on the approach followed thus far by the Commission and the Special Rapporteur. As several comments by international organizations during the course of the project have revealed, the latter are keen to ensure that any codification of the law on the responsibility of international organizations fully reflects their characteristics as subjects of international law and is not detrimental to the full and unimpeded discharge of their respective constitutional functions. This concern is particularly relevant since the Commission has followed the approach of modelling the draft articles on the articles on the responsibility of States for internationally wrongful acts (*Yearbook ... 2001*, vol. II (Part Two), p. 26, para. 76), even though the practice available on many aspects of the responsibility of international organizations is scarce or non-existent and the status of the law in this area is less settled than in the case of States.

B. Invocation of the responsibility of an international organization: general considerations

International Maritime Organization

1. We are pleased to note that the International Law Commission considered the sixth report by G. Gaja, Special Rapporteur on the topic of the responsibility of international organizations (*Yearbook ... 2008*, vol. II (Part One), document A/CN.4/507), and has provisionally adopted eight draft articles, thus making substantial progress on this topic. We congratulate the Commission on its achievement and, in particular, pay tribute to Mr. Gaja for the work he has done.

2. We would like to make the following brief comments of a general nature.

3. We note that these draft articles follow, by analogy and *mutatis mutandis*, the wording of corresponding provisions on State responsibility, supplemented with the views and practices of some international organizations, such as the European Union.

4. We believe that, in principle, the established rules governing State responsibility might be applied to the responsibility of international organizations, under similar circumstances. However, the European Union, as a regional economic integration organization to which exclusive competence over certain matters has been transferred by its members, is completely different in nature from a United Nations specialized agency such as the International Maritime Organization. Accordingly, the principles that might be applicable to the European Union may not be suitable for IMO.

5. IMO is a regulatory agency of the United Nations, established to perform certain functions provided for in its constitution for the common interest of its member States and the maritime industry. Whether this organization can take certain actions depends, in the main, on its constitution, the applications of the treaty and non-treaty instruments adopted under its auspices, and the decisions taken by its governing bodies. The latter also exert strict oversight over the activities of the organization.

6. At this stage, it is still unclear to us how the draft provisions would apply to the activities undertaken by IMO, and what the relationship will be between the draft provisions and the Vienna Convention on the Law of Treaties as well as the Convention on the Privileges and Immunities of the Specialized Agencies. It is also difficult to imagine scenarios that would give rise to the possible application of the draft provisions by our organization.

7. We would therefore support the suggestion that a meeting be organized between the Commission and the legal advisers of international organizations in order to engage in a concrete discussion of the issues raised by the draft articles, including the question of countermeasures.

Organization for the Prohibition of Chemical Weapons

We find chapters III.B and VII of the report quite wide-ranging, as they include a variety of issues that arise in the context of the international responsibility of international organizations that were dealt with in a similar manner in the articles on responsibility of States for internationally wrongful acts (*Yearbook ... 2001*, vol. II (Part Two), p. 26, para. 76). Regarding draft articles 46 to 53, we noticed that they were modelled, with some adjustments, on the corresponding provisions on State responsibility. In our view, these adjustments are appropriate.

World Health Organization

Concerning draft articles 46 to 53, most of them do not raise particular issues, as they replicate the corresponding articles on the responsibility of States on issues for which no particular distinction between States and international organizations seems to be warranted. At the same time, the applicability of some of the articles to international organizations may be difficult in practice.

C. Draft article 46. Invocation of responsibility by an injured State or international organization

Draft article 46, as provisionally adopted by the Commission at its sixtieth session, reads as follows:

Article 46. Invocation of responsibility by an injured State or international organization

A State or an international organization is entitled as an injured State or an injured international organization to invoke the responsibility of another international organization if the obligation breached is owed to:

(*a*) that State or the former international organization individually;

(*b*) a group of States or international organizations including that State or the former international organization, or the international community as a whole, and the breach of the obligation:

(i) specially affects that State or that international organization; or

(ii) is of such a character as radically to change the position of all the other States and international organizations to which the obligation is owed with respect to the further performance of the obligation.

United Nations Educational, Scientific and Cultural Organization

Article 46 (*b*) envisages a situation in which a breached obligation is owed to a group of States *or* international organizations *or* the international community. In this respect, UNESCO considers that the breach of obligation provided for in article 46 (*b*) (ii) should be "of such a nature to change the position of all the other States *or* international organizations" rather than of "all the other States *and* international organizations".

D. Draft article 48. Admissibility of claims

Draft article 48, as provisionally adopted by the Commission at its sixtieth session, reads as follows:

Article 48. Admissibility of claims

1. An injured State may not invoke the responsibility of an international organization if the claim is not brought in accordance with any applicable rule relating to nationality of claims.

2. When a rule requiring the exhaustion of local remedies applies to a claim, an injured State or international organization may not invoke the responsibility of another international organization if any available and effective remedy provided by that organization has not been exhausted.

Organization for the Prohibition of Chemical Weapons

We noticed that the Commission decided not to include a provision similar to article 44 on State responsibility (*Yearbook ... 2001*, vol. II (Part Two), p. 26, para. 76) regarding the nationality of claims. In its analysis of the issue, the Commission may wish to consider the practical consequences of the absence of such a rule. This rule could be of particular significance when the individuals of a State are injured by acts contrary to international law committed by an international organization from which the State has been unable to obtain satisfaction through the ordinary channels. We believe that this matter is not only relevant to questions of jurisdiction or to the admissibility of claims before judicial bodies, but is also a general condition for the invocation of responsibility in those cases where it is applicable.

E. Draft article 49. Loss of the right to invoke responsibility

Draft article 49, as provisionally adopted by the Commission at its sixtieth session, reads as follows:

Article 49. Loss of the right to invoke responsibility

The responsibility of an international organization may not be invoked if:

(*a*) the injured State or international organization has validly waived the claim;

(*b*) the injured State or international organization is to be considered as having, by reason of its conduct, validly acquiesced in the lapse of the claim.

World Health Organization

The valid waiver of a claim by an international organization under draft article 49, or its acquiescence, may be difficult to ascertain due to the potential complexity of the attribution of competence to the various organs of an organization under its relevant rules. We note that the commentary to that article acknowledges such difficulties.

F. Draft article 50. Plurality of injured States or international organizations

Draft article 50, as provisionally adopted by the Commission at its sixtieth session, reads as follows:

Article 50. Plurality of injured States or international organizations

Where several States or international organizations are injured by the same internationally wrongful act of an international organization, each injured State or international organization may separately invoke the responsibility of the international organization for the internationally wrongful act.

United Nations Educational, Scientific and Cultural Organization

UNESCO notes that there seems to be a contradiction between the commentary of the International Law Commission and the wording of this article. Indeed, the Commission specified in its commentary that this article envisages situations where (*a*) there is a plurality of injured States; (*b*) there is a plurality of injured international organizations; and (*c*) there are one or more injured States and one or more injured organizations. Yet article 50, in its current wording, does not foresee a situation in which there are one or more injured States and one or more injured organizations. UNESCO is therefore of the view that if the latter situation is to be envisaged in this article, the wording of the first part of the sentence should be changed to "Where several States *and/or* international organizations". If, however, the intent is to envisage only situations where there are a plurality of injured States or a plurality of injured organizations, then the comments of the Commission should be modified as to exclude the third possible situation.

G. Draft article 51. Plurality of responsible States or international organizations

Draft article 51, as provisionally adopted by the Commission at its sixtieth session, reads as follows:

Article 51. Plurality of responsible States or international organizations

1. Where an international organization and one or more States or other organizations are responsible for the same internationally wrongful act, the responsibility of each State or international organization may be invoked in relation to that act.

2. Subsidiary responsibility, as in the case of draft article 29, may be invoked insofar as the invocation of the primary responsibility has not led to reparation.

3. Paragraphs 1 and 2:

(*a*) do not permit any injured State or international organization to recover, by way of compensation, more than the damage it has suffered;

(*b*) are without prejudice to any right of recourse that the State or international organization providing reparation may have against the other responsible States or international organizations.

United Nations Educational, Scientific and Cultural Organization

According to the Commission, this article envisages a situation in which an international organization is responsible for a wrongful act along with one or more other entities, either international organizations or States. In the view of UNESCO, even though the term "other" in article 51, paragraph 1, could imply "international" organizations, it would be preferable to specify that these "other organizations" must be international.

H. Draft article 52. Invocation of responsibility by a State or an international organization other than an injured State or international organization

Draft article 52, as provisionally adopted by the Commission at its sixtieth session, reads as follows:

Article 52. Invocation of responsibility by a State or an international organization other than an injured State or international organization

1. A State or an international organization other than an injured State or international organization is entitled to invoke the responsibility of another international organization in accordance with paragraph 4 if the obligation breached is owed to a group of States or international organizations, including the State or organization that invokes responsibility, and is established for the protection of a collective interest of the group.

2. A State other than an injured State is entitled to invoke the responsibility of an international organization in accordance with paragraph 4 if the obligation breached is owed to the international community as a whole.

3. An international organization that is not an injured international organization is entitled to invoke the responsibility of another international organization in accordance with paragraph 4 if the obligation breached is owed to the international community as a whole and safeguarding the interest of the international community underlying the obligation breached is included among the functions of the international organization invoking responsibility.

4. A State or an international organization entitled to invoke responsibility under paragraphs 1 to 3 may claim from the responsible international organization:

(*a*) cessation of the internationally wrongful act, and assurances and guarantees of non-repetition in accordance with draft article 33; and

(*b*) performance of the obligation of reparation in accordance with Part Two, in the interest of the injured State or international organization or of the beneficiaries of the obligation breached.

5. The requirements for the invocation of responsibility by an injured State or international organization under draft articles 47; 48, paragraph 2; and 49 apply to an invocation of responsibility by a State or international organization entitled to do so under paragraphs 1 to 4.

World Health Organization

Similar practical and conceptual difficulties characterize in our view also the applicability of draft article 52 to international organizations. For example, it is difficult to identify obligations owed indistinctly to a group of international organizations in view of their status as international entities with limited and different functions, besides cases in which international organizations are parties to the same treaty, as well as the unlikely case of a breach by an international organization of a peremptory norm of such a character as to be generally applicable to any subject of international law. It is therefore quite possible that, as in this case, provisions taken from the context of the responsibility of States which seem on their face easily transposable to international organizations may turn out to be of questionable applicability or of marginal practical relevance.

I. Countermeasures

United Nations Educational, Scientific and Cultural Organization

1. UNESCO does not have any objection to the inclusion of draft articles on countermeasures. UNESCO will, however, respond to various issues raised in the report of the International Law Commission at its sixtieth session.

2. Draft article 52 on object and limits of countermeasures[1] raises no particular objection for UNESCO. In particular, UNESCO agrees with the terms "only if this is not inconsistent with the rules of the … organization", used in draft article 52, paragraphs 4 and 5. UNESCO supports not only the reference to the rules of the organization but also, considering that often countermeasures are not specifically provided for by the rules of international organizations, the possibility for an injured member of an international organization to resort to countermeasures which are not explicitly allowed by the rules of the organization.

3. As regards draft article 55, paragraph 3 (*b*),[2] concerning conditions relating to resort to countermeasures, UNESCO would agree with the proposals made to extend the exception to disputes pending before a body other than a court or a tribunal provided it has the capacity to make decisions binding on the parties.

4. As regards draft article 57,[3] UNESCO agrees with the proposals to redraft this article and considers that for a matter of clarity the provisions for "lawful measures" and for "countermeasures" should not be dealt with in the same article.

World Health Organization

1. Concerning the delicate topic of countermeasures, the World Health Organization shares the views of those members of the Commission that called for particular caution in introducing draft articles on countermeasures against international organizations. In principle, WHO agrees with the statement by the Special Rapporteur that there is no cogent reason why an international organization that breaches an international obligation should be exempted from countermeasures taken by an injured State or international organization to bring about compliance by the former organization with its obligations. Conversely, it would seem illogical to deprive an international organization injured by a breach of an international obligation by another international organization of the possibility of taking retaliatory measures to induce the latter organization to comply with its obligations.

2. Having said that, it should be noted that for international organizations of quasi-universal membership such as those of the United Nations system, the possibility for their respective member States to take countermeasures against them would either be severely limited by the operation of the rules of those organizations, rendering it largely virtual, or would be subject to a *lex specialis*—thus outside of the scope of the draft articles—to the extent that the rules of the organization concerned do not prevent the adoption of countermeasures by its member States.

3. With regard to the actual countermeasures that international organizations could adopt against other organizations, WHO shares the views of those members of the Commission who would limit them to withholding the performance of contractual obligations under existing treaty relationships. These would often consist of obligations to cooperate with the responsible organizations in various respects, either by implementing joint activities, financing certain activities of the other organizations, providing data and information or consulting on matters of common interest. At the same time, while such measures are theoretically possible, the fact that those obligations are provided not for the benefit of the responsible organizations but rather for the discharge by both organizations of their respective constitutional functions for the benefit of their member States or their populations, should be taken into account. It would be rather difficult for an international organization to suspend its compliance with such obligations in view of their public and functional nature.

[1] For the text of draft article 52 as proposed by the Special Rapporteur, see *Yearbook … 2008*, vol. II (Part Two), para. 141, footnote 481.

[2] *Ibid.*, footnote 484, for the text of draft article 55 as proposed by the Special Rapporteur.

[3] *Ibid.*, para. 142, footnote 486, for the text of draft article 57 as proposed by the Special Rapporteur.

4. Finally, any provision on countermeasures that may be included in the draft articles should minimize the possibility of abuse, considering in particular the different position of States and international organizations from both a legal and a political point of view. It would arguably be easier in practice for States, whether members or not of an international organization, to impose measures presented as countermeasures against it than the reverse. An example could be the refusal of a donor Government to continue financing certain activities of an international organization under a donation or project agreement in response to the non-compliance by the organization of some of its obligations under the same agreement. That measure could have severe repercussions on the possibility for the organization to continue to carry out activities which are of a public nature and in the public interest. It would be legally and practically more difficult for an organization to envisage retaliation against a donor Government which is breaching its obligations to fund certain activities beyond the sanction provided by the constitution of several international organizations, consisting of the loss of the right to vote in case of non-payment of assessed contribution. The suspension by the organization concerned of its activities would normally be the result of the lack of financial resources; should it be taken as a countermeasure, it would probably be ineffective to induce the donor to honour its obligations and would negatively affect the interests of the beneficiaries of those activities.

SHARED NATURAL RESOURCES

[Agenda item 5]

DOCUMENT A/CN.4/608

Paper on oil and gas prepared by Mr. Chusei Yamada, Special Rapporteur on shared natural resources

[*Original: English*]
[*18 February 2009*]

1. The present informal paper has been prepared for the members of the Working Group on Shared Natural Resources, which might be established at the sixty-first session of the International Law Commission in 2009 to consider the question of oil and natural gas within the wider topic of shared natural resources.

2. The Commission began its work on shared natural resources in 2002. It was generally understood that the topic covered three kinds of natural resources: groundwaters, oil and natural gas, as indicated in the syllabus prepared by Robert Rosenstock.[1] The Commission adopted a step-by-step approach, beginning with groundwaters. It completed the second reading of the draft articles on the law of transboundary aquifers in 2008 and transmitted them to the General Assembly with the recommendation that the Assembly: (*a*) take note of the draft articles in a resolution and annex them to the resolution; (*b*) recommend to States to make appropriate bilateral or regional arrangements for the proper management of their transboundary aquifers on the basis of the principles enunciated in the articles; and (*c*) consider at a later stage the elaboration of a convention on the basis of the articles.[2] By adopting its resolution 63/124 of 11 December 2008, the General Assembly acted along the lines of the Commission's recommendation.[3]

3. During the Commission's work on transboundary aquifers, questions on the possible work on oil and natural gas and its relevance to the work on groundwater were often raised, not only in the Commission, but also in the Sixth Committee of the General Assembly. In 2007, while the Commission was awaiting comments and observations from States on its first-reading draft articles on the law of transboundary aquifers, which had been adopted in 2006, it received the fourth report of the Special Rapporteur.[4] The report covered the questions of oil and natural gas, including a preliminary study of oil and natural gas resources, their similarities and dissimilarities with groundwaters, management practice and environmental implications. Following the plenary debate, the Working Group on Shared Natural Resources, chaired by Enrique Candioti, was established to consider various issues raised in the report.

4. On the basis of considerations by the Working Group,[5] the Commission decided to proceed to the second reading of the law on transboundary aquifers independently of any possible work on oil and natural gas, it being understood that the latter two resources would be considered together, and also to circulate a questionnaire on oil and natural gas to States. Such a questionnaire would, *inter alia*, seek to determine whether there were any agreements, arrangements or practice regarding the exploration and exploitation of transboundary oil and natural gas resources or for any other cooperation for such resources, including maritime boundary delimitation agreements, as well as unitization and joint development agreements or other arrangements.

5. Pursuant to the decision of the Commission, the secretariat of the Commission circulated the following questionnaire, to which 35 States have so far responded:[6]

> 1. Do you have any agreement(s), arrangement(s) or practice with your neighbouring State(s) regarding the exploration and exploitation of transboundary oil and gas resources or for any other cooperation for such oil and gas?

[1] *Yearbook ... 2000*, vol. II (Part Two), p. 141, annex.

[2] *Yearbook ... 2008*, vol. II (Part Two), para. 49.

[3] In resolution 63/124 the General Assembly:

"4. *Takes note* of the draft articles on the law of transboundary aquifers, presented by the Commission, the text of which is annexed to the present resolution, and commends them to the attention of Governments without prejudice to the question of their future adoption or other appropriate action;

"5. *Encourages* the States concerned to make appropriate bilateral or regional arrangements for the proper management of their transboundary aquifers, taking into account the provisions of these draft articles;

"6. *Decides* to include in the provisional agenda of its sixty-sixth session an item entitled "The law of transboundary aquifers" with a view to examining, *inter alia*, the question of the form that might be given to the draft articles."

[4] *Yearbook ... 2007*, vol. II (Part One), document A/CN.4/580.

[5] See A/CN.4/L.717 (mimeographed). See also *Yearbook ... 2007*, vol. II (Part Two), paras. 178–183.

[6] Algeria, Argentina, Australia, Austria, the Bahamas, Bosnia and Herzegovina, Canada, Chile, Cuba, Cyprus, the Czech Republic, Guyana, Hungary, Iraq, Ireland, Jamaica, Kuwait, Lebanon, Mali, Mauritius, Myanmar, the Netherlands, Norway, Oman, Portugal, the Republic of Korea, Saint Vincent and the Grenadines, Slovakia, Tajikistan, Thailand, Tunisia, Turkey, the United Kingdom of Great Britain and Northern Ireland, the United States of America and Uruguay (see document A/CN.4/607 and Add.1 in the present volume).

2. Are there any joint bodies, mechanisms or partnerships (public or private) involving exploration, exploitation or management of transboundary oil or gas?

3. If the answer to question 1 is yes, please answer the following questions on the content of agreements or arrangements and regarding the practice:

(*a*) Are there any specific principles, arrangements or understandings regarding allocation or appropriation of oil and gas, or other forms of cooperation? Please provide a description of the principles, provisions, arrangements or understandings;

(*b*) Are there any arrangements or understandings or is there any practice regarding prevention and control of pollution or regarding other environmental concerns, including mitigation of accidents? Please provide further description.

4. Please provide any further comments or information, including legislation, judicial decisions, which you consider to be relevant or useful to the Commission in the consideration of issues regarding oil and gas.

5. Are there any aspects in this area that may benefit from further elaboration in the context of the Commission's work? Please indicate those aspects.

6. Although it will be necessary to encourage the further submission of responses to the questionnaire from the States concerned, the replies so far received are useful in identifying the problems of oil and natural gas. There exist many bilateral agreements and arrangements between the States concerned and between their national oil and gas companies. The texts of these agreements should be carefully analysed. They generally provide for cooperation, exchange of information, effective exploitation, equitable sharing, protection of environment, etc. There also exist joint mechanisms but they are as yet rather informal and embryonic. Unlike the case of transboundary aquifers, oil and natural gas reserves are often located on the continental shelf. In such situations, the maritime boundary delimitation is the prerequisite for determining the existence of transboundary resources. However, most of the coastal States have the firm position that that is a matter to be decided solely by those States concerned. Some States also hold that the question of oil and natural gas is bilateral, highly technical and politically sensitive and that it must be dealt with case by case. Accordingly they urge the Commission to take a cautious approach.

7. States made oral comments on the possible work by the Commission on oil and natural gas during the debate in the Sixth Committee in 2007 and 2008. One State consistently held that the work on groundwater and oil and natural gas must be conducted together.[7] Some other States supported the Commission's approach of treating groundwater independently of oil and natural gas, but their positions on the possible work on oil and natural gas were diverse. Some States doubted the need for any universal rules on oil and natural gas and advised the Commission not to proceed with the codification work,[8] pointing out mainly that the question of oil and natural gas is bilateral, highly technical and politically sensitive and that it must be dealt with on a case-by-case basis, while also stressing the need to avoid any encroachment into questions of maritime delimitation. Some other States favoured the Commission proceeding with the work.[9] Yet others were not decided but favoured either further study or a cautious approach.[10] Some States also stressed the importance of the concept of unitization, which implies the consideration of the transboundary oil and natural gas field as one unit with a single operator but where earnings and costs are shared.[11]

8. In the absence of consensus among States on the question of possible work on oil and natural gas, it is the view of the Special Rapporteur that the Commission must make further studies before making any definitive decision whether to proceed with the codification process of oil and natural gas. It is advisable that the Commission establish a programme of work for the studies for the next several years. The Commission would need further inputs from States. The Commission must also consider ways and means to seek assistance from the relevant international organizations, such as the Economic Commission for Europe, and from scientific, technical, administrative, commercial and legal experts.

---

[7] The Netherlands, *Official Records of the General Assembly, Sixty-second Session, Sixth Committee*, 24th meeting (A/C.6/62/SR.24) and *ibid., Sixty-third Session, Sixth Committee*, 19th meeting (A/C.6/63/SR.19).

[8] Sweden, on behalf of the Nordic countries, *ibid., Sixty-second Session, Sixth Committee*, 22nd meeting (A/C.6/62/SR.22) and *ibid., Sixty-third Session, Sixth Committee*, 16th meeting (A/C.6/63/SR.16); United Kingdom, *ibid.*; Australia, *ibid.*, 17th meeting (A/C.6/63/SR.17); Canada, *ibid.*; Greece, *ibid.*; United States of America, *ibid., Sixty-second Session, Sixth Committee*, 22nd meeting (A/C.6/62/SR.22) and *ibid., Sixty-third Session, Sixth Committee*, 18th meeting (A/C.6/63/SR.18); Islamic Republic of Iran, *ibid., Sixty-second Session, Sixth Committee*, 25th meeting (A/C.6/62/SR.25).

[9] Poland, *ibid., Sixty-third Session, Sixth Committee*, 17th meeting (A/C.6/63/SR.17); Uruguay, *ibid.*, 18th meeting (A/C.6/63/SR.18); Democratic Republic of the Congo, *ibid., Sixty-second Session, Sixth Committee*, 24th meeting (A/C.6/62/SR.24).

[10] China, *ibid., Sixty-second Session, Sixth Committee*, 22nd meeting (A/C.6/62/SR.22); Republic of Korea, *ibid., Sixty-third Session, Sixth Committee*, 16th meeting (A/C.6/63/SR.16); Germany, *ibid.*; Mexico, *ibid.*, 17th meeting (A/C.6/63/SR.17); Russian Federation, *ibid.*, 18th meeting (A/C.6/63/SR.18); Lebanon, *ibid.*; Italy, *ibid., Sixty-second Session, Sixth Committee*, 22nd meeting (A/C.6/62/SR.22); Romania, *ibid.*, 24th meeting (A/C.6/62/SR.24); Bolivarian Republic of Venezuela, *ibid.*, 25th meeting (A/C.6/62/SR.25); New Zealand, *ibid.*

[11] Norway, on behalf of the Nordic countries, *ibid., Sixty-third Session, Sixth Committee*, 16th meeting (A/C.6/63/SR.16); Mexico, *ibid.*, 17th meeting (A/C.6/63/SR.17); Indonesia *ibid., Sixty-second Session, Sixth Committee*, 25th meeting (A/C.6/62/SR.25).

SHARED NATURAL RESOURCES

[Agenda item 5]

DOCUMENT A/CN.4/607* and Add.1

Comments and observations received from Governments

[Original: English]
[29 January and 17 June 2009]

CONTENTS

Multilateral instruments cited in the present report

	Source
Convention on the Continental Shelf (Geneva, 29 April 1958)	United Nations, *Treaty Series*, vol. 499, No. 7302, p. 311.
Convention for the Protection of the Mediterranean Sea against Pollution (Barcelona, 16 February 1976)	*Ibid.*, vol. 1102, No. 16908, p. 27.
Convention on Wetlands of International Importance especially as Waterfowl Habitat (Ramsar, 2 February 1971)	*Ibid.*, vol. 996, No. 14583, p. 245.
International Convention for the prevention of pollution from ships, 1973 (MARPOL Convention) (London, 2 November 1973)	*Ibid.*, vol. 1340, No. 22484, p. 184.
Protocol of 1978 relating to the International Convention for the prevention of pollution from ships, 1973 (London, 17 February 1978)	*Ibid.*, vol. 1340, No. 22484, p. 61.
Convention on the Conservation of Migratory Species of Wild Animals (Bonn, 23 June 1979)	*Ibid.*, vol. 1651, No. 28395, p. 333.
United Nations Convention on the Law of the Sea (Montego Bay, 10 December 1982)	*Ibid.*, vol. 1833, No. 31363, p. 396.
Vienna Convention for the Protection of the Ozone Layer (Vienna, 22 March 1985)	*Ibid.*, vol. 1513, No. 26164, p. 293.
Montreal Protocol on Substances that Deplete the Ozone Layer (Montreal, 16 September 1987)	*Ibid.*, vol. 1522, No. 26369, p. 28.
Convention on Environmental Impact Assessment in a Transboundary Context (Espoo, 25 February 1991)	*Ibid.*, vol. 1989, No. 34028, p. 309.

* Incorporating A/CN.4/607/Corr.1.

	Source
United Nations Framework Convention on Climate Change (New York, 9 May 1992)	*Ibid.*, vol. 1771, No. 30822, p. 107.
Kyoto Protocol to the United Nations Framework Convention on Climate Change (Kyoto, 11 December 1997)	*Ibid.*, vol. 2303, No. 30822, p. 162.
Convention on Biological Diversity (Rio de Janeiro, 5 June 1992)	*Ibid.*, vol. 1760, No. 30619, p. 79.
Convention for the Protection of the Marine Environment of the North-East Atlantic (Paris, 22 September 1992)	*Ibid.*, vol. 2354, No. 42279, p. 67.
Stockholm Convention on Persistent Organic Pollutants (Stockholm, 22 May 2001)	*Ibid.*, vol. 2256, No. 40214, p. 119.

Introduction

1. At its fifty-ninth session, in 2007, the International Law Commission requested the Secretariat to circulate to Governments a questionnaire, prepared by the Working Group on Shared Natural Resources, seeking information on State practice, in particular treaties or other arrangements existing regarding oil and gas.[1] In a circular note dated 17 October 2007, the Secretariat transmitted the questionnaire to Governments.

2. Responses to the questionnaire were received from the following 35 States: Algeria, Argentina, Australia, Austria, the Bahamas, Bosnia and Herzegovina, Canada, Chile, Cuba, Cyprus, the Czech Republic, Guyana, Hungary, Iraq, Ireland, Jamaica, Kuwait, Lebanon, Mali, Mauritius, Myanmar, the Netherlands, Norway, Oman, Portugal, the Republic of Korea, Saint Vincent and the Grenadines, Slovakia, Tajikistan, Thailand, Tunisia, Turkey, the United Kingdom of Great Britain and Northern Ireland, the United States of America and Uruguay. The responses are organized, to the extent possible, on the basis of the questions contained in the questionnaire.

[1] *Yearbook ... 2007*, vol. II (Part Two), p. 56, para. 159.

Comments and observations on the questionnaire on oil and gas received from Governments

A. General comments

1. Canada

1. A number of bilateral maritime delimitation agreements concluded internationally incorporate provisions regarding the possibility of finding a natural resource that straddles across a maritime boundary, as well as a procedure to be followed in the event of such a discovery. The obligations generally focus firstly on advising the other State that a transboundary field has been discovered, and secondly, on the necessity for States to seek to reach an agreement on some form of joint exploitation.

2. For the purposes of the present questionnaire, however, Canada will focus on the *only* agreement that Canada has entered into relating to the exploration and exploitation of transboundary hydrocarbons, entitled the Agreement between the Government of Canada and the Government of the French Republic relating to the Exploration and Exploitation of Transboundary Hydrocarbon Fields (signed in Paris, 17 May 2005). The Agreement governs the apportion of the reserves found in transboundary hydrocarbon fields straddling the maritime boundary between Canada and France.

3. Canada would like to note that providing answers to the Commission should not be interpreted as either agreement or acquiescence by Canada for the Commission to provide a set of draft articles on a subject matter, such as oil and gas, that is essentially bilateral in nature, highly technical, politically sensitive, encompasses diverse regional situations and requires a case-by-case solution.

4. Canada considers that any matters relating to offshore boundary delimitation should not be considered by the Commission.

2. Guyana

1. Exploration for oil and gas in Guyana dates back to early Dutch colonial explorers. The structure of a still-emerging oil and gas sector has its roots in near pre-independence arrangements, which have evolved to what currently prevails. Guyana has an undisputable petroleum discovery in the Takutu Basin of no commercial consequence. There is no oil and gas production from Guyana.

2. The frontiers for oil and gas exploration in Guyana are: (*a*) the extent of Guyana's maritime area, which is part of the regional geological feature referred to as the Guyana-Suriname Basin; (*b*) the extension of the same basin onto the coastal onshore; and (*c*) the section of the Takutu Basin in Rupununi Guyana.

3. The States that share boundaries with Guyana's oil and gas frontiers are: (*a*) in the maritime area: Barbados, the Bolivarian Republic of Venezuela, Suriname, and Trinidad and Tobago; (*b*) in the coastal extension onshore: Suriname and the Bolivarian Republic of Venezuela; and (*c*) in the Takutu Basin, Rupununi District: Brazil.

3. Republic of Korea

1. The Republic of Korea considers that the valuable work on this topic (Shared natural resources) by the International Law Commission represents a timely

contribution to the progress development through codification in this field of law.[1]

2. An important decision is before the Commission as to whether it needs to move beyond transboundary aquifers and then to deal also with other shared natural resources. It is advisable that the Commission exercise caution in this matter. States and industries have immense economic and political stakes in the allocation and regulation of oil and gas resources, and any proposal by the Commission is likely to be highly controversial. States in the international community already have considerable experience and practices in dealing with transboundary oil and gas reservoirs. It is doubtful whether the Commission should go beyond the issue of transboundary aquifers.

3. The Republic of Korea entered "none" on comments and observations on the questionnaire on shared resources.

[1] The reply by the Republic of Korea also included comments on the Commission's draft articles on the law of transboundary aquifers, which have been omitted.

B. Question 1

Do you have any agreement(s), arrangement(s) or practice with your neighbouring State(s) regarding the exploration and exploitation of transboundary oil and gas resources or for any other cooperation for such oil or gas?

Such agreements or arrangements should include, as appropriate, maritime boundary delimitation agreements, as well as unitization and joint development agreements or other arrangements.

Please provide a copy of the agreement(s) or arrangement(s) or describe the practice.

1. Algeria

There are no agreements regarding the exploration and exploitation of transboundary deposits. However, on 29 December 2005 a framework agreement was signed between the Algerian national company Sonatrach and the Libyan national company, the National Oil Corporation, to launch a joint study on the exploitation of the deposits at Alrar in Algeria and Wafa in the Libyan Arab Jamahiriya.

2. Argentina

Agreements in force for the Argentine Republic that relate to oil and gas within the "Shared natural resources" framework include:[1]

(*a*) Supplementary Agreement to the Treaty concerning the Río de la Plata and the Corresponding Maritime Boundary (signed in Montevideo, 19 November 1973, United Nations, *Treaty Series*, vol. 295, No. 21424, p. 293) regarding the line marking the maritime lateral limit, the common fishing zone and the common area within which the discharge of hydrocarbons and other polluting actions are prohibited, signed: Montevideo, 15 July 1974; entry into force: 15 July 1974;

[1] The texts of the agreements, in Spanish, are available for consultation at the Codification Division of the Office of Legal Affairs.

(*b*) Cooperation Agreement between the Argentine Republic and the Eastern Republic of Uruguay to prevent and combat incidents of contamination of the aquatic environment by hydrocarbons and other harmful substances, signed: Buenos Aires, 16 September 1987; enactment: Act No. 23,829; entry into force: 29 October 1993;

(*c*) Specific Additional Protocol on the protection of the Antarctic environment between the Argentine Republic and the Republic of Chile, signed: Buenos Aires, 2 August 1991; entry into force: 17 November 1992;

(*d*) Treaty between the Argentine Republic and the Republic of Bolivia on the environment, signed: Buenos Aires, 17 March 1994; enactment: Act No. 24,774; entry into force: 1 June 1997;

(*e*) Agreement between the Argentine Republic and the Federative Republic of Brazil on cooperation in environmental matters (with Annex A), signed: Buenos Aires, 9 April 1996; enactment: Act 24,930; entry into force: 18 March 1998;

(*f*) Additional Protocol to the Treaty on the Environment between the Government of the Argentine Republic and the Government of the Republic of Bolivia, signed: Tarija, 22 July 2004; entry into force: 22 July 2004;

(*g*) Memorandum of Understanding between the Argentine Republic, the Republic of Bolivia and the Eastern Republic of Uruguay on energy and economic integration, signed: Brasilia, 20 August 2004; entry into force: 20 August 2004;

(*h*) Additional Protocol to the Agreement of Partial Scope on energy integration between Argentina and Bolivia for the supply of natural gas from the Republic of Bolivia to the north-east Argentina gas pipeline, signed: Sucre, 14 October 2004; entry into force: 27 May 2005;

(*i*) Framework Agreement between the Argentine Republic and the Republic of Bolivia for the sale of natural gas and the realization of energy integration projects, signed: Buenos Aires, 29 June 2006; entry into force: 29 June 2006 (United Nations, *Treaty Series*, vol. 2446, No. 44022, p. 129);

(*j*) Agreement for work to be started on the north-east Argentina gas pipeline and natural gas liquids plant (Republic of Bolivia), signed: Santa Cruz de la Sierra, 26 March 2007;

(*k*) Framework Agreement between the Argentine Republic and the Republic of Bolivia on energy integration, signed: Tarija, 10 August 2007;

(*l*) Financing Agreement between the Argentine Republic and the Republic of Bolivia: Pre-investment and construction studies for the natural gas liquids plant and associated distribution and marketing system, signed: Tarija, 10 August 2007; entry into force: 10 August 2007;

(*m*) Organization of South American Gas Producing and Exporting Countries (OPPEGASUR): Tarija agreement on gas integration between the Bolivarian Republic of Venezuela, the Argentine Republic and the Republic of Bolivia, within the framework of OPPEGASUR, signed: Tarija, 10 August 2007;

(*n*) Cooperation Agreement between the Eastern Republic of Uruguay and the Argentine Republic on energy-related matters, signed: Buenos Aires, 5 July 2007.

3. Australia

1. Australia is an island State with a lengthy coastline. It has a number of bilateral maritime delimitations with its neighbouring States. Several of these delimitation treaties include a provision that deals with the possibility of finding a natural resource that straddles across a boundary. The provisions are all similar to the following:

> If any single accumulation of petroleum, whether in a gaseous, liquid or solid state, or if any other mineral deposit beneath the seabed, extends across the lines described in [the] Treaty, and the part of such accumulation or deposit that is situated on one side of the line is recoverable wholly or in part from the other side of the line, the two Parties will seek to reach agreement on the manner in which the accumulation or deposit shall be most effectively exploited and on the equitable sharing of the benefits arising from such exploitation.

2. The bilateral treaties between Australia and its neighbours and their relevant provisions include the following (together with links to websites where the treaties can be found online):

(*a*) Treaty between the Government of Australia and the Government of New Zealand establishing Certain Exclusive Economic Zone Boundaries and Continental Shelf Boundaries (art. 4), done at Adelaide on 25 July 2004 (entry into force: 25 January 2006), United Nations, *Treaty Series*, vol. 2441, No. 43985, p. 235 (also available from www.austlii.edu.au/au/other/dfat/treaties/2006/4.html);

(*b*) Agreement between the Government of the Commonwealth of Australia and the Government of the Republic of Indonesia establishing Certain Seabed Boundaries (art. 7), done at Canberra on 18 May 1971 (entry into force: 8 November 1973), *ibid.*, vol. 974, No. 14122 (also available from www.austlii.edu.au/au/other/dfat/treaties/1973/31.html);

(*c*) Agreement between the Government of the Commonwealth of Australia and the Government of the Republic of Indonesia establishing Certain Seabed Boundaries in the Area of the Timor and Arafura Seas, supplementary to the Agreement of 18 May 1971 (art. 7), done at Jakarta on 9 October 1972 (entry into force: 8 November 1973), *ibid.*, vol. 974, No. 14123 (also available from www.austlii.edu.au/au/other/dfat/treaties/1973/32.html);

(*d*) Treaty between Australia and the Independent State of Papua New Guinea concerning Sovereignty and Maritime Boundaries in the area between the two Countries, including the area known as Torres Strait, and Related Matters (art. 6), done at Sydney on 18 November 1978 (entry into force: 15 February 1985) ("Torres Strait Treaty"), *ibid.*, vol. 1429, No. 24238 (also available from www.austlii.edu.au/au/other/dfat/treaties/1985/4.html);

(*e*) Agreement between the Government of Australia and the Government of Solomon Islands establishing Certain Sea and Seabed Boundaries (art. 2), done at Honiara on 13 September 1988 (entry into force: 14 April 1989), *ibid.*, vol. 1536, No. 26661 (also available from www.austlii.edu.au/au/other/dfat/treaties/1989/12.html);

(*f*) Treaty between the Government of Australia and the Government of the Republic of Indonesia establishing an Exclusive Economic Zone Boundary and Certain Seabed Boundaries (art. 9), done at Perth on 14 March 1997 (not yet in force) ("Perth Treaty"), ILM, vol. 36, p. 1053 (also available from www.austlii.edu.au/au/other/dfat/treaties/notinforce/1997/4.html).

3. There are currently no known offshore oil and gas resources that exist across the boundaries established by the treaties mentioned above.

4. Australia and Timor-Leste have not established permanent maritime boundaries but have a number of interim treaties in force that provide for practical maritime arrangements between them. The Timor Sea Treaty, done at Dili on 20 May 2002 (entry into force: 2 April 2003), United Nations, *Treaty Series*, vol. 2258, No. 40222, p. 3, establishes an area of joint petroleum development in the Timor Sea. The Treaty provides that Australia and Timor-Leste are to jointly control, manage and facilitate the exploration, development and exploitation of the petroleum resources of the joint area for the benefit of the peoples of Australia and Timor-Leste. The Treaty can be found at: www.austlii.edu.au/au/other/dfat/treaties/2003/13.html.

5. Australia and Timor-Leste have a unitization agreement between them that applies to the "Greater Sunrise" field that lies in both the joint development area and an area in which Australia regulates activities in relation to the resources of the seabed and subsoil: Agreement between the Government of Australia and the Government of the Democratic Republic of Timor-Leste relating to the Unitisation of the Sunrise and Troubador Fields, done at Dili on 6 March 2003 (entry into force: 23 February 2007). The Agreement can be found at: www.austlii.edu.au/au/other/dfat/treaties/2007/11.html.

6. Further information on the maritime arrangements between Australia and Timor-Leste can be found at: www.dfat.gov.au/geo/timor-leste/fs_maritime_arrangements.html.

4. Austria

1. Austria has concluded only one agreement on the exploration of transboundary oil and gas resources: the Agreement between the Austrian Federal Government and the Government of Czechoslovakia on the exploitation of the common oil and gas deposits (Prague, 23 January 1960), United Nations, *Treaty Series*, vol. 495, No. 7242, p. 134, now being in force between Austria and the Czech Republic, and Austria and the Slovak Republic.

2. The cooperation with the Czech Republic has already come to an end, since the oil and gas resources have already been fully exploited. The cooperation with the Slovak Republic will come to an end within the next few years, since these resources are about to be fully exploited.

5. Bahamas

Presently the Bahamas does not have any such agreements or arrangements with neighbouring States, but it realizes the true importance of having such legally binding treaties. The Bahamas commenced work on its archipelagic baseline with the use of United Nations-approved software (CARISLOTS), which would produce the median line between the Bahamas and its neighbouring States. The Government's intention is to submit these baseline coordinates to the United Nations by April 2008.

6. Bosnia and Herzegovina

Bosnia and Herzegovina responded "No". At the moment there is no such agreement or arrangement between Bosnia and Herzegovina and the neighbouring States.

7. Canada

1. Pursuant to the decision of the Arbitral Tribunal in the case concerning the *Delimitation of Maritime Areas between Canada and the French Republic of June 10, 1992*, Court of Arbitration, UNRIAA, vol. XXI, p. 265, Saint-Pierre-et-Miquelon only has jurisdiction over a narrow strip of maritime area that is 10 nautical miles in width and extends 200 nautical miles south of the islands, which is completely enclosed by Canada's exclusive economic zone.

2. As the 1992 Arbitral Tribunal definitively decided the permanent boundary between Canada and France (for Saint-Pierre-et-Miquelon) for all purposes, a need was felt for an agreement triggered by the possibility of petroleum fields straddling the Canadian-French boundary. Canada approached France in 1998 to suggest that both sides enter into a treaty to manage possible transboundary fields. Finally, in 2005, Canada and France signed an agreement to provide a management regime for hydrocarbon exploration and exploitation offshore Newfoundland, Nova Scotia and Collectivité de Saint-Pierre-et-Miquelon. The Agreement between the Government of Canada and the Government of the French Republic relating to the Exploration and Exploitation of Transboundary Hydrocarbon Fields, containing 21 articles and 6 annexes, recognizes the need for a common approach to oil and gas management to ensure the conservation and management of hydrocarbon resources that straddle the maritime boundary, to apportion between the two countries the reserves found in transboundary fields and to promote safety and the protection of the environment.

3. The Agreement acknowledges that nothing is to prejudice or restrict the sovereignty or jurisdiction of either party over their respective internal waters and territorial seas, or the exercise of sovereign rights, in accordance with international law, over their respective exclusive economic zones.

4. The Agreement was inspired by the 1976 Markham Agreement, United Nations, *Treaty Series*, vol. 1098, No. 16878, p. 4, which was used as a "framework" arrangement adapted to Canadian and French respective circumstances.

5. The Agreement has yet to enter into force, and Canada would therefore refrain from disclosing it at this time. That said, the relevant paragraphs will provide a general outline of the Agreement.

8. Chile

1. The only international agreement concluded by the Republic of Chile in relation to this subject area is the Treaty with the Argentine Republic on Mining Integration and Complementarity, signed on 29 December 1997 and currently in force.[1]

2. While the Treaty was not intended to address integration or complementarity in relation to hydrocarbons, its content does not exclude that possibility. In any event, it should be noted that the treatment of hydrocarbons exploitation in the domestic legislation of Chile differs from the regime governing metallic and some non-metallic minerals. Whereas hydrocarbons are subject to State concessions or special operating contracts, minerals can be subject to mining concessions under the Chilean Mining Code.

3. In addition, it should be noted that the scope of application of the above-mentioned Treaty is geographically limited to the area defined by the set of coordinates listed in annex I to the Treaty and represented on the reference map contained in annex II. This area excludes any and all maritime areas and island territories, as well as the coastline as defined in each State party's domestic legislation.

[1] The text of the treaty, in Spanish, is available for consultation at the Codification Division of the Office of Legal Affairs.

9. Cuba

1. Cuba has no agreements, arrangements or practices with neighbouring States related to prospecting for or exploitation of transboundary oil and gas resources, or to their distribution, because to date there is no evidence of any transboundary oil and gas resources shared with Haiti, Jamaica, Mexico or the United States of America.

2. There are bilateral maritime delimitation agreements between Cuba and Haiti, Jamaica, Mexico and the United States, but they do not refer to transboundary oil and gas resources or any other kind of cooperation regarding such resources.

10. Cyprus

1. Cyprus has signed the following agreements:

(*a*) Agreement between the Republic of Cyprus and the Arab Republic of Egypt on the Delimitation of the Exclusive Economic Zone (ratified);

(*b*) Agreement between the Republic of Cyprus and the Republic of Lebanon on the Delimitation of the Exclusive Economic Zone (not yet ratified);

(*c*) Framework Agreement between the Republic of Cyprus and the Arab Republic of Egypt concerning the Development of Cross-Median Line Hydrocarbon Resources (not yet ratified).

2. A copy of the Agreement between the Republic of Cyprus and the Arab Republic of Egypt on the Delimitation of the Exclusive Economic Zone is provided, as it has been ratified by the House of Representatives.[1] Copies of the other two agreements are not provided as they have not yet been ratified by the House of Representatives (they are in the process of ratification).

[1] Text available for consultation at the Codification Division of the Office of Legal Affairs.

11. Czech Republic

1. An Agreement between the Government of the Czechoslovak Republic and the Austrian Federal Government on the Exploitation of Shared Natural Gas and Oil Deposits, negotiated in 1960, United Nations, *Treaty Series*, vol. 495, No. 7242, p. 125, specified the international legal and technical parameters for the exploitation of deposits of these raw materials. The shared deposits concerned were at Vysoká pri Morave (now in the territory of Slovakia), Zwerndorf (in the territory of Austria), and in Nový Přerov (now in the territory of the Czech Republic) and Altprerau (in the territory of Austria).

2. After its establishment in 1993, the Czech Republic succeeded to the 1960 Agreement between the Government of the Czechoslovak Republic and the Austrian Federal Government on the Exploitation of Shared Natural Gas and Oil Deposits.

12. Guyana

1. The Guyana Geology and Mines Commission, as the Government agency responsible for the regulation of petroleum operations, is unaware of any Government agreements or practice with neighbouring States regarding oil and gas exploration and exploitation of transboundary oil and gas resources. The Commission for and/or on behalf of the Government of Guyana has not entered into agreements with sister agencies of neighbouring States or companies operating under the jurisdiction of neighbouring States.

2. The Commission is aware that, within the purview of the Ministry of Foreign Affairs, there is an initiative for cooperation between Suriname and Guyana, which includes technical cooperation in the petroleum sector. The Petroleum Division of the Commission and Staatsolie of Suriname have visited each other and Petroleum Division staff have had exchanges of a technical nature for capacity-building of skills. No understanding is in place to deal with possible transboundary oil and gas resources, such as unitization and joint development arrangements. Technical cooperation in the petroleum sector ceased following the maritime dispute between Guyana and Suriname, and has not been revived since.

13. Iraq

Iraq has several oil fields shared with its neighbouring States, some of which are in production and some of which are partially non-producing. Shared hydrocarbons with the Islamic Republic of Iran, Kuwait, Saudi Arabia and the Syrian Arab Republic also appear to exist. Nevertheless, Iraq has not concluded any agreement regarding the exploration and exploitation of the shared oil fields.

14. Ireland

1. Ireland responded "Yes"—article 3 of the Agreement between the Government of Ireland and the Government of the United Kingdom concerning the Delimitation of Areas of the Continental Shelf between the Two Countries, United Nations, *Treaty Series*, vol. 1564, No. 27204, p. 217, signed at Dublin on 7 November 1988, and entered into force on 11 January 1990, specifically deals with cross-boundary fields.

2. This Agreement was supplemented by the Protocol supplementary to the Agreement between the Government of Ireland and the Government of the United Kingdom concerning the Delimitation of Areas of the Continental Shelf between the Two Countries of 7 November 1988, done at Dublin on 8 December 1992, United Nations, *Treaty Series*, vol. 1745, No. 27204, p. 473. The Agreement referred to above, as supplemented, is a Maritime Boundary Delimitation Agreement. No unitization or joint development agreements have been necessary to date. Drilling in the Irish sector is not permitted within 125m of any boundary line.

3. An oil and gas discovery (named Dragon) in the St. George's Channel area was for a time a candidate for development, and part of the structural closure was mapped as crossing the agreed continental shelf boundary between Ireland and the United Kingdom. Preliminary discussions were held with counterparts in the United Kingdom prior to appraisal drilling but since the appraisal drilling was not successful no further discussions took place and Ireland understands there are currently no plans for further drilling or development.

15. Jamaica

1. The Maritime Delimitation Treaty between the Government of Jamaica and the Government of Colombia, signed on 12 November 1993, United Nations, *Treaty Series*, vol. 1776, No. 30943, p. 18, provides, *inter alia*, for the exploitation, management and conservation of the maritime areas between the two countries. Pursuant to article 3 of the Treaty, the parties established a "joint regime area", pending the determination of their jurisdictional limits in the area designated in that article. Under article 3, the joint regime area is designated as a zone of joint management, control, exploration and exploitation of the living and non-living resources.

2. In the joint regime area, either party may, *inter alia*, carry out activities for the exploration and exploitation of the natural resources, whether living or non-living, and other activities for the economic exploitation and exploration of the joint regime area.

3. Under the Treaty, activities relating to exploration and exploitation of non-living resources must be carried out on a joint basis agreed by both parties.

16. Kuwait

1. *Wafra Joint Operations*. There is a divided zone marked between Saudi Arabia and Kuwait where the oil and gas resources are shared 50 per cent by each State.

2. *Khafji Joint Operations.* There are agreements, arrangements and practices with neighbouring States regarding the exploration and exploitation of transboundary oil and gas resources or for any other cooperation in respect of such oil and gas. There is a Joint Petroleum Production Operations Agreement for the shareholders, which lays down the principles and guidelines for the management and operations of the oil and gas fields within the offshore divided zone. This Agreement also stipulates the formation and functioning of two high-level committees, the Joint Executive Committee and the Joint Operating Committee, which are the main authorities for strategic and operating decisions in the offshore divided zone for the exploration and exploitation of transboundary oil and gas resources. The Agreement defines and describes the roles and authority of these Committees.

17. Lebanon

The Government of Lebanon signed an agreement with the Government of Cyprus in 2007 concerning the joint economic border. This agreement has not yet been ratified.

18. Mali

With the exception of the Framework Agreement on Cooperation signed with Mauritania, which covers, among other things, exploration, production, transport, storage and refining activities in the sedimentary basins shared by the two countries (Nara and Taoudéni), no other such agreement or arrangement has been signed or concluded between Mali and its other neighbours. A framework agreement covering only training and exchanges of information and experience has been signed with Senegal.

19. Mauritius

Mauritius responded "No".

20. Myanmar

As Myanmar does not have transboundary oil and gas resources with neighbouring States, presently there are no agreements, arrangements or practices with neighbouring States regarding the exploration and exploitation of transboundary oil and gas resources.

21. Netherlands

The Netherlands has concluded the following bilateral agreements relating to shared natural resources:

(*a*) Supplementary Agreement between the Kingdom of the Netherlands and Federal Republic of Germany of 14 May 1962 to the Treaty of 8 April 1960 concerning arrangements for cooperation in the Ems Estuary (Ems-Dollard Treaty) (United Nations, *Treaty Series*, vol. 509, No. 7404, p. 140);

(*b*) Agreement between the Government of the Kingdom of the Netherlands and the Government of the United Kingdom of Great Britain and Northern Ireland of 6 October 1965 relating to the exploitation of single geological structures extending across the dividing line on the continental shelf under the North Sea (*ibid.*, vol. 595, No. 8615, p. 105);

(*c*) Agreement between the Kingdom of the Netherlands and the United Kingdom of Great Britain and Northern Ireland of 26 May 1992 relating to the exploitation of the Markham Field Reservoirs and the offtake of petroleum therefrom (*ibid.*, vol. 1731, No. 30235, p. 155);

(*d*) Memorandum of Understanding between the Government of the United Kingdom of Great Britain and Northern Ireland and the Kingdom of the Netherlands of 25 July 2007 concerning the Minke Main Development (not published).

22. Norway

Norway has entered into the following agreements:

(*a*) Agreement between Norway and the United Kingdom relating to the exploitation of the Frigg Field Reservoir and the transmission of gas therefrom to the United Kingdom, 10 May 1976 (United Nations, *Treaty Series*, vol. 1098, No. 16878, p. 3);

(*b*) Agreement relating to the amendment of the Agreement between Norway and the United Kingdom relating to the exploitation of the Frigg Field Reservoir and the transmission of gas therefrom to the United Kingdom, 25 August 1998 (*ibid.*, vol. 2210, No. 16878, p. 94);

(*c*) Exchange of notes regarding the amendment of the Agreement between Norway and the United Kingdom relating to the exploitation of the Frigg Field Reservoir and the transmission of gas therefrom to the United Kingdom, 21 June 2001 (United Kingdom, *Treaty Series*, No. 43 (2001), cm 5258);

(*d*) Agreement between Norway and the United Kingdom relating to the exploitation of the Statfjord Field Reservoirs and the offtake of petroleum therefrom, 16 October 1979 (United Nations, *Treaty Series*, vol. 1254, No. 20551, p. 379);

(*e*) Amendments to the Agreement between Norway and the United Kingdom relating to the exploitation of the Statfjord Field Reservoirs and the offtake of petroleum therefrom, 24 March 1995 (*ibid.*, vol. 1914, No. 20551, p. 509);

(*f*) Agreement between Norway and the United Kingdom relating to the exploitation of the Murchison Field Reservoir and the offtake of petroleum therefrom, 16 October 1979 (*ibid.*, vol. 1249, No. 20387, p. 173);

(*g*) Agreement supplementary to the Agreement between Norway and the United Kingdom relating to the exploitation of the Murchison Field Reservoir and the offtake of petroleum therefrom, 22 October 1981 (*ibid.*, vol. 1288, No. 20387, p. 447);

(*h*) Second agreement supplementary to the Agreement between Norway and the United Kingdom relating to the exploitation of the Murchison Field Reservoir and the offtake of petroleum therefrom, 22 June 1983 (*ibid.*, vol. 1352, No. 20387, p. 357);

(*i*) Amendments to the Agreement between Norway and the United Kingdom relating to the exploitation of the Murchison Field Reservoir and the offtake of petroleum therefrom, 9 August 1999 (*ibid.*, vol. 2142, No. 20387, p. 215);

(*j*) Agreement between Norway and the United Kingdom relating to the delimitation of the continental shelf between the two countries, 10 March 1965 (*ibid.*, vol. 551, No. 8043, p. 213);

(*k*) Protocol supplementary to the Agreement between Norway and the United Kingdom relating to the delimitation of the continental shelf between the two countries, 22 December 1978 (*ibid.*, vol. 1202, No. 8043, p. 363);

(*l*) Agreement between Norway and the United Kingdom concerning the Playfair and Boa petroleum fields, 4 October 2004 (*ibid.*, vol. 2309, No. 41167, p. 217);

(*m*) Framework Agreement between Norway and the United Kingdom concerning cross-boundary petroleum cooperation, 4 April 2005 ;

(*n*) Agreement between Norway and Iceland concerning transboundary hydrocarbon deposits, 3 November 2008 (not yet in force as at 17 March 2009);

(*o*) Agreement relating to the delimitation of the continental shelf between Norway and Denmark, signed at Oslo on 8 December 1965 (United Nations, *Treaty Series*, vol. 634, No. 9052, p. 71);

(*p*) Exchange of notes of 24 April 1968 constituting an agreement amending the agreement relating to the delimitation of the continental shelf between Norway and Denmark of 8 December 1965 (*ibid.*, vol. 643, No. 9052, p. 414);

(*q*) Exchange of notes of 4 June 1974 constituting an agreement amending the agreement relating to the delimitation of the continental shelf between Norway and Denmark of 8 December 1965 (*ibid.*, vol. 952, No. 9052, p. 390);

(*r*) Agreement between Norway and Sweden relating to the delimitation of the continental shelf, 24 July 1968 (*ibid.*, vol. 968, No. 14015, p. 235);

(*s*) Agreement between Norway and Denmark concerning the delimitation of the continental shelf in the area between Norway and the Faroe Islands and concerning the boundary between the fishery zone near the Faroe Islands and Norwegian Economic Zone, 15 June 1979 (*ibid.*, vol. 1211, No. 19512, p. 163);

(*t*) Agreement between Norway and Denmark concerning the delimitation of the continental shelf in the area between Jan Mayen and Greenland and concerning the boundary between the fishery zones in the area, 18 December 1995 (*ibid.*, vol. 1903, No. 32441, p. 171);

(*u*) Additional Protocol to the agreement of 18 December 1995 between Norway and Denmark concerning the delimitation of the continental shelf in the area between Jan Mayen and Greenland and the boundary between the fishery zones in the area, 11 November 1997 (*ibid.*, vol. 2100, No. 32441, p. 180);

(*v*) Agreement between Norway on the one hand, and Denmark together with the Home Rule Government of Greenland on the other hand, concerning the delimitation of the continental shelf and the fisheries zones in the area between Greenland and Svalbard, 20 February 2006 (*ibid.*, vol. 2378, No. 42887, p. 21);

(*w*) Agreement between the Russian Federation and the Kingdom of Norway on the maritime delimitation in the Varangerfjord area, 11 July 2007 (*ibid.*, vol. 2526, No. 45114, p. 33).

23. Oman

1. Oman responded "Yes". There are arrangements regarding oil, gas and minerals between the Government of the Sultanate of Oman, represented by the Ministry of Oil and Gas, and some neighbouring States, such as the United Arab Emirates, Yemen and the Islamic Republic of Iran. However, no agreements have yet been signed regarding the joint utilization or development of any shared fields.

2. There are maritime boundary delimitation agreements, but such agreements are within the purview of the Ministry of the Interior.

24. Portugal

Portugal responded "No".

25. Saint Vincent and the Grenadines

Saint Vincent and the Grenadines responded "Nil" with respect to oil exploitation.

26. Slovakia

Slovakia has concluded two agreements regarding the exploration and the exploitation of transboundary resources:

(*a*) Agreement concerning the principles of geological co-operation between the Czechoslovak Republic and the Republic of Austria (with exchange of notes) of 23 January 1960, United Nations, *Treaty Series*, vol. 495, No. 7241, p. 99. Slovakia is a successor State in respect of this agreement, which determines the exchange of geological records and their common review as well as the coordination of common geological exploration in the border areas;

(*b*) Agreement concerning the working of common deposits of natural gas and petroleum between the Czechoslovak Socialist Republic and the Republic of Austria, signed in 1960, United Nations, *Treaty Series*, vol. 495, No. 7242, p. 125 (Slovakia is a successor State in respect of this agreement). It determines the conditions of exploitation and sharing of gas.

27. Tajikistan

Tajikistan has no agreements, arrangements, or practices with its neighbouring States regarding the exploration and exploitation of transboundary oil and gas resources or for any other cooperation for such oil and gas.

28. Thailand

Thailand has entered into the Agreement between the Government of the Kingdom of Thailand and the Government of Malaysia on the Constitution and other Matters relating to the Establishment of the Malaysia-Thailand Joint Authority.

29. Turkey

Turkey does not have any agreement, arrangement or practice with its neighbouring States regarding the exploration and exploitation of transboundary oil/gas resources.

30. United Kingdom

The United Kingdom has entered into the following agreements:

(*a*) 1965, United Kingdom-Norway agreement on delimitation of the continental shelf (United Kingdom, *Treaty Series*, No. 71 (1965), Cmnd 2757), signed in London, 10 March 1965;

(*b*) 1965, United Kingdom-Netherlands agreement on delimitation of the continental shelf under the North Sea (*ibid.*, No. 23 (1967) Cmnd 3253), signed in London, 6 October 1965;

(*c*) 1965, United Kingdom-Netherlands agreement on exploitation of single geological structures extending across the dividing line on the North Sea continental shelf (*ibid.*, No. 24 (1967) Cmnd 3254), signed in London, 6 October 1965;

(*d*) 1966, United Kingdom-Denmark agreement on delimitation of areas of the continental shelf (*ibid.*, No. 35 (1967) Cmnd 3278), signed in London, 3 March 1966;

(*e*) 1971, United Kingdom-Netherlands protocol amending the agreement on delimitation of the continental shelf under the North Sea agreement (*ibid.*, No. 130 (1972) Cmnd 5173), signed in London, 25 November 1971;

(*f*) 1971, United Kingdom-Denmark agreement on the delimitation of areas of the continental shelf (*ibid.*, No. 6 (1973) Cmnd 5193), signed in London, 25 November 1971;

(*g*) 1971, United Kingdom-Germany agreement on the delimitation of the continental shelf (*ibid.*, No. 7 (1973) Cmnd 5192), signed in London, 25 November 1971;

(*h*) 1973, United Kingdom-Norway agreement on the transmission of petroleum by pipeline from Ekofisk and neighbouring areas (*ibid.*, No. 101 (1973) Cmnd 5423), signed in Oslo, 22 May 1973;

(*i*) 1976, United Kingdom-Norway agreement on the exploitation of the Frigg Field Reservoir and the transmission of gas therefrom (*ibid.*, No. 113 (1977) Cmnd 7043), signed in London, 10 May 1976;

(*j*) 1978, United Kingdom-Norway protocol supplementary to the agreement on the delimitation of the continental shelf (*ibid.*, No. 31 (1980) Cmnd 7853), signed in Oslo, 22 December 1978;

(*k*) 1979, United Kingdom-Norway agreement on the exploitation of the Statfjord Field Reservoirs (*ibid.*, No. 44 (1981) Cmnd 8282), signed in Oslo, 16 October 1979;

(*l*) 1979, United Kingdom-Norway agreement on the exploitation of the Murchison Field Reservoir (*ibid.*, No. 39 (1981) Cmnd 8270), signed in Oslo, 16 October 1979;

(*m*) 1981, United Kingdom-Norway agreement supplementary to the Murchison Field Reservoir agreement (*ibid.*, No. 25 (1982) Cmnd 8577), signed in Oslo, 22 October 1981;

(*n*) 1982, United Kingdom-France agreement on the delimitation of the continental shelf in the area east of 30 minutes west of the Greenwich Meridian (*ibid.*, No. 20 (1983) Cmnd 8859), signed in London, 24 June 1982;

(*o*) 1983, United Kingdom-Norway second agreement supplementary to the Murchison Field Reservoir agreement (*ibid.*, No. 71 (1983) Cmnd 9083), signed in Oslo, 22 June 1983;

(*p*) 1985, United Kingdom-Norway Heimdal treaty (*ibid.*, No. 39 (1987) Cm 201), signed in Oslo, 21 November 1985;

(*q*) 1988, United Kingdom-Ireland agreement on the delimitation of areas of the continental shelf (*ibid.*, No. 20 (1990) Cm 990), signed in Dublin, 7 November 1988;

(*r*) 1991, United Kingdom-Belgium agreement on the delimitation of the continental shelf (*ibid.*, No. 20 (1994) Cm 2499), signed in Brussels, 29 May 1991;

(*s*) 1991, United Kingdom-France agreement on the completion of the delimitation of the continental shelf in the southern North Sea (*ibid.*, No. 46 (1992) Cm 1979), signed in London, 23 July 1991;

(*t*) 1992, United Kingdom-Netherlands agreement on the exploitation of the Markham Field Reservoirs (*ibid.*, No. 39 (1993) Cm 2254), signed in The Hague, 26 May 1992;

(*u*) 1992, United Kingdom-Ireland protocol supplementary to the agreement on the delimitation of areas of the continental shelf (*ibid.*, No. 47 (1993) Cm 2302), signed in Dublin, 8 December 1992;

(*v*) 1993, United Kingdom-Ireland agreement on the transmission of natural gas by pipeline (*ibid.*, No. 73 (1993) Cm 2377), signed in Dublin, 30 April 1993;

(*w*) 1995, United Kingdom-Norway exchange of notes on the amendment of the agreement on the exploitation of the Statfjord Field Reservoir (*ibid.*, No. 57 (1995) Cm 2941), signed in Oslo, 24 March 1995;

(*x*) 1997, United Kingdom-Belgium agreement on the transmission of natural gas by pipeline (*ibid.*, No. 3 (2003) Cm 5738), signed in Brussels, 10 December 1997;

(*y*) 1998, United Kingdom-Norway agreement on the amendment of the agreement on the exploitation of the Frigg Field Reservoir and the transmission of gas therefrom to the United Kingdom (*ibid.*, No. 21 (2002) Cm 5513), signed in Stavanger, 25 August 1998;

(*z*) 1998, United Kingdom-Norway framework agreement on the laying, operation and jurisdiction of interconnecting submarine pipelines (*ibid.*, No. 9 (2003) Cm 5762), signed in Stavanger, 25 August 1998;

(*aa*) 1999, United Kingdom-Denmark agreement on the delimitation of areas of the continental shelf in the area between the United Kingdom and the Faroe Islands (*ibid.*, No. 76 (1999) Cm 4514), signed in Tórshavn Faroe Islands, 18 May 1999;

(*bb*) 1999, United Kingdom-Norway exchange of notes amending the agreement on the Murchison Field Reservoir (*ibid.*, No. 110 (2000) Cm 4857), signed in Oslo, 9 August 1999;

(*cc*) 2001, United Kingdom-Norway exchange of notes on the amendment of the agreement on the exploitation of the Frigg Field Reservoir and the Transmission of Gas therefrom to the United Kingdom (*ibid.*, No. 43 (2001) Cm 5258), signed in Oslo, 21 June 2001;

(*dd*) 2004, United Kingdom-Netherlands exchange of notes amending the agreement on the delimitation of the continental shelf under the North Sea (as amended) (*ibid.*, No. 2 (2006) Cm 6749), signed in The Hague, 28 January and 7 June 2004;

(*ee*) 2004, United Kingdom-Ireland agreement on the transmission of natural gas through a second pipeline (*ibid.*, No. 2 (2005) Cm 6674, not yet in force), signed in Gormanstown, 24 September 2004;

(*ff*) 2004, United Kingdom-Norway exchange of notes on the Playfair and Boa petroleum fields (*ibid.*, No. 48 (1999) Cm 6412), signed in Oslo, 4 October 2004;

(*gg*) 2004, United Kingdom-Norway agreement on the amendment of the Heimdal treaty (*ibid.*, No. 1 (2005) Cm 6694, not in force), signed in Oslo,1 November 2004;

(*hh*) 2005, United Kingdom-Netherlands agreement on the transmission of natural gas through a pipeline (*ibid.*, No. 2 (2005) Cm 6675, not yet in force), signed in The Hague, 21 March 2005;

(*ii*) 2005, United Kingdom-Norway framework agreement concerning cross-boundary petroleum co-operation (*ibid.*, No. 20 (2007) Cm 7206, not yet in force), signed in Oslo, 4 April 2005;

(*jj*) 2005, United Kingdom-Belgium exchange of notes amending the agreement on the delimitation of the continental shelf under the North Sea (*ibid.*, No. 18 (2007) Cm 7204), signed in Brussels, 21 March and 7 June 2005.

31. United States

1. Aside from certain provisions in one maritime boundary treaty with Mexico (described below), the United States has not entered into any international agreements or arrangements, nor established any practice with neighbouring States, in relation to transboundary oil and gas reservoirs along the United States maritime or continental shelf boundaries with Mexico or Canada. The United States is not aware that any such transboundary reservoirs have been identified. The United States also has identified no agreements, arrangements or established practice with its neighbouring States specific to the exploration and exploitation of transboundary oil and gas resources along its land boundaries.

2. The United States has two maritime boundary and delimitation agreements with Mexico. The first is the United States-Mexico Treaty on Maritime Boundaries (signed at Mexico City on 4 May 1978 and entered into force on 13 November 1997), United Nations, *Treaty Series*, vol. 2143, No. 37399, p. 405, which establishes the maritime boundary between the United States and Mexico out to 200 miles in the Gulf of Mexico and the Pacific Ocean, using the principle of equidistance. The agreement does not address the exploration or exploitation of transboundary oil and gas resources. In addition, the agreement left two "gaps", or areas outside the exclusive economic zone of either State: one in the eastern Gulf, which concerned Cuba, Mexico and the United States, and one in the western Gulf, which concerned Mexico and the United States.

3. To address the gap in the western Gulf, the United States and Mexico concluded the Treaty on the Delimitation of the Continental Shelf in the Western Gulf of Mexico beyond 200 Nautical Miles, with annexes (signed at Washington, D.C., on 9 June 2000 and entered into force on 17 January 2001) (the Western Gap Treaty), United Nations, *Treaty Series*, vol. 2143, No. 37400, p. 417. Again applying the principle of equidistance, the Treaty allots 62 per cent of the 17,190 km² area to Mexico and 38 per cent to the United States. The Treaty also established a buffer zone extending 1.4 nautical miles on either side of the boundary in the Western Gap, within which neither party may engage in drilling or exploitation of the continental shelf for a period of 10 years.

4. While unitization and joint development arrangements were not part of the Western Gap Treaty, it does address the subject of possible oil and gas transboundary reservoirs. In particular, the Treaty requires each party, in accordance with its national laws and regulations, to facilitate requests from the other party to authorize geological and geophysical studies to help determine the possible presence and distribution of transboundary reservoirs. In addition, each party is required to share geological and geophysical information in its possession in order to determine the possible existence and location of transboundary reservoirs. In the event any transboundary reservoir is identified, the Treaty obligates the parties "to seek to reach agreement for the

efficient and equitable exploitation of such transboundary reservoirs" (see article V, paragraph 1 (*b*)).

32. Uruguay

Uruguay has no knowledge of the existence of any treaties or other agreements, arrangements or practices subscribed to or undertaken by Uruguay with neighbouring countries in relation to the exploration and exploitation of transboundary oil and gas resources.

C. Question 2

Are there any joint bodies, mechanisms or partnerships (public or private) involving exploration, exploitation or management of the transboundary oil or gas? Please provide information describing the nature and functioning of such arrangements, including governing principles.

1. Australia

1. The Timor Sea Treaty establishes a joint management and regulation regime for the joint development area in the Timor Sea. The Timor Sea Designated Authority is the day-to-day regulator of the joint area and is based in Dili.

2. The Designated Authority is responsible to a Joint Commission, currently constituted by two Timor-Leste officials and one Australian official, which oversees the work of the Designated Authority and establishes policies and regulations relating to petroleum activities in the joint area. The ultimate decision-making body established by the Timor Sea Treaty is a Ministerial Council, constituted by an equal number of ministers from Australia and Timor-Leste. The Designated Authority, Joint Commission and Ministerial Council operate in accordance with the terms of the Timor Sea Treaty.

2. Austria

The above-mentioned agreement (see section B above) provides for a "mixed committee" which is composed of a representative of the Austrian Federal Ministry of Economics and Labour and a representative of the OMV oil and gas corporation on the Austrian side, and a representative of the Slovak Ministry of Economics and a representative of the NAFTA company on the Slovak side. This committee decides, among others, on the share of the oil and gas—which is exploited exclusively on Austrian territory—to be given to the Slovak side.

3. Bahamas

There are no such joint programmes, mechanisms or partnerships concerning exploration or management of transboundary oil or gas in the Bahamas.

4. Bosnia and Herzegovina

Bosnia and Herzegovina does not have any local or transboundary sources of gas or oil, or contract related to that issue. There were certain researches regarding sources of crude oil in Bosnia and Herzegovina by 1990, but they have never been exploited.

5. Canada

1. The Agreement between the Government of Canada and the Government of the French Republic relating to the Exploration and Exploitation of Transboundary Hydrocarbon Fields envisages the creation of a joint Technical Working Group to examine technical issues that arise from the implementation of the Agreement or from any Exploitation Agreement (explained further below), including information related to the regional geological setting and geological basins as well as any question related to the implementation of the Development Plan or Benefits Plan (explained further below). The Working Group must allow the parties to review information related to the regional geological setting and, at the request of one party, meet to facilitate approval of a Development Plan or Benefits Plan by reviewing concerns or issues regarding such a plan or a preliminary version of it. The Unit Operator is normally to be invited to all or part of any such meetings.

2. The Working Group consists of individuals nominated by each party (two chairs and two secretaries), as well as other persons which either party considers should be present at any Working Group meeting.

6. Cuba

Cuba has no joint body, mechanism or partnership for transboundary oil and gas resource prospecting, exploitation or management with neighbouring States.

7. Cyprus

The Framework Agreement between the Republic of Cyprus and the Arab Republic of Egypt concerning the Development of Cross-Median Line Hydrocarbon Resources provides that when a cross-median line hydrocarbon reservoir is identified and may be exploited, each party (the Republic of Cyprus and the Arab Republic of Egypt) shall require the concerned licensees to meet and reach a unitization agreement for the joint development and exploitation of the said reservoir. The unitization agreement shall define the cross-median line hydrocarbon reservoir taking into account the following elements: (*a*) the geographical extent and the geological features of the cross-median line reservoir and the proposed area for joint development and exploitation of the said reservoir (the "unit area"); (*b*) the total amount of the hydrocarbons in place and reserves, and the methodology used for the calculations; (*c*) the apportionment of reserves between each side of the median line; (*d*) the procedure for the determination of any of the above items, where appropriate, by an independent third-party expert; and (*e*) the procedure for periodical redetermination of the above items, where appropriate. The unitization agreement shall be submitted to the parties for their approval.

8. Czech Republic

1. In conformity with the 1960 Agreement between the Government of the Czechoslovak Republic and the Austrian Federal Government on the Exploitation of Shared Natural Gas and Oil Deposits, there existed a Czechoslovak-Austrian Mixed Commission defined in article 2 of the said Agreement. The Mixed Commission

was composed of representatives of the two Contracting Parties. The task of the Mixed Commission was to calculate the total reserves in individual deposits and to specify the share of each Contracting Party, to specify the conditions for exploitation, in particular to establish long-term exploitation programmes, as well as the ways of removing potential difficulties that might arise within the implementation of the Agreement.

2. The Czechoslovak side was represented in the Mixed Commission by representatives of the competent ministry and by the Nafta Hodonín mining company. After the disintegration of Czechoslovakia, a Czech-Austrian Mixed Commission was set up to continue to fulfil the tasks arising from the 1960 Agreement between the Government of the Czechoslovak Republic and the Austrian Federal Government on the Exploitation of Shared Natural Gas and Oil Deposits. Participating in the work of the Mixed Commission on the Czech side are representatives of the Ministry of Industry and Trade and of the Moravské naftové doly mining company.

9. Guyana

The Guyana Geology and Mines Commission has no joint body convened for the purpose of exploration, exploitation or management of transboundary oil or gas.

10. Hungary

The Hungarian Oil and Gas Company (MOL) has concluded two partnership agreements with the Croatian National Oil and Gas Company (INA) to jointly explore cross-border Croatian-Hungarian plays. One of the agreements covers the Podravska Slatina-Zalata area (signed in 2006), the other agreement concerns the Novi Gradac-Potony area (signed in 2007). Both companies have 50–50 share in the exploration projects. The partnership is governed by the Management Committee, which consists of the representatives of MOL and INA, and all decisions are made on a consensual basis. The Steering Committee decides on the annual work programme and the necessary budget. INA is the operator on the Croatian side, and MOL undertakes the responsibilities and tasks of the operator on the Hungarian side. The agreements are governed by English law.

11. Iraq

Technical committees have been formed and are working to establish formulas for joint cooperation between Iraq and its neighbouring countries.

12. Ireland

Not at the moment. However, Ireland is in regular contact with its counterparts in the United Kingdom (Department for Business, Enterprise and Regulatory Reform (BERR, formerly Department of Trade and Industry)) regarding issues of mutual interest. Ireland responded "Not applicable" to the question "Please provide information describing the nature and functioning of such arrangements, including governing principles".

13. Jamaica

Pursuant to article 4 of an agreement with Colombia, the parties have established a joint commission to develop the modalities for activities for the exploration and exploitation of natural resources, whether living or non-living; ensure compliance with regulations and measures adopted by the parties for exploration and exploitation activities in the joint regime area; and carry out any functions assigned to the commission by the parties to implement the agreement. The joint commission consists of one representative of each party, who may be assisted by such advisers as considered necessary. The commission makes recommendations to the parties, which become binding when adopted by the parties.

14. Kuwait

1. *Wafra Joint Operations*. Exploration, exploitation and management of oil and gas resources is the joint responsibility of two companies, the Kuwait Gulf Oil Company and Saudi Arabian Chevron, with joint operations performed by Wafra Joint Operations, organized by the Joint Operations Committee. The Joint Operations Committee consists of representatives from both companies with equal voting rights. It provides guidance to asset management teams in joint operations and approves business plans and budgets.

2. *Khafji Joint Operations*. Joint bodies, mechanisms and partnerships exist for the exploration, exploitation and management of transboundary oil and gas. In the offshore divided zone, Khafji Joint Operations is the entity established to operate and manage the oil and gas field on behalf of both shareholders in an equal partnership. The Joint Executive Committee and Joint Operations Committee are two high-level committees, with equal representation by both shareholders, which act as the main authority to approve and monitor all major activities within the joint operations and to ensure that best practices are used for the exploration, exploitation and management of the oil and gas reserves in the offshore divided zone.

15. Mali

1. A steering committee comprising representatives of Mali and Mauritania has been established to implement the Framework Agreement on oil-related activities in the shared sedimentary basins.

2. The steering committee meets at least twice annually or as necessary to consider project and budget proposals for activities within a mutually agreed area.

16. Mauritius

Mauritius responded "No".

17. Myanmar

Since Myanmar does not have any agreements, arrangements or practices with neighbouring States regarding the exploration and exploitation of transboundary oil and gas resources, there are no joint bodies, mechanisms or partnerships (public or private) involving exploration, exploitation or management of transboundary oil and gas.

18. Netherlands

The Netherlands responded "No".

19. Norway

Any transboundary oil and gas resources belonging partly to Norway are exploited as a unit by commercial companies having been awarded exclusive rights to do so by the Government of Norway and the Government on the other side of the delimitation line respectively. Such exploitation is subject to a unit agreement being entered into by the relevant companies on both sides of the delimitation line and to such unit agreement being approved by the two relevant Governments. Upon receipt of such approval, the relevant companies on both sides of the delimitation line form a joint venture for the purpose of exploiting the transboundary oil and gas deposit as a unit.

20. Oman

1. The Ministry of Oil and Gas is not involved with any joint bodies, mechanisms or partnerships (public or private) engaged in the exploration, exploitation or management of transboundary oil or gas.

2. However, there are understandings on bilateral exchange of technical information. Such understandings are implemented as needed by companies on both sides under the supervision of the Ministry.

21. Portugal

Portugal responded "No".

22. Slovakia

A bilateral commission has been established under the provisions of the Common Oil and Gas Resources Exploitation Agreement between the Czechoslovak Republic and the Republic of Austria. The Commission calculates the capacity of all underground fields and the amounts of each participant's share. The Commission also sets the conditions for exploitation.

23. Tajikistan

There are no joint bodies, mechanisms or partnerships (public or private) involving exploration, exploitation or management of transboundary oil or gas in Tajikistan.

24. Thailand

The Malaysia-Thailand Joint Authority has been established as a statutory body to assume all rights and responsibilities on behalf of the two Governments (Thailand and Malaysia) to explore and exploit non-living resources, particularly petroleum, in the offshore overlapping continental shelf area claimed by the two countries and known as the "joint development area" for a period of 50 years commencing from the date the memorandum of understanding came into force (22 February 1979). The Joint Authority consists of two joint-chairpersons, one from each country, and an equal number of members from each country.

25. Turkey

Turkey does not have joint bodies, mechanisms or partnerships involving exploration, exploitation or management of the transboundary oil or gas.

26. United Kingdom

Bilateral agreements for the exploitation of transboundary structures or fields on the United Kingdom continental shelf usually include provisions for the Governments to meet, as required, in a consultative commission or other forum to facilitate the implementation of the agreement, address matters that may be raised by either Government, or consider licensee disputes raised under the licensee agreements. The commission or forum will generally be limited to a specified number of Government representatives, but the agreements may also provide for reference to external arbitration. An example can be found in the new framework agreement between the United Kingdom and Norway.

27. United States

The United States has identified no joint bodies, partnerships or formal mechanisms with Mexico or Canada to address exploration, exploitation and management of transboundary oil or gas. Along its maritime boundary, the United States itself does not engage in these forms of activity, but instead issues outer continental shelf leases within United States jurisdiction on a competitive basis to private oil and gas companies. These leases and their operators must adhere to United States laws and regulations and to the terms of the lease. (See the Outer Continental Shelf Lands Act and its implementing regulations, the most pertinent of which are found at Code of Federal Regulations, Title 30, parts 250, 256 and 260.)

D. Question 3

If the answer to question 1 is yes, please answer the following questions on the content of the agreements or arrangements and regarding the practice:

***(a)* Are there any specific principles, arrangements or understandings regarding allocation or appropriation of oil and gas, or other forms of cooperation? Please provide a description of the principles, provisions, arrangements or understandings;**

***(b)* Are there any arrangements or understandings or is there any practice regarding prevention and control of pollution or regarding other environmental concerns, including mitigation of accidents? Please provide further description.**

1. Algeria

1. There is an agreement of friendship and cooperation between the Algerian and Libyan Arab Jamahiriya Governments regarding the development and exploitation of the deposits at Alrar and Wafa.

2. The firm Oil Spill Response Company (OSPREC) was created in January 2007. Its shareholders include

Algeria and Morocco, soon to be joined by Tunisia. The firm's objective is to prevent and combat hydrocarbon pollution in an area extending from the southern Mediterranean coast to the west coast of Africa.

2. Australia

1. In relation to question 3 (*a*), the provisions quoted above (see paragraph 1 of Australia's response to question 1 above) in several of Australia's delimitation agreements make it clear that for any transboundary petroleum resource found, the two parties are to seek to reach agreement on the manner in which the resource is to be most effectively exploited and on the equitable sharing of the benefits arising from such exploitation.

2. In relation to question 3 (*b*):

(*a*) In those areas where Australia exercises seabed jurisdiction and Indonesia exercises water column jurisdiction, the parties will be required by article 7 of the Perth Treaty, when it enters into force, to take effective measures as may be necessary to prevent, reduce and control pollution of the marine environment;

(*b*) Article 13 of the Torres Strait Treaty between Australia and Papua New Guinea provides obligations on the parties to protect and preserve the marine environment in and in the vicinity of the Protected Zone. Under article 15, Australia and Papua New Guinea have agreed to extend a moratorium on mining and drilling of the seabed and subsoil for the exploration or exploitation of the resources within the Protected Zone for an indefinite period;

(*c*) Article 10 of the Timor Sea Treaty places obligations on Australia and Timor-Leste to cooperate to protect the marine environment of the joint petroleum development area, so as to prevent and minimize pollution and other environmental harm from petroleum activities. In the Greater Sunrise unit area, article 21 of the unitization agreement between Australia and Timor-Leste provides that certain specified Australian environmental protection legislation will apply and will be administered by the regulatory authorities designated by the unitization agreement;

(*d*) The Australian Maritime Safety Authority, responsible for maritime safety, marine environment protection, and maritime and aviation search and rescue in Australia, has several memorandums of understanding with Australia's neighbours (New Caledonia, New Zealand, Papua New Guinea and Indonesia) which relate to responses to major oil spills.

3. Austria

1. Since the gas is exploited exclusively on Austrian territory, Austrian laws and regulations apply.

2. There are no specific arrangements.

4. Bahamas

The Bahamas indicated that the question was "Not applicable".

5. Canada

1. The Agreement between the Government of Canada and the Government of the French Republic relating to the Exploration and Exploitation of Transboundary Hydrocarbon Fields is a framework arrangement which does not contemplate a single unified regime but instead is a means to facilitate the requirements of French and Canadian legislation to be fulfilled for any transboundary field.

2. In addition to reiterating the definitive boundary between Canada and France for all purposes, the Agreement's preamble recognizes proportionality based on respective share of reserves in a transboundary field as the basis of the Agreement and highlights the importance of good oil field practice, safety, protection of the environment and the conservation of resources in transboundary fields.

3. The following are the main features of the Agreement regarding allocation or appropriation of oil and gas, or other forms of cooperation:

(*a*) The Agreement envisages provision of information with a more comprehensive exchange once accumulation has been determined to be transboundary. The Agreement imposes a requirement for information exchange upon the drilling of any well within 10 nautical miles of the maritime boundary. Information exchanged cannot be further disclosed without the consent of the party that provided it;

(*b*) The Agreement speaks about the notice to be given to the other party, with evidence, if data shows that accumulation is (or is not) transboundary. If the other party is not convinced, that party can: (*i*) request a meeting of the Technical Working Group; and/or (*ii*) send the disagreement to a single expert for determination in accordance with procedure and timelines for using the expert outlined in the Agreement;

(*c*) The Agreement provides for determination and redetermination of hydrocarbon reserves in a transboundary field. Indeed, the Unit Operator is to submit specific proposals on which both parties shall agree upon in a specific time frame. Should such an agreement not be reached, the disagreement is submitted to a single expert for determination, in accordance with procedure and timelines for using the expert outlined in the Agreement;

(*d*) Once agreement is reached or the expert determines that the accumulation is transboundary, the parties must delineate an area for the exchange of comprehensive data. If a Holder of Mineral Titles, meaning a person or firm to whom one of the parties has granted a subsisting mineral title or exclusive right to explore or exploit hydrocarbons in a particular area, is interested in production from the transboundary field, the parties will start negotiation of an Exploitation Agreement. The Exploitation Agreement is defined as any agreement entered into between Canada and the French Republic in respect of a transboundary field;

(*e*) The Agreement envisages a separate Exploitation Agreement for each transboundary field. It imposes a time limit for the parties to enter into an Exploitation Agreement since any commercial production in a transboundary field cannot commence until an Exploitation Agreement has been concluded. If the parties are unable to conclude an Exploitation Agreement within a particular time frame, either party may refer the finalization of the Exploitation Agreement to arbitration, in accordance with the arbitration procedure outlined in the Agreement. This provides certainty as to time frames in which the Exploitation Agreement will be finalized;

(*f*) The Agreement requires that Mineral Title Holders conclude a Unitization Agreement that provides for: (i) combining respective rights in the transboundary field's hydrocarbon resources; (ii) sharing costs and benefits; (iii) operating the field as a single unit. The Unitization Agreement is subject to the prior written approval of both parties. This is an operator-led confidential arrangement which incorporates provisions to ensure that, in the event of a conflict between the Unitization Agreement and the Exploitation Agreement, the terms of the Exploitation Agreement shall prevail;

(*g*) Exploitation of any transboundary field is to be undertaken in accordance with the Exploitation Agreement and the Unitization Agreement;

(*h*) A Development Plan and a Benefits Plan must be agreed upon for a particular transboundary field before production can commence. A Development Plan sets out in detail the approach to the development and operation of the transboundary field while a Benefits Plan ensures that, in developing the transboundary field, and subject to all applicable domestic and international legal obligations of the parties, best efforts are made to ensure economic benefits are shared between Canada and France, taking into account the apportionment of hydrocarbon reserves as between the parties. Upon submission from the Unit Operator, parties have a specific time frame in which to approve a Development Plan and a Benefits Plan. Should the time period expire, either party can refer the matter to arbitration, in accordance with the arbitration procedure outlined in the Agreement;

(*i*) The parties must ensure that exploitation of the transboundary field is in accordance with approved Development and Benefits Plans;

(*j*) The Agreement provides that all disputes are to be resolved through negotiation except for disputes which are specifically to be submitted to an expert or to arbitration.

4. The Agreement contains provisions that address environmental considerations, including transboundary environmental impact assessments. The Agreement provides for parties to conclude arrangements or agreements dealing with search and rescue, marine pollution and transboundary impact environmental assessments. For instance, the parties are required to enter into a side arrangement on implementation of the Convention on Environmental Impact Assessment in a Transboundary Context, Espoo, Finland, 1991.

5. The parties have a duty to take all necessary measures to minimize adverse impact on the environment. The Agreement imposes a requirement for Mineral Title Holders to provide security, as determined by the party having jurisdiction over them, to meet environmental damage caused by any hydrocarbon exploration or exploitation activity.

6. On a separate note, environmental considerations are part of the approval process for oil and gas activities under Canada's domestic legislation, and this would be true in the case of transboundary fields as well.

6. Cuba

There is no arrangement or practice with Cuba's neighbouring States (Mexico and the United States) for the prevention or control of pollution or other environmental problems. To date, no agreements on cooperation in salvage rescue or intervention in the case of accidents have been signed.

7. Cyprus

1. The apportionment of reserves on each side of the median line and the allocation or appropriation of oil and gas is determined by the licensees in the unitization agreement and is subject to the approval of the States. The assistance of an independent, third-party expert may be called upon.

2. The framework agreement provides that the States shall take all necessary measures so that the concerned licensees comply with the health, safety and environmental requirements provided for in their respective applicable legislation and shall in particular ensure that the performance of the relevant activities, including the construction and operation of facilities and pipelines, shall prevent damage to the marine environment, and that relevant procedures are established for the safety of navigation and the safety and health of personnel. Furthermore, there are provisions in national legislation (the Hydrocarbons [Prospecting, Exploration and Exploitation] Law and the Hydrocarbons [Prospecting, Exploration and Exploitation] Regulations) for the protection of the environment. Cyprus has also conducted a strategic environmental assessment concerning the hydrocarbon activities within its exclusive economic zone, in which the likely significant environmental effects of implementing hydrocarbon exploration and exploitation activities are identified, described and evaluated. The licensees are bound to follow and comply with the recommendations of the study and must prepare an environmental impact assessment prior to the granting of an exploitation licence. The strategic environmental assessment was conducted in accordance with the relevant European Union directive (2001/42/EC), *Official Journal of the European Communities*, L 197 (27 June 2001), pp. 30–37. Cyprus is a party to a number of international conventions and protocols, such as the International Convention for the Prevention of Pollution from Ships (MARPOL), 1973 and its Protocol of 1978; the Convention for the Protection of the Mediterranean Sea against Pollution; the Convention on Wetlands of International Importance, especially as Waterfowl Habitat; the Convention on the Conservation of Migratory Species of Wild Animals;

the United Nations Convention on the Law of the Sea; the Vienna Convention for the Protection of the Ozone Layer; the Montreal Protocol on Substances that Deplete the Ozone Layer; the United Nations Framework Convention on Climate Change; Agenda 21, adopted at the United Nations Conference on Environment and Development [Rio de Janerio, Brazil, 3 to 14 June 1992 (A/CONF.151/26/Rev.1)(vol.I/Corr.1, vol. II, vol. III/Corr.1)], the Convention on Biological Diversity; the Kyoto Protocol to the United Nations Framework Convention on Climate Change and the Stockholm Convention on Persistent Organic Pollutants.

8. Czech Republic

1. A specific feature of the 1960 Agreement between the Government of the Czechoslovak Republic and the Austrian Federal Government on the Exploitation of Shared Natural Gas and Oil Deposits was that the raw material was used only by one Contracting Party (Austria) with regard to the technically rational system of mining. The other Contracting Party (Czechoslovakia/Czech Republic) had at its disposal an observation well to monitor the observation of technical parameters. As the raw material comes also from the Czechoslovak/Czech territory, Czechoslovakia/the Czech Republic was entitled to certain financial compensation. The recipient of the compensation was the mining company that had the mining licence for the area, namely, the Nafta Hodonín company (now the Moravské naftové doly mining company).

2. The 1960 Agreement provides for the duty of notification in the event of any special circumstances requiring immediate measures (art. 4). The mining companies of the Contracting Parties cooperate in the exploitation and are expected to exchange information also on the environmental impacts of the exploitation.

9. Ireland

1. Ireland responded "Yes"—article 3 of the Agreement between the Government of Ireland and the Government of the United Kingdom concerning the Delimitation of Areas of the Continental Shelf between the Two Countries, as supplemented, reads as follows:

> "If any oil, gas or condensate field extends across Line A or Line B and the part of such field which is situated on one side of the line is exploitable, wholly or in part, from the other side of the line, the two Governments shall make determined efforts to reach agreement as to the exploitation of such field."

2. Ireland indicated that question 3 (*a*) was "Not applicable".

3. As regards, question 3 (*b*) an Oil Spill Contingency Plan is put in place before any drilling takes place. Strategic environmental assessments also include a section on transboundary impact assessment.

10. Jamaica

1. There are no express provisions in the Maritime Delimitation Treaty between Jamaica and Colombia concerning specific principles, arrangements or understandings in respect of the allocation or appropriation of oil or gas in the joint regime area. Article 3 of the Treaty provides, however, that activities in the area shall be carried out on a joint basis as agreed by both parties.

2. Under article 3 of the Treaty, the parties may carry out activities in the joint regime area for the protection and preservation of the marine environment. The article further provides that this shall be done on a joint basis as agreed by both parties. There are no current arrangements regarding the prevention and control of pollution in the joint regime area. Both parties are, however, engaged in ongoing discussions on the exploration and exploitation of non-living resources in the area and will begin discussions on modalities for the preservation and protection of the environment in the area.

11. Kuwait

1. For Wafra Joint Operations, the Kuwait Gulf Oil Company and Saudi Arabian Chevron share 50 per cent in all aspects related to expenses, manpower and all produced fluids.

2. Specific principles, arrangements and understandings regarding allocation of appropriation of oil and gas are in place for the Khafji Joint Operations.

3. Under the terms of the Joint Petroleum Production Operations Agreement, both partners have an equal and undivided 50 per cent interest in all petroleum acquired or produced in connection with the joint operations. The Agreement also states that each party shall have the right to receive in kind its proportionate share of each grade and quality of crude oil and natural gas acquired or produced through the joint operations.

4. Wafra Joint Operations, a joint venture of the Kuwait Gulf Oil Company and Saudi Arabian Chevron, complies with the Kuwait Petroleum Corporation health, safety and environment management system and the Kuwait Environment Public Authority and Chevron Operational Excellence standards, which are aimed at controlling pollutants and reducing the release of environmental hazards into the atmosphere. For example, Wafra Joint Operations has started projects to recycle paper and control hazardous material as part of its waste management systems. In addition, to reduce oil leaks, Wafra Joint Operations has been implementing a project to replace flow lines. There is also a project on pit remediation as part of a zero discharge project. The Wafra Central Gas Utilization Project is under study to reduce gas flaring.

5. There are arrangements, understandings and practices in respect of Khafji Joint Operations regarding prevention and control of pollution or regarding other environmental concerns, including mitigation of accidents. Khafji Joint Operations complies with relevant environmental regulations and other requirements applicable to its operating activities. In particular, Khafji Joint Operations complies with the environmental standards specified by Saudi Arabia and Kuwait and has developed appropriate guidelines and an environment management system compatible with the objectives of environmental protection prevailing in the region.

6. Khafji Joint Operations has a well-defined performance management system to monitor and mitigate issues pertaining to environment, health and safety incidents. It has also implemented ISO 14001 for its environment management system to establish international standards for management of the environment in its operations.

12. Mali

Mali responded "No"—the Framework Agreement with Mauritania does not include any specific principles or arrangements regarding allocation or appropriation of oil and gas, nor does the Framework Agreement include any such understandings or arrangement.

13. Mauritius

Mauritius indicated that the question was "Not applicable".

14. Netherlands

1. In relation to question 3 (*a*):

(*a*) Articles 5 to 9 of the 1962 Supplementary Agreement to the Ems-Dollard Treaty;

(*b*) Articles 5 and 6 of the 1992 Markham Agreement (United Nations, *Treaty Series*, vol. 1731, No. 30235, p. 156);

(*c*) Paragraph (*f*) of the Minke Main Memorandum of Understanding.

2. As regards question 3 (*b*):

(*a*) Article 17 of the 1992 Markham Agreement;

(*b*) Paragraph (*d*) of the Minke Main Memorandum of Understanding.

15. Norway

1. Any exclusive right to explore for and produce oil and gas on the Norwegian continental shelf is subject to a production licence being awarded to eligible companies. This licence is exclusive and gives the holders the right, within a specified time limit, to explore for and produce any oil and gas discovered in the area covered by the licence.

2. Any production of oil and gas from a transboundary deposit is subject to a unit agreement being entered into by the relevant companies on both sides of the delimitation line and to such unit agreement being approved by the two relevant Governments. Upon receipt of such approval, the relevant companies on both sides of the delimitation line form a joint venture for the purpose of exploiting the transboundary oil and gas deposit as a unit.

3. Any profits resulting from the exploitation of transboundary oil and gas deposits are, in the case of Norway, subject to taxation of the individual companies holding the relevant production licence on the Norwegian side of the delimitation line.

4. The legal basis for the joint operations is always a unitization agreement between the two or more Governments on each side of the delimitation line. In the case of Norway, its delimitation agreements with Denmark, the United Kingdom and Iceland all foresee that transboundary oil and gas deposits will be exploited on the basis of unitization agreements between the Governments in question.

5. Norway and its neighbouring countries all have national legislation providing that pollution resulting from oil and gas activities is subject to strict liability on the oil companies holding the exclusive rights to conduct exploration for and exploitation of oil and gas in the area where the pollution occurred. These oil companies are also strictly liable to mitigate the effects of accidents resulting in such pollution. Other kinds of accidents shall be mitigated and compensated as far as the oil company holding the relevant exclusive right is responsible and liable for the accident.

16. Oman

1. In relation to question 3 (*a*), there are arrangements to foster cooperation in the oil and gas sectors between the Sultanate and some neighbouring States. For example, there is a joint Omani-Yemeni technical committee on oil and gas. That committee has held four meetings since its creation in 1993. The most important things that were agreed on during that period are:

(*a*) Exchange of information and maps on common border zones in relation to oil and gas;

(*b*) Bilateral exchange of technical information on areas adjoining the borders and the provision of facilities to Omani and Yemeni companies wishing to invest in the oil and gas sectors; such investment must take place in accordance with the procedures followed in both countries;

(*c*) Training of Yemeni technicians in various areas by Petroleum Development Oman (PDO) and Occidental Petroleum Corporation in the year 2000;

(*d*) Exchange of visits between officials and technical personnel from both countries as well as visits to oil facilities and companies operating in the country.

2. The committee met most recently in Sana'a from 1 to 4 July 2007. Many important matters were discussed at the meeting, such as the formation of a joint working group of the Petroleum Exploration and Production Authority (PEPA) of Yemen and the Oman Oil Company (OOC) to study the possibility of investing in available areas in Yemen. Also discussed was Omani use of Yemeni expertise in the development of a centralized database, which the Ministry intends to create in the near future. A delegation from the Ministry recently visited Yemen to discuss the matter.

3. In relation to question 3 (*b*), in respect of environmental affairs, the Ministry of the Environment and Climate Affairs is the competent body.

17. Portugal

Portugal responded "Not applicable".

18. Saint Vincent and the Grenadines

A draft energy policy has been adopted by Cabinet for discussions with stakeholders.

19. Slovakia

Slovakia has no arrangements, understandings or practices regarding the prevention and control of pollution or regarding other environmental concerns, including mitigation of accidents.

20. Thailand

1. All costs incurred and benefits to be derived by the Malaysia-Thailand Joint Authority from activities carried out in the joint development area are to be equally borne and shared by the two Governments (Malaysia and Thailand).

2. Under the Malaysia-Thailand Joint Authority Agreement, the Malaysia-Thailand Joint Authority Act 1990 and relevant petroleum income tax acts, the Joint Authority is empowered to award, with the approval of the Governments, contracts for the exploration and exploitation of petroleum resources in the joint development area. Contracts have to be in the form of a production-sharing contract.

3. Further information is available in the Agreement between the Government of the Kingdom of Thailand and the Government of Malaysia on the Constitution and other Matters relating to the Establishment of the Malaysia-Thailand Joint Authority, article 9, finance, chapter III: financial provisions.

4. In relation to question 3 (*b*), the Procedures for Drilling Operations and Procedures for Production Operations of the Malaysia–Thailand Joint Authority contain further information.[1]

[1] The texts of the agreements are available for consultation at the Codification Division of the Office of Legal Affairs.

21. United Kingdom

1. A common feature of bilateral agreements delimiting the United Kingdom continental shelf is a requirement to reach further agreement on the manner in which a transboundary petroleum field or structure shall be effectively exploited and the costs and proceeds apportioned. These further agreements provide for both Governments to approve matters relating to development. These will usually include commercial agreements between the appropriate licensees of each State that are relevant to exploitation of the structure/field; technical arrangements for determining the geological extent of the field or structure and for apportionment between the licence groups; appointment of the operator for any field development and decommissioning plans; the role of the Governments and the extent that each Government has jurisdiction over installations and field facilities; the arrangements for measuring petroleum produced; arrangements for maintaining the safety of installations and pipelines; arrangements for third party use of the field and associated facilities; arrangements for environmental protection; and arrangements for dispute settlement.

2. Under Council Directive 85/337/EEC of 27 June 1985 on the assessment of the effects of certain public and private projects on the environment (*Official Journal of the European Communities*, L 175/40, 5 July 1985) and the Directive of the European Parliament and the Council concerning integrated pollution prevention and control (15 January 2008) (2008/1/EC) (*Official Journal of the European Communities*, L 24/8, 29 January 2008), member States of the European Union are obliged to advise bordering States of any proposals that could have an impact on the environment in those States and there is therefore a formal procedure for exchanging applications relating to environmental impact assessments and atmospheric emissions. A similar, though less formal, exchange procedure is also in force in relation to discharges to the marine environment controlled under binding agreements made under the Convention for the Protection of the Marine Environment of the North-East Atlantic. In addition to these agreements, the United Kingdom regulators meet with the regulators of bordering States on a regular basis, to discuss general policy issues and specific development proposals.

3. As regards other environmental concerns, including mitigation of accidents, the United Kingdom is party to several international agreements that provide for cooperation in dealing with major marine pollution incidents. Appendix B of the National Contingency Plan provides details of these agreements, which set out roles and responsibilities with regard to notification and response to marine pollution incidents (see www.mcga.gov.uk). United Kingdom offshore oil and gas operators are required to notify regulatory authorities in the event of any oil or chemical spill in the sea, regardless of volume. The Maritime Coastguard Agency has the responsibility, through the previously mentioned international agreements, to notify border States if any pollution is likely to enter their waters.

22. United States

1. There are no principles, arrangements or understandings regarding allocation or appropriation of oil and gas production from transboundary reservoirs, as no transboundary reservoirs have been identified along the United States maritime boundary. The only forms of cooperation concern data sharing and other limited forms of cooperation described in the Western Gap Treaty with regard to possible transboundary reservoirs.

2. Because the United States has no arrangements or practices regarding the exploration and exploitation of transboundary oil and gas resources, there are no related arrangements or understandings regarding pollution prevention and control or other environmental concerns. As a domestic matter, oil and gas operators operating in areas under United States jurisdiction are required to follow all United States laws and regulations, many

of which relate to pollution and environmental issues. For example, see generally the Outer Continental Shelf Lands Act, and specifically its implementing regulations at the Code of Federal Regulations, Title 30, Part 250. In addition, United States Government inspectors visit and inspect offshore facilities regularly to ensure that all equipment and facilities comply with regulatory requirements.

E. Question 4

Please provide any further comments or information, including legislation or judicial decisions, which you consider to be relevant or useful to the Commission in the consideration of issues regarding oil and gas.

1. Australia

Australia responded "No response".

2. Bahamas

Bahamas indicated that the question was "Not applicable".

3. Bosnia and Herzegovina

Bosnia and Herzegovina cited the following:

(*a*) Decision of the Council of Ministers of Bosnia and Herzegovina on the quality of oil products (2002);

(*b*) Decree on the organization and regulation of the gas sector in the Federation of Bosnia and Herzegovina (2007); and the Gas Law relating to the Republic of Srpska (2007). Activities are ongoing on drafting of the national gas law and improving of the existing legislation on the entity level.

4. Canada

1. The Canadian area covered by the Agreement between the Government of Canada and the Government of the French Republic relating to the Exploration and Exploitation of Transboundary Hydrocarbon Fields is governed domestically by the Canada-Newfoundland Offshore Petroleum Board, an independent body that regulates the offshore area on behalf of Canada and the Province of Newfoundland and Labrador. The pertinent legislation is the Canada-Newfoundland Atlantic Accord Implementation Act, available from: http://laws.justice.gc.ca/en/C-7.5/index.html.

2. In addition, there is a small transboundary area that could be subject to the Canada-Nova Scotia Offshore Petroleum Resources Accord Implementation Act.

3. Both pieces of legislation provide for the management of offshore oil and gas resources on behalf of the federal and provincial governments.

5. Cuba

By decision of the Government of Cuba, the State Commission on the Outer Limit of the Continental Shelf was established to extend the present maritime limit beyond the 200 nautical miles from the baselines from which the breadth of the territorial sea is measured, in accordance with article 76 of the United Nations Convention on the Law of the Sea and, therefore, beyond Cuba's exclusive economic zone in the Gulf of Mexico. That Commission is currently in the process of organizing its submission to the United Nations Commission on the Limits of the Continental Shelf, which will in the future examine oil and gas prospecting and exploitation.

6. Cyprus

The following national legislation has been harmonized with Directive 94/22/EC of the European Parliament and of the Council of 30 May 1994 on the conditions for granting and using authorizations for the prospection, exploration and production of hydrocarbons (*Official Journal of the European Communities*, L 164/3, 30 June 1994):

(*a*) Hydrocarbons (Prospecting, Exploration and Exploitation) Law of 2007 (Law 4(I)/2007);

(*b*) Hydrocarbons (Prospecting, Exploration and Exploitation) Regulations of 2007 (Regulatory Administrative Act 51/2007).

7. Czech Republic

The Czech Republic has oil and natural gas deposits only in a small part of its territory, practically only in the southern and northern border areas in the east of the Czech Republic. Therefore, what is taken into consideration are the transboundary oil and natural gas deposits shared only with Austria and possibly perhaps carboniferous gas deposits shared with Poland. With regard to the really thorough (unique in the world) geological exploration of the territory of the Czech Republic, no new oil or natural gas deposits are likely to be found and requiring a new international agreement that would regulate their shared exploitation and/or use.

8. Hungary

There are only few precedents of cross-border development of petroleum resources; therefore Hungary is not aware of relevant treaties or judicial decisions. However, the adaptation of the unitization principles elaborated by the international oil and gas industry is worth considering.

9. Ireland

Ireland indicated that the question was "Not applicable".

10. Jamaica

Legislation has been enacted in Jamaica only in respect of areas within Jamaica's exclusive jurisdiction[1] and the legislation is not, therefore, applicable to the joint regime area.

[1] The Maritime Areas Act (1996) and the Exclusive Economic Zone Act (1991).

11. Mali

In preparation for the possible discovery of hydrocarbon reserves, the question of its transport in border areas is currently being studied. The Government is seeking to define an appropriate legal framework for this activity.

12. Mauritius

Mauritius responded "None".[1]

[1] However, the Government of Mauritius annexed to its response the Petroleum Act, Act No. 6 of 16 April 1970, the text of which, in English, is available for consultation at the Codification Division of the Office of Legal Affairs.

13. Netherlands

1. The 1962 Supplementary Agreement to the 1960 Ems-Dollard Treaty on the allocation of oil and gas is an exceptional agreement in that it provides for the division of oil and gas reserves in an area where no inter-State boundary exists. In the 1960 Ems-Dollard Treaty, the Netherlands and Germany "agreed to disagree" with regard to a boundary in the Ems-Dollard area, which had been under dispute for several hundred years. Taking into account this exceptional situation, it was agreed in 1962 to equally divide the oil and gas reserves between the two countries in an area defined as the "border area". The agreements that have been concluded with respect to the Ems-Dollard estuary are regarded by many as exemplary of how to deal with a situation where no agreement concerning a boundary can be reached between two countries.

2. The 1992 Markham Agreement was a specific agreement for a specific situation, which resulted in an elaborate and detailed agreement.

14. Norway

Reference was made above to the texts of relevant agreements with neighbouring countries.

15. Oman

Oman responded that no information relevant to question 4 was currently available.

16. Portugal

1. As far as is known, there is no agreement on maritime boundaries delimitation with Spain. An agreement with Spain on the definition of the maritime boundaries is important, but it should not prejudice Portugal as far as current legislation is concerned, i.e. it should take into account the Portuguese legislation in force and keep the median line criterion. The 1958 Convention on the Continental Shelf, which uses the median line for the delimitation of the maritime boundary in areas in dispute, was ratified by Portugal and Spain.

2. Portuguese Act No. 33/77 of 28 May 1977 establishes the width and the limits of the territorial sea and a 200-mile exclusive economic zone. It also stipulates that in case of lack of formally valid agreement between both countries, the limit of the zone is the median line. This law is in accordance with the rule established in the Convention on the Continental Shelf. Subsequently, Portuguese Decree Law No. 119/78 of 1 June 1978 settled the external limits of the exclusive economic zone based on the geographic coordinates of the points that determine the limits, defining the median lines between Portugal and the countries with which it has boundaries (Spain and Morocco) (see map No. 1001-E at the Institute Hidrográfico).

3. The rights that result from the Portuguese legislation were reaffirmed in the decree of the President of the Republic of Portugal No. 67–A/97 of 14 October 1997 for ratification of the United Nations Convention on the Law of the Sea.

4. In 2002, in accordance with Portuguese legislation, a bidding round was opened for the concession of oil (liquid and/or gas) exploration and production rights in 14 blocks of the deep offshore (published in the Portuguese *Official Gazette* and in the *Official Journal of the European Union*). Block 14 is limited on the east side by the exclusive economic zone line, in accordance with the above-referenced Decree Law No. 119/78.

5. The blocks were defined in the Universal Transverse Mercator-European Datum 1950 reference system, which is also used in Spain.

6. The Repsol/RWE group made applications for blocks 13 and 14. This group did not just accept and fulfil all requirements but exceeded them. The two blocks were awarded, the contract drafts were initialled and the contracts are expected to be signed.

17. Saint Vincent and the Grenadines

Availability of the Petroleum Stabilization Fund of the Caribbean Community was established in 2004. The Energy Cooperation Agreement (PetroCaribe) was established in 2005.

18. Tajikistan

The Republic of Tajikistan would like to draw the attention of the International Law Commission to the situation in the southern part of Tajikistan, in the Amu Darya District, bordering the Republic of Uzbekistan. There are 16 oil deposits which, due to unresolved demarcation problems, are being used by the Uzbek side. In this regard, Tajikistan is expecting the Commission to propose the best ways for addressing the existing dispute.

19. Turkey

1. According to international law, the delineation of the continental shelf, as well as the exclusive economic zone in semi-enclosed seas such as the Eastern Mediterranean could only be possible through arrangements to be made among all the countries concerned and by observing the rights and interests of all the parties.

2. In this respect, Turkey's views regarding the Greek Cypriot attempts that are contrary to international law and legitimacy, to delimit maritime jurisdiction areas and

to issue licences for exploring oil and gas in the Eastern Mediterranean Sea have been duly conveyed to the United Nations and other relevant international organizations, as well as to the international community, on every occasion.

3. In this context, following the signing of a delimitation agreement between Egypt and the Greek Cypriot side on 17 February 2003, it has been registered with the letter of the Permanent Mission of Turkey dated 2 March 2004, which was also circulated as a United Nations document (published in the *Law of the Sea Bulletin*, No. 54), that the attempts of the Greek Cypriot side to delimit maritime jurisdiction areas are unacceptable, and that Turkey also has legitimate rights and jurisdiction in areas to the west of the Island of Cyprus beyond the longitude 32° 16' 18" East. In this vein, it has been stated that the Greek Cypriot endeavours to create *de facto* situations through unilateral acts in the Eastern Mediterranean would not be accepted.

20. United Kingdom

The United Kingdom responded that it had no further comments.

21. United States

There is no United States legislation or judicial decision specifically addressing transboundary reservoirs at this time and the relevant agency in the federal Government currently lacks domestic legislative authority to enter into a cooperative development arrangement (such as a joint plan, allocation or unitization arrangement) with a neighbouring State. United States outer continental shelf operators are subject to a number of laws and regulations, including provisions for domestic unitization arrangements between leaseholders in certain circumstances. In general, operators are allowed to explore, develop and produce hydrocarbons from their leased acreage pursuant to the "modern rule of capture", which requires, for example, resource conservation practices and maximizing ultimate recovery from resource reservoirs.

F. Question 5

Are there any aspects in this area that may benefit from further elaboration in the context of the Commission's work? Please indicate those aspects.

1. Australia

1. Australia feels that the Commission should approach with caution any examination of areas of international law that directly engage matters that are essentially bilateral in nature. Australia acknowledges the valuable work undertaken by the Commission and especially the Special Rapporteur, Mr. Chusei Yamada, on the general topic of shared natural resources and, in particular, shared underground aquifers.

2. With respect to the Commission's proposed consideration of shared oil and gas, this is one of essential bilateral interest—that is, one to be resolved by negotiation between the particular States involved. The topic is already adequately covered by international law principles and dealt with by States on a bilateral basis.

3. If the Commission proceeds with its consideration of shared oil and gas resources, Australia considers that it should not examine matters relating to offshore boundary delimitation. Whether such resources are in fact physically shared is first and foremost a question of delimitation of territory or maritime jurisdictions. Individual circumstances will impact on each situation and States will want to resolve any differences on a case-by-case approach. These differing circumstances will throw up a degree of complexity that would be difficult to succinctly distil. Maritime delimitation, and assessment of offshore resources, are matters for the States concerned and this is made clear by the 1982 United Nations Convention on the Law of the Sea. In addition, in Australia's experience delimitation agreements generally contain unitization clauses that deal with petroleum resources that straddle the agreed boundary.

2. Bahamas

There is the issue of horizontal drilling regarding transboundary oil and gas resources that requires further dilation.

3. Bosnia and Herzegovina

Bosnia and Herzegovina responded "Not defined".

4. Canada

1. While there is a growing demand for rules governing the use of shared or transboundary natural resources, Canada believes that the oil and gas issue is essentially bilateral in nature, highly technical and politically sensitive and encompasses diverse regional situations. As such, it should be left for resolution by negotiation between States involved. As a result, Canada is not persuaded by the need for the Commission to develop any framework or model agreement(s) or arrangement(s) or draft articles on oil and gas.

2. However, Canada does see the benefit of the Commission outlining elements that could guide States when negotiating agreements on partition of oil and gas. A "template of elements" on the practice applicable, including a review of the existing agreements and State practice, along with an identification of common principles and features, best practices and lessons learned, would be very useful, not only to Canada, but also internationally. Such a template could separate (*a*) circumstances where there is no delimitation agreement in place; and (*b*) circumstances where a delimitation agreement is already in place.

3. Should the Commission proceed with the consideration of the topic of shared oil and gas resources, Canada would not endorse the Commission examining matters relating to offshore boundary delimitation.

5. Cuba

Currently, Cuba considers the Commission's work in the examination of the matter in question to be adequate.

6. Cyprus

With regard to the exploration and exploitation of transboundary oil and gas resources, one aspect that may benefit from further elaboration in the context of the Commission's work is that Israel, the Syrian Arab Republic and Turkey should sign the United Nations Convention on the Law of the Sea, which has been signed by more than 150 countries. The situation in the eastern Mediterranean would be much clearer if those States signed the Convention, since the relevant business environment would benefit from efforts by other States for exploration and exploitation of hydrocarbons in this region.

7. Ireland

Ireland responded "No", and in relation to indicating those aspects, Ireland responded, "Not applicable".

8. Mali

Certain aspects of the transport of Malian oil and gas to terminals in neighbouring countries need more detailed study, namely: integration and harmonization of the regulations of the different countries; and understandings and/or arrangements with neighbouring countries with which Mali shares sedimentary basins.

9. Mauritius

Mauritius responded "No".

10. Myanmar

Regarding additional information in the context of the Commission's work, Myanmar is pleased to inform the Commission of the current status of cooperation with neighbouring States on a bilateral basis. Myanmar is presently selling around 1.2 billion cubic feet of natural gas to Thailand from the Yadana and Yetagun gas fields in the Myanmar offshore Moattama area via pipeline to the Myanmar-Thailand border and sold at the border to Thailand in accordance with an export gas sales agreement, since 1998 and 2000 respectively. In addition, oil companies from neighbouring States have signed production-sharing contracts with the Myanmar Oil and Gas Enterprise, the national oil company, to explore and develop the oil and gas resources of Myanmar onshore, offshore and in deepwater blocks. Plans are also under way to sell natural gas from Myanmar's Rakhine-specified offshore blocks via pipeline to China. Feasibility studies and front-end engineering and design are in progress.

11. Norway

Legal certainty is a key factor in dealing with transboundary oil and gas resources, and this is provided for as according to international law States have a sovereign right to the exploitation of these resources and, to the extent necessary, have entered into bilateral treaties made to handle the individual cases specifically.

12. Oman

Oman responded that no information relevant to question 5 was currently available.

13. United Kingdom

The United Kingdom responded "Not in the view of the United Kingdom".

14. United States

The United States believes that State practice in the area of transboundary oil and gas resources is divergent and relatively sparse, and that specific resource conditions likewise vary widely. In addition, development of oil and gas resources, including transboundary resources, entails very sensitive political and economic considerations. Given these factors, the United States does not believe it would be helpful or wise for the Commission to study this area further or attempt to extrapolate rules of customary international law from limited practice.

EXPULSION OF ALIENS

[Agenda item 6]

DOCUMENT A/CN.4/611*

Fifth report on the expulsion of aliens, by Mr. Maurice Kamto, Special Rapporteur

[Original: French]
[27 March 2009]

CONTENTS

* Incorporating A/CN.4/611/Corr.1.

** Continuation of *Yearbook ... 2007*, vol. II (Part One), document A/CN.4/581 (section title revised).

Multilateral instruments cited in the present report

	Source
American Declaration of the Rights and Duties of Man (Bogota, 2 May 1948)	O.A.S. Res. XXX, adopted by the Ninth International Conference of American States (1948), reprinted in *Basic Documents Pertaining to Human Rights in the Inter-American System*, OEA/Ser.L.V/II.82 doc.6 rev.1 at 17 (1992).
Geneva Conventions for the protection of war victims (Geneva, 12 August 1949)	United Nations, *Treaty Series*, vol. 75, Nos. 970–973, pp. 31 *et seq.*
Geneva Convention for the Amelioration of the Condition of the Wounded and Sick in Armed Forces in the Field	*Ibid.*, No. 970, p. 31.
Geneva Convention for the Amelioration of the Condition of Wounded, Sick and Shipwrecked Members of Armed Forces at Sea	*Ibid.*, No. 971, p. 85.
Geneva Convention relative to the Treatment of Prisoners of War	*Ibid.*, No. 972, p. 135.
Geneva Convention relative to the Protection of Civilian Persons in Time of War	*Ibid.*, No. 973, p. 287.
Convention for the Protection of Human Rights and Fundamental Freedoms (European Convention on Human Rights) (Rome, 4 November 1950)	*Ibid.*, vol. 213, No. 2889, p. 221.
Protocol No. 6 to the Convention for the Protection of Human Rights and Fundamental Freedoms, concerning the Abolition of Death Penalty (Strasbourg, 28 April 1983)	*Ibid.*, vol. 1496, No. 2889, p. 281.
Protocol No. 7 to the Convention for the Protection of Human Rights and Fundamental Freedoms (Strasbourg, 22 November 1984)	*Ibid.*, vol. 1525, No. 2889, p. 195.
Protocol No. 12 to the Convention for the Protection of Human Rights and Fundamental Freedoms (Rome, 4 November 2000)	Council of Europe, *European Treaty Series,* No. 177.
Convention relating to the Status of Refugees (Geneva, 28 July 1951)	United Nations, *Treaty Series*, vol. 189, No. 2545, p. 137.
European Convention on Establishment (with Protocol) (Paris, 13 December 1955)	*Ibid.*, vol. 529, No. 7660, p. 141.
International Convention on the Elimination of All Forms of Racial Discrimination (New York, 21 December 1965)	*Ibid.*, vol. 660, No. 9464, p. 212.
International Covenant on Civil and Political Rights (New York, 16 December 1966)	*Ibid.*, vol. 999, No. 14668, p. 171.
Second Optional Protocol to the International Covenant on Civil and Political Rights, aiming at the abolition of the death penalty (New York, 15 December 1989)	*Ibid.*, vol. 1642, Annex A, No. 14668, p. 414.
International Covenant on Economic, Social and Cultural Rights (New York, 16 December 1966)	*Ibid.*, vol. 993, No. 14531, p. 3.
American Convention on Human Rights: "Pact of San José, Costa Rica" (San José, 22 November 1969)	*Ibid.*, vol. 1144, No. 17955, p. 143.
Convention on the Elimination of All Forms of Discrimination against Women (New York, 18 December 1979)	*Ibid.*, vol. 1249, No. 20378, p. 13.
African Charter on Human and Peoples' Rights (Nairobi, 27 June 1981)	*Ibid.*, vol. 1520, No. 26363, p. 217.
Convention against Torture and Other Cruel, Inhuman or Degrading Treatment or Punishment (New York, 10 December 1984)	*Ibid.*, vol. 1465, No. 24841, p. 112.
Convention on the Rights of the Child (New York, 20 November 1989)	*Ibid.*, vol. 1577, No. 27531, p. 3.
African Charter on the Rights and Welfare of the Child (Addis Ababa, 11 July 1990)	*Human Rights: A Compilation of International Instruments, vol. II, Regional Instruments* (United Nations publication, Sales No. E.97.XIV.1), sect. C, No. 39.
Charter of Fundamental Rights of the European Union (Nice, 7 December 2000)	*Official Journal of the European Communities*, No. C 364 (18 December 2000), p. 1.

Works cited in the present report

ABRAHAM, Ronny

"Article 25" in Louis-Edmond PETTITI, Emmanuel DECAUX and Pierre-Henri IMBERT, eds., *La Convention européenne des droits de l'homme: Commentaire article par article.* Paris, Economica, 1995, pp. 579–590.

ALLAND, Denis, ed.

Droit international public. Paris, Presses universitaires de France ("Droit fondamental" collection), 2000.

BENNOUNA, Mohamed

"Remise en cause et contestations de principe", *La Déclaration universelle des droits de l'homme, 1948–98: Avenir d'un idéal commun.* Paris, La Documentation française, 1999, pp. 243–245.

BOSSUYT, Marc

"Article 14", in Louis-Edmond PETTITI, Emmanuel DECAUX and Pierre-Henri IMBERT, eds., *La Convention européenne des droits de l'homme: Commentaire article par article.* Paris, Economica, 1995, pp. 475–488.

BREITENMOSER, Stephan and Gunter E. WILMS

"Human rights v. extradition: the *Soering* case", *Michigan Journal of International Law*, vol. 11, No. 3, 1990, pp. 845–886.

CABRILLAC, Rémy, and others

Libertés et droits fondamentaux. 14th ed. Paris, Dalloz, 2008.

CALVO, Charles

Le droit international théorique et pratique précédé d'un exposé historique des progrès de la science du droit des gens. 2nd ed. Paris, A. Durand et Pedone-Lauriel, 1870.

CARLIER, Jean-Yves

"Et Genève sera ... la définition du réfugié: bilan et perspectives", *La Convention de Genève du 28 juillet 1951 relative au statut des réfugiés 50 ans après: bilan et perspectives.* Brussels, Bruylant, 2001, pp. 63–89.

CARRILLO-SALCEDO, Juan Antonio

"Article 1", in Louis-Edmond PETTITI, Emmanuel DECAUX and Pierre-Henri IMBERT, eds., *La Convention européenne des droits de l'homme: commentaire article par article.* Paris, Economica, 1995, pp. 135–141.

CHAMPEIL-DESPLATS, Véronique

"La notion de droit 'fondamental' et le droit constitutionnel français", *Recueil Dalloz Sirey de doctrine, de jurisprudence et de législation.* Cahier No. 42, Chronique, 1995, pp. 323–329.

CHETAIL, Vincent

"Le droit des réfugiés à l'épreuve des droits de l'homme: bilan de la jurisprudence de la Cour européenne des droits de l'homme sur l'interdiction du renvoi des étrangers menacés de torture et de traitements inhumains et dégradants", *Belgian Review of International Law,* vol. XXXVII, 2004–1, pp. 155–210.

COHEN-JONATHAN, Gérard

La Convention européenne des droits de l'homme. Paris, Economica, 1989.

"La responsabilité pour atteinte aux droits de l'homme", *La responsabilité dans le système international, Colloque de la Société française pour le droit international.* Paris, Pedone, 1991, pp. 101–135.

"Les droits de l'homme, une valeur internationalisée", *Droits fondamentaux.* No. 1. July–December 2001, pp. 157–164 (www.droits-fondamentaux.org).

COT, Jean-Pierre and Alain PELLET

"Préambule", in Jean-Pierre COT, Alain PELLET and Matias FORTEAU, eds., *La Charte des Nations Unies: commentaire, article par article*, 3rd ed. Paris, Economica, 2005.

COUTURIER, Gérard, Mireille DELMAS-MARTY and Claude LUCAS DE LEYSSAC, eds.

Libertés et droits fondamentaux. Paris, Seuil, 1996.

DE VATTEL, Emer

Le Droit des gens, ou principes de la loi naturelle, appliqués à la conduite et aux affaires des Nations et des Souverains, reproduction of first edition (1758), in James Brown SCOTT, ed., *The Classics of International Law*, vol I. Washington, D.C., Carnegie Institution, 1916.

DECAUX, Emmanuel (ed.)

Le droit face au racisme. Paris, Pedone, 1999.

DELMAS-MARTY, Mireille and Claude LUCAS DE LEYSSAC, eds.

Libertés et droits fondamentaux. 2nd ed. Paris, Seuil, 2002.

DORMENVAL, Agnès

"UN Committee against Torture: practice and perspectives", *Netherlands Quarterly of Human Rights.* vol. 8, No. 1, 1990, pp. 26–44.

DUPUY, Pierre-Marie

Droit international public. 8th ed. Paris, Dalloz, 2006.

EDELMAN, Bernard

"La dignité de la personne humaine, un concept nouveau", *Recueil Dalloz Sirey de doctrine, de jurisprudence et de législation.* Cahier No. 23, Chronique, 1997, pp. 185–188.

FAVOREU, Louis

"Rapport général introductif", *Revue internationale de droit comparé*, vol. 33, No. 2, April–June 1981, pp. 255–281.

FAVOREU, Louis and Loïc PHILIP

Les grandes décisions du Conseil constitutionnel. 9th ed. Paris, Dalloz, 1997.

FIALAIRE, Jacques and Eric MONDIELLI

Droits fondamentaux et libertés publiques. Paris, Ellipses, 2005.

FREDMAN, Sandra, ed.

Discrimination and Human Rights: The Case of Racism. Oxford, Oxford University Press, 2001.

GENEVOIS, Bruno and Robert BADINTER

"Normes de valeur constitutionnelle et degré de protection des droits fondamentaux", *Revue française de droit administratif.* No. 6 (3), May–June 1990, pp. 317–335.

HOLMSTRÖM, Leif, ed.

Conclusions and Recommendations of the UN Committee against Torture: Eleventh to Twenty-Second Sessions (1993–1999). The Hague/Boston/London, Martinus Nijhoff, 2000.

INGELSE, Chris

The UN Committee against Torture: An Assessment. The Hague, Kluwer, 2001.

INSTITUTE OF INTERNATIONAL LAW

"Règles internationales sur l'admission et l'expulsion des étrangers" adoptées, *Annuaire de l'Institut de droit international*, vol. XII, 1892–1894, Session de Genève, pp. 218 *et seq*.

"The protection of human rights and the principle of non-intervention in internal affairs of States", resolutions adopted, *Yearbook*, vol. 63 (II), session of Santiago de Compostela, 1989, pp. 338–345.

JARREAU, Brigitte

"L'éloignement des étrangers: interdiction définitive du territoire français (arrêts Ezzouhdi et Abdouni des 13 et 27 février 2001)", *Centre de recherches et d'études sur les droits de l'homme et le droit humanitaire.* Proceedings of the eighth information session, 2008, accessed 10 January 2013.

KAYSER, Pierre

"Essai de contribution au droit naturel à l'approche du troisième millénaire", *Revue de la Recherche Juridique: Droit prospectif* (Aix-en-Provence), 1998–1, No. XXIII–72, pp. 387–432.

KOLB, Robert

"La jurisprudence internationale en matière de torture et de traitement inhumains ou dégradants", *Revue universelle des droits de l'homme.* vol. 15, No. 7–10, 15 December 2003, pp. 254–287.

LABORDE, Jean-Pierre

"Conclusion: les principes et droits fondamentaux en matière sociale en Espagne et en France", *Bulletin de Droit Comparé du Travail et de la Sécurité Sociale* (Pessac), 1994, No. 2, pp. 119–120.

LE GUYADER, Alain

"La question philosophique d'un noyau dur des droits de l'homme", in Denis MAUGENEST and Paul-Gérard POUGOUÉ, eds., *Les droits de l'homme en Afrique centrale.* Paris, Karthala, 1995, pp. 249–265.

LE POURHIET, Anne-Marie

"Le Conseil constitutionnel et l'éthique bio-médicale", *Études en l'honneur de Georges Dupuis.* Paris, LGDJ, 1997, pp. 213–225.

LILLICH, Richard B.

"The *Soering* case", AJIL, vol. 85, No. 1, January 1991, pp. 128–149.

MARCOUX, Laurent

"Le concept de droits fondamentaux dans le droit de la Communauté économique européenne", *Revue internationale de droit comparé*, vol. 35, No. 4, 1983. pp. 691–733.

MATHIEU, Bertrand

"La dignité de la personne humaine, quel droit? Quel titulaire?" *Recueil Dalloz Sirey de doctrine, de jurisprudence et de législation.* Cahier No. 33, Chronique, 1996, pp. 282–286.

"La supra-constitutionnalité existe-t-elle? Réflexions sur un mythe et quelques réalités", *Les Petites Affiches*, No. 29, 1995, pp. 12–17.

MCKEAN, Warwick

Equality and Discrimination Under International Law. Oxford, Clarendon Press, 1983.

MCRAE, Donald M.

"The contribution of international trade law to the development of international law", *Collected Courses of The Hague Academy of International Law,* vol. 260, Leiden, Nijhoff, 1996, p. 166.

MEYER-BISCH, Patrice

"Le problème des limitations du noyau intangible des droits et d'un droit de l'homme", in Patrice MEYER-BISCH, ed., *Le noyau intangible des droits de l'homme.* Fribourg, Editions universitaires, 1991, pp. 97–121.

NEIRINCK, Claire

"La dignité humaine ou le mauvais usage d'une notion philosophique", in Philippe PEDROT, ed., *Ethique, droit et dignité de la personne.* Paris, Economica, 1999, pp. 39–50.

NOWAK, Manfred

"The implementation functions of the United Nations Committee against Torture", in Manfred NOWAK, Dorothea STEURER and Hannes TRETTER, eds., *Progress in the Spirit of Human Rights.* Kehl/Strasbourg/Arlington, N.P. Engel, 1988, pp. 493–526.

OPSAHL, Torkel

Law and Equality: Selected Articles on Human Rights. Oslo, Ad Notam Gyldendal, 1996, p. 171.

PAVIA, Marie-Luce

"Eléments de réflexion sur la notion de droit fondamental", *Les Petites Affiches*, No. 54, 1994, pp. 6–13.

PHILLIMORE, Robert

Commentaries upon International Law. Philadelphia, T. & J.W. Johnson, Law Booksellers, vols. 1–4, 1854–1861.

PILLET, Antoine

"Recherches sur les droits fondamentaux des États dans l'ordre des rapports internationaux et sur la solution des conflits qu'ils font naitre", RGDIP, vol. 5, 1898, pp. 66 and 236.

PONTIER, Jean-Marie

Droits fondamentaux et libertés publiques. 3rd ed. Paris, Hachette Supérieur, 2007.

RICHER, Laurent

Editorial, "Les droits fondamentaux: une nouvelle catégorie juridique?" *L'Actualité juridique: Droit administratif,* special edition of 20 July–20 August 1998, p. 1.

ROUCOUNAS, Emmanuel

"Facteurs privés et droit international public", *Collected Courses of The Hague Academy of International Law*, vol. 299, 2002, pp. 9–419.

RUSSO, Carlo

"Article 8 § 1" in Louis-Edmond PETTITI, Emmanuel DECAUX and Pierre-Henri IMBERT, eds., *La Convention européenne des droits de l'homme: commentaire article par article.* Paris, Economica, 1995, pp. 305–321.

SAINT-JAMES, Virginie

"Réflexions sur la dignité de l'être humain en tant que concept juridique du droit français", *Recueil Dalloz Sirey de doctrine, de jurisprudence et de législation.* Cahier No. 10, Chronique, 1997, pp. 61–66.

SILVERS, Samuel M.

"The exclusion and expulsion of homosexual aliens", *Columbia Human Rights Law Review*, vol. 15, No. 2, 1983–1984, pp. 295–332.

SUDRE, Frédéric

"La notion de 'peines et traitements inhumains ou dégradants' dans la jurisprudence de la Commission et de la Cour européenne des droits de l'homme", RGDIP, vol. 88, No. 4, 1984, pp. 866–868.

"Extradition et peine de mort: arrêt *Soering* de la Cour européenne des droits de l'homme du 7 juillet 1989", RGDIP, vol. 94, 1990, pp. 103 *et seq.*

"Quel noyau intangible des droits de l'homme?", in Denis MAUGENEST and Paul-Gérard POUGOUÉ, eds., *Les droits de l'homme en Afrique centrale.* Paris, Karthala, 1995, pp. 267–275.

"Article 3", in Louis-Edmond PETTITI, Emmanuel DECAUX and Pierre-Henri IMBERT, eds., *La Convention européenne des droits de l'homme: commentaire article par article.* Paris, Economica, 1995, pp. 155–175.

Droit international et européen des droits de l'homme. 4th rev. ed. Paris, Presses universitaires de France, 1999.

TCHAKOUA, Jean-Marie

Dignité et droits fondamentaux des salariés: réflexion à partir des droits camerounais et français. University of Yaoundé II Law School (dissertation), 1999.

THERON, Jean-Pierre

"Dignité et liberté: propos sur une jurisprudence contestable", *Pouvoir et liberté. Études offertes à Jacques Mourgeon.* Brussels, Bruylant, 1988, pp. 295–306.

VAN BOVEN, Théo

"Convention de sauvegarde des droits de l'homme et des libertés fondamentales: commentaire du préambule", in Louis-Edmond PETTITI, Emmanuel DECAUX and Pierre-Henri IMBERT, eds., *La Convention européenne des droits de l'homme: commentaire article par article.* Paris, Economica, 1995, pp. 125–134.

VAN DEN WYNGAERT, Christine

"Applying the European Convention on Human Rights to extradition: opening Pandora's box?" *International and Comparative Law Quarterly*, vol. 39, No. 4, 1990, pp. 757–779.

VAN MUYLDER, Céline

"Le droit au respect de la vie privée des étrangers", *Revue française de droit administratif*, No. 17 (4), July–August 2001, pp. 797–806.

VEGLÉRIS, Phedon

"Le principe d'égalité dans la Déclaration universelle et la Convention européenne des droits de l'homme", *Miscellanea W. J. Ganshof van der Meersch*, vol. I, Brussels, Bruylant, 1972, pp. 565–588.

VIERDAG, E. W.

The Concept of Discrimination in International Law: with special reference to human rights. The Hague, Nijhoff, 1973.

WARBRICK, Colin

"Coherence and the European Court of Human Rights: the adjudicative background to the *Soering* case", *Michigan Journal of International Law*, vol. 11, No. 4, 1990, pp. 1073–1096.

WILT, Harmen G. VAN DER

"Après *Soering*: the relationship between extradition and human rights in the legal practice of Germany, the Netherlands and the United States", *Netherlands International Law Review*, vol. 42, No. 1, 1995, pp. 53–80.

ZÜHLKE, Susanne and Jens-Christian PASTILLE

"Extradition and the European Convention—*Soering* revisited", *Heidelberg Journal of International Law*, vol. 59, No. 3, 1999, pp. 749–784.

Introduction

1. In his fourth report,[1] the Special Rapporteur considered the issue of expulsion in cases of dual or multiple nationality and that of loss of nationality or denationalization. While his analysis of these issues gave rise to heated discussion by the Commission, most of its members shared the Special Rapporteur's conclusion that it would not be worthwhile for the Commission to set out draft rules specific to these issues, even in the interest of progressive development of international law,[2] since the topic dealt not with the nationality regime but with the expulsion of aliens.

2. It should also be recalled that the working group established in 2008, at the sixtieth session of the Commission, in order to consider the issues raised by the expulsion of persons having dual or multiple nationality and by denationalization in relation to expulsion concluded that: (*a*) "the commentary to the draft articles should indicate that, for the purposes of the draft articles, the principle of the non-expulsion of nationals applies also to persons who have legally acquired one or several other nationalities"; and that (*b*) the commentary should include "wording to make it clear that States should not use denationalization as a means of circumventing their obligations under the principle of the non-expulsion of nationals". These conclusions were approved by the Commission, which requested the Drafting Committee to take them into consideration in its work.[3]

3. States' representatives took a variety of positions on the topic in general, and on the questions addressed in the fourth report in particular, during the Sixth Committee's consideration, at the sixty-third session of the United Nations General Assembly, of the report of the International Law Commission on the work of its sixtieth session. Ultimately, however, it was clear from the discussion that most of the delegations that spoke on this topic shared the Special Rapporteur's view that the Commission would be unwise to undertake the preparation of draft articles on the issues of dual or multiple nationality, loss of nationality and denationalization in the context of expulsion.[4]

4. With regard to general comments on the topic, its scope of application, the definitions proposed by the Special Rapporteur and the right of expulsion and its limitations, a few States, even at this stage, expressed doubts as to whether the topic of the expulsion of aliens lent itself to codification and progressive development.[5] Other States said that there appeared to be no need for codification in certain areas, such as that of migrant workers,[6] while still others stated, concerning the scope of the topic, that questions relating to non-admission, extradition and other forms of movement of persons,[7] to expulsion in situations of armed conflict[8] or to the status of refugees, non-refoulement and movement of populations[9] should be excluded. With regard to definitions, some States considered that the term "territory" was vague[10] or that there was no need for a separate definition of the term "conduct".[11] Another delegation

[1] *Yearbook ... 2008*, vol. II (Part One), document A/CN.4/594.

[2] *Ibid.*, para. 35.

[3] *Ibid.*, vol. II (Part Two), para. 171.

[4] See, in particular, the statements made by Canada (*Official Records of the General Assembly, Sixty-third Session, Sixth Committee*, 20th meeting (A/C.6/63/SR.20), para. 34), France (*ibid.*, 19th meeting (A/C.6/63/SR.19), para. 17), Greece (*ibid.*, 24th meeting (A/C.6/63/SR.24), para. 5), the Islamic Republic of Iran (*ibid.*, para. 39), Israel (*ibid.*, para. 77), Italy (*ibid.*, 19th meeting (A/C.6/63/SR.19), para. 98), New Zealand (*ibid.*, 22nd meeting (A/C.6/63/SR.22), para. 9), the Netherlands (*ibid.*, 20th meeting (A/C.6/63/SR.20), para. 16), Romania (*ibid.*, 21st meeting (A/C.6/63/SR.21), para. 57) and the United Kingdom (*ibid.*, para. 25).

[5] See the statement made by the United Kingdom (A/C.6/63/SR.21), para. 25.

[6] See the statement made by Denmark on behalf of the Nordic countries (*ibid.*, 20th meeting (A/C.6/63/SR.20), para. 2).

[7] See the statement made by the United States (*ibid.*, 21st meeting (A/C.6/63/SR.21), para. 9).

[8] See the statements made by the United States (*ibid.*, 21st meeting (A/C.6/63/SR.21), para. 9) and Israel (*ibid.*, 24th meeting (A/C.6/63/SR.24), para. 76).

[9] See the statement made by Israel (*ibid.*).

[10] See the statements made by the representatives of the United States (*ibid.*, 21st meeting (A/C.6/63/SR.21), para. 12) and Israel (*ibid.*, 24th meeting (A/C.6/63/SR.24), para. 76).

[11] See the statement made by Israel (*ibid.*).

proposed that the Commission should make it clear that the term "refugee" should be defined in accordance with each country's obligations in that regard.[12] Several States stressed the need to strike a balance between the sovereign right of States to expel aliens and the limits imposed by international law, particularly the rules relating to the protection of human rights and the treatment of aliens;[13] in that spirit, some States made it clear that the right of expulsion implied, conversely, the obligation of States to readmit their own nationals.[14] In addition, one State noted that expulsion should be based on legitimate grounds such as public safety and national security, as defined in the domestic law,[15] while another maintained that it should be possible to expel aliens not lawfully present for that reason alone.[16]

5. Clearly, these comments and observations by States concerned issues that had already been hotly debated by the Commission. These debates allowed the Special Rapporteur to provide the necessary clarification and explanations and allowed the Commission to develop a general approach to the topic, to which it can make any necessary modifications as the process continues. For this reason, the Special Rapporteur will not dwell further on the matter, particularly as most of the concerns were taken duly into account in the second report on the expulsion of aliens (*Yearbook ... 2006*, vol. II (Part One), document A/CN.4/573).

6. With regard, more specifically, to comments made on the issues of expulsion in cases of dual or multiple nationality and denationalization followed by expulsion, which were the subject of the Special Rapporteur's fourth report,[17] various concerns were expressed in connection with different aspects of the Special Rapporteur's analysis. One State expressed doubts as to the appropriateness of including a draft article on non-expulsion of nationals.[18] However, several other States stressed that the expulsion of nationals was prohibited by international law[19] since the principle of non-expulsion of nationals was a basic human right recognized under customary international law.[20] However, while some States considered that this was an absolute principle,[21] others believed that it may be subject to certain derogations under exceptional circumstances[22] but that any exception to the principle must be carefully drafted and narrowly construed.[23] Several States endorsed the Commission's position that the principle of non-expulsion of nationals applied also to persons who had legally acquired more than one nationality.[24] One of those States suggested that this should be explicitly reflected in draft article 4[25] and others proposed that the matter should be clarified in the commentary.[26] Similarly, it was noted that the criterion of "effective" or "dominant" nationality could not justify a State's treating its nationals as aliens for the purposes of expulsion.[27] However, one State supported the opposite point of view, maintaining that the principle of non-expulsion of nationals did not typically apply to persons with dual or multiple nationality and that it was necessary to clarify what was meant by "effective" nationality.[28]

7. Concerning the possible relationship between, on the one hand, loss of nationality and denationalization, and, on the other, expulsion, some States reaffirmed the right of every person to a nationality and the right not to be arbitrarily deprived of one's nationality.[29] One State considered that denationalization was prohibited by international law,[30] while others felt that denationalization was permissible under certain circumstances[31]—on condition,

[12] See the statement made by the United States (*ibid.*, 21st meeting (A/C.6/63/SR.21), para. 14). Surprisingly, the same country suggested that the language of draft article 5, on refugees, should more consistently track the provisions of the 28 July 1951 Convention relating to the Status of Refugees (arts. 32 and 33) and should take the distinction between legal and illegal refugees into account (*ibid.*).

[13] See the statements made by Denmark on behalf of the Nordic countries (*ibid.*, 20th meeting (A/C.6/63/SR.20), para. 3), Japan (*ibid.*, 22nd meeting (A/C.6/63/SR.22), para. 18), New Zealand (*ibid.*, para. 9), El Salvador (*ibid.*, 23rd meeting (A/C.6/63/SR.23), para. 48) and the Islamic Republic of Iran (*ibid.*, 24th meeting (A/C.6/63/SR.24), para. 73).

[14] See the statement made by Denmark on behalf of the Nordic countries (*ibid.*, 20th meeting (A/C.6/63/SR.20), para. 3).

[15] See the statement made by Islamic Republic of Iran (*ibid.*, 24th meeting (A/C.6/63/SR.24), para. 37).

[16] See the statement made by United States (*ibid.*, 21st meeting (A/C.6/63/SR.21), para. 10).

[17] *Yearbook ... 2008*, vol. II (Part One), document A/CN.4/594.

[18] See the statement made by the United Kingdom (*Official Records of the General Assembly, Sixty-third Session, Sixth Committee*, 21st meeting (A/C.6/63/SR.21), para. 25).

[19] See, in particular, the statements made by the Czech Republic (*ibid.*, 19th meeting (A/C.6/63/SR.19), para. 93), Hungary (*ibid.*, 20th meeting (A/C.6/63/SR.20), para. 30), the Islamic Republic of Iran (*ibid.*, 24th meeting (A/C.6/63/SR.24), para. 37) and Israel (*ibid.*, para. 76).

[20] See the statement made by Hungary (*ibid.*, 20th meeting (A/C.6/63/SR.20), para. 30).

[21] See the statements made by the Republic of Korea (*ibid.*, 19th meeting (A/C.6/63/SR.19), para. 65), the Czech Republic (*ibid.*, para. 93), Portugal (*ibid.*, 20th meeting (A/C.6/63/SR.20), para. 26), the Islamic Republic of Iran and El Salvador (*ibid.*, 23rd meeting (A/C.6/63/SR.23), para. 49).

[22] See the statements made by Romania (*ibid.*, 21st meeting (A/C.6/63/SR.21), para. 57) and Qatar (*ibid.*, 24th meeting (A/C.6/63/SR.24), para. 77).

[23] See the statement made by Greece (*ibid.*, 24th meeting (A/C.6/63/SR.24), para. 4).

[24] See the statements made by France (*ibid.*, 19th meeting (A/C.6/63/SR.19), para. 17), the Czech Republic (*ibid.*, para. 93), the Netherlands (*ibid.*, 20th meeting (A/C.6/63/SR.20), para. 13), Portugal (*ibid.*, para. 26), Hungary (*ibid.*, para. 30), the United States (*ibid.*, 21st meeting (A/C.6/63/SR.21), para. 13), Poland (*ibid.*, para. 33), the Russian Federation (*ibid.*, para. 43), Chile (*ibid.*, 22nd meeting (A/C.6/63/SR.22), para. 17), India (*ibid.*, 23rd meeting (A/C.6/63/SR.23), para. 23), El Salvador (*ibid.*, paras. 48–49), Greece (*ibid.*, 24th meeting (A/C.6/63/SR.24), para. 4) and the Islamic Republic of Iran (*ibid.*, para. 38).

[25] See the statement made by the Netherlands (*ibid.*, 20th meeting (A/C.6/63/SR.20), para. 16).

[26] See the statements made by France (*ibid.*, 19th meeting (A/C.6/63/SR.19), para. 17) and Chile (*ibid.*, 22nd meeting (A/C.6/63/SR.22), para. 17).

[27] See the statements made by the Czech Republic (*ibid.*, 19th meeting (A/C.6/63/SR.19), para. 93), the Netherlands (*ibid.*, 20th meeting (A/C.6/63/SR.20), para. 14), Portugal (*ibid.*, para. 26), Greece (*ibid.*, 24th meeting (A/C.6/63/SR.24), para. 4) and the Islamic Republic of Iran (*ibid.*, para. 38).

[28] See the statement made by Cuba (24th meeting (A/C.6/63/SR.24), para. 27).

[29] See the statements made by Portugal (*ibid.*, 20th meeting (A/C.6/63/SR.20), para. 26) and Romania (*ibid.*, 21st meeting (A/C.6/63/SR.21), para. 57).

[30] See the statement made by the Islamic Republic of Iran (*ibid.*, 24th meeting (A/C.6/63/SR.24), para. 37).

[31] See the statements made by the Netherlands (*ibid.*, 20th meeting (A/C.6/63/SR.20), para. 15) and Israel (*ibid.*, 24th meeting (A/C.6/63/SR.24), para. 76).

said some, that it did not lead to statelessness,[32] that it was done in accordance with domestic law[33] and that it was non-discriminatory,[34] and on the understanding that it must not be done arbitrarily or unlawfully.[35] On this point, a number of States agreed with the Commission's conclusion that States should not use denationalization as a means of circumventing the principle of non-expulsion of nationals,[36] and the inclusion of a draft article to that effect was proposed.[37]

[32] See the statements made by the Netherlands (*ibid.*, 20th meeting (A/C.6/63/SR.20), para. 15), Greece and Cuba (24th meeting (A/C.6/63/SR.24), para. 27).

[33] See the statement made by Greece.

[34] *Ibid.*

[35] See the statements made by Greece and Israel (*ibid.*, 24th meeting (A/C.6/63/SR.24), para. 76).

[36] See the statements made by Portugal (*ibid.*, 20th meeting (A/C.6/63/SR.20), para. 26), the United States (*ibid.*, 21st meeting (A/C.6/63/SR.21), para. 13), Poland (*ibid.*, para. 33), the Russian Federation (*ibid.*, para. 43), Chile (*ibid.*, 22nd meeting (A/C.6/63/SR.22), para. 11), India (*ibid.*, 23rd meeting (A/C.6/63/SR.23), para. 23) and El Salvador (*ibid.*, para. 48).

[37] See the statement made by Italy (*ibid.*, 19th meeting (A/C.6/63/SR.19), para. 98).

8. Bearing all this in mind, it is now time to pursue the study of the rules that limit the right of expulsion, which was begun in the third report.[38] As stated in that report, the right to expel must be exercised with respect for the *rules of international law*[39] that limit it. The third report examined the limits relating to the person to be expelled and identified, in turn, the principles of non-expulsion of nationals, non-expulsion of refugees, non-expulsion of stateless persons and prohibition of collective expulsion.

9. The present report will pursue this study by considering, on the one hand, the limits relating to the obligation to respect the human rights of persons being expelled and, on the other, some practices that are prohibited by international law on expulsion.

[38] *Yearbook ... 2007*, vol. II (Part One), document A/CN.4/581.

[39] In his previous reports, the Special Rapporteur spoke of the "fundamental rules of international law". In the light of the merits of the comments made both within and outside the Commission, he decided to delete the word "fundamental", which restricts the scope of the relevant rules of international law and which, moreover, is likely to give rise to controversy as to which rules of international law are, or are not, considered fundamental.

GENERAL RULES

General principles

A right to be exercised subject to respect for the rules of international law

Limits relating to the requirement of respect for fundamental human rights

(a) *Preliminary considerations*

(i) *Protection of the rights of all human beings*

10. Persons being expelled, for whatever reason, remain human beings who, as such, must continue to enjoy all their fundamental rights. Such persons have the same attributes and aspire to the same freedoms, regardless of their race, ethnicity, sex, beliefs or nationality; this is what has been called the universal identity of human beings.[40] A tendency to place humankind at the centre of international ethics has made the protection of these fundamental rights a major concern of contemporary international law. As is well known, this protection is no longer left to the discretion of States, a practice justified by the domestic jurisdiction doctrine on the dubious grounds of absolute State sovereignty. Persons whom a State has decided to expel must be protected, particularly as such persons are made vulnerable by their status as aliens and by the prospect of their expulsion. They are guaranteed this protection under international law and under the law of the expelling State, regardless of their legal status and of the conditions under which they entered the territory of that State, whether as legal or illegal aliens; nationals are not concerned owing to the principle that a State may not expel its own nationals.

[40] Dupuy, *Droit international public*, p. 214.

11. This equal protection of all people is the cornerstone of all human rights regimes. It derives from both the universal human rights instruments and the regional legal instruments. For example, the Universal Declaration of Human Rights (1948)[41] proclaims in the first paragraph of its preamble that "recognition of the inherent dignity and of the equal and inalienable rights of all members of the human family is the foundation of freedom, justice and peace in the world". More specifically, article 2 of this founding document states, in language that merits quotation *in extenso*:

> Everyone is entitled to all the rights and freedoms set forth in this Declaration, without distinction of any kind, such as race, colour, sex, language, religion, political or other opinion, national or social origin, property, birth or other status. Furthermore, no distinction shall be made on the basis of the political, jurisdictional or international status of the country or territory to which a person belongs, whether it be independent, trust, non-self-governing or under any other limitation of sovereignty.

12. In the same spirit, the High Contracting Parties to the Convention for the Protection of Human Rights and Fundamental Freedoms of 4 November 1950, hereinafter the "European Convention on Human Rights", in article 1 thereof—significantly entitled "Obligation to

[41] General Assembly resolution 217 (III), 10 December 1948. The texts of the legal instruments cited in this report are published in *Human Rights: A Compilation of International Instruments*, vols. I and II (First Part) (United Nations publication, Sales No. E.02.XIV.4 and E.97. XIV.1) (New York and Geneva, 2002).

respect human rights"—undertook to "secure to everyone within their jurisdiction the rights and freedoms defined in … this Convention". This provision not only recalls the general obligation of respect for human rights; it internalizes that obligation by guaranteeing enjoyment of the rights and freedoms set forth in the Convention to anyone within the jurisdiction of the High Contracting Parties.[42] In a similar vein, article 1 of the 1969 American Convention on Human Rights ("Pact of San José, Costa Rica"), "Obligation to Respect Rights", provides as follows:

> The States Parties to this Convention undertake to respect the rights and freedoms recognized herein and to ensure to all persons subject to their jurisdiction the free and full exercise of those rights and freedoms, without any discrimination for reasons of race, colour, sex, language, religion, political or other opinion, national or social origin, economic status, birth, or any other social condition.

In articles 1 and 2, the African Charter on Human and Peoples' Rights states, in different words:

> Every individual shall be entitled to the enjoyment of the rights and freedoms recognized and guaranteed in the present Charter without distinction of any kind such as race, ethnic group, colour, sex, language, religion, political or any other opinion, national and social origin, fortune, birth or other status

and that the States members of the Organization of African Unity, who are automatically parties to the Charter, "shall recognize the rights, duties and freedoms enshrined in this Chapter and shall undertake to adopt legislative or other measures to give effect to them". The protection of rights and freedoms is extremely broad and comprehensive, and States' obligation is both specific and extensive.

13. From these legal instruments, a principle of non-discrimination among the beneficiaries of the rights and freedoms set forth therein emerges; this principle is expressed differently according to whether the instrument is universal or regional in nature. The universal instruments concern all human beings, wherever they may be and whatever their origin. In the regional instruments, the reference to persons "subject to the jurisdiction" of the State, particularly in the European Convention on Human Rights, appears to limit the number of beneficiaries of the rights and freedoms set forth in the Convention since the principle of universality is maintained *ratione personae* rather than *ratione loci*; everyone, regardless of legal status or condition, has the benefit of the rights and freedoms set forth in these regional instruments.

14. Thus, the status of national confers no more rights than that of alien. By the same token, alien status does not create a situation of inferiority with regard to the protection required by human rights; in fact, even unlawful residence in the territory of a State cannot justify a lessening of these fundamental rights, even during expulsion proceedings. In its judgement in *Mubilanzila Mayeka and Kaniki Mitunga v. Belgium*,[43] the European Court of Human Rights recalled that in exercising their sovereign right to control their borders and the entry and stay of aliens, States must comply with their international obligations, including those established in the European Convention on Human Rights (arts. 3, 5 and 8) and the Convention on the Rights of the Child of 20 November 1989 (arts. 3, 10 and 37)—in other words, they must respect the fundamental rights of aliens and, in particular, those of children. According to the Court, "the States' interest in foiling attempts to circumvent immigration rules must not deprive aliens of the protection afforded by these conventions or deprive foreign minors, especially if unaccompanied, of the protection their status warrants".[44]

15. Protection of the rights of aliens has been of special concern to the United Nations General Assembly since the 1970s. A subcommission was established to consider the matter; it concluded its work in 1977.[45] On the basis of the outcome of this work, the General Assembly adopted the Declaration on the Human Rights of Individuals Who are not Nationals of the Country in which They Live.[46] The Declaration covers all the individuals in question and calls for respect for the human rights of aliens, specifically the right to life; the right to privacy; the right to be equal before courts and tribunals; the right to freedom of opinion and religion; and the right to retain their own language, culture and tradition.[47] The Declaration also prohibits individual or collective expulsion on discriminatory grounds[48] and establishes the right to join trade unions and the right to safe and healthy working conditions, the right to medical care, the right to social security and the right to education.[49] However, the Declaration remains quite general with regard to the scope of the rights protected. Thus, closer study is needed in order to try to identify, through international human rights instruments and the judicial practices of universal and regional monitoring bodies and national courts, the specific human rights rules that must particularly be respected during expulsions.

(ii) *Concept of "fundamental rights"*

16. The question is whether aliens being expelled are entitled to enjoy all human rights, or whether the specific nature of their status requires that only their fundamental rights be guaranteed in this instance.

17. The Special Rapporteur considers it unrealistic to require that a person being expelled be able to benefit from all the human rights guaranteed by international instruments and by the domestic law of the expelling State. For example, how would it be possible to guarantee, throughout the expulsion process, the exercise of their right to education, to freedom of assembly and association and to free enterprise; their freedom to choose a profession; and their right to work, to marry and to found a family? It seems more realistic and more consistent with State practice to limit the rights guaranteed during expulsion to the *fundamental* human rights.

---

[42] See Carrillo-Salcedo, "Article 1", p. 135.

[43] ECHR, application No. 13178/03, Judgement of 12 October 2006, *Reports of Judgments and Decisions 2006–XI*.

[44] *Ibid.*, p. 254, para. 81.

[45] Report prepared by Baroness Elles, "The Problem of the Applicability of Existing International Provisions for the Protection of Human Rights to Individuals Who Are Not Citizens of the Country in Which They Live" (E/CN.4/Sub.2/L.628 and Add. 1).

[46] Declaration on the Human Rights of Individuals Who are not Nationals of the Country in which They Live, General Assembly resolution 40/144 of 13 December 1985.

[47] *Ibid.*, art. 5.

[48] *Ibid.*, art. 7.

[49] *Ibid.*, art. 8.

18. While this concept of fundamental rights has its basis in legal language, its meaning is remarkably confused by the use of other concepts that are considered to be related or equivalent. For example, the legal literature includes examples of a failure to distinguish between the concepts of human rights, civil liberties, fundamental freedoms, fundamental rights and freedoms and fundamental principles, and it is not clear that they refer to the same legal reality.[50]

19. The concept of fundamental rights corresponds to several domestic law models. First, some rights are considered fundamental owing to their place in the hierarchy of law; constitutionally protected rights and freedoms fall into this category.[51] It has even been argued that fundamental rights are essentially constitutional[52] and that this distinguishes them from the broader category of civil liberties. The fundamental rights would thus be those that are expressed or guaranteed by the higher laws of a given legal system or that are essential to the existence and content of other such rights.[53]

20. Both of these models draw upon the legal system for elements of a definition of "fundamental rights"; they are therefore subject to the vagaries of the legal edifice and to the arbitrariness of lawmakers. The question of the contingency of fundamental rights lies at the heart of a major controversy. According to some authors, these rights are superior to legal systems because they represent higher values.[54] This position recalls the idea of natural law, which is continually laid to rest and then resurrected.[55] Opposing this model are those who believe that the existence of supra-constitutional rules of domestic law is a virtually ontological or absolute impossibility,[56] especially since their existence would deprive the people of their (lawmaking) sovereignty. The French Constitutional Council shares this view[57] although, on close examination, its words suggest[58] that by repeating the language of the Constitution, the Council, perhaps unconsciously, was merely taking note of (pre)-existing rules rather than drawing attention to the rules established by the regulatory authorities. It is thus understandable that the Constitutional Court of Germany should take the view that the substance of fundamental rights lies beyond the scope of any constituent power, even the drafters of a new constitution.[59] This position is comparable to the one expressed in a judgement of the Constitutional Court of Italy, which specifically stated:

> The Italian Constitution includes several supreme principles which cannot be overturned or modified in their essential content, even through a constitutional review act or other constitutional legislation.[60]

21. This debate—which is, moreover, a classic one—between the supporters of legal positivism and the defenders of natural law is not unrelated to international human rights law, but the discussion has been less heated in this area; as we shall see, despite some reluctance, the idea that a category of inviolable human rights exists ultimately prevailed.

22. The fundamental-rights-based approach is not without problems; the question is to determine what is meant by "fundamental rights". The terminology is well established in legal theory, which has endorsed it without always being able to find a precise definition of the concept.[61] Similarly, the word "fundamental" is included in the titles of a few international human rights instruments, such as the aforementioned European Convention for the Protection of Human Rights and Fundamental Freedoms and the 11 protocols thereto; the Declaration on the Right and Responsibility of Individuals, Groups and Organs of Society to Promote and Protect Universally Recognized Human Rights and Fundamental Freedoms[62] and the Basic Principles for the Treatment of Prisoners.[63]

23. The concept of the "fundamental rights" of human beings vaguely recalls the theory of the fundamental rights of States, which appeared in the eighteenth-century legal theory of de Vattel.[64] The concept of the fundamental rights of States, which is a direct offshoot of de Vattel's theory of the perfect rights and obligations of States, was systematized in the nineteenth century by authors such as Argentinean diplomat Carlos Calvo,[65] French

[50] See Tchakoua, *Dignité et droits fondamentaux des salariés: réflexion à partir des droits camerounais et français*, p. 5.

[51] See Favoreu, "Rapport général introductif", p. 671.

[52] See Genevois, "Normes de valeur constitutionnelle et degré de protection des droits fondamentaux", p. 317.

[53] Marcoux, "Le concept de droits fondamentaux dans le droit de la Communauté économique européenne", p. 691.

[54] See, in particular, Laborde, "Conclusions", pp. 119–120.

[55] See Kayser, "Essai de contribution au droit naturel à l'approche du troisième millénaire", p. 287.

[56] See Mathieu, "La supra-constitutionnalité existe-t-elle? Réflexions sur un mythe et quelques réalités", p. 12.

[57] See, for example, its Decision No. 92–312 DC of 2 September 1992, *Recueil*, p. 94.

[58] The 1958 French Constitution, like those of several other countries, uses the verbs "recognize" (*reconnaître*) and "proclaim" (*proclamer*) in setting forth fundamental rights. These two verbs do not convey the idea of (normative) creation; according to the usual French-language dictionaries (*Le Petit Robert*, *Larousse*), "to proclaim" means "to announce or recognize by an official instrument" and "recognize" means "to acknowledge as true or real", "to take note of, to reveal".

[59] See the Court's decision of 23 April 1991.

[60] Judgement cited by Favoreux and Philip, *Les grandes décisions du Conseil constitutionnel*, p. 826.

[61] The search engine Google finds several thousand hits for "droits fondamentaux" (fundamental rights). See, for example, the quarterly online journal *Droits fondamentaux* (www.droits-fondamentaux.org), No. 1 (July–December 2001). An editorial in this volume by Emmanuel Decaux uses the term only once, stating that today, as in the past, the fundamental rights remain a challenge. But he explains neither the meaning of this concept nor his choice, stating only that "the universal and indivisible rights proclaimed by the Charter of the United Nations in 1945 deserve more than lip service"; only this sentence vaguely suggests his position on the matter; Cabrillac and others, *Libertés et droits fondamentaux*; Pontier, *Droits fondamentaux et libertés publiques*; Delmas-Marty and Lucas de Leyssac, eds., *Libertés et droits fondamentaux*; Couturier, Delmas-Marty and Lucas de Leyssac, eds., *Libertés et droits fondamentaux*; and Fialaire and Mondielli, *Droits fondamentaux et libertés publiques*; see also, *inter alia*, Carlier, "Et Genève sera ... La définition du réfugié: bilan et perspectives", which mentions the contextualization of fundamental rights, p. 79.

[62] Adopted by General Assembly in its resolution 53/144 of 9 December 1998.

[63] Adopted and proclaimed by General Assembly in its resolution 45/111 of 14 December 1990.

[64] See de Vattel, *Le Droit des gens ou principes de la loi naturelle, appliqués à la conduite et aux affaires des Nations et des Souverains*, 1758.

[65] See Calvo, *Le droit international théorique et pratique.*

university professor Antoine Pillet[66] and British judge Robert Philimore.[67] This theory is based on the idea that States, by the mere fact of their existence, have inherent, permanent and fundamental rights in their relations with other States. It is imperative for all States to respect these rights, which are thus at the root of the law of nations and of all international relations, both in peacetime and in wartime; similarly, violation of these rights justifies the use of force. The content of these fundamental rights of States varies from one author to another, but most of them refer to what was known at that time as the right to self-preservation: the right to respect for sovereignty, to trade and to equality. The earliest legal theorists considered that these fundamental rights of States arose from natural law. For that reason, this theory was abandoned under the deep and lasting influence of positivism on international legal theory.[68]

24. This theory cannot be transferred mechanically to the field of human rights, but it is clear that the two situations share the dominant idea of a set of rights that are essential to the very existence of both the State and the individual. Moreover, it was the Charter of the United Nations that officially introduced the concept of the "fundamental rights" of persons by proclaiming, in its Preamble, that "the peoples of the United Nations … reaffirm faith in fundamental human rights, in the dignity and worth of the human person, in the equal rights of men and women …".[69] Such a statement is also found in the International Covenant on Civil and Political Rights and the International Covenant on Economic, Social and Cultural Rights; article 5, paragraph 2, of the former instrument states that "there shall be no restriction upon or derogation from any of the *fundamental human rights** recognized or existing in any State Party to the present Covenant …". Moreover, the Charter of the United Nations states that one of the purposes of the United Nations is "to achieve international co-operation" in, *inter alia*, "encouraging respect for human rights and for *fundamental freedoms** for all without distinction as to race, sex, language, or religion".[70] The words "human rights and fundamental freedoms" also appear in Article 55 (*c*) of the Charter.[71]

25. Clearly, the vocabulary is somewhat inconsistent. The reference is either to "fundamental rights" or to "human rights and fundamental freedoms"; "fundamental" modifies "freedoms", which shows that rights are not at issue here. The expression "fundamental rights" is not used in Article 1, paragraph 3, or Article 55 (*c*), of the Charter of the United Nations. While the authors of commentaries on the Preamble to the Charter take note of this fact, they do not discuss it or draw any conclusions.[72] However, the two expressions cannot be said to be synonymous. Is this shift from "fundamental human rights" to "human rights and fundamental freedoms" a sign that the framers of the Charter wished to limit the scope of the fundamental norms in question to those that touched on freedoms?

26. There is nothing to support such a conclusion. The truth is that no international instrument provides a definition of the concept of "fundamental rights", or even that of "fundamental freedoms", which appears—as we have seen—in the wording of several international conventions. We might have hoped for clarification from the Commission or the European Court of Human Rights, at least with regard to the "fundamental freedoms" mentioned in the 1950 European Convention on Human Rights. The Commission and the Court have indeed referred explicitly or implicitly to the fifth paragraph of the preamble to this Convention as a reflection of one of its essential characteristics, the attempt to strike "a just balance between the protection of the general interest of the Community and the respect due to fundamental human rights while attaching particular importance to the latter".[73] While specifically entitled the "Charter of Fundamental Rights of the European Union",[74] the instrument adopted on 7 December 2000 at the Nice Summit by the European Parliament, the Council of the European Union and the European Commission provides no assistance in defining the concept of "fundamental rights"; neither its preamble nor its articles have anything to offer in that regard. We might conclude from this that all the rights set forth in the 54 articles of the European Charter are the "fundamental rights" to which it refers. The title of the instrument supports this theory, but was that really the intention of its drafters?

27. The judgement handed down by the European Court of Human Rights in *Golder* followed a logic that might be helpful in determining the meaning of the concept of "fundamental rights". In that case, the Court did not ignore the British Government's comment that the drafters of the European Convention on Human Rights had taken a "selective approach" and that the Convention did not seek to protect human rights in general, but merely "certain of the Rights stated in the Universal Declaration".[75] This leads to the following conclusion: just as each international human rights instrument targets a particular aspect of human rights (such as the rights of the child, the rights of women, the rights of migrant workers or slavery) or targets only certain rights and freedoms, it will easily be agreed that all human rights cannot be exercised simultaneously at all times. The range of fundamental rights may vary according to the status and current situation of individuals; however, these variations must occur around what is held to be a "hard core" regarded as inviolable. Rarely have jurists addressed this issue squarely.

---

[66] See Pillet, "Recherches sur les droits fondamentaux des états dans l'ordre des rapports internationaux …".

[67] See Philimore, *Commentaries upon International Law*, 1854–1861.

[68] For a recent summary of this theory, see Alland, ed., *Droit international public*, pp. 78–79.

[69] Preamble to the Charter of the United Nations.

[70] Article 1, paragraph 3, of the Charter.

[71] Without claiming to be exhaustive, we might also mention paragraph 15 of the Vienna Declaration and Programme of Action, adopted in Vienna on 25 June 1993 at the World Conference on Human Rights.

[72] See the commentary by Cot and Pellet in Cot, "Preamble", p. 290.

[73] *Case "relating to Certain Aspects of the Laws on the Use of Languages in Education in Belgium" (merits)*, Judgement of 23 July 1968, *Series A, No. 6*, para. 5; see also the judgement of 7 July 1989 in *Soering v. United Kingdom*, *Series A, No. 161*, para. 87; and Van Boven, "Convention de sauvegarde des droits de l'homme et des libertés fondamentales: commentaire du préambule", p. 130.

[74] See the *Official Journal of the European Communities*, 18 December 2000 (2000/C 364/01).

[75] Judgement of 21 February 1975, *Series A: Judgments and Decisions*, vol. 18, para. 34.

(iii) *Fundamental rights and the "inviolable" or "non-derogable core" of human rights*

a. Definition

28. There is no legal definition of the concept of "fundamental human rights". Legal theorists sometimes appear to confuse it with the concept of "human rights"[76] and therefore conclude that it refers to all the rights and freedoms of the individual that are recognized in States' constitutions and in international instruments and are protected by the relevant national and international bodies. In the context of this and subsequent reports, the term "fundamental rights" will be understood as synonymous with the "hard core" of human rights.

29. In legal theory, establishing a hierarchy of human rights makes it easier to ensure respect for the core rights that the international community considers fundamental. This concept of a "hard core" is used in both international human rights law and international humanitarian law to refer to "a set of human rights from which there can be no derogation. The list of these rights varies from one convention to another, but they all include a few rights that are the minimum needed to protect physical safety and integrity. These are also referred to as 'inviolable rights'; we therefore speak of an 'inviolable core'".[77] In the same vein, another writer states that "some rules have been accorded particular authority and customary recognition; they form the 'hard core' of human rights. These include the so-called 'inviolable rights' from which no derogation is permitted, even in wartime".[78] Still another writer concludes that "there is, in any event, a hard core of human rights that ensure respect for individuals' dignity and physical integrity and that are binding everywhere and on every authority. In reality, this is a guarantor of the values that are the basis for universal civilization, for what the Statute of the International Criminal Court (Rome, 17 July 1998) calls 'a shared heritage [and a] delicate mosaic [that] may be shattered at any time'".[79]

30. The idea of a hard core of non-derogable rights is not, however, above criticism. The classic objection is that it would amount to establishing a hierarchy among human rights, thereby violating the principle of their indivisibility. But some consider that the concept has a "subjective, evolving and even contingent nature that is in clear contradiction to universality",[80] while others believe that it endorses a reality of relations between States and thus that it "simply expresses a positivist prejudice".[81]

31. This criticism seems ideological rather than legal or technical in nature. It is based on the principles of the universality and indivisibility of human rights, which convey the dubious idea that all rights are equally important and have equal legal status. As has rightly been noted, the idea of a hard core is "a response to the individualist proliferation of rights, which may pose a threat to the idea of human rights".[82]

32. Contrary to initial assumption, this idea makes it easier to address the use of cultural relativism to justify derogations from, and even violations of, universal human rights standards and challenges to the universal concept of human rights. In this context, the universal appears as the hard core.[83] The crucial problem here is to find an operative identification criterion so that this hard core can be defined. On this point, Frédéric Sudre has provided useful clarification; he writes that "the term 'hard core' necessarily implies a 'soft envelope' and a distinction between rights that are fundamental and rights that are less so, between priority rights and secondary rights, between first-tier and second-tier rights. In short, the hypothesis of a 'hard core' raises the inescapable question, in law, of the hierarchy of human rights".[84]

33. Many critics consider such an approach shocking and, in any event, blasphemous because it is contrary to the founding principles of the indivisibility and interdependence of human rights.[85]

34. The idea of the possible existence of a hard core of human rights is not, however, groundless from the legal point of view. Beyond the philosophical language and the ideological and essentially moral approach to the issue, it is clear that "human rights law does not protect all rights in the same manner". If *lex ferenda* is not confused with *lex lata*, as it often is by some militant human rights activists, it will be seen that human rights law "does not place all proclaimed rights within the same legal regime and that it is possible to agree on the principle of cumulative, complementary application of proclaimed rights".[86]

35. If it is considered that there is general agreement regarding the legal and practical usefulness of the hard core, what identification criteria should be used?

36. The concept of *jus cogens* cannot be a satisfactory criterion.[87] On the one hand, despite its acceptance in treaties and case law, it remains controversial because of the indeterminacy of its content. On the other hand, with regard to human rights, it is the subject of contrary interpretations: a broad interpretation under which human

[76] For example, when we speak of the online journal *Droits fondamentaux* or of the research network *Droits fondmentaux*, we mean nothing less than the entire body of human rights, without exception. The same is true of the many studies of "fundamental rights and freedoms", several of which are mentioned in footnote 61 above.

[77] Le Guyader, "La question philosophique d'un noyau dur des droits de l'homme", p. 249. However, the philosopher takes exception to this definition, which he describes as "narrowly legal", and his philosophical reflections make a valuable contribution to the discussion of this concept. It goes without saying that the Special Rapporteur will focus on the legal definition.

[78] Cohen-Jonathan, "Les droits de l'homme, une valeur internationalisée", p. 159 (www.droits-fondamentaux.org).

[79] Bennouna, "Remise en cause et contestations de principe" (lecture given at the Sorbonne at a (French) National Consultative Commission on Human Rights conference held on the occasion of the fiftieth anniversary of the Universal Declaration of Human Rights), p. 245.

[80] Dupuy, *op. cit.* (footnote 40 above), p. 225.

[81] Le Guyader, *loc. cit.* (footnote 77 above), p. 254.

[82] *Ibid.*, p. 255.

[83] *Ibid.*, p. 266.

[84] Sudre, "Quel noyau intangible des droits de l'homme?", p. 271.

[85] See, for example, Meyer-Bisch, "Le problème des limitations du noyau intangible des droits et d'un droit de l'homme", p. 101.

[86] Sudre, "Quel noyau intangible des droits de l'homme?", p. 271.

[87] *Ibid.*, p. 272; by the same author, *Droit international et européen des droits de l'homme*, Nos. 42–44, pp. 59–60.

rights in general form part of *jus cogens*, as suggested by the Commission's articles on the responsibility of States for internationally wrongful acts and its Code of Crimes against the Peace and Security of Mankind; and a restrictive interpretation under which only a few human rights form part of it. Sudre notes that an examination of international human rights instruments, with the sole exception of the African Charter on Human and Peoples' Rights, reveals a "duality of the legal regime for human rights": certain rights, which Sudre calls "*conditional rights*"*,[88] "may be subject to restrictions and/or derogation and may therefore be imperfectly applied and/or temporarily not applied, while other rights—*inviolable rights*—are not subject to these restrictions; they are absolute rights applicable to everyone at all times and in all places".[89]

37. The operative criterion for identifying the hard core of human rights is therefore the *inviolability* of the rights concerned. It cannot be denied that this concept of a "hard" or "inviolable" core introduces a hierarchy of human rights. However, it is clearly a *de facto* hierarchy deriving from the analysis of international legal instruments rather than from a formal rule: a hard core of inviolable rights enjoying absolute protection derives from the major human rights instruments, such as the European Convention on Human Rights (art. 15), the American Convention on Human Rights (art. 27, para. 2) and the International Covenant on Civil and Political Rights (art. 4, para. 2). The African Charter on Human and People's Rights is the only exception.

38. It is indeed the "universal" rights which underlie this concept of a "hard core" of human rights: "the question of the 'hard core' presupposes the existence of a common irreducible base on which there would be general agreement, but which would implicitly allow for diverse interpretations of human rights …".[90] And from the point of view of human rights implementation, the concept of a hard core is the practical result of the fact that the constantly evolving list of human rights is ignored by many States or regarded as a mere *petitio principii* and that therefore an essential minimum should be "guaranteed, a sort of standard below which it is not possible to speak of 'human rights'".[91]

b. Content

39. The issue here is to determine, within the corpus of human rights, which rights constitute the hard core. The content of this hard core may not be identified in exactly the same way from one author to another.

40. In general, it is considered that the fundamental rights forming the "hard core" of human rights comprise the right to life and the prohibition of torture, inhuman treatment or punishment, slavery and servitude. Some authors add to these the principles of equality and non-retroactivity of the law. However, the content is likely to vary with regard to time and even space. In this regard, Protocol No. 7 to the European Convention on Human Rights, adopted on 22 November 1984, adds a new right to the list of inviolable rights contained in the 1950 Convention: the principle *non bis in idem* (art. 4). Similarly, it has been noted that the list of rights forming the "hard core" differs from one continent to another. While the African Charter on Human and Peoples' Rights contains no non-derogable rights, there are 5 such rights in Europe, 11 in the Americas and 7 at the universal level.[92]

41. Cohen-Jonathan proposes an even more extensive list. He believes that a comparison of article 4, paragraph 2, of the International Covenant on Civil and Political Rights and article 15, paragraph 2, of the European Convention on Human Rights indicates that the right to life, the prohibition of torture and inhuman or degrading treatment or punishment, and the prohibition of slavery constitute "inviolable" rights; this corresponds approximately to the content of common article 3 of the four Geneva Conventions of 12 August 1949.[93] However, he adds that, in accordance with international case law, prohibition of the flagrant denial of justice and of arbitrary detention should be added to these. Moreover, he considers that the prohibition of racial discrimination and discrimination against women, already mentioned specifically in Article 55 (*c*) of the Charter of the United Nations, should be included in this list, not to mention freedom of thought, conscience and religion, which is considered an equally inviolable right under article 4 of the International Covenant on Civil and Political Rights.[94]

42. In this context, the question of the universality of the "hard core" arises. An analysis shows that a number of these rights constitute a common irreducible base in all lists of "hard core" rights. This "hard core of the hard cores", to quote Sudre, consists of four rights: the right to life, the right not to be subjected to torture or to inhuman or degrading treatment, the right not to be held in slavery or servitude, and the right to the non-retroactivity of criminal law.[95]

43. To these may be added, as fundamental rights associated with the specific situation of a person being expelled: the principle of non-discrimination; the right to respect for the physical integrity of the person being expelled; the right to respect for family life; and the right of a person not to be expelled to a country where his or her life is in danger.

44. The protection afforded by respect for these rights should bring about the implementation of the overarching human right, which is the right to dignity.

(b) *General obligation to respect human rights*

45. There is agreement today on the existence of a general international obligation to respect human rights.[96]

[88] Sudre, *Droit international et européen des droits de l'homme*, No. 120, p. 167.

[89] Sudre, "Quel noyau intangible des droits de l'homme?", p. 272.

[90] *Ibid.*, p. 267.

[91] *Ibid.*

[92] *Ibid.*, p. 274.

[93] See Cohen-Jonathan, "Les droits de l'homme, une valeur internationalisée", p. 159.

[94] *Ibid.*, p. 160.

[95] Sudre, *op. cit.* (footnote 89 above); Meyer-Bisch, *op. cit.* (footnote 85 above); Dupuy, *op. cit.* (footnote 39 above), p. 226.

[96] See Alland, *op. cit.* (footnote 67 above), pp. 577–593; Cohen-Jonathan, *loc. cit.* (footnote 93 above), pp. 160–161.

This is an obligation *erga omnes*, according to the judgment of the International Court of Justice in its famous dictum in the *Barcelona Traction* case. The Court stated:

> In particular, an essential distinction should be drawn between the obligations of a State towards the international community as a whole, and those arising *vis-à-vis* another State in the field of diplomatic protection. By their very nature the former are the concern of all States. In view of the importance of the rights involved, all States can be held to have a legal interest in their protection; they are obligations *erga omnes*.
>
> Such obligations derive, for example, in contemporary international law, from the outlawing of acts of aggression, and of genocide, as also from the principles and rules concerning the basic rights of the human person, including protection from slavery and racial discrimination. Some of the corresponding rights of protection have entered into the body of general international law (*Reservations to the Convention on the Prevention and Punishment of the Crime of Genocide, Advisory Opinion, I.C.J. Reports 1951*, p. 23); others are conferred by international instruments of a universal or quasi-universal character.[97]

46. In the same vein, the Court noted, in its judgment of 27 June 1986 in *Military and Paramilitary Activities in and against Nicaragua*, that "the absence of ... a commitment [with regard to human rights] would not mean that [a State] could with impunity violate human rights".[98]

47. Reproducing the wording used by the Court in *Barcelona Traction*, the Institute of International Law, in its resolution of 13 September 1989,[99] stated with regard to the general international obligation to respect human rights that "it is incumbent upon every State in relation to the international community as a whole, and every State has a legal interest in the protection of human rights".

48. The draft articles on the responsibility of States for internationally wrongful acts, as adopted by the Commission on first reading in 1996, set out very clearly this concept of obligations *erga omnes* with regard to norms for "the protection of human rights and fundamental freedoms", and the possibility of the public right of action that this concept implies. Draft article 40[100] stated that "injured State" meant, "... (*e*) if the right infringed by the act of a State arises from a multilateral treaty or from a rule of customary international law, any other State party to the multilateral treaty or bound by the relevant rule of customary international law, if it is established that: ... (iii) the right has been created or is established for the protection of human rights and fundamental freedoms". In the final version of the draft articles, adopted by the Commission on second reading in 2001, and of which the General Assembly "took note" in its resolution 56/83 of 12 December 2001, fundamentally the same approach seems to have been taken, even though the expression "injured State" is no longer used in relation to such cases, and despite the fact that the articles no longer contain, in this context, an explicit reference to human rights and fundamental freedoms. Pursuant to the 2001 version of article 48, paragraph 1, "any State other than an injured State" is entitled to invoke the responsibility of another State in accordance with paragraph 2 of the article if "(*a*) the obligation breached is owed to a group of States including that State, and is established for the protection of a collective interest of the group; or (*b*) the obligation breached is owed to the international community as a whole". And in this regard, it should be noted that the commentary to paragraph 1 (*a*) of the article mentions as an example the case of "a regional system for the protection of human rights",[101] while the commentary to paragraph 1 (*b*) refers in particular to the part of the judgment of the International Court of Justice in *Barcelona Traction* which cites as examples of obligations *erga omnes* "the principles and rules concerning the basic rights of the human person, including protection from slavery and racial discrimination".[102]

49. It may be inferred from the above provisions that the breach by a State of its obligations relating to human rights protection may entail the responsibility of that State *vis-à-vis* all the other States parties to the treaty in question in the case of a treaty obligation, or *vis-à-vis* all States where the obligation breached is governed by general international law and is owed to the international community as a whole.

50. This general international obligation to respect human rights is all the more imperative with regard to persons whose legal situation makes them vulnerable, as is the case with regard to aliens being expelled. For this reason, on the strength of the elements of international case law mentioned above and the degree of agreement on the subject in the legal literature, which is widely supported by the work of authoritative codification bodies, the following draft article is proposed:

"*Draft article 8. General obligation to respect the human rights of persons being expelled*"

"Any person who has been or is being expelled is entitled to respect for his or her fundamental rights and all other rights the implementation of which is required by his or her specific circumstances."

(c) *Specially protected rights of persons being expelled*

51. As a human being, an alien present in the territory of a State enjoys the protection of his or her human rights. As an alien being expelled, he or she enjoys, in addition to this general protection, specific protection of some of these rights. As the Institute of International Law had already proposed in the late nineteenth century in article 17 of its Geneva resolution of 9 September 1892 on the International Rules on the Admission and Expulsion of Aliens, "expulsion is not a punishment and must therefore be executed with the utmost consideration and taking into account the individual's particular situation".[103]

52. Special protection of the rights in question of the person being expelled is afforded through the "hard core"

---

[97] Judgment of 5 February 1970, *I.C.J. Reports 1970*, p. 32, paras. 33–34.

[98] *I.C.J. Reports 1986*, p. 134, para. 267.

[99] Institute of International Law, "The protection of human rights and the principle of non-intervention in internal affairs of States", p. 341; see, on this aspect of the Institute's work, Cohen-Jonathan, "La responsabilité pour atteinte aux droits de l'homme", p. 120.

[100] *Yearbook ... 1996*, vol. II (Part Two), pp. 62–63.

[101] *Yearbook ... 2001*, vol. II (Part Two), p. 320, para. (7) of the commentary.

[102] *Ibid.*, p. 322, para. (9) of the commentary.

[103] Institute of International Law, "Règles internationales sur l'admission et l'expulsion des étrangers", p. 222.

rights—the inviolable rights of the expelled person that derive from international legal instruments and are reinforced by international case law. These are:

—The right to life;

—The right to dignity;

—The right to the integrity of the person;

—Non-discrimination;

—The right not to be subjected to torture or to inhuman or degrading treatment or punishment;

—The right to family life.

(i) *The right to life*

53. The right to life, which, under article 6, paragraph 1, of the International Covenant on Civil and Political Rights, is "inherent" to "every human being", is enshrined, albeit in a variety of wordings, in the main international human rights instruments, both universal[104] and regional.[105]

54. What is the substance of this right? The Universal Declaration of Human Rights (1948) gives no indication; article 3 merely affirms laconically that "everyone has the right to life, liberty and security of person". The American Declaration of the Rights and Duties of Man (1948) merely reproduces this wording *in extenso* in article 1.

55. It was the European Convention on Human Rights that first set out detailed provisions regarding the right to life which tell us about the substance of that right. Article 2 of the Convention states:

> 1. Everyone's right to life shall be protected by law. No one shall be deprived of his life intentionally save in the execution of a sentence of a court following his conviction of a crime for which this penalty is provided by law.
>
> 2. Deprivation of life shall not be regarded as inflicted in contravention of this article when it results from the use of force which is no more than absolutely necessary:
>
> a. In defence of any person from unlawful violence;
>
> b. In order to effect a lawful arrest or to prevent the escape of a person lawfully detained;
>
> c. In action lawfully taken for the purpose of quelling a riot or insurrection.

56. It can be seen that this interpretation of the right to life does not rule out the death penalty as a possible punishment for certain criminal offences imposed by a court in accordance with the law. This approach is followed in the International Covenant on Civil and Political Rights, through the wording of the third sentence of article 6, paragraph 1, which states: "No one shall be arbitrarily deprived of his life." This means, in non-negative wording, that a person may be deprived of his or her life provided that this is not done in an arbitrary manner. This wording from the Covenant is reproduced to the letter in article 4 of the American Convention on Human Rights (1969) and article 4 of the African Charter on Human and Peoples' Rights (1981).

57. It was the Second Optional Protocol of 1989 to the International Covenant on Civil and Political Rights, aiming at the abolition of the death penalty, that radically changed the scope of the rule affirming the right to life, by providing in article 1 that:

> 1. No one within the jurisdiction of a State Party to the present Protocol shall be executed.
>
> 2. Each State Party shall take all necessary measures to abolish the death penalty within its jurisdiction.

Similarly, article 1 of Protocol No. 6 of 28 April 1983 to the European Convention on Human Rights provides:

> 1. The death penalty shall be abolished. No one shall be condemned to such penalty or executed.

The structure of article 2 of the Charter of Fundamental Rights of the European Union demonstrates that the prohibition of the death penalty and of execution is understood as the corollary of the right to life. Thus, after the statement in article 2, paragraph 1, that "everyone has the right to life", paragraph 2 of the article provides that "no one shall be condemned to the death penalty, or executed". Therefore, pursuant to this Charter, the right to life entails the prohibition of capital punishment and of execution.

58. However, this prohibition is still constrained by conflicting legislation in many countries outside Europe and is by no means a universal customary rule, despite the moratorium on the use of the death penalty adopted by the General Assembly in its resolution 62/149 of 18 December 2007.[106] It is true that the United Nations Commission on Human Rights had, during the 10 years preceding the resolution in question, adopted resolutions at all its sessions calling upon "States that still maintain the death penalty to abolish [it] completely and, in the meantime, to establish a moratorium on executions".[107] However, this resolution, like that of the General Assembly itself, is merely a set of recommendations that are not legally binding and do not represent an *opinio juris communis* on the subject: resolution 62/149 was not adopted unanimously.

59. With regard to case law, the question of expulsion, extradition or refoulement of a person to a State where his or her right to life may be violated has been considered both at the international level and at the regional level.

---

[104] See, in particular, article 3 of the Universal Declaration of Human Rights (1948) and article 6 of the International Covenant on Civil and Political Rights.

[105] See article 2 of the European Convention on Human Rights (1950); article 2 of the Charter of Fundamental Rights of the European Union; article 4 of the American Convention on Human Rights (1969); article I of the American Declaration of the Rights and Duties of Man (1948); and article 4 of the African Charter on Human and Peoples' Rights (1981).

[106] In which the Assembly "calls upon all States that still maintain the death penalty", *inter alia*, "(*c*) to progressively restrict the use of the death penalty and reduce the number of offences for which it may be imposed; (*d*) to establish a moratorium on executions with a view to abolishing the death penalty" (para. 2). In addition, the Assembly "calls upon States which have abolished the death penalty not to reintroduce it" (para. 3).

[107] Commission on Human Rights, *Report on the Sixty-First Session, Supplement No. 3* (E/2005/23–E/CN.4/2005/135). The Commission's last resolution before the adoption of the General Assembly resolution of 18 December 2007 was that of 20 April 2005 (resolution 2005/59).

60. At the international level, the Human Rights Committee considered the question in a well-known case, *Ng v. Canada* (1993),[108] which, although it relates to an issue of extradition rather than expulsion, may nonetheless illuminate the point under discussion. Mr. Ng was a detainee who had committed a series of murders. He was totally without scruples and was considered particularly dangerous. The United States of America had requested Canada to extradite Mr. Ng because of the murders he had committed on United States soil. The problem was therefore that of extradition to a State where the author would be subject to the death penalty. Knowing that the International Covenant on Civil and Political Rights permitted the death penalty (or in any case did not prohibit it), Canada extradited Mr. Ng to the United States. Although it had not violated article 6 of the Covenant, Canada was nonetheless held to have violated its obligations under article 7 because, in this case, it was possible that the execution would be carried out by means of gas asphyxiation, which causes pain and prolonged agony and does not result in death as swiftly as possible. It was therefore the risk of cruel treatment that was condemned in this case.

61. However, in 2003, the Human Rights Committee in *R. Judge v. Canada* overturned its jurisprudence in this matter. The case concerned a man sentenced to death in the United States for murder, who then escaped to Canada. He contested his extradition to the United States, citing the risk he ran in the United States of being executed. The Committee reversed its earlier jurisprudence and came up with a new interpretation of article 6, paragraph 1, of the International Covenant on Civil and Political Rights in which, after a lengthy argument, it concluded:

> For these reasons, the Committee considers that Canada, as a State party which has abolished the death penalty, irrespective of whether it has ratified the Second Optional Protocol to the Covenant, aiming at the abolition of the death penalty, violated the author's right to life under article 6, paragraph 1, by deporting him to the United States, where he is under sentence of death, without ensuring that the death penalty would not be carried out. The Committee recognizes that Canada did not itself impose the death penalty on the author. But by deporting him to a country where he was under sentence of death, Canada established the crucial link in the causal chain that would make possible the execution of the author.[109]

62. It follows from this decision that:

(*a*) A State that abolishes the death penalty may not extradite or expel, or in a general sense hand over, a person sentenced to death in a State which has the death penalty without having previously obtained a guarantee that the death penalty will not be imposed or carried out;

(*b*) States that have not yet abolished the death penalty and that continue to impose it in accordance with the provisions of article 6, paragraph 2, of the International Covenant on Civil and Political Rights are not subject to this obligation, which applies only to abolitionist States.

63. With regard to the jurisprudence of regional human rights bodies, the European Court of Human Rights first considered this question in the well-known case of *Soering v. United Kingdom*.[110] The applicant, who had committed a murder, contested his extradition to the United States, where he was liable to the death penalty. He argued that his extradition would violate article 3 of the European Convention on Human Rights, in view, in particular, of the conditions he would face during a long period on death row before his execution. The question was thus not the possibility of execution in the event of extradition—the death penalty as such not being prohibited by the Convention—but the circumstances attending the death penalty in the United States. This nuance led the Court to consider the question of whether there would be a real risk of torture or of inhuman or degrading treatment, and thus a violation of article 3, in the event that the applicant was extradited. Thus, the Court did not base its decision on the death penalty but on the conditions attending its imposition.

64. Several petitions have recently been lodged with the Inter-American Commission on Human Rights against States members of OAS concerning either violations of the American Convention on Human Rights: Pact of San José, Costa Rica or violations of the 1948 American Declaration of the Rights and Duties of Man. Thus, in *Hugo Armendáriz v. United States*,[111] the applicant argued that his deportation from the United States to Mexico violated several provisions of the Declaration, article 1 of which protects the right to life. In *Marino López et al. (Operation Genesis) v. Colombia*,[112] the applicants cited, *inter alia*, a violation of article 4, paragraph 1, of the American Convention enshrining the same right. The Commission found the petitions admissible, without, however, considering the merits.

65. On the other hand, the Inter-American Court of Human Rights ruled on the obligation to protect the lives and integrity of persons subjected to expulsion in *Haitians and Dominicans of Haitian origin in the Dominican Republic*. In its order of 2 February 2006 in this case, the Court decided, in view of its order of 18 August 2000 requiring the Dominican Republic to take whatever measures were necessary "to protect the lives and personal integrity" of Benito Tide-Méndez, Antonio Sension, Andrea Alezy, Janty Fils-Aime and William Medina-Ferreras, and also of Father Pedro Ruquoy and Ms. Solange Pierre; its order of 12 November 2000 ratifying the order of 14 September 2000 by which the President of the Court required the same country to adopt "the necessary measures to protect

---

[108] Report of the Human Rights Committee, *Official Records of the General Assembly, Forty-ninth Session, Supplement No. 40* (A/49/40), vol. II, annex IX, sect. CC, communication No. 469/1991. *Ibid., Forty-eight Session, Supplement No. 40* (A/48/40), vol. II, annex XII, sect. U, *Kindler v. Canada* (1993), communication No. 470/1991; and *ibid., Fiftieth Session, Supplement No. 40* (A/50/40), annex X, sect. M, *Cox v. Canada* (1995), communication No. 539/1993. See also the commentaries of these cases in *Revue universelle des droits de l'homme*, 1994, p. 150; *ibid.*, p. 165; and *ibid.*, 1995, p. 13, respectively.

[109] Report of the Human Rights Committee, *Official Records of the General Assembly, Fifty-eighth Session, Supplement No. 40* (A/58/40), vol. II, annex VI, sect. G, communication No. 829/1998, decision of 5 August 2003, p. 93, para. 10.6.

[110] Application No. 14038/88, *Series A*, no. 161, Judgement of 7 July 1989.

[111] Report No. 57/06, Petition 526–03, Admissibility, 20 July 2006, *Annual Report of the Inter-American Commission on Human Rights*, 563, OEA/Ser.L/V/II.127 doc. 4, para. 2.

[112] Report No. 86/06, Petition 499–04, Admissibility, 21 October 2006, *Annual Report of the Inter-American Commission on Human Rights*, 273, OEA/Ser.L/V/II.127 doc. 4, para. 2.

the life and personal integrity" of Rafaelito Pérez Charles and Berson Gelim; and its order of 26 May 2001 recalling the two previous orders:[113]

> 1. To ratify the Order of the President of the Inter-American Court of Human Rights of October 5, 2005, wherein the State was instructed to extend and implement whatever measures are necessary to protect the life and personal integrity of Ms. Solain Pie or Solain Pierre or Solange Pierre's four children.
>
> 2. To reiterate what was expressed in the Orders of the Inter-American Court of Human Rights of August 18, 2000, November 12, 2000 and May 26, 2001, in the sense that the State must maintain whatever measures it may have adopted and immediately provide for those that prove necessary to effectively protect the life and personal integrity of Messrs. Benito Tide-Méndez, Antonio Sension, Janty Fils-Aime, William Medina-Ferreras, Rafaelito Pérez-Charles, Berson Gelim, Father Pedro Ruquoy and Mss. Andrea Alezy and Solain Pie or Solain Pierre or Solange Pierre.
>
> 3. To call upon the State to create due conditions for Solain Pie or Solain Pierre or Solange Pierre and her four children to return to their home in the Dominican Republic and, as soon as this happens, to adopt whatever measures are necessary to protect their lives and personal integrity[114].

66. The following conclusions may be drawn from the foregoing analyses:

(*a*) First, the right to life of every human being is an inherent right, formally enshrined in international human rights law. As such, it applies to persons in a vulnerable situation such as aliens who are the subject of extradition, expulsion or refoulement. In this regard, it may be understood as an obligation on the part of the expelling State to protect the lives of the persons in question, both in the host country and the State of destination. Such is the tenor of article 22, paragraph 8, of the American Convention on Human Rights, which imposes significant restrictions on expulsion and places an obligation on the expelling State to protect the right to life of the alien. The article provides:

> In no case may an alien be deported or returned to a country, regardless of whether or not it is his country of origin, if in that country his right to life or personal freedom is in danger of being violated because of his race, nationality, religion, social status or political opinions;

Article 33, paragraph 1, of the Convention relating to the Status of Refugees contains the same provision;

(*b*) Secondly, the right to life does not necessarily imply the prohibition of the death penalty and of executions. It is certainly the case in terms of treaty law and regional jurisprudence in Europe that any extradition (or expulsion) to a State where the person concerned may suffer the death penalty is in and of itself prohibited. But it would not be appropriate to generalize the rule, since it is not a customary norm;

(*c*) Thirdly, a State that has abolished the death penalty may not extradite or expel to another country a person sentenced to death without having previously obtained guarantees that the death penalty will not be carried out in this instance; however, this obligation applies only to States that have abolished the death penalty.

67. The following draft article is proposed:

"Draft article 9. Obligation to protect the right to life of persons being expelled

"1. The expelling State shall protect the right to life of a person being expelled.

"2. A State that has abolished the death penalty may not expel a person who has been sentenced to death to a State in which that person may be executed without having previously obtained a guarantee that the death penalty will not be carried out."

(ii) *The right to dignity*

68. The concept of dignity has been the subject of great interest in recent juridical writings.[115] In domestic law in particular, there is no doctrinal consensus as to whether the question should be the subject of legislation: some authors have pointed out the danger, even impossibility, of incorporating it in a juridical concept;[116] others have concluded that dignity has acquired juridical status and that this constitutes the basis for a new right.[117] There is, however, no doubt that dignity is a concept of positive law in many national legal systems.[118]

69. At the international level, the concepts of human dignity and fundamental rights have emerged and developed concomitantly. In this process dignity is both a justification and a framework principle within which other rights are forged. As the ethical and philosophical foundation of fundamental rights, the principle of respect for human dignity provides the basis for all other individual rights. The Charter of the United Nations, in its second preambular paragraph, contains the earliest reference to these two concepts, affirming the determination of the "peoples

[113] Order of 2 February 2006, paras. 1–3.

[114] *Ibid.*, decision (excerpt).

[115] See, in particular, Mathieu, "La dignité de la personne humaine, quel droit? quel titulaire?", pp. 282 *et seq.*; Saint-James, "Réflexions sur la dignité humaine en tant que concept juridique du droit français", pp. 61 *et seq.*; Edelman, "La dignité de la personne humaine, un concept nouveau", pp. 185 *et seq.*; Richer, "Les droits fondamentaux: une nouvelle catégorie juridique?", pp. 1 *et seq.*; Champeil-Desplats, "La notion de 'droit fondamental' et le droit constitutionnel français", pp. 323 *et seq.*; Pavia, "Eléments de réflexion sur la notion de droit fondamental", pp. 6 *et seq.*; Marcoux, "Le concept de droits fondamentaux dans le droit de la Communauté économique européenne"; and Tchakoua (*op. cit.*, footnote 50 above), pp. 11 *et seq.*

[116] See, in particular, Theron, "Propos sur une jurisprudence contestable", pp. 295 *et seq.*; Le Pourhiet, "Le Conseil constitutionnel et l'éthique bio-médicale", pp. 213 *et seq.*; and Neirinck, "La dignité humaine ou le mauvais usage d'une notion philosophique".

[117] See, in particular, Edelman (*loc. cit.*, footnote 115 above) and Mathieu (*loc. cit.*, footnote 115 above).

[118] There are increasingly common references to dignity in both legal instruments and judicial decisions. With regard to instruments, see, for example in the case of France, the Criminal Code, chapter V, title III, which is entitled "Violations of dignity", the Code of Medical Ethics and the law on bio-ethics in the Civil Code; in the case of Cameroon, the preamble to the Constitution incorporating the international human rights instruments to which Cameroon is party (see, in this regard, the African Charter on Human and Peoples' Rights, art. 5). With regard to court decisions, see the decisions of the French Constitutional Council of 27 July 1994 and 25 January 1995 (*Recueil*, 1994 and 1995), of the French Council of State of 25 October 1995 (*Recueil*, 1995) and of the Paris Court of Appeal of 28 May 1996 (Dalloz, *Jurisprudence*, 1996, pp. 617 *et seq.*, note, B. Edelman). On the emergence of dignity as a new right and its impact on the French legal system, see Tchakoua, *op. cit.* (footnote 50 above), pp. 12–26.

of the United Nations … to reaffirm [their] faith in fundamental human rights, in the dignity and worth of the human person, in the equal rights of men and women …". Following on from the Charter, the Universal Declaration of Human Rights (1948) states, in its very first preambular paragraph, "*Whereas* recognition of the inherent dignity and of the equal and inalienable rights of all members of the human family is the foundation of freedom, justice and peace in the world".

70. It may be observed that, notwithstanding the force with which it has been enunciated, the reference to human dignity had previously remained at a preambular level, although there is no need here to join the debate on the value of the preamble to a legal instrument.[119] The concept is formulated more robustly in the operative part of the African Charter on Human and Peoples' Rights, article 5, which provides that: "Every individual shall have the right to the respect of the dignity inherent in a human being and to the recognition of his legal status." More recently, the Charter of Fundamental Rights of the European Union, adopted in 2000, begins with this concept. Article 1, entitled "Human dignity", states that: "Human dignity is inviolable. It must be respected and protected."

71. International jurisprudence has reinforced the positive quality of the concept of human dignity in international human rights law and, in addition, provided some elements of its content. The decision rendered by the Trial Chamber of the International Tribunal for the Former Yugoslavia in *Furundžija* is particularly interesting in this regard. The Chamber:

> … holds that the forced penetration of the mouth by the male sexual organ constitutes *a most humiliating and degrading attack upon human dignity**. The essence of the whole corpus of international humanitarian law as well as human rights law lies in the protection of the human dignity of every person, whatever his or her gender. The general principle of respect for human dignity is the basic underpinning and indeed the very raison d'être of international humanitarian law and human rights law; indeed in modern times it has become of such paramount importance as to permeate the whole body of international law. This principle is intended to shield human beings from outrages upon their personal dignity, whether such outrages are carried out by unlawfully attacking the body or by humiliating and debasing the honour, the self-respect or the mental well-being of a person. It is consonant with this principle that such an extremely serious sexual outrage as forced oral penetration should be classified as rape.[120]

72. A fundamental precept in human axiology is that dignity is priceless; it conveys the concept of the absolute inviolability of fundamental rights, or the "hard core" of human rights. It is thus, in addition to the right to life, which is a basic right, a fundamental right of every human being. This right is of particular importance to persons being expelled owing to the risk of abuse to which aliens, especially those whose status in the expelling State is illegal, are exposed. This is why there is a need to reformulate this right in terms that are specific to the situation of an alien being expelled. The draft article below is based on article 1 of the Charter of Fundamental Rights of the European Union, the first clause of which is reproduced *in extenso* in paragraph 1 and the second is reflected in paragraph 2, supplemented to strengthen protection for a person who has been or is being expelled.

"Draft article 10. Obligation to respect the dignity of persons being expelled

"1. Human dignity is inviolable.

"2. The human dignity of a person being expelled, whether that person's status in the expelling State is legal or illegal, must be respected and protected in all circumstances."

(iii) *Prohibition of torture and of cruel, inhuman or degrading treatment or punishment*

73. This prohibition is reflected in a wide range of treaty instruments. Thus, article 5 of the Universal Declaration of Human Rights provides that: "No one shall be subjected to torture or to cruel, inhuman or degrading treatment or punishment." This provision is echoed in article 3 of the European Convention on Human Rights,[121] in the first sentence of article 5, paragraph 2, of the American Convention on Human Rights, and in the first sentence of article 7 of the International Covenant on Civil and Political Rights. The Convention against Torture and Other Cruel, Inhuman or Degrading Treatment or Punishment incorporates this same provision in its fourth preambular paragraph, by which States parties declare that they have regard to article 5 of the Universal Declaration of Human Rights and article 7 of the International Covenant on Civil and Political Rights. The African Charter on Human and Peoples' Rights enshrines the same rule, but in a formulation associating it with other categories of prohibited violations of human dignity. The second sentence of article 5 provides that "[a]ll forms of exploitation and degradation of man particularly slavery, slave trade, torture, cruel, inhuman or degrading punishment and treatment shall be prohibited".[122]

74. This general wording does not allow the precise content of the rule to be determined. International jurisprudence provides valuable assistance in this regard. In particular, the jurisprudence of the European Court of Human Rights in this area is extensive and well established.[123] On the basis of this long-standing and consistent jurisprudence, article 3 of the European Convention on Human Rights implies an obligation not to expel a person

---

[119] On this issue, see, in particular, Cot and Pellet in Cot, "Preamble", pp. 287–312; van Boven, "Convention de sauvegarde des droits de l'homme et des libertés fondamentales: commentaire du préambule", pp. 125–134.

[120] International Tribunal for the Former Yugoslavia, *Prosecutor v. Furundžija* (case No. IT–95–17/1–T), Trial Chamber, Judgement, 10 December 1998, *Judicial Reports 1998*, vol. 1, p. 593, para. 183.

[121] "No one shall be subjected to torture or to inhuman or degrading treatment or punishment."

[122] In the same vein, the Declaration on the Human Rights of Individuals Who are not Nationals of the Country in which They Live provides, in its article 6, that "[N]o alien shall be subjected to torture or to cruel, inhuman or degrading treatment or punishment …".

[123] The Inter-American Commission on Human Rights has found admissible several applications impugning States members of OAS for ill-treatment (violation of the Pact of San José, Costa Rica, art. 5), without, however, considering the merits: see *Sebastián Echaniz Alcorta and Juan Víctor Galarza Mendiola v. Venezuela*, Report No. 37/06, Petition 562–03, 15 March 2006, *Annual Report of the Inter-American Commission on Human Rights*, 607, OEA/Ser.L/V/II.127 doc. 4, para. 2; *Jesús Tranquilino Vélez Loor v. Panama*, Report No. 95/06, Petition 92–04, 23 October 2006, *Annual Report of the Inter-American Commission on Human Rights*, 500, OEA/Ser.L/V/II.127 doc. 4, para. 1; *Hugo Armendáriz v. United States and Marino López et al. v. Colombia* (footnotes 111–112 above).

to a country in which that person may be subjected to torture or to inhuman or degrading treatment.[124]

75. It is apparent from this wide-ranging, teleological interpretation of the obligations on States parties to this Convention that article 3 not only prohibits contracting States from inflicting torture or any other inhuman or degrading treatment, but also imposes the related obligation not to place an individual under their jurisdiction in a situation in which that person could be a victim of such a violation, even if committed by a third State.[125] According to the European Commission of Human Rights in *Kirkwood v. United Kingdom*, this interpretation "... is based upon the unqualified terms of article 3 of the Convention, and the requirement which this read in conjunction with Article 1 imposes upon the Contracting Parties to the Convention to protect 'everyone within their jurisdiction' from the real risk of such treatment, in the light of its irremediable nature".[126]

76. The Court's reasoning has been absorbed into doctrine by means of the "protection by ricochet" theory,[127] by which reliance may be had on the "rights arising under the Convention, not guaranteed as such by it but benefiting from its indirect protection as an associated guaranteed right".[128] The prohibition on returning an alien to that person's torturers or to a country where he or she may be subjected to torture or to cruel or inhuman or degrading treatment is an implicit obligation stemming from the nature of the right protected.

77. The European Court of Human Rights, in *Soering v. United Kingdom*,[129] found occasion to clarify its reasoning. It seems to have based itself on three principles, namely:

(*a*) The irrelevance of the international responsibility of the third State, since this is not an extraterritorial application of article 3 with a view to securing compliance by a third State with the provisions of a treaty to which it is not necessarily a party;

(*b*) The primacy of the European Convention over the other treaty obligations of States parties; (*c*) The implicit obligation contained in article 3 to oppose the extradition or expulsion of a person exposed to the risk of torture or inhuman or degrading treatment.

[124] ECHR, *Chahal v. United Kingdom*, Judgement of 15 November 1996, *Reports of Judgments and Decisions 1996–V, Series A*, No. 22, p. 1853, paras. 73–74.

[125] See Chetail, "Le droit des réfugiés à l'épreuve des droits de l'homme: bilan de la jurisprudence de la Cour européenne des droits de l'homme sur l'interdiction du renvoi des étrangers menacés de torture et de traitement inhumains ou dégradants", p. 161.

[126] European Commission of Human Rights, *Kirkwood v. United Kingdom*, application No. 10479/83, decision of 12 March 1984, *Decisions and Reports*, vol. 37 (July 1984), p. 183. For commentary on the grounds underpinning the interpretation in this case, see Chetail, *loc. cit.* (footnote 125 above), pp. 161–162.

[127] Sudre, "La notion de 'peines et traitements inhumains ou dégradants' dans la jurisprudence de la Commission et de la Cour européenne des droits de l'homme", pp. 866–868; see also Cohen-Jonathan, *La Convention européenne des droits de l'homme*, pp. 84 and 304.

[128] Sudre, "Extradition et peine de mort: arrêt *Soering* de la Cour européenne des droits de l'homme du 7 juillet 1989", p. 108.

[129] ECHR, *Soering v. United Kingdom*, Judgement of 7 July 1989, *Series A: Judgments and Decisions*, vol. 161, p. 33, para. 86.

78. Some 20 years later, the debate over the European Court's reasoning in *Soering* does not appear to have been exhausted.[130] There is, however, no doubt that, even if the investigation is confined solely to conventions, article 3 of the Convention gives rise to a peremptory norm, given the provision of article 15, paragraph 2, of the Convention that there shall be no derogation from the prohibition of torture and inhuman or degrading treatment, even in time of war or other public emergency threatening the life of the nation. This is, moreover, the reasoning most frequently invoked in the legal literature to justify measures for the expulsion (in the broad sense in which it is understood here) of aliens. From the standpoint of international responsibility, the expelling State would become complicit in the actions of the receiving State, in that, through the expulsion, it would have enabled the latter to commit the unlawful act.

79. It is now time to examine in greater depth the predicate conduct prohibited by the norm. It should be pointed out first that, as has been seen, article 3 of the European Convention prohibits "inhuman or degrading treatment or punishment". The International Covenant on Civil and Political Rights adds a word to the second part of the proscribed behaviour, referring to cruel, inhuman or degrading treatment or punishment; this wording from article 7 of the Covenant is reproduced in the American Convention (art. 5, para. 2) and the African Charter (art. 5). It is therefore this formulation which will be used in the present report.

a. Torture

80. Torture is regarded as the most serious act in the hierarchy of forms of violation of the physical integrity of the human person.[131]

81. Under the terms of article 1, paragraph 1, of the 1984 Convention against Torture and Other Cruel, Inhuman or Degrading Treatment or Punishment:

> The term "torture" means any act by which severe pain or suffering, whether physical or mental, is inflicted on a person for such purposes as obtaining from him or a third person information or a confession, punishing him for an act he or a third person has committed or is suspected of having committed, or intimidating or coercing him or a third person, or for any reason based on discrimination of any kind, when such pain or suffering is inflicted by or at the instigation of or with the consent or acquiescence of a public official or other person acting in an official capacity. It does not include pain or suffering arising only from, inherent in or incidental to lawful sanctions.

82. As the Trial Chamber of the International Tribunal for the Former Yugoslavia noted in *Furundžija*,[132] this legal definition of torture rests on four essential elements:

[130] Apart from the references already cited, see also Van Den Wyngaert, "Applying the European Convention on Human Rights to extradition: opening Pandora's box?", pp. 757–779; Warbrick, "Coherence and the European Court of Human Rights: the adjudicative background to the *Soering* case", pp. 1073–1096; Breitenmoser and Wilms, "Human rights v. extradition: The *Soering* case", pp. 845–886; Richard, "The *Soering* case", pp. 128–149; Wilt, "*Après Soering*: the relationship between extradition and human rights in the legal practice of Germany, the Netherlands and the United States", pp. 53–80; Zühlke and Pastille, "Extradition and the European Convention: *Soering* revisited", pp. 749–784; see also Chetail, *loc. cit.* (footnote 125 above), p. 165.

[131] See Kolb, "La jurisprudence internationale en matière de torture et de traitement inhumains ou dégradants", p. 225.

[132] *Furundžija* (footnote 120 above), para. 162.

(*a*) A material or physical element: the infliction, by act or omission, of severe pain or suffering, whether physical or mental;

(*b*) A psychological element: the act or omission must be intentional;

(*c*) A purpose: the torture must aim at obtaining information or a confession, or at punishing, intimidating, humiliating or coercing the victim or a third person, or at discrimination on any ground against the victim or a third person;

(*d*) An element of instrument or agency: at least one of the persons involved in the torture process must be a public official or must act in a non-private capacity, e.g., as a *de facto* organ of a State or any other authority-wielding entity.

83. In the light of these elements, there is no doubt that a person who has been, or is in the process of being, expelled may be a victim of acts of torture, whether in the expelling State or in the State of destination. Moreover, the Committee against Torture established by the 1984 Convention against Torture, which began its operations only in 1991, has received several hundred individual communications, virtually all of which relate to cases of expulsion or extradition of an individual to a State where he or she risks being subjected to torture or ill-treatment.[133] The solutions adopted by the Committee in these cases are more or less identical and somewhat repetitive.[134] It will thus suffice to refer to a number of cases by way of illustration.[135]

84. In *Mutombo v. Switzerland* (1994), the author of the application clandestinely became a member of a political movement in Zaire, the *Union pour la démocratie et le progrès social*. He was arrested shortly afterwards, in 1989, and locked up in a one-metre square cell, and for four days he was subjected to electric shocks, beaten with a rifle butt and struck on the testicles until he lost consciousness. During his imprisonment, he received no medical treatment for a head injury caused by the torture inflicted on him. On being released in 1990, he fled to Switzerland. Despite medical certificates indicating that his scars corresponded with the alleged maltreatment (torture), an expulsion order was issued against him by Switzerland.

85. Against this decision to expel him, he claimed a violation of article 3 of the Convention against Torture, which provides that:

> 1. No State party shall expel, return ("refouler") or extradite a person to another State where there are substantial grounds for believing that he will be in danger of being subjected to torture.
>
> 2. For the purpose of determining if there are such grounds, the competent authorities shall take into account all relevant considerations including, where applicable, the existence in the State concerned of a consistent pattern of gross, flagrant, or mass violations of human rights.

86. After indicating that it needed to determine whether there were substantial grounds for believing that Mr. Mutombo would be in danger of being subjected to torture, the Committee stated that:

> The aim of the determination, however, is to establish whether the individual concerned would be personally at risk of being subjected to torture in the country to which he would return. It follows that the existence of a consistent pattern of gross, flagrant or mass violations of human rights in the country does not as such constitute a sufficient ground for determining that a person would be in danger of being subjected to torture upon his return to that country; additional grounds must exist that indicate that the individual concerned would be personally at risk. Similarly, the absence of a consistent pattern of gross violations of human rights does not mean that the person cannot be considered to be in danger of being subjected to torture in his specific circumstances.[136]

87. According to the Committee, there was no doubt that in the case in question substantial grounds existed for believing that the author was in danger of being subjected to torture in his country of origin. Among the many elements supporting this belief were his ethnic background, his political affiliation, his detention history, his desertion from the army in order to flee the country and the arguments adduced by him in his request for asylum, which could be considered defamatory towards Zaire, together with a situation of systematic human rights violations in that country.[137]

88. The same criteria were applied in *Alan v. Switzerland* (1996). The author of the communication was a sympathizer of an outlawed Kurdish-Marxist/Leninist organization. In 1983, he was arrested in Turkey; he stated that he had been brutally tortured for 36 days by electric shocks. After having been arrested again several times in 1988 and 1989, he fled to Switzerland. Despite a medical report which confirmed that scars on his body were compatible with the torture described, Switzerland decided to expel him.[138] The Committee stated that:

> In the instant case, the Committee considers that the author's ethnic background, his political affiliation, his detention history, and his internal exile should all be taken into account when determining whether he would be in danger of being subjected to torture upon his return. The State party has pointed to contradictions and inconsistencies in the author's story, but the Committee considers that complete accuracy is seldom to be expected by victims of torture and that such inconsistencies as may exist in the author's presentation of the facts are not material and do not raise doubts about the general veracity of the author's claims.[139]

89. Next, recalling a number of cases of ill-treatment referred to by Mr. Alan, the Committee stated that, under the circumstances, it "finds that the author has

---

[133] See Kolb, *loc. cit.* (footnote 131 above), pp. 261 and 266.

[134] On the work of this Committee, see, *inter alia*, Ingelse, *The United Nations Committee Against Torture. An Assessment*; Holmström, ed., *Conclusions and Recommendations of the United Nations Committee Against Torture: Eleventh to Twenty-Second Session (1993–1999)*; see also Dormenval, "United Nations Committee against Torture: practice and perspectives", pp. 26 *et seq.*; Nowak, "The implementation functions of the United Nations Committee against Torture", pp. 493–526.

[135] Kolb summarizes them in his study cited above (footnote 131 above; see, in particular, pages 268–273), and this is drawn on in the present analysis.

[136] Report of the Committee against Torture, *Official Records of the General Assembly, Forty-ninth Session, Supplement No. 44* (A/49/44), annex V, sect. B, *Mutombo v. Switzerland*, communication No. 13/1993, para. 9.3.

[137] *Ibid.*, para. 9.4.

[138] *Ibid., Fifty-first session, Supplement No. 44* (A/51/44), annex V, sect. A, communication No. 21/1995, paras. 11.2–11.6.

[139] *Ibid.*, para. 11.3.

sufficiently substantiated that he personally is at risk of being subjected to torture if he returned to Turkey".[140] It "concluded that the expulsion of return of the author to Turkey in the prevailing circumstances would constitute a violation of article 3 of the Convention against Torture and Other Cruel, Inhuman or Degrading Treatment or Punishment".[141]

90. In *Aemei v. Switzerland* (1997), the Committee followed a line of reasoning that was subsequently confirmed by international courts. It affirmed the *jus cogens* nature of the norm set forth in article 3. The Committee:

> ... would recall that the protection accorded by article 3 of the Convention is absolute. Whenever there are substantial grounds for believing that a particular person would be in danger of being subjected to torture if he was expelled to another State, the State party is required not to return that person to that State. The nature of the activities in which the person engaged is not a relevant consideration in the taking of a decision in accordance with article 3 of the Convention.[142]

91. This unequivocal legal precedent by non-jurisdictional oversight bodies is well established, given the abundance of consistent decisions by jurisdictional bodies.[143]

92. We will begin with the case law of the International Tribunal for the Former Yugoslavia. The Tribunal stated its opinion on torture for the first time in *Delalić (Čelebići)* (1998). While, where the definition is concerned, the Tribunal's Trial Chamber relied on that contained in the 1984 Convention against Torture[144], its decision is particularly noteworthy in that it asserts that the prohibition of torture is customary in nature and applies both in peacetime and in times of armed conflict, whether internal or international.[145] The Chamber confirmed this some months later in *Furundžija*[146] after clearly recalling the doctrine governing this rule:

> Firstly, given the importance that the international community attaches to the protection of individuals from torture, the prohibition against torture is particularly stringent and sweeping. States are obliged not only to prohibit and punish torture, but also to forestall its occurrence: it is insufficient merely to intervene after the infliction of torture, when the physical or moral integrity of human beings has already been irremediably harmed. Consequently, States are bound to put in place all those measures that may pre-empt the perpetration of torture. As was authoritatively held by the European Court of Human Rights in *Soering*, international law intends to bar not only actual breaches but also potential breaches of the prohibition against torture (as well as any inhuman and degrading treatment. It follows that international rules prohibit not only torture but also (i) the failure to adopt the national measures necessary for implementing the prohibition and (ii) the maintenance in force or passage of laws which are contrary to the prohibition.[147]

93. This decision of the Trial Chamber was confirmed by the Appeals Chamber, which "finds it inconceivable that it could ever be argued that the acts charged in paragraph 25 of the Amended Indictment, namely, the rubbing of a knife against a woman's eyes and stomach, coupled with the threat to insert the knife into her vagina, once proven, are not serious enough to amount to torture".[148]

94. The rule prohibiting torture has a special legal consequence in the contact of the law of State responsibility. The Tribunal notes that:

> Normally, the maintenance or passage of national legislation inconsistent with international rules generates State responsibility and consequently gives rise to a corresponding claim for cessation and reparation (*lato sensu*) only when such legislation is concretely applied. By contrast, in the case of torture, the mere fact of keeping in force or passing legislation contrary to the international prohibition of torture generates international State responsibility. The value of freedom from torture is so great that it becomes imperative to preclude any national legislative act authorizing or condoning torture or at any rate capable of bringing about this effect.[149]

95. Moreover, in the wake of *Delalić*, the Trial Chamber stated:

> 151. Furthermore, the prohibition of torture imposes upon States obligations *erga omnes*, that is, obligations owed towards all the other members of the international community, each of which then has a correlative right. In addition, the violation of such an obligation simultaneously constitutes a breach of the correlative right of all members of the international community and gives rise to a claim for compliance accruing to each and every member, which then has the right to insist

---

[140] *Ibid.*, para. 11.4.

[141] *Ibid.*, para. 11.6.

[142] *Ibid., Fifty-second session, Supplement No. 44* (A/52/44), annex V, sect. B.2, *Aemei v. Switzerland*, communication No. 34/1995, para. 9.8.

[143] *Ibid., Fifty-fifth session, Supplement No. 44* (A/55/44), *A.D. v. Netherlands*, communication No. 96/1997; *G.T. v. Switzerland*, communication No. 137/1999, annex VIII, sect. A, p. 147; *H.A.D. v. Switzerland*, communication No. 126/1999, annex VIII, sect. A, p. 125; *J.A. Arana v. France*, communication No. 63/1997, annex VIII, sect. A, p. 77; *K.M. v. Switzerland*, communication No. 107/1998, annex VIII, sect. A, p. 109; *K.T. v. Switzerland*, communication No. 118/1998, annex VIII, sect. A, p. 121; *S.C. v. Denmark*, communication No. 143/1999, annex VIII, sect. A, p. 154; *T.P.S. v. Canada*, communication No. 99/1997, annex VIII, sect. A, p. 94; *V.X.N. and H.N. v. Sweden*, communications No. 130 and 131/1999, annex VIII, sect. A, p. 135; *ibid., Fifty-fourth session, Supplement No. 44* (A/54/44), *C. R. Núñez Chipana v. Venezuela*, communication No. 110/1998, annex VII, sect. A, p. 96; *H.D. v. Switzerland*, communication No. 112/1998, annex VII, sect. A, p. 101; *J.U.A. v. Switzerland (1)*, communication No. 100/1997, annex VII, sect. A, p. 63; *M.B.B. v. Sweden (2)*, communication No. 104/1998, annex VII, sect. A, p. 82; *N.P. v. Australia*, communication No. 106/1998, annex VII, sect. A, p. 89; *S.M.R. and M.M.R. v. Sweden*, communication No. 103/1998, annex VII, sect. A, p. 73; *ibid., Fifty-third session, Supplement No. 44* (A/53/44), *A.L.N. v. Switzerland*, communication No. 90/1997, annex X, sect. A, p. 106; *E.A. v. Switzerland*, communication No. 28/1995, annex X, sect. A, p. 54; *I.A.O. v. Sweden*, communication No. 65/1997, annex X, sect. A, p. 82; *K.N.C. v. Switzerland*, communication No. 94/1997, annex X, sect. A, p. 111; *P.Q.L. v. Canada*, communication No. 57/1996, annex X, sect. A, p. 60; *X., Y. and Z. v. Sweden*, communication No. 61/1996, annex X, sect. A, p. 75; ibid., *Fifty-second session, Supplement No. 44* (A/52/44), *X. v. Switzerland*, communication No. 27/1995, annex V, sect. B, p. 64; *X. v. Switzerland*, communication no. 38/1995, annex V, sect. B, p. 80; *ibid., Fifty-first session, Supplement No. 44* (A/51/44), *X. v. Netherlands*, communication No. 36/1995, annex V, sect. A, p. 76.

[144] The Tribunal's Trial Chamber revised its jurisprudence relating to the definition of torture in *Kunarac et al.*: "In view of the international instruments and jurisprudence reviewed above, the Trial Chamber is of the view that the definition of torture contained in the torture convention cannot be regarded as the definition of torture under international customary law which is binding regardless of the context. ... The Trial Chamber, therefore, holds that the definition of torture contained in article 1 of the torture convention can only serve, for present purposes, as an interpretational aid." (*Kunarac, Kovac and Vukovic* case No. IT–96–23–T & IT–96–23/1–T, 22 February 2001, paragraph 482; see also paragraph 496).

[145] *Delalić (Čelebići)*, Judgement of 16 November 1998, *Judicial Reports 1998*, vol. 2, paras. 446 and 454.

[146] *Furundžija* (footnote 120 above), para. 155.

[147] *Ibid.*, para. 148.

[148] *Furundžija (Appeal, 2000)*, Appeals Chamber Judgement of 21 July 2000, para. 114.

[149] *Furundžija* (footnote 120 above), para. 150.

on fulfilment of the obligation or in any case to call for the breach to be discontinued.

152. Where there exist international bodies charged with impartially monitoring compliance with treaty provisions on torture, these parties enjoy priority over individual States in establishing whether a certain State has taken all the necessary measures to prevent and punish torture and, if they have not, in calling upon that State to fulfil its international obligations. The existence of such international mechanisms makes it possible for compliance with international law to be ensured in a mutual and impartial manner.

...

153. While the *erga omnes* nature just mentioned appertains to the area of international enforcement (*lato sensu*), the other major feature of the principle proscribing torture relates to the hierarchy of rules in the international normative order. Because of the importance of the values it protects, this principle has evolved into a peremptory norm or *jus cogens*, that is, a norm that enjoys a higher rank in the international hierarchy than treaty law and even "ordinary" customary rules. The most conspicuous consequence of this higher rank is that the principle at issue cannot be derogated from by States through international treaties or local or special customs or even general customary rules not endowed with the same normative force.

154. Clearly, the *jus cogens* nature of the prohibition against torture articulates the notion that the prohibition has now become one of the most fundamental standards of the international community. Furthermore, this prohibition is designed to produce a deterrent effect, in that it signals to all members of the international community and the individuals over whom they wield authority that the prohibition of torture is an absolute value from which nobody must deviate.[150]

96. This position that the prohibition of torture is a peremptory norm was also taken by the European Court of Human Rights in *Al-Adsani v. United Kingdom*. The Court notes that "there have been a number of judicial statements to the effect that the prohibition of torture has attained the status of a peremptory norm or *jus cogens*"; it states "on the basis of [the] authorities, that the prohibition of torture has achieved the status of a peremptory norm in international law".[151]

97. Well before that case, the European Court of Human Rights had had occasion to rule on the prohibition of the expulsion of an asylum seeker on grounds of risk of torture in *Cruz Varas and others v. Sweden* (1991). The case related to the expulsion of Chilean nationals to their country of origin at the time when General Pinochet was still in power there. Transposing the wording of *Soering* to the case in question, the Court accepted that a decision to expel an asylum seeker could engage the responsibility of the expelling State under the 1984 Convention against Torture where there were "substantial grounds" for believing that the person concerned would face, in the country of destination, "a real risk of being subjected to torture or to inhuman or degrading treatment or punishment".[152] In the case before it, the Court considered that the expulsion of the applicant to his country of origin had not exposed him to a real risk of being subjected to such treatment on his return to Chile in October 1989. Accordingly, there had been no violation by Sweden of the obligations under article 3 of the European Convention on Human Rights.

98. The European Court confirmed this precedent in *Vilvarajah and others v. United Kingdom* (1991). At issue was the United Kingdom's decision to return five Sri Lankan asylum seekers to their country. The Court recalled that article 3 of the above-mentioned Convention prohibits the return of a refugee who would be at real risk of being subjected to ill-treatment in his or her country, while nevertheless considering that in the case in question the persons being returned would not run such a risk. Applying here a "national standard" rather than a "minimum" international standard, the Court considered that it was not established that the applicants' "personal position was any worse than the generality of other members of the Tamil community or other young male Tamils who were returning to their country". Admittedly, given the unsettled situation, "there existed the possibility that they might be detained and ill-treated, as appears to have occurred previously in the cases of some of the applicants"; but their expulsion did not constitute a breach of article 3 of the European Convention on Human Rights.[153]

99. These precedents have been summarized as follows:

First: there must be substantial grounds for believing that expulsion exposes the person concerned to a real risk of treatment contrary to article 3. Second: the approach is subjective, in that what counts is that the person concerned personally runs this risk. Third: the objective situation in the third State has indicative value, as the widespread practice of maltreatment also makes the risk to the person concerned more probable. The contrary is true if the position of the person concerned does not appear to be distinguished from that of all members of the community to which he or she belongs on the soil of the State to which expulsion is to take place; this constitutes an argument against sufficient objective risk.[154]

100. From these international precedents, of which *Furundžija* constitutes the most advanced illustration, three major findings emerge.[155] First, the prohibition of torture extends not only to actual violations but also to potential violations of the physical and moral (or mental) integrity of the human person; consequently, the State has not only an obligation to intervene after the event to remedy it, but also the duty to pre-empt it through diligent action, including the prompt elimination of laws contrary to the rule of prohibition.[156] Next, the prohibition of torture imposes obligations *erga omnes*; all States have a right to act and an interest in acting pursuant to this rule.[157] Lastly, the prohibition is a rule of *jus cogens*, a peremptory norm that cannot be derogated from under any circumstances. It occupies a high rank commensurate with the supreme values it protects.[158]

[150] *Ibid.*, paras. 151–154.

[151] ECHR, *Al-Adsani v. United Kingdom*, Judgement of 21 November 2001, *Reports of Judgements and Decisions, 2001–XI*, paras. 60–61.

[152] ECHR, *Cruz Varas and Others v. Sweden*, Judgement of 20 March 1991, *Series A: Judgments and Decisions*, vol. 201, p. 28, para. 69; see also judgement published in *Revue universelle des droits de l'homme*, 1991, vol. 3, No. 6, at pp. 209–222, at p 217.

[153] ECHR, *Vilvarajah and others v. United Kingdom*, Judgement of 30 October 1991, *Series A: Judgments and Decisions*, vol. 215, paras. 104 *et seq.*, particularly para. 111. See also judgement published in *Revue universelle des droits de l'homme*, 1991, pp. 537–551, at pp. 548–549.

[154] Kolb, *loc. cit.* (footnote 131 above), p. 270. The author recalls that this criterion of "non-discrimination" has been criticized in the legal literature; see, *inter alia*, Sudre, "Article 3", p. 174.

[155] See Kolb, *loc. cit.* (footnote 131 above), p. 273.

[156] *Furundžija* (footnote 120 above), paras. 148–150.

[157] *Ibid.*, paras. 151–153.

[158] *Ibid.*, paras. 153–157.

b. Cruel, inhuman or degrading treatment

i. Overview

101. As already indicated, the prohibition of "cruel, inhuman or degrading treatment or punishment" (the wording of the Universal Declaration of Human Rights) is embodied, with a few slight variations in wording, in the formulations used in the main international human rights instruments.

102. The legal instruments in question do not define the various categories that make up this part of the norm prohibiting violation of the rights of the person and limiting the State's right of expulsion. International jurisprudence has filled this gap, notably through the ruling by the International Tribunal for the Former Yugoslavia in *Delalić (Čelebići)*, cited above. The Trial Chamber defines "inhuman treatment" as follows:

> ...acts or omissions that cause serious mental or physical suffering or injury or constitute a serious attack on human dignity... In sum, the Trial Chamber finds that inhuman treatment is an intentional act or omission, that is an act which, judged objectively, is deliberate and not accidental, which causes serious mental or physical suffering or injury or constitutes a serious attack on human dignity.[159]

103. The fundamental difference from the definition of torture is, on the one hand, that inhuman (cruel or degrading) treatment is not necessarily administered for the purpose of obtaining information or a confession; and, on the other, that such treatment must not be necessarily or exclusively inflicted by agents of the State acting under cover of it.

104. As for "cruel treatment", the Chamber, in the same case, gives the following definition:

> [C]ruel treatment constitutes an intentional act or omission, that is an act which, judged objectively, is deliberate and not accidental, which causes serious mental or physical suffering or injury or constitutes a serious attack on human dignity. As such, it carries an equivalent meaning and therefore the same residual function for the purposes of common article 3 of the Statute as inhuman treatment does in relation to grave breaches of the Geneva Conventions. Accordingly, the offence of torture under common article 3 of the Geneva Conventions is also included within the concept of cruel treatment. Treatment that does not meet the purposive requirement for the offence under common article 3, constitutes cruel treatment.[160]

105. In the light of these two definitions, it would appear that the concept of "cruel treatment" is more comprehensive, including both inhuman treatment and certain aspects of the crime of torture, although it is not fully coterminous with that crime. Nevertheless, all these acts or forms of treatment constitute attacks on human dignity. Subsequent to the *Delalić* judgement, the Tribunal referred to outrage upon human dignity as a consequence of inhuman treatment in *Aleksovski* (1999).[161]

106. The list of acts characterized as cruel, inhuman or degrading treatment is long and varied, and it would be tedious to make an inventory here of those that emerge from the jurisprudence. More worthwhile is to identify the criteria for the characterization. In its case law, the European Court of Human Rights has consistently held that:

> … ill-treatment must attain a minimal level of severity if it is to fall in the scope of Article 3 (art. 3). The assessment of this minimum is, in the nature of things, relative; it depends on all the circumstances of the case, such as the duration of the treatment, its physical or mental effects, and in some cases, the sex, age and state of health of the victim, etc.[162]

107. It was in *Soering* that the European Court of Human Rights began to establish its case law in relation to the prohibition of extradition, and by extension expulsion, on the grounds of the risk of cruel, inhuman or degrading treatment. The central issue the Court had before it was whether the extradition of an individual by a State party to the European Convention on Human Rights to a third State can engage the responsibility of the State party under article 3 of the Convention by reason of the ill-treatment the person extradited may face in the country of destination. To this question the Court responded, in its judgement of 7 July 1989, that no right not to be extradited is as such protected by the Convention; nevertheless:

> … insofar as a measure of extradition has consequences adversely affecting the enjoyment of the Convention right, it may, assuming that the consequences are not too remote, attract the obligations of a Contracting State under the relevant Convention guarantee.[163]

108. As already indicated in paragraph 76 of the present report, the legal literature gives this mechanism the name "protection by ricochet",[164] the principle of which may be presumed to have originated in article 1 of the Convention and the general obligation of the High Contracting Parties to accord the rights defined in the Convention to "all persons under their jurisdiction".[165]

109. One could argue, as the respondent Government did in *Soering*, that the State which deports or extradites a person is not responsible as such for the violation which is only opposable to the receiving State where the ill-treatment takes place. That was not the view of the European Commission on Human Rights, which, in its report, acknowledged that the deportation or extradition would under certain circumstances involve the responsibility of the deporting or extraditing Convention State if, for example, that State deported or extradited a person to a country where it was certain or where there was a serious risk that the person would be subjected to torture or inhuman treatment. The basis of State responsibility, the report of the Commission stressed, "lies in the exposure

[159] *Delalić (Čelebići)* (footnote 145 above), paras. 442 and 543; see also *Blaskić* (2000), International Tribunal for the former Yugoslavia, *Judicial Reports 2000,* vol. 1, para. 154.

[160] *Delalić (Čelebići)* (footnote 145 above), para. 552.

[161] *Prosecutor v. Zlatko Aleksovski*, Trial Chamber, case No. IT–95–14/1–T, Judgement of 25 June 1999, *Judicial Reports 1999*, para. 56; see also *Blaskić* (footnote 159 above), para. 681.

[162] European Court of Human Rights, *Ireland v. United Kingdom*, Judgement of 18 January 1978, *Series A: Judgments and Decisions*, vol. 25, para. 162; see also, in the context of extradition and expulsion, *Soering v. United Kingdom* (footnote 129 above), para. 100; *Cruz Varas and others v. Sweden* (footnote 152 above), para. 83.

[163] *Soering v. United Kingdom*, (footnote 129 above), para. 85.

[164] Cohen-Jonathan, *La Convention européenne des droits de l'homme*, pp. 84 and 304; see also Sudre, "Extradition et peine de mort: arrêt *Soering* de la Cour européenne des droits de l'homme du 7 juillet 1989", p. 108.

[165] Sudre, "Extradition et peine de mort", p. 109.

of a person by way of deportation or extradition to inhuman or degrading treatment in another country".[166] In so stating, the Commission was consistent with its previous case law, which it cited in its report.[167]

110. The *Soering* precedent was subsequently confirmed in other judgements of the Court,[168] one of the most recent of which is that handed down on 26 July 2005 in *N. v. Finland*, concerning the expulsion of a former member of the special forces of Mobutu, the former Head of State of Zaire, now the Democratic Republic of the Congo. The Court considered that the person concerned took part "in various events during which dissidents seen as a threat to … Mobutu were singled out", and that "there is reason to believe that the applicant's situation could be worse than that of most other former Mobutu supporters"; moreover, in view of possible "feelings of revenge" in relatives of dissidents affected by his actions, there were "substantial grounds for believing that the applicant would be exposed to a real risk of treatment contrary to Article 3 [of the European Convention on Human Rights (prohibition of inhuman treatment)], if expelled". The Court therefore enjoined Finland not to expel the person concerned.[169]

111. The obligation thus asserted rests on the axiological foundations of the Convention. As a former judge of the European Court of Human Rights wrote:

> The absolute prohibition of torture and inhuman or degrading treatment or punishment in the European Convention on Human Rights embodies the fundamental values of democratic societies. Consequently, a State party would be behaving in a manner incompatible with the underlying values of the Convention if it knowingly returned a fugitive, heinous though the crime he is alleged to have committed might be, to another State where there were substantial grounds for believing that the person concerned faced a risk of torture [or maltreatment].[170]

This opinion matches the conclusion the Court reached in *Soering*, when it decided that despite the absence of an explicit reference in the text of article 3 of the Convention:

> this inherent obligation not to extradite also extends to cases in which the fugitive would be faced in the receiving State by a real risk of exposure to inhuman or degrading treatment or punishment proscribed by that Article (art. 3).[171]

112. The rule applies to expulsion,[172] whether or not the expulsion or extradition decided upon is carried out, as one author has written: "following the Commission, the Court so decided in its *Soering* decision of 7 July 1989 (para. 90). After the judgements in *Soering* (decision to extradite to the United States not carried out), *Cruz Varas* of 20 March 1991 (expulsion to Chile, Series ANl. 201, para. 70) *Vilvarajah* of 30 October 1991 (return of Tamils to Sri Lanka; series ANl. 215, paras. 102–103), the approach under European law is perfectly clear: once they have been the subject of a decision, expulsions, extraditions or returns, whether carried out or not, are capable of constituting inhuman or degrading treatment."[173]

113. This is not the case when no expulsion order has been made, as is apparent moreover from *Vijayanathan and Pusparajah v. France*.[174] Even where the oversight bodies of the European Convention on Human Rights develop case law on "imminent violation" in the context of expulsion, they limit it to cases of forced removal measures for aliens which have already been decided upon but not yet carried out.[175]

114. What about a case where an individual is expelled to a State where he or she risks facing violence committed not by organs of the State but by individuals acting in a private capacity?

115. The European Court of Human Rights had such a case before it in *H.L.R. v. France* (1997). The applicant, who was being expelled to Colombia, argued the risk of being subjected in that country to acts of torture or inhuman acts committed by private groups, namely the drug traffickers who had recruited him as a courier. Since *Soering*, the scope of article 3 of the European Convention has been extended to acts by State authorities which could lead to torture in the third State by authorities of that State. In *H.L.R. v. France*, the Court further expanded it to cover non-State risks on the assumption that the third State was not in a position to protect the person concerned: it considered that there was a breach of article 3 of the 1950 Convention if a State exposed an individual to a real danger of inhuman treatment committed by persons acting in a private capacity. The Court wrote:

> Owing to the absolute character of the right guaranteed, the Court does not rule out the possibility that Article 3 of the Convention (art. 3) may also apply where the danger emanates from persons or groups of persons who are not public officials. However, it must be shown that the risk is real and that the authorities of the receiving State are not able to obviate the risk by providing appropriate protection.[176]

116. The European case law on prohibition of the expulsion of an individual to a State where he or she is at risk of ill-treatment is followed by the oversight bodies of the universal human rights instruments. The United Nations Committee against Torture has ruled to this effect, as we have seen, in *Mutombo v. Switzerland* (1994), where it considered that "substantial grounds exist for believing that the author would be in danger of being subjected

---

[166] *Soering v. United Kingdom*, application No. 14038/88, Report of the Commission, 19 January 1989, published in ECHR, *Series A: Judgments and Decisions*, vol. 161, Annex, p. 55, para. 96.

[167] See decision of 3 May 1983 in *Altun v. Federal Republic of Germany*, application No. 10308/83, European Commission of Human Rights, *Decisions and Reports*, vol. 36, pp. 209–235; decision of 12 March 1984 in *Kirkwood v. United Kingdom* (footnote 126 above), application No. 10479/83, *Decisions and Reports*, vol. 37, pp. 158–191.

[168] See, for example, *D. v. United Kingdom*, in which the Court found that there was a risk of the applicant's being exposed to inhuman treatment (and hence a breach of article 3 of the Convention) if he was expelled to Saint Kitts and Nevis despite his critical state of health and the lack of appropriate medical equipment on the island.

[169] Source: *Agence France-Presse*, 27 July 2005. See ECHR, *N. v. Finland*, application No. 38885/02, Judgement of 26 July 2005 (English only).

[170] Carrillo-Salcedo, *loc. cit.* (footnote 42 above), p. 140.

[171] *Soering v. United Kingdom* (footnote 129 above), para. 88.

[172] See Sudre, "Article 3", p. 163.

[173] *Ibid.*, p. 173.

[174] See application Nos. 17550/90 and 17825/91, Opinion of the European Commission of Human Rights, as expressed in their report of 5 September 1991, published in ECHR, *Series A: Judgments and Decisions*, vol. 241-B.

[175] See Abraham, "Article 25", p. 588.

[176] *Reports of Judgments and Decisions*, 1997–III, No. 36, para. 40; *Revue universelle des droits de l'homme*, vol. 9, No. 1–4, 28 November 1997, p. 60.

to torture".[177] With regard to the risk of ill-treatment in general, i.e. including torture and cruel, inhuman or degrading treatment or punishment, the Human Rights Committee expressed an opinion on this subject in *Alzery v. Sweden*.[178]

117. The applicant, a chemistry and physics teacher at Cairo University, had been active in an organization involved in Islamist opposition. Using a false visa, he managed to enter Saudi Arabia, where he lived until his departure for the Syrian Arab Republic. He was forced to leave that country since it had extradited a number of Egyptian nationals back to their country of origin. Using a false Danish passport, he was able to enter Sweden, where he immediately sought asylum and admitted having used a false passport to enter the country. In support of his application for asylum, he reported that he had been physically assaulted and tortured in Egypt; that he had felt that he was being watched and that his home had been searched; that after his departure from Egypt he had been sought at his parents' home; that he feared being brought before a military court if he returned to Egypt; and that he was afraid of being arrested and tortured.[179]

118. The first substantive issue before the Committee was whether the applicant's expulsion from Sweden to Egypt exposed him to a real risk of torture or other ill-treatment in the receiving State, in breach of article 7 of the International Covenant on Civil and Political Rights:

> 11.4 The Committee notes that, in the present case, the State party itself has conceded that there was a risk of ill-treatment that—without more—would have prevented the expulsion of the author consistent with its human rights obligations. The State party in fact relied on the diplomatic assurances alone for its belief that the risk of proscribed ill-treatment was sufficiently reduced to avoid breaching the prohibition on refoulement.
>
> 11.5 The Committee notes that the assurances procured contained no mechanism for monitoring of their enforcement. Nor were any arrangements made outside the text of the assurances themselves which would have provided for effective implementation. The visits by the State party's ambassador and staff commenced five weeks after the return, neglecting altogether a period of maximum exposure to risk of harm. The mechanics of the visits that did take place, moreover, failed to conform to key aspects of international good practice by not insisting on private access to the detainee and inclusion of appropriate medical and forensic expertise, even after substantial allegations of ill-treatment emerged. In light of these factors, the State party has not shown that the diplomatic assurances procured were in fact sufficient in the present case to eliminate the risk of ill-treatment to a level consistent with the requirements of article 7 of the Covenant. The author's expulsion thus amounted to a violation of article 7 of the Covenant.[180]

119. The Special Rapporteur felt that it was mainly this development in case law, in particular with respect to the European Court of Human Rights, which Europe wished to reflect in article 19, paragraph 2, of the Charter of Fundamental Rights of the European Union, entitled "Protection in the event of removal, expulsion or extradition". This paragraph states that:

> No one may be removed, expelled or extradited to a State where there is a serious risk that he or she would be subjected to the death penalty, torture or other inhuman or degrading treatment or punishment.

120. In view of the foregoing analysis relating to the prohibition of torture and of cruel, inhuman or degrading treatment and the consequent obligation of States to protect all persons from such ill-treatment, including resident aliens or persons being expelled, the following draft article is proposed:

"Draft article 11. Obligation to protect persons being expelled from torture and cruel, inhuman or degrading treatment

"1. A State may not, in its territory, subject a person being expelled to torture or to cruel, inhuman or degrading treatment.

"2. A State may not expel a person to another country where there is a serious risk that he or she would be subjected to torture or to cruel, inhuman or degrading treatment.

"3. The provisions of paragraph 2 of this article shall also apply when the risk emanates from persons or groups of persons acting in a private capacity."

ii. Specific case of children

121. A final aspect of the protection of aliens being expelled from the risk of ill-treatment concerns the protection of children. The Convention on the Rights of the Child of 20 November 1989, which entered into force on 2 September 1990, establishes the general framework for the protection of these rights in a manner which encompasses the risks of ill-treatment mentioned above. Article 2 of the Convention provides that:

> 1. States Parties shall respect and ensure the rights set forth in the present Convention to each child within their jurisdiction without discrimination of any kind, irrespective of the child's or his or her parent's or legal guardian's race, colour, sex, language, religion, political or other opinion, national, ethnic or social origin, property, disability, birth or other status.
>
> 2. States Parties shall take all appropriate measures to ensure that the child is protected against all forms of discrimination or punishment on the basis of the status, activities, expressed opinions, or beliefs of the child's parents, legal guardians, or family members.

As a supplement to article 2 (cited above), article 3, paragraph 1, sets out a standard which summarizes the finalist philosophy that should underpin the implementation of all obligations of States under the Convention:

> In all actions concerning children, whether undertaken by public or private social welfare institutions, courts of law, administrative authorities or legislative bodies, the best interests of the child shall be a primary consideration.

In addition, article 37 provides as follows:

> States Parties shall ensure that:
>
> (*a*) No child shall be subjected to torture or other cruel, inhuman or degrading treatment or punishment. Neither capital punishment nor life imprisonment without possibility of release shall be imposed for offences committed by persons below eighteen years of age;

[177] Decision of 27 April 1994, (A/49/44), annex V, sect. B, communication No. 13/1993, para. 9.3.

[178] Report of the Human Rights Committee, *Official Records of the General Assembly, Sixty-second Session, Supplement No. 40* (A/62/40), vol. II, annex VII, sect. II, decision of 25 October 2006, communication No. 1416/2005; *Revue universelle des droits de l'homme*, 2006, vol. 27, Nos. 9–12, pp. 391 *et seq.*

[179] Report of the Human Rights Committee, p. 333, para. 3.2.

[180] *Ibid.*, pp. 406–407, paras. 11.4 and 11.5.

(b) No child shall be deprived of his or her liberty unlawfully or arbitrarily. The arrest, detention or imprisonment of a child shall be in conformity with the law and shall be used only as a measure of last resort and for the shortest appropriate period of time;

(c) Every child deprived of liberty shall be treated with humanity and respect for the inherent dignity of the human person, and in a manner which takes into account the needs of persons of his or her age. In particular, every child deprived of liberty shall be separated from adults unless it is considered in the child's best interest not to do so and shall have the right to maintain contact with his or her family through correspondence and visits, save in exceptional circumstances;

(d) Every child deprived of his or her liberty shall have the right to prompt access to legal and other appropriate assistance, as well as the right to challenge the legality of the deprivation of his or her liberty before a court or other competent, independent and impartial authority, and to a prompt decision on any such action.

122. In terms of case law, the European Court of Human Rights accords a wide scope to the protection afforded under article 3 of the European Convention on Human Rights: on the one hand, as the Judges' Council Chamber of the Brussels Criminal Court recalled in *Ana Arízaga Cajamarca and her daughter Angélica Loja Cajamarca v. Belgium*, this protection "is absolute and does not allow for any exception, even when the attitude of the alien invoking it might be open to criticism"; on the other hand, such protection extends to every human being, whether an adult or a child. In the aforementioned case, the applicants argued at the factual level that Angélica Loja Cajamarca, aged 11 years, had been severely traumatized by her arrest and detention. They referred to "serious violations" of the European Convention on Human Rights and of the Convention on the Rights of the Child. In fact, the applicants had been taken to the airport and held at the INAD detention centre. Ms. Cajamarca stated that she had been handcuffed and separated from her daughter, which increased the psychological trauma suffered by the latter. The Zaventem police categorically refused the applicants access to their legal counsel and a doctor, although the Office for Aliens had authorized this.

123. From a legal standpoint, the applicants maintained that the ill-treatment to which they were subjected constituted inhuman and degrading treatment, even torture, particularly in view of the young age and extreme vulnerability of Angélica; that the right to physical integrity was a fundamental right whose violation must cease immediately; and that the judge could therefore raise a motion to ensure the protection of this civil right without the need for a party to invoke such protection itself.

124. In this regard, in the *Mubilanzila Mayeka and Kaniki Mitunga v. Belgium* judgement on which the aforementioned Belgian court based its verdict, the European Court of Human Rights found Belgium guilty of inhuman and degrading treatment for the two-month detention of a five-year-old child in Transit Centre No. 127. The Court also found that the detention of a child in the same conditions as adults, namely in a closed centre initially designed for adults that was consequently not adapted to the needs of a child that age, constituted inhuman and degrading treatment contrary to article 3 of the European Convention on Human Rights. The Court emphasized the extreme vulnerability of children and noted that it was the responsibility of the Belgian State to take adequate measures to provide protection and care for them as part of its positive obligations under the aforementioned article 3.[181] It clarified that "the vulnerability of children must take precedence over their administrative status".[182] The Court's reasoning was as follows:

In view of the absolute nature of the protection afforded by article 3 of the Convention, it is important to bear in mind that this [the extremely vulnerable situation of the child] is the decisive factor and it takes precedence over considerations relating to the ... applicant's status as an illegal immigrant.[183]

125. The Judges' Council Chamber of the Brussels Criminal Court produced the following wording in this regard: "Children must be considered, treated and protected as children, irrespective of their immigration status."[184] This is the quintessence of the European Court's jurisprudence, which enriches the scope of article 3 of the European Convention on Human Rights and also indirectly specifies the provisions of article 37 of the Convention on the Rights of the Child, referred to above.

126. While nothing to date indicates that such wording expresses a customary rule, it can be said that such wording reflects a marked tendency in this area. In any event, it may be assumed that there is little overt opposition to the protective philosophy that underpins the Convention on the Rights of the Child and appears in various forms in regional instruments such as the African Charter on the Rights and Welfare of the Child, adopted in 1990.

127. In the light of these considerations, a specific norm is needed to protect children from the risk of torture and cruel, inhuman or degrading treatment irrespective of their immigration status.

"Draft article 12. Specific case of the protection of children being expelled

"1. A child being expelled shall be considered, treated and protected as a child, irrespective of his or her immigration status.

"2. Detention in the same conditions as an adult or for a long period shall, in the specific case of children, constitute cruel, inhuman and degrading treatment.

"3. For the purposes of the present article, the term "child" shall have the meaning ascribed to it in article 1 of the Convention on the Rights of the Child of 20 November 1989."

(iv) *Respect for the private and family life of persons being expelled*

128. Another limitation on the State's right of expulsion is the obligation to respect the right of individuals to

[181] The Court dismissed Belgium's claims that the child's family was at the origin of, and thus responsible for, the alleged harm caused. The Court's reasoning was followed by the Judges' Council Chamber of the Brussels Criminal Court in its decision of 4 July 2007 in *Ana Arízaga Cajamarca and her daughter Angélica Loja Cajamarca v. Belgium*.

[182] Wording of the Judge's Council Chamber of the Brussels Criminal Court.

[183] ECHR, *Mubilanzila Mayeka and Kaniki Mitunga v. Belgium*, (see footnote 43 above), para. 55.

[184] See footnote 181 above.

a private and family life, including aliens in the process of expulsion. This right is enshrined in both international instruments and regional conventions for the protection of human rights. At the international level, while the 1948 Universal Declaration of Human Rights is silent on this issue, article 17 of the International Covenant on Civil and Political Rights provides that:

> 1. No one shall be subjected to arbitrary or unlawful interference with his privacy, family …
>
> 2. Everyone has the right to the protection of the law against such interference or attacks.

129. Similarly, under the terms of article 5, paragraph 1 (*b*), of the Declaration on the Human Rights of Individuals Who are not Nationals of the Country in which They Live, aliens enjoy "the right to protection against arbitrary or unlawful interference with privacy, family, home or correspondence".

130. At the regional level, article 8, paragraph 1, of the European Convention on Human Rights provides that "Everyone has the right to respect for his private and family life …". Article 7 of the Charter of Fundamental Rights of the European Union reproduces this provision *in extenso*. While the African Charter on Human and Peoples' Rights does not contain this right, in other respects it is deeply committed to the protection of the family (see article 18). Article 11, paragraph 2, of the American Convention on Human Rights establishes this right in the same terms as article 17 of the International Covenant on Civil and Political Rights, cited above. Under section III (*c*) of the Protocol to the European Convention on Establishment, the contracting States, in exercising their right of expulsion, must in particular take due account of family ties and the period of residence in their territory of the person concerned.

131. International jurisprudence has provided clarifications both on the content of the right to a private and family life and on the limitations on this right. In *Canepa v. Canada*, the Human Rights Committee provided a criterion to assess a violation of the right to family life. It declared:

> The separation of a person from his family by means of his expulsion could be regarded as an arbitrary interference with the family and as a violation of article 17 if in the circumstances of the case the separation of the author from his family and its effects on him were disproportionate to the objectives of removal.[185]

132. Thus, through a process of deduction or reasoning *a contrario*, the criterion that emerges is one of proportionality between the interests of the expelling State—which, in expulsion cases, are public order and security—and the interests of the family, which, in this case, is the need to preserve the family life of the person being expelled. This was more clearly expressed in the position taken in a previous case, *Stewart v. Canada*, in which the Committee found that:

> … the interference with Mr. Stewart's family relations that will be the inevitable outcome of his deportation cannot be regarded as either unlawful or arbitrary when the deportation order was made under law in furtherance of a legitimate state interest and due consideration was given in the deportation proceedings to the deportee's family connections.[186]

133. The practice of the European Court of Human Rights, in which the importance of respect for family life has increased, is moving in the same direction. In *Abdulaziz, et al. v. United Kingdom* (1985), the Court found that:

> This is an area in which the Contracting Parties enjoy a wide margin of appreciation in determining the steps to be taken to ensure compliance with the Convention with due regard to the needs and resources of the community and of individuals.[187]

However, in *C. v. Belgium* (1996), just over 10 years later, the Court decided that the essential question was:

> … whether the deportation in issue struck a fair balance between the relevant interests, namely the applicant's right to respect for his private and family life, on the one hand, and the prevention of disorder or crime, on the other.[188]

134. The expelling State's interest in maintaining public order and security therefore seems to serve as the yardstick against which jurisprudence evaluates whether or not there has been a violation of the right to private or family life. In line with this criterion, in *Moustaquin*,[189] *Beldjoudi*[190] and *Nasri*,[191] the Court found that, irrespective of the crime of which the individual was accused, the expulsion was illegal if it violated his or her right to private and family life. The Court had already reached a similar decision in *Berrehab*. In that case, the issue at stake was whether the decision to repatriate a father to Morocco despite his right to visit his 14-year-old daughter, custody of whom had been awarded to his Dutch ex-wife, constituted a violation of his right to respect for family life. In view of the difficulties for the applicant to visit the Netherlands from Morocco in order to exercise his visiting rights, the Court concluded that the expulsion measure prevented, in practice, the exercise of these rights and thus violated article 8 of the European Convention on Human Rights.[192]

135. However, in *Boughanemi*,[193] *C. v. Belgium*,[194] *Bouchelkia*[195] and *Boujlifa*, following a proportionality

---

[185] Report of the Human Rights Committee, *Official Records of the General Assembly, Fifty-second Session, Supplement No. 40* (A/52/40), vol. II, annex VI.K, communication No. 558/1993, *Giosue Canepa v. Canada*, views adopted on 3 April 1997, para. 11.4.

[186] *Ibid.*, annex VI.G, communication No. 538/1993, *Charles E. Stewart v. Canada*, views adopted on 1 November 1996, fifty-eighth session, para. 12.10.

[187] ECHR, *Abdulaziz, Cabales and Balkandali v. the United Kingdom,* Judgement of 28 May 1985, *Series A: Judgments and Decisions*, vol. 94, pp. 33–34, para. 67.

[188] *C. v. Belgium*, Judgement of 7 August 1996, *Reports of Judgments and Decisions* (1996–III), No. 12, p. 924, para. 32.

[189] *Moustaquim v. Belgium*, Judgement of 18 February 1991, *Series A : Judgments and Decisions*, vol. 193, pp. 18–20, paras. 4146.

[190] *Beldjoudi v. France*, Judgement of 26 March 1992, *Series A: Judgments and Decisions*, vol. 234, pp. 26–28, paras. 71–80.

[191] *Nasri v. France*, Judgement of 13 July 1995, *Series A: Judgments and Decisions*, vol. 320–B, pp. 23–26, paras. 34–46.

[192] *Berrehab v. the Netherlands*, Judgement of 21 June 1988, *Series A: Judgments and Decisions*, vol. 138, p. 16, para. 29; and the comments of Carlo Russo, a former judge at the European Court of Human Rights, "Article 8 § 1", p. 318.

[193] *Boughanemi v. France*, Judgement of 24 April 1996, *Reports of Judgments and Decisions* (1996–II), No. 8, p. 610.

[194] *C. v. Belgium*, Judgement of 7 August 1996 (see footnote 188 above), pp. 924–925, para. 35.

[195] *Bouchelkia v. France*, Judgement of 29 January 1997, *Reports of Judgments and Decisions* (1997–I), No. 28, p. 63, para. 41.

test between the interests of the family and the interests of the expelling State with respect to public order and security, the Court appears to have given decisive weight to offences committed by the applicants in assessing the decision to expel. In *Boujlifa*, which is particularly illustrative of the predominant trend in the Court's jurisprudence, the applicant was a Moroccan national who had been living in France since the age of 5, together with his parents and eight brothers and sisters, and had been educated there. He had been convicted of robbery and armed robbery and the French authorities had decided to expel him to Morocco. Despite his long residence in France and the fact that his entire family was living there, the European Court of Human Rights considered that "the requirements of public order outweighed the personal considerations which prompted the application".[196] In other words, any infringement of the right to respect for the private and family life of an individual—in this case, a person being expelled—must be proportionate to the aims pursued by the expelling State.[197]

136. The Court went much further in *Boughanemi* by finding that the applicant's expulsion was not contrary to article 8 of the European Convention on Human Rights on the grounds that Mr. Boughanemi had kept his Tunisian nationality and had apparently never sought French nationality; that he had retained links with Tunisia that went beyond the mere fact of his nationality, as the Government of the expelling country had claimed; and that he had not claimed before the European Commission of Human Rights that he could not speak Arabic, or that he had cut all ties with his country of birth, or that he had not returned there.[198]

137. Should the conclusion drawn from this be that aliens must break all ties and social and cultural links with their countries in order to protect themselves from expulsion? That question can be answered by analysing developments in the case law of the Court. Some of the major milestones have already been mentioned.

138. Until the *Ezzouhdi* judgement of 2001, to which we shall return, many comments concerning this issue fell into two distinct periods of the Court's jurisprudence. The first period began with the *Moustaquim v. Belgium* judgement,[199] which was the first to consider the expulsion of an alien as a violation of article 8. This was followed by the *Beldjoudi v. France*[200] and *Nasri*[201] judgements, which reached similar conclusions. At the time, the Court was considered to be particularly sympathetic to second-generation immigrants, who therefore enjoyed its protection from expulsion.

139. The second period in the development of the Court's jurisprudence began in 1996 with the aforementioned *Boughanemi* judgement, which ruled out any violation of article 8 by reason of expulsion. This was followed by judgements and decisions on admissibility in *C. v. Belgium*,[202] *Boulchekia*,[203] *El Boujaïdi*,[204] *Boujlifa*,[205] *Dalia*,[206] *Benrachid*,[207] *Baghli*,[208] *Farah v. Sweden*[209] and *A. v. Norway*,[210] which all reached similar conclusions. The implication was that the Court had taken a tougher line. However, this ignores the fact that, in the course of this trend in case law, the Court had upheld a violation of article 8 in the *Mehemi v. France* (*Reports of Judgments and Decisions, 1997–VI*) judgement of 26 September 1997 concerning an application submitted by a foreign national born in France, with a wife and three children, who had been sentenced to six years' imprisonment and permanent exclusion from French territory for smuggling hashish. In this instance, the Court clearly made a distinction between cannabis and hashish, on the one hand, and heroin, on the other. The latter substance was involved in the *El Boujaïdi*, *Dalia*, *Baghli*, *Farah* and *A. v. Norway* cases cited above.

140. The judgement delivered on 13 February 2001 in *Ezzouhdi v. France*[211] enabled the Court to supplement its case law on the issue of expulsion in relation to respect for the right to private and family life while also demonstrating the consistency of a jurisprudence that had been considered inconsistent when, in fact, it was merely highly nuanced.[212] Mr. Ezzouhdi, a Moroccan national born in 1970, had lived in France since the age of 5. He had received an education in France until leaving school at 16 years of age. His father had died in 1995 but his mother and two sisters lived in France. Between 1993 and 1997, he had received three criminal convictions, including one for the possession, acquisition and use of narcotic drugs: more specifically, cannabis. In 1997, he had been sentenced by the Bourg-en-Bresse Criminal Court to 18 months'

[196] ECHR, *Boujlifa v. France*, Judgement of 21 October 1997, *Reports of Judgments and Decisions* (1997–VI), No. 54, p. 2265, para. 44.

[197] A judge appointed to replace the President of the Brussels Court of First Instance has adhered strictly to the practice of the European Court of Human Rights in this regard. In his order of 30 July 2007 concerning *Cajamarca and her daughter*, he underlined: "... that any violation of law with respect to the private and family life of an individual must, *inter alia*, be necessary in a democratic society, i.e. be proportionate to the aims pursued, in accordance with article 8 of the European Convention on Human Rights" (Case No. 07/5726/B, applicant: Ana Cajamarca Arízaga).

[198] ECHR, Judgement of 24 April 1996 (footnote 193 above), p. 610, para. 44. See also the decision of the Human Rights Committee, *Ngoc Si Truong v. Canada*, communication No. 743/1997: Canada 05/05/2003, CCPR/C/77/D/743/1997 (Jurisprudence); and *Benjamin Ngambi and Marie-Louise Nebol v. France*, communication No. 1179/2003: France 16/07/2004, CCPR/C/81/D/1179/2003, in which a violation of the right to family life could not be claimed owing to the lack of a family in this case: since the applicant's claim was based on a false marriage certificate, the family reunification sought could not take place.

[199] See footnote 189 above.

[200] See footnote 190 above.

[201] See footnote 191 above.

[202] See footnote 188 above.

[203] See footnote 195 above.

[204] ECHR, *El Boujaïdi v. France*, Judgement of 26 September 1997, *Reports of Judgments and Decisions, 1997–VI*.

[205] See footnote 196 above.

[206] *Dalia v. France*, Judgement of 19 February 1998, *Reports of Judgments and Decisions, 1998–I*.

[207] *Benrachid v. France*, Decision of 8 December 1998, *ibid.*, *1999–II*.

[208] *Baghli v. France*, Judgement of 30 November 1999, *ibid.*, *1999–VIII*.

[209] *Farah v. Sweden*, Judgement of 24 August 1999.

[210] Judgement of 21 March 2000.

[211] ECHR, application No. 471160/99, Judgement of 13 February 2001.

[212] On this judgement, see particularly the comments of Jarreau, "L'éloignement des étrangers: interdiction définitive du territoire français (arrêts Ezzouhdi et Abdouni des 13 et 27 février 2001)".

imprisonment and permanent exclusion from French territory for the acquisition and use of heroin, cocaine and hashish. The Court of Appeal had upheld his exclusion from French territory and had increased his term of imprisonment to two years. Mr. Ezzouhdi had filed an application for judicial review but this had been rejected. He had therefore submitted his case to the European Court of Human Rights, claiming that France had violated article 8 of the European Convention on Human Rights.

141. In its Judgement of 13 February 2001, the Court handed down successive rulings with respect to the two paragraphs of article 8.

142. With regard to paragraph 1, the question was whether the applicant could claim to have a private and family life in France that had been disrupted by the expulsion order. The Court answered this question in the affirmative, recalling the date of Mr. Ezzouhdi's arrival in France, his age at that time and the fact that he had been educated in France and that he worked there. In reality, until that stage, the only question posed by the French Government had been whether an unmarried man with no children had a family life under the terms of article 8, paragraph 1. In other words, was the application related to a violation of the applicant's private and family life or only to a violation of his private life? The Court found that the applicant's family ties with his mother, brothers and sisters living in France were sufficient to constitute a family life. It should be recalled that, according to the Human Rights Committee, the term "family", for the purposes of the International Covenant on Civil and Political Rights:

> ... must be understood broadly as to include all those comprising a family as understood in the society concerned. The protection of such family is not necessarily obviated, in any particular case, by the absence of formal marriage bonds, especially where there is a local practice of customary or common law marriage. Nor is the right to protection of family life necessarily displaced by geographical separation, infidelity, or the absence of conjugal relations. However, there must first be a family bond to protect.[213]

In the case in question, there can be no doubt that such a family bond existed between the applicant and his mother, brothers and sisters.

143. Another argument in the applicant's favour that was accepted by the Court was the absence of any tie other than that of nationality between Mr. Ezzouhdi and his native country: he had lived in Morocco only in his early youth and said he did not speak Arabic, and the French Government did not provide evidence that he had any other ties to that country.

144. The Court then embarked on a proportionality test that consisted of ascertaining whether the expulsion measure struck a fair balance between the relevant interests, namely the applicant's right to respect for his private and family life, on the one hand, and the protection of public order, the prevention of crime and the protection of health, on the other. In the Court's view, the seriousness of the offences committed by the applicant was a crucial factor in assessing this proportionality. In this case, it regarded the offences of which Mr. Ezzouhdi stood accused as being of limited impact, noting that he had been convicted of using and consuming drugs, not of selling them. The Court was thus of the opinion that those acts did not constitute a serious threat to public order, despite the finding of recidivism. The Court concluded that there was a lack of proportionality between the offences committed by the applicant and the harm done to his private and family life as a result of the expulsion measure, and found, lastly, that "the definitive nature of the exclusion seems unusually harsh".

145. Thus, the *Ezzouhdi* judgement represented a return, some three years after the aforementioned *Mehemi* judgement, to the European Court's position in previous cases in which it had found an expulsion measure to be in violation of article 8 of the European Convention on Human Rights. Nonetheless, it is not certain that this judgement truly marks a development, much less a break, in the Court's jurisprudence in a manner favourable to applicants. It is essentially "a decision consistent with previous ones that has the opposite effect, but only because the facts of the case so required".[214] What the Court requires in all cases—without distinguishing between "legitimate" and "illegitimate" families—is that, regardless of the extent of the relationships concerned, the resulting "family life" be pre-existing and effective, and marked by real and sufficiently close relations between its members:[215] such relations may take the form of shared living quarters, financial dependence (as in the case of minor children),[216] regularly exercised visiting rights,[217] or ongoing relations between a father and his illegitimate children.[218]

146. With respect to article 8, paragraph 2, certain authors[219] and some judges of the Court, in their dissenting opinions, have raised the question of how the right to respect for private life is related to the right to family life. In its judgement of 21 October 1997 in *Boujlifa*, cited above, the Court dealt specifically with the right to private life, although its conclusions were of little avail to the applicant. The question thus remains: is there an overlap between private life and family life? Is the latter simply a component of the former? The *Ezzouhdi* judgement confirmed the formulation of the aforementioned *Baghli* judgement in this regard, without really settling the issue. Yet it is undeniable that private life and family life do not always coincide, since an unmarried adult, for example, may have a private life apart from his or her family life, which exists despite his or her unmarried status, as shown in *Ezzouhdi*. This suggests that equal weight should be

[213] *Benjamin Ngambi and Marie-Louise Nébol v. France* (footnote 198 above), para. 6.4.

[214] Jarreau, *loc. cit.* (footnote 212 above), p. 3.

[215] See Russo, *loc. cit.*, p. 316.

[216] Application No. 2991/66, *Alam and Khan v. United Kingdom, Yearbook of the European Convention on Human Rights,* No. 2 (1968), p. 789; application No. 8244/78, *Singh Uppal v. United Kingdom, Decisions and Reports* 17, p. 149, and *Decisions and Reports* 20, p. 29.

[217] *Berrehab and Koster v. the Netherlands*, application No. 10730/84, decision of 8 March 1985, p. 196, report of 7 October 1986, Judgement of 21 June 1988, *Series A*, No. 138.

[218] *X. v. Federal Republic of Germany*, application No. 3110/67, *Decisions and Reports* 27, pp. 77–91; *X. v. Switzerland*, application No. 8924/80, *Decisions and Reports* 24; *X. and Y. v. Switzerland*, application Nos. 7289/75 and 7349/76, *Decisions and Reports* 9, p. 57.

[219] See, for example, Van Muylder, "Le droit au respect de la vie privée des étrangers", p. 797.

given to these two components of the rights referred to in article 8, paragraph 1, in the proportionality test in expulsion cases.

147. Thus, it does not seem possible, given the current state of international human rights law, to consider the requirement of respect for private and family life in expulsion cases as a rule of customary law. Inferred from the right to private and family life enshrined, as seen above, in some of the principal international human rights instruments, this requirement appears, in the light of the still-incipient case law of the Human Rights Committee and the more substantial case law of the European Court of Human Rights, as an obligation that may be generalized and extended to expulsion cases. On this basis, and in view of the developments outlined above, the following draft article is proposed:

"Draft article 13. Obligation to respect the right to private and family life

"1. The expelling State shall respect the right to private and family life of the person being expelled.

"2. It may not derogate from the right referred to in paragraph 1 of the present article except in such cases as may be provided for by law and shall strike a fair balance between the interests of the State and those of the person in question."

(v) *Non-discrimination*

148. Unlike the rules discussed above, non-discrimination "does not originate from the hard core of human rights".[220] Found in various spheres of international law, this "principle" has different constituent elements and modes of application depending on whether it is applied to relations between States, relations between States and private individuals or relations between private individuals. The relevant situation in expulsion cases concerns relations between States and private individuals. In the context of such relations, the principle of non-discrimination first appeared in peace treaties in the form of standards for the protection of minorities and of populations and territories under mandate. In this regard, the Permanent Court of International Justice stated, in its advisory opinion on *Settlers of German origin in Poland*, that "[t]here must be equality in fact as well as ostensible legal equality in the sense of the absence of discrimination in the words of the law".[221] The Court further clarified its position in its judgment in *Minority Schools in Albania*, adding that "[e]quality in law precludes discrimination of any kind; whereas equality in fact may involve the necessity of different treatment in order to attain a result which establishes an equilibrium between different situations".[222]

149. In the field of human rights and civil liberties, the non-discrimination rule appears as a corollary to the general principle of equality in law between individuals,[223] although the two concepts are different.[224] The non-discrimination rule has thus been established, in varying formulations, in a number of international human rights instruments. For example, article 7 of the Universal Declaration of Human Rights provides that "All are equal before the law and are entitled without any discrimination to equal protection of the law. All are entitled to equal protection against any discrimination in violation of this Declaration and against any incitement to such discrimination". Under article 2, paragraph 1, of the International Covenant on Civil and Political Rights, each State party to the Covenant "undertakes to respect and to ensure to all individuals within its territory and subject to its jurisdiction the rights recognised in the present Covenant, without distinction of any kind, such as race, colour, sex, language, religion, political or other opinion, national or social origin, property, birth or other status". Article 2, paragraph 1, of the Convention on the Rights of the Child is substantially similar, although paragraph 2 of that article provides that States parties "shall take all appropriate measures to ensure that the child is protected against all forms of discrimination or punishment on the basis of the status, activities, expressed opinions, or beliefs of the child's parents, legal guardians, or family members". Under article 2 of the Convention on the Elimination of All Forms of Discrimination against Women,[225] States parties "condemn discrimination against women in all its forms" and undertake to implement a variety of measures to prohibit, eliminate or punish such discrimination. The term "discrimination against women" is defined in article 1 of that Convention as "any distinction, exclusion or restriction made on the basis of sex which has the effect or purpose of impairing or nullifying the recognition, enjoyment or exercise by women, irrespective of their marital status, on a basis of equality of men and women, of human rights and fundamental freedoms in the political, economic, social, cultural, civil or any other field". The other international legal instruments for the protection of specific categories of people against discrimination reflect the same spirit: they are intended to guard against actions or conduct that aim at or result in discrimination. Such instruments include the Declaration on the Elimination of All Forms of Intolerance and of Discrimination Based on Religion or Belief[226] and the International Convention on the Elimination of All Forms of Racial Discrimination.[227]

---

[220] Roucounas, "Facteurs privés et droit international public", p. 159.

[221] *P.C.I.J., Series B, No. 6*, advisory opinion of 10 September 1923, p. 24.

[222] *P.C.I.J., Series A/B*, Judgment of 6 April 1935, p. 19.

[223] See Vegléris, "Le principe d'égalité dans la Déclaration universelle et la Convention européenne des droits de l'homme", pp. 565 *et seq.*; Mekean, *Equality and Discrimination under International Law*; Vierdag, *The Concept of Discrimination in International Law*; and Roucounas (footnote 220 above), pp. 160–161.

[224] See McRae, "The contribution of international trade law to the development of international law", p. 166; Opsahl, *Law and Equality: Selected Articles on Human Rights*, pp. 171 *et seq.*

[225] Adopted and opened for signature, ratification and accession by the General Assembly in its resolution 34/180 of 18 December 1979; entered into force on 3 September 1981.

[226] Proclaimed by the General Assembly on 25 November 1981 (resolution 36/55), art. 2.

[227] Adopted by the General Assembly on 21 December 1965 (resolution 2106 (XX)) and entered into force on 4 January 1969, art. 2. On this Convention and the non-discrimination rule, see, in particular, Decaux, ed., *Le droit face au racisme*, and Fredman, ed., *Discrimination and Human Rights: The Case of Racism*.

150. The non-discrimination rule also appears in the principal regional human rights instruments. These include the European Convention on Human Rights, whose article 14 expresses the idea without using the word; Protocol No. 12 to the European Convention, which was opened for signature on 4 November 2000, broadens the scope of application of article 14. The Charter of Fundamental Rights of the European Union, in a formulation that differs from those in the European Convention and Protocol No. 12, which establish the right to the enjoyment, without discrimination, of the rights and freedoms set forth in those instruments, immediately highlights the idea of prohibiting discrimination. The Charter's article 21, paragraph 1, provides that "[a]ny discrimination based on any ground such as sex, race, colour, ethnic or social origin, genetic features, language, religion or belief, political or any other opinion, membership of a national minority, property, birth, disability, age or sexual orientation shall be prohibited". It may be noted that, with respect to sexual orientation, the current state of the law of Western countries is far from reflecting the general situation.[228] Lastly, the African Charter on Human and Peoples' Rights takes an original approach to non-discrimination that seems to be based more on values than on legal considerations. Article 28 of that Charter provides that "[e]very individual shall have the duty to respect and consider his fellow beings without discrimination, and to maintain relations aimed at promoting, safeguarding and reinforcing mutual respect and tolerance". Of all the provisions referred to above, this is the only one that clearly and positively indicates what conduct should be adopted in order to ensure non-discrimination. Accordingly, it is of interest in connection with the rights to be preserved in cases involving the expulsion of aliens.

151. The question is how the non-discrimination rule can be applied to expulsion cases, given the acceptance of the principle of non-expulsion of nationals. The possibility that the expulsion of an alien may be due to discrimination *vis-à-vis* nationals cannot be discounted. This is why article 7 of the Declaration on the Human Rights of Individuals Who are not Nationals of the Country in which They Live prohibits "[i]ndividual or collective expulsion of [aliens lawfully in the territory of a State] on grounds of race, colour, religion, culture, descent or national or ethnic origin". But it seems quite evident that non-discrimination should also apply in such cases between the aliens being expelled. The idea is that in expulsion cases there should be no discrimination not only between aliens and nationals, but also between different categories of aliens, on grounds such as those of race, sex, language, religion, political or other opinion, national or social origin, property, birth or other status (International Covenant on Civil and Political Rights, art. 2, para. 1), with the European Convention on Human Rights adding, as seen above, "membership of a national minority" (art. 14 of the Convention and art. 1, para. 1, of Protocol No. 12).

[228] There are numerous precedents in this regard in European and North American case law, particularly in the United States (see Silvers, "The exclusion and expulsion of homosexual aliens", pp. 295–332). At the same time, many countries in Africa, the Arab world and Asia have retained their laws penalizing homosexuality, and such laws have even been introduced in some countries where homosexuality had not been penalized before, such as Burundi, which adopted a law on this subject in March 2009.

152. Thus, in *Mauritian Women*, the Human Rights Committee considered that the expulsions concerned were illegal because legislation had given rise to discrimination on the ground of sex by protecting the wives of Mauritian men against expulsion while not affording such protection to the husbands of Mauritian women.[229] Non-discrimination between aliens with respect to expulsion may be considered to have a relevant legal basis in the different international instruments cited above, which establish this rule as one of the elements of protection afforded to the specific categories of people to which they refer.

153. The European Court of Human Rights, in its judgement of 28 May 1985 in *Abdulaziz, Cabales and Balkandali*,[230] echoed the Human Rights Committee's views on *Mauritian Women*, cited above. The Court held unanimously that article 14 of the European Convention on Human Rights had been violated by reason of discrimination against each of the applicants on the ground of sex: unlike male immigrants settled in the United Kingdom, the applicants did not have the right, in the same situation, to obtain permission for their non-national spouses to enter or remain in the country for settlement. After noting that "the advancement of the equality of the sexes is today a major goal in the member States of the Council of Europe", the Court expressed the view that "very weighty reasons would have to be advanced before a difference of treatment on the ground of sex could be regarded as compatible with the Convention".[231] It went on to stress that article 14 "is concerned with the avoidance of discrimination in the enjoyment of the Convention rights in so far as the requirements of the Convention as to those rights can be complied with in different ways".[232] On the other hand, it considered that, in the case in question, the fact that the applicable rules affected "fewer white people than others" was not a sufficient reason to consider them as racist in character, since they "did not contain regulations differentiating between persons or groups on the ground of their race or ethnic origin".[233]

154. The developments described above indicate that:

(*a*) The non-discrimination rule is widely established in written human rights law and the very nature of those rights requires that they be applied without discrimination to the categories of people concerned;

(*b*) This rule is established, with respect to expulsion, by the jurisprudence of the bodies responsible for monitoring the implementation of human rights instruments, although such jurisprudence is still based on a very limited number of cases;

[229] Report of the Human Rights Committee, *Official Records of the General Assembly, Thirty-sixth Session, Supplement No. 40* (A/36/40), annex XIII, views adopted on 9 April 1981, communication No. R.9/35, pp. 134 *et seq.*, reproduced in part in *Human Rights Law Journal*, vol. 2 (1981), p. 139, para. 9.2.

[230] ECHR, *Abdulaziz, Cabales and Balkandali v. United Kingdom*, Judgement of 28 May 1985, *Series A, No. 94* (footnote 187 above); relevant parts of the judgement are recalled by Bossuyt in "Article 14", pp. 482–483.

[231] *Abdulaziz* (footnote 187 above), para. 78.

[232] *Ibid.*, para. 82.

[233] *Ibid.*, para. 85.

(*c*) The prohibition of discrimination with respect to human rights in general, and expulsion in particular, "does not exist independently"[234] in that it is meaningful only when it is observed in relation to a given right or freedom;

(*d*) The legal instruments and case law considered do not attempt to provide an exhaustive listing of the different factors that may serve as grounds for discrimination.

155. Here again, the relevant rule should be formulated not in terms of rights which all beneficiaries should enjoy without discrimination, but in terms of the State's obligation not to apply the rights in question in a discriminatory fashion.

[234] Bossuyt, "Article 14", p. 478.

156. In the light of the foregoing analyses and observations, the following draft article is proposed:

"Draft article 14. Obligation not to discriminate

"1. The State shall exercise its right of expulsion with regard to the persons concerned without discrimination of any kind, on grounds such as race, colour, sex, language, religion, political or other opinion, national or social origin, property, birth or other status.

"2. Such non-discrimination shall also apply to the enjoyment, by a person being expelled, of the rights and freedoms provided for in international human rights law and in the legislation of the expelling State."

EXPULSION OF ALIENS

[Agenda item 6]

DOCUMENT A/CN.4/604

Comments and observations received from Governments

[*Original: English*]
[*26 August 2008*]

CONTENTS

Multilateral instruments cited in the present report

	Source
Geneva Conventions for the protection of war victims (Geneva, 12 August 1949)	United Nations, *Treaty Series*, vol. 75, Nos. 970–973, pp. 31 *et seq.*
Geneva Convention relative to the Treatment of Prisoners of War (Geneva Convention III)	*Ibid.*, No. 972, p. 135.
Geneva Convention relative to the Protection of Civilian Persons in Time of War (Geneva Convention IV)	*Ibid.*, No. 973, p. 287.
Convention for the Protection of Human Rights and Fundamental Freedoms (European Convention on Human Rights) (Rome, 4 November 1950)	*Ibid.*, vol. 213, No. 2889, p. 221.
Protocol No. 4 to the Convention of 4 November 1950 for the Protection of Human Rights and Fundamental Freedoms, securing certain rights and freedoms other than those already included in the Convention and in the first Protocol thereto (Strasbourg, 16 September 1963)	*Ibid.*, vol. 1496, No. 2889, p. 263.
Protocol No. 7 to the Convention for the Protection of Human Rights and Fundamental Freedoms (Strasbourg, 22 November 1984)	*Ibid.*, vol. 1525, No. 2889, p. 195.
Convention relating to the Status of Refugees (Geneva, 28 July 1951)	*Ibid.*, vol. 189, No. 2545, p. 137.
Convention relating to the Status of Stateless Persons (New York, 28 September 1954)	*Ibid.*, vol. 360, No. 5158, p. 117.
European Convention on Establishment (Paris, 13 December 1955)	*Ibid.*, vol. 529, No. 7660, p. 141.
Convention on the Reduction of Statelessness (New York, 30 August 1961)	*Ibid.*, vol. 989, No. 14458, p. 175.
International Covenant on Civil and Political Rights (New York, 16 December 1966)	*Ibid.*, vol. 999, No. 14668, p. 171.
American Convention on Human Rights: "Pact of San José, Costa Rica" (San José, 22 November 1969)	*Ibid.*, vol. 1144, No. 17955, p. 143.
African Charter on Human and Peoples' Rights (Nairobi, 27 June 1981)	*Ibid.*, vol. 1520, No. 26363, p. 217.
The Schengen acquis – Agreement between the Governments of the States of the Benelux Economic Union, the Federal Republic of Germany and the French Republic on the gradual abolition of checks at their common borders (Schengen, 14 June 1985)	*Official Journal of the European Communities*, No. L 239, 22 September 2000, pp. 13–18.
Convention determining the State responsible for examining applications for asylum lodged in one of the Member States of the European Communities—Dublin Convention (Dublin, 15 June 1990)	*Ibid.*, No. C 254, 19 August 1997, pp. 1–12.
International Convention on the Protection of the Rights of All Migrant Workers and Members of their Families (New York, 18 December 1990)	United Nations, *Treaty Series*, vol. 2220, No. 39481, p. 3.

Introduction

1. At its fifty-seventh session, in 2005, the International Law Commission decided, in accordance with article 19, paragraph 2, of its statute, to request, through the Secretary-General, Governments to submit any information concerning the practice of States, including national legislation, relating to the topic "Expulsion of aliens".[1]

2. In paragraph 4 of resolution 60/22 of 23 November 2005, the General Assembly invited Governments to provide information to the Commission, as requested in chapter III of the Commission's report on its fifty-seventh session,[2] regarding, *inter alia*, the topic "Expulsion of aliens".

3. At its fifty-ninth session, in 2007, the Commission reiterated its request for information regarding the practice of States under the topic "Expulsion of aliens", including examples of domestic legislation. The Commission welcomed in particular observations and comments on specific issues relating to this topic.[3]

4. In paragraph 3 of its resolution 62/66 of 6 December 2007, the General Assembly drew the attention of Governments to the importance for the Commission of having their views on the various aspects involved in, *inter alia*, the topic "Expulsion of aliens", in particular on all the specific issues identified in chapter III of the Commission's report on the work of its fifty-ninth session.[4] In paragraph 4 of the same resolution, the General Assembly

[1] *Yearbook ... 2005*, vol. II (Part Two), para. 27.

[2] *Ibid.*

[3] *Yearbook ... 2007*, vol. II (Part Two), para. 27. The issues on which the Commission invited Governments to submit comments and observations are listed in section A below.

[4] *Ibid.*

invited Governments, within the context of paragraph 3, to provide information regarding practice concerning, *inter alia*, the topic "Expulsion of aliens".

5. As at 29 August 2008, written replies had been received from Germany (27 May 2008), Mauritius (12 November 2007), the Russian Federation (30 April 2008) and Switzerland (22 July 2008). These replies are reproduced below. Section A contains comments and observations on the specific issues (or aspects thereof) identified by the Commission, while section B contains comments and observations on other issues relating to this topic.

Comments and observations received from Governments

A. Comments and observations on the specific issues identified by the Commission

1. State practice with regard to the expulsion of nationals. Is it allowed under domestic legislation? Is it permissible under international law?

RUSSIAN FEDERATION

According to article 61, paragraph 1, of the Constitution of the Russian Federation, "A citizen of the Russian Federation may not be deported from the Russian Federation or extradited to another State."

SWITZERLAND

National legislation

1. The expulsion of nationals is not permitted under Swiss law. This prohibition is provided for by the Federal Constitution: "Swiss citizens may not be expelled from Switzerland and may only be extradited to a foreign authority with their consent" (art. 25, para. 1).

International law

2. States are prohibited from expelling their nationals by various international and regional human rights instruments.

3. The International Covenant on Civil and Political Rights of 16 December 1966 (160 States parties and 67 signatories) provides, in article 12, paragraph 4, that "[n]o one shall be arbitrarily deprived of the right to enter his own country". Although the Covenant does not explicitly mention a prohibition against expulsion, but rather a right to enter, the Human Rights Committee, in its general comment No. 27, notes that the right enshrined in article 12, paragraph 4, of the Covenant implicitly includes the right to remain in one's own country and, consequently, not to be expelled.[5] The term "arbitrarily" appears to suggest that only arbitrary expulsions would be prohibited by the Covenant. The Human Rights Committee specifies that the term "arbitrarily" is intended to emphasize that the principle applies to all State action, whether legislative, administrative or judicial, and that interference, even where provided for by law, should be in accordance with the spirit of the Covenant and reasonable in view of the circumstances.[6] Thus, the prohibition against depriving an individual of the right to enter his own country (and, thereby, the prohibition against expelling him from it) is conditional and implies that the expulsion of a national, depending on the circumstances, could be considered reasonable and admissible. Furthermore, it should be noted that the right enshrined in article 12 is derogable under article 4 of the Covenant, namely in times of public emergency threatening the life of the nation. Such derogation is subject to the conditions provided for by article 4.

4. At the regional level, Protocol No. 4 of 16 September 1963[7] to the European Convention for the Protection of Human Rights and Fundamental Freedoms (41 States parties, 4 signatories and 2 non-signatory States, including Switzerland) provides that "[n]o one shall be expelled ... from the territory of the State of which he is a national" (art. 3, para. 1). Like the European human rights regime, the American Convention on Human Rights of 22 November 1969 (24 States parties, 1 signatory and 7 non-signatory States) prohibits the expulsion of nationals (art. 22, para. 5). However, it should be noted that the European and American conventions both allow States the option, in exceptional cases of war or public danger, of derogating from the prohibition against the expulsion of their own nationals, in accordance with articles 15 and 27, respectively. Article 12, paragraph 2, of the African Charter on Human and Peoples' Rights of 27 June 1981 also provides that every individual has the right to return to his country. However, this right may be subject to restrictions for reasons of national security, public order, health or morality, where provided for by law.

5. In the light of the above, it appears that the general principle of non-expulsion of nationals is largely recognized in international law, although opinions differ as to its scope and definition.

[5] General comment No. 27 (1999), *Official Records of the General Assembly, Fifty-fifth Session, Supplement No. 40* (A/55/40), vol. I, annex VI, sect. A, para. 19: "The right has various facets. It implies the right to remain in one's own country."

[6] *Ibid.*, para. 21: "The reference to the concept of arbitrariness in this context is intended to emphasize that it applies to all State action, legislative, administrative and judicial; it guarantees that even interference provided for by law should be in accordance with the provisions, aims and objectives of the Covenant and should be, in any event, reasonable in the particular circumstances."

[7] Switzerland has not signed Protocol No. 4 for reasons unrelated to the article on expulsion of nationals.

2. The manner in which persons having two or more nationalities are dealt with under expulsion legislation. Can such persons be considered aliens in the context of expulsion?

RUSSIAN FEDERATION

Under Russian legislation, a citizen of the Russian Federation possessing the nationality of another State is considered by the Russian Federation only as a citizen of the Russian Federation unless otherwise provided for by an international treaty of the Russian Federation or federal law" (art. 6, para. 1, of the Federal Law on Citizenship of the Russian Federation). Thus, the prohibition on expelling Russian nationals also covers those who possess the nationality of other States.

SWITZERLAND

The Swiss Federal Constitution provides that "Swiss citizens may not be expelled from Switzerland".[1] It therefore appears that even if the individual in question has one or more other nationalities in addition to Swiss nationality, he cannot be expelled. A double national (one of whose nationalities is Swiss) therefore cannot be considered to be an alien as far as expulsion is concerned.

[1] Federal Constitution of the Swiss Confederation of 18 April 1999, art. 25, para. 1.

3. The question of deprivation of nationality as a possible precondition for a person's expulsion. Is such a measure allowed under domestic legislation? Is it permissible under international law?

RUSSIAN FEDERATION

1. In accordance with the Constitution of the Russian Federation, Russian citizens shall not be deprived of nationality (art. 6, para. 3). The Federal Law mentioned above also provides for such a ban (art. 4, para. 4). In the Russian Federation, the prohibition against depriving a citizen of his or her nationality is one of the principles of the institution of citizenship as a whole.

2. At the same time, the deprivation of nationality should be clearly distinguished from the annulment of a decision on granting nationality when it is established that an applicant has provided false data or forged documents. The annulment of a decision on granting nationality acquired by fraud is an inherent sovereign right of a State. In the Russian Federation, the procedure of annulment of a decision on granting nationality is regulated by the Federal Law on Citizenship of the Russian Federation (chap. IV).

SWITZERLAND

National legislation

1. Under Swiss law, the competent federal office may revoke Swiss nationality if three conditions have been met. First, the person in question must have dual nationality. Secondly, the person must have caused serious harm to the interests or standing of Switzerland. Thirdly, the authority of the canton of origin must have given its consent.[1]

2. Furthermore, Swiss law also provides for Swiss nationality to be revoked in the five years following naturalization or reinstatement obtained by false declarations or by concealment of vital facts, even if the person becomes stateless as a result.[2]

3. Once an individual has been deprived of Swiss nationality, he becomes a foreign national and, consequently, may be subject to the expulsion procedure. Theoretically, it is therefore possible to deprive a person who has caused serious harm to the interests or standing of Switzerland of his Swiss nationality and then to expel that person on the grounds that he represents a threat to national security. However, the intention to expel a person is not a valid ground for revoking Swiss nationality from an individual.

International law

4. The conferment and deprivation of nationality fall within the exclusive jurisdiction of States. General international law therefore does not govern questions relating to this field. However, it attempts to minimize statelessness.[3]

5. States also have exclusive jurisdiction to determine the rules governing the grounds and procedures for the expulsion of aliens, provided that they respect their international obligations, including in the area of human rights.

6. This being the case, it is understandable that international law remains silent on the issue of whether or not the deprivation of nationality can be used as a prelude to the expulsion of an individual.

7. However, it should be noted that even the Convention on the Reduction of Statelessness of 30 August 1961 provides that States may formulate a declaration (at the time of signature or ratification) enabling them to derogate from the principle of non-deprivation of nationality resulting in statelessness, if an individual "[h]as conducted himself in a manner seriously prejudicial to the vital interests of the State".[4] While this international convention aimed at limiting statelessness provides the possibility for States to render an individual stateless, it becomes clear that there is little or no limitation on the deprivation of nationality on the grounds of national interest. It may therefore be supposed that it would be permissible, under international law, for a State to deprive one of its nationals of his nationality on the grounds of occasioning serious harm to its national interests and, on the same grounds (national security), to expel him once his nationality had been revoked.

[1] Federal Act on the acquisition and loss of Swiss nationality of 29 September 1952 (Nationality Act), RS 141.0, art. 48. A parliamentary initiative was submitted in December 2006 proposing an amendment to the Nationality Act so that aliens with dual nationality could, at least temporarily, be deprived of Swiss nationality if they seriously or repeatedly endangered public safety or violated the law. The competent parliamentary commission did not propose to take further action on that initiative, but the National Council has still not discussed the issue.

[2] Ibid., art. 41. Regarding the cancellation of naturalization, even in the case of statelessness, see judgement No. 5A.22/2006 of the Federal Court of 13 July 2006, grounds 4.4 (unpublished).

[3] See the Convention on the Reduction of Statelessness. It should be noted that to date this Convention has only 34 States parties and 3 signatories (Switzerland is not among these States). This reveals the reluctance of States to see questions of nationality governed by international law.

[4] Art. 8, para. 3 (*a*) (ii). Four States parties out of 26 have made use of the possibility provided for by this provision to formulate such a reservation.

4. The question of the collective expulsion of aliens who are nationals of a State involved in an armed conflict with the host State. In such a situation, should a distinction be drawn between aliens living peacefully in the host State and those involved in activities hostile to it?

Switzerland

1. The question of collective expulsion in cases of armed conflicts is not addressed by national legislation in Switzerland. However, at the level of international law, several human rights and international humanitarian law instruments may help to answer this question.

2. First of all, it is important to consider the issue of collective expulsion in the light of the principle of non-refoulement. Indeed, the prohibition of torture and inhuman or degrading treatment or punishment—which is enshrined in article 7 of the International Covenant on Civil and Political Rights of 16 December 1966 and article 3 of the European Convention on Human Rights, and which is recognized as a peremptory norm of international law—is closely linked to the issue of expulsion. A State may not expel or return a person to a country if he or she is in danger in that country of being subjected to acts of torture or inhuman or degrading treatment or punishment, in times of peace as in times of war, irrespective of the offence with which the person concerned is charged.[1] This means that, at all times, a State must examine each case of expulsion individually in order to ensure that the expulsion under consideration does not violate the absolute prohibition of torture or inhuman or degrading treatment or punishment. Since a State is obliged to examine expulsions on a case-by-case basis, collective expulsion is strictly prohibited in times of peace as in times of war, irrespective of the offence with which the person concerned is charged.

3. Although the very principle of non-refoulement excludes collective expulsion in absolute terms, in the interest of completeness it is worth examining specific international humanitarian law and human rights provisions on collective expulsion.

4. Article 13 of the International Covenant on Civil and Political Rights stipulates that a person lawfully in the territory of a State party may not be expelled without having access to due process of law. This implies an individual examination of each case of expulsion and, consequently, the prohibition of collective expulsion. However, a State is not obliged to comply with this provision if "compelling reasons of national security" otherwise require.

5. Protocol No. 4 of 16 September 1963 to the European Convention for the Protection of Human Rights and Fundamental Freedoms also prohibits the collective expulsion of aliens (art. 4).[2] The Protocol remains silent on the prohibition against derogating from the rights and obligations contained within it. It therefore follows that derogating from the prohibition against collective expulsion is permissible under article 15 of the Convention (Protocol 4, art. 6). Consequently, the collective expulsion of aliens would be permitted in times of war, to the extent strictly required by the situation and provided that the measures undertaken were not inconsistent with other obligations under international law.

6. In implementing this provision of the Convention, it appears relevant to make a distinction between aliens living peacefully in the host State and those engaged in activities hostile to it. In fact, it would be difficult to argue that the expulsion of peaceful aliens would be required by the situation pursuant to article 15. A State expelling nationals from a State with which it is in conflict, irrespective of their involvement in the conflict, would certainly find itself in violation of article 4 of Protocol No. 4 and article 15 of the Convention. The same argument applies to the American Convention on Human Rights, which prohibits the collective expulsion of aliens (art. 22, para. 9) in the same terms as the European Convention and also provides for the option of derogation in time of war (art. 27).

7. Unlike the European and American regimes, the African Charter on Human and Peoples' Rights of 27 June 1981 states that the prohibition of the collective expulsion of aliens, enshrined in article 12, may not be subject to derogation.[3] Under the African regime, the question of the distinction between aliens living peacefully in the host State and those engaged in activities hostile to it therefore does not arise.

8. International humanitarian law also tends to support the principle of the prohibition of collective expulsion. Indeed, despite the fact that the Geneva Conventions of 12 August 1949 do not explicitly mention the prohibition of collective expulsion, it is clear from all of the provisions that each State is obliged to examine expulsions of aliens on a case-by-case basis in order to ensure that the person concerned would not be in any danger in the country of destination.

9. Also noteworthy is article 44 of the Geneva Convention relative to the Protection of Civilian Persons in Time of War (Geneva Convention IV), of 12 August 1949, which provides that refugees may not be treated as enemy aliens exclusively on the basis of their juridical attachment to an enemy State. It follows that the expulsion of a category of refugees based solely on their nationality would not be permissible. Moreover, article 12 of the Geneva Convention relative to the Treatment of Prisoners of War (Geneva Convention III) and article 45 of Geneva Convention IV provide that prisoners of war and civilians "may only be transferred by the Detaining Power to a Power which is a party to the Convention and after the Detaining Power has satisfied itself of the willingness and ability of such transferee Power to apply

[1] European Court of Human Rights: *Saadi v. Italy*, Grand Chamber, Judgment of 28 February 2008, para. 127. Human Rights Committee, general comment No. 20, para. 9; *Official Records of the General Assembly, Forty-ninth Session, Supplement No. 40* (A/49/40), vol. II, annex IX, sect. CC, communication No. 469/1991, *Chitat Ng v. Canada*; *ibid., Fiftieth Session, Supplement No. 40* (A/50/40), vol. II, annex X, sect. M, communication No. 539/1993, *Cox v. Canada*; and *ibid., Fifty-third Session, Supplement No. 40* (A/53/40), vol. II, annex XI, sect. U, communication No. 706/1996, *G.T. v. Australia.*

[2] Switzerland has not signed Protocol No. 4 for reasons unrelated to the article on collective expulsion.

[3] Art. 12, para. 5.

the Convention". Furthermore, article 45 of the Geneva Convention IV contains a non-refoulement clause. Lastly, it is worth noting the commentary to article 45 of the Geneva Convention IV, which clarifies the term "transfer" and establishes that: "In the absence of any clause stating that deportation is to be regarded as a form of transfer, this article would not appear to raise any obstacle to the right of parties to the conflict to deport aliens in individual cases when State security demands such action.[4] However, practice and theory both make this right a limited one: the mass deportation, at the beginning of a war, of all the foreigners in the territory of a belligerent cannot, for instance, be permitted."[5]

10. It follows from the above that collective expulsion, whether in times of peace or war, is excluded under international law. That being the case, the issue of whether a distinction should be made between peaceful and hostile aliens is no longer relevant in the context of collective expulsions. However, that does not mean that the criterion of the peaceful or hostile characteristics of the person concerned should not be taken into consideration in the procedure for the expulsion of an individual.

[4] The French version of the commentary, published in 1956, appears to be more restrictive on this point. The corresponding passage reads: "… et lorsque la sécurité de l'État l'exige *absolument**".

[5] Jean S. Pictet, ed., *Commentary on the Geneva Convention relative to the Protection of Civilian Persons in Time of War (Fourth Geneva Convention)* (Geneva, ICRC, 1956), p. 286.

5. The question of whether an alien who has had to leave the territory of a State under an expulsion order that is subsequently found by a competent authority to be unlawful has the right of return

Russian Federation

A priori, the alien has such a right [of return] provided that the legal grounds for his or her stay in the territory of a State are still in force. Otherwise, the right to return seems to depend on the ground on which an expulsion order is found to be unlawful. If, for example, expulsion of an alien has led to a violation of his or her right to respect for family life, the readmission of the individual appears to be an adequate "compensation". On the other hand, if an order of expulsion is found to be unlawful on account of a failure to comply with certain formalities, the only duty of the expelling State is to grant compensation for the damage caused to the alien expelled, without this necessarily entailing a right to return.

Switzerland

1. In accordance with the Federal Act on Aliens,[1] legal remedies are governed by general provisions on federal procedure. According to these general provisions, the competent authority may execute its decision only when this can no longer be contested through a legal remedy, when the possible legal remedy does not have a suspensive effect, or when the suspensive effect attributed to a legal remedy has been withdrawn (Federal Act on Administrative Procedure, art. 39). Federal procedure stipulates that appeals have a suspensive effect, save in a few exceptional cases or unless otherwise provided for by law (Federal Act on Administrative Procedure, art. 55).

[1] Federal Act on Aliens of 16 December 2005, RS 142.20, art. 112.

2. When no exceptions are foreseen and the Federal Act on Aliens does not provide otherwise, an expulsion will not be executed if it can be contested and the appeal has a suspensive effect. An alien subject to an expulsion order will therefore be present on Swiss territory while awaiting the decision of the competent authority.[2] In such a case, the question of a right of return therefore does not arise.

3. Nevertheless, in some cases of removal or expulsion, such as the immediate removal of an alien occasioning serious harm to public safety and order, the appeal does not have a suspensive effect. In such a case, the outcome of any appeal must be awaited while the appellant is outside the territory of Switzerland. If the appeals authority decides that the expulsion order has been unlawfully adopted, it may annul the contested decision and issue another ruling. In such a case, depending on the decision of the appeals authority, the alien may be granted the right of return.

4. It should also be mentioned that when an application against an expulsion order is lodged with the European Court of Human Rights, this appeal does not have a suspensive effect. The Swiss authorities therefore remove the alien before a judgement is delivered by the Strasbourg Court. If the Court concludes that an expulsion was executed in violation of the European Convention on Human Rights, the alien in question will not be granted an automatic right of return. However, the competent cantonal authorities will generally issue a new authorization to enter Switzerland, provided that there is no other reason to deny it.

5. Lastly, although strictly speaking this is not a right of return resulting from the acknowledgement of an unlawful expulsion, it should be mentioned that the readmission agreements that Switzerland has concluded with other States generally include a provision whereby the State requesting the readmission of a person to his (presumed) country of origin is obliged to readmit him to its territory if it is subsequently established that the person does not hold the nationality of the country in question (i.e., "readmission").

[2] It should be noted that the procedure for removal will be amended following the implementation of the Schengen and Dublin Agreements in Switzerland. Indeed, pursuant to the provisions of the Dublin Association Agreements, the removal will be immediately enforceable and the appeal against the order for removal will not have a suspensive effect.

6. Criteria that could be used to distinguish between the expulsion of an alien and the question of non-admission; more specifically, determining the point at which the removal of an illegal immigrant is governed by the expulsion procedure and not by the non-admission procedure

Russian Federation

1. A main criterion for drawing a distinction between these two procedures seems to be the "territorial" one, since it is not feasible to expel a person who is not present

in the territory of the expelling State. Such a person can only be denied admission. Thus, non-admission means preventing a person who is actually outside the territory of a State from entering that State, while expulsion means forcing a person who is actually in the territory of a State to leave that territory.

2. Given that, it would be justifiable to exclude the territorial sea, the internal waters and the frontier zone from the definition of "territory" for the purposes of the draft articles under consideration. With a special regime applied to aliens in the areas mentioned above, such aliens are unlikely to be subject to expulsion. The Russian Federation is not convinced that this situation should be within the scope of the draft articles.

SWITZERLAND

1. The provisions of the Federal Act on Aliens always address issues relating to the denial of a residency permit and the non-extension of a residency permit within the same context. This implies that, generally speaking, no distinction is made between removal within the context of the non-admission procedure (denial of a residency permit) and removal within the context of the expulsion procedure (non-extension of a residency permit).

2. However, the Federal Act on Aliens contains a clause on the special case of return at the airport.[1] This clause is applicable when an immigrant is refused entry to Switzerland during border controls at the airport. In such a case, the alien is required to leave Swiss territory without delay. The competent office issues a decision within 48 hours. This decision is subject to appeal within a very short period (48 hours) after notification is given. The appeals authority is required to issue its ruling within 72 hours. Until the forced return of the alien is ordered, he may be held for up to 15 days in the transit zone in order to prepare for his departure. Up to that point, this is a non-admission procedure.

3. In cases where an alien cannot be returned, owing to the risk of torture or any other cruel or inhuman treatment or punishment, for example, he is granted temporary admission. The alien in question is therefore no longer an "illegal immigrant". Consequently, the person concerned is no longer subject to the non-admission procedure. His case will periodically be examined to determine whether the person may remain in Swiss territory or whether he or she will be returned (under the expulsion procedure).

4. On the other hand, if the person concerned intends to apply for asylum and satisfies the requirements contained in the Asylum Act,[2] his or her entry into Switzerland will be permitted so that he or she may submit an application for asylum. The alien will therefore no longer be subject to the non-admission procedure. If the competent authorities proceed to take removal measures, this will be under the removal or expulsion procedure and not the non-admission procedure.

[1] Federal Act on Aliens of 16 December 2005, RS 142.20, art. 65.

[2] Asylum Act of 26 June 1998, RS 142.31.

7. The legal status of illegal immigrants located in the territorial sea or in internal waters, or in the frontier zone excluding port and airport areas. Specifically, apart from port and airport areas, is there an international zone within which an alien would be considered as not having yet entered the territory of the State? If so, how is the extent and breadth of such a zone determined?

RUSSIAN FEDERATION

Apart from port and airport areas, the following territories may well be considered as international zones in the given sense (i.e., zones within which an alien would be considered as not having yet entered the territory of the State): the territories of railway or car stations/terminals open for international traffic as well as of other specifically designated localities in immediate proximity to the State border where admission to the territory of a State is exercised according to the national legislation. The extent and breadth of these zones are determined by domestic legislation.

SWITZERLAND

Not applicable to Switzerland.

8. State practice in relation to grounds for expulsion, and the question of whether and, where appropriate, the extent to which such grounds are restricted by international law

GERMANY

The German Residence Act (*Aufenthaltsgesetz, AufenthG*) sets out various grounds for expulsion. These include grounds based on the commission of criminal offences or convictions, as well as those related to terrorist or extremist activities and regulatory offences.

MAURITIUS

The Deportation Act of 1968 of the Republic of Mauritius governs the expulsion of aliens. Section 4 of the Act empowers the Minister of Defence and Security to make a deportation order in respect of: (*a*) a convicted person; (*b*) an undesirable person; (*c*) a destitute person; or (*d*) a prohibited immigrant. These categories of individuals are defined under the Act.

RUSSIAN FEDERATION

Question of whether the grounds for expulsion are restricted by international law

1. It seems pertinent to talk about the grounds only with regard to the expulsion of aliens lawfully present in the territory of a State (in respect of illegal aliens, the grounds are evident). General international law is unlikely to restrict the grounds for the expulsion of "lawful" aliens, save for those enjoying special status: refugees and stateless persons as well as migrant workers and their family members who are documented or in a regular status.

2. Specific rules with regard to their expulsion are established by the Convention relating to the Status of Refugees of 28 July 1951 (arts. 32–33), the Convention

relating to the Status of Stateless Persons of 28 September 1954 (art. 31) and the International Convention on the Protection of the Rights of All Migrant Workers and Members of their Families of 18 December 1990 (art. 56, para. 3), respectively.

3. The regional level is characterized by a differentiated approach to restricting the grounds for expelling an alien. For instance, under article 1 of Protocol 7 to the European Convention on Human Rights of 22 November 1984, the grounds for the expulsion of "lawful aliens" are restricted to the considerations of national security and public order. Such a restriction, however, applies only in cases of expulsion before the exercise of the procedural safeguards laid down in this article. The European Convention on Establishment of 13 December 1955 restricts the grounds for expulsion of residing aliens, including long-term residents (art. 3).

4. At the same time, grounds for the expulsion of aliens—at least of those who do not enjoy any special status—are, as a rule, at the discretion of a State, this principle being based on the very nature of the right to expel. Obviously, the grounds for expulsion shall not be discriminatory.

The practice of the Russian Federation with regard to the grounds for expulsion

5. Under the national legislation of the Russian Federation, there are two procedures relating to expulsion. These are: administrative removal of an alien or a stateless person and deportation.

6. Administrative removal is a measure of administrative responsibility of an alien or a stateless person for administrative offences. The latter are connected mainly with the breaching of the regime for stay of foreigners (stateless persons) in the territory of the Russian Federation, including the immigration regime and that relating to labour activity. The list of offences entailing administrative removal, as well as the procedure of assigning responsibility and execution of punishment, are clearly governed by the Russian Code of Administrative Offences.

7. Deportation is applied to persons if the grounds for their legal stay (residence) in the territory of the Russian Federation have ceased and such persons do not leave the territory voluntarily. The cessation of the grounds mentioned above may follow the decision of competent authorities to reduce the term of stay (residence) of an alien (stateless person) or to annul the permission for his or her temporary or permanent residence in the Russian Federation. The list of instances in which such a decision may be rendered is exhaustive. It is contained in the Federal Law on Legal Status of Aliens in the Russian Federation.

8. Moreover, Russian legislation provides for a mechanism under which the competent authorities may decide on the undesirability of staying in respect of an alien (stateless person) lawfully staying in the territory of the Russian Federation. Such a decision may be rendered if the stay (residence) of a person creates a real threat to the defence or security of the State, or to public order or public health, as well as for reasons relating to the protection of the constitutional order, morality, or rights and legal interests of other persons. Aliens (stateless persons) whose staying is found to be undesirable should leave the territory of the Russian Federation voluntarily. Otherwise, they are subject to deportation.

Switzerland

Grounds for expulsion under Swiss law

(*a*) The alien has been denied a residency permit, or the permit has been revoked or has not been extended ("ordinary return", Federal Act on Aliens,[1] art. 66);

(*b*) The alien does not have the required authorization ("return without a formal decision", Federal Act on Aliens, art. 64, para. 1 (*a*));

(*c*) The alien, during a stay that does not require authorization, no longer satisfies the conditions required by law to remain on Swiss territory without authorization ("return without a formal decision", Federal Act on Aliens, art. 64, para. 1 (*b*));

(*d*) The alien seriously or repeatedly causes harm to or endangers public order and safety, or represents a threat to internal or external safety (Federal Constitution, art. 121; "return without a formal decision", Federal Act on Aliens, art. 64, para. 3; "ordinary return", Federal Act on Aliens, art. 66, para. 3; and "expulsion", Federal Act on Aliens, art. 68, paras. 1 and 4).

Restrictions on the grounds for expulsion under international law and, where appropriate, their extent

1. Since Switzerland is a country that applies the monist theory, international law (conventional international law, since its entry into force in Switzerland, and customary international law) forms part of its domestic legal order. A law will therefore be interpreted in the light of both national law and international law. In principle, international law will have primacy over national law. Thus, international law may restrict the application of national law, including legislation governing the expulsion of aliens. The competent judicial authorities will consequently examine each case of expulsion in the light of customary international law and the conventions and treaties to which Switzerland is a party.

2. In addition, the Federal Act on Aliens applies to aliens "to the extent that their legal status is not governed by other provisions of federal law or by international treaties concluded by Switzerland".[2] Consequently, the provisions of this Act, which include grounds for expulsion, are applicable only when no other federal act or provision of international law (such as the Convention relating to the Status of Refugees, of 28 July 1951) is applicable.

3. While the grounds for the expulsion of aliens are not restricted by international law today, the enforcement of expulsions is more broadly restricted by the obligations binding upon Switzerland under international law (see section below).

---

[1] Federal Act on Aliens of 16 December 2005, RS 142.20.

[2] *Ibid.*, art. 2, para. 1.

B. Comments and observations on other issues

Germany

1. The two-step process for ending residence in Germany must be taken into account when considering the question of restrictions imposed by international law. An alien's residence permit expires upon expulsion and his/her right of residence in Germany is thus terminated. He/she is therefore required to leave the country (sect. 50 of the Residence Act). Only once the requirement to leave the country has become enforceable, and it is not assured that the alien will leave voluntarily or reasons of public security and order make the supervision of the departure seem necessary, is the requirement to leave enforced by means of deportation (sect. 58 of the Residence Act).

2. International obligations may militate against both expulsion and deportation. For example, the considerations mentioned in article 8 of the European Convention on Human Rights of 4 November 1950 and article 6 of the German Basic Law (Constitution) have been incorporated into the Residence Act in section 56 (special protection from expulsion in the case of family ties in Germany). Section 60 (2) and (5) of the Residence Act prohibits deportation (also because of the obligation under art. 3 of the European Convention) if there is a danger that the alien, once deported, would be subject to torture or inhumane or degrading treatment or punishment. These restrictions apply no matter what grounds for expulsion exist.

Mauritius

1. Under the Mauritius Citizenship Act of 1968, an alien is defined as a person who is not a Commonwealth citizen or a British protected person. An alien may, subject to certain conditions, qualify for residency in the Republic of Mauritius: section 5 (1)(*b*) of the Immigration Act of 1973 provides that subject to its section 6, any person, not being a citizen, shall have the status of a resident for the purposes of this Act where, in the case of an alien, he has, before 10 December 1966, been ordinarily resident in Mauritius continuously for a period of seven years or more and has since the completion of that period of residence not been absent from Mauritius for a period of three years or more.

2. The Deportation Act of 1968 of the Republic of Mauritius governs the expulsion of aliens. Section 4 of the Act empowers the Minister of Defence and Security to make a deportation order in respect of: (*a*) a convicted person; (*b*) an undesirable person; (*c*) a destitute person; or (*d*) a prohibited immigrant. These categories of individuals are defined under the Act. Upon contemplation of the issue of a deportation order, the deportee must be served with a notice containing the reasons for his proposed deportation. Further, said notice shall require him to show cause before a Magistrate in Chambers as to why the order should not be made. The Minister will then consider the Magistrate's report and decide whether or not to issue the deportation order. If the Minister decides that one should be issued, the deportee will have a second opportunity to show cause in writing as to why the order should not be made.

3. The Immigration Act of 1973 of the Republic of Mauritius is mostly concerned with the question of the non-admission of persons as opposed to expulsion/deportation. Section 8 of the Act sets out a list of persons classified as "prohibited immigrants" for whom there is no right of admission to Mauritius. However, under section 8 (2) and (3), the Immigration Minister has the discretionary power to grant conditional admission to a person classified as a "prohibited immigrant". Furthermore, in some cases, section 13 (6)(*b*) of the Immigration Act gives a right of appeal to a passenger who has been refused admission to Mauritius. It provides that where a passenger to whom the Minister has refused admission to Mauritius claims to be a citizen, permanent resident or resident, an appeal shall lie with the Supreme Court against the decision of the Minister.

4. Lastly, the Passport Act of the Republic of Mauritius contains a section on the non-admissibility of persons to Mauritius: section 12 (1) provides that the Minister may prescribe the countries, the nationals or citizens of which shall obtain a visa before entering Mauritius, and section 12 (2) states that a stateless person, or, where regulations are made under subsection (1), a national or citizen of a country specified in the regulations shall not be allowed to enter Mauritius unless he has previously obtained a visa from the passport authorities.

Switzerland

1. While the grounds for the expulsion of aliens are not restricted by international law today, the enforcement of expulsions is more broadly restricted by the obligations binding upon Switzerland under international law. In particular, Switzerland may not enforce an expulsion if this violates its human rights obligations, including the principle of non-refoulement. Switzerland has codified these obligations in its domestic law. For example, the Swiss Federal Constitution provides that no one may be returned to the territory of a State where he or she is in danger of being subjected to torture or any other cruel or inhuman treatment or punishment (see article 25, paragraph 3). In more general terms, the Federal Act on Aliens[1] establishes that the enforcement of an expulsion or removal order "is unlawful when the return of the alien to his State of origin, to the State from which he came, or to a third State, is contrary to the obligations binding upon Switzerland under international law" (Federal Act on Aliens, art. 83). The removal consequently cannot be enforced and the alien is granted temporary admission authorization.

2. Another example of a restriction on the enforcement of an expulsion arises from the primacy of the extradition procedure over the expulsion procedure. If an extradition request is submitted to Switzerland pursuant to mutual legal assistance in criminal matters, the person will be transferred to the requesting State in accordance with the applicable extradition procedure and not the expulsion procedure. Furthermore, it would not be permissible to use a readmission agreement for the purpose of extraditing the person concerned.

[1] Federal Act on Aliens of 16 December 2005, RS 142.20, art. 121.

EXPULSION OF ALIENS

[Agenda item 6]

DOCUMENT A/CN.4/617

Draft articles on protection of the human rights of persons who have been or are being expelled, as restructured by the Special Rapporteur, Mr. Maurice Kamto, in the light of the plenary debate during the first part of the sixty-first session

[*Original: French*]
[*21 July 2009*]

Multilateral instruments cited in the present document

	Source
Geneva Convention relative to the Protection of Civilian Persons in Time of War (Geneva, 12 August 1949)	United Nations, *Treaty Series*, vol. 75, No. 973, p. 287.
Convention for the Protection of Human Rights and Fundamental Freedoms (European Convention on Human Rights) (Rome, 4 November 1950)	*Ibid.*, vol. 213, No. 2889, p. 221.
Convention relating to the Status of Refugees (Geneva, 28 July 1951)	*Ibid.*, vol. 189, No. 2545, p. 137.
Final Act of the Convention relating to the Status of Stateless Persons (New York, 28 September 1954)	*Ibid.*, vol. 360, No. 5158, p. 117.
Agreement relating to Refugee Seamen (The Hague, 23 November 1957)	*Ibid.*, vol. 506, No. 7384, p. 125.
International Covenant on Civil and Political Rights (New York, 16 December 1966)	*Ibid.*, vol. 999, No. 14668, p. 171.
OAU Convention Governing the Specific Aspects of Refugee Problems in Africa (Addis Ababa, 10 September 1969)	*Ibid.*, vol. 1001, No. 14691, p. 45.
American Convention on Human Rights: "Pact of San José, Costa Rica" (San José, 22 November 1969)	*Ibid.*, vol. 1144, No. 17955, p. 123.
African Charter on Human and Peoples' Rights (Nairobi, 27 June 1981)	*Ibid.*, vol. 1520, No. 26363, p. 217.
Convention against Torture and Other Cruel, Inhuman or Degrading Treatment or Punishment (New York, 10 December 1984)	*Ibid.*, vol. 1465, No. 24841, p. 85.
Arab Charter on Human Rights (Tunis, 22 May 2004)	CHR/NONE/2004/Rev.1.

---

1. When the fifth report on the expulsion of aliens (document A/CN.4/611, reproduced in the present volume) was considered during the first part of the sixty-first session of the International Law Commission, in 2009, it appeared that a large majority of the members of the Commission did not understand what the Special Rapporteur meant to say about protection of the human rights of persons who had been or were being expelled as a limitation on the State's right of expulsion. Most members wanted the principle of full protection of the rights of persons who had been or were being expelled to be clearly stated in the context of the expulsion of aliens and therefore requested that draft article 8 should be reformulated in that sense.

2. Following the same logic, the Commission also requested a restructuring of draft articles 9 to 14 to take into account the changes proposed to some of those draft articles during the debate, so that the set of draft articles 8 to 14 contained in the fifth report could be referred to the Drafting Committee.

3. The present document represents an effort to respond to the concerns expressed. The set of draft articles has been restructured into four sections dealing, respectively, with "General rules", "Protection required from the expelling State", "Protection in relation to the risk of violation of human rights in the receiving State" and "Protection in the transit State".

CHAPTER 4

Protection of the human rights of persons who have been or are being expelled[1]

A. General rules

Draft article 8.[2] *General obligation to respect the human rights of persons who have been or are being expelled*

Any person who has been or is being expelled is entitled to respect for his or her human rights, *in particular those mentioned in the present draft articles.*

Draft article 9.[3] *Obligation to respect the dignity of persons who have been or are being expelled*

The dignity of a person who has been or is being expelled must be respected and protected in all circumstances.

Draft article 10.[4] *Obligation not to discriminate [Non-discrimination rule]*

1. The State shall exercise its right of expulsion with regard to the persons concerned without discrimination of any kind on grounds such as race, colour, sex, language, religion, political or other opinion, national or social origin, property, birth or other status.

2. Such non-discrimination among persons who have been or are being expelled shall also apply to the enjoyment of the rights and freedoms provided for in international human rights law and in the legislation of the expelling State.

B. Protection required from the expelling State

Draft article 11.[5] *Obligation to protect the lives of persons who have been or are being expelled*

1. The expelling State shall protect the right to life of a person *who has been or is being expelled.*

2. A State may not, in its territory *or in a territory under its jurisdiction*, subject a person who has been or is being expelled to torture or to inhuman or degrading treatment.

Draft article 12.[6] *Obligation to respect the right to family life*

1. The expelling State shall respect the right to family life of a person who has been or is being expelled.

2. It may not derogate from the right referred to in paragraph 1 of the present article except in such cases as may be provided for by *international law* and shall strike a fair balance between the interests of the State and those of the person in question.

Draft article 13.[7] *Specific case of vulnerable persons*

1. Children, older persons, *persons with disabilities and pregnant women* who have been or are being expelled shall be considered, treated and protected as such, irrespective of their immigration status.

2. In particular, any measure concerning a child who has been or is being expelled must be taken in the best interests of the child.

---

[1] The numbering and title of chapter 4 are taken from the new workplan for the entire topic of the expulsion of aliens as proposed by the Special Rapporteur in document A/CN.4/618, reproduced in the present volume. Chapter 4 therefore replaces the text entitled, "Limits relating to the requirement of respect for fundamental human rights", contained in the fifth report (document A/CN.4/611, reproduced in the present volume).

[2] Draft article 8 incorporates the following changes proposed during the discussions in the plenary meetings of the Commission: the term "fundamental rights" has been replaced by the broader and non-limitative term "human rights"; the phrase "in particular those mentioned in the present draft articles" was inspired by the plenary debate; the purpose is to emphasize not only that there is no intention to establish a hierarchy among the human rights to be respected in the context of expulsion but also that the rights specifically mentioned in the draft articles are neither exhaustive nor exclusive.

[3] This provision corresponds to former draft article 10 but has been moved forward into section A, "General rules", relating to the protection of the human rights of persons who have been or are being expelled, in order to emphasize that it is general in scope.

Paragraph 1 of former draft article 10 setting forth the general rule that human dignity is inviolable has been eliminated in order to indicate that the right to dignity is being considered here in the specific context of expulsion rather than in a general context.

[4] This provision corresponds to former draft article 14. It has also been moved forward into section A, "General rules", in order to emphasize that it is general in scope.

In paragraph 2, the words "among persons who have been or are being expelled" have been added to take into account the comments of several Commission members who stressed that in the context the discrimination prohibited was discrimination among the aliens subject to expulsion, not discrimination between such aliens and the nationals of the expelling State.

[5] This draft article combines paragraph 1 of former draft article 9 and paragraph 1 (which here becomes paragraph 2) of former draft article 11. This rearrangement is in response to the strongly expressed desire of some Commission members to differentiate the obligations of the expelling State from those of the receiving State.

The phrase "in a territory under its jurisdiction" has been added in paragraph 2 in order to take into account the concerns expressed by other Commission members.

[6] This provision corresponds to former draft article 13.

The phrase "to private life" has been eliminated from the title and from paragraph 1 of the draft article, as some Commission members wished; moreover, in paragraph 2 the words "by law" have been changed to read "by international law", as other Commission members requested.

[7] This provision is taken from former draft article 12 on the "specific case of the protection of children being expelled". It has now been expanded to all "vulnerable persons", as the title indicates.

Paragraph 1 specifies what persons are meant. Paragraph 2, on the other hand, is a new provision, which replaces paragraph 2 of the former draft article. It stresses that where a child is involved in expulsion the child's best interests must prevail; in some cases the child's best interests may require the child to be detained in the same conditions as an adult so that the child is not separated from the adult.

Draft article (X). Conditions of detention and treatment of persons who have been or are being expelled

[To be formulated.]

C. Protection in relation to the risk of violation of human rights in the receiving State

Draft article 14.[8] *Obligation to ensure respect for the right to life and personal liberty in the receiving State of persons who have been or are being expelled*

1. No one may be expelled or returned (*refoulé*) to a State where his or her right to life or personal liberty is in danger of being violated because of his or her race, religion, nationality, membership of a particular social group or political opinions.

2. A State that has abolished the death penalty may not expel an alien who is under a death sentence to a State in which that person may be executed without having previously obtained an assurance that the death penalty will not be carried out.

3. The provisions of paragraphs 1 and 2 of this article shall also apply to the expulsion of a stateless person who is in the territory of the expelling State.

Draft article 15.[9] *Obligation to protect persons who have been or are being expelled from torture and inhuman or degrading treatment*

1. A State may not expel a person to another country where there is a real risk that he or she would be subjected to torture or to inhuman or degrading treatment.

2. The provisions of paragraph 1 of this article shall also apply when the risk emanates from persons or groups of persons acting in a private capacity and when the authorities of the receiving State are not able to obviate the risk by providing appropriate protection.

D. Protection in the transit State

Draft article 16.[10] *Application of the provisions of this chapter in the transit State*

The provisions of this chapter shall also apply in the transit State to a person who has been or is being expelled.

---

[8] This draft article is a reformulation of former draft article 9, particularly paragraph 1 thereof. The new formulation seeks to take into account the desire expressed by some Commission members to extend the scope of protection of the right to life to all expelled persons. This provision of general scope also covers the situation of asylum seekers, which therefore does not require special treatment.

(1) Some Commission members would prefer to generalize the principle of *non-refoulement* so that the protection thus afforded would be extended to all persons who have been or are being expelled, whether or not they are lawfully present.

On this point, it should be recalled that the principle of *non-refoulement* is a fundamental principle of international refugee law. Since the Convention relating to the Status of Refugees, it has been incorporated in many conventions and declarations of principle at both the universal and regional levels (such as the Final Act of the Convention relating to the Status of Stateless Persons of 23 September 1954; article 10 of the Agreement relating to Refugee Seamen of 23 November 1957; article III, paragraph 3, of the Principles concerning Treatment of Refugees adopted in 1966 by the Asian-African Legal Consultative Committee (*Yearbook ... 1967,* vol. II, p. 331); resolution (67) 14 on asylum to persons in danger of persecution adopted by the Committee of Ministers of the Council of Europe; article 3 of the United Nations Declaration on Territorial Asylum adopted by the General Assembly on 14 December 1967; article II, paragraph 3, of the OAU Convention Governing the Specific Aspects of Refugee Problems in Africa of 10 September 1969; the many conclusions announced by the Executive Committee of the United Nations High Commissioner for Refugees (UNHCR) Programme since 1977; and the Cartagena Declaration on Refugees of 22 November 1984, which sought "to reiterate the importance and meaning of the principle of *non-refoulement* (including the prohibition of rejection at the frontier) as a cornerstone of the international protection of refugees" (conclusion 5).

However, the principle of *non-refoulement* has passed beyond the bounds of international refugee law and has become part of international humanitarian law (see article 45 of the Geneva Convention relative to the Protection of Civilian Persons in Time of War of 12 August 1949); it is also deemed to be an integral part of international human rights protection.

With specific reference to human rights, the principle was introduced through a number of international instruments, notably in article 22, paragraph 8, of the American Convention on Human Rights of 22 November 1969 and in article 3, paragraph 1, of the Convention against Torture and Other Cruel, Inhuman or Degrading Treatment or Punishment.

However, only the provisions of the American Convention on Human Rights expressly accord the principle of non-refoulement general scope with respect to human rights. Article 22, paragraph 8, of the Convention provides: "In no case may an alien be deported or returned to a country, regardless of whether or not it is his country of origin, if in that country his right to life or personal freedom is in danger of being violated because of his race, nationality, religion, social status, or political opinions." This provision echoes article 3 of the Universal Declaration of Human Rights, which states: "Everyone has the right to life, liberty and security of person." That provision has been taken up, with differences or nuances of formulation, in a variety of international human rights instruments both universal and regional (article 6 of the International Covenant on Civil and Political Rights; art. 2, para. 1, of the Convention for the Protection of Human Rights and Fundamental Freedoms (European Convention on Human Rights); art. 4 of the African Charter on Human and Peoples' Rights; see also the Arab Charter on Human Rights). The arguments drawn from universal instruments and convergent regional rights offer a sufficient basis for codifying this rule in the context of the law on the expulsion of aliens.

(2) The Special Rapporteur, while noting the preference expressed by some Commission members for a formulation tending towards abolition of the death penalty, did not believe that he should make changes in that sense to the provision now contained in paragraph 2 of draft article 14 for the reasons explained in paragraph 58 of his fifth report (document A/CN.4/611 of the present volume).

(3) The Special Rapporteur added paragraph 3 to address a concern expressed by the Drafting Committee when it considered draft article 6 on non-expulsion of stateless persons.

[9] Draft article 15 corresponds to former draft article 11, which has been divided in two because of the need, strongly expressed by some Commission members, to draw a distinction, when restructuring former draft articles 8 to 14, between the protection of the human rights of an alien who has been or is being expelled required in the expelling State and the protection required in the receiving State.

The present draft article 15 draws on paragraphs 2 and 3 of former draft article 11. To former paragraph 3 have been added the words "and when the authorities of the receiving State are not able to obviate the risk by providing appropriate protection", in order to reflect the jurisprudence of the European Court of Human Rights in the case of *H.L.R. v. France* (*Reports* 1997–III, fasc. 36, para. 40).

[10] The Special Rapporteur has added this provision to complete the set of provisions governing the rights of the expelled person during the entire process and the whole of the journey from the expelling State to the receiving State.

EXPULSION OF ALIENS

[Agenda item 6]

DOCUMENT A/CN.4/618

New draft workplan presented by the Special Rapporteur, Mr. Maurice Kamto, with a view to structuring the draft articles

[Original: French]
[21 July 2009]

1. During the plenary debate on the third (*Yearbook ... 2007*, vol. II (Part One), document A/CN.4/581) and fifth reports (document A/CN.4/611 of the present volume) on the expulsion of aliens, although the Special Rapporteur had submitted a workplan in his preliminary report (*Yearbook ... 2005*, vol. II (Part One), document A/CN.4/554, annex I), it happened on occasion that members' comments anticipated questions that were to be examined by the Special Rapporteur in his future reports, thereby complicating the discussion. No doubt the nature of the topic accentuates the desire to deal with all the issues involved simultaneously.

2. Moreover, any workplan on a topic is necessarily provisional, and adjustments are always necessary as treatment of the topic progresses.

3. For these different reasons, the Special Rapporteur has decided to present to the Commission a new, completely restructured workplan, which nonetheless remains provisional, since the final outline will only take shape once the study of the topic is completed.

4. The purpose of the new workplan is to present all the ramifications of the topic as clearly as possible, not from an analytical standpoint, but with a view to providing a framework for the draft articles already produced or yet to be produced on the topic of the expulsion of aliens.

RESTRUCTURED WORKPLAN

PART ONE

GENERAL RULES

CHAPTER 1

Introduction

Draft article 1. Scope

Draft article 2. Definitions

Draft article 3. Right of expulsion

CHAPTER 2

Persons whose expulsion is prohibited

Draft article 4. Non-expulsion by a State of its nationals

Draft article 5. Non-expulsion of refugees

Draft article 6. Non-expulsion of stateless persons

CHAPTER 3

Expulsion practices prohibited

Draft article 7. Prohibition of collective expulsion

Draft article 8. Prohibition of disguised expulsion

Draft article 9. Prohibition of expulsion on grounds contrary to the rules of international law

CHAPTER 4

Protection of the human rights of persons who have been or are being expelled

A. General rules

Draft article 10 [8].[1] *General obligation to respect the human rights of persons who have been or are being expelled*

Draft article 11 [9]. Obligation to respect the dignity of persons who have been or are being expelled

Draft article 12 [10]. Obligation not to discriminate [Non-discrimination rule]

B. Protection in the expelling State

Draft article 13 [11]. Obligation to protect the lives and liberty of persons who have been or are being expelled

[1] The number in brackets indicates the current number of the draft article as it appears in document ILC(XLI)/EA/CRD.1.

Draft article 14 [12]. Obligation to respect the right to family life of persons who have been or are being expelled

Draft article 15 [13]. Specific case of vulnerable persons

Draft article (X ...). Conditions of detention and treatment of persons who have been or are being expelled

[To be formulated.]

C. Protection in relation to the receiving State

Draft article 16 [14]. Obligation to ensure respect for the right to life and liberty in the receiving State of persons who have been or are being expelled

Draft article 17 [15]. Obligation to protect persons who have been or are being expelled from torture and inhuman or degrading treatment

D. Protection in the transit State

Draft article 18 [16]. Application of the provisions of chapter 4 in the transit State to persons who have been or are being expelled

PART TWO

EXPULSION PROCEDURES

CHAPTER 5

Due process guarantees for persons who have been or are being expelled

CHAPTER 6

Remedies

CHAPTER 7

Relations among the expelling, transit and receiving States

PART THREE

LEGAL CONSEQUENCES OF EXPULSION

CHAPTER 8

Rights of expelled persons

—Protection of the property rights of an expelled person

—Right of return in the case of unlawful expulsion

CHAPTER 9

Responsibility of the expelling State for unlawful expulsion

—Affirmation of the principle of the responsibility of the expelling State

—Reparation for the injury suffered as a result of an unlawful expulsion

THE OBLIGATION TO EXTRADITE OR PROSECUTE (*AUT DEDERE AUT JUDICARE*)

[Agenda item 7]

DOCUMENT A/CN.4/612

Comments and observations received from Governments

[*Original: Arabic/English/French/Spanish*]
[*26 March 2009*]

CONTENTS

Multilateral instruments cited in the present report

	Source
Convention on Extradition (Montevideo, 26 December 1933)	League of Nations, *Treaty Series*, vol. CLXV, No. 3803, p. 45.
Convention on the Prevention and Punishment of the Crime of Genocide (Paris, 9 December 1948)	United Nations, *Treaty Series*, vol. 78, No. 1021, p. 277.
Geneva Conventions for the protection of war victims (Geneva, 12 August 1949)	*Ibid.*, vol. 75, Nos. 970–973, pp. 31 *et seq.*
Geneva Convention for the Amelioration of the Condition of the Wounded and Sick in Armed Forces in the Field	*Ibid.*, No. 970, p. 31.
Geneva Convention for the Amelioration of the Condition of the Wounded, Sick and Shipwrecked Members of the Armed Forces at Sea	*Ibid.*, No. 971, p. 85.
Geneva Convention relative to the Treatment of Prisoners of War	*Ibid.*, No. 972, p. 135.
Geneva Convention relative to the Protection of Civilian Persons in Time of War	*Ibid.*, No. 973, p. 287.
Protocol additional to the Geneva Conventions of 12 August 1949, and relating to the protection of victims of international armed conflicts (Protocol I) (Geneva, 8 June 1977)	*Ibid.*, vol. 1125, No. 17512, p. 3.
Protocol additional to the Geneva Conventions of 12 August 1949, and relating to the protection of victims of non-international armed conflicts (Protocol II) (Geneva, 8 June 1977)	*Ibid.*, No. 17513, p. 609.
European Convention on Extradition (Paris, 13 December 1957)	*Ibid.*, vol. 359, No. 5146, p. 273.
Single Convention on Narcotic Drugs (New York, 30 March 1961)	*Ibid.*, vol. 520, No. 7515, p. 151.

	Source
Single Convention on Narcotic Drugs, 1961, as amended by the Protocol amending the Single Convention on Narcotic Drugs, 1961 (with annexes) (New York, 8 August 1975)	*Ibid.*, vol. 976, No. 14152, p. 105.
Convention on offences and certain other acts committed on board aircraft (Tokyo, 14 September 1963)	*Ibid.*, vol. 704, No. 10106, p. 219.
Convention for the suppression of unlawful seizure of aircraft (The Hague, 16 December 1970)	*Ibid.*, vol. 860, No. 12325, p. 105.
Convention on Psychotropic Substances (Vienna, 21 February 1971)	*Ibid.*, vol. 1019, No. 14956, p. 175.
Convention for the suppression of unlawful acts against the safety of civil aviation (Montreal, 23 September 1971)	*Ibid.*, vol. 974, No. 14118, p. 177.
Protocol for the suppression of unlawful acts of violence at airports serving international civil aviation, supplementary to the Convention for the suppression of unlawful acts against the safety of civil aviation (Montreal, 24 February 1988)	*Ibid.*, vol. 1589, No. 14118, p. 474.
Convention on the Prevention and Punishment of Crimes against Internationally Protected Persons, including Diplomatic Agents (New York, 14 December 1973)	*Ibid.*, vol. 1035, No. 15410, p. 167.
European Convention on the Suppression of Terrorism (Strasbourg, 27 January 1977)	*Ibid.*, vol. 1137, No. 17828, p. 93.
Convention on the physical protection of nuclear material (Vienna, 26 October 1979)	*Ibid.*, vol. 1456, No. 24631, p. 101.
International Convention against the taking of hostages (New York, 17 December 1979)	*Ibid.*, vol. 1316, No. 21931, p. 205.
United Nations Convention on the Law of the Sea (Montego Bay, 10 December 1982)	*Ibid.*, vol. 1833, No. 31363, p. 3.
Riyadh Arab Agreement for Judicial Cooperation (Riyadh, 6 April 1983)	*A Collection of the Council's documents.* Rabat, Council of Arab Ministers of Justice, vol. 2 (1988), p. 96.
Convention against Torture and Other Cruel, Inhuman or Degrading Treatment or Punishment (New York, 10 December 1984)	United Nations, *Treaty Series*, vol. 1465, No. 24841, p. 85.
Inter-American Convention to Prevent and Punish Torture (Cartagena de Indias, 9 December 1985)	OAS, *Treaty Series*, No. 67.
Convention for the Suppression of Unlawful Acts against the Safety of Maritime Navigation (Rome, 10 March 1988)	United Nations, *Treaty Series*, vol. 1678, No. 29004, p. 201.
Protocol for the Suppression of Unlawful Acts against the Safety of Fixed Platforms Located on the Continental Shelf (Rome, 10 March 1988)	*Ibid.*
United Nations Convention against Illicit Traffic in Narcotic Drugs and Psychotropic Substances (Vienna, 20 December 1988)	*Ibid.*, vol. 1582, No. 27627, p. 95.
Inter-American Convention on International Traffic in Minors (Mexico City, 18 March 1994)	OAS, *Treaty Series*, No. 79.
Inter-American Convention on Forced Disappearance of Persons (Belém, Brazil, 9 June 1994)	ILM, vol. 33, No. 6 (November 1994), p. 1529.
Convention on the Safety of United Nations and Associated Personnel (New York, 9 December 1994)	United Nations, *Treaty Series*, vol. 2051, No. 35457, p. 363.
Inter-American Convention against Corruption (Caracas, 29 March 1996)	ILM, vol. 35, No. 3 (May 1996), p. 727.
Inter-American Convention against the Illicit Manufacturing of and Trafficking in Firearms, Ammunition, Explosives and Other Related Materials (Washington, D.C., 14 November 1997)	United Nations, *Treaty Series*, vol. 2029, No. 35005, p. 55.
International Convention for the Suppression of Terrorist Bombings (New York, 15 December 1997)	*Ibid.*, vol. 2149, No. 37517, p. 256.
Convention on Combating Bribery of Foreign Public Officials in International Business Transactions (Paris, 17 December 1997)	ILM, vol. 37, No. 1 (January 1998), p. 4.
Arab Convention on the Suppression of Terrorism (Cairo, 22 April 1998)	United Nations, *International Instruments Related to the Prevention and Suppression of International Terrorism*. Sales No. E.08.V.2, p. 178.
Rome Statute of the International Criminal Court (Rome, 17 July 1998)	United Nations, *Treaty Series*, vol. 2187, No. 38544, p. 3.
International Convention for the Suppression of the Financing of Terrorism (New York, 9 December 1999)	*Ibid.*, vol. 2178, No. 38349, p. 197.
United Nations Convention against Transnational Organized Crime (New York, 15 November 2000)	*Ibid.*, vol. 2225, No. 39574, p. 209.
Protocol to Prevent, Suppress and Punish Trafficking in Persons, Especially Women and Children, supplementing the United Nations Convention against Transnational Organized Crime (New York, 15 November 2000)	*Ibid.*, vol. 2237, No. 39574, p. 319.
Protocol against the Smuggling of Migrants by Land, Sea and Air, supplementing the United Nations Convention against Transnational Organized Crime (New York, 15 November 2000)	*Ibid.*, vol. 2241, No. 39574, p. 480.
Protocol against the Illicit Manufacturing of and Trafficking in Firearms, Their Parts and Components and Ammunition, supplementing the United Nations Convention against Transnational Organized Crime (New York, 31 May 2001)	*Ibid.*, vol. 2326, No. A-39574, p. 211.

	Source
Convention on cybercrime (Budapest, 23 November 2001)	*Ibid.*, vol. 2296, No. 40916, p. 167.
Additional Protocol to the Convention on cybercrime, concerning the criminalization of acts of a racist and xenophobic nature committed through computer systems (Strasbourg, 28 January 2003)	*Ibid.*, vol. 2466, No. A-40916, p. 205.
United Nations Convention against Corruption (New York, 31 October 2003)	*Ibid.*, vol. 2349, No. 42146, p. 41.
International Convention for the Suppression of Acts of Nuclear Terrorism (New York, 13 April 2005)	*Ibid.*, vol. 2445, No. 44004, p. 89.
International Convention for the Protection of All Persons from Enforced Disappearance (New York, 20 December 2006)	*Ibid.*, vol. 2716, No. 44088, p. 3.

Works cited in the present report

Pictet, Jean Simon, ed.

The Geneva Conventions of 12 August 1949—Commentary: Geneva Convention relative to the Protection of Civilian Persons in Time of War. Geneva, International Committee of the Red Cross, vol. IV, 1958.

Princeton Project on Universal Jurisdiction

The Princeton Principles on Universal Jurisdiction. Princeton, New Jersey: Program in Law and Public Affairs, 2001.

Introduction

1. The present report has been prepared pursuant to General Assembly resolution 62/66 of 6 December 2007, which, *inter alia*, invited Governments to provide to the International Law Commission information on practice regarding the topic "The obligation to extradite or prosecute (*aut dedere aut judicare*)".

2. At its fifty-eighth session, in 2006, the Commission decided in accordance with article 19, paragraph 2, of its statute to request Governments, through the Secretary-General, to submit information concerning their legislation and practice, particularly more contemporary ones, with regard to this topic. More specifically, Governments were requested to provide information concerning:

(*a*) International treaties by which a State is bound, containing the obligation to extradite or prosecute, and reservation made by that State to limit the application of this obligation;

(*b*) Domestic legal regulation adopted and applied by a State, including constitutional provisions and penal codes of criminal procedures, concerning the obligation to extradite or prosecute (*aut dedere aut judicare*);

(*c*) Judicial practice of a State reflecting the application of the obligation *aut dedere aut judicare*;

(*d*) Crimes or offences to which the principle of the obligation *aut dedere aut judicare* is applied in the legislation or practice of a State.[1]

3. At its fifty-ninth session in 2007, the Commission further requested Governments to submit information concerning their relevant legislation and practice, particularly more contemporary ones, more specifically on:

(*a*) International treaties by which a State is bound, containing the principle of universal jurisdiction in criminal matters; is it connected with the obligation *aut dedere aut judicare*?

(*b*) Domestic legal regulations adopted and applied by a State, including constitutional provisions and penal codes or codes of criminal procedures, concerning the principle of universal jurisdiction in criminal matters; is it connected with the obligation *aut dedere aut judicare*?

(*c*) Judicial practice of a State reflecting the application of the principle of universal jurisdiction in criminal matters; is it connected with the obligation *aut dedere aut judicare*?

(*d*) Crimes or offences to which the principle of universal jurisdiction in criminal matters is applied in the legislation and practice of a State; is it connected with the obligation *aut dedere aut judicare*?[2]

4. At the same session, the Commission also indicated that it would appreciate information on the following questions:

(*a*) Whether the State has authority under its domestic law to extradite persons in cases not covered by a treaty or to extradite persons of its own nationality?

(*b*) Whether the State has authority to assert jurisdiction over crimes occurring in other States that do not involve one of its nationals?

(*c*) Whether the State considers the obligation to extradite or prosecute as an obligation under customary international law and if so to what extent?[3]

5. Comments received at the sixtieth session of the Commission were reproduced in *Yearbook . . . 2008*, vol. II (Part One), document A/CN.4/599. Since then, and as at 30 March 2009, written observations have been received from the following six States: Argentina, Belgium, Canada, Mexico,[4] South Africa and Yemen.

[1] See *Yearbook . . . 2006*, vol. II (Part Two), para. 30.

[2] *Ibid.*, para. 31.

[3] *Ibid.*, para. 32.

[4] The comments received from Mexico contained the statement delivered in the Sixth Committee on 3 November 2008 and are not reproduced in the present document. For a summary of that statement, see *Official Records of the General Assembly, Sixty-third Session, Sixth Committee*, 23rd meeting (A/C.6/63/SR.23), paras. 58–60.

Comments and observations received from Governments

A. Argentina

1. With reference to the Commission's question reproduced in paragraph 3 (*a*) above, Argentina is a party to the following multilateral treaties containing the obligation *aut dedere aut judicare*, in respect of which it has not made any reservations or declarations to limit the application of the obligation: Convention on Extradition adopted by the Seventh International Conference of American States, 1933; Convention for the suppression of unlawful seizure of aircraft, 1970; Convention for the suppression of unlawful acts against the safety of civil aviation, 1971; Convention on the Prevention and Punishment of Crimes against Internationally Protected Persons, including Diplomatic Agents, 1973; International Convention against the taking of hostages, 1979; Convention on the physical protection of nuclear material, 1980; Convention against Torture and Other Cruel, Inhuman or Degrading Treatment or Punishment, 1984; Inter-American Convention to Prevent and Punish Torture, 1985; Protocol for the suppression of unlawful acts of violence at airports serving international civil aviation, supplementary to the Convention for the suppression of unlawful acts against the safety of civil aviation, 1988; Convention for the Suppression of Unlawful Acts against the Safety of Maritime Navigation, 1988; Protocol for the Suppression of Unlawful Acts against the Safety of Fixed Platforms Located on the Continental Shelf, 1988; United Nations Convention against Illicit Traffic in Narcotic Drugs and Psychotropic Substances, 1988; Convention on the Safety of United Nations and Associated Personnel, 1994; Inter-American Convention on International Traffic in Minors, 1994; Inter-American Convention on Forced Disappearance of Persons, 1994; Inter-American Convention against Corruption, 1996; Convention on Combating Bribery of Foreign Public Officials in International Business Transactions, 1997; International Convention for the Suppression of Terrorist Bombings, 1997; International Convention for the Suppression of the Financing of Terrorism, 1999; United Nations Convention against Transnational Organized Crime, 2000; United Nations Convention against Corruption, 2003.

2. Argentina has concluded bilateral extradition treaties containing the obligation *aut dedere aut judicare* with the following countries: Australia, 1988; Belgium, 1886; Bolivia, 1898; Brazil, 1961; Colombia, 1922; Italy, 1987; the Netherlands, 1893; Paraguay, 1996; the Republic of Korea, 1995; Spain, 1987; and Switzerland, 1906. These bilateral treaties provide for the person whose extradition is sought to be prosecuted by the courts of the requested State, if that State does not grant extradition on the grounds that the person in question is one of its nationals.

3. With reference to the Commission's question reproduced in paragraph 3 (*b*) above, in the legal system of Argentina, Act No. 24,767 governs international cooperation in criminal matters, including extradition proceedings (*Boletín Oficial de la República Argentina*, No. 28565, 16 January 1997). This legislation does not make general provision for the obligation *aut dedere aut judicare* but provides for this obligation only where the person whose extradition is sought is an Argentine national. Thus, according to article 12:

> If the person sought for prosecution is an Argentine national, that person may opt to be placed on trial by the Argentine courts, unless a treaty providing for the compulsory extradition of nationals is applicable to the case … If the national exercises this option, the extradition will be refused. The national will then be placed on trial in Argentina, in accordance with Argentine criminal law, provided that the requesting State consents, waiving its jurisdiction, and provides all background information and evidence needed for the trial …

It should be noted that, although Act No. 24,767 does not make general provision for the obligation to extradite or prosecute, the application of this obligation may derive from any of the treaties mentioned in paragraphs 1 and 2 above, since the same Act establishes that "if a treaty exists between the requesting State and the Argentine Republic, its provisions shall govern the assistance procedure".

4. Furthermore, Act No. 26,200 (*Boletín Oficial de la República Argentina*, No. 31069, 9 January 2007), which incorporates the provisions of the Rome Statute of the International Criminal Court into the Argentine legal system, expressly provides for the application of the *aut dedere aut judicare* principle in the case of crimes within the Court's jurisdiction. According to article 4 of the Act: "Where a person suspected of having committed a crime as defined in this Act is in the territory of the Argentine Republic or in a place subject to its jurisdiction and that person is not extradited or handed over to the International Criminal Court, the Argentine Republic shall take all necessary steps to exercise its jurisdiction with respect to that crime."

5. With regard to the Commission's question reproduced in paragraph 3 (*c*) of the above introduction, Argentine courts strictly apply the provisions of Act No. 24,767 in extradition cases. Under this law, if an extradition treaty exists between the requesting State and the Argentine Republic, the extradition is governed by the provisions of that treaty. If no such treaty exists, the Argentine Republic makes extradition contingent on the existence or offer of reciprocity. Extradition is also subject to other rules, both formal and substantive, laid down in Act No. 24,767.

6. According to the records of the national body designated as the central authority with regard to international legal cooperation, the obligation *aut dedere aut judicare* has been applied in Argentine judicial practice only in cases where extradition has been refused on the grounds of the nationality of the person sought. This has occurred in a limited number of cases since Act No. 24,767 came into force, none of which have reached judgement, owing to the failure on the part of the requesting foreign courts to provide the relevant background information.

7. It should be noted that the obligation *aut dedere aut judicare* would be enforceable in Argentina only in the case of passive extradition requests where the person sought was an Argentine national and where no treaty was applicable. This is pursuant to the provisions of article 12

of Act No. 24,767, which sets out three possible scenarios regarding the extradition of a national: (*a*) no treaty is applicable; (*b*) the treaty applicable does not provide for an extradition request to be refused on the grounds of the nationality of the person sought; and (*c*) the extradition of nationals is optional under the applicable treaty, in which case the decision is taken by the Argentine executive branch. Among these three possible scenarios, the obligation to extradite or prosecute is, in practice, relevant only to the first: in cases where the national opts for trial by the Argentine courts, the extradition request must be refused. The obligation could also be applicable in the third scenario although, in the cases decided to date, the principle of the surrender of nationals has been applied as it is more consistent with modern extradition practice and the spirit of international cooperation in criminal matters.

8. With reference to the Commission's question reproduced in paragraph 3 (*d*) of the above introduction, Act No. 24,767 lists only those offences for which extradition will not be granted, namely political offences and offences that are recognized solely under military criminal law. All other offences recognized under Argentine criminal law are therefore extraditable offences, provided that the general rules laid down in Act No. 24,767 are followed. It should be noted that article 9 (*g*) of Act No. 24,767 specifies that "offences in respect of which the Argentine Republic has assumed an international treaty obligation to extradite or prosecute" shall not be considered as political offences for extradition purposes.

B. Belgium

1. With reference to the Commission's question reproduced in paragraph 3 (*a*) of the above introduction, in the view of Belgium, the issue is to determine which of the treaties by which Belgium is bound contain the obligation *aut dedere aut judicare* and to what extent that obligation implies universal jurisdiction. The answer varies from treaty to treaty.

2. At the outset, however, it is necessary to make a distinction between two types of provision on the basis of which a State's universal jurisdiction may be established:

(*a*) Treaties which make the obligation to prosecute conditional upon refusal of a request for extradition of the alleged perpetrator of an offence. These treaties contain an *aut dedere aut judicare* clause in the classic sense of the word;

(*b*) Treaties which require States to exercise universal jurisdiction over perpetrators of the serious offences covered by these conventions, without making this obligation conditional upon refusal to honour a prior extradition request. These treaties contain a *judicare vel dedere* clause.

3. The following is a non-exhaustive list of treaties with an *aut dedere aut judicare* clause and the condition of a refusal to extradite:

(*a*) The Convention for the suppression of unlawful seizure of aircraft (Hague Convention) of 16 December 1970 (ratified by Belgium on 24 August 1973), article 7 of which contains an obligation *aut dedere aut judicare* [Belgium then reproduced a portion of the text of this article];

(*b*) The Convention for the suppression of unlawful acts against the safety of civil aviation (Montreal Convention) of 23 September 1971, ratified by Belgium on 13 August 1976, art. 5, para. 2;

(*c*) The European Convention on the Suppression of Terrorism of 27 January 1977, ratified by Belgium on 31 October 1985, article 7.

4. The following is a non-exhaustive list of treaties with a *judicare vel dedere* clause without the condition of a refusal to extradite:

(*a*) The Geneva Conventions of 12 August 1949 (ratified by Belgium on 3 September 1952) establish this in their common articles 40, 50, 129 and 146 [text of the common articles omitted]. In other words, the Geneva Conventions do not make the obligation to prosecute conditional upon a prior unmet extradition request. The State party must prosecute perpetrators of serious crimes who are in its territory. The State party may also elect not to prosecute if it prefers to extradite the person to a requesting State. Thus, the Conventions establish not an obligation *aut dedere aut judicare*, but what might be termed an obligation *judicare vel dedere*. The International Committee of the Red Cross jurists' commentary on the Geneva Conventions confirms this interpretation:

> The obligation on the High Contracting Parties to search for persons accused of having committed grave breaches imposes an active duty on them. As soon as a Contracting Party realizes that there is on its territory a person who has committed such a breach, its duty is to ensure that the person concerned is arrested and prosecuted with all despatch. The necessary police action should be taken spontaneously, therefore, and not merely in pursuance of a request from another State.[1]

(*b*) The Convention against Torture and Other Cruel, Inhuman or Degrading Treatment or Punishment of 10 December 1984 (ratified by Belgium on 25 June 1999) appears, at first sight, to base the obligation to exercise universal jurisdiction on *aut dedere aut judicare*. Article 5, paragraph 2, tends to confirm the establishment of universal jurisdiction on the basis of *aut dedere aut judicare*. Yet the Committee against Torture has considered that the obligation to prosecute was related to what Belgium has called an obligation *judicare vel dedere* rather than an obligation *aut dedere aut judicare*; on 17 May 2006, the Committee stated that "the obligation to prosecute the alleged perpetrator of acts of torture does not depend on the prior existence of a request for his extradition".[2] This interpretation of article 5, paragraph 2, of the 1984 Convention is an official interpretation of the Convention and, moreover, is consistent with the International Law Commission's statement in its draft Code of Crimes against the Peace and Security of Mankind concerning the suppression of such crimes;[3]

---

[1] Pictet, ed., *Commentary on the Geneva Conventions of 12 August 1949 relative to the Protection of Civilian Persons in Time of War*, p. 621.

[2] Communication No. 181/201, *Suleymane Guengueng et al. v. Senegal*, 17 May 2006, para. 9.7 (CAT/C/36/D/181/2001).

[3] *Yearbook . . . 1996*, vol. II (Part Two), pp. 31–32.

(*c*) The International Convention for the Protection of All Persons from Enforced Disappearance of 20 December 2006 also provides for universal criminalization of the *judicare vel dedere* type.

5. To summarize, it is clear from these examples that the principle of universal jurisdiction is not necessarily connected with the *aut dedere aut judicare* rule and that for a number of international crimes, particularly crimes of international humanitarian law, universal jurisdiction takes the form of a *judicare vel dedere* rule instead.

6. Furthermore, in addition to these treaty obligations, which Belgium assumed by ratifying and implementing these instruments, Belgium considers that there are customary obligations which require States to incorporate universal jurisdiction rules into their domestic law in order to prosecute the alleged perpetrators of crimes so serious that they pose a threat to the international community as a whole, such as serious crimes of international humanitarian law (crimes against humanity and the crime of genocide). In Belgium's view, this treaty obligation to prosecute the perpetrators of serious crimes of international humanitarian law exists only where the alleged perpetrators are present in its territory.

7. Concerning the Commission's question reproduced in paragraph 3 (*b*) of the above introduction, while Belgium has universal jurisdiction over certain crimes, this is not always related to *aut dedere aut judicare.*

8. For some of these offences, there is no international rule that requires the exercise of universal jurisdiction based on *aut dedere aut judicare*. This has not prevented Belgium from assuming universal jurisdiction so that its courts can investigate the crimes in question. As noted in the reply to the first question, the principle of universal jurisdiction is, therefore, not inextricably connected with the *aut dedere aut judicare* rule.

9. In addition, Belgium was a pioneer in establishing universal jurisdiction over serious crimes of international humanitarian law. The very broad universal jurisdiction regime established in this area by the Act of 16 June 1993, which essentially incorporated into Belgian law four Geneva Conventions and two protocols on war victims and was further expanded to include the crime of genocide and crimes against humanity by the Act of 10 February 1999, has nonetheless had to be restricted owing to abuse of this legislation. Wherever possible, however, the principles underlying the Acts of 1993 and 1999 have been maintained and the jurisdiction rules remain very broad since the ordinary law governing the exterritorial jurisdiction of Belgian courts has been adapted to the realities of modern international crime.

10. The following forms of extraterritorial jurisdiction are recognized by Belgian judges:

(*a*) Active personal jurisdiction: Belgian courts have jurisdiction over foreign nationals who have their primary residence in Belgium and who have committed an act defined as a crime or misdemeanour under Belgian law (Code of Criminal Procedure, Preliminary Title, arts. 6–7); in the case of ordinary law crimes or misdemeanours other than those that threaten the State's external security, serious violations of international humanitarian law, terrorist acts or counterfeiting, the exercise of criminal jurisdiction is subject to the condition that the act in question must also be criminalized in the country in which the offence was committed (Code of Criminal Procedure, Preliminary Title, art. 7);

(*b*) Passive personal jurisdiction: Belgian courts have jurisdiction over:

(i) Foreign nationals who have perpetrated, against a Belgian, an act defined as a crime in Belgium, provided that it is subject, in the country where the crime was committed, to a maximum sentence of more than five years' imprisonment (Code of Criminal Procedure, Preliminary Title, art. 10, para. 5);

(ii) Foreign nationals who have perpetrated a crime of international humanitarian law against a Belgian, a person recognized as a refugee in Belgium or a foreign national who has effectively, habitually and legally resided in Belgium for at least three years (Code of Criminal Procedure, Preliminary Title, art. 10, para. 1 *bis*);

(*c*) Protective jurisdiction: Belgian courts have jurisdiction over foreign nationals who have committed, while abroad, a crime or misdemeanour against the State's external security (Code of Criminal Procedure, Preliminary Title, art. 10, para. 1);

(*d*) Universal jurisdiction: Belgian courts have jurisdiction over foreign nationals who have committed, while abroad, some of the offences established in Belgian criminal law (some of which have been mentioned above). These include:

(i) Sexual offences perpetrated against minors, exploitation of prostitution or trafficking in persons (Code of Criminal Procedure, Preliminary Title, art. 10, para. 3, referring to articles 379 to 381 and 381 *bis*, paras. 1 and 3, of the Penal Code);

(ii) Female genital mutilation (Code of Criminal Procedure, Preliminary Title, art. 10, para. 3 (2), referring to article 409 of the Penal Code);

(iii) Failure to comply with some of the rules governing the activities of marriage brokers (Code of Criminal Procedure, Preliminary Title, art. 10, para. 3 (3), referring to articles 10 to 13 of the Act of 9 March 1993);

(iv) Acts of corruption (Code of Criminal Procedure, Preliminary Title, art. 10, para. 4, referring to articles 246–250 of the Penal Code);

(v) Acts of marine pollution (Act of 6 April 1995, art. 17 *bis*);

(vi) Counterfeiting (Code of Criminal Procedure, Preliminary Title, art. 10, paras. 2 and 3);

(vii) Serious violations of international humanitarian law (Code of Criminal Procedure, Preliminary Title, art. 10, para. 1 *bis*);

(viii) Terrorist acts (Code of Criminal Procedure, Preliminary Title, art. 10, para. 6); and

(ix) Any offence which, under international treaty law or international customary law, must be prosecuted regardless of the country in which it was committed and of the nationality of its perpetrator(s) (Code of Criminal Procedure, Preliminary Title, art. 12 *bis*). Belgian courts have jurisdiction on the basis of this provision even where Belgium has not refused an extradition request.

11. Concerning the Commission's question reproduced in paragraph 3 (*c*) of the above introduction, Belgium's judicial practice in the area of universal jurisdiction is not connected with the obligation *aut dedere aut judicare*. Thus, when a Belgian judge was assigned to the criminal trials of individuals accused of having participated in the massacres committed in Rwanda from April to June 1994, this was done on the basis of jurisdiction established in the Act of 16 June 1993 on the punishment of serious violations of the Geneva Conventions of 12 August 1949 and the 1977 Additional Protocols thereto, regardless of any extradition request made by another State.

12. Concerning the Commission's question reproduced in paragraph 3 (*d*) of the above introduction, the reply is contained in the preceding paragraphs: universal jurisdiction is sometimes expressed not by *aut dedere aut judicare* but by *judicare vel dedere*.

13. Concerning the Commission's question reproduced in paragraph 4 (*a*) of the above introduction, Belgium referred to its Extradition Act of 15 March 1874 (art. 1, para. 1), as amended by the Acts of 28 June 1899, 31 July 1985 and 14 January 1999, which do not provide for extradition in cases not covered by a treaty. Furthermore, the law (art. 1, para. 1) permits the extradition only of foreign nationals. Belgium therefore refuses to extradite its own nationals and agrees to extradite a foreign national only pursuant to a treaty between Belgium and the requesting State.

14. Concerning extradition for offences not covered by a treaty between Belgium and the requesting State, article 1, paragraph 2, of the Extradition Act states that only acts which are criminalized under both Belgian law and the law of the other country and which are subject to a prison sentence of more than one year may give rise to extradition. In accordance with modern extradition law, this means that the offences that can give rise to extradition are those which, on the one hand, are criminalized both in Belgium and in the requesting State and which, on the other hand, are subject to a fairly serious sentence (more than one year's imprisonment) both in Belgium and in the requesting State. Thus, the determining factor is not the nature of the offence but its dual criminalization and the gravity of the sentence envisaged in the two States. Belgium would therefore refuse any request for extradition of the alleged perpetrator of an offence which was not criminalized both in Belgium and in the requesting State or which was not subject to a sentence of more than one year's imprisonment.

15. Concerning the extradition of nationals, although, as indicated above, the practice is prohibited under its extradition law, Belgium is bound by the Council of the European Union's framework decision of 13 June 2002, which established a European arrest warrant (*Official Journal of the European Communities*, L 190, vol. 45, 18 July 2002). This framework decision was implemented in Belgium through the Act of 19 December 2003. The 2002 framework decision and the 2003 Act call for the surrender of a person for whom a European arrest warrant has been issued by a State member of the European Union. That person may be a national of the State in which the arrest warrant is to be executed; this is, therefore, an exception to the principle that a State shall not extradite its own nationals. However, the framework decision and the Act provide that the executing State may make the surrender of its nationals subject to the condition that they are returned to their State of origin in order to serve there the custodial sentence or detention order passed against them in the State that issued the arrest warrant (framework decision, art. 5, para. 3; Act of 2003, art. 8).

16. In other words, Belgium agrees that, within the framework of the European Union, a Belgian national shall be surrendered to a European Union member State pursuant to an arrest warrant issued for that person, but Belgium may make the surrender of its national to the State that issued the arrest warrant subject to the condition that the person must be returned to Belgium in order to serve there the sentence passed by the court of the State that issued the arrest warrant.

17. Concerning the Commission's question reproduced in paragraph 4 (*b*) of the above Introduction, if, by crimes "that do not involve one of its nationals", the question means crimes committed in other States by a foreign national, the answer is "yes": in the context of the extraterritorial jurisdiction recognized by Belgian law, Belgian judges may exercise jurisdiction, under various conditions established in Belgian criminal law, over crimes committed in other States by persons who are not Belgian nationals (see paragraphs 7 to 10 above).

18. Lastly, concerning the Commission's question reproduced in paragraph 4 (*c*) of the above introduction, it has sometimes been maintained that the obligation to extradite or prosecute was a customary obligation. For example, in the *Lockerbie* case, which the Libyan Arab Jamahiriya, as claimant State, brought against the United Kingdom and the United States of America as respondents, Judge Weeramantry, in his dissenting opinion to the order on provisional measures, mentioned the "rule of customary international law, *aut dedere aut judicare*";[4] however, Judges Evensen, Tarassov, Guillaume and Aguilar Mawdsley, in a joint declaration on the same order, stated:

> Moreover, in general international law there is no obligation to prosecute in default of extradition. Although since the days of Covarruvias and Grotius such a formula has been advocated by some legal scholars, it has never been part of positive law.[5]

---

[4] *Questions of Interpretation and Application of the 1971 Montreal Convention arising from the Aerial Incident at Lockerbie*, order of 14 April 1992, Provisional Measures, dissenting opinion by Judge Weeramantry, pp. 69 (United Kingdom order) and 179 (United States of America order).

[5] *Ibid.*, joint declaration by Judges Evensen, Tarassov, Guillaume and Aguilar Mawdsley, pp. 24 (United Kingdom order) and 135 (United States of America order).

Belgium shares this opinion with respect to the criminal prosecution of the perpetrators of customary law crimes.

19. Concerning crimes of international law, Belgium considers the obligation to extradite or prosecute to be, in essence, a treaty obligation. It is, in fact, envisaged in a number of treaties that establish certain crimes as international offences (see the examples mentioned in paragraphs 1 to 6 above) and more generally, for offences under domestic law, in the European Convention on Extradition of 13 December 1957 (art. 6, para. 2), in cases involving refusal to extradite a national.

20. However, Belgium considers that all States must cooperate in suppressing certain extremely serious crimes—particularly crimes of international humanitarian law (crimes against humanity, genocide and war crimes)—since such crimes pose a threat, both qualitatively and quantitatively, to the most fundamental values of the international community. This contribution to the suppression effort may take the form of direct prosecution of the alleged perpetrators of such crimes or of extradition of those responsible to any State that wishes to prosecute them. Thus, there is indeed an obligation to prosecute, but of a *judicare vel dedere* rather than an *aut dedere aut judicare* nature. This is a customary obligation which has numerous sources:

(*a*) The draft Code of Crimes against the Peace and Security of Mankind, prepared by the International Law Commission (see paragraph 4 above);

(*b*) Various General Assembly resolutions on the suppression of war crimes and crimes against humanity (i.e., resolutions 2840 (XXVI) of 18 December 1971, paras. 1, 2 and 4, and 3074 (XXVIII) of 3 December 1973, paras. 1–9);

(*c*) The many positions taken by the General Assembly and the Security Council concerning the need to combat impunity. See, for example, the General Assembly resolutions which require that the perpetrators of crimes of international humanitarian law be brought to justice in the case of, *inter alia*, Iraq (resolution 54/178 of 17 December 1999, para. 3 (*d*)), the Democratic Republic of the Congo (resolution 54/179 of 17 December 1999, para. 3 (*d*)), Haiti (resolution 54/187 of 17 December 1999, para. 8) and Rwanda (resolution 54/188 of 17 December 1999, para. 8). The Security Council has taken similar positions. For example, on the occasion of the Millennium Summit, the Council:

> Stresse[d] that the perpetrators of crimes against humanity, crimes of genocide, war crimes, and other serious violations of international humanitarian law should be brought to justice (resolution 1318 (2000) of 7 September 2000, sect. VI; see also, *inter alia*, resolutions 1120 (1997) of 14 July 1997, para. 7, and 1325 (2000) of 31 October 2000, para. 11);

(*d*) The fourth through sixth paragraphs of the preamble to the Rome Statute of the International Criminal Court, in which the States parties to the Statute affirm the need for the international community as a whole to combat impunity for the most serious crimes and recall the duty of every State to exercise its criminal jurisdiction over those responsible for international crimes.

21. For all these reasons, Belgium considers that there is a universal obligation to suppress crimes of international humanitarian law. This obligation is customary in the light of the many consistent positions expressed by the international community on this issue. It takes the form of "prosecute or extradite" rather than "extradite or prosecute". However, for serious offences other than crimes of international humanitarian law, there is only the obligation either to extradite or to prosecute, and this is solely a treaty obligation.

C. Canada

1. Canada supports the work of the International Law Commission in this area. It remained interested in the potential scope of the topic, as it is of the view that the obligation to extradite or submit the matter for prosecution does not apply to all crimes. Canada welcomes further discussion of the source of the obligation and suggests that a systematic survey of the treaties that contain an obligation to extradite or prosecute would be useful. Canada also welcomes the Special Rapporteur's decision to refrain from further examination of the "triple alternative", as Canada considers surrender to an international criminal tribunal to differ substantively from an act of extradition, the latter involving bilateral State-to-State action.

2. In Canada, the obligation to extradite or prosecute applies to crimes of universal jurisdiction where provided by treaty and Canada has the capacity to extradite or prosecute for non-treaty based crimes of universal jurisdiction. As has been noted by the Special Rapporteur and in the submissions of other Governments, the alternative obligation to extradite or to prosecute assumes different forms in the multilateral treaties in which it has been embodied.

3. *Universal jurisdiction*. Where crimes are so serious and on such a scale that they can justly be regarded as an attack on the international legal order, the principle of universality provides jurisdiction for offences anywhere in the world. For example, the Geneva Conventions of 12 August 1949 and the 1977 Additional Protocol provide for mandatory universal jurisdiction over grave breaches and require a party to either bring alleged offenders before its courts or else surrender them to another party for trial. In addition, piracy, serious violations of the laws and customs of war, crimes against humanity and genocide are generally recognized as subject to the universality principle.

4. Similarly, a number of multilateral anti-terrorism conventions require the parties to extradite or to exercise jurisdiction in cases where extradition is not granted (submit the case "without exception whatsoever" to the competent authorities, with the qualification that those authorities must act as they would with any other "ordinary offence of a serious nature"), as appears in the Convention for the suppression of unlawful seizure of aircraft, adopted in 1970. This structure of the obligation has been replicated in a series of subsequent agreements on the repression of international offences concluded under the auspices of the United Nations or its specialized agencies and also appears in the Convention against Torture and Other Cruel, Inhuman or Degrading Treatment or Punishment, adopted in 1984.

5. *Permissive exercise of extraterritorial jurisdiction over non-nationals where extradition is refused.* In other multilateral conventions, the alternative obligation to prosecute where extradition is refused is subject to the State's general posture with respect to the propriety of exercising extraterritorial jurisdiction. This framework is premised on the assumption that States which refuse to extradite their nationals will have no difficulty in trying them and provide, generally, that where the only reason for refusing extradition is the offender's nationality he should be punishable at home for the offence committed abroad. This formulation of the obligation may be found, for example, in the multilateral drug conventions, the United Nations Convention against Transnational Organized Crime, adopted in 2000, and the United Nations Convention against Corruption, adopted in 2003.

6. The latter framework, as with bilateral extradition treaties that provide an alternative obligation to extradite or prosecute, primarily addresses the concern that States who refuse to extradite their own nationals will offer a safe haven to alleged offenders who would otherwise escape prosecution for offences committed abroad.

7. Canada would caution against the adoption of an overly broad conception of the obligation to extradite or prosecute. It is Canada's view that, for the vast majority of crimes, the obligation to extradite or prosecute does not and should not apply and, where applicable, the scope of the obligation should be defined by treaty. In this regard, Canada supports the inclusion of such provisions in multilateral treaties as part of the international community's collective efforts to deny a safe haven to terrorists and other criminals.

8. In Canada, extradition to another State is governed by the Extradition Act, Statutes of Canada, 1999, chap. 18, which came into force on 17 June 1999, and the Canadian Charter of Rights and Freedoms, Part I of the Constitution Act, 1982, being Schedule B to the Canada Act 1982 (U.K.), 1982, chap. 11 (available from http://laws.justice.gc.ca/en/Charter/index.html). The Extradition Act, in tandem with the Charter, governs domestic proceedings for the extradition of an individual from Canada to another State and provides for three distinct extradition regimes: (*a*) pursuant to a bilateral or multilateral treaty; (*b*) to an extradition partner designated in the Schedule to the Extradition Act; or (*c*) on an exceptional basis to a non-designated, non-treaty partner in relation to a specific extradition request. The extradition of a person from another State at the request of Canada is dealt with pursuant to the provisions of any bilateral or multilateral treaty in force between Canada and the requested State, and the law of the requested State.

9. Canada is currently bound by 51 bilateral extradition treaties.[1] Although many bilateral treaties provide for the discretionary refusal of an extradition request where both Canada and the requesting State have jurisdiction to prosecute the offence for which extradition is sought, where there are ongoing proceedings in Canada against the individual for the offence for which extradition is requested and/or where the competent authorities in Canada have decided not to prosecute or to terminate a prosecution that had been initiated, none of Canada's bilateral treaties contain an obligation to extradite or submit the matter for prosecution. The Extradition Act also provides grounds on which the Minister of Justice may or must refuse extradition requests that apply when an extradition request is made in the absence of a treaty, including that surrender may be refused when there are criminal proceedings in Canada against the individual for the offence for which extradition is requested (subsect. 47(*d*)). Canada also identified in its observations its extradition partners designated as such in the Schedule to the Extradition Act. The texts of Canada's bilateral extradition treaties are available on the Government of Canada's treaty information website (available from www.treaty-accord.gc.ca/).

10. Canada is also party to a number of multilateral treaties that contain an obligation to extradite or prosecute, including:

(*a*) *Universal*: Geneva Convention for the Amelioration of the Condition of the Wounded and Sick in Armed Forces in the Field (Geneva I), adopted in 1949; Geneva Convention for the Amelioration of the Condition of the Wounded, Sick and Shipwrecked Members of the Armed Forces at Sea (Geneva II), adopted in 1949; Geneva Convention relative to the Treatment of Prisoners of War (Geneva III), adopted in 1949; Geneva Convention relative to the Protection of Civilian Persons in Time of War (Geneva IV), adopted in 1949; Protocol additional to the Geneva Conventions of 12 August 1949, and relating to the protection of victims of international armed conflicts (Protocol I), adopted in 1977; Convention for the suppression of unlawful seizure of aircraft, adopted in 1970; Convention for the suppression of unlawful acts against the safety of civil aviation, adopted in 1971; Convention on the Prevention and Punishment of Crimes against Internationally Protected Persons, including Diplomatic Agents, adopted in 1973; International Convention against the taking of hostages, adopted in 1979; Convention on the physical protection of nuclear material, adopted in 1980; United Nations Convention on the Law of the Sea, adopted in 1982; Convention Against Torture and Other Cruel, Inhuman or Degrading Treatment or Punishment, adopted in 1984; Protocol for the suppression of unlawful acts of violence at airports serving international civil aviation, supplementary to the Convention for the suppression of unlawful acts against the safety of civil aviation, adopted in 1988; Convention for the Suppression of Unlawful Acts against the Safety of Maritime Navigation, adopted in 1988; Protocol for the Suppression of Unlawful Acts against the Safety of Fixed Platforms Located on the Continental Shelf, adopted in 1988; Convention on the Safety of United Nations and Associated Personnel, adopted in 1994; International Convention for the Suppression of Terrorist Bombings, adopted in 1997; International Convention for the Suppression of the Financing of Terrorism, adopted in 1999;

(*b*) *Permissive*: Single Convention on Narcotic Drugs, adopted in 1961; Convention on Psychotropic Substances, adopted in 1971; Protocol amending the Single Convention on Narcotics Drugs, 1961, adopted in

[1] A list of such bilateral treaties was enclosed and is available from the Codification Division of the Office of Legal Affairs.

1972; United Nations Convention against Illicit Traffic in Narcotic Drugs and Psychotropic Substances, adopted in 1988; Inter-American Convention against Corruption, adopted in 1996; Convention on Combating Bribery of Foreign Public Officials in International Business Transactions, adopted in 1997; United Nations Convention against Transnational Organized Crime, adopted in 2000; Protocol to Prevent, Suppress and Punish Trafficking in Persons, Especially Women and Children, supplementing the United Nations Convention against Transnational Organized Crime, adopted in 2000; Protocol against the Smuggling of Migrants by Land, Sea and Air, supplementing the United Nations Convention against Transnational Organized Crime, adopted in 2000; and United Nations Convention against Corruption, adopted in 2003.

11. Canada is also a party to the Convention on the Prevention and Punishment of the Crime of Genocide, adopted in 1948, and the Convention on offences and certain other acts committed on board aircraft, adopted in 1963. While Canada recognizes that these two Conventions do not contain an explicit obligation to extradite or prosecute, it notes that they do require States to establish jurisdiction in respect of certain offences.

12. Canada has not sought to limit the application of this obligation in any of these multilateral treaties.

13. Canada has also signed, but has not yet ratified, the following treaties: Inter-American Convention against the Illicit Manufacturing of and Trafficking in Firearms, Ammunition, Explosives, and Other Related Materials, adopted in 1997; Convention on cybercrime, adopted in 2001; Protocol against the Illicit Manufacturing of and Trafficking in Firearms, Their Parts and Components and Ammunition, supplementing the United Nations Convention against Transnational Organized Crime, adopted in 2001; Additional Protocol to the Convention on cybercrime, concerning the criminalization of acts of a racist and xenophobic nature committed through computer systems, adopted in 2003; and International Convention for the Suppression of Acts of Nuclear Terrorism, adopted in 2005.

14. In Canada, the obligation to extradite or submit the matter for prosecution applies to crimes of universal jurisdiction, whether recognized as such by treaty or by customary international law. Although there are no statutory or constitutional rules which directly address the obligation to extradite or prosecute, statutory provisions establishing extraterritorial jurisdiction for specified crimes enabling prosecution in Canada are included in the Criminal Code, Revised Statutes of Canada 1985, chap. 46, the Crimes Against Humanity and War Crimes Act, Statutes of Canada 2000, chap. 24 (available from http://laws.justice.gc.ca/en/showdoc/cs/C-45.9/) and the National Defence Act, Revised Statutes of Canada 1985, chap. N–5.

15. Where the applicable legislation does not extend jurisdiction extraterritorially, Canada's courts have determined that it is sufficient if there is a "real and substantial link" between the offence and Canada for Canadian courts to have jurisdiction (see further *Libman v. The Queen*, [1985] 2 *Supreme Court Reports* 178 (Canada), available from www.canlii.org/en/ca/scc/doc/1985/1985canlii51/1985canlii51.html).

16. Section 6(2) of the Criminal Code states the general rule that the territorial application of Canadian criminal law is limited to those offences committed in Canada, unless Canadian jurisdiction is specifically extended by federal law. Exceptions to the general rule that provides for trial in Canada of offences committed outside Canada are primarily outlined in section 7 of the Criminal Code. Section 7 of the Criminal Code extends Canadian criminal law jurisdiction to cover a number of offences which often have international law implications such as air piracy, offences against diplomats, terrorist offences, protection of nuclear material and torture. A number of the offences referred to in section 7 of the Criminal Code, such as torture (sect. 269.1), crimes against internationally protected persons (sect. 431) and terrorism offences (part II.1) were created to fulfil Canada's obligations under the international conventions listed above aimed at preventing and suppressing certain types of offences. Canadian jurisdiction is also extended in some circumstances in relation to the International Space Station (subsects. 7(2.3) to 7(2.34)); defined circumstances relating to, among other things, internationally protected persons, United Nations personnel and terrorism offences (subsects. 7(3) to 7(3.75)); offences committed outside Canada by Canadian public service employees (subsect.. 7(4)); and certain sexual offences when committed outside Canada by Canadian citizens or permanent residents (subsects. 7(4.1) to 7(4.3)). However, the expanded jurisdiction provided in the Criminal Code is qualified by the requirement to obtain the consent of the Attorney General of Canada to institute proceedings against non-citizens (subsect. 7(7)).

17. Sections 6, 7 and 8 of the Crimes Against Humanity and War Crimes Act also provide that the offences of genocide, crimes against humanity, war crimes, and breach of command responsibility in relation to genocide, a crime against humanity or a war crime committed outside Canada, may be prosecuted in Canada if, at the time the offence is alleged to have been committed, (*a*) the person was a Canadian citizen or was employed by Canada in a civilian or military capacity, (*b*) the person was a citizen of a State that was engaged in an armed conflict against Canada, or was employed in a civilian or military capacity by such a State, (*c*) the victim of the alleged offence was a Canadian citizen or (*d*) the victim of the alleged offence was a citizen of a State that was allied with Canada in an armed conflict. In addition, such offences may be prosecuted in Canada if, after the time the offence is alleged to have been committed, the person is present in Canada.

18. Canada also asserts specific extraterritorial jurisdiction in other limited circumstances, including offences committed by Canadian military personnel and other persons subject to the Code of Service Discipline (sects. 67, 130 and 132 of the National Defence Act).

19. Canada notes that the obligation to submit a matter for prosecution, as the alternative where extradition is not possible, remains chiefly a concern for those States that refuse to extradite their own nationals. Canada allows, and regularly authorizes, the extradition of its own nationals; therefore, the application of this principle rarely, if ever, surfaces in Canada. As such, there is no particular practice concerning the obligation to extradite or prosecute in Canada, be it from a judicial, prosecutorial or law enforcement perspective, nor are there any particular crimes or

offences to which this obligation is applied or not applied, as the Canadian courts only become seized of criminal matters once the relevant law enforcement authorities decide to lay charges and the Attorney General of Canada, or the relevant provincial Attorney General, undertakes a prosecution. The Government of Canada is not aware of any judicial decisions in Canada that specifically apply the principle of the obligation to extradite or prosecute.

20. Where an extradition request is deemed deficient on evidentiary grounds, or owing to a lack of dual criminality from Canada's perspective, it follows that the relevant Canadian authorities would not be able to proceed with a prosecution for the same reasons. Where, on the other hand, the offence at issue in any extradition request is alleged to have occurred outside Canadian territory, Canada would, except in certain exceptional circumstances, not be able to lay charges or proceed with a prosecution for want of jurisdiction.

21. Finally, decisions to initiate prosecutions, stay proceedings or launch appeals in Canada may take into account the public interest, but must not include any consideration of the political implications of the decision. No investigative agency, Government department or Minister of the Crown may issue instructions for the pursuit or discontinuance of a particular prosecution or to undertake a specific appeal. These decisions rest solely with the Attorney General (and his or her counsel) who must for these purposes be regarded as an independent officer, exercising responsibilities in a manner similar to that of a judge.

D. South Africa

1. Before dealing with the specific questions asked by the International Law Commission, South Africa pointed out that it would have found an exposition on the Commission's understanding of the principles of universal jurisdiction, as well as its link, if any, with the principle of *aut dedere aut judicare* useful. It would also be useful to know how the study of universal jurisdiction will be incorporated into the Commission's project on *aut dedere aut judicare*.

2. In the absence of such an explanation, and for the purposes of its comments, South Africa explained that it had utilized the principle of universal jurisdiction as set out in the *Princeton Principles on Universal Jurisdiction*:

> 1. … Universal jurisdiction is criminal jurisdiction based solely on the nature of the crime, without regard to where the crime was committed, the nationality of the alleged or convicted perpetrator, the nationality of the victim, or any other connection to the state exercising such jurisdiction.
>
> 2. Universal jurisdiction may be exercised by a competent and ordinary judicial body of any state in order to try a person duly accused of committing serious crimes under international law as specified in Principle 2(1), provided the person is present before such a judicial body. …[1]

It further noted that the serious crimes under international law specified in principle 2(1) include piracy, slavery, war crimes, crimes against peace, crimes against humanity, genocide and torture.

3. South Africa is of the view that the extent to which universal jurisdiction is part of customary international law needs to be explored further, but at this stage it is probably only in relation to obligations *erga omnes*. For the rest, it is the Government's view that universal jurisdiction or even quasi-universal jurisdiction is treaty-based.

4. It is also the view of the Government that universal jurisdiction and *aut dedere aut judicare* are not automatically linked. As evidenced in the definition above, universal jurisdiction enables a State to establish jurisdiction—it does not create an obligation to prosecute or extradite. It is acknowledged that universal, or quasi-universal, jurisdiction and the principle of *aut dedere aut judicare* are often linked, especially in a treaty framework, but this does not necessarily mean that they are always linked, and certainly there is no link in terms of customary international law.

5. With reference to the Commission's question reproduced in paragraph 3 (*a*) of the above introduction, in view of the fact that there seems to be some disagreement about which treaties establish universal jurisdiction, it would be useful to have an indication from the Commission in this regard. Some of the treaties which do have a concept of universal jurisdiction linked with the principle of *aut dedere aut judicare* are the 13 United Nations counter-terrorism treaties.

6. With reference to the Commission's question reproduced in paragraph 3 (*b*) of the above introduction, South Africa is a party to the 13 United Nations counter-terrorism treaties mentioned in the previous paragraph. The *aut dedere aut judicare* principle has been given effect through, for example, the Civil Aviation Offences Act 10 of 1972 and the Protection of Constitutional Democracy against Terrorist and Related Activities Act 33 of 2004.

7. While the Rome Statute on the International Criminal Court does not confer universal jurisdiction on the Court, individual States have enacted legislation to give some form of universal jurisdiction to their own courts to try international crimes recognized by the Rome Statute—genocide, crimes against humanity and war crimes. In South Africa, the Implementation of the Rome Statute of the International Criminal Court Act 27 of 2002 empowers a South African court to exercise jurisdiction over a person who has committed such crimes outside South Africa if "that person, after the commission of the crime is present in the territory of the Republic". The incorporation legislation, Act 27 of 2002, enables the National Prosecuting Authority of the Republic to prosecute and the High Courts of the Republic to adjudicate in cases brought against any person accused of having committed a crime in the Republic and beyond the borders of the Republic in certain circumstances. "Crime" is defined as genocide, war crimes and crimes against humanity. It appears that these crimes are incorporated into South African domestic law irrespective of who has committed them and irrespective of where. There will also be jurisdiction if the crimes are committed in the territories of States not parties to the Statute.

8. With reference to the Commission's question reproduced in paragraph 3 (*c*) of the above introduction, so far, no cases specifically referring to the obligation *aut dedere aut judicare* have been located.

[1] *The Princeton Principles on Universal Jurisdiction*, p. 28 (available from http://lapa.princeton.edu/hosteddocs/unive_jur.pdf, accessed 31 July 2015).

9. With reference to the Commission's question reproduced in paragraph 4 (*a*) of the above introduction, the Extradition Act 67 of 1962 contains no exemption for nationals. South Africa's approach towards nationality (citizenship) and extradition was examined by the Constitutional Court in *Geuking v. President of the Republic of South Africa* 2003 (3) SA 34 (CC), in which it was argued that the President, in exercising his power to surrender a person to the Federal Republic of Germany under section 3(2) of the Act, had failed to have regard to the fact that the person was a South African national (citizen). Justice Goldstone, speaking for the court, said:

> In the present case, the President stated in the affidavit he filed in the High Court that in deciding whether to grant his consent under section 3(2) of the Act the citizenship of the appellant would not have been a relevant consideration. I can find no constitutional ground for attacking that policy decision. Unlike the Federal Republic of Germany and many other civil law jurisdictions, South Africa does not ordinarily prosecute its citizens for crimes committed beyond its borders. Criminal conduct would go unpunished if South African citizens were not extradited to face prosecution in the country where the crime was committed. The President is therefore entitled to adopt a policy that is in the interests of the Republic to consent to a request for extradition proceedings against a person, regardless of his or her citizenship.

10. South Africa has the authority under domestic law to extradite persons in situations not covered by a treaty. Section 3(2) of the Act provides:

> Any person accused or convicted of an extraditable offence committed within the jurisdiction of a foreign State which is not a party to an extradition agreement shall be liable to be surrendered to such foreign State, if the President has in writing consented to his or her being so surrendered.

The existence of a treaty is not necessary for extradition in terms of section 3(2) of the Act. This principle was confirmed in *Harksen v. President of the Republic of South Africa and Others* 2000 (2) SA 825 (CC). In that case, the Constitutional Court confirmed the legality of extradition of the applicant to Germany notwithstanding the fact that there was no treaty.

11. In the context of the questions raised, however, all the requirements of extradition law must be adhered to. The Extradition Act therefore does not automatically provide authority to extradite on the principle of universal jurisdiction unless the particular crime has been incorporated into South African domestic law.

12. In reply to the Commission's question reproduced in paragraph 4 (*b*) of the above introduction, South Africa referred to its observations contained above.

13. With reference to the Commission's question reproduced in paragraph 4 (*c*) of the above introduction, South Africa does not believe that the principle of *aut dedere aut judicare* has reached sufficient international recognition and widespread practice to be considered as part of international customary law and at this stage its legal status is still reliant on a treaty basis.

E. Yemen

1. Yemen stressed its respect for the international agreements, conventions and instruments to which it is a party and indicated that it fulfils its obligations thereunder. Article 6 of its Constitution provides as follows:

> The Republic of Yemen confirms its adherence to the Charter of the United Nations, the Universal Declaration of Human Rights, the Charter of the League of Arab States and the generally recognized rules of international law.

2. While article 45 of the Constitution states that no Yemeni citizen may be extradited, the relevant laws affirm that criminals shall be prosecuted and sentenced fairly. Article 3 of the Penal Code that was promulgated by Republican Decree No. 12 of 1994 provides as follows:

> This law shall apply to all crimes that are perpetrated within the State, whatever the nationality of the perpetrator. The crime shall be considered as perpetrated within the State if any of its constituent parts takes place within the State; when all or part of the crime is perpetrated within the State, this law shall apply to anyone who participated therein, even if their participation did not take place within the State. This law shall also apply to crimes that are perpetrated beyond the State and shall be dealt with by the Yemeni courts in accordance with the Law of Criminal Procedure.

3. Yemen has signed with a number of fraternal and friendly countries the following bilateral agreements on the extradition and prosecution of criminals: agreement on cooperation in the field of internal and public security concluded with Jordan; security cooperation agreement concluded with the Libyan Arab Jamahiriya; bilateral cooperation agreement between the Ministries of the Interior of Yemen and Djibouti, with executive programme; agreement concluded with Egypt on the transfer of imprisoned convicted criminals; and security cooperation agreements concluded bilaterally with Algeria, Egypt, Ethiopia and Saudi Arabia.

4. Yemen is also a party to the following international agreements on the extradition and prosecution of criminals: the Riyadh Arab Agreement for Judicial Cooperation, signed by Yemen and ratified by Law No. 36 of 1983; and the Arab Anti-Terrorism Agreement, signed in 1998 in Cairo and ratified by Yemen by Law No. 34 of 1999.

PROTECTION OF PERSONS IN THE EVENT OF DISASTERS

[Agenda item 8]

DOCUMENT A/CN.4/615*

Second report on the protection of persons in the event of disasters, by Mr. Eduardo Valencia-Ospina, Special Rapporteur

[*Original: English*]
[*7 May 2009*]

CONTENTS

Multilateral instruments cited in the present report

	Source
Convention on the Prevention and Punishment of the Crime of Genocide (Paris, 9 December 1948)	United Nations, *Treaty Series*, vol. 78, No. 1021, p. 277.
Vienna Convention on Consular Relations (Vienna, 24 April 1963)	*Ibid.*, vol. 596, No. 8638, p. 261.
International Covenant on Economic, Social and Cultural Rights (New York, 16 December 1966)	*Ibid.*, vol. 993, No. 14531, p. 3.
African Charter on Human and Peoples' Rights (Nairobi, 27 June 1981)	*Ibid.*, vol. 1520, No. 26363, p. 217.
Vienna Convention for the Protection of the Ozone Layer (Vienna, 22 March 1985)	*Ibid.*, vol. 1513, No. 26164, p. 293.
Convention on Assistance in the Case of a Nuclear Accident or Radiological Emergency (Vienna, 26 September 1986)	*Ibid.*, vol. 1457, No. 24643, p. 133.

* Incorporating A/CN.4/614/Corr.1.

	Source
Montreal Protocol on Substances that Deplete the Ozone Layer (Montreal, 16 September 1987)	*Ibid.*, vol. 1522, No. 26369, p. 3. For the final amended version of the Protocol, see *Handbook for the Montreal Protocol on Substances that Deplete the Ozone Layer*, 8th ed. (UNEP, 2009), sect. 1.
Agreement establishing the Caribbean Disaster Emergency Response Agency (Port of Spain, 26 February 1991)	*Ibid.*, vol. 2256, No. 40212, p. 53.
Inter-American Convention to Facilitate Disaster Assistance (Santiago, 7 June 1991)	OAS, *Official Documents*, OEA/Ser.A/49 (SEPF), p. 13.
Tampere Convention on the Provision of Telecommunication Resources for Disaster Mitigation and Relief Operations (Tampere, 18 June 1998)	United Nations, *Treaty Series*, vol. 2296, No. 40906, p. 5.
Framework Convention on Civil Defence Assistance (Geneva, 22 May 2000)	*Ibid.*, vol. 2172, No. 38131, p. 213.
ASEAN Agreement on Disaster Management and Emergency Response (Vientiane, 26 July 2005)	*ASEAN Documents Series 2005*, p. 157.
Convention on the Rights of Persons with Disabilities (New York, 13 December 2006)	United Nations, *Treaty Series*, vol. 2515, No. 44910, p. 3.

Works cited in the present report

BABOVIĆ, Bogdan

"The duty of States to cooperate with one another in accordance with the Charter", in Milan ŠAHOVIĆ, ed., *Principles of International Law Concerning Friendly Relations and Cooperation.* Belgrade, Institute of International Politics and Economics, 1972, pp. 277–321.

BECK, Ulrich

Risk Society: Towards a New Modernity. Translated by Mark Ritter. London, Sage Publications, 1992. 266 p.

BERNARD, Mountague

"On the principle of non-intervention". A lecture delivered in the hall of All Souls' College. Oxford, Parker, 1860. 36 p.

FISCHER, Horst

"International disaster response law treaties: trends, patterns, and lacunae", *International Disaster Response Laws, Principles and Practice: Reflections, Prospects and Challenges.* Geneva, International Federation of Red Cross and Red Crescent Societies, 2003, pp. 24–44.

GIDDENS, Anthony

"Affluence, poverty and the idea of a post-scarcity society". Discussion Paper No. 63. UNRISD, 1995.

HART, Herbert Lionel Adolphus and Tony HONORÉ

Causation in the Law. 2nd ed. Oxford, Clarendon Press, 1985. 516 p.

HUME, David

A Treatise of Human Nature. 2nd ed. Oxford, Clarendon Press, 1978 (reprint of 1739). 743 p.

INSTITUTE OF INTERNATIONAL LAW

Yearbook. Vol. 70, Part II, session of Bruges, 2003, second part, Paris, Pedone.

MACDONALD, Ronald St. John

"The principle of solidarity in public international law", in C. DOMINICÉ, R. PATRY and C. REYMOND, eds., *Études de droit international en l'honneur de Pierre Lalive.* Basel, Helbing & Lichtenhahn, 1993, pp. 275–307.

MILL, John Stuart

A System of Logic, Ratiocinative and Inductive, being a Connected View of the Principles of Evidence and the Methods of Scientific Investigation. Book III, chap. V, p. 327, para. 3, in J. M. ROBSON, ed., *Collected Works of John Stuart Mill*, vol. VII. Toronto, University of Toronto, 1974. 638 p.

UVIN, Peter

Human Rights and Development. Bloomfield (Connecticut), Kumarian Press, 2004. 241 p.

WERNER, Wouter G.

"State sovereignty and international legal discourse", in Ige F. DEKKER and Wouter G. WERNER, eds., *Governance and International Legal Theory.* Leiden, Nijhoff, 2004. pp. 125–157.

Introduction*

1. The present report on the protection of persons in the event of disasters is preceded by a preliminary report on the same topic,[1] submitted by the Special Rapporteur at the sixtieth session of the International Law Commission in May 2008, following the Commission's decision at its fifty-ninth session in 2007[2] to include the topic in its current programme of work.

2. The preliminary report dealt in a general way with the scope of the topic, in order to properly circumscribe

* The Special Rapporteur expresses his appreciation for their assistance in the preparation of the present report to: Arjen Vermeer, PhD candidate, T.M.C. Asser Institute, The Hague; René Urueña, PhD candidate, and J. Benton Heath, JD candidate, New York University Law School, New York.

[1] *Yearbook ... 2008*, vol. II (Part One), document A/CN.4/598.

[2] *Yearbook ... 2007*, vol. II (Part Two), p. 98, para. 375.

it.[3] To that effect, it presented a broad outline of the most relevant legal questions involved, clustering the discussion around three axes: *ratione materiae* (including the concept and classification of disasters[4] and the concept of protection of persons[5]), *ratione personae*[6] and *ratione temporis*.[7] Of special interest was the possibility of a rights-based approach to the topic, which the Special Rapporteur examined without prejudice to the outcome of further debates.[8] Applicable sources of law for international disaster protection and assistance were also assessed,[9] and some preliminary ideas regarding the appropriate final form of the work were presented.[10]

3. The preliminary report was considered by the Commission at its 2978th to 2982nd meetings, in July 2008.[11] Discussion among members of the Commission focused on the advantages and challenges featured by a rights-based approach to the topic.[12] The appropriate limits of its scope were also thoroughly discussed in reference to the three mentioned axes,[13] as was the right to humanitarian assistance as an important element to be considered in subsequent stages of the debates.[14]

4. The Commission gave attention to the notion of "responsibility to protect", whose relevance for the present topic remained unclear for some members, particularly in the context of disasters.[15] Sources relevant to the consideration of the topic were finally examined, highlighting the importance for the Commission's work of not duplicating prior work on the topic done elsewhere,[16] for example, the Guidelines for the Domestic Facilitation and Regulation of International Disaster Relief and Initial Recovery Assistance, adopted by the International Federation of Red Cross and Red Crescent Societies (IFRC) at its 30th Conference in 2007.[17]

5. In October and November 2008, at the sixty-third session of the General Assembly, the Sixth Committee further considered the preliminary report and the debate held thereon in the Commission. In connection with the discussion of chapter IX of the Commission's report on the work of its sixtieth session (*Yearbook ... 2008*, vol. II (Part Two)), more than 20 States and IFRC presented their views on the issues put forward by the Special Rapporteur's preliminary report. All delegations shared the view of the Special Rapporteur on the importance and timeliness of the general undertaking, and all agreed on the topic's particular complexities, which warrant special care in its treatment by the Commission. A provisional understanding was reached regarding the final outcome of the work: while some States favoured non-binding guidelines,[18] there was no objection to the suggestion that work should proceed in the form of draft articles, whose ultimate binding force could be decided at a later stage.

6. A similar understanding emerged with regard to some limitations of the scope *ratione materiae*. The exclusion of armed conflict from the subject matter to be studied was supported by all delegations that referred to the issue.[19] Likewise, to draw a strict line between man-made and natural disasters seemed unnecessary to various delegations, particularly if both causes would produce similar effects.[20] Nonetheless, some of those delegations proposed that, as a question of methodology, work could start by considering natural disasters and then move on to other types of disaster.[21]

7. Limitations on the scope *ratione temporis* were also discussed in the Sixth Committee. In various interventions,[22] the idea was put forward of limiting, in principle, the Commission's work to two phases of a disaster situation: the disaster proper (response) and post-disaster (early recovery), without prejudice as to the further consideration of issues of preparedness at the pre-disaster phase in the future.

8. Finally, a rights-based approach to the topic was supported by various delegations,[23] while some expressed

[3] *Yearbook ... 2008*, vol. II (Part One), document A/CN.4/598, p. 146, para. 9.

[4] *Ibid.*, pp. 152–153, paras. 44–49.

[5] *Ibid.*, pp. 153–154, paras. 50–55.

[6] *Ibid.*, p. 154, para. 56.

[7] *Ibid.*, paras. 57–58.

[8] *Ibid.*, paras. 12, 26 and 51.

[9] *Ibid.*, pp. 148–151, paras. 21–42.

[10] *Ibid.*, p. 155, paras. 59–60.

[11] *Ibid.*, vol. II (Part Two), para. 216.

[12] *Ibid.*, paras. 227–229.

[13] *Ibid.*, paras. 230–240.

[14] *Ibid.*, paras. 241–246.

[15] *Ibid.*, paras. 247–250, especially 248.

[16] *Ibid.*, paras. 251–256.

[17] Introduction to the Guidelines for the Domestic Facilitation and Regulation of International Disaster Relief and Initial Recovery Assistance (Geneva, IFRC, 2008).

[18] For example, Germany (*Official Records of the General Assembly, Sixty-third Session, Sixth Committee*, 22nd meeting (A/C.6/63/SR.22), para. 60), India (*ibid.*, 23rd meeting (A/C.6/63/SR.23), para. 21) and the United Kingdom (*ibid.*, para. 64).

[19] For example, Finland (on behalf of the Nordic States) (*ibid.*, 22nd meeting (A/C.6/63/SR.22), para. 54), India (*ibid.*, 23rd meeting (A/C.6/63/SR.23), para. 19), Japan (*ibid.*, para. 41), Republic of Korea (*ibid.*, para. 24), Poland (*ibid.*, 24th meeting (A/C.6/63/SR.24), para. 55), Spain (*ibid.*, 23rd meeting (A/C.6/63/SR.23), para. 37) and the United Kingdom (*ibid.*, para. 63).

[20] For example, Austria (*ibid.*, 23rd meeting (A/C.6/63/SR.23), para. 7), Chile (*ibid.*, 22nd meeting (A/C.6/63/SR.22), para. 14), Finland (on behalf of the Nordic States) (*ibid.*, para. 54), France (*ibid.*, 24th meeting (A/C.6/63/SR.24), para. 81), Germany (*ibid.*, 22nd meeting (A/C.6/63/SR.22), para. 60), Greece (*ibid.*, 24th meeting (A/C.6/63/SR.24), para. 6), Republic of Korea (*ibid.*, 23rd meeting (A/C.6/63/SR.23), para. 24) and the United Kingdom (*ibid.*, para. 63). See also Argentina (*ibid.*, 24th meeting (A/C.6/63/SR.24), para. 64) (drawing a sharp line between natural and man-made disasters would be difficult).

[21] For example, Japan (*ibid.*, 23rd meeting (A/C.6/63/SR.23), para. 41), Republic of Korea (*ibid.*, para. 24), Mexico (*ibid.*, para. 61), Portugal (*ibid.*, 25th meeting (A/C.6/63/SR.25), para. 6) and Spain (*ibid.*, 23rd meeting (A/C.6/63/SR.23, para. 37).

[22] For example, Austria (*ibid.*, A/C.6/63/SR.23, para. 9), France (*ibid.*, 24th meeting (A/C.6/63/SR.24), para. 80), Republic of Korea (*ibid.*, 23rd meeting (A/C.6/63/SR.23), para. 24) and New Zealand (*ibid.*, 24th meeting (A/C.6/63/SR.24), para. 11).

[23] For example, Chile (*ibid.*, 22nd meeting (A/C.6/63/SR.22), para. 16), Finland (on behalf of the Nordic States) (*ibid.*, para. 53), France (*ibid.*, 24th meeting (A/C.6/63/SR.24), para. 81), Poland (*ibid.*, para. 55), Portugal (*ibid.*, 25th meeting (A/C.6/63/SR.25), para. 6), Spain (*ibid.*, 23rd meeting (A/C.6/63/SR.23), para. 37) and Thailand (*ibid.*, para. 90). See also Austria (*ibid.*, para. 10) (elements of human rights law will have a bearing on the topic).

doubts as to whether such was the correct path to be followed in this case.[24] Similarly, while the relevance of a "responsibility to protect" still remained unclear for several delegations,[25] some delegations considered that the Commission should not find itself prevented from considering that notion, should the logic of its undertaking propel it in that direction.[26]

9. In the report on the work of its sixtieth session, the Commission indicated that it would welcome any information concerning the practice of States under this topic, including examples of domestic legislation. It would welcome in particular information and comments on specific legal and institutional problems encountered in dealing with or responding to disasters.[27] Replies to the Commission's concern were given orally by El Salvador in its statement in the Sixth Committee[28] and in writing by Mexico on 5 November 2008 and Germany on 26 February 2009. The written replies have been circulated as internal documents of the Commission.

10. Also at its sixtieth session, the Commission decided to pose a question to the United Nations system, in the following terms:

> How has the United Nations system institutionalized roles and responsibilities, at global and country levels, with regard to assistance to affected populations and States in the event of disasters—in the disaster response phase but also in pre- and post-disaster phases—and how does it relate in each of those phases with actors such as States, other intergovernmental organizations, the Red Cross movement, non-governmental organizations, specialized national response teams, national disaster management authorities and other relevant actors?[29]

The Commission likewise decided to seek information from IFRC on the basis of a similar inquiry adjusted as appropriate.[30]

11. By letters dated 6 November 2008 the Secretary of the Commission transmitted the question to the two addressees. Replies were received on 10 March 2009 from IFRC and on 17 April from the Office for the Coordination of Humanitarian Affairs (OCHA) of the Secretariat. These replies have been circulated as internal documents of the Commission.

12. During the sixtieth session of the Commission and afterwards, the Special Rapporteur continued his contacts with representatives of interested governmental and non-governmental organizations. He met in July of 2008 with Mr. Sálvano Briceño, Director of the Inter-Agency Secretariat of the International Strategy for Disaster Reduction (UNISDR). He also held a separate meeting with OCHA, chaired by Mr. Dusan Zupka (Emergency Preparedness Section) and attended by 14 officials of the Office; a meeting with IFRC chaired by Mr. Ibrahim Osman, Deputy Secretary-General, and attended by six Federation officials; and a meeting with the Protection Cluster Working Group chaired by Mr. Walter Kälin, Representative of the Secretary-General on human rights of internally displaced persons and attended by four other members of the Working Group, mainly officials from the Office of the United Nations High Commissioner for Refugees (UNHCR).

13. For the benefit of the Special Rapporteur, a round-table meeting on the topic was convened in Geneva in December 2008, presided over by the Representative of the Secretary-General on human rights of internally displaced persons and attended by 14 officials from his office, OHCHR, IFRC, OCHA, UNHCR, the United Nations Children's Fund (UNICEF) and members of the Protection Cluster Working Group.

Recent developments

14. In the period following the end of the Commission's sixtieth session, a number of documents have been issued that are of relevance to the consideration of the present topic. They include:

(*a*) The report of the independent expert on human rights and international solidarity submitted to the Human Rights Council by the High Commissioner for Human Rights;[31]

(*b*) The Manual on International Law and Standards Applicable in Natural Disaster Situations prepared and published by the International Development Law Organization. As explained in the foreword, the Manual provides a comprehensive analysis of the international legal standards pertaining to five key aspects of disaster response: human rights, the rights of vulnerable groups, the rights of children, land and property management, and anti-corruption/funds management;

(*c*) The report of the Secretary-General on implementing the responsibility to protect.[32] Referring to paragraphs 138 and 139 of the 2005 World Summit Outcome,[33] the report explains in paragraph 10 (*b*) that

> [t]he responsibility to protect applies, until Member States decide otherwise, only to the four specified crimes and violations: genocide, war crimes, ethnic cleansing and crimes against humanity. To try to extend it to cover other calamities, such as HIV/AIDS, climate change or the response to natural disasters, would undermine the 2005 consensus and stretch the concept beyond recognition or operational utility.

[24] For example, China (*ibid.*, A/C.6/63/SR.23, para. 29), New Zealand (*ibid.*, 24th meeting (A/C.6/63/SR.24), para. 11) and the Netherlands (*ibid.*, 22nd meeting (A/C.6/63/SR.22), para. 62).

[25] For example, China (*ibid.*, 23rd meeting (A/C.6/63/SR.23), para. 31), India (*ibid.*, para. 20) and Japan (*ibid.*, para. 42).

[26] For example, Finland (on behalf of the Nordic States) (*ibid.*, 22nd meeting (A/C.6/63/SR.22), para. 55), Poland (*ibid.*, 24th meeting (A/C.6/63/SR.24), para. 53) and Portugal (*ibid.*, 25th meeting (A/C.6/63/SR.25), para. 6).

[27] *Yearbook ... 2008*, vol. II (Part Two), para. 31.

[28] *Official Records of the General Assembly, Sixty-third Session, Sixth Committee*, 23rd meeting (A/C.6/63/SR.23), paras. 56–57.

[29] *Yearbook ... 2008*, vol. II (Part Two), para. 32.

[30] *Ibid.*, para. 33.

[31] A/HRC/9/10.

[32] A/63/677.

[33] General Assembly resolution 60/1 of 16 September 2005.

Chapter I

Defining the scope of the topic

15. The valuable guidance of the Commission and the Sixth Committee allows the Special Rapporteur to advance with the definition of the topic's scope. Once again, to facilitate the discussion, three aspects of scope are treated below: *ratione materiae*, *ratione personae* and *ratione temporis*.

A. *Ratione materiae*

1. Rights and needs in the protection of persons in the event of disasters

16. An important aspect of the preliminary report and the debate that ensued was the scope to be given to the protection of persons in the present undertaking, specifically in relation to the "rights-based" approach to the topic. "Rights-based" approaches emerged during the late 1980s as a conceptual change from previous paradigms of development studies.[34] The shift of language implied that development policy could and should be seen as a matter of rights, thus orienting the established regulatory and judicial machinery of human rights towards the achievement of development goals. As a result, rights standards would become crucial criteria to assess development agendas and, perhaps more importantly, rights-based reasoning would become an important part of the conceptual framework for understanding development policy.[35]

17. Rights-based approaches have, since then, expanded as a methodology for understanding the most varied aspects of development. More than a normative statement with claims of exclusivity, the approach is a useful departing position that carries the all-important baggage of rights-based language, and needs to be complemented by other views of relevance to the specific subject matter to be understood. IFRC has suggested that a rights-based approach to the topic may be complemented by considering the relevance of needs in the protection of persons in the event of disasters.[36] The Special Rapporteur believes that such an exercise can be usefully undertaken in this context. There is no stark opposition between needs and a rights-based approach to the protection of persons in the event of disasters. On the contrary, a reasonable, holistic approach to the topic seems to require that both rights and needs enter the equation, complementing each other when appropriate.

18. One further rationale to be considered when defining the scope of the topic is risk. Risk management is a crucial consideration that informs all aspects of disaster policy,[37] and it is possible to understand it in reference to two different moments of the disastrous event: first, risk as a fundamental element of disaster prevention and, secondly, risk as a variable in the protection of persons at the disaster proper and post-disaster phases. UNISDR in Geneva is currently working for increased awareness of the importance of disaster reduction as an integral component of sustainable development.[38] In order to avoid unnecessary duplication of efforts, it seems reasonable to the Special Rapporteur that the Commission should at the present stage follow the efforts of UNISDR on disaster prevention, leaving a risk-informed paradigm for later debates on disaster preparedness.

2. The dual nature of the protection of persons in the event of disasters

19. In his preliminary report, the Special Rapporteur concluded, *inter alia*, that "[w]ork on the topic can be undertaken with a rights-based approach that will inform the operational mechanisms of protection" (*Yearbook ... 2008*, vol. II (Part One), document A/CN.4/598, para. 62). In this connection, the Special Rapporteur notes that the kind of international regulation that would constitute a significant contribution to the subject matter can be usefully understood in reference to two different axes: the rights and obligations of States in relation to one another; and the rights and obligations of States in relation to persons in need of protection.

20. The notion that these two axes are intimately linked to, yet conceptually distinct from, one another is not new in international law. A case in point is the 1948 Convention on the Prevention and Punishment of the Crime of Genocide, whereby the Contracting Parties undertake obligations to one another, yet whose ultimate beneficiaries are human beings. In giving its advisory opinion on *Reservations to the Convention*, ICJ identified with clarity the premise that informs the Special Rapporteur's approach, by holding:

> The Convention was manifestly adopted for a purely humanitarian and civilizing purpose. It is indeed difficult to imagine a convention that might have this dual character to a greater degree, since its object on the one hand is to safeguard the very existence of certain human groups and on the other to confirm and endorse the most elementary principles of morality. In such a convention the contracting States do not have any interests of their own; they merely have, one and all, a common interest, namely, the accomplishment of those high purposes which are the *raison d'être* of the convention. Consequently, in a convention of this type one cannot speak of individual advantages or disadvantages to States, or of the maintenance of a perfect contractual balance between rights and duties. The high ideals which inspired the Convention provide, by virtue of the common will of the parties, the foundation and measure of all its provisions.[39]

21. This premise has also informed further interpretation of the Convention on the Prevention and Punishment

[34] Debates in development studies led in 1986 to the first formal evidence of a paradigm shift, with the adoption of the Declaration on the Right to Development (General Assembly resolution 41/128, annex).

[35] See Uvin, *Human Rights and Development*, p. 165.

[36] *Official Records of the General Assembly, Sixty-third Session, Sixth Committee*, 22nd meeting (A/C.6/63/SR.22), para. 68.

[37] See UNISDR, *Living with risk: a global review of disaster reduction initiatives*, 2004, available from www.unisdr.org/we/inform/publications/657 (accessed 24 October 2014).

[38] See www.unisdr.org.

[39] *Reservations to the Convention on the Prevention and Punishment of the Crime of Genocide, Advisory Opinion, I.C.J. Reports 1951*, p. 15, at p. 23.

of the Crime of Genocide. Under article 1, the Contracting Parties confirm that genocide, whether committed in time of peace or in time of war, is a crime under international law which they undertake to prevent and to punish. While both the perpetrators and victims of the crime are likely to be individuals, they are not direct subjects of the Convention. And yet, it seems hard to understand the legal regime established by the Convention if individuals are not included in the reasoning. An expression of this tension appeared in the *Bosnia and Herzegovina v. Serbia and Montenegro* judgment of 26 February 2007,[40] where the Respondent argued that the condition *sine qua non* for establishing State responsibility for the crime of genocide is the prior establishment, according to the rules of criminal law, of the individual responsibility of a perpetrator engaging the State's responsibility. The Court, mindful of the distinction between the two axes presented here, held:

> The different procedures followed by, and powers available to, this Court and to the courts and tribunals trying persons for criminal offences, do not themselves indicate that there is a legal bar to the Court itself finding that genocide or the other acts enumerated in Article III have been committed
>
> …
>
> Any other interpretation could entail that there would be no legal recourse available under the Convention in some readily conceivable circumstances: genocide has allegedly been committed within a State by its leaders but they have not been brought to trial because, for instance, they are still very much in control of the powers of the State including the police, prosecution services and the courts and there is no international penal tribunal able to exercise jurisdiction over the alleged crimes; or the responsible State may have acknowledged the breach. The Court accordingly concludes that State responsibility can arise under the Convention for genocide and complicity, without an individual being convicted of the crime or an associated one.[41]

22. A parallel situation is that of article 36 of the 1963 Vienna Convention on Consular Relations, which provides certain rights and obligations with a view to facilitating the exercise of consular functions relating to nationals of the sending State. Specifically, article 36, paragraph 1 (*b*) and paragraph 2 provide that:

> (*b*) If he so requests, the competent authorities of the receiving State shall, without delay, inform the consular post of the sending State if, within its consular district, a national of that State is arrested or committed to prison or to custody pending trial or is detained in any other manner. Any communication addressed to the consular post by the person arrested, in prison, custody or detention shall be forwarded by the said authorities without delay. The said authorities shall inform the person concerned without delay of his rights under this subparagraph.
>
> …
>
> 2. The rights referred to in paragraph 1 of this article shall be exercised in conformity with the laws and regulations of the receiving State, subject to the proviso, however, that the said laws and regulations must enable full effect to be given to the purposes for which the rights accorded under this article are intended.

23. In the *LaGrand* decision, ICJ considered whether the reference to "rights" in the foregoing provision "applies only to the rights of the sending State and not also to those of the detained individual",[42] and concluded that "Article 36, paragraph 1, creates individual rights for the detained person in addition to the rights accorded the sending State, and that consequently the reference to 'rights' in paragraph 2 must be read as applying not only to the rights of the sending State, but also to the rights of the detained individual".[43] The Special Rapporteur notes that the Court understood article 36 in reference to two different axes: on the one hand, rights and obligations of States in relation to one another; and on the other, the rights and obligations of States in relation to the individual detainee. Such an approach is the one followed by the Special Rapporteur concerning the protection of persons in the event of disasters.

24. This approach was taken by ICJ in the *Avena and other Mexican Nationals* judgment.[44] When addressing the adequate reparations for the violation of article 36, the Court drew a difference between the obligations among Contracting Parties and the obligations in relation to an individual detainee.[45] Following this differentiation, the Court concluded,

> the remedy to make good these violations should consist in an obligation on the United States to permit review and reconsideration of these nationals' cases by the United States courts … with a view to ascertaining whether in each case the violation of Article 36 committed by the competent authorities caused actual prejudice to the defendant in the process of administration of criminal justice.[46]

25. Approaching a subject in consideration of the two axes referred to above does not imply any prior assessment of the status of the rights and obligations clustered around each axis. In the *Avena and other Mexican Nationals* decision, ICJ pondered whether the right of consular notification and communication was to be considered a fundamental human right. The Court held that it was unnecessary for it to decide on the status of that right:

> Whether or not the Vienna Convention rights are human rights is not a matter that this Court need decide. The Court would, however, observe that neither the text nor the object and purpose of the Convention, nor any indication in the *travaux préparatoires*, support the conclusion that Mexico draws from its contention in that regard.[47]

26. The approach adopted in the present report is also present in the practice of the Dispute Settlement Body of the World Trade Organization (WTO). A case in point is the panel report in the case of *United States—Sections 301–310*,[48] where the panel analysed the implications of a certain domestic legal act for the application of article 23.1 of the Dispute Settlement Understanding. The panel considered the issue by seeking to identify the objects and purposes of the Dispute Settlement Understanding, and WTO more generally, that are relevant to a construction of article 23. For the panel, the most relevant were "those which relate to the creation of market conditions conducive to individual economic activity in national and global markets and to the provision of a secure and predictable multilateral trading system".[49] The panel noted

---

[40] *I.C.J. Reports 2007*, p. 43.

[41] *Ibid.*, paras. 181–182.

[42] *LaGrand Case (Germany v. United States of America), Judgment, I.C.J. Reports 2001*, p. 466, para. 89.

[43] *Ibid.*

[44] *Case concerning Avena and other Mexican Nationals (Mexico v. United States), Judgment, I.C.J. Reports 2004*, p. 12.

[45] *Ibid.*, paras. 121–122.

[46] *Ibid.*, para. 121.

[47] *Ibid.*, para. 124.

[48] *United States—Sections 301–310 of the Trade Act of 1974*, panel report, document WT/DS152/R (22 December 1999).

[49] *Ibid.*, para. 7.71.

that these goals are only achievable through the actions of private actors, which are not part of the multilateral trading regime, as "the GATT/WTO did *not* create a new legal order the subjects of which comprise both contracting parties or Members and their nationals".[50] However, for the panel,

> It would be entirely wrong to consider that the position of individuals is of no relevance to the GATT/WTO legal matrix. Many of the benefits to Members which are meant to flow as a result of the acceptance of various disciplines under the GATT/WTO depend on the activity of individual economic operators in the national and global market places. The purpose of many of these disciplines, indeed one of the primary objects of the GATT/WTO as a whole, is to produce certain market conditions which would allow this individual activity to flourish.[51]

27. Such reasoning, and the aforementioned examples, reflect the approach adopted by the Special Rapporteur with regard to the protection of persons in the event of disasters. Firstly, rights and obligations of States in relation to one another may be discussed, in order to define at a later stage the rights and obligations of States in relation to persons in need of protection.

B. *Ratione personae*: States and non-State actors

28. Post-disaster relief commonly involves the participation of numerous actors, including several governmental agencies, the military, international and domestic non-governmental organizations, IFRC, national Red Cross and Red Crescent societies and the private sector. Through its Guidelines (see paragraph 4 above), IFRC has already made a substantial contribution to the domestic legal regime applicable to several of these actors, as it tries to improve the domestic legal, policy, and institutional frameworks concerning international disaster relief and initial recovery assistance.[52] In that context, defining a new, comprehensive legal framework for all actors involved in a post-disaster response would seem unnecessary, for it could overlap with work already done in the Guidelines. Moreover, and as significantly, such an effort would exceed what may be plausibly asked from the present undertaking. It seems, thus, of importance to prioritize the addressees of the Commission's work on the topic. The Special Rapporteur is of the opinion, *prima facie*, that the Commission could usefully start by focusing its efforts on rights and duties of States for guaranteeing the protection of persons in the event of disasters. This would be without prejudice to specific provisions that the Commission would discuss at a later stage, applicable to non-State actors.

C. *Ratione temporis*: pre-disaster, disaster proper and post-disaster action

29. Intimately related to the prior points is the limitation of the topic *ratione temporis*. During the discussions in the Sixth Committee, a number of delegates suggested that work on the topic could be limited to the disaster proper and post-disaster phases.[53] Disaster risk reduction features an agenda that, according to the Hyogo Framework for Action, includes providing frameworks to (*a*) ensure that disaster risk reduction is a national and a local priority with a strong institutional basis for implementation; (*b*) identify, assess and monitor disaster risks and enhance early warning; (*c*) use knowledge, innovation and education to build a culture of safety and resilience at all levels; (*d*) reduce the underlying risk factors; and (*e*) strengthen disaster preparedness for effective response at all levels.[54] The scope of these tasks could be overly ambitious to be appropriately covered in the present stage of work on the topic and may undermine more limited (yet relevant) contributions by the Commission to the protection of persons in the event of disasters. However, preparedness or action prior to the disaster should actively enhance the protection of persons in the ulterior phases. The Special Rapporteur is of the opinion that the way to reconcile such complementary needs is to follow the cited members' suggestion for the present phase of the work, and limit the scope of this topic, *ratione temporis*, to the disaster proper and post-disaster phases. This is without prejudice to the Commission addressing, at a later stage, preparedness at the pre-disaster phase.

30. Having considered the foregoing, it is possible to propose the following wording for a draft article on the scope of the draft articles:

"*Draft article 1. Scope*

"The present draft articles apply to the protection of persons in the event of disasters, in order for States to ensure the realization of the rights of persons in such an event, by providing an adequate and effective response to their needs in all phases of a disaster."

D. Defining disaster

31. The Special Rapporteur notes that "disaster" is not a term of art and, as such, lacks one single accepted definition; consequently, as noted in the preliminary report (*Yearbook ... 2008*, vol. II (Part One), document A/CN.4/598), some international instruments have forgone a definition altogether.[55] Yet, a definition seems of essential importance in the present context. Such a definition will help identify the situations in which protection may or shall be invoked, as well as the circumstances under which protection will no longer be necessary. Describing the contours of "disaster" will also help identify the persons in need of protection and thus ascertain who is entitled to protection. A definition should also fix reasonable limits on the scope of the topic, excluding events such as armed conflict.

32. The term "disaster" has been defined through two different methodologies in international law. The first is a specific approach, which does not dwell in an abstract definition of the term but understands it as a specific kind of event that warrants emergency treatment in and of itself. Following this approach, the question of whether an event falls under the definition of "disaster" becomes

[50] *Ibid*., para. 7.72.

[51] *Ibid*., para. 7.73.

[52] See Guidelines (footnote 17 above), para. 3.

[53] See footnote 22 above.

[54] Hyogo Framework for Action 2005–2015: building the resilience of nations and communities to disasters (A/CONF.206/6 and Corr.1, chap. I, resolution 2), para. 14.

[55] See, for example, the Inter-American Convention to Facilitate Disaster Assistance of the Organization of American States, which entered into force on 16 October 1996.

moot. That is the case of the 1986 Convention on Assistance in the Case of a Nuclear Accident or Radiological Emergency, which avoids a definition of "disaster" but establishes the kind of cooperation to be undertaken by the Contracting Parties in case of a nuclear accident or radiological emergency, events that are deemed to be disasters in and of themselves.

33. The second alternative is a broader definition of disaster, not restricted to a single kind of event. Considering that the topic is framed so as not to address the protection of persons in a specific hypothesis of disaster, but rather to codify and develop rules or guidelines that may be usefully applicable to all kinds of disasters, it seems appropriate to opt for this second methodology, that is, to propose a general definition establishing the necessary elements that characterize an event as a "disaster". To this effect, a good point of departure is the 1998 Tampere Convention on the Provision of Telecommunication Resources for Disaster Mitigation and Relief Operations, pointed out by the delegation of Finland in the Sixth Committee,[56] whose article 1.6 provides that:

> "Disaster" means a serious disruption of the functioning of society, posing a significant, widespread threat to human life, health, property or the environment, whether caused by accident, nature or human activity, and whether developing suddenly or as the result of complex, long-term processes.

The same definition was used by IFRC in its Guidelines, though excluding armed conflicts.[57] This definition, including the latter caveat, provides a good basis at the start of work on the present topic.

34. Building on this basis, several aspects of the foregoing definition deserve the Commission's attention. The first refers to the requirement of harm (or lack thereof) in the definition of disaster: would the mere threat to human life be enough to consider an event a disaster? The Framework Convention on Civil Defence Assistance, for example, requires only threatened losses, defining in article 1 (*c*) disaster as "an exceptional situation in which life, property or the environment may be at risk". A possible alternative would be to consider language that requires the existence of actual losses in the definition of disaster. An example of the latter may be the "Internationally agreed glossary of basic terms related to Disaster Management", developed by the Department of Humanitarian Affairs of the United Nations in 1992,[58] which defines disaster as:

> A serious disruption of the functioning of society, causing widespread human, material or environmental losses which exceed the ability of [the] affected society to cope using only its own resources. Disasters are often classified according to their cause (natural or man-made).

35. In addition to foreseeing actual losses, this definition and others require that the disaster overwhelm the affected region's response capacity. Another example of such a requirement may be found in the Agreement Establishing the Caribbean Disaster Emergency Response Agency:

> "Disaster" means a sudden event attributable directly and solely either to the operation of the forces of nature or to human intervention or to both of them and characterized by widespread destruction of lives or property accompanied by extensive dislocation of public services, but excluding events occasioned by war, military confrontation or mismanagement.

36. Moreover, the Tampere definition includes a reference to the causal element of disasters, in order to underscore that the definition covers both man-made and natural events. Reference to causation in the definition of "disaster" may fail to consider the problem of complex causation—that is, the problem that one condition can hardly be described as being the only and sufficient cause of a given consequence.[59] This obstacle seems of crucial importance today more than ever, when natural phenomena merge with human agency in the complex birth and expansion of disastrous events.[60] In this context, explicit reference to causation may be unnecessary in a definition of disaster. The Code of Conduct for the International Red Cross and Red Crescent Movement and Non-Governmental Organizations in Disaster Relief,[61] for example, does not employ a causal element, defining disaster as "a calamitous event resulting in loss of life, great human suffering and distress, and large-scale material damage".

37. This point leads to a more general conclusion. Several delegations in the Sixth Committee suggested that the definition of disaster may be usefully restricted to the impact of the event, and not necessarily to its origins.[62] This suggestion points in the correct direction. It seems of limited use to insist on a strict separation between natural and man-made disasters when, on the one hand, it is singularly difficult to establish a clear causal relation and, on the other, such a test would not imply a substantive contribution to the definition of the term. That is, though, without prejudice to the use of said distinction in contexts other than the definition of disaster, as the Commission may find useful or necessary in its future work.

38. Furthermore, the present topic relates specifically to protection of persons in the event of disasters. The Tampere and most other definitions include threat of harm not only to persons, but also to property and the environment. Should the definition of disaster in the present report be limited to loss of human life or health? That would not appear to be the case. While, as it currently stands, the topic is limited to the protection of persons, losses amounting to a disaster that would trigger such protection are not thus limited. An environmental disaster calls for the protection of persons for, in the words of ICJ, "the environment is not an abstraction but represents

[56] *Official Records of the General Assembly, Sixty-third Session, Sixth Committee*, 22nd meeting (A/C.6/63/SR.22), para. 54.

[57] See section 2.1 of the Guidelines, (footnote 17 above).

[58] Document DHA/93/36 (1992).

[59] In Hume's words, causation "belongs entirely to the soul which considers the union of two or more objects in all past instances" (Hume, *Treatise of Human Nature,* p. 166). On the problematic relation between causes and conditions, see generally Mill, *A System of Logic Ratiocinative and Inductive*, at p. 327. On the same problem in legal reasoning, see Hart and Honoré, *Causation in the Law*, at II.

[60] See generally Beck, *Risk Society: Towards a New Modernity*, p. 21; Giddens, "Affluence, poverty and the idea of a post-scarcity society", at p. 4.

[61] Annex VI to the report entitled "Principles and response in international humanitarian assistance and protection", document 95/C. II/2/1, 26th International Conference of the Red Cross and Red Crescent, Geneva, 3–7 December 1995.

[62] See footnote 20 above.

the living space, the quality of life and the very health of human beings, including generations unborn".[63] Similarly, widespread material destruction could also warrant protection of persons. Drawing strict conceptual lines in the context of disastrous situations may be undesirable, as material and environmental losses are inextricably linked to human life and health, warranting, as a unit, the protection of persons in the aftermath of a disaster. While this seems clear in the context of a definition, in view of the topic's limitation it remains subject to guidance by the Commission whether further work should assess in detail the protection of property or the environment in the event of a disaster.

39. Among the instruments that do not limit their definitions of disaster to those that directly affect human life or health is the Charter on Cooperation to Achieve the Coordinated Use of Space Facilities in the Event of Natural or Technological Disasters (also known as the International Charter on Space and Major Disasters).[64] Article I of the Charter states:

> The term "natural or technological disaster" means a situation of great distress involving loss of human life or large-scale damage to property, caused by a natural phenomenon, such as a cyclone, tornado, earthquake, volcanic eruption, flood or forest fire, or by a technological accident, such as pollution by hydrocarbons, toxic or radioactive substances.

40. It should be noted that the International Charter on Space and Major Disasters also includes a detailed contemplation of the causes of disasters. Similarly, the Framework Convention on Civil Defence Assistance, an instrument intended to promote effective disaster prevention and crisis management, deals with environmental and material threats, but does not include a causal element:

> "Disaster" is an exceptional situation in which life, property or the environment may be at risk.[65]

41. The Red Cross/Red Crescent code of conduct, issued in 1995, appears to take a much more restrictive approach, requiring both loss of life and material damage. The code defines disaster as:

> A calamitous event resulting in loss of life, great human suffering and distress, and large scale material damage.[66]

42. An alternate approach embraces disasters that cause either loss of life, property damage or environmental degradation, but contains an additional restrictive requirement that the event be of such scale that the local community is incapable of adequately responding. Consider a definition of natural disaster offered by the Operational Guidelines on Human Rights and Natural Disasters adopted by the Inter-Agency Standing Committee:

> "Natural disaster" refers to the consequences of events triggered by such natural hazards as earthquakes, volcanic eruptions, landslides, tsunamis, floods and drought that overwhelm local response capacity. Such disasters seriously disrupt the functioning of a community or a society causing widespread human, material, economic or environmental losses, which exceed the ability of the affected community or society to cope by using its own resources.[67]

43. UNISDR has adopted similar language in its own definition, defining disaster as:

> A serious disruption of the functioning of a community or a society causing widespread human, material, economic or environmental losses which exceed the ability of the affected community or society to cope using its own resources.[68]

44. After reviewing such definitions, among others, the Special Rapporteur is of the opinion that the Tampere Convention appears to provide the best guidance for this topic. The convention's definition considers natural and man-made phenomena and acknowledges the reality that disasters often result from a complex web of factors, where no single sufficient cause may be identified. In addition, the convention's definition includes events that threaten not only human life, but also property and the environment. As noted above, each of such threats is severe enough to give rise to a need for protection.

45. Considering the foregoing, it seems possible to conclude this section with the following draft language of a definition of disaster:

"Draft article 2. Definition of disaster

"'Disaster' means a serious disruption of the functioning of society, excluding armed conflict, causing significant, widespread human, material or environmental loss."

46. This definition adopts the basic characterization of disaster as a "serious disruption", a term employed by the Tampere Convention of 1998 and other recent definitions.[69] This usage reflects the general understanding that the threshold in determining the existence of a disaster should be the degree of dysfunction of the society in which it occurs. This definition does not, however, demand that the event "overwhelm a society's response capacity".[70] Such a requirement would shift the present topic's focus from the persons in need of protection.

47. Moreover, the Special Rapporteur underscores that some actual loss is required, as opposed to the mere threat of harm. This sits most comfortably with the common understanding of disaster as a calamitous event, and it refers to those situations that would call for the protection of persons. The type of harm, however, is not limited to loss of life or health, reflecting the fact that severe environmental degradation or property damage will warrant certain protections.

---

[63] *Legality of the Threat or Use of Nuclear Weapons, Advisory Opinion, I.C.J. Reports 1996*, p. 241, para. 29.

[64] Available from www.disasterscharter.org/.

[65] Art. 1 (*c*).

[66] See footnote 61 above.

[67] Brookings-Bern Project on Internal Displacement, *Human Rights and Natural Disasters: Operational Guidelines and Field Manual on Human Rights Protection in Situations of Natural Disaster* (2008).

[68] UNISDR, UNISDR *Terminology on Disaster Risk Reduction*, available from www.unisdr.org/we/inform/publications/7817.

[69] See IFRC, (footnote 17 above), and Department of Humanitarian Affairs definition, (footnote 58 above). See also the International Charter on Space and Major Disasters ("situation of great distress") (footnote 64 above), and the Agreement Establishing the Caribbean Disaster Emergency Response Agency ("accompanied by extensive dislocation of public services").

[70] See Brookings-Bern Project, (footnote 67 above). See also Department of Humanitarian Affairs, (footnote 58 above).

48. Similarly, the definition does not distinguish between natural and man-made events, recognizing that disasters often arise from complex sets of causes that may include both wholly natural elements and contributions from human activities. Armed conflicts are expressly excluded, with the understanding that a well-developed body of law exists to cover such situations.

49. Finally, the definition excludes an inquiry into causation. Disasters generally arise from a complex set of factors, making virtually impossible any effort to identify a single sufficient cause. Furthermore, in the light of this topic's focus on protection of persons, the inquiry into a calamity's root cause is immaterial. The disruption itself, not the originating causal phenomena, gives rise to the need for protection. This definition, focusing on the disruption and its particular harms, builds the most appropriate framework to explore the rights and obligations relating to protection of persons.

Chapter II

Solidarity and cooperation

50. The underlying principles in the protection of persons in the event of disasters are those of solidarity and cooperation, both among nations and among individual human beings. It is in the solidarity inspired by human suffering that the Commission's mandate finds *telos*, as an expression of our common heritage in a global context.

51. In such a context, effective international cooperation is indispensable for the protection of persons in the event of disasters. As has been observed by the Secretary-General:

> The belief in the dignity and value of human beings as expressed in the preamble of the Charter of the United Nations is and must be the prime motive for the international community to give humanitarian assistance. The concept of international solidarity so often evoked following major emergencies and understood as a feeling of responsibility towards people in distress equally has its roots in the ethical principles of the Charter. Solidarity in this sense is not charity.[71]

More recently, the independent expert on human rights and international solidarity held that:

> International solidarity and international cooperation are based on the foundation of shared responsibility. In the broadest sense, solidarity is a communion of responsibilities and interest between individuals, groups and States, connected by the ideal of fraternity and the notion of cooperation. The relationship between international solidarity and international cooperation is an integral one, with international cooperation as a core vehicle by which collective goals and the union of interests are achieved.[72]

An expression of the principle of solidarity can be found in the 2005 Hyogo Declaration:

> We are determined to reduce disaster losses of lives and other social, economic and environmental assets worldwide, mindful of the importance of international cooperation, solidarity and partnership, as well as good governance at all levels.[73]

52. The duty to cooperate is well established as a principle of international law and can be found in numerous international instruments. The Charter of the United Nations enshrines it, not least with reference to the humanitarian context in which the protection of persons in the event of disasters places itself.[74] Article 1, paragraph 3, of the Charter clearly spells out as one of the purposes of the Organization:

> To achieve international cooperation in solving international problems of an economic, social, cultural, or humanitarian character, and in promoting and encouraging respect for human rights and for fundamental freedoms for all without distinction as to race, sex, language, or religion.

Articles 55 and 56 of the Charter elaborate on Article 1, paragraph 3, with respect to international cooperation. Article 55 of the Charter reads:

> With a view to the creation of conditions of stability and well-being which are necessary for peaceful and friendly relations among nations based on respect for the principle of equal rights and self-determination of peoples, the United Nations shall promote:
>
> a. Higher standards of living, full employment, and conditions of economic and social progress and development;
>
> b. Solutions of international economic, social, health, and related problems; and international cultural and educational cooperation; and
>
> c. Universal respect for, and observance of, human rights and fundamental freedoms for all without distinction as to race, sex, language, or religion.

Article 56 of the Charter reads:

> All Members pledge themselves to take joint and separate action in cooperation with the Organization for the achievement of the purposes set forth in Article 55.

53. The general duty to cooperate was reiterated as one of the principles of international law in the Declaration on Principles of International Law concerning Friendly Relations and Cooperation among States in accordance with the Charter of the United Nations in the following terms:

> States have the duty to cooperate with one another, irrespective of the differences in their political, economic and social systems, in the various spheres of international relations, in order to maintain international peace and security and to promote international economic stability and progress, the general welfare of nations and international cooperation free from discrimination based on such differences.[75]

---

[71] A/45/587, para. 5.

[72] A/HRC/9/10, para. 6. See also General Assembly resolution 46/182 of 19 December 1991, annex, guiding principles, para. 5.

[73] A/CONF.206/6 and Corr.1, chap. I, resolution 1, fifth preambular paragraph.

[74] See *Yearbook ... 2008*, vol. II (Part One), document A/CN.4/590, para. 17 and footnote 57.

[75] General Assembly resolution 2625 (XXV) of 24 October 1970, annex, para. 1.

As interpreted by one author, this obligation "consecrat[es] the solidarity of nations".[76]

54. Solidarity as an international legal principle, and distinct from charity, gives rise to a system of cooperation in furtherance of the notion that justice and the common good are best served by policies that benefit all nations.[77] Seen in this light, it can also be traceable in the context of international environmental law, in relation to the role of the developing world. Thus, the Stockholm Declaration proclaimed that nations must undertake a coordinated effort to preserve and safeguard natural resources, insofar as environmental protection "affects the well-being of peoples and economic development throughout the world".[78] Recognizing that "environmental deficiencies generated by the conditions of under-development and natural disaster pose grave problems", the Declaration calls for accelerated development through financial and technological assistance.[79] The Declaration further provides that developed countries shall provide, and developing countries shall assist in promoting, scientific information and expertise relevant to mitigating environmental degradation.[80] The duties placed on developed and developing States alike are premised on the recognition that global environmental problems "will require extensive cooperation among nations"[81] with the specific understanding that "industrialized countries should make efforts to reduce the gap [between] themselves and the developing countries".[82] Moreover, the Rio Declaration on Environment and Development, reaffirming Stockholm, prioritizes the concerns of developing countries, stating that the "special situation and needs of developing countries, particularly the least developed and those most environmentally vulnerable, shall be given special priority".[83]

55. Subsequent instruments implemented this obligation to cooperate, establishing mechanisms to share information, finances and scientific resources. The Vienna Convention for the Protection of the Ozone Layer, for example, mandates cooperative research and information-sharing among all States parties to the Convention. In 1990, the amending Montreal Protocol on Substances that Deplete the Ozone Layer fulfilled the Vienna Convention's promise to take into account the "circumstances and particular requirements of developing countries". Developing countries are given leniency with respect to certain proscribed or regulated chemicals,[84] and the Protocol mandates that developed nations shall provide financial assistance and technology to less-developed nations.[85] The Protocol establishes a multilateral fund to motivate participation by developing countries.[86] In turn, developing nations are bound to pollution control measures, and the parties to the Convention are empowered to invoke non-compliance procedures where appropriate.[87]

56. As noted above, solidarity is an important element of cooperation towards solving economic problems, as put forward in Article 1, paragraph 3, of the Charter of the United Nations and in the 1970 Friendly Relations Declaration.[88] The Declaration recognizes a duty of States to cooperate with one another, and provides that "States should cooperate in the promotion of economic growth throughout the world, especially that of the developing countries".[89] This concept was brought to the fore and expanded by the Declaration on the Establishment of a New International Economic Order.[90] The Declaration is based upon a duty of States to cooperate "in the solving of world economic problems ... bearing in mind the necessity to ensure accelerated development of all the developing countries".[91] And further holds that "cooperation for development is the shared goal and common duty of all countries".[92]

57. Solidarity as an international legal principle found reflection beyond the 1974 Declaration. The Declaration of International Economic Cooperation, adopted by the General Assembly in 1990, notes the interdependence of the international community[93] and recognizes that reviving growth in developing countries requires "a concerted and committed effort by all countries".[94] Most recently, the United Nations Millennium Declaration places solidarity among the fundamental values essential to international relations.[95] The declaration further elaborates on its invocation of solidarity:

> Global challenges must be managed in a way that distributes the costs and burdens fairly in accordance with basic principles of equity and social justice. Those who suffer or who benefit least deserve help from those who benefit most.[96]

58. Solidarity is also reflected in regional instruments. The African Charter on Human and Peoples' Rights establishes that individuals and groups should dispose of their wealth "with a view to strengthening African unity and solidarity"[97] and guarantees the right to social and

[76] B. Babović, "The duty of States to cooperate with one another in accordance with the Charter", at p. 289.

[77] See generally MacDonald, "Solidarity in the practice and discourse of public international law", at p. 275.

[78] Declaration of the United Nations Conference on the Human Environment, *Report of the United Nations Conference on the Human Environment, Stockholm, 5–16 June 1972* (United Nations publication, Sales No. E.73.II.A.14), and corrigendum, chap. I.

[79] *Ibid.*, principle 9.

[80] *Ibid.*, principle 20.

[81] *Ibid.*, para. 7.

[82] *Ibid.*, para. 4.

[83] Report of the *United Nations Conference on Environment and Development Rio de Janeiro, 3–14 June 1992* (United Nations publication, Sales No. E.93.I.8 and corrigenda), principle 6.

[84] Art. 5, paras. 1–3.

[85] Arts. 10 and 10A; see also article 5, paragraph 5 (noting that developing nations' compliance with the Protocol's control measures will be contingent on developed countries' willingness to provide financial and technological assistance).

[86] Art 10.

[87] Art 5.

[88] General Assembly resolution 2625 (XXV) of 24 October 1970, annex.

[89] *Ibid.*

[90] General Assembly resolution 3201 (S–VI) of 1 May 1974.

[91] *Ibid.*, para. 4 (c).

[92] *Ibid.*, para. 3.

[93] General Assembly resolution S–18/3 of 1 May 1990, annex, para. 12.

[94] *Ibid.*, para. 21.

[95] See General Assembly resolution 55/2 of 8 September 2000, para. 6.

[96] *Ibid.*

[97] African Charter on Human and Peoples' Rights, art. 21, para. 4.

economic development.[98] It also establishes a right to a "satisfactory environment"[99] and the duty of the individual to promote social and national solidarity.[100]

59. The international cooperation imperative is firmly rooted in international instruments of a humanitarian character. As noted above, the duty to cooperate in the context of human rights has been explicitly embodied in Article 1, paragraph 3, of the Charter of the United Nations. Likewise, it has been reiterated in numerous General Assembly declarations and resolutions. Thus, for example, the Friendly Relations Declaration proclaims:

> States shall cooperate in the promotion of universal respect for, and observance of, human rights and fundamental freedoms for all, and in the elimination of all forms of racial discrimination and all forms of religious intolerance.[101]

And in its resolution 56/152, entitled "Respect for the purposes and principles contained in the Charter of the United Nations to achieve international cooperation in promoting and encouraging respect for human rights and for fundamental freedoms and in solving international problems of a humanitarian character", the General Assembly affirmed:

> The solemn commitment of all States to enhance international cooperation in the field of human rights and in the solution to international problems of a humanitarian character in full compliance with the Charter of the United Nations.

60. As has been pointed out in the preliminary report on this topic, international human rights law takes on special significance in this context.[102] The International Covenant on Economic, Social and Cultural Rights refers explicitly to international cooperation as a means of realizing the rights contained therein.[103] This has been reiterated by the Committee on Economic, Social and Cultural Rights in its general comments relating to the implementation of specific rights guaranteed by the Covenant.[104] In a recent resolution, the Economic and Social Council encouraged:

> Member States and, where applicable, regional organizations to strengthen operational and legal frameworks for international disaster relief, [to take] into account, as appropriate, the Guidelines for the Domestic Facilitation and Regulation of International Disaster Relief and Initial Recovery Assistance, adopted at the thirtieth International Conference of the Red Cross and Red Crescent held in Geneva in November 2007.[105]

And, in the same resolution, the Council:

> *Recognizes* the benefits of engagement of and coordination with relevant humanitarian actors to the effectiveness of humanitarian response, and encourages the United Nations to continue to pursue efforts to strengthen partnerships at the global level with the International Red Cross and Red Crescent Movement, relevant humanitarian non-governmental organizations and other participants of the Inter-Agency Standing Committee.[106]

61. International cooperation gained particular prominence in the 2006 Convention on the Rights of Persons with Disabilities which is, *inter alia*, applicable "in situations of risk, including situations of armed conflict, humanitarian emergencies and the occurrence of natural disasters".[107] In a separate article of that Convention, international cooperation is dealt with in the following terms:

> States Parties recognize the importance of international cooperation and its promotion, in support of national efforts for the realization of the purpose and objectives of the present Convention, and will undertake appropriate and effective measures in this regard, between and among States and, as appropriate, in partnership with relevant international and regional organizations and civil society, in particular organizations of persons with disabilities.[108]

62. There is a vast number of instruments of specific relevance to the protection of persons in the event of disasters which demonstrate the importance of the imperative of international cooperation in combating the effects of disasters. Not only are these instruments in themselves expressions of cooperation, they generally reflect the principle of cooperation relating to specific aspects of disaster governance in the text of the instrument. Typically in bilateral agreements, this has been reflected in the title given to the instrument, denoting either cooperation or (mutual) assistance.[109] Moreover, the cooperation imperative, usually laid down in the preamble of a particular instrument, in the vast majority of cases is framed as one of the objectives of the instrument or is attributed positive effects towards their attainment. Again, the Tampere Convention is of relevance in this respect as it indicates in paragraph 21 of its preamble that the parties wish "to facilitate international cooperation to mitigate the impact of disaster". Another example, very much in line with the scope of the present topic, can be found in an agreement between France and Malaysia:

> Convinced of the need to develop cooperation between the competent organs of both Parties in the field of the prevention of grave risks and the protection of populations, property and the environment.[110]

---

[98] *Ibid.*, art. 22.

[99] *Ibid.*, art. 24.

[100] *Ibid.*, art. 29, para. 4.

[101] See footnote 75 above.

[102] See *Yearbook ... 2008*, vol. II (Part One), document A/CN.4/598, paras. 25–26.

[103] General Assembly resolution 2200 A (XXI), annex, arts. 11, 15, 22 and 23.

[104] See, in particular, general comments No. 2 (Report on the fourth session, Committee on Economic, Social and Cultural Rights, *Official Records of the Economic and Social Council, 1990, Supplement No. 3* (E/1990/23), annex III, p. 86); No. 3 (Report on the fifth session, *ibid., Supplement No. 3* (E/1991/23), annex III, p. 83; No. 7 (Report on the sixteenth and seventeenth sessions, *ibid., Supplement No. 2* (E/1998/22), annex IV, p. 113; No. 14 (Report on the twenty-second, twenty-third and twenty-fourth sessions, *ibid., Supplement No. 2* (E/2001/22), annex IV, p. 128; and No. 15 (Report on the twenty-eighth and twenty-ninth sessions, *ibid., Supplement No. 2* (E/2003/22), annex IV, p. 120.

[105] Resolution 2008/36 of the Economic and Social Council, of 25 July 2008, para. 5.

[106] *Ibid.*, para. 7.

[107] Art. 11.

[108] Art. 32.

[109] See *Yearbook ... 2008*, vol. II (Part One), addendum I, document A/CN.4/590 and Add.1–3, paras. 25–26, for a comprehensive list of relevant instruments. For a further typology of instruments for the purposes of international disaster response law, see Fischer, "International disaster response law treaties: trends, patterns, and lacunae" ("Despite the fact that in all cases the specific purpose is different, the underlying rationale is the need to increase capacities to deal with the effects of disaster", p. 33).

[110] Agreement between the Government of the French Republic and the Government of Malaysia on Cooperation in the Field of Disaster Prevention and Management and Civil Security, 25 May 1998, preambular paragraph 4: *Journal officiel de la République française*, 9 December 1998, p. 18519.

63. Cooperation should, however, not be interpreted as diminishing the prerogatives of a sovereign State within the limits of international law. On the contrary, the principle underlines respect for the sovereignty of States and its corollary, non-intervention and the primary role of State authorities in the initiation, organization, coordination and implementation of the measures relevant to the protection of persons in the event of disasters. Sovereignty may be conceived as "a concept to describe a pre-existing reality, a scheme of interpretation, used to organize and structure our understanding of political life".[111] Non-intervention is a well-established principle of international law, dating from the early stages of that body of law,[112] whose substantive contents need not be restated here. Suffice it to point out that the protection of persons in the event of disasters will often involve the adoption of political, regulatory, administrative and juridical measures by the affected State, including the deployment of its armed forces within its own territory, which are expressions of the "right of every sovereign State to conduct its affairs without outside interference", as ICJ defined said principle in its 1986 judgment in the *Case concerning Military and Paramilitary Activities in and against Nicaragua*.[113]

64. It is the primary duty of the authorities of the affected State to take care of the victims of natural disasters and similar emergencies occurring in its territory.[114] In the words of the General Assembly, "the abandonment of the victims of natural disasters and similar emergency situations without humanitarian assistance constitutes a threat to human life and an offence to human dignity".[115]

65. Cooperation complements the primary duty of States. However, this primary duty concerns not only Governments and governmental authorities, but also competent international organizations and elements of civil society, such as national Red Cross and Red Crescent societies. The position has been characterized with clarity by the Secretary-General as early as 1971 in the comprehensive report entitled "Assistance in cases of natural disaster":

> While a Government should be able to count on the help of the international community, provided through Governments, the League of Red Cross Societies and other voluntary agencies or the United Nations organizations, in its preparations against or its efforts to meet such emergencies, the primary responsibility for protecting the life, health and property of people within its frontiers and for maintaining the essential public services rests with that Government. International assistance can only supplement, and will depend very largely for its effectiveness on, the efforts of the country itself through its Government or through such organizations as its national Red Cross society.[116]

66. The 2008 Secretariat memorandum points out the link between the principle of cooperation as a *sine qua non* for this topic and the multiple actors involved, listing not only State actors but also non-State actors, that is, relief organizations.[117] The involvement of, and cooperation with, non-State actors has thus gradually found its way into the international legal discourse which recognizes that the increasing interdependence within international society necessitates international cooperation including actors other than States. In the words of the Independent expert on human rights and international solidarity:

> From a global perspective, interdependence, by its very nature, exists not only between States, but also between other international actors, and these relationships require international cooperation.[118]

67. The role of those actors has been recognized as essential for combating the effects of disasters. The duty of States to cooperate with the United Nations is expressed in Article 56 of the Charter and the Organization has, in turn, emphasized the need to work in close cooperation with IFRC[119] and with non-governmental organizations and civil society as a whole.[120]

68. In addition, a number of treaties between States and international organizations[121] have been concluded that acknowledge the importance of international cooperation between State actors and non-State actors at the international level.[122] Other international instruments do likewise. The preamble to the 1992 Rio Declaration on Environment and Development cites the goal of "establishing a new and equitable global partnership through the creation of new levels of cooperation among States, key sectors of societies and people".[123] The concept of global partnership is then repeated in principles 7, 21 and 27. Cooperation is expressed in a number of ways. With regard to the present topic, principle 18 provides:

> States shall immediately notify other States of any natural disasters or other emergencies that are likely to produce sudden harmful effects on the environment of those States. Every effort shall be made by the international community to help States so afflicted.

The ASEAN Agreement on Disaster Management and Emergency Response of 2005 states that:

---

[111] Werner, "State sovereignty and international legal discourse", p. 155.

[112] For an early exposition of its origins, see Bernard, "On the principle of non-intervention. a lecture delivered in the hall of all Souls' College".

[113] *Case Concerning Military and Paramilitary Activities in and against Nicaragua (Nicaragua v. United States of America), I.C.J. Reports 1986*, para. 202.

[114] Resolution 46/182 of 19 December 1991, annex, para. 4. See also Hyogo Declaration 2005 (footnote 73 above), para. 4.

[115] Resolution 45/100 of 14 December 1990, sixth preambular paragraph.

[116] E/4994, para. 100. This point was reaffirmed by the General Assembly in resolution 43/131 of 8 December 1988.

[117] *Yearbook ... 2008*, vol. II (Part One), addendum I, document A/CN.4/590 and Add.1–3, para. 18.

[118] A/HRC/4/8, para. 11.

[119] See, *inter alia*, resolutions 2435 (XXIII) of 19 December 1968, 2816 (XXVI) of 14 December 1971, 36/225 of 17 December 1981, 46/182 of 19 December 1990, 57/150 of 16 December 2002 and 63/139 of 11 December 2008.

[120] Resolutions 63/139 of 11 December 2008 and 63/141 of 11 December 2008.

[121] The Special Rapporteur follows the definition provisionally adopted by the Commission under the topic of "Responsibility of international organizations". Draft article 2 defines an international organization for the purposes of the draft articles as "an organization established by a treaty or other instrument governed by international law and possessing its own international legal personality. International organizations may include as members, in addition to States, other entities" (*Yearbook ... 2008*, vol. II (Part Two), para. 164).

[122] See the list of instruments between States and international organizations in *Yearbook ... 2008*, vol. II (Part One), addendum I, document A/CN.4/590 and Add.1–3.

[123] *Report of the United Nations Conference on Environment and Development* ... (see footnote 83 above).

The Parties, in addressing disaster risks, shall involve, as appropriate, all stakeholders including local communities, non-governmental organizations and private enterprises, utilizing, among others, community-based disaster preparedness and early response approaches.[124]

The 1986 Convention on Assistance in the Case of Nuclear Accident or Radiological Emergency provides in its first article:

The States Parties shall cooperate between themselves and with the International Atomic Energy Agency.

The Hyogo Declaration expresses the value of non-State actor involvement in the context of disaster reduction in terms of "cooperation, including partnerships".[125] Likewise, the Institute of International Law, in its resolution on humanitarian assistance, has recognized the "essential role played by the United Nations, intergovernmental organizations, the International Committee of the Red Cross and non-governmental organizations".[126]

69. The concept of civil society does not necessarily carry a transnational connotation. Rather, it emphasizes local civil society. The working definition proposed by the London School of Economics Centre for Civil Society is illustrative:

Civil society refers to the arena of uncoerced collective action around shared interests, purposes and values. In theory, its institutional forms are distinct from those of the state, family and market, though in practice, the boundaries between state, civil society, family and market are often complex, blurred and negotiated. Civil society commonly embraces a diversity of spaces, actors and institutional forms, varying in their degree of formality, autonomy and power. Civil societies are often populated by organizations such as registered charities, development non-governmental organizations, community groups, women's organizations, faith-based organizations, professional associations, trade unions, self-help groups, social movements, business associations, coalitions and advocacy groups.[127]

70. In the light of the foregoing, the Special Rapporteur proposes the following draft article on the duty of cooperation:

"Draft article 3. Duty to cooperate

"For the purposes of the present draft articles, States shall cooperate among themselves and, as appropriate, with:

"(*a*) Competent international organizations, in particular the United Nations;

"(*b*) The International Federation of Red Cross and Red Crescent Societies; and

"(*c*) Civil society."

[124] Art. 3, para. 6.

[125] Hyogo Declaration 2005 (footnote 73 above), para. 4. See also paragraph 2 in which "the importance of involving all stakeholders" is underlined.

[126] Resolution adopted on 2 September 2003 (Institute of International Law, *Yearbook*, p. 263).

[127] "What is civil society?", Centre for Civil Society, London School of Economics, 2004.

Chapter III

Future work

71. The present report has focused on the scope of the protection of persons in the event of disasters and proposed a definition of disaster. It has stressed the conceptual approach to guide further developments, and has put forward a draft article on the basic principle that inspires work on the topic. As the next step, work shall be directed towards complementing the first axis, namely, that of the rights and obligations of States in relation to one another, and identifying the principles that inspire the protection of persons in the event of disaster, in its aspect related to persons in need of protection. Further work will concentrate on the operational aspects of disaster relief and assistance.

CHECKLIST OF DOCUMENTS OF THE SIXTY-FIRST SESSION

Document	*Title*	*Observations and references*
A/CN.4/604	Expulsion of aliens: comments and information received from Governments	Reproduced in the present volume.
A/CN.4/605	Provisional agenda for the sixty-first session	Mimeographed. For agenda as adopted, see *Yearbook ... 2009*, vol. II (Part Two).
A/CN.4/606 and Add.1	Topical summary of the discussion held in the Sixth Committee of the General Assembly during its sixty-third session, prepared by the Secretariat	Mimeographed.
A/CN.4/607 [and Corr.1] and Add.1	Shared natural resources: comments and observations received from Governments	Reproduced in the present volume.
A/CN.4/608	Shared natural resources: paper on oil and gas prepared by Mr. Chusei Yamada, Special Rapporteur on shared natural resources	*Idem.*
A/CN.4/609	Responsibility of international organizations: comments and observations received from international organizations	*Idem.*
A/CN.4/610	Seventh report on responsibility of international organizations, by Mr. Giorgio Gaja, Special Rapporteur	*Idem.*
A/CN.4/611 [and Corr.1]	Fifth report on expulsion of aliens, by Mr. Maurice Kamto, Special Rapporteur	*Idem.*
A/CN.4/612	The obligation to extradite or prosecute (*aut dedere aut judicare*): comments and information received from Governments	*Idem.*
A/CN.4/613 and Add.1	Filling of casual vacancies in the Commission: note by the Secretariat	A/CN.4/613, reproduced in the present volume. A/CN.4/613/Add.1 mimeographed.
A/CN.4/614 [and Corr.1] and Add.1–2	Fourteenth report on reservations to treaties, by Mr. Alain Pellet, Special Rapporteur	Reproduced in the present volume.
A/CN.4/615 [and Corr.1]	Second report on the protection of persons in the event of disasters, by Mr. Eduardo Valencia-Ospina, Special Rapporteur	*Idem.*
A/CN.4/616	Reservations to treaties in the context of succession of States: memorandum by the Secretariat	*Idem.*
A/CN.4/617	Expulsion of aliens: draft articles on protection of the human rights of persons who have been or are being expelled, as restructured by the Special Rapporteur, Mr. Maurice Kamto, in the light of the plenary debate during the first part of the sixty-first session	*Idem.*
A/CN.4/618	Expulsion of aliens: new draft workplan presented by the Special Rapporteur, Mr. Maurice Kamto, with a view to structuring the draft articles	*Idem.*
A/CN.4/L.743 and Add.1	Responsibility of international organizations: restructuring of the draft articles and text of draft articles 2, 4, 8, 15, paragraph 2, (*b*), 15 *bis*, 18, 19 and 55, adopted by the Drafting Committee on 25, 26, 27 May and 2 June 2009	Mimeographed.
A/CN.4/L.744 [and Corr.1–2] and Add.1	Reservations to treaties: text and title of the draft guidelines provisionally adopted by the Drafting Committee on 5, 6, 18, 19, 27, 28 and 29 May 2009	*Idem.*
A/CN.4/L.745	Draft report of the International Law Commission on the work of its sixty-first session: chapter I (Organization of the work of the session)	*Idem.* See the text approved in *Official Records of the General Assembly, Sixty-fourth Session, Supplement No. 10* (A/64/10). The final text appears in *Yearbook ... 2009*, vol. II (Part Two).

Document	*Title*	*Observations and references*
A/CN.4/L.746	*Idem*: chapter II (Summary of the work of the Commission at its sixty-first session)	*Idem.*
A/CN.4/L.747 and Add.1	*Idem*: chapter III (Specific issues on which comments would be of particular interest to the Commission)	*Idem.*
A/CN.4/L.748 and Add.1–2 [and Add.2/Corr.1]	*Idem*: chapter IV (Responsibility of international organizations)	*Idem.*
A/CN.4/L.749 and Add.1–7	*Idem*: chapter V (Reservations to treaties)	*Idem.*
A/CN.4/L.750 [and Corr.1] and Add.1	*Idem*: chapter VI (Expulsion of aliens)	*Idem.*
A/CN.4/L.751	*Idem*: chapter VII (Protection of persons in the event of disasters)	*Idem.*
A/CN.4/L.752	*Idem*: chapter VIII (Shared natural resources)	*Idem.*
A/CN.4/L.753	*Idem*: chapter IX (The obligation to extradite or prosecute (*aut dedere aut judicare*))	*Idem.*
A/CN.4/L.754	*Idem*: chapter X (Immunity of State officials from foreign criminal jurisdiction)	*Idem.*
A/CN.4/L.755	*Idem*: chapter XI (The most-favoured-nation clause)	*Idem.*
A/CN.4/L.756	*Idem*: chapter XII (Treaties over time)	*Idem.*
A/CN.4/L.757	*Idem*: chapter XIII (Other decisions and conclusions of the Commission)	*Idem.*
A/CN.4/L.758	Protection of persons in the event of disasters: text and title of draft articles 1, 2, 3, 4 and 5 as provisionally adopted by the Drafting Committee	Mimeographed.
A/CN.4/L.759	Report of the Planning Group	*Idem.*
A/CN.4/SR.2998–A/CN.4/SR.3035	Provisional summary records of the 2998th to 3035th meetings	*Idem.* The final text appears in *Yearbook ... 2009*, vol. I.